The Globe Edition

THE POETICAL WORKS

OF

WILLIAM COWPER

MACMILLAN AND CO., Limited
LONDON . BOMBAY . CALCUTTA
MELBOURNE

THE MACMILLAN COMPANY
NEW YORK . BOSTON . CHICAGO
ATLANTA . SAN FRANCISCO

THE MACMILLAN CO. OF CANADA, Ltd.
TORONTO

The Globe Edition

THE POETICAL WORKS

OF

WILLIAM COWPER

EDITED

WITH NOTES AND BIOGRAPHICAL INTRODUCTION

BY

WILLIAM BENHAM, B.D.

MACMILLAN AND CO., LIMITED
ST. MARTIN'S STREET, LONDON
1908

RICHARD CLAY AND SONS, LIMITED,
BREAD STREET HILL, E.C., AND
BUNGAY, SUFFOLK.

First Edition, 1870.
Reprinted 1874, 1879, 1889, 1902, 1908.

TO THE

MOST REVEREND R. C. TRENCH, D.D.

LORD ARCHBISHOP OF DUBLIN.

MY DEAR LORD ARCHBISHOP,

When I asked leave to dedicate to you this Edition of Cowper's Poems, I wished to express, in the only way that lies in my power, my gratitude for past kindnesses, and for all that I have learned from you. But, independently of these feelings, I know that all readers of this volume will recognize a fitness in the offering for your acceptance the Works of one whose writings were so natural and pure and good, and whose command of his mother-tongue was so complete. With deep feelings of affection and sympathy,

I remain,

MY DEAR LORD ARCHBISHOP,

Your Grace's faithful Servant,

W. BENHAM.

ADDINGTON VICARAGE,
July 9, 1870.

CONTENTS.

TRANSLATIONS FROM MILTON.

I.—THE LATIN.

Elegies.

Epigrams.

Miscellaneous Poems.

II.—THE ITALIAN POEMS.

III.—COMPLIMENTARY POEMS TO MILTON,

FROM THE LATIN AND ITALIAN.

TRANSLATIONS FROM VINCENT BOURNE.

TRANSLATIONS FROM THE LATIN CLASSICS.

EPIGRAMS, TRANSLATED FROM THE LATIN OF OWEN.

INDEX TO FIRST LINES.

PREFACE.

THE works which have formed the materials for this volume are the following, named in the order of their publication :—

    1. Olney Hymns : 1779. (See Memoir, p. xxxvii.)

    2. Poems by William Cowper : 1782. (See p. 45.)

    3. The Task, with three other pieces, by the same : 1785. (See p. 181.)

    4. The above volumes were published distinctly, No. 3 offering no indication that the author had appeared in print before. But always afterwards Nos. 2 and 3 were issued together, and numbered "Cowper's Poems, Vols. i. and ii." New editions were published in 1786, 1787, 1788, 1793, 1794, 1798 (*two* editions in this year, very different in form and appearance), and 1800. The foregoing were all that were printed in the author's lifetime. The various editions contained fresh poems from time to time.

    5. Poems translated from the French of Madame de la Mothe Guyon by the late William Cowper, Esq., Author of "The Task," to which are added some Original Poems of Mr. Cowper, not inserted in his Works. Newport-Pagnel, 1801.

    6. The Life and Letters of William Cowper, Esq., with Remarks on Epistolary Writers. By William Hayley, Esq. : 4 vols. 1803.

    This work contained many additional poems which had been sent to friends, but not published by the author among his works. These will be found, with others, in pp. 327—402. A brief notice of each poem is given in the Notes at the end. During Cowper's later life, beginning with 1791, Hayley was intimately connected with him and his friends. It was a priceless boon to give Cowper's Letters to the public ; two brother poets have pronounced him "the best letter-writer in the English language."* Hayley's work therefore was highly interesting, but it had many serious faults. Not only is its style windy and tiresome, but the writer was so anxious not to give offence to any one, that in dealing with the more painful passages of Cowper's life, he contrives to leave us in utter uncertainty of what the *facts* were, and invariably assures us that if we knew everything we should see that everybody concerned acted in the most exemplary manner possible. With the same end in view he has made large omissions from the letters, without giving any indication of having done so. The originals of many of the letters which he printed are in the Manu-script Room of the British Museum (Addl. MSS. 24,154 and 21,556), and the omitted passages are mostly crossed with pencil-marks, I presume by his hand. The few passages not so crossed were probably struck out in the proofs. All these letters I have carefully compared with the printed copies.

    Hayley's knowledge of Cowper, moreover, was confined to his later life. In the earlier part of the biography he has made several mistakes, and to one of the most interesting portions of Cowper's life, his only love affair, he makes no allusion. The references to Hayley's work in the present volume are to the edition of 1812.

---

* Southey in Life, p. 1, and Alex. Smith in "Encyclopædia Britannica."

b

7. Latin and Italian Poems of Milton.   Translated by Cowper.   1808.

This work was published by Hayley for the benefit of Cowper's godson, W. C. Rose, See p. lxiv.

8. Memoir of the Early Life of William Cowper.   Written by Himself.   With an Appendix containing some of Cowper's Religious Letters, and other Documents. London, 1816.

This was written at Huntingdon for the private reading of his friends the Unwins, and its publication was never dreamt of. It was written just when Cowper was in the full conviction of his conversion, and in consequence speaks most severely of his previous life, and rails (it is not too strong a word) against the acquaintances of his youth. Written with all the exaggeration of excitement, and with a morbid dwelling upon the details of his madness, it is a painful work to read, and it is to be regretted that it was ever published. A lady who was on a visit to Newton saw the MS. on his table, unjustifiably took a copy, and lent it to a friend. Of course, it soon found its way into a publisher's hands, through the instrumentality of a " pious character," to use the expression of one of Cowper's biographers (Grimshawe, v. 262).

9. Adelphi.   A Sketch of the Character, and an Account of the Last Illness of the late Rev. John Cowper, who finished his course with joy, March 20, 1770. Written by William Cowper ; transcribed from his original MS. by J. Newton. London, 1816.

10. Private Correspondence of William Cowper with several of his most intimate Friends, now first published from the Originals in the possession of John Johnson.   2 vols.   London, 1814.

11. Poems by William Cowper, in three volumes, by his Kinsman, John Johnson, LL.D., Rector of Yaxham with Welborne in Norfolk.

The 3d volume comprised "his Posthumous Poetry, with a Sketch of his Life," and contained a few pieces which had not yet appeared. Dr. Johnson was, as will be seen in the Life, a relative very dear to Cowper, and made it his pious care to tend him in his last years. It may be well to mention here that he was no connexion of the Johnson who will also appear often in the memoir as the original publisher of Cowper's works.

12. Poems, the Early Productions of William Cowper, now first published from the Originals in the possession of James Croft.   With anecdotes of the Poet, collected from Letters of Lady Hesketh, written during her residence at Olney. London, 1825.

This volume was a deeply interesting one, for in it the public was informed for the first time that the Poet in his early days had been deeply in love with his cousin Theodora Jane Cowper, and had addressed to her verses enough to make a small volume. The editor, Mr. Croft, was the son of Sir Archer Croft, who married the youngest sister of Harriet (Lady Hesketh) and Theodora Cowper. The editing of the volume is very bad. The poems are full of misprints, and the prose part consists of extracts from Lady Hesketh's letters without arrangement or dates, or any indication of the quantity of her correspondence. If these letters are still in existence, the possessor would confer a great boon on literature by publishing them, for the great want in the materials for Cowper's life are the letters of his friends. He appears not to have preserved them ; not above two or three have been published. And this volume of Mr. Croft's is still the only one which contains any letters of his cousin and faithful friend, Lady Hesketh.

In 1835 was published Southey's Life of Cowper.   At that time the " Private Correspondence " above mentioned (No. 10) was a copyright property, though an unsaleable one.   Southey's publishers applied to the possessor of it for leave to purchase both copyright and remaining stock.   Instead of granting it, they commissioned a Mr. Grimshawe (brother-in-law of Dr. John Johnson) to prepare a rival edition to Southey's. Both works therefore came out almost together. Grimshawe's contained the copyright correspondence, but beyond this had no merit. Southey, debarred from printing the correspondence, wove the gist of it into his biographical narrative. There was some disadvantage in this, for it sometimes makes his narrative long and tedious. As soon as the copyright in the Private Correspondence ceased it was placed at the end of Southey's edition as a supplement.

Since Southey's there have been many lives written, the only ones calling for special remark being those of Robert Bell and of Mr. John Bruce. The latter is prefixed to the Aldine Edition. Though it proves that he had taken great pains with his subject, and is written in a vigorous, tasteful style, it does not contain much that is new. But he had collected much fresh matter in the way of letters, which he was preparing to publish when his lamented death took place suddenly, in the autumn of 1869.

Great light has been thrown upon some of the most difficult passages in Cowper's life by a series of papers in the *Sunday at Home* (1866) by the Rev. William Bull, of Newport-Pagnell. The same gentleman has also published the life of his grandfather, Josiah Bull, one of Cowper's intimate friends, and "Memorials of John Newton" (Religious Tract Society, 1869). I have largely availed myself of the facts which he has brought to light ; they will be noticed in their proper place.

The present edition contains some new and interesting matter.

[1] Some lines written on the margin of the *Monthly Review.* My authority for them is an anonymous correspondent of the *Record* newspaper of Feb. 20, 1867. Minute examination leaves no doubt of their genuineness. P. 356, and *note.*

[2] "To a Young Lady, with a Present of two Cockscombs." P. 347.

[3] "To a Lady who wore a Lock of his Hair." P. 355.

For the two last we are indebted to Mr. Charles Stuart. The MSS. are pasted inside the lid of an edition of 1793, which was given to him by Mrs. Lyon. She vouched for their genuineness, having received them from the Rev. J. A. Knight, to whom they had been given by Lady Austen. The former of them had already reached Mr. Bruce from another source, which is of course an additional proof of genuineness. Of the deep interest attaching to the last piece I have spoken in the Memoir, p. liv.

The arrangement of the Poems in the present edition is as follows :—

1. Those written in youth, comprising No. 11, as above named, along with a few others (indicated in the Notes), taken from other sources, but placed here as belonging to the same period. This division occupies pp. 1–23 of the present volume.

2. The Olney Hymns, pp. 24–44.

3. The first published volume, pp. 45–179.

4. The second published volume, pp. 181–309.

5. Poems added by the Author in later editions of his works, pp. 311–325.

6. Poems written in middle and later life, but never published by the Author among his works, pp. 327–400.

7. Translations, pp. 403–512.

No notes are placed at the foot of the page, except those that were written by the Author himself. It was thought better to put my own Notes at the end, so as to present an unbroken page—easy to do in this case, because, except in the translations from Milton, there are few recondite allusions in Cowper's works. But I hope it will be found that all needful explanations have been given, and that the Notes are more complete than in any other edition. I have not burdened them with discussion of every variation in reading, only naming these in special cases. But all the editions have been most scrupulously and carefully collated, and each reading has been duly weighed.

In my frequent references to Macaulay's Essays and Mahon's (Lord Stanhope's) History, necessary to explain Cowper's allusions, it may save time to mention that I have always used the "People's Edition" of Macaulay, and the "Cabinet" of Mahon.

INTRODUCTORY MEMOIR.

BOTH by father and mother Cowper was of gentle blood. His father's family is traced back without interruption to the time of Edward IV., when the Cowpers were possessors of land at Strode, in the parish of Slinfold, in Sussex. His mother was Ann, daughter of Roger Donne of Ludham Hall, Norfolk, of the same family as Dr. Donne, the Dean of St. Paul's, and said to be "descended through four different lines from King Henry III."[*]

A younger member of the Cowper family, leaving Strode in the possession of his elder brother, settled in London in the reign of Henry VIII., married an heiress, Margaret Spencer, and bought an estate at Nonington, in Kent. His son John,[†] Alderman of London, who died in 1609, was the father of Sir William, the first baronet. Sir William is noteworthy for his love and reverence for Hooker, "his spiritual father," as Walton calls him. It was he who erected the monument to the great divine in Bishopsbourne Church, and composed the epitaph for it, which will not be out of place here.

> " Though nothing can be spoke worthy his fame,
> Or the remembrance of that precious name,
> Judicious HOOKER ; though this cost be spent
> On him that hath a lasting monument
> In his own books ; yet ought we to express,
> If not his worth, yet our respectfulness.
> Church ceremonies he maintain'd ; then why
> Without all ceremony should he die ?
> Was it because his life and death should be
> Both equal patterns of humility ?
> Or that, perhaps, this only glorious one
> Was above all, to ask, why had he none ?
> Yet he that lay so long obscurely low,
> Doth now preferr'd to greater honours go.
> Ambitious men, learn hence to be more wise,
> Humility is the true way to rise :
> And God in me this lesson did inspire,
> To bid this humble man, ' Friend, sit up higher.' "

Sir William was an ardent Churchman and Royalist, and was imprisoned with his son John during the Commonwealth. The latter died in prison, leaving an

---

[*] Johnson's Memoir, p. xii.
[†] Up to this time the name was spelt *Cooper*, and it has never been pronounced otherwise by the family. He altered it, probably in affectation of the Norman spelling "Cupere," or "Coupre," as the names appear in the roll of Battle Abbey. Many of the family, however, retained the old spelling for some time after. In Lord Campbell's Life of Chancellor Cowper, we have one or two letters signed "Wm. Cooper."

infant son, who on Sir William's death in 1664 succeeded to the title, and by his marriage with one Sarah Holled became father of two sons, William and Spencer. The former became Lord Chancellor, and an Earl, in 1706. Spencer having been tried for murder and acquitted,* became Chief Justice of Chester, and a Judge of the Common Pleas. He died in 1728, leaving three sons, William, John, and Ashley, and several daughters. One of these married Colonel Madan, and became the mother of Martin Madan, whose name will occur several times in this volume, and of Frances Maria, who married her cousin Major Cowper, and became one of Cowper's constant correspondents.

The second of the three sons became the Rev. John Cowper, Chaplain to King George II., and Rector of Great Berkhamstead. He married Ann Donne ; and at the rectory (or as her son afterwards called it, "the pastoral house") she gave birth to the future poet on the 26th of November (O. S. 15th), 1731. The house was pulled down to make room for a new rectory about thirty years ago. His parents had five other children, all of whom died in infancy except John. He lived until manhood, but his birthday was a heavy day for Berkhamstead parsonage. The mother died at the age of thirty-four.† It was the 14th of November, 1737. William therefore was just six years old. In what sacred remembrance the gentle child held her love and care of him we shall find in more than one passage of his life. When heavy clouds gathered round his spirit in years after, and seemed altogether to hide the blessing of God from him, the image of his mother remained clear in his memory, one bright spot which told him that there was a Heaven above. The gift of her picture, which he received fifty-three years after her death, gave him the occasion to pour out all his love and gratitude in what is probably the most touching elegy in the English language.

The death of his mother, generally the heaviest loss which a child can have, was a more than ordinary calamity here. He was delicate in body, sensitive and nervous in mind. His father, zealous towards his flock, and, according to his son's testimony, labouring to do them good, appears not to have understood his child's extreme need of sympathy and care. Within a year of his mother's death the poor boy was sent to school at a Dr. Pitman's, at Markyate Street, a straggling, unattractive village between St. Alban's and Dunstable. There he remained for two years, the victim of systematic bullying from some of his school companions. His shyness, sensibility, ill-health, were all converted into means of tormenting him. There was one boy in particular who persecuted him so relentlessly that Cowper writes in his autobiography, "I had such a dread of him, that I did not dare lift my eyes to his face. I

---

* Lord Campbell gives the case at length (Chancellors, iv. 260). He decides that the verdict was a righteous one, though the case was not without suspicion. Macaulay (History of England, chapter xxv.) holds the charge to be absolutely groundless, got up out of nothing but political spite.
† She is buried within the altar-rails of Berkhamstead Church.

knew him best by his shoe-buckle." This cruelty was at length discovered, the brute was expelled, and Cowper was removed from the school.

Meanwhile another trouble had fallen upon the child, inflammation of the eyes. Accordingly, he spent the next two years in the house of an oculist, leading a dull, and apparently not a healthy, life. However, his sight became better, and at ten years of age his father sent him to Westminster.

Cowper has spoken at great length in his autobiography of the religious feelings and fancies of his boyish days. These need not detain us. Most children have strong though often transient religious impressions, and there is little in his account of his own which has not probably befallen other boys. Later in life he looked back upon his feelings through the light of his morbid fancies, and exaggerated their significance.

It would be more to the purpose if we could discover anything concerning the religious teaching which he received in his childhood, for unquestionably it left its mark upon him for many a year. All writers agree in holding that it was an evil time both in faith and practice. The company in which Mr. Pattison found himself in his excellent *Essay on the Religious Thought of the* 18th *Century,** has somewhat discredited that essay. But it is at any rate valuable for our present purpose, as gathering up into short compass the characteristics of the time in which young Cowper was brought up. "It was a period," writes Mr. Pattison in the opening of his essay, "of decay of religion, licentiousness of morals, public corruption, profaneness of language,—a day of rebuke and blasphemy. Even those who look with suspicion on the contemporary complaints from the Jacobite clergy of 'decay of religion,' will not hesitate to say that it was an age destitute of depth and earnestness ; an age whose poetry was without romance, whose philosophy was without insight, and whose public men were without character ; an age of 'light without love,' whose very merits were of the earth, earthy."

This is certainly true in the general, though there are certain qualifications which the author makes in the course of his essay. Our concern at this moment is with the *theology* of the period. And that may be summed up in a word—it was the period of the *Evidences.* Let us hear Mr. Pattison once more. "Dogmatic theology had ceased to exist ; the exhibition of religious truth for practical purposes was confined to a few obscure writers. Every one who had anything to say on sacred subjects drilled it into an array of arguments against a supposed objector. Christianity appeared made for nothing else but to be 'proved ;' what use to make of it when it was proved was not much thought about. The only quality in Scripture which was dwelt on was its *credibility.*"

We may, then, fairly suppose that the worthy Rector of Berkhamstead was on a par with his brother clergy—that he would preach against the Deists, and marshal his arguments as well as he could ; but that he would not go beyond

* No. VI. in "Essays and Reviews."

this, nor exhibit in his sermons the depth and experience of the Christian life. If we add to this the tenderness and gentle piety of his wife, with little knowledge of religious differences or dogmatics, we shall probably be very near the mark in estimating the influences under which the child received his first religious instruction. That the Established religion was the true one, and could be proved so, that it promoted virtue and morality, this the boy must have been taught from the beginning; and probably not much beyond it. The death of his mother removed the last chance which remained of anything beyond intellectual teaching. And that this is not theology, but only the surrounding of it, that it cannot satisfy the spirit of man, many a one besides Cowper has found. He mentions in one of his letters, that when he was eleven years old his father gave him a treatise in favour of Suicide, and requested him to give his opinions upon it. It does not seem a high proof of parental wisdom. The oculist's household too, if the autobiography is not hard upon him, was unfavourable to religious feeling, and the atmosphere of Westminster School not much less so. The head master, Dr. Nicholls, in preparing him for Confirmation, made some impression upon him, he says, but it was transient. It had no root, and withered away. He did not apparently commit any great acts of sin, but he grew careless about religious things, and ceased to pray. Let it be considered that the mocking laughter of Fielding was now in full vigour, in entire harmony with a wide-spread public opinion, and that it was holding up to unsparing ridicule what the boy had been taught to look upon as religion, and we shall hardly wonder that he was fascinated by the daring and recklessness of it, and, conscious of that, began to look upon himself as a young reprobate, at enmity with God.

Such thoughts, however, would be soon done with, and his life at Westminster seems to have been a very happy one. He not only became an excellent scholar, but was a good cricketer and football player ; * and was popular both with masters and boys. The usher of his form was Vincent Bourne (celebrated for his Latin poetry),† another usher was Dr. Pierson Lloyd. Among his schoolfellows were Robert Lloyd (son of the doctor), Warren Hastings and his future enemy Impey, George Colman, Charles Churchill, George Cumberland, and William Russell. His intimacy with these at school was for the most part brought to an end, as is usual in such cases, by their parting. But we shall see how various passages in the course of his life brought back the memory of old times. Of all his friendships here the warmest were those with Russell and Lloyd. The former was, a few years later, drowned while bathing, at a time when Cowper was in deep distress from another cause. He has blended both sorrows together in an effusion which shows how deep the love between them was (p. 15).

Lloyd was a clever, showy youth, who in due course graduated at Cambridge, and became, like his father, an usher at Westminster. But the irregularities of his life,

---

* See *Tirocinium*, p. 294.   † See pp. 172 and 472, and notes on them.

and his impatience of steady work, brought this to an end, and he betook himself to the precarious profession of literature. A clever poem called "The Actor" gained a very favourable reception ; and Cowper, who made swans, not unfrequently, of very small geese, called him "the successor of Prior." Public taste has not ratified the verdict, and Lloyd is no longer reckoned among the English poets. His poetical abilities were undoubtedly good, but his habitual indolence, which prevented him from seeking worthy materials, as well as from bestowing the needful labour upon what he wrote, blighted his hopes.

Churchill's poems were of a much higher order. What can be said in mitigation of the follies and excesses of his life has been said admirably by Mr. Forster.* Lloyd, who is said to have been attached to Churchill's sister, took to his bed on hearing of his death, saying, "Ah! I shall soon follow poor Charles." The one died in November, the other in December, 1764. The way in which Cowper afterwards spoke of these friends is very characteristic of him. In the abstract he was not only most indignant at wrong-doing, but he was censorious ; ready to take an unfairly bad view of motives, as well as to condemn trivial faults without measure. He denounces oratorios, chess, whist-playing, and smoking, as severely as he does breaches of the moral law. But when he afterwards came across a smoker in the person of his friend Bull, his anger and scorn were over and done with directly. In the estimate of all his personal acquaintants he was the most charitable of men. And so when the voice of society pronounced Churchill only a good-for-nothing rake, Cowper took occasion to express his hearty admiration of the man.† Macaulay, speaking of his chivalrous sonnet to Warren Hastings, attributes it to Cowper's partiality.‡ No doubt ; yet Cowper's estimate is still, not improbably, a righteous one. Intimate knowledge of men shows that none are devils, and the tone of affection which comes natural to us need not be out of unison with the voice of heavenly love, which has bidden us judge none, but hope the best of all. So different as these two men were, Cowper learned his poetic style from the works of Churchill. The versification is very similar, and the realism which Churchill revived with such felicitous results to our literature was taken up by Cowper. It may be mentioned here that his first poem (p. 1), written while he was still at Westminster, was an imitation of John Philips' "Splendid Shilling." Its easy and finished rhythm proves that it was by no means the only attempt of the kind. He says in one of his letters, that he translated an elegy of Tibullus when he was fourteen. He also read the English poets with delight, especially Milton and Cowley. With regard to Milton, he says that he was quite unhappy because he had not made his acquaintance till he was fourteen, and so the previous years had suffered a loss which could never be made up. He appears to have known Milton nearly by heart.

* "Defoe and Churchill." Two Essays, by John Forster.
† Table Talk, p. 62.   ‡ Essays, vol. ii. p. 183.

He left Westminster in 1748, and was entered of the Middle Temple. After spending nine months in his father's house, he was articled for three years to a solicitor, Mr. Chapman, of Ely Place, Holborn. Not far off, in Southampton Row, lived his uncle Ashley, afterwards Clerk of the Parliaments.* He had three daughters; two of them, Harriet and Theodora, were ripening into womanhood. It was arranged that William was to visit them every Sunday, and this soon led to his being there continually on week-days. He was "to be found there," he said afterwards, "from morning to night, giggling and making giggle." In this pleasant occupation he was much assisted by a fellow-clerk at Mr. Chapman's, whom he had introduced at his uncle's house. This clerk, Edward Thurlow by name, was Cowper's junior by a few months. He had been educated at the King's School, Canterbury, and afterwards at Cambridge; and though wayward, and given to continual breaches of discipline, had been able, by fits of application and hard work, to make himself a good scholar. In like manner now, though he lounged about places of amusement and drank much punch, he contrived to give himself a good knowledge of law. Cowper saw the young man's great powers, and his knack of turning to account everything that he acquired, and one day said to him: "Thurlow, I am nobody, and shall always be nobody, and you will be Lord Chancellor. You shall provide for me when you are!" Thurlow smiled and said, "I surely will!" "These ladies are witnesses," said Cowper. "Let them be," answered Thurlow, "for I will certainly do it." The same prophecy had been made to Thurlow when a little boy, by a clergyman named Leach, and possibly the repetition of it by Cowper led to this lightly-made compact now. Cowper's prophecy was fulfilled, but not Thurlow's promise.

Thus, pleasantly rather than profitably, the three years of clerkship went by, and when they were ended Cowper was deeply in love with Theodora, and his love was as tenderly returned. The progress of this courtship, the quarrels and renewals of love, the young gentleman's bashfulness, and his increased care for his personal appearance,—all these things are described for us, as well as such matters can be, in the poems which courtship produced. I cannot at all agree with Mr. Bell's judgment of them. "Cowper," he says, "was not capable of very strong emotions. The shadow of love seems to have hovered about him, but he was indifferent to the reality. We look in vain for the fervour of a youthful devotion." Whilst the young poet was pluming his wings, consciously imitating others, it is no wonder that some of these early love pieces are artificial. To me at least it is evident that his passion became anything but a shadow "which made no lasting impression upon him." Cowper was very reserved all his life on other matters

---

* Ashley Cowper was a very little man, and he used to wear a white hat lined with yellow. On which two facts Cowper once expressed his opinion that it would not be surprising if some day he should be "picked" by mistake for a mushroom, and popped into a basket.

besides this, but I believe that his love-affair affected the whole of his life very deeply.

For a while the course of love ran tolerably smooth. But when, on the expiration of his clerkship, he went into residence at the Temple, in 1752, a fresh shadow soon fell upon his course. Seclusion had its natural effect upon the nervous sensitive youth, and he had hard work to drive melancholy away. He tried first medicine, then religiosity, reading George Herbert, and "composing a set of prayers." Herbert, he says, relieved him a good deal: "I found in him a strain of piety which I could not but admire." But "a very near and dear relation" (probably Madan) disapproved of Herbert, and he was laid aside. His friends found a better cure for morbidness in taking him away for change of scene. He went with Mr. Hesketh, the affianced lover of his cousin Harriet, to Southampton, and remained some months there. In his autobiography he gives more of his morbid feelings and thoughts here, which we again pass by. At length, much relieved, he returned to London in 1754, and was called to the Bar. But Ashley Cowper soon saw, or had already seen, enough of his nephew's aptitude for business to induce him to take an important step. He refused to sanction his daughter's engagement. The young lady pleaded with such earnestness as to shake his resolution for a while, but he returned to it, and after a considerable interval, during which some communication was still allowed, he forbade the lovers from meeting. The young lady regretfully submitted, and they never saw each other again. And Cowper never mentions her in any of his poems or letters. Nor does he write of love in any of his future poems. That he was mortified and angry appears from several slight but unmistakeable proofs. Meanwhile few will read without pity the effusions belonging to the latter part of his courtship, evidently the faithful picture of his alternating hopes and fears, until all hope was at an end.* The effect upon Theodora was deep and lasting. She never loved again, but always took the deepest interest in hearing about him. She read his poems with eagerness, and afterwards, as we shall see, showed her unaltered affection in a more substantial way. The verses which he had written to her she treasured up until the close of her life. Then, at a time when she also had apparently sunk into melancholy, she gave them in a sealed packet, for reasons which can only be guessed at, to a friend, directing that the packet should be opened after her death. The friend and she died nearly together, in 1824, and the sealed packet was then sent to her nephew Mr. Croft. He published them the following year, as we have already told.†

Other sorrows had fallen on Cowper besides the loss of his love. His father died in July 1756; and although Cowper's connexion with Berkhamstead had never been continuous since his mother's death, he had always retained a warm affection for it. The connexion now ceased entirely; and he says the parting with it was most bitter to him. His father had married again, and the widow

---

* Pages 11—15.   † P. xviii. No. 12.

continued to reside there. But her stepson and she, though friendly, were not intimate, and he never visited her, though they occasionally corresponded. She died not very long afterwards. His brother John was now at Cambridge, studying for holy orders.

The profession of a barrister is generally more honourable than lucrative for the first few years. It certainly was so in Cowper's case, for it is doubtful whether he ever had a brief.[*] He moved from the Middle to the Inner Temple, and bought chambers there for £250. The little money which he had was fast diminishing, and his father's death warned him that this was a matter which would have to be attended to without loss of time. One or two of his letters exist, written at this time; he speaks lightly on the matter,[†] but one may say with tolerable certainty that a very anxious heart lay beneath the jesting manner, and that the anxiety increased every day. Though this may not have been the cause of the melancholy which soon after appeared, the forced hilarity is painful enough when one knows what followed. He was made a Commissioner of Bankrupts about this time through family influence, which brought him £60 a year.

He was now a member of the _Nonsense Club_,[‡] consisting of some old "West-minsters," among them Robert Lloyd and Colman. The leading member was Bonnell Thornton, another old Westminster boy, but much Cowper's senior. He had already made several essays in authorship, before he started, in company with Colman, the _Connoisseur_. The first number was published January 31, 1754, and it was continued weekly, until September 30, 1756. Cowper contributed a few papers to the last volume. The following were his.[§] I take the titles from the table of contents to the volumes.

> No. 111.—_Letter, containing the character of the delicate Billy Suckling._
>
> No. 115.—_Letter from Christopher Ironside, an old Bachelor, complaining of the indignities received by him from the ladies._
>
> No. 119.—_Of keeping a secret.—Characters of faithless confidantes._
>
> No. 134.—_Letter from Mr. Village, giving an account of the present state of Country Churches, their Clergy, and their Congregations._
>
> No. 138.—_On Conversation. The chief pests of Society pointed out. Those who converse irrationally, considered as imitating the language of different animals._

[*] A letter to Hill, dated October 10, 1767, after asking a law question, contains the following: "You are a better counsellor than I was, but I think you have much such a client in me as I had in Dick Harcourt."

[†] "This provokes me, that a covetous dog who will work by candlelight in the morning, to get what he does not want, shall be praised for his thriftiness, while a gentleman shall be abused for submitting to his wants, rather than work like an ass to relieve them. . . There are some sensible folks, who, having great estates, have wisdom enough to spend them properly; there are others, who are not less wise, perhaps, as knowing how to shift without 'em. . . This is a strange epistle, nor can I imagine how the devil I came to write it."—_Letter to Rowley_, September 2, 1762.

[‡] The Nonsense Club originated the "Exhibition of Sign Painters," a piece of drollery which, without giving offence, made much fun of the newly-opened Royal Academy. It consisted of a number of daubs, with humorous descriptions in the catalogue, and was very successful.

[§] The evidence of their authorship is as follows: Southey says they are "all attributed to the same author in the concluding pages of the volume." (Life, vol. i. p. 325.) But this is a mistake, for the words at the end of the volume are, "From a friend, a gentleman of the Temple, we

More than this, he "produced several half-penny ballads, two or three of which had the honour to become popular."* It is unfortunate that they are lost, for half-penny ballads by the Author of "John Gilpin" would certainly have been worth preserving. He also contributed a few papers to the *St. James's Chronicle*, of which Thornton and Colman were part proprietors. He kept up his classical studies also, especially that of Homer, and translated two books of Voltaire's " Henriade," said to have been published in a magazine in 1759. The humorous ode given at p. 21 of this volume was printed in the *St. James's Chronicle*. It was not signed with his name, and there is no direct evidence to prove that it was his; but as Southey thought it to be so, all succeeding editions have included it. (See *note* on it.)

But by the time that ode was published, a dreadful calamity had fallen upon Cowper. He had gone mad. We have seen already that he had had melancholy fits at school. The opening lines of his Epistle to Lloyd (p. 9), written in 1754, show that these fits had taken an intenser form, and, as we have said, his fears of poverty probably made matters worse. An event which happened in 1763, which for the moment filled him with joy, brought the catastrophe. The Clerk of the Journals of the House of Lords died, and the gentleman who held the two offices of Reading Clerk and Clerk of Committees resigned at the same time. The right of presentation to all the appointments belonged to Major Cowper, who immediately offered the two most lucrative of them to his cousin. The offer was no sooner accepted, than Cowper began to reproach himself with having wished for the former holder's death, and therefore being a murderer. First one fancy, then another. After a week he begged his cousin to give the more lucrative places to a friend, a Mr. Arnold, and the poorest, the Clerkship of the Journals, to himself. With a little demur (for in the eyes of the world, which did not know the circumstances, there would be some suspicion of bribery) the Major consented to this, and for a week or two there was calm.

But very soon came another obstacle. A powerful party in the Lords contested the Major's right to nominate. An inquiry was begun, and the new clerk was told that he must give evidence of qualification at the bar of the House. At this news he broke down again, not immediately, for he tried and tried again for more than half a year to prepare for examination, but all was of no use. Each day his terrors increased; a visit to Margate checked them, for a letter exists written

---

received Nos. 111, 115, and 119." The other two are not referred to. They, with No. 119, are given as Cowper's by Hayley, whose authority in this matter is conclusive. He says, "During Cowper's visit to Eartham, he kindly pointed out to me three of his papers in the last volume of the *Connoisseur*. I inscribed them with his name at the time, and find other numbers of that work ascribed to him, but the three following I print as his, on his own explicit authority." (Vol. iv. p. 384.) No. 119 is also mentioned by Cowper himself, in one of his letters, as having been written by him. He says that the writing of it had a good effect upon him: " I have never broken a secret since."

* Letter to Newton, Dec. 4, 1781.

to his cousin Harriet, now become Lady Hesketh, in which he is fairly cheerful. But on his return the evil spirit returned once more. His cousin came to the Temple to see him, but he would not speak to her nor look at her. He has written down a long account of these days in his autobiography, but one's memory recoils from it,— from the attempts upon his life with laudanum and knife and cord. The last time his purpose hardly failed. On that occasion he so far recovered from his dream as to be conscience-stricken ; but this brought no relief, nothing but the conviction that he was damned beyond hope.

God knows whether any human means could have drawn him forth out of this horrible pit ; but we who behold in Christ the healer of all infirmities, the caster-forth of devils, must believe that to have followed His steps by telling of the infinite love of God to His creatures might have brought the blessing of health. But no such message reached poor Cowper. His cousin Martin Madan, chaplain of the Lock Hospital, and a strong Calvinist, came to visit him. He spoke of the efficacy of Christ's blood for justification ; and the poor sufferer, as he says, began to feel his heart burn within him, and the tears which he had just before declared impossible flowed freely, as hope sprung up in his heart. But when Madan began with his restrictions, the necessity of certain feelings, the hopelessness of the case in which they were absent, this hope was again thrown away. All the confusions and fancies of vague thoughts and opinions tossed and surged around him, and that faith in God's everlasting love which might have guided him safely was not there. He was at the mercy of every wind of vain doctrine. Every text of the Bible, and every religious word, was turned into fresh proof that the mouth of hell was opened upon him, and he wrote the awful sapphics which are given at p. 23. His relatives, rightly judging that there was no other resource left to them, placed him in a lunatic asylum at St. Alban's. This was on December 7, 1763.

The proprietor of this asylum, Dr. Nathanael Cotton, possessed a high name for his professional skill, and was also a man of great moral worth.* He had also won considerable popularity as a writer of verse. His "Visions" passed through many editions ; and though they are no longer read, they contain a good deal of sound sense and practical benevolence. He died in 1788. Under his judicious care Cowper slowly recovered. The physician saw this before the patient, and summoned his brother. The first meeting was a disappointment, for Cowper put on a stiff reserve, but he recovered himself, and improved daily. He was now filled with religious fervour ; he had received from his heavenly Father, he said, the full assurance of faith, and out of his stony heart had been raised up a child unto Abraham. It was a good and righteous conviction, but it did not go far enough. It made its foundation upon his own feelings, and not upon God's love. His is not the only case where such ecstasy breaks down. In some it is followed by desperate plunges into sin again ; in this, despair again after a

* Notice of his life in Anderson's "Poets," vol. xi. p. 1105.

while supervened. Yet transient feelings of such joy are feelings to be thankful for, when we regard them as God's testimony of a love which is *not* transient, of an eternal mercy and loving-kindness.*

Immediately after his recovery he wrote the hymn at p. 37 :

"How blessed thy creature is, O God."

What a contrast to the production which he had last written, "Hatred and Vengeance " !

Though his recovery took place within three or four months after he was sent to Dr. Cotton's, Cowper continued there for a year, apparently dreading a relapse, and unequal to the task of facing the rough world. But he was very poor, and already owed Dr. Cotton money, and so determined to remove to some quiet home. The hymn at p. 37—

"Far from the world, O Lord, I flee "—

was written while thinking over this matter. London he would see no more, and he threw up his Commissionership of Bankrupts, and with it nearly all his income —to wit, £60 a year. His relations, feeling that this was unavoidable, subscribed together to make him an annual allowance.

His brother was now Fellow of St. Benet's College, Cambridge, and he wished to find lodgings near him. But none suitable could be found nearer than Huntingdon, and hither he moved in June 1765, accompanied by a lad who had waited on him at Dr. Cotton's. With this exception he was entirely surrounded by strangers ; but the quiet tranquil town suited him well. " I do really think it the most agreeable neighbourhood I ever saw," he wrote. There were morning and evening prayers daily in the church, which he always attended ; there was the Ouse for him to bathe in, and many pleasant walks. Some of the residents used to send him books and newspapers. The Rector, Mr. Hodgson, and Curate, Mr. Nicholson, called upon him, and he liked them both.† Then the brothers met every week, at Cambridge and Huntingdon alternately, and this caused him to become a horseman.

Soon after his arrival he was visited by an old London friend, whose name has hitherto not been mentioned, but who always held one of the foremost places in his affection, Joseph Hill. Nothing is known of his early life, except that he had been an old Westminster boy, and also one of the members of the Nonsense Club. He was an attorney, living in George Street, Westminster. Cowper had introduced him to Thurlow, who, on his appointment to the Chancellorship afterwards, made him his secretary. He had kindly managed Cowper's

---

* Maurice's " Prophets and Kings of the Old Testament," pp. 33, 34.

† " Another acquaintance I have lately made is with a Mr. Nicholson, a north-country divine, very poor, but very good and very happy. He reads prayers here twice a day all the year round, and travels on foot to serve two churches every Sunday ; his journey out and home again being sixteen miles. I supped with him last night. He gave me bread and cheese, and a black jug of ale brewed with his own hands."—*To Lady Hesketh*, September 14, 1765.

affairs during his illness, and now gratuitously made himself his general agent in town, disposing of his rooms in the Temple, arranging his money matters, and receiving the bounty of his kinsmen. With him and with Lady Hesketh Cowper now began that regular correspondence which has won for him the praise of being "the best letter writer in the English language." His letters to Hill are playful, and relate mostly to his finances; those to Lady Hesketh are entirely of a religious character. He is still enraptured with his own religious condition, and hints that he would fain see her even as himself. It is evident that though no one could have had a higher regard for him, she had little sympathy with his religious fervour. We note in passing that she sent him "Hervey's Meditations," and that he was delighted with it. Besides these, he opened correspondence next year with Major Cowper and his wife. The latter, it will be remembered, was also his first cousin, sister to Martin Madan, and therefore, in Cowper's present state of feeling, a peculiarly acceptable correspondent. Several of his letters to her are a discussion of the question of mutual recognition in heaven, he holding the affirmative against her negative. From one of them we learn that he had formed an idea of taking orders. Fortunately he abandoned it. Meanwhile his finances became embarrassed. The following extract from a letter, written less than a fortnight after he got to Huntingdon, is amusing, but very much to the purpose. It is addressed to Hill.

"DEAR JOE,—Whatever you may think of the matter, it is no such easy thing to keep house for two people. A man cannot always live upon sheeps' heads, and liver and lights, like the lions in the Tower; and a joint of meat, in so small a family, is an endless encumbrance. My butcher's bill for last week amounted to four shillings and tenpence. I set off with a leg of lamb, and was forced to give part of it away to a washerwoman. Then I made an experiment upon a sheep's heart, and that was too little. Next I put three pounds of beef into a pie, and this had like to have been too much, for it lasted three days, though my landlord was admitted to a share in it. Then as to small-beer, I am puzzled to pieces about it. I have bought as much for a shilling as will serve us at least a month, and it is grown sour already. In short, I never knew how to pity poor housekeepers before; but now I cease to wonder at that politic cast which their occupation usually gives to their countenance, for it is really a matter full of perplexity." *

This prepares us for the announcement by and by that he has "contrived, by the help of good management and a clear notion of economical affairs, to spend the income of a twelvemonth" between June and September. His relatives wrote to scold him for what they considered extravagance, and a few months later Colonel (late Major) Cowper threatened to give him nothing more. While this correspondence was going on, he received an anonymous letter, telling him that if the threatened withdrawal should take place, he had one who loved and admired him, who would supply the deficiency. He thought that Lady Hesketh was the writer, but it is more likely, as will be seen hereafter, that it was her sister, Cowper's former love. His anxiety was naturally returning. Besides, Huntingdon shows to less advantage in the decline of the year than in June, and his outdoor pursuits were becoming circumscribed. But at this critical moment a happy accident came to his relief. His daily attendance at church, his solitariness, his

* July 3, 1765.

quiet and thoughtful face, strongly attracted the notice of a young man who had just returned home after graduating at Cambridge. He wished to call on Mr. Cowper, but his mother was against it, having heard that the stranger did not care for company. However, he addressed him one morning after church, and was cordially met. They took a walk together, were mutually delighted, and Cowper invited him to tea that afternoon. The new acquaintance was named William Cawthorne Unwin.

His father, the Rev. Morley Unwin, had some years before been master of the Free School at Huntingdon, but in 1742 had received the college living of Grimston, in Norfolk. On this appointment he had married Mary Cawthorne (much younger than himself), the pretty, clever daughter of a draper at Ely. Their son was baptized at Grimston, March 15, 1744. But Mrs. Unwin did not like Grimston,* and persuaded her husband to become non-resident. He returned with his two children (for they had now also a daughter) to Huntingdon, where he took pupils. Cowper, writing to Hill, describes this family, into which he was now introduced, as " the most agreeable people imaginable, quite sociable, and free from the ceremonious civility of country gentlefolks. The old gentleman is a man of learning and sense, and as simple as Parson Adams." He tells Lady Hesketh that he has just come from a two hours' walk with Mrs. U., and that "the conversation has done him more good than an audience of the first prince in Europe." He finds that they "have one faith, and have been baptized with the same baptism," and "gives God thanks, *who has brought him into the society of Christians.*"

The intimacy increased, and Cowper found himself there constantly. In a few weeks (Nov. 1765) a pupil left Mr. Unwin. Cowper then begged to be taken as their lodger, and they gladly consented. The first agreement was that he should pay them eighty guineas a year ; but when his means threatened to fall short, she offered to take half this sum. The following extract from a letter to his cousin, Mrs. Cowper, describes their manner of life together :—

"I am obliged to you for the interest you take in my welfare, and for your inquiring so particularly after the manner in which my time passes here. As to amusements, I mean what the world calls such, we have none—the place indeed swarms with them ; and cards and dancing are the professed business of almost all the *gentle* inhabitants of Huntingdon. We refuse to take part in them, or to be accessaries

---

* From a kind and interesting letter which I have received from the Rev. J. Rowlands, the present Rector of Grimston, it appears that Mr. Unwin resided at Grimston from 1742 to 1748, though it is startling to find that his signature never appears in the church registers before 1765. This does not prove that he did nothing, for in old registers the Occasional Offices are not each attested by the signature of the officiating minister. But the absence of his name altogether, and the appearance of his curate's where a signature is needed, proves that the curate did the greater part of the work. On his return to Huntingdon he became lecturer at the parish church. The parish books contain several resolutions of censure upon him for neglect of his duty, and once he was nearly dismissed. Mr. Rowlands gives me reasons for supposing that he resigned Grimston in 1766.

to this way of murdering our time, and by so doing have acquired the name of Methodists.   Having told you how we *do not* spend our time, I will next say how we do.   We breakfast commonly between eight and nine; till eleven we read either the Scriptures or the sermons of some faithful preacher of those holy mysteries; at eleven we attend Divine Service, which is performed here twice every day; and from twelve to three we separate and amuse ourselves as we please. During that interval I either read in my own apartment, or walk, or ride, or work in the garden.*   We seldom sit an hour after dinner, but, if the weather permits, adjourn to the garden, where, with Mrs. Unwin and her son, I have generally the pleasure of religious conversation till tea-time.   If it rains, or is too windy for walking, we either converse within-doors, or sing some hymns of Martin's† collection, and by the help of Mrs. Unwin's harpsichord make up a tolerable concert, in which our hearts, I hope, are the best and most musical performers.   After tea we sally forth to walk in good earnest.   Mrs. Unwin is a good walker, and we have generally travelled about four miles before we see home again.   When the days are short, we make this excursion in the former part of the day, between church-time and dinner.   At night we read and converse, as before, till supper, and commonly finish the evening either with hymns or a sermon, and, last of all, the family are called to prayers.   I need not tell *you* that such a life as this is consistent with the utmost cheerfulness; accordingly we are all happy, and dwell together in unity as brethren."

We must give one more extract—a proof of his sensitiveness, or rather of his high-minded conscientiousness.   William Unwin was going to London, and Cowper gave him an introduction to Mrs. Cowper.   In writing afterwards to thank her for her courteous reception of his friend, he goes on to denounce his own vile and deceitful heart.   He had wanted Unwin to call on her, because there were people who looked down upon him, and had even gone the length of calling him "that fellow Cowper;" so he could not resist the opportunity of furnishing the Unwins with ocular demonstration of his high connexion.   Upon this discovery of his own heart he bursts out:

"Oh Pride! Pride! it deceives with the subtlety of a serpent, and seems to walk erect, though it crawls upon the earth.   How will it twist and twine itself about to get from under the Cross which it is the glory of our Christian calling to be able to bear with patience and good-will.   They who can guess at the heart of a stranger, and you especially, who are of a compassionate temper, will be more ready, perhaps, to excuse me, in this instance, than I can be to excuse myself.   But, in good truth, it was abominable pride of heart, indignation, and vanity, and deserves no better name.   How should such a creature be admitted into those pure and sinless mansions, where nothing shall enter that defileth, did not the blood of Christ, applied by the hand of faith, take away the guilt of sin, and leave no spot or stain behind it?   Oh what continual need have I of an Almighty, All-sufficient Saviour!"   (April 3, 1767.)

---

* He says in another letter: "I am become a great florist and shrub-doctor. If the Major can make up a small packet of seeds for a garden where there is little but jessamine and honey-suckle, I will promise to take great care of them."

† Martin Madan, Mrs. Cowper's brother.   He had some musical skill.   The popular tune *Helmsley*, "Lo! He comes with clouds descending," was composed by him.

The tranquil life at Huntingdon was destroyed by a sudden blow. On the 28th June, 1767, Mr. Unwin, while riding to church, was thrown from his horse, fractured his skull, and died four days afterwards. The two children were started in life. William was ordained to a curacy, and his sister* was soon afterwards married to the Rev. Matthew Powley, Vicar of Dewsbury. It was necessary for Mrs. Unwin to remove, and Cowper determined to go with her, as her behaviour to him had " always been that of a mother to a son," and, moreover, " Mr. Unwin had intimated to his wife his desire that if she survived him, Mr. Cowper might still dwell with her." †

A few days after Unwin's death, the Rev. John Newton, Curate of Olney, on his way thither from Cambridge, had stayed at Huntingdon, and called on Mrs. Unwin, at the request of a friend. Much interested both in her and Cowper, he agreed, at their request, to look out for a house for them. He soon found them one at Olney, and they removed thither on the 14th of September, 1767.

The Rev. John Newton, under whose influence Cowper was thus brought, was about five years his senior. He had passed through the strangest vicissitudes of fortune. In his youth he had been a sailor of idle and vicious habits, had been flogged for desertion, and was only prevented from drowning himself by fearing that the lady whom he afterwards married would form a bad opinion of him. He suffered frightful miseries in a slave plantation at Sierra Leone, and after being released was shipwrecked on his way home, and barely saved his life. This event, which he was always wont to call his "Great Deliverance," changed his character altogether. He resolved to lead a new life, and kept the resolution. Looking upon this as a special interposition of Providence on his behalf, he was a Calvinist from that time. He soon became master of a vessel, and for the next four years was engaged on the sea. From this time until his death, he kept a diary, of which the following passage is the opening, dated Dec. 22, 1751 :—

" I dedicate unto Thee, most blessed God, this clean, unsullied book : and at the same time renew my tender of a foul, blotted, corrupt heart. Be pleased, O Lord, to assist me with the influences of Thy Spirit to fill the one in a manner agreeable to Thy will, and by Thy all-sufficient grace to overpower and erase the ill impressions sin and the world have from time to time made in the other, so that both my public converse and retired meditation may testify that I am indeed Thy servant, redeemed, renewed, and accepted in the sufferings, merit, and mediation of my Lord and Saviour Jesus Christ, to whom, with the Father and the Holy Spirit, be glory, honour, and dominion, world without end. Amen."

Then he goes on to detail the holy resolutions which he has made; amongst them is one to set apart a special day " to recommend himself and his concerns, his journey and his voyage," to the blessing of God. He speaks of his devotions with his crew, and ever and anon writes down prayers of intense and unquestionable earnestness. And at the end of his voyage he expresses his thankfulness to God for having prospered him so well. It may not have occurred to the reader to ask what was the business in which he was engaged. But it was the slave-trade.

---

* She lived till 1835, dying at the age of eighty-nine.
† This latter statement is made by Newton. (Bull's Memorials, p. 157.)

Forty years later, when Wilberforce was moving heaven and earth for abolition, Newton preached on the same side, and wrote his "Thoughts upon the African Slave-Trade," denouncing it unsparingly. "I am bound in conscience," he says, "to take shame to myself by a public confession, which, however sincere, comes too late to prevent or repair the misery and mischief to which I have formerly been accessory." And he adds,—what is probably just,—"Perhaps what I have said of myself may be applicable to the nation at large. The slave-trade was always unjustifiable, but inattention and self-interest prevented for a time the evil from being perceived." Newton's religiousness was unquestionably sincere and real, but his morality in this matter cannot be said to be of the highest kind, and both now and after he displays a want of deep reflection, as well as some selfishness of character. His "Cardiphonia" contains passages which are hardly surpassed for their beauty and earnest zeal towards God. And there, more than anywhere else that I know of, the large-heartedness of the man appears. He has come to the conclusion, even in the first letter (1775), that "observation and experience contribute, by the grace of God, gradually to soften and sweeten our spirits;" that Protestants, Papists, Socinians, are all his neighbours; and that he must not expect them to see with his eyes. Here speaks the man, not the theologian; for his sight was narrow as his heart was large. He is always seeking to interpret every "dispensation;" if he cannot do it at the moment, he is sure the interpretation will soon come. He cannot understand why Molly P. should have the small-pox at such an inconvenient time, and is surprised that his prayers for her have not yet been heard. In short, no man perhaps ever had a stronger faith in God's personal love for him; but that "the earth is the Lord's and the fulness thereof," was more apparently than had taken possession of his mind. The same kind of spirit is shown in his taking a lottery ticket some years afterwards, supposing that "his vow and his design of usefulness therein sanctioned his hope that the Lord would give him a prize."[*]

Severe illness brought Newton's seafaring life to an end, and he obtained the post of tide surveyor at Liverpool. During the time that he held it he was brought much into contact with Whitefield, and to some degree also with Wesley. In 1764, after difficulties which he showed great courage in overcoming, he was ordained to the curacy of Olney. There can be no question that the step was taken from a love for the souls of men, and that it was done at a great personal sacrifice. The same year he made the acquaintance of Wilberforce, and of John Thornton.[†]

[*] I cannot forbear referring to Sir James Stephen's wise and weighty words concerning Newton. I had not read them until the above was in type, but it is gratifying to be able to claim him in support of my view. Essay on *the Evangelical Succession*, p. 114.

[†] John Thornton was born in 1720, and succeeded his father as a Russian merchant. He was remarkably keen and skilful in business, and to the end of his life was always on the look-out for good investments. There is a story that he strolled along Cork harbour, when an old man, saw a freight of tallow come in, and made a vast sum by buying it at once, then strolled into a nursery ground, and with the profits he had just made set an impoverished man on his feet. But his greatest acts of generosity, whether wise or unwise, were towards ministers of religion. He

The latter formed so high an opinion of him that he made him an allowance of £200 a year, mainly with the view of enabling him to keep open house, and so to influence the more people for good.

The labours of Newton (who lived till 1807) are of course no part of our subject, except so far as they illustrate Cowper's life. To the latter we therefore now pass on.

The house in which he now took up his residence is in the market-place at Olney. It was called Orchard Side. The vicarage, in which Newton lived, was close by, and he said afterwards that for twelve years he and Cowper were hardly ever twelve hours apart. "The first six," he adds, "were spent in admiring and trying to imitate him; during the second six I walked with him in the shadow of death."

Olney lies on the Ouse at the northern extremity of Buckinghamshire.* It is not an attractive town, and the staple occupations of its inhabitants, and whole neighbourhood, lacemaking and strawplaiting, were, and still are, very prejudicial to health, wealth, and godliness. The vicar, Moses Browne, was an absentee through debt, and there were no gentry. Cowper was commonly known there as "Sir Cowper." Newton fell in with the popular appellation, and calls him so often in his letters. Cowper says, later, in one of his letters, "We have

> "One parson, one poet, one bellman, one crier,
> And the poor poet is the only squire."

To minister among the poor here was a task requiring great energy and courage, arduous and, as far as this world is concerned, thankless. Newton, who had wonderful bodily strength and nerve, enjoyed it thoroughly, but certainly it was not suitable labour for the nervous, sensitive invalid, who now under Newton's guidance undertook it. He visited indefatigably, and read and prayed with the sick. Newton had started prayer-meetings at an uninhabited house in the town belonging to Lord Dartmouth,—the "Great House" it was called,—and the heat and excitement of these may be judged by any one who reads Newton's account. We need not say what a contrast such devotions were to the daily prayers in Huntingdon Church, and few will doubt that the change was not for the better to Cowper. But who would not tremble for the result when we add to this that he himself was called to take part in, sometimes to lead, the extempore prayers—he who had said of himself, when called on to qualify for his clerkship, "that doing anything in public was mortal poison" to him! Mr. Bull quotes the saying of some one who was there, that he "never heard praying that equalled Mr. Cowper's." But it was at a terrible cost. Nor was this all. He lost his regular exercise. He had been accustomed to a quiet evening walk, but "now," he says to Lady Hesketh, "we have sermon or lecture every evening, which lasts till supper-time."

bought up livings, and bestowed them on "truly religious" ministers. His sister married Wilberforce's uncle, and the Evangelicalism of Wilberforce was owing to this connexion. Thornton died in 1790. It was his brother-in-law, Dr. Conyers, who introduced Newton to Cowper.
* The most interesting description which has been written of Olney and its neighbourhood is that of Hugh Miller, in his "First Impressions of England."

Mr. Bull gives several letters from Mr. Newton belonging to this period. That they breathe real piety needs not to be said; but they are not altogether pleasing to read. Instead of enlarging upon God's care for His creatures, and His mercy toward every soul which seeks after Him, he gives highly-wrought pictures of particular providences, and searches after God's love in religious excitement. The Lord is to be found not in the still small voice, but in the wind, the earthquake, and the fire. Where these are not, so it might seem, God is not. As long as these feelings were kept alive by the unhealthful religious stimulants, Cowper could boast of his "decided Christian happiness." But a time comes when stimulants fail to act, and then reaction comes, and ruin with it.

Threatenings appeared from a very early period of his residence at Olney. In a letter to Hill, for instance, dated June 16, 1768, he expresses his belief that his life is drawing to an end. All his letters are upon religious topics, and generally gloomy in tone; he drops his old friends, and even writes chilling letters to Hill—one declining an invitation, another in reply to the announcement of his marriage. The common idea that his first years at Olney were happy ones is certainly not well-founded.

His melancholy was greatly increased by the death of his brother, which took place at Cambridge in March 1770. Their affection from infancy had been unbroken, and Cowper mourned for him deeply. He gave expression to his feelings by writing a memoir of him, which was afterwards published by Newton. (No. 9 in List of Works, p. xviii. See also the "Time Piece," 780—787.) His brother left £700, but £350 were owed to his college; the rest was transferred to Cowper's account by Hill. But he speaks of himself as being a considerable loser by his brother's death. He must therefore have received a regular allowance from him as well as from his other relatives.[*]

In 1771 Mr. Newton proposed that they should jointly compose a volume of hymns, partly "for the promotion of the faith and comfort of sincere Christians," partly to perpetuate the memory of their friendship. The work was undertaken, but not completed for 8 years. It was then published with this title :—

OLNEY HYMNS. IN THREE BOOKS.

Book I.—On Select Texts of Scripture.
II.—On Occasional Subjects.
III.—On the Spiritual Life.

Cantabitis, Arcades, inquit,
Montibus hæc vestris ; soli cantare periti
Arcades. O mihi tum quam molliter ossa quiescant,
Vestra meos olim si fistula dicat amores.
VIRG. *Ecl.* x. 31.

Rev. xiv. 3.
2 Cor. vi. 10.

[*] See letters to Hill, Nov. 5 and 17, 1772.

The volume is dated Olney, February 15, 1779, and contains 348 hymns, Cowper's being distinguished by a C.

Many of these compositions have become so popular, that a collection of hymns without them would seem incomplete. Such, for example, is Newton's "How sweet the name of Jesus sounds." There are others which are not in the least suited for congregational worship. Poems, for example, like the seventh in the present volume are not acts of worship, but diatribes. Some begin as prayers, but trail off into sermons, like the 22d. But all Cowper's hymns throw light upon his mental state at the time, and there are several allusions to the circumstances of his life. Such compositions as Nos. 8 and 9, — the one written in joy, the other in sadness,—are not only beautiful, but such as probably all faithful Christians at one time or another are ready to adopt. But it is different with such pieces as Nos. 37—44. The expressions of assurance are hardly to be distinguished from cries of despair. "Assurance of salvation" is a cardinal point in the Calvinist's creed, and it would not be difficult to lay one's hand upon a remarkable case in which great physical energy and exuberant animal spirits joined with this assurance have given wonderful life and power to a preacher. Preaching comes so easy in such a case, there is no attempt to grapple with the hard problems which perplex more subtle and thoughtful minds, there is an impatience of them ; the creed is an easy one to its holder, and he goes on his way rejoicing. But Cowper's mind was a delicate one, his brain restless and busy ; the full assurance which on Newton's word he held to be necessary was a physical impossibility with him, and thereof came despondency and sadness. The high wave is not more naturally followed by the deep trough. Brooding over his morbid sensations increased them ; his mind oscillated fearfully on the balance between assurance of salvation, and assurance of perdition, till his whole being reeled and tottered. Before the work had proceeded very far, he was a second time insane. This accounts for the fact that eight years elapsed between the projection of the Olney Hymns and their publication. The return of his malady also put a stop to his intended marriage with Mrs. Unwin. Their engagement has been warmly denied. Southey writes : "I believe it to be utterly unfounded ; for that no such engagement was either known or suspected by Mr. Newton I am enabled to assert, and who can suppose that it would have been concealed from him ?" On what ground he makes this assertion he does not say, but there is an assertion on the other side, lately made known, of which the truth cannot be doubted. Mr. Bull, in his Memorials of Newton, declares that again and again he had heard his father say that they were about to be married when Cowper's malady returned in 1773, and that Bull knew this from Mrs. Unwin herself. And then he adds the following extract from Newton's hitherto unpublished diary :—

"They were congenial spirits, united in the faith and hope of the gospel, and their intimate and growing friendship led them in the course of four or five years to an engagement of marriage, which was well known to me, and to most of their and my friends, and was to have taken place in a few months, but was prevented by the terrible malady which seized him about that time."

This settles the question, and shows that Southey was mistaken. The evidence from Cowper's own letters is too slight to build upon, but, viewed in the light of the positive statement, it is confirmatory. Cowper must have known that, as far as society is concerned, he was in a false position with regard to Mrs. Unwin. He could hardly expect that his excellent and pure life would secure them from ill-natured remarks, nor did it; but it is moreover natural to suppose that their feelings towards each other had changed. Her kindness at first had recalled to his memory the love of his long-lost mother; he had leaned upon her and admired her. But after her husband's death her kindness was no longer that of the wife of an old man, it was that of a woman only four or five years his senior. And thus friendship, trust, and admiration, ended in marriage engagement. Cowper's condition from this time forward was not such as to render a renewal of their hopes possible, and there is no further evidence upon the subject. But the fact as now stated throws light upon a matter which will find its due place in our history, and which has caused much perplexity.

The second attack of insanity came on by degrees. His letters at this time, as well as the Olney Hymns, show his oscillations of spirit.

The following extracts from the Memorials of Newton are painfully expressive :—

"Tuesday, July 7 [1772].—Time fully taken up in visiting and receiving visits. Preached at the Great House from Heb. ii. 18, to which I was led by Mr. Cowper's prayer."

Next day, in a letter to his wife, he says :—

"Dear Sir Cowper is in the depths as much as ever. The manner of his prayer last night led me to speak from Heb. ii. 18. I do not think he was much the better for it, but perhaps it might suit others."

Not the better for it! No, for most unwittingly Newton has created a Frankenstein, and is now sorrowing that he cannot control it.*

On January 2, 1773, Newton writes thus :—

"My time and thoughts much engrossed to-day by an afflicting and critical dispensation at Orchard Side. I was sent for early this morning, and returned astonished and grieved."

There was too sad reason for grief. The poor lunatic had again attempted his life, and he repeated the attempt more than once. He became persuaded that it was the sovereign will of God that he should do so, and because he failed, he believed himself condemned to double perdition. He ceased not only from public worship,

---

* " I believe my name is up about the country for preaching people mad ; for whether it is owing to the sedentary life the women lead here, poring over their [lace] pillows for ten or twelve hours every day, and breathing confined air in their crowded little rooms, or whatever may be the immediate cause, I suppose we have near a dozen in different degrees disordered in their heads, and most of them, I believe, truly gracious people."—*Letter of Newton to Thornton.*

but from private prayer. "For him to implore mercy," he said, "would only anger God the more."

In order to be out of hearing of the noise of the annual fair, which was held in April, he visited Newton at the vicarage, and being there, entreated not to be sent away. There he remained till May in the following year; so piteous were his tears and entreaties to be suffered to remain, that Newton had not the heart to remove him. His malady, on the whole, was still increasing upon him. Yet it was not till October 1773 that Newton thought of consulting Dr. Cotton. It was too late then; perhaps it would have been of no use earlier. Some years later the unhappy patient described the thousand fancies which beset him; but there is no good in repeating a sick man's dreams. Mrs. Unwin watched over him all this time with the most tender solicitude. She undertook the care of him single-handed, and shared her diminished income with him. The expense of his living fell heavily also on Newton, as appears from a letter to his benefactor Thornton; but Newton's affection was too unselfish to allow him to put his poor friend from his house. During this sad time Cowper employed himself in gardening. He spoke little,— never except when questioned. The first signs of improvement were seen in the garden; he began to make remarks on the state of the trees, and the growing of them. One day when feeding the chickens some trifle made him smile. "That is the first smile for sixteen months," said Newton. His companion, taking courage from this, proposed to return home. He consented, and having done so, was impatient of the few days' necessary delay. At home he again took to gardening, and also to carpentering. A friend gave him three hares, which he may be said to have immortalised. Ten years later he wrote his famous article in the *Gentleman's Magazine* [June, 1784], giving an account of these animals, and his arrangements for their health and comfort. His friends, pleased with his interest, gave him other animals—five rabbits, two guinea-pigs, two dogs, a magpie, a jay, a starling, and some pigeons, canaries, and goldfinches. The interest he took in them shows that his mind was partially recovering itself, though the clouds still hung heavily upon it. "As long as he is employed," says Newton of this period, "he is tolerably easy; but as soon as he leaves off, he is instantly swallowed up by the most gloomy apprehensions, though in everything that does not concern his own peace he is as sensible and discovers as quick a judgment as ever."[*]

What I have already said will indicate the opinion to which I have been brought on the relation of his religious views to his madness. I have never forgotten—who could, in reading this strange and melancholy life?—that insanity is verily an inscrutable mystery, on which it behoves our words at all times to be wary and few. I do not believe certainly that religious opinions were the original cause of the madness. When I began the study of this life I believed that I should find that the views were merely the form which the madness happened to

---

[*] Bull, p. 202.

take. But this belief I cannot now hold. It became as clear to me as any demonstration could make it, that the Calvinistic doctrine and religious excitements threw an already trembling mind off its balance, and aggravated a malady which but for them might probably have been cured.

In 1776 he recommenced correspondence, as well as reading, and his letters are even playful. He had written none since 1772. One of the first was to Hill, thanking him for a present of fish.* He also took to sketching, and drew "mountains, valleys, woods, streams, ducks, and dabchicks." But this employment hurt his eyes. He formed a plan of taking three or four boys into his house as pupils,† but none offered. Several friends, Hill especially, lent him books, on which he sent back criticisms. In one letter he asks especially for a work on the microscope, and Vincent Bourne's Poems. But his letters as yet were few.

In September 1779 Mr. Newton, who was disappointed and out of heart at his ill-success with the people of Olney, was presented by Thornton to the living of St. Mary Woolnoth, and left Olney at the end of the year. His last act before doing so was the publication of the Olney Hymns, by which Cowper was first introduced to the world. His departure naturally made great changes in Cowper's habits and doings, the chief being that he had much time thrown on his hands. In order to fill up the gap in his small circle of acquaintance, Newton, on leaving, introduced him to the Rev. W. Bull, an Independent minister residing at Newport-Pagnell, five miles from Olney. This choice was a happy one, and they became fast friends. Cowper had a knack of giving all his friends nicknames, and Mr. Bull become "Carissime Taurorum." But the distance between their homes, and Bull's hard work, prevented them from being much together, and Cowper was thrown on his own resources. He worked at his garden with more energy than ever, built frames for pine plants, and glazed the kitchen windows. Of his last achievement he gives a very humorous account in one of his letters. He revived his law studies a little, and gave advice gratis in a few cases. But, happily for English literature, he began to betake himself regularly to poetical composition. It is noticeable that "Nose v. Eyes," as well as the lines "On the Burning of Lord Mansfield's Library," were written now. Speaking of the first of these, —"Happy is the man," says he, "who knows just so much law as to make himself a little merry now and then with the solemnity of judicial proceedings." But in a letter to Newton a few days later, he uses a ghastly similitude about this jocularity. He compares himself to harlequin dancing round a corpse.

His prophecy concerning Thurlow had been fulfilled in June 1778, when the latter succeeded Earl Bathurst as Lord Chancellor of England. Cowper's friends hoped that this would bring some preferment to him, and William Unwin, now

* Cowper was remarkably fond of fish. "The most ichthyophagous of Protestants" he called himself. It is most amusing, in turning over his letters, to find him asking for fish over and over.
† Letter to Hill, July 6, 1776.

become Rector of Stock, in Essex, urged him to write to Thurlow. But Cowper was much too sensitive to do so. "He is very liberal, generous, and discerning," he replied, "but he is well aware of the tricks that are played upon such occasions, and after fifteen years' interruption of all intercourse between us, would translate my letter into this language—Pray remember the poor." But he was not without great hope that Thurlow would do something for him unasked, and it is not impossible that the latter had the will to do so, but lacked opportunity. At any rate he appointed, without solicitation, his and Cowper's friend Hill as his secretary. There seems an expression of disappointment in the end of a letter of Cowper to Hill, dated February 15, 1781. "Farewell, my friend, better than any I have to boast of either among the Lords—or gentlemen of the House of Commons." The latter clause probably refers to his cousin, Colonel Cowper, judging from some expressions in the earlier part of the letter. The letters written at this period are among the most delightful of his compositions, full of kindly humour, and rarely morbid. Even those to Newton—there are not many—avoid religious discussion. He encloses to whomsoever he may be writing the last new poem he has thrown off, apparently with no thought but that of amusing his friends.

One piece written now requires special mention, and that not of a pleasant character. Martin Madan's name has occurred more than once in this biography; it will be remembered that he was Cowper's first cousin, and chaplain of the Lock Hospital. In 1781 he published a work in two large octavos, to which he afterwards added a third as supplement, entitled "*Thelyphthora; or a Treatise on Marriage*," and the estimate which he made of his performance may be judged by the first sentence which it contains :—"The Author doth not scruple to call this Treatise one of the most important and interesting Publications that have appeared since the days of the Protestant Reformation." The substance of it is that Polygamy is a state which was not only allowed by the Most High to the Jews, but spoken of in His law in such a manner as to show that it received His sanction to the end of the world. There is an abundance of learned discussion of the sacred languages, and many quotations from the Fathers, the author throughout taking his position upon the strictest literalism, and holding himself bound by every word of the Sacred Book, but rejecting every other ground of argument. The book has never been reprinted,—not even by Brigham Young. But it is a work which has left its mark. It is no wild guess to say that it had much to do with John Henry Newman's growing disgust towards, and final rejection of, Protestantism. "Protestantism," he said, long before quitting the English Church, "has sometimes developed into Polygamy." When one remembers what the tone of his mind was from youth, what a high store he set upon the celibate life, it will be felt with what shuddering he must have penned that sentence. And when it is compared with his renewed and distinct reference to Madan's book in his celebrated correspondence with Mr. Kingsley (pp. 17, 18), there can be no question that a system which could have produced such a book must long have raised an antagonism in his mind.

Cowper and Newton would of course have no such thought as this. Instead of generalizing upon it, they came to the conclusion that it was simply the work of a vicious and immorally-minded man. To one who knows so little of Madan as I have been able to discover, it is impossible to give any judgment on this point. But internal evidence does not support such a view. If Madan ever looked sorrowfully upon his charge at the Lock, and thought how each fallen woman had been once an innocent child, and might have been a happy wife with children round her knees, is it to be wondered at that he pondered on the question "On what theory *might* these have been wives?" Dwelling upon this,—being (let it be remembered) a Puritan in theology, and Judaizing in his view of the Scriptures,—one is not surprised that he rushed into the notion that the polygamy of the Mosaic days is not contrary to the will of God, and that by the restoration of it harlotry might be put an end to. If we start with the assumption that the law of the Pentateuch is the basis and limit of all moral legislation whatsoever,—and such an assumption should scarcely appear startling to many Protestants, —then the whole of Madan's doctrine follows as a matter of course, for no one disputes the minor premiss, that Polygamy was allowed and practised. But those who hold that the world has been under a Divine Education, that the Christian Church has mounted on the stepping-stones of Judaism to higher things, will hold the theory to be an outrage on religion,— on the whole Bible. The consensus of Christian nations, of *all* nations indeed which have emerged out of barbarism, has a far higher authority in this matter than texts out of Leviticus.* It is not wonderful that the righteous instincts of Cowper revolted at the theory. But considering his kinship with Madan, and their former intercourse, his course is certainly much to be regretted. His epigrams upon the book, poor enough, were only written for Newton's eye ; but he wrote, and printed anonymously (1781), a long Poem entitled " Antithelyphthora," † and a wretched production it is. It seems almost incredible that such a foolish straining after the comic, such a coarse and vulgar effusion, could have proceeded from so delightful a humorist and such a thorough gentleman. It may be said in excuse that he was now only a novice in the art of Poetry, and that as most of the poets that he had read were coarse, he may have thought it a necessity to be the same, just as Waller could not get on without an imaginary Saccharissa.

Cowper appears to have been somewhat ashamed of the production himself, for neither he nor his executors ever included it in his works. It was only by a curious accident that its authorship was discovered. Southey found, in a book which he had borrowed, a note from Samuel Rose—a friend of Cowper's of whom mention

---

* For some thoughts in this criticism I am indebted to my friend Professor Plumptre.
† See page 330.

will hereafter be made,—to Isaac Reid, shut between the leaves as a marker. In this note Rose, in answer to a question, gives the name of the poem, and speaks of it as Cowper's. Southey made inquiry at the British Museum, and found the work, printed in quarto. Allusions in Cowper's letters confirm the proof of its authorship, and it has ever since been included in his works. If his own wishes could have been consulted, I cannot help thinking that it would have continued buried in the Museum.

It was Mrs. Unwin who first proposed to him some work of greater importance, and on his acquiescence suggested "The Progress of Error," to be made the subject of a moral satire. He found the new occupation so congenial to his taste, and so successful in dispelling his melancholy, that he worked at it incessantly. When that was finished, he wrote "Truth," "Table-Talk," "Expostulation," all in such rapid succession, that these four poems, begun in December 1780, were finished in the following March. He had acquainted Newton with what he was doing, and now requested him to find a publisher. His intention was to add a few of his smaller pieces to these large ones, and so to make a moderate-sized volume. Newton went to his own publisher, Joseph Johnson, who at once consented, and took all the risk. The volume was sent to the publisher in April 1781, and he, on the ground that the publishing season was over, proposed to Cowper to enlarge the volume. He accordingly wrote " Hope," and soon afterwards " Charity." The latter occupied him about a fortnight ; it was finished on the 12th of July. Whilst the book was being printed, he began once more, and wrote "Conversation," and "Retirement." He also called upon Newton to assist him further by writing a preface. After some demur, Newton consented. When it was written, Johnson was frightened at the serious tone of it, and, though Cowper was still willing to let it appear, both he and Newton agreed to its being withdrawn, though the latter was somewhat displeased. It was first printed in the fifth edition at his request. It will be found in p. 47 of the present volume ; in all other respects pp. 45—179 contain a reprint of the first edition.

On the eve of publication Cowper disclosed it for the first time to Unwin. The latter, who had been the recipient of all his small pieces as they were produced, was hurt at his friend's reticence, and Cowper, evidently conscious that he had ground for annoyance, laboured, not with the best grace, to remove it. He was, however, successful, and friendship continued uninterrupted. A few stanzas were hastily written, and placed at the end of the volume, in order that if this should be the author's last publication, a memorial of his friendship with Unwin might be preserved.

All this while he was very happy, kept so by employment and by hope. It was while he was correcting his proofs, during what he called an African summer, that he hit upon a simple means of comfort. He had previously built himself a greenhouse, which a gardener, he said, would think nothing of carrying away on his back. He now converted it into a summerhouse, hanging mats all round to keep out the sun, and carpeting the floor. Here now most of his time was spent, with myrtles in the window, and birds and rustling foliage making melody all around, and the letter describing it is perhaps the most beautiful of all his beautiful letters.* This summerhouse is now classic ground, and the care of each successive owner has preserved it to this day in its original state.

Cowper says, in one of his letters written at this period, that he has only read one English poet for the last twenty years ; a statement sufficient to justify me in not comparing him with other writers of the time. He had nothing to do with them. He may have read Percy's Reliques (published the same year that he removed to Huntingdon), but it is not very likely. The author whose style he imitated most was Churchill. But his position was a new one in literature. His foremost idea when he began "The Progress of Error" was to be, not merely a Poet, but a teacher,—a *Vates*. The title which Hayley gives him, " The Bard of Christianity," expresses what he sought after for himself. " Table Talk " was not the first written of the long poems, but he placed it first, as explaining his aims. As its name implies, it is a somewhat desultory production. A. and B. begin to converse about true and false Glory, then pass on to the duties, difficulties, and shortcomings of kings.   A. hints that B. might turn his verse to useful account by propounding therein some plan for paying the national debt, but is told that even the engineering skill of Brindley could not turn Helicon to such a purpose.   "Let us, at all events," says A. "have something practical. Why does a Briton love liberty?" This leads to a discussion of the English character, and of the use and abuse of liberty. B. takes a gloomy view of the present position of England, but A. reminds him that a like view was widely prevalent just when Lord Chatham's wonderful successes began.   "Yet that view was correct," replies B., "and if Sin get the mastery of the nation the gloomy prognostications will yet come true." The growing passion of the verses excites A.'s notice, and this leads to a descant upon the functions of the Poet, and this again to the present condition of English Poetry. The bard holds that there is one new field into which the Poet may enter, namely, Religion.

> "All other themes are sped,
> Hackneyed and worn to the last flimsy thread."

It were indeed, he exclaims, a noble aim for one to entrance his hearers by singing the love of Christ. Better even doggrel verse on high topics than flowing numbers on base ones. This is the author's preface, in fact, to the rest. What was the character of the religion which he thus set himself to expound we need hardly say. It was " Evangelicalism," the form which all earnestness took at that period in the history of the Church of England, the reaction against the " Evidential " and " Moral " Theology of the years preceding. Its defects as well as

---

* To Newton, Aug. 16, 1781.

excellences are faithfully reflected in the poems of Cowper. "Experimental" was one of Newton's favourite words, and the religion taught by him was too much based upon experiences and thoughts and feelings, and thus often fell short of the fulness and breadth of the Gospel. The morbid self-consciousness which is often so painful in Cowper is certainly owing, in some degree, to the same cause. The two quiet recluses at Olney, spending half their time in reading Evangelical sermons, and discussing them afterwards,* never brought into contact with active men of the world, became unable to make allowance, or to view charitably opinions which did not coincide with their own. But, on the other hand, Cowper's natural kindliness and generosity caused his narrowness of view to vanish directly he came into contact with good people who thought differently. The indignation which flashes along his lines is directed against an *abstract* "Mr. Legality;" had he met with him in the flesh, he would have shown more consideration for him. The only personalities in these poems are the attacks upon "Occiduus" and Madan, both in "The Progress of Error." Had he known a live bishop, he might even have shown some mercy to *his* order. Certainly no man ever disliked bishops more cordially ;† and as one looks over the list of that period there seems little reason why he should have held them in veneration. Thomas Newton and Lowth are the only names which have any claim to be remembered. A curious instance of what we have been saying is furnished by the fact that in his poem of "Expostulation" Cowper spoke severely of the Roman Catholics, but, after it was printed off, cancelled the leaf.‡ It has been commonly asserted and denied that he did so out of respect to the Throckmortons, who were Roman Catholics, and whose acquaintance he had made in the interval.§ It is not unlikely that there is some truth in this statement. They came into his neighbourhood just at the time when the poem was being printed, and though there was no intimacy till two years after, there were civilities between them. But it was probably simple good taste which led him to make the cancel. One thing we never lose sight of in reading Cowper—he is a gentleman, well-bred, scholarly, pure-minded, sincere, and without offence. When he exchanged a harsh view for a more charitable one, it was not through policy, but because experience had modified his opinion.

His political views also smack of his retirement. He had no books of his own, and was dependent upon loans from his friends. His knowledge of history was very slight. For example, he thought that the Latin element in our language was owing to the Roman conquest. He sat at home and read Mrs. Macaulay and the *St. James's Chronicle,* and prophesied without a misgiving of error that the

---

* See page xxxiv.

† I do not know whether the following expression of opinion has ever appeared in print. I copied it from his MS.: "Bishops are κακα θηρια, γαστερες αργοι." Dated Sept. 24, 1786. It is characteristic of him that on renewing acquaintance, years afterwards, with his old friend Walter Bagot, he went somewhat out of his way to speak a civil word of his brother, who had been made Bishop of Norwich (Tirocinium, p. 290, l. 435).

‡ See note on Expostulation, l. 390. § See hereafter, page lv.

moment the Americans gained their independence England would fall to utter destruction.

The titles of his poems are somewhat misleading. "The Progress of Error," for example, leads us to expect a philosophical disquisition, whereas we find that the sum of this poem is that operas, card-playing, intemperance, gluttony, reading of bad novels, are the causes of Error; that they who hate truth shall be the dupe of lies. Quite true, of course; but who supposes that this is an adequate account of the progress of Error? In like manner "Truth" is not an essay upon Truth in the abstract, but an assertion of the sinfulness of man, the perfection of God, and hence the need of the propitiation of Christ.

The author improves in his style by practice. The versification of the "Progress of Error" is harsh, but that of "Expostulation" is highly finished. The latter is throughout a beautiful poem. It is an impassioned address to England to avoid the sin, and the consequent ruin, of the Jews, and is said to have been suggested by a fast-sermon of Newton's. Cowper himself liked it better than those which preceded it.* So, too, although "Hope" is based on the same idea as that which forms the subject of "Truth," and contains nothing that has not been said before, it is much more pleasing and kindly in expression. "Charity" really concludes this series of Poems; "Conversation" and "Retirement" are quite distinct from it. "Conversation" is the lightest in tone of all; its versification, too, is delightful, while the whole piece is full of wisdom and goodness. "Retirement" has been called the most *poetical* piece, being rich in illustration, as well as graceful and picturesque. There is less satire in it than in the other pieces. But taken as a whole, the stinging satire is the most telling feature of the whole series of Poems. The sketches of the fox-hunting clergyman and of the travelling youth in the "Progress of Error," of "the ancient prude" in "Truth," of the proser in "Conversation," and, best of all, of Sir Smug in "Hope" are wonderfully pointed and vigorous. The force and severity, joined to good humour and freedom from coarseness and offensiveness, have never been excelled unless by the lamented author of the "Book of Snobs." His language is always well chosen, always the handmaid of the sense. Sometimes he bursts out into impassioned earnestness, as in "Expostulation," and at the end of "Hope." But he falls back into placid smoothness. To use his own simile, he always rides Pegasus with a curb. His rhymes are very frequently indeed inexact, more so than those of any English poet.† It would be hard to find a page without a false rhyme or a prosaic line. He intended to produce *variety*, but when we find him expressing his belief that he has removed all inaccuracies, we can only say that his ear was at fault.

---

* " I have written it with tolerable ease to myself, and in my own opinion (for an opinion I am bound to have about what I write whether I will or no), with more emphasis and energy than in either of the others."

† See note on page 3.

Such was his first volume. It appeared in March 1782; its price was 3s. He sent copies to a few only of his friends. Among them were the Chancellor and Colman, now manager of the Haymarket theatre. The copy to Thurlow was accompanied by the following letter:—

"Olney, Bucks, Feb. 25, 1782.

"MY LORD,—I make no apology for what I account a duty; I should offend against the cordiality of our former friendship should I send a volume into the world, and forget how much I am bound to pay my particular respects to your Lordship upon that occasion. When we parted you little thought of hearing from me again; and I as little that I should live to write to you, still less that I should wait on you in the capacity of an author.

"Among the pieces I have the honour to send, there is one for which I must entreat your pardon. I mean that of which your Lordship is the subject. The best excuse I can make is, that it flowed almost spontaneously from the affectionate remembrance of a connexion that did me so much honour.

"As to the rest, their merits, if they have any, and their defects, which are probably more than I am aware of, will neither of them escape your notice. But where there is much discernment, there is generally much candour; and I commit myself into your Lordship's hands, with the less anxiety, being well acquainted with yours.

"If my first visit, after so long an interval should prove neither a troublesome nor a dull one, but especially if not altogether an unprofitable one, *omne tuli punctum.*

"I have the honour to be, though with very different impressions of some subjects, yet with the same sentiments of affection and esteem as ever, your Lordship's faithful and most obedient, humble servant,

"W. C."

Neither Thurlow nor Colman acknowledged the gift; and Hill, who of course was much with Thurlow, and had mentioned Cowper's name to him, never heard a word from him on this subject. Colman, too, on publishing his translation of the *Ars Poetica* soon after, hurt Cowper's feelings by not sending him a copy. Some months after, the poor Poet, who had hitherto hoped against hope, gave vent to his wounded feelings in his indignant "Valediction."*

Striving to be unconcerned, he now watched to see his volume running the gauntlet of the critics. The *Critical Review* immediately fell foul of the volume. Southey has disinterred and gibbeted the article, which is evidently the work of some pert and ignorant youth—"nothing more nor less than a pompous noodle," as Thackeray said of one of *his* critics. A few excerpts will suffice:—"Not possessed of any abilities or power of genius;" "weak and languid verses;" "neither novelty, spirit, or animation;" "flat and tedious;" "no better than a dull sermon;" "very indifferent verse;" "coarse, vulgar, and unpoetical." Other magazines, the *Gentleman's* and the *London*, spoke in approbation; and Dr. Benjamin Franklin delighted the Poet by writing to Mr. Thornton, who sent him the volume, a discriminating and highly favourable opinion. The *Monthly*, the chief of the reviews, delayed a long time, but at length spoke in praise. But though the critics admitted him as a poet, they could not make him a popular one. People apparently made up their minds that he was a very good sort of a man, who wrote nice verses on the Evangelical side, and troubled themselves no more about him. The volume did not sell. Another lady became the means of making him popular.

* P. 354. See note on it.

Lady Austen was the widow of a baronet, and sister-in-law of a clergyman named Jones, residing at Clifton, near Olney, with whom Cowper had a slight acquaintance. In the summer of 1781, whilst he was preparing his first volume for press, Cowper saw the two sisters shopping in the street at Olney. He was so struck with Lady Austen's appearance that he persuaded Mrs. Unwin to invite them to tea. They came; then he was so shy that Mrs. Unwin had difficulty in bringing him to meet them. But as soon as they met all reserve vanished, and they were "like old friends together." Lady Austen and he soon came to address each other as "William" and "Sister Ann." For a while all went delightfully. She was lively and full of anecdote, and sang and played well; and she was pleased with him, the well-bred, interesting, thoughtful man. The party dined, walked, pic-nicked together constantly, and Lady Austen announced her intention of taking a house at Olney, as the lease of her town house was nearly out. When she returned to town in October, both Cowper and Mrs. Unwin felt the blank. The "Poetical Epistle" at p. 337 was addressed to her during this absence, and may be read with interest here. It will be seen that he anticipated great results from the new acquaintance, though what they are to be does not exactly appear. It was written in December 1781, yet in the following February a fracas had taken place which nearly brought the acquaintance to an end. The circumstances are unknown, the only account being contained in a letter from Cowper to Unwin. "The lady, in her correspondence," he says, "expressed a sort of romantic idea of our merits, and built such expectations of felicity upon our friendship, as we were sure that nothing human can possibly answer, and I wrote to her not to think more lightly of us than the subject would warrant; and intimating that when we embellish a creature with colours taken from our own fancy, and so adorned, admire and praise it beyond its real merits, we make it an idol, and have nothing to expect in the end but that it will deceive our hopes, and that we shall derive nothing from it but a painful conviction of our error. Your mother heard me read the letter; she read it herself, and honoured it with her warm approbation. But it gave mortal offence. It received, indeed, an answer, but such a one as I could by no means reply to." What are we to make of all this? Had Lady Austen fallen in love with him, and been repelled in this letter of his at Mrs. Unwin's instigation? Or was Mrs. Unwin jealous without cause? If so, no wonder that Lady Austen was angry. Probability, considering events which followed, inclines to the former view. That it was a quarrel between the ladies especially, appears from an expression of Hayley, who had seen the correspondence. He calls it "a trifling feminine discord."

Meanwhile Cowper might with advantage have learned from this, that two persons who are not brother and sister had better not call themselves so. However, the breath was soon healed. She sent him some worked ruffles as a present, got a civil message in return, and soon afterwards they met. After a few minutes' awkwardness they were all as friendly as ever. Before long she had taken up her residence in the vicarage at Olney. And now began the most sunny period in Cowper's life. His letters are full of fun and frolic, and comparatively free from melancholy. The trio were constantly together, engaged in quiet amusements, "Lady Austen playing on the harpsichord," as he says in one letter, "Mrs. Unwin and himself playing battledore and shuttlecock, and the little dog under the chair howling to admiration." "In the morning," says another letter, "I walk with one or other of the ladies, and in the afternoon wind thread. Thus did Hercules, and thus probably did Samson, and thus do I."

When low spirits overtook him, Lady Austen's sprightliness was generally able to exorcise them. One afternoon when he was in this condition, she told him the story of John Gilpin. He lay awake half the night convulsed with laughter, and by the next morning had turned it into a ballad. It was sent to Unwin, who sent it on to the *Public Advertiser*, where it appeared anonymously. It attracted no special notice, until three years afterwards it came under the eye of Richard Sharp—"Conversation Sharp" as he was commonly known to the literary society of the period. He showed it to Henderson, a first-class actor of the time, who was then giving public readings at Freemasons' Hall. He read "John Gilpin," and electrified the audience, Mrs. Siddons among them. The ballad was reprinted again and again, and the famous horseman was seen in all the printshops. Some other smaller pieces were owing to Lady Austen, being written for her to sing. But they were trifles indeed compared with the poem which placed him in the first place among the authors of his time, namely, "THE TASK."

Lady Austen had often begged him to try his hand at blank verse. "I will," he answered one day, "if you will give me a subject." "Oh, you can write upon any subject," said she: "write upon this *Sofa*." And so he began; hence the great poem, and hence its title. It was begun in the summer of 1783, and completed in about twelve months. But before it was finished another breach had taken place between him and Lady Austen, and this time it was final. Of this separation we have notices from two hands—very slight, it is true, but pointing to a definite conclusion. The first is Cowper's. In a letter to Unwin, dated July 12, 1784, after discussing other topics, he writes:

"You are going to Bristol. A lady, not long since our near neighbour, is probably there; she *was* there very lately. If you should chance to fall into her company, remember, if you please, that we found the connexion on some accounts an inconvenient one; that we do not wish to renew it; and conduct yourself accordingly. A character with which we spend all our time should be made on purpose for us; too much or too little of any ingredient spoils all. In the instance in question, the dissimilitude was too great not to be felt continually, and consequently made our intercourse unpleasant. We have reason, however, to believe that she has given up all thoughts of a return to Olney."

And eighteen months after, he writes to Lady Hesketh as follows:—

"There came a lady into this country, by name and title Lady Austen, the widow of the late Sir Robert Austen. At first she lived with her sister, about a mile from Olney; but in a few weeks took lodgings at the vicarage here. Between the vicarage and the back of our house are interposed our garden, an orchard, and the garden belonging to the vicarage. She had lived much in France, was very sensible, and had infinite vivacity. She took a great liking to us, and we to her. She had been used to a great deal of company, and we fearing that she would find such a transition into silent retirement irksome, contrived to give her our agreeable company often. Becoming continually more and more intimate, a practice obtained at length of our dining with each other alternately every day, Sundays excepted. In order to facilitate our communication, we made doors in the two garden walls abovesaid, by which means we considerably shortened the way from one house to the other, and could meet when we pleased without entering the town at all; a measure the rather expedient, because the town is abominably dirty, and she kept no carriage. On her first settlement in our neighbourhood, I made it my own particular business (for at that time I was not employed in writing, having published my first volume and not begun my second) to pay my devoirs to her ladyship every morning at eleven. Customs very soon become laws. I began *The Task*; for she was the lady who gave me the Sofa for a subject. Being once engaged in the work, I began to feel the inconvenience of my morning attendance. We had seldom breakfasted ourselves till ten; and the intervening hour was all the time that I could find in the whole day for writing, and occasionally it would happen that the half of that hour was all that I could secure for the purpose. But there was no remedy. Long usage had made that which at first was optional a point of good manners, and consequently of necessity, and I was forced to neglect *The Task*, to attend upon the Muse who had inspired the subject. But she had ill health, and before I had quite finished the work was obliged to repair to Bristol. Thus, as I told you, my dear, the cause of the many interruptions that I mentioned was removed, and now, except the Bull that I spoke of [Mr. Bull], we seldom have any company at all. After all that I have said upon this matter, you will not completely understand me, perhaps, unless I account for the remainder of the day. I will add, therefore, that having paid my morning visit, I walked; returning from my walk, I dressed: we then met and dined, and parted not till between ten and eleven at night."

This is Cowper's account of the fracas. The other is by Hayley, and shall be given at full length.

"The year 1784 was a memorable period in the life of the poet, not only as it witnessed the completion of one extensive performance, and the commencement of another (his translation of Homer), but as it terminated his intercourse with that highly pleasing and valuable friend, whose alacrity of attention and advice had induced him to engage in both.

"Delightful and advantageous as his friendship with Lady Austen had proved, he now began to feel that it grew impossible to preserve that triple cord, which his own pure heart had led him to suppose not speedily to be broken. Mrs. Unwin, though by no means destitute of mental accomplishments, was eclipsed by the brilliancy of the Poet's new friend, and naturally became uneasy under the apprehension of being so; for to a woman of sensibility, what evil can be more afflicting than the fear of losing all mental influence over a man of genius and virtue, whom she has been long accustomed to inspirit and to guide?

"Cowper perceived the painful necessity of sacrificing a great portion of his present gratifications. He felt that he must relinquish that ancient friend, whom he regarded as a venerable parent; or the new associate, whom he idolised as a sister, of a heart and mind peculiarly congenial to his own. His gratitude for past services of unexampled magnitude and weight would not allow him to hesitate; with a resolution and delicacy, that do the highest honour to his feelings, he wrote a farewell letter to Lady Austen, explaining and lamenting the circumstances that forced him to renounce the society of a friend, whose enchanting talents and kindness had proved so agreeably instrumental to the revival of his spirits, and to the exercise of his fancy.

"In those very interesting conferences with which I was honoured by Lady Austen, I was irresistibly led to express an anxious desire for the sight of a letter written by Cowper in a situation that must have called forth all the finest powers of his eloquence as a monitor and a friend. The lady confirmed me in my opinion, that a more admirable letter could not be written; and had it existed at that time, I am persuaded, from her noble frankness and zeal for the honour of the departed poet, she would have given me a copy; but she ingenuously confessed that in a moment of natural mortification she burnt this very tender, yet resolute letter. I mention the circumstance, because a literary correspondent, whom I have great reason to esteem, has recently expressed to me a wish (which may perhaps be general) that I could introduce into this compilation the letter in question. Had it been confided to my care, I am persuaded I should have thought it very proper for publication, as it displayed both the tenderness and the magnanimity of Cowper; nor could I have deemed it a want of delicacy towards the memory of Lady Austen to exhibit a proof that, animated by the warmest admiration of the great poet, whose fancy she could so successfully call forth, she was willing to devote her life and fortune to his service and protection. The sentiment is to be regarded as honourable to the lady; it is still more honourable to the Poet, that with such feelings, as rendered him perfectly sensible of all Lady Austen's fascinating powers, he could return her tenderness with innocent gallantry, and yet resolutely preclude himself from her society, when he could no longer enjoy it without appearing deficient in gratitude towards the compassionate and generous guardian of his sequestered life. No person can justly blame Mrs. Unwin for feeling apprehensive that Cowper's intimacy with a lady of such extraordinary talents might lead him into perplexities, of which he was by no means aware. This remark was suggested by a few elegant and tender verses, addressed by the Poet to Lady Austen, and shown to me by that lady.

"Those who were acquainted with the unsuspecting innocence and sportive gaiety of Cowper, would readily allow, if they had seen the verses to which I allude, that they are such as he might have addressed to a real sister; but a lady only called by that endearing name may be easily pardoned, if she was induced by them to hope that they might possibly be a prelude to a still dearer alliance. To me they appeared expressive of that peculiarity in his character, a gay and tender gallantry, perfectly distinct from amorous attachment. If the lady, who was the subject of the verses, had given them to me with a permission to print them, I should have thought the Poet himself might have approved of their appearance, accompanied with such a commentary."

The endeavours to make everything pleasant all round are very characteristic of Hayley, and in this case ludicrous. He softens here and subdues there, and, where this is impossible, makes omissions which leave the matter almost unintelligible. But the substance of the whole apparently is that Lady Austen was in love with Cowper, and believed him to be so with her; that Mrs. Unwin was jealous, and that Cowper thereupon broke off the connexion. Then was Lady Austen's belief right, or had she misunderstood him? That she would gladly have married him is unquestionable, and I cannot doubt that a tender feeling towards her was growing up in his mind also, but that, as he looked back on the past and upon Mrs. Unwin's kindness and tenderness (although his intended marriage with her was probably quite abandoned by this time), he felt that it would be ungrateful on his part to forsake her for another. That he should write of Lady Austen, as we have seen, with something like asperity, is easily intelligible, especially when we remember that his letters were only intended for the sight of William Unwin.

The "elegant and tender verses" of which Hayley speaks are printed for the first time in the present volume; and one is constrained to say that a woman who was not an actual sister could only put one interpretation upon them. And if they were not intended to bear this interpretation, they seem to me to be a thoughtless sporting with a woman's peace.

The loss of Lady Austen's friendship was a serious one for him.* He had need of such friends. Melancholy was increasing upon him again, and this breach seems to have deepened it greatly. "When I was writing 'The Task,'" he said afterwards, "I was often supremely unhappy." And in a letter written at the time

---

* Lady Austen afterwards married a Frenchman, M. de Tardiff. She died in 1802, whilst Hayley's first volume was going through the press.

he said, "The grinners at 'John Gilpin' little think what its writer sometimes suffers. How I hated myself last night for having written it!"

It is grievous to read the quiet matter-of-fact way in which he puts aside all attempts at consolation. "Your arguments [against his belief in his final perdition] are quite reasonable," he says quietly to Newton, "but the event will prove them false." And in the same way he treated Mrs. Unwin's reasonings. Sometimes he would make her no answer, at others would sharply tell her she was wrong. "It was no use reasoning in this case," he said; "reasoning might say one thing, but fact said another." And all this while his letters are expressed as vigorously and strongly as ever, his humour and clearness of thinking are as unclouded. His madness has such method in it that his destruction is clear before his eyes; he contemplates it *ab extra* as if he were looking at the ruin of a building, or a falling tree. "You will think me mad," he says, in one most gloomy letter; "but I am not mad, most noble Festus, I am only in despair."

Meanwhile he had made fresh acquaintances, not without influence on his life. Bull we have already mentioned. Before "The Task" was begun he had given Cowper the Poems of Madame Guyon, that he might amuse himself in his sad hours with translating them. He did it in a month, copying them into a "Lilliputian book," as he called it, and then gave the little volume to his friend. Bull some time after suggested that he should publish them, and he consented, but the idea was not carried out during his lifetime.

Another acquaintance, made about the time of the separation from Lady Austen, was with the Throckmortons. They lived at Weston Underwood, a village about two miles from Olney. Cowper had always been allowed a key of their park, but no intercourse had taken place with the family, who were Roman Catholics. The possessor dying in 1782, a younger brother came to live at Weston,* and Cowper sent his card and asked for a continuance of the favour, which was readily granted. The Throckmortons had been grossly affronted on account of their religion by some of their neighbours, and were naturally shy of seeking acquaintance. However, in May 1784, they invited Cowper and Mrs. Unwin to see an attempt to send up a balloon from Weston.† The gentle, refined poet found himself the object of his host's special attention, and acquaintance soon ripened into intimacy. From this time the Throckmortons appear among his correspondents—he addresses them as "Mr. and Mrs. Frog"—and several of his smaller poems relate to incidents connected with them.

We have seen how Cowper, on the publication of his first volume, concealed his intention from his friend Unwin. He acted in the same way with Newton on the publication of his second. Though in constant correspondence with him he

* John Throckmorton; he was the son of Sir Robert, who was 84 years old, living in Oxfordshire. The old baronet lived till 1791, and Cowper's friend then succeeded to the title.
† Balloons were all the rage just then. Montgolfier made his in 1783. The first aeronaut in England, Lunardi, ascended from Moorfields, September 15, 1784.

avoided even a hint. He sent the volume to Unwin, desiring him to offer it to his former publisher Johnson ; if he should refuse, or stroke his chin and look up to the ceiling and cry " Humph ! " then to take it to Longman, or to Nichols, the printer of the *Gentleman's Magazine.* However, Johnson spared Unwin any further trouble, for he accepted it directly. At length * Cowper announced the volume to Newton. He did so in a constrained manner, betraying his feeling that his friend had some ground of complaint. Newton had evidently lost considerable hold of his affections. His letters to him are colder, and he makes no allusion to him in his manifold letters to Unwin at this period. The day following his announcement to Newton, Cowper writes to Unwin : "I wrote to Mr. Newton by the last post to tell him I was gone to press again. He will be surprised, and perhaps not pleased. But I think he cannot complain, for he keeps his own authorly secrets without participating them with me."

Newton was evidently much mortified, though he wrote back a kind answer. He asked to see the proof-sheets, but Cowper, " for many reasons," as he told Unwin, refused them.† He sent him, however, a title, list of headings, and specimen extract. ‡ Newton sent back a carping criticism, objecting to title, headings, metre, and phraseology. And Cowper returned answer, verbally civil, but steeped in irony.§

His publisher, as before, wanted more matter to make up the volume. Cowper accordingly completed "Tirocinium," which he had begun two years previously and laid aside. He also wrote the Epistle to Hill, partly with the hope of giving him an agreeable surprise, partly from the feeling that, having mentioned by name several of his friends, it would be unjustifiable to omit one whose conduct towards him had been so helpful and generous.‖ It was written at a single sitting. He then proposed to add "John Gilpin." Johnson doubted, and Cowper left it to his judgment, but it was eventually resolved to put it in. They thought, and rightly, that a poem which had become so famous (for it was while "The Task" was in the press that Henderson made the hit with it that has been previously described), and of which the author's name had not yet transpired, would stimulate curiosity and recommend the volume. It was therefore not only inserted, but put in the title. Besides, Cowper was desirous of showing that, though he wrote seriously, he could be sometimes merry. Above all, it would refute the *Critical* reviewer, who had charged him with a vain attempt at humour.

The new volume was published in June 1785, and public opinion immediately placed its author at the head of the poets of the age. The first volume had sold so slowly, that it was judged desirable to make no mention of it in the new title-page (see p. 181) ; but an advertisement of the previous volume, with table of contents, was inserted at the end. People were attracted to the new book solely by the name of "John Gilpin," eager to see the other works of

---

* October 30, 1784.   † November 29.   ‡ Lines 729–817 of the last book (p. 279).
        § December 13 and 24, 1784.   ‖ Letter to Hill, Oct. 11, 1785.

one who had made such a sensation. They were astonished to find a volume of serious poetry, but not the less delightful. When once opened, "The Task" needed no other recommendation, and more than that, it led them to seek out the previously neglected volume. The success was triumphant ; a new edition was called for, and next year the two volumes were published together.

The great beauties of "The Task," and its pure and elevated feeling, can hardly be said to make it a poem of the highest class. The very method of its origin was some bar to success. The author began it without a definite purpose ; in fact, changed his views as he went along, for he began it to please Lady Austen, and continued in such a way as to please Mrs. Unwin.* The graceful address to Mrs. Unwin in the First Book, lines 144-162, may very probably have been inserted as a compliment, to wipe away any unpleasantness after the rupture with Lady Austen, but, on the other hand, it is not impossible that the author's leaving "The Sofa" for other subjects may synchronize with the breach. It is curious to mark his mode of transition. He hopes he shall never have to lie on the sofa through gout, because he likes walking. When he walks, he sees rural scenes. And there-upon he goes off into rural scenes, and the Sofa is quite done with and forgotten. Of course it is the scenery of Olney which occupies him wholly, and the description of his walks is as beautiful as any poetry can make it. Towards the end of the First Book he again changes his subject, for the purpose of moralizing. The country and the life therein are contrasted with the town, and this affords the opening for satire, which is just touched in the end of the First Book, but forms the staple of the Second. And splendid satire it is, full of vigour, and energy, and point, sometimes mere good-humoured badinage, sometimes full of burning indignation. It is satire of a different kind from that of his former poems ; it is less bilious, more free from personality. Yet, Antæus-like, the author loses all his power when he ceases to touch his proper sphere. His faculty of keen observation enables him to lash effectively the false pretensions and follies which he sees. But his reflections upon the world without are of the poorest kind. He foresees the end of the world close at hand. He rails at the natural philosopher who attempts to discover the causes of physical calamities, such as earthquakes and diseases ; at the historian who takes the trouble to investigate the motives of remarkable men ; at the geologist and the astronomer. For the last especially there is nothing but contempt. It would be hard to find a more foolish and mischievous piece of rant than that contained in "The Garden," lines 150-190. But no man ought to sit in judgment as he has done who lives in retirement. We have already spoken of his censoriousness. It came from his want of knowledge of men. The hard and revolting view of religion which he took from his theological friends was not corrected by any experience of those at whom he railed. His indiscriminate abuse of pursuits that did not interest him might just as fairly be

* See p. 285, lines 1,006-1,011.

applied to his own ; fiddling or chess-playing, to say nothing of natural history studies, need not be less innocent than growing cucumbers or making rabbit-hutches. It is strange that he did not see that his vaunted method of securing peace of mind failed in his own case. He mocked at the folly of others for seeking happiness in other pursuits than the simple ones in which he was engaged, and yet he was "supremely unhappy" the whole time. A more charitable method, if he had been taught it, might have wrought a happy change upon him.

It is not until we come to the Third Book, "The Garden," that the plan of the poem becomes definite. As the author expresses it, he has been winding

> . . . now this way, and now that,
> His devious course uncertain."

Now, however, he settles quietly down to his subject of domestic happiness. Many flit to and fro in vain quest of happiness ; he lives at home engaged in simple occu-pations. And here we come to one of the chief excellences of the volume, that which was lacking in the first volume, and which now had the chief part in winning popularity. "The Task" is all about himself. He takes you into his con-fidence, and his artless blank verse seems more like a flowing and melodious conversation with some dear friend than a service of the Muses. His religious thoughts and meditations, his friends, his ill-health, his walks, his tame hares, he tells you all about them in a simple straightforward way, as though he were quite aware that he is able to interest you in every one of them. There is not a piece of description anywhere in which he himself is not in the foreground of the landscape, though he never seems intrusive or egotistical. There are some fine pieces of description in "The Garden," and the satire upon the gaieties and extravagances of London life is pungent and well-deserved. But his attempt to make poetry out of minute directions for the raising of a cucumber is not very successful.

"The Winter Evening" is delightful throughout ; the interest never flags at all. It is the best of his poems. The description of the old postman, of the approach of evening, of the Poet's "brown study," of the suffering poor, are all perfect. "The Winter Morning Walk," too, begins with pictures equally good,—the slanting winter sun, the feeding of the cattle, the woodman toiling through the snow, with "pipe in mouth and dog at heels." But the greater part of this poem is occupied with a disquisition on Liberty, which the author brings in oddly. The icicles remind him of the Russian ice-palace, which leads on to the amuse-ments of monarchs, and these to a discussion on monarchy in general, which affords the Poet an opportunity of stating his moderate Whig views.

Though necessarily traversing the same subjects as Thomson, and writing in the same metre, Cowper is not at all like him. Thomson is sometimes sublime. But he knows less of his subject than Cowper, and is often vague, indistinct, and untrue. Cowper never is. Every picture is clear and minute. As he says in one of his letters, he describes only what he sees, and takes nothing at second-hand. As he had never seen a mountain or a lake in his life, never listened to the roar of a torrent, nor slept at sea, nor visited a foreign country, and knew next to nothing of his own, it is not to be wondered at that he was wedded to his own haunts as closely as a snail to its shell, and not a trait of beauty escaped his notice. Ignorance of any other language is said to give a great reader unusual command of his own; and Cowper's case was like this. Grand scenery would have weakened his powers; he was not physically capable of enjoying it. Bodily and mental powers alike were best suited by the Buckinghamshire lanes and pastures. One may know what Olney scenery is like by "The Task" better than by a set of photographs.* Nor is this minuteness the work of a mere close observer; he observes as an artist. The description of the flowers in "The Garden," lines 560–595, is very pretty and natural; but that in "The Winter Walk at Noon," lines 141–180, is far more than this. The author is not there describing what is before him, but his imagination sees the flowers as they will be in the coming summer, and the group of colours is as rich and warm as ever was painted by artist. Towards the end of the poem he aims at a higher flight than he has ever aimed at before, and foretells the final victory of the Kingdom of God (pp. 280–282). Herein he reaches, for the first and only time, sublimity.

One of the first results of the success of "The Task" was the renewal of intimacy between the Poet and his relations. He had said to Unwin at the time of publication, "I have had more comfort in the connexions that I have formed within the last twenty years, than in the more numerous ones that I had before. Memorandum, the latter are almost all Unwins or Unwinisms." Several causes had concurred to break off the intimacy between him and his relatives. Lady Hesketh had been repelled by the religious tone of his letters at Huntingdon, and although she retained an unwavering feeling of kindness towards him, she suffered the correspondence to drop when she left England with her husband in 1767. She was now a widow, Sir Thomas having died in 1782. Her father and General Cowper had continued their allowance to him with kindly feeling enough, but with pity, as for one who was useless in the world. He did not send any of them his first volume. But "The Task" and "John Gilpin" soon found its way to them, and Cowper was nearly wild with delight when, on coming down to breakfast one morning, he found a letter in the well-remembered hand of Lady Hesketh, franked by his uncle Ashley. It broke a silence of nineteen years. Her letter is not in existence; scarcely any addressed to Cowper are. In his answer he declares that she has made them all young again, and brought back their happy days as freshly as ever. But he rejoices in her letter most of all because it gives him an opportunity of telling her that neither years nor interrupted intercourse have abated his affection for her. He does not mention

---

* It has been said, I forget by whom, that "he is to Buckinghamshire what Cuyp is to Holland."

Theodora, but says that any father is happy who has three such daughters as his uncle has.*

The correspondence thus begun was continued busily. Lady Hesketh soon inquired into his money matters, and offered him assistance. He replied with frankness. He had always been poor, he said, but Mrs. Unwin, whose income had been double his, had shared alike with him. But latterly her income had become reduced, and they had been obliged to forego some of their wonted comforts. He therefore freely accepted her proffered kindness. "I know you thoroughly, and have that consummate confidence in the sincerity of your wish to serve me, that delivers me from all awkward restraint, and from all fear of trespassing by acceptance. To you, therefore, I reply, yes. Whensoever, and whatsoever, and in what manner soever you please; and add, moreover, that my affection for the giver is such as will increase to tenfold the satisfaction that I shall have in receiving. . . . . . Strain no points to your own inconvenience or hurt, for there is no need of it, but indulge yourself in communicating (no matter what) that you can spare without missing it." † How liberally she responded to this will presently appear; and she gave him additional pleasure by causing him to renew his correspondence with the General.

Very soon he entrusts to her "a great secret, so great that she must not even whisper it to her cat." He is engaged in translating Homer, and has done twenty-one books of the Iliad.

He had always been fond of Homer. In the Temple he had gone all through it with Pope's translation, and had been thoroughly dissatisfied, discovering, as he said, that there was nothing in the world of which Pope was so destitute as a taste for Homer. Homer and a Clavis were the only Greek books he had kept since. Three or four days after finishing "Tirocinium," ‡ whilst suffering from an insupportable attack of melancholy, he took up the "Iliad" as a diversion. With no other thought than this he translated the first twelve lines, and on the next attack did some more. Finding the work pleasant, he soon took it up as a regular employment, and worked at it assiduously. He had been engaged just twelve months with it when he made the announcement to Lady Hesketh. He soon after removed his injunction of secresy, and asked her to get him subscribers. He also communicated his design to Newton, not without apprehension of objections, but determined not to heed them if any came. However, Newton approved. Cowper, moreover, inserted a long letter, signed "Alethes," in the *Gentleman's Magazine,* pulling Pope's translation to pieces, and maintaining that a translation ought to be in blank verse, because otherwise the translator must be continually obliged to depart from the meaning of the original in order to bring in his rhymes. He ended by saying, that while Homer is grand and sublime, Pope

* October 12, 1785.   † November 9, 1785.   ‡ November 12, 1784.

is only stiff and pompous, and that while scholars delight in the original, English readers have found the translation turgid, wearisome, and intolerable.

Having thus prepared the way for himself he wrote to his publisher, announcing his intention of publishing by subscription. Johnson endeavoured to dissuade him from this, adding that he would make him liberal offers. But Cowper held to his purpose, finding that friends to whom he began to communicate his design entered into it warmly. One of these was the Rev. Walter Bagot, an old schoolfellow, whom he had scarcely seen since leaving Westminster, but who had recently taken an opportunity of renewing the acquaintance. He now sent him £20 beforehand, and asked for a parcel of the subscription papers. At the same time a correspondence was renewed with his old friends Colman and Thurlow. His angry feelings had passed away after writing the "Valediction," and he seized at a kind expression of Colman's repeated to him by Hill to write him a warm and affectionate letter, which received a like response.

Colman proved useful at this moment. He had won much credit by his translation of Terence, and his criticism was therefore valuable. His encouraging remarks on the specimen which Cowper sent him comforted him for many of a contrary kind which he had received. Another favourable judge, for a long time unknown to him, proved to be the painter Fuseli, to whom Johnson had shown a portion.

And now, for a while, his peace of mind in great measure returned to him. In a letter to his cousin, written in January 1786, after giving an account of his late malady, he adds: "Methinks I hear you ask—your affection for me will, I know, make you wish to do so,—Is it quite removed? I reply, In great measure, but not quite. Occasionally I am much distressed, but that distress becomes continually less frequent, and I think less violent. I find writing, and especially poetry, my best remedy. Perhaps, had I understood music, I had never written verse, but had lived on fiddle strings instead. It is better, however, as it is." And here again: "He who hath preserved me hitherto, will still preserve me. All the dangers that I have escaped are so many pillars of remembrance, to which I shall hereafter look back with comfort. . . My life has been a life of wonders for many years, and a life of wonders I believe in my heart it will be to the end. Wonders I have seen in the great deep, and wonders I shall see in the paths of mercy also." *

Yet this was the time that Newton thought that he was growing worldly, and thought proper to warn him about renewing his intercourse with his family! Cowper answered him with warmth, not to say bitterness. The following words are significant: "I could show you among them two men, whose lives, though they have but little of what we call evangelical light, are ornaments to a Christian country—men who fear God more than some who profess to love Him."

* January 28, 1786.

In the spring of this year Lady Hesketh wrote, proposing to visit him in June. His delight knew no bounds; he could talk, write, think of nothing else: "June," he said, "was never so wished for before since June was made." And at the same time he received an anonymous letter, beseeching him not to overstrain his powers, nor be distressed if Homer did not sell to his expectations, and announcing the intention of sending him £50 a year. He poured out his feelings in a letter to Lady Hesketh. He had spent hours and hours examining the handwriting. First he thought it hers; then he was confident, from the method of underscoring, and the forms of the letters, that it was her father's disguised. The writer has never been made known. Lady Hesketh knew, and she seems to have told him that it was neither she nor her father. He responded gratefully and touchingly, and added that he would not attempt further to penetrate the secret. Though he made pretence to talk of his benefactor as _he_, he must have felt sure, as every one else must, that it was Theodora, faithful to her young love. All this will explain the following extract from a letter to Unwin, dated "Olney, July 10, 1786:"—

"Within this twelvemonth my income has received an addition of a clear £100 per annum. For a considerable part of it I am indebted to my dear cousin now on the other side of the Orchard. At Florence she obtained me £20 a year from Lord Cowper; since he came home she has recommended me with such good effect to his notice that he has added twenty more; twenty she has added herself, and ten she has procured me from the William of my name whom you saw at Hertingfordbury. From my anonymous friend who insists on not being known or guessed at, and never shall by me, I have an annuity of £50. All these sums have accrued within this year, except the first, making together, as you perceive, an exact century of pounds annually poured into the replenished purse of your once poor poet of Olney."

The "dear cousin" is, of course, Lady Hesketh. She had come in June, according to appointment, and taken lodgings at the vicarage, now occupied by a bachelor, who only wanted two rooms. The first meeting was too much for Cowper, and he fell into an alarming fit of melancholy. But it did not last, and they were soon all happy together. She was pleased with Mrs. Unwin, and it is to this period that her letters to her sister belong. He wrote to Hill that he was happier than he had ever been since he had come to Olney. He even wrote cheerfully to Newton, once or twice; but as time went on his brighter hopes faded, and he again spoke of himself as vainly seeking communion with God. He had hoped, he said, that he was coming out of the Red Sea, and was preparing to sing the song of Moses, but the comfort had once more been wrested from him. Still he was hopeful that it might yet come, and embraced every promise of it with alacrity. Especially he took hold of a thought which Lady Hesketh's liveliness inspired,—_Olney was dull!_ The floods and the mud kept him a prisoner; both he and Mrs. Unwin were feeling the want of exercise tell upon their health and spirits,—their house was not very convenient, and it was tumbling down, and Lady Hesketh urged them to change. A house at Weston Underwood, belonging to Mr. Throckmorton, was vacant; there would be pleasant society in their friends; the house was offered to them on very liberal terms, and Lady Hesketh furnished the means of removal. In November 1786 they left Olney, after a residence of nineteen years.

Will it be believed that Newton again interfered in a most intolerable manner, accusing him of deviating into forbidden paths, and leading a life so unbecoming the Gospel as to grieve his London friends and amaze the people of Olney? He doubted more than ever, he said, whether he would ever be restored to Christian privileges again, and added that there was still intercourse between London and Olney, and that he should be sure to hear of any fresh evil doings. The sins which called forth this solemn warning were that he was, of course, more intimate with the Throckmortons, and that he sometimes even took a walk with Lady Hesketh, or by himself, on Sunday evenings.* It is only fair to Newton to suppose that some slanderous tongue had spread false reports; but he might at least have inquired before writing. Even Mr. Bull thinks that in this he "might have been a little precipitate." †

They had only been a fortnight at Weston when a sore trial fell upon them. William Unwin, while on a tour through the southern counties with Henry Thornton, the son of their kind friend, sickened and died of typhus fever at Winchester. Of all Cowper's friends he had been the dearest. Of all the affectionate letters which Cowper wrote, those to Unwin are the most affectionate. He deserved to be loved. From the day that they met under the trees at Huntingdon, his affection had never known change. He is buried in the south aisle of Winchester Cathedral.

Cowper's grief was great, not only for his own loss, but for the mother, the widow, and the orphans. But he was perfectly assured of his friend's gain, and the habitual composure of Mrs. Unwin also taught him to control his sorrow. His letters to his cousin, after the first outburst of sorrow, were as playful as ever, and he worked at Homer with unabated zeal. But the clouds were gathering again. A month later he had "had a little nervous feeling lately." In two months he had only done thirty lines of Homer. He fought hard against his terror, as his letters show, but in vain; and for a while—from January to June 1787—he was again in a terrible state. He again attempted self-destruction, and very nearly succeeded. He would see no one, nor have any one near him but Mrs. Unwin. He recovered almost suddenly, and immediately resumed his correspondence. His first letter was to a new friend, from that time onward a regular and valued one. This was Samuel Rose, a young man of twenty, who, being on his way from Glasgow University to London, turned aside to Olney,

* Cowper to Unwin, September 24, 1786.   † Memorials, p. 285.

partly to gratify his curiosity, partly to bring him the thanks of some Scotch professors. This was on the very eve of his mental attack. On his recovery, Cowper hastened to acknowledge the attention. This visit is noteworthy, because Rose took occasion of it to present him with the Poems of Burns. When he wrote to Rose he had read them all twice, and though the Scotch tongue had been somewhat troublesome to him, he was satisfied that the work was "a very extraordinary production." [*] Rose was invited to Weston, and the more Cowper saw of him the better he liked him, and the feeling was entirely reciprocated, as is shown by Rose's own letters to his sister, still in existence. He proved very useful, for he was never better pleased than in transcribing the translation of Homer from Cowper's rough copy. Cowper's mind seemed now at ease again. He still suffered a good deal from headache and giddiness, [†] but was in great hopes of ultimate recovery. He stood godfather to one of Rose's children, who was accordingly christened "William Cowper." Another point which was noticed by Lady Hesketh was that he said grace at his dinner. In his darkest moods he used, while grace was being said, to play with his knife and fork ostentatiously, as proving that he had no part nor lot in worshipping God. Mr. Throckmorton gave him the run of his library, and seeing, as he often said, that he had no books of his own, [‡] this was a great benefaction. It is remarkable that the only letters of his at this time which are dark and sad are those to Newton. Though he esteemed him as highly as ever, many of his former illusions had been connected with him, and, conscious of that, Cowper always dreaded the time when friendship required him to write.

Lady Hesketh was to visit him in the spring of 1788, but the continued illness of her father, now eighty-six years old, forced her to put off the visit from time to time. In one of his letters to her Cowper enclosed a poem, which he entitled "Benefactions ; a poem in Shenstone's manner. Addressed to my dearest Coz, April 14, 1788." This poem he afterwards altered into the form in which it will be found in p. 357 of this volume. But the two last stanzas as they stood originally, bearing so entirely on his present condition, ought not to be lost. They ran thus :—

> " These items endear my abode,
>   Disposing me oft to reflect
> By whom they were kindly bestowed,
>   Whom here I impatient expect.
> But hush !   She a parent attends,
>   Whose dial hand points to eleven,
> Who, oldest and dearest of friends,
>   Waits only a passage to heaven.

---

[*] July 24, 1787.

[†] "The jarrings make my skull feel like a broken egg-shell. . . . I have a perpetual din in my head, and though I am not deaf, hear nothing aright, neither my own voice, nor that of others. I am under a tub, from which tub accept my best love.—Yours, W.C."—*To Lady Hesketh*, Sept. 29, 1787.

[‡] He says in one letter that he has bought a Latin dictionary, and now, perhaps, will buy more Latin books to make it useful, for that at present he has only a Virgil.

> " Then willingly want her awhile,
>   And, sweeping the cords of your lyre,
> The gloom of her absence beguile,
>   As now, with poetical fire.
> 'Tis yours, for true glory athirst,
>   In high-flying ditty to rise
> On feathers renown'd from the first
>   For bearing a goose to the skies."

The old man died in the following June. The letters of consolation which Cowper wrote to Lady Hesketh are very beautiful. He says in one : " I often think what a joyful interview there has been between him and some of his contemporaries who went before him. The truth of the matter is, my dear, that they are the happy ones, and that we shall never be such ourselves until we have joined the party." It is sad after reading this to come upon a letter to Mr. Newton, written after a visit from him in the following August, marked by the old despair.

The beginning of 1790 found him still renewing old acquaintances and making fresh ones. This time it was his mother's relatives, of whom he had heard nothing since his childhood. John Johnson was the grandson of his mother's brother, Roger Donne, rector of Catfield, in Norfolk. He was a Cambridge undergraduate, who had written a poem, and brought it to his relative for his opinion. It was not very favourable,[*] but the youth still rejoiced in his visit, for Cowper's heart yearned towards him. He went back quite delighted, with an introduction to Lady Hesketh, and much Homer to transcribe. On telling his aunt, Mrs. Bodham, how Cowper had received him, and how warmly he had expressed his affection for her (for they had been playfellows as children), she sent him an affectionate letter, and with it a portrait of his mother. He acknowledged the gift in one of the most charming of his letters, and wrote upon it the beautiful elegy of which we have already spoken. We see in it how the memory of the touch of her vanished hand, of the sound of her stilled voice, *almost* gave him peace of mind. Had anything earthly been able to do so, it would have been the memory of his mother's love. But his desire was unto that which is eternal and immortal, and until this desire was fulfilled, even until mortality was swallowed up of life, darkness rested upon his soul. This poem will always testify, not only the earnestness of his love and the strength of his faith in God, but also the truth that—

> " Nor man, nor nature, satisfy whom only God created."

Another correspondent was Clotworthy Rowley, of Stoke-by-Nayland, with whom he had been intimate in the Temple, but whom he had not seen since. Rowley opened correspondence on the occasion of returning half a dozen books, which

---

[*] Cowper's advice to him is worth repeating, whether sound or not : " Remember that in writing, perspicuity is always more than half the battle. The want of it is the ruin of more than half the poetry that is published. A meaning that does not stare you in the face is as bad as no meaning, because nobody will take the pains to poke for it."

Cowper had lent him twenty-five years before. A Mrs. King also, wife of a friend of his brother, introduced herself on the strength of that, and was kindly received. Last, not least, Thurlow, whom Lady Hesketh had found means to reach, interested himself in the subscription to his Homer (August 1788), and they exchanged some letters on the relative merits of rhyme and blank verse. It is noticeable that Cowper, who wrote the first letter, begins "My Lord," and Thurlow with "Dear Cowper." But Cowper sticks to his original form of address.

Whilst engaged busily on Homer, he was constantly throwing off small pieces, as relaxations. Amongst them were the poems on the slave trade,* which Lady Hesketh asked him to write. He also composed a few review articles. The poem on the Queen's visit to London (p. 370) was written at Lady Hesketh's request, she probably hoping that he would succeed Warton as Poet Laureate. But when the latter died in the following year Cowper begged her not to think of it. "He should never," he said, "write anything more worth reading if he were appointed." So the honour was not asked for, and Pye † was appointed.

The Homer was published in the summer of 1791. His illness and long-continued intervals of incapacity for work had occasioned the delay. Johnson took all expenses, and paid him £1,000, the copyright remaining Cowper's. It was pub-

---

* Pp. 363 – 365.
† I cannot resist the temptation of laying a specimen of his productions before the reader :—

"AN ODE ON HER MAJESTY'S BIRTHDAY.

" Britannia hail the blessed day,
　Ye smiling seasons sing the same,
　The birth of *Albion*'s Queen proclaim,
　Great *Cæsar*'s fame and regal sway,
　Ye gentle tides and gales convey
　To foreign lands, that sink with fear ;
　While victories and laurels come
　To heighten joy and love at home :
　Can Heaven greater gifts confer?
　Can more success a monarch share?
　　Ye songsters of the ærial tribe,
　Break forth in sweet melodious sounds ;
　Ye flowery fields and fertile grounds,
　Rich treasures yield for *Cæsar*'s bride.
　　Ye autumns and ye winters sing,
　Due praise and honour to our king.

A I R.

" The heavens to ease a monarch's care,
　Benignly gave *Charlotte* the fair ;
　Who adds such lustre to the crown,
　Such strong alliance, great renown,
　By royal birth and noble mind,
　As claim no wonder from mankind,
　That so much worth and goodness prove,
　An object fit for *Cæsar*'s love.

lished in two volumes, quarto, at three guineas. I do not feel competent to criticize it. It seems to me dreary and dull, but not more so than other translations of Homer. He was qualified by his scholarship, which Pope was not. The translation, therefore, is probably as accurate as any translation can be. But he had no sympathy for the wars and battles. Arthur Clough's commentary on it is, after all, the most exhaustive—"Where is the man who has ever read it?" His undertaking it at all seems to me one of the misfortunes arising from the breach with Lady Austen. She might have suggested something better than the wasting of five years in such profitless labour.

What next? For both he and his friends had learned that continual occupation was necessary to his well-being. Lady Hesketh was for another long poem, and proposed to him "The Mediterranean" as a subject. He replied, truly, that he did not know history enough, and that, moreover, it seemed a subject not for one poem, but for twenty. A neighbouring clergyman, Mr. Buchanan, proposed "The Four Ages of Man." He liked the idea extremely, and began upon it. He began also "Yardley Oak," keeping it apparently as a secret with which to surprise his friends when it was finished. But Johnson invited him to undertake an edition of Milton, as a match for Boydell's Shakespeare, Cowper to write notes and translate the Latin and Italian poems, and Fuseli to do the illustrations. He undertook this, and did the work of translation with great pleasure, as well as success. But the

RECITATIVO.

" *Britons*, with heart-felt joy, with decent mirth,
Hail now your Queen, hail now the day of birth ;
Send voice for blessings, send wishes to the sky,
For peace, long life, and numerous progeny.

AIR.

" See envy's self is fain to own
Those virtues which adorn the throne ;
While home-bred faction droops her head,
See liberty and justice spread
Their happy influence around,
The land where plenteous stores abound,
Of wealth and grain, where arts and science
To every nation bid defiance.

RECITATIVO.

" Fly hence, ye gloomy cares,
For you here's no employ ;
Here sweetest ease appears,
With real love and joy.

CHORUS.

" While *George* and *Charlotte* rule the land,
Nor storms nor threats we'll fear,
Their names our seas and coasts defend,
And drive our foes afar ;
Each season, and each year, shall roll
Their fame and power from pole to pole.'

e 2

notes were irksome to him; oftentimes he would sit down and be unable to write anything, and it became clear, after long effort, that the engagement must be given up.

For not only was his spirit becoming darkened again, but another great sorrow was impending over him. Mrs. Unwin, who had never recovered a fall on some ice in the winter of 1788-9, was seized with paralysis in December 1791. She recovered slowly as the spring came on, but the effect upon Cowper's spirits could not but be severe.

He had taken the fancy that he heard voices speaking to him on waking in the morning. Sometimes he understood them, but more often they were unintelligible. A schoolmaster at Olney, Samuel Teedon (whether knave or fool may be doubtful), whose uncouth compliments and heavy-witted opinions Cowper had often quizzed, undertook to interpret these voices. Mrs. Unwin at first appears to have humoured his fancy, but as her disease grew upon her, she too fell in with the insanity, and now nothing was done until the voices had spoken, and Teedon had interpreted. The balderdash was all written down, and volumes were filled with it. No one but themselves were made acquainted with these miserable proceedings. Sir John Throckmorton too, on succeeding to the baronetcy, left the neighbourhood for his late father's residence in Oxfordshire, and this must have been a great loss at such a trying time, though his successor afterwards proved equally kind to them. He was Sir John's younger brother, George, but had taken the name of Courtenay.*

The Milton engagement brought Cowper one pleasure before it came to an end. It was the cause of his friendship with Hayley. The latter had been engaged by Boydell to write a life for a sumptuous edition of Milton, and the public were thus led to believe that Hayley and Cowper were engaged as rivals. Hayley was much distressed, and wrote to Cowper, hitherto a stranger to him, to assure him that he had no idea that the latter was so engaged, and pointing out that their two works would be so different in character that they would not clash. He added the warmest expressions of respect and admiration, and enclosed also a sonnet to him. Cowper responded in a like spirit; the correspondence thus begun was carried on with energy, and in May 1791 Hayley visited him at Weston. But before he had been there long Mrs. Unwin had a second and more severe attack of paralysis. Hayley's kindness and usefulness under this trial endeared him to Cowper for life; and on Mrs. Unwin's partial recovery, the two recluses, in the following July, returned his visit at his residence at Eartham in Sussex. Cowper might well call such a journey a "tremendous exploit" for them, considering what their life for twenty years had been.

No one reads Hayley's plays or poems now, but he was an amiable and remarkable man. His domestic life was unhappy and irregular, and some of his writings

---

* He had, on previous visits to his brother, been one of the most ardent transcribers of Homer, and his wife had been dubbed "my lady of the ink-bottle."

are prurient, but he was most unselfish and generous towards his friends; his reading was extensive, and his critical power considerable. Gibbon visited Eartham, and called it a little paradise, but declared that its owner's mind was even more elegant than it. Thurlow, Flaxman, Warton, all loved and admired him, and Miss Seward poured forth admiring verses upon him.

Cowper, who had hardly ever seen a hill in his life, was of course delighted with the South Downs, the wide landscape, the sea, and the Isle of Wight. He could not write, however; all was so strange to him. "I am like the man in the fable," he said, "who could leap nowhere but at Rhodes." He gave some help to Hayley in translating "Adam," an Italian dramatic poem, a wretchedly poor work, not worth reprinting. Poor Charlotte Smith was staying there, writing "The Old Manor House." She was wonderfully rapid, and used each evening to read to them what she had written in the day. On this occasion, too, Romney, who was Hayley's dearest friend, took the portrait by which Cowper is so well known to us. The portrait by Abbot had been taken just before starting for Eartham.

Six weeks were spent here—happy weeks; but Cowper began to pine for quiet Weston again. Repose and seclusion had always suited him best; he felt them indispensable to him now. Mrs. Unwin's continued infirmities, and the declining season of the year, concurred in making him anxious to be gone, and they returned to Weston in September. How he wrote to Teedon day after day, and week after week, we pause not to relate; it is most distressing to read the letters. Newton never exercised a greater power over him than this man, who received all his confidences, prescribed to him what prayers to use, and how long a time to spend in them, and prognosticated his future. Cowper paid him from time to time much more money than he could afford, even while, sound in all respects but one, he was making hearty fun of his absurdity and vanity. Mrs. Unwin, too, got worse; and he who had been the object of her care so long now became her tender and attentive nurse. The poor woman became so irritable and exacting that his health, comfort, and peace of mind were sacrificed to her fancies. She sat silent, looking into the fire, unable to work or to read; under such circumstances he had little heart to write. His state became more wretched and dark than ever. Small doses of James' powders, or a small quantity of laudanum taken at night, were the best remedies that he had found, he says. "I seem to myself," he wrote to Newton,[*] "to be scrambling always in the dark, among rocks and precipices, without a guide, but with an enemy ever at my heels, prepared to push me head-long. Thus I have spent twenty years, but thus I shall not spend twenty years more. Long ere that period arrives, the grand question concerning everlasting weal or woe will be decided." Lady Hesketh might have wrought him good, perhaps, but she had fallen out of health, and was ordered to Bath. Besides, she

* Nov. 11, 1792.

knew nothing of the Teedon delusion, and was quite abroad in her thoughts of the doings at Weston. The schoolmaster's promises of relief within a specified period failed, and, as a matter of course, Cowper, who had trusted to them implicitly, came to the conclusion that God had finally forsaken him and cast him off.

But what is so especially touching in the history of this sad period is that he fought so hard against his insanity. His letters to his friends are still playful and witty, and a great number of his smaller poems belong to this year. He worked at Milton as long as it was possible, and he studied the old commentaries on Homer, with a view of improving his second edition when it should be called for. There are passages in his letters which lead one to believe that if he had only had a fair chance his mind might have recovered itself. But what chance was there, with Teedon on one side and poor Mrs. Unwin on the other? In one of his letters he says that while he is writing it, she is sitting in her corner, sometimes bursting into a laugh at nothing, sometimes talking nonsense, to which no one thinks of paying attention. And yet this was, for months, the only "conversation" that he had; and she would not even let him read, except aloud to her. The only way by which he could gain any leisure was to rise at six, begin work at once, and breakfast at eleven; and this he did in winter as well as in summer. In the autumn of 1793 Lord Spencer invited him to Althorpe to meet Gibbon, who was making a long stay there, and he was much tempted to go. But the state of his spirits, as well as Mrs. Unwin's infirm condition, unhappily compelled him to decline the invitation.

Towards the end of the year 1793, just after he had dropped the Miltonic engagement, Lady Hesketh came to Weston. Hayley had been there a few weeks before; but in April 1794 received a message from her entreating him to come again, for that the unhappy patient had become much worse. He came at once. It was evidently a terrible sight to them; Hayley's unaffected description is most pathetic. The poor sufferer would hardly eat anything, and refused all medicine, walking backwards and forwards incessantly in his bedroom, believing from hour to hour that the devil was coming to carry him away. At Thurlow's request, Dr. Willis, whose success in the king's insanity had made his name renowned, came to Weston, but found the case past his skill. A letter came from Lord Spencer, announcing that the king granted Mr. Cowper a pension of £300 a year, but he was not in a condition to receive the announcement. Whilst he was worn out with fatigue, anguish, and fasting, Mrs. Unwin would insist on his dragging her round the garden. She persisted too in keeping the management of the household, and the reckless extravagance below stairs amazed and horrified Lady Hesketh, who, however, bravely struggled on for more than a year, vainly hoping to relieve him. She then wrote to his cousin Johnson, who had been recently ordained, urging the necessity of removal, and he came and succeeded in persuading Cowper to consent to it. It was spoken of as temporary, otherwise the consent would never have been given; but when it came to the last Cowper felt that he should never return.   He wrote, unseen by any one, these lines on a window-shutter :—

> " Farewell, dear scenes, for ever closed to me ;
> Oh ! for what sorrows must I now exchange ye."

It was the 30th of July, 1795.   He saw the Ouse once more, at St. Neots, on his journey.   And as he walked with Johnson through the churchyard in the moonlight, he talked with cheerfulness.   It was the last time that he was ever to do so.   They went first to North Tuddenham, then to Mundsley, on the coast, where Johnson noticed that the monotonous sound of the breakers seemed to soothe him, and finally they settled at Dunham Lodge, near Swaffham.   Johnson tried to coax him into composition or correspondence, but without avail.   The only thing that seemed to please him was being read to, and they read Richardson's novels to him.   This was evidently successful, and novel-reading was accordingly persisted in.   Presently Johnson spoke in his hearing of some criticisms on his Homer, and laid the volumes where he could see them.   They soon found that he had sought out the passages, and had made some corrections in his translation in consequence.   But Dunham proving inconvenient, they moved to a house in the little town of East Dereham in October 1796.   Two months afterwards (Dec. 17) Mrs. Unwin was released from her sufferings.   Johnson took Cowper to see her corpse.   He gazed for a minute or two, then uttered some half-finished exclamation of sorrow, and was led away.   He regained his calmness down-stairs, asked for a glass of wine,* and from that time never alluded to her again.   She was buried by torchlight, that he might not know the time of the funeral.

His friends hoped that Mrs. Unwin's release might allow of Cowper's restoration.   But the hope was vain.   The gloom which rested upon him was dark as ever.   Means, wise and unwise, were tried to dispel it †—the only one which at all succeeded being the attempt to interest him in his Homer.   In September 1797 Johnson placed the revised copy open before him at the place where he had left it off twelve months before, and opened all the commentaries at the same place.   Then after talking upon other subjects to him he led up to this.   After a while the Poet took up one of the books and sat down on the sofa, saying in a low and plaintive voice, " I may as well do this, for I can do nothing else."   And from that time he continued steadily at the work.   There were few outward signs of any alleviation of his misery, but he was always more composed when thus engaged ; and his letters to Lady Hesketh, though appalling in their fixed despair, occasionally contain "dear cousin," and "yours affectionately," both of which expressions he had quite dropped.   Old friends

---

* " He is wonderfully calm now, and made me give him a glass of wine the moment he got down, and took two pinches of snuff, which he had not done for nearly a week."—*Extract from Johnson's letter announcing the death.*
† One of them was the clandestine insertion of tubes into his bedroom, through which messages were spoken, professing to be supernatural, and intended to nullify the Teedon " voices " !

who came to see him, though he would not speak to them, nor appear to notice them, evidently were of some comfort to him, for he spoke of them afterwards. In March 1799 he finished with Homer. Johnson then put the unfinished "Four Ages of Man" before him. He altered a few lines, and added two or three more. But he was evidently past this. Easier subjects were mentioned. At length he said that he had thought of some Latin verses which he thought he might do, and next day he wrote "Montes Glaciales." The story had been read to him at Dunham Lodge, but he had not appeared to take any notice. A few days afterwards he translated it into English, and the next day wrote "The Castaway," founded upon a story in "Anson's Voyages," which he had heard read some months before. This was his last original poem. He still seemed to like being read to, and he listened to Gibbon's Miscellaneous Works and to his own poems, except "John Gilpin," which he forbade. Vincent Bourne was brought to him again, and he translated a few more of the poems, as well as some Fables from Gay. This was in Jan. 1800. The last words which he ever wrote were a correction of a mistranslation in Homer, which Hayley in a letter had pointed out. Two days afterwards (Feb. 1) signs of dropsy appeared in his feet, and a physician was called in. On his asking him how he felt, "I feel unutterable despair," was the answer. The last visitor who came to see him was Rose. Cowper showed evident regret at his departure.

There was a Miss Perowne, a friend of Miss Johnson, who was staying with them, who had more influence with him than any one. She only, and she not always, could persuade him to take any medicine. Mr. Johnson took courage, on one occasion, to speak to him of death as the deliverance from misery. He seemed to listen, but made no answer. Then Johnson spoke yet more encouragingly—spoke of the unutterable blessedness which God has prepared for those who love Him, and therefore for him. He was quiet until the last four words, then he passionately entreated that no such words should be spoken more. And so the sad days passed on, and no comfort appeared. So near was he to the eternal sunrise now, and yet not a ray of its light appeared to herald the day-dawn. Not an echo reached the dying man's ear of the voice of the Good Shepherd who walked by his side through that horrible valley. The ship was in the midst of the sea, all the waves and storms of despair beating and surging over it, and the Saviour was not yet visible, though He was walking on the waters.

Miss Perowne offered the sufferer a cordial. He refused it, saying, "What can it signify?" Those were his last words. Soon after, the tranquillity of unconsciousness came on, and lasted for some hours. It was five o'clock in the evening of St. Mark's Day, 1800, when the happy change came. Even so we must all be changed, in a moment, in the twinkling of an eye. Thank God.

"From that moment," says the relative who loved him so well, "until the coffin was closed, the expression into which his countenance had settled was that of calmness and composure, mingled as it were with holy surprise." A pretty fancy we may call this; but who can doubt that it symbolized the simple truth? All who had ever known him loved him; but the love of the best of us grows cold before the might of Thine, O most merciful Father of us all. Thy judgments are like the great deep; but Thy righteousness standeth like the strong mountains.

O poets! from a maniac's tongue, was poured the deathless singing!
O Christians! at your cross of hope, a hopeless hand was clinging!
O men! this man, in brotherhood, your weary paths beguiling,
Groaned inly while he taught you peace, and died while ye were smiling!

And now, what time ye all may read through dimming tears his story,
How discord on the music fell, and darkness on the glory,
And how, when one by one, sweet sounds and wandering lights departed,
He bore no less a loving face because so broken-hearted;

He shall be strong to sanctify the poet's high vocation,
And bow the meekest Christian down in meeker adoration:
Nor ever shall he be, in praise, by wise or good forsaken;
Named softly, as the household name of one whom God hath taken.

ELIZABETH BARRETT-BROWNING.

He was buried on Saturday, May 2, in Dereham Church, in St. Edmund's Chapel: Mrs. Unwin is buried in the north aisle. Lady Hesketh had a monument erected to him, for which Hayley wrote the following inscription:—

IN MEMORY
OF WILLIAM COWPER, ESQ.
Born in Hertfordshire 1731.
Buried in this Church 1800.

Ye, who with warmth the public triumph feel
Of talents, dignified by sacred zeal,
Here, to devotion's bard devoutly just,
Pay your fond tribute due to Cowper's dust!
England, exulting in his spotless fame,
Ranks with her dearest sons his favourite name:
Sense, fancy, wit, suffice not all to raise
So clear a title to affection's praise:
His highest honours to the heart belong;
His virtues form'd the magic of his song.

THE POETICAL WORKS

OF

WILLIAM COWPER

EARLY POEMS.

(PUBLISHED POSTHUMOUSLY.)

VERSES,

WRITTEN AT BATH IN HIS 17TH YEAR, ON FINDING THE HEEL OF A SHOE.

FORTUNE! I thank thee: gentle Goddess, thanks!
Not that my Muse, though bashful, shall deny
She would have thanked thee rather hadst thou cast
A treasure in her way; for neither meed
Of early breakfast, to dispel the fumes
And bowel-raking pains of emptiness,
Nor noontide feast, nor evening's cool repast,
Hopes she from this, presumptuous,—though perhaps
The cobbler, leather-carving artist, might.
Nathless she thanks thee, and accepts thy boon,
Whatever; not as erst the fabled cock,
Vain-glorious fool, unknowing what he found,
Spurned the rich gem thou gavest him. Wherefore, ah!
Why not on me that favour (worthier sure!)
Conferredst thou, Goddess? Thou art blind, thou say'st:
Enough! thy blindness shall excuse the deed.
   Nor does my Muse no benefit exhale
From this thy scant indulgence;—even here,
Hints, worthy sage Philosophy, are found,
Illustrious hints, to moralize my song.
This ponderous heel of perforated hide
Compact, with pegs indented many a row,
Haply (for such its massy form bespeaks)
The weighty tread of some rude peasant clown
Upbore: on this supported oft he stretched,
With uncouth strides, along the furrowed glebe,
Flattening the stubborn clod, till cruel Time,
(What will not cruel Time?) on a wry step,
Severed the strict cohesion; when, alas!
He, who could erst with even equal pace
Pursue his destined way with symmetry
And some proportion formed, now on one side,
Curtailed and maimed, the sport of vagrant boys,
Cursing his frail supporter, treacherous prop!
With toilsome steps, and difficult, moves on.
Thus fares it oft with other than the feet
Of humble villager: the statesman thus,
Up the steep road where proud ambition leads,

B

Aspiring, first uninterrupted winds
His prosperous way; nor fears miscarriage foul,
While policy prevails and friends prove true:
But that support soon failing, by him left
On whom he most depended,—basely left,
Betrayed, deserted,—from his airy height
Headlong he falls, and through the rest of life
Drags the dull load of disappointment on.

1748

TRANSLATION OF PSALM CXXXVII.

To Babylon's proud waters brought,
  In bondage where we lay,
With tears on Sion's Hill we thought,
  And sighed our hours away;
Neglected on the willows hung
Our useless harps, while every tongue
  Bewailed the fatal day.

Then did the base insulting foe
  Some joyous notes demand,
Such as in Sion used to flow
  From Judah's happy band:
Alas! what joyous notes have we,
Our country spoiled, no longer free,
  And in a foreign land?
O Solyma! if e'er thy praise
  Be silent in my song,
Rude and unpleasing be the lays,
  And artless be my tongue!

Thy name my fancy still employs;
To thee, great fountain of my joys,
  My sweetest airs belong.

Remember, Lord! that hostile sound,
  When Edom's children cried,
"Razed be her turrets to the ground,
  And humbled be her pride!"
Remember, Lord! and let the foe
The terrors of thy vengeance know,
  The vengeance they defied!

Thou too, great Babylon, shalt fall
  A victim to our God;
Thy monstrous crimes already call
  For heaven's chastising rod.
Happy who shall thy little ones
Relentless dash against the stones,
  And spread their limbs abroad.

SONG.

No more shall hapless Celia's ears
  Be fluttered with the cries
Of lovers drowned in floods of tears,
  Or murdered by her eyes;
No serenades to break her rest,
Nor songs her slumbers to molest,
          With my fa, la, la.

The fragrant flowers that once would
  And flourish in her hair,   [bloom
Since she no longer breathes perfume
  Their odours to repair,
Must fade, alas! and wither now,
As placed on any common brow,
          With my fa, la, la.

Her lip, so winning and so meek,
  No longer has its charms;
As well she might by whistling seek
  To lure us to her arms;

Affected once, 'tis real now,
As her forsaken gums may show,
          With my fa, la, la.

The down that on her chin so smooth
  So lovely once appeared,
That, too, has left her with her youth,
  Or sprouts into a beard;
As fields, so green when newly sown,
With stubble stiff are overgrown,
          With my fa, la, la.

Then, Celia, leave your apish tricks,
  And change your girlish airs,
For ombre, snuff, and politics,
  Those joys that suit your years;
No patches can lost youth recall,
Nor whitewash prop a tumbling wall,
          With my fa, la, la.

THE CERTAINTY OF DEATH.

MORTALS! around your destined heads
    Thick fly the shafts of Death,
And lo! the savage spoiler spreads
    A thousand toils beneath.

In vain we trifle with our fate;
    Try every art in vain;
At best we but prolong the date,
    And lengthen out our pain.

Fondly we think all danger fled,
    For Death is ever nigh;
Outstrips our unavailing speed,
    Or meets us as we fly.

Thus the wrecked mariner may strive
    Some desert shore to gain,
Secure of life, if he survive
    The fury of the main.

But there, to famine doomed a prey,
    Finds the mistaken wretch
He but escaped the troubled sea,
    To perish on the beach.

Since then in vain we strive to guard
    Our frailty from the foe,
Lord, let me live not unprepared
    To meet the fatal blow!

OF HIMSELF.

WILLIAM was once a bashful youth;
    His modesty was such,
That one might say (to say the truth)
    He rather had too much.

Some said that it was want of sense,
    And others want of spirit,
(So blest a thing is impudence,)
    While others could not bear it.

But some a different notion had,
    And at each other winking,
Observed, that though he little said,
    He paid it off with thinking.

Howe'er, it happened, by degrees,
    He mended and grew perter;
In company was more at ease,
    And dressed a little smarter;

Nay, now and then would look quite gay,
    As other people do;

And sometimes said, or tried to say,
    A witty thing or so.

He eyed the women, and made free
    To comment on their shapes;
So that there was, or seemed to be,
    No fear of a relapse.

The women said, who thought him rough,
    But now no longer foolish,
"The creature may do well enough,
    But wants a deal of polish."

At length, improved from head to heel,
    'Twere scarce too much to say,
No dancing bear was so genteel,
    Or half so *dégagé*.

Now that a miracle so strange
    May not in vain be shown,
Let the dear maid who wrought change
    E'er claim him for her own.

THE SYMPTOMS OF LOVE.

WOULD my Delia know if I love, let her take
My last thought at night, and the first when I wake;
When my prayers and best wishes preferred for her sake.

Let her guess what I muse on, when, rambling alone,
I stride o'er the stubble each day with my gun,
Never ready to shoot till the covey is flown.

Let her think what odd whimsies I have in my brain,
When I read one page over and over again,
And discover at last that I read it in vain.

Let her say why so fixed and so steady my look,
Without ever regarding the person who spoke,
Still affecting to laugh, without hearing the joke.

Or why when with pleasure her praises I hear
(That sweetest of melody sure to my ear),
I attend, and at once inattentive appear.

And lastly, when summoned to drink to my flame,
Let her guess why I never once mention her name,
Though herself and the woman I love are the same.

AN APOLOGY

FOR NOT SHOWING HER WHAT I HAD WROTE.

DID not my Muse (what can she less?)
Perceive her own unworthiness,
Could she by some well-chosen theme
But hope to merit your esteem,
She would not thus conceal her lays,
Ambitious to deserve your praise.
But should my Delia take offence,
And frown on her impertinence,
In silence, sorrowing and forlorn,
Would the despairing trifler mourn,
Curse her ill-tuned, unpleasing lute,
Then sigh and sit for ever mute.
In secret therefore let her play,
Squandering her idle notes away
In secret as she chants along,
Cheerful and careless in her song ;
Nor heeds she whether harsh or clear,
Free from each terror, every fear,
From that, of all most dreaded, free,
The terror of offending Thee.

Cutfield, July 1752.

At the same place.

DELIA, the unkindest girl on earth,
    When I besought the fair,
That favour of intrinsic worth,
    A ringlet of her hair,

Refused that instant to comply
    With my absurd request,
For reasons she could specify,
    Some twenty score at least.

Trust me, my dear, however odd
    It may appear to say,
I sought it merely to defraud
    Thy spoiler of his prey.

Yes ! when its sister locks shall fade,
    As quickly fade they must,
When all their beauties are decayed,
    Their gloss, their colour, lost—

Ah then ! if haply to my share
    Some slender pittance fall,
If I but gain one single hair,
    Nor age usurp them all ;—

When you behold it still as sleek,
    As lovely to the view,
As when it left thy snowy neck, —
    That Eden where it grew,—

Then shall my Delia's self declare
    That I professed the truth,
And have preserved my little share
    In everlasting youth.

AN ATTEMPT AT THE MANNER OF WALLER.

Did not thy reason and thy sense,
With most persuasive eloquence,
Convince me that obedience due
None may so justly claim as you,
By right of beauty you would be
Mistress o'er my heart and me.

Then fear not I should e'er rebel,
My gentle love! I might as well
A froward peevishness put on,
And quarrel with the mid-day sun;

Or question who gave him a right
To be so fiery and so bright.

Nay, this were less absurd and vain
Than disobedience to thy reign;
His beams are often too severe;
But thou art mild, as thou art fair;
First from necessity we own your sway,
Then scorn our freedom, and by choice
    obey.

Drayton, March 1753.

A SONG.

The sparkling eye, the mantling cheek,
The polished front, the snowy neck,
  How seldom we behold in one!
Glossy looks, and brow serene,
Venus' smiles, Diana's mien,
  All meet in you, and you alone.

Beauty like other powers maintains
Her empire, and by union reigns;
  Each single feature faintly warms:

But where at once we view displayed
Unblemished grace, the perfect maid
  Our eyes, our ears, our heart alarms.

So when on earth the god of day
Obliquely sheds his tempered ray,
    Through convex orbs the beams
      transmit,
The beams that gently warmed before,
Collected, gently warm no more,
  But glow with more prevailing heat.

A SONG.

On the green margin of the brook
  Despairing Phyllida reclined,
Whilst every sigh and every look
  Declared the anguish of her mind.
"Am I less lovely then? (she cries,
  And in the waves her form surveyed;)
Oh yes, I see my languid eyes,
  My faded cheek, my colour fled:
These eyes no more like lightning pierced,
These cheeks grew pale, when Damon first
  His Phyllida betrayed.

"The rose he in his bosom wore,
  How oft upon my breast was seen!

And when I kissed the drooping flower
  'Behold,' he cried, 'it blooms again!'
The wreaths that bound my braided
    hair,
Himself next day was proud to wear
  At church, or on the green."

While thus sad Phyllida lamented,
  Chance brought unlucky Thyrsis on;
Unwillingly the nymph consented,
  But Damon first the cheat begun.
She wiped the fallen tears away,
Then sighed and blushed, as who
    should say,
  "Ah! Thyrsis, I am won."

UPON A VENERABLE RIVAL.

FULL thirty frosts since thou wert young
  Have chilled the withered grove,
Thou wretch! and hast thou lived so long,
  Nor yet forgot to love !

Ye Sages ! spite of your pretences
  To wisdom, you must own
Your folly frequently commences
  When you acknowledge none.

Not that I deem it weak to love,
  Or folly to admire ;
But ah ! the pangs we lovers prove
  Far other years require.

Unheeded on the youthful brow
  The beams of Phœbus play ;
But unsupported Age stoops low
  Beneath the sultry ray.

For once, then, if untutored youth,
  Youth unapproved by years,
May chance to deviate into truth,
  When your experience errs ;

For once attempt not to despise
  What I esteem a rule :
Who early loves, though young, is wise,—
  Who old, though grey, a fool.

AN ODE

ON READING MR. RICHARDSON'S HISTORY OF SIR CHARLES GRANDISON.

SAY, ye apostate and profane,
Wretches who blush not to disdain
    Allegiance to your God,
Did e'er your idly-wasted love
Of virtue for her sake remove
    And lift you from the crowd ?

Would you the race of glory run ?
Know, the devout, and they alone,
    Are equal to the task :
The labours of the illustrious course
Far other than the unaided force
    Of human vigour ask,

To arm against repeated ill
The patient heart, too brave to feel
    The tortures of despair ;
Nor safer yet high-crested Pride,
When wealth flows in with every tide
    To gain admittance there.

To rescue from the tyrant's sword
The oppressed ;—unseen and unim-
    plored,
    To cheer the face of woe ;

From lawless insult to defend
An orphan's right, a fallen friend,
    And a forgiven foe ;—

These, these distinguish from the crowd,
And these alone, the great and good,
    The guardians of mankind ;
Whose bosoms with these virtues heave,
Oh, with what matchless speed they
    leave
    The multitude behind !

Then ask ye, from what cause on earth
Virtues like these derive their birth ?
    Derived from Heaven alone,
Full on that favoured breast they shine,
Where Faith and Resignation join
    To call the blessing down.

Such is that heart ;—but while the Muse
Thy theme, O Richardson, pursues,
    Her feebler spirits faint ;
She cannot reach, and would not wrong,
That subject for an angel's song,
    The hero, and the saint !

IN A LETTER TO C. P., ESQ.

ILL WITH THE RHEUMATISM.

GRANT me the Muse, ye gods! whose humble flight
Seeks not the mountain-top's pernicious height;
Who can the tall Parnassian cliff forsake,
To visit oft the still Lethean lake;
Now her slow pinions brush the silent shore,
Now gently skim the unwrinkled waters o'er,
There dips her downy plumes, thence upward flies,
And sheds soft slumbers on her votary's eyes.

IN A LETTER TO THE SAME.

IN IMITATION OF SHAKESPEARE.

TRUST me, the meed of praise, dealt thriftily
From the nice scale of judgment, honours more
Than does the lavish and o'erbearing tide
Of profuse courtesy. Not all the gems
Of India's richest soil at random spread
O'er the gay vesture of some glittering dame,
Give such alluring vantage to the person,
As the scant lustre of a few, with choice
And comely guise of ornament disposed.

At Cutfield.

THIS evening, Delia, you and I
Have managed most delightfully,
    For with a frown we parted;
Having contrived some trifle that
We both may be much troubled at,
    And sadly disconcerted.

Yet well as each performed their part,
We might perceive it was but art;
    And that we both intended
To sacrifice a little ease;
For all such petty flaws as these
    Are made but to be mended.

You knew, dissembler! all the while,
How sweet it was to reconcile
    After this heavy pelt;
That we should gain by this allay
When next we met, and laugh away
    The care we never felt.

Happy! when we but seek to endure
A little pain, then find a cure
    By double joy requited;
For friendship, like a severed bone,
Improves and gains a stronger tone
    When aptly reunited.

WRITTEN IN A QUARREL.

(THE DELIVERY OF IT PREVENTED BY A RECONCILIATION.)

THINK, Delia, with what cruel haste
    Our fleeting pleasures move,
Nor heedless thus in sorrow waste
    The moments due to love;

Be wise, my fair, and gently treat
    These few that are our friends;
Think, thus abused, what sad regret
    Their speedy flight attends!

Sure in those eyes I love so well,
  And wished so long to see,
Anger I thought could never dwell,
  Or anger aimed at me.

No bold offence of mine I knew
  Should e'er provoke your hate ;
And, early taught to think you true,
  Still hoped a gentler fate.

SEE where the Thames, the purest
    stream
That wavers to the noon-day beam,
  Divides the vale below ;
While like a vein of liquid ore
His waves enrich the happy shore,
  Still shining as they flow !

Nor yet, my Delia, to the main
Runs the sweet tide without a stain,
  Unsullied as it seems ;
The nymphs of many a sable flood
Deform with streaks of oozy mud
  The bosom of the Thames.

Some idle rivulets, that feed
And suckle every noisome weed,
  A sandy bottom boast ;
For ever bright, for ever clear,
The trifling shallow rills appear
  In their own channel lost.

Thus fares it with the human soul,
Where copious floods of passion roll,
  By genuine love supplied ;

How blest the youth whom Fate ordains
A kind relief from all his pains,
  In some admired fair ;
Whose tenderest wishes find expressed
Their own resemblance in her breast,
  Exactly copied there !

What good soe'er the gods dispense,
The enjoyment of its influence
  Still on her love depends ;
Her love, the shield that guards his
    heart,
Or wards the blow, or blunts the dart
  That peevish Fortune sends.

Thus, Delia, while thy love endures,
The flame my happy breast secures
  From Fortune's fickle power ;

With kindness bless the present hour,
  Or oh ! we meet in vain !
What can we do in absence more
  Than suffer and complain?

Fated to ills beyond redress,
  We must endure our woe ;
The days allowed us to possess,
  'Tis madness to forego.

Fair in itself the current shows,
But ah ! a thousand anxious woes
  Pollute the noble tide.

These are emotions known to few ;
For where at most a vapoury dew
  Surrounds the tranquil heart,
There as the triflers never prove
The glad excess of real love,
  They never prove the smart.

Oh then, my life, at last relent !
Though cruel the reproach I sent,
  My sorrow was unfeigned :
Your passion, had I loved you not,
You might have scorned, renounced,
    forgot,
  And I had ne'er complained.

While you indulge a groundless fear,
The imaginary woes you bear
  Are real woes to me :
But thou art kind, and good thou art,
Nor wilt, by wronging thine own heart,
  Unjustly punish me.

Change as she list, she may increase,
But not abate my happiness,
  Confirmed by thee before.

Thus while I share her smiles with thee,
Welcome, my love, shall ever be
  The favours she bestows ;
Yet not on those I found my bliss,
But in the noble ecstasies
  The faithful bosom knows.

And when she prunes her wings for
    flight,
And flutters nimbly from my sight,
  Contented I resign
Whate'er she gave ; thy love alone
I can securely call my own,
  Happy while that is mine.

AN EPISTLE TO ROBERT LLOYD, ESQ.

'TIS not that I design to rob
Thee of thy birthright, gentle Bob,
For thou art born sole heir and single
Of dear Mat Prior's easy jingle;
Nor that I mean, while thus I knit
My threadbare sentiments together,
To show my genius or my wit,
When God and you know I have
    neither;
Or such, as might be better shown
By letting poetry alone.
'Tis not with either of these views
That I presume to address the Muse:
But to divert a fierce banditti
(Sworn foes to every thing that's witty),
That, with a black infernal train,
Make cruel inroads in my brain,
And daily threaten to drive thence
My little garrison of sense:
The fierce banditti which I mean,
Are gloomy thoughts led on by Spleen.
Then there's another reason yet,
Which is, that I may fairly quit
The debt which justly became due
The moment when I heard from you:
And you might grumble, crony mine,
If paid in any other coin;
Since twenty sheets of lead, God knows,
(I would say twenty sheets of prose,)
Can ne'er be deemed worth half so much
As one of gold, and yours was such.
Thus the preliminaries settled,
I fairly find myself pitch-kettled;
And cannot see, though few see better,
How I shall hammer out a letter.
    First, for a thought—since all agree—
A thought—I have it—let me see—
'Tis gone again—plague on't! I thought
I had it—but I have it not.
Dame Gurton thus, and Hodge her son,
That useful thing, her needle, gone,
Rake well the cinders, sweep the floor,
And sift the dust behind the door;
While eager Hodge beholds the prize
In old grimalkin's glaring eyes;
And Gammer finds it on her knees
In every shining straw she sees.
This simile were apt enough,

But I've another, critic-proof.
The virtuoso thus at noon,
Broiling beneath a July sun,
The gilded butterfly pursues
O'er hedge and ditch, through gaps and
    mews,
And after many a vain essay
To captivate the tempting prey,
Gives him at length the lucky pat,
And has him safe beneath his hat:
Then lifts it gently from the ground;
But ah! 'tis lost as soon as found;
Culprit his liberty regains;
Flits out of sight and mocks his pains.
The sense was dark, 'twas therefore fit
With simile to illustrate it;
But as too much obscures the sight,
As often as too little light,
We have our similes cut short,
For matters of more grave import.
That Matthew's numbers run with ease
Each man of common sense agrees;
All men of common sense allow,
That Robert's lines are easy too;
Where then the preference shall we
    place,
Or how do justice in this case?
"Matthew," says Fame, "with endless
    pains
Smoothed and refined the meanest
    strains,
Nor suffered one ill-chosen rhyme
To escape him at the idlest time;
And thus o'er all a lustre cast,
That while the language lives shall
    last."
"An't please your ladyship," quoth I,
(For 'tis my business to reply,)
"Sure so much labour, so much toil,
Bespeak at least a stubborn soil.
Theirs be the laurel-wreath decreed,
Who both write well and write full speed;
Who throw their Helicon about
As freely as a conduit spout!
Friend Robert, thus like *chien sçavant*,
Lets fall a poem *en passant*,
Nor needs his genuine ore refine;
'Tis ready polished from the mine."

ODE, SUPPOSED TO BE WRITTEN ON THE MARRIAGE OF A FRIEND.

Thou magic lyre, whose fascinating sound
  Seduced the savage monsters from their cave,
Drew rocks and trees, and forms uncouth around,
  And bade wild Hebrus hush his listening wave;
No more thy undulating warblings flow
O'er Thracian wilds of everlasting snow!

Awake to sweeter sounds, thou magic lyre,
  And paint a lover's bliss—a lover's pain!
Far nobler triumphs now thy notes inspire,
  For see, Eurydice attends thy strain;
Her smile, a prize beyond the conjurer's aim,
Superior to the cancelled breath of fame.

From her sweet brow to chase the gloom of care,
  To check the tear that dims the beaming eye,
To bid her heart the rising sigh forbear,
  And flush her orient cheek with brighter joy,
In that dear breast soft sympathy to move,
And touch the springs of rapture and of love.

Ah me! how long bewildered and astray,
  Lost and benighted, did my footsteps rove,
Till sent by Heaven to cheer my pathless way,
  A star arose—the radiant star of love.
The God propitious joined our willing hands,
And Hymen wreathed us in his rosy bands.

Yet not the beaming eye, or placid brow,
  Or golden tresses, hid the subtle dart;
To charms superior far than those I bow,
  And nobler worth enslaves my vanquished heart;
The beauty, elegance, and grace combined,
Which beam transcendent from that angel mind.

While vulgar passions, meteors of a day,
  Expire before the chilling blasts of age,
Our holy flame with pure and steady ray,
  Its glooms shall brighten, and its pangs assuage;
By Virtue (sacred vestal) fed, shall shine,
And warm our fainting souls with energy divine.

ON HER ENDEAVOURING TO CONCEAL HER GRIEF AT PARTING.

Ah! wherefore should my weeping maid suppress
  Those gentle signs of undissembled woe?
When from soft love proceeds the deep distress,
  Ah! why forbid the willing tears to flow?

Since for my sake each dear translucent drop
  Breaks forth, best witness of thy truth sincere,
My lips should drink the precious mixture up,
  And, ere it falls, receive the trembling tear.

Trust me, these symptoms of thy faithful heart
  In absence shall my dearest hopes sustain;
Delia! since such thy sorrow that we part,
  Such when we meet thy joy shall be again.

Hard is that heart and unsubdued by love
  That feels no pain, nor ever heaves a sigh;
Such hearts the fiercest passions only prove,
  Or freeze in cold insensibility.

Oh! then indulge thy grief, nor fear to tell
  The gentle source from whence thy sorrows flow;
Nor think it weakness when we love to feel,
  Nor think it weakness what we feel to show.

Bid adieu, my sad heart, bid adieu to thy peace!
Thy pleasure is past, and thy sorrows increase;
See the shadows of evening how far they extend,
And a long night is coming, that never may end;
For the sun is now set that enlivened the scene,
And an age must be past ere it rises again.

Already deprived of its splendour and heat,
I feel thee more slowly, more heavily beat;
Perhaps overstrained with the quick pulse of pleasure,
Thou art glad of this respite to beat at thy leisure;
But the sigh of distress shall now weary thee more
Than the flutter and tumult of passion before.

The heart of a lover is never at rest,
With joy overwhelmed, or with sorrow oppressed:
When Delia is near, all is ecstasy then,
And I even forget I must lose her again:
When absent, as wretched as happy before,
Despairing I cry, "I shall see her no more!"

Berkhamstead.

WRITTEN AFTER LEAVING HER AT NEW BURNS.

How quick the change from joy to woe!
How chequered is our lot below!
Seldom we view the prospect fair,
Dark clouds of sorrow, pain, and care
(Some pleasing intervals between,
Scowl over more than half the scene.
Last week with Delia, gentle maid,
Far hence in happier fields I strayed,
While on her dear enchanting tongue
Soft sounds of grateful welcome hung,
For absence had withheld it long.
"Welcome, my long-lost love," she said,
"E'er since our adverse fates decreed
That we must part, and I must mourn
Till once more blessed by thy return,

Love, on whose influence I relied
For all the transports I enjoyed,
Has played the cruel tyrant's part
And turned tormentor to my heart.
But let me hold thee to my breast,
Dear partner of my joy and rest,
And not a pain, and not a fear
Or anxious doubt, shall enter there."
Happy, thought I, the favoured youth,
Blessed with such undissembled truth !
Five suns successive rose and set,
And saw no monarch in his state,
Wrapped in the blaze of majesty,
So free from every care as I.

Next day the scene was overcast ;
Such day till then I never passed,
For on that day,—relentless fate !—

At Berkhamstead.

Delia and I must separate.
Yet ere we looked our last farewell,
From her dear lips this comfort fell :
" Fear not that time, where'er we rove,
Or absence, shall abate my love."
And can I doubt, my charming maid,
As unsincere what you have said ?
Banished from thee to what I hate,
Dull neighbours and insipid chat,
No joy to cheer me, none in view,
But the dear hope of meeting you ;
And that through passion's optic scene,
With ages interposed between ;
Blessed with the kind support you give,
'Tis by your promised truth I live ;
How deep my woes, how fierce my flame,
You best may tell who feel the same.

R. S. S.

ALL-WORSHIPPED Gold ! thou mighty mystery !
Say by what name shall I address thee rather,
Our blessing, or our bane ? Without thy aid,
The generous pangs of pity but distress
The human heart, that fain would feel the bliss
Of blessing others ; and, enslaved by thee,
Far from relieving woes which others feel,
Misers oppress themselves.   Our blessing then
With virtue when possessed ; without, our bane.
If in my bosom unperceived there lurk
The deep-sown seeds of avarice or ambition,
Blame me, ye great ones (for I scorn your censure),
But let the generous and the good commend me
That to my Delia I direct them all,
The worthiest object of a virtuous love.
Oh ! to some distant scene, a willing exile
From the wild uproar of this busy world,
Were it my fate with Delia to retire ;
With her to wander through the sylvan shade,
Each morn, or o'er the moss-imbrownèd turf,
Where, blessed as the prime parents of mankind
In their own Eden, we would envy none ;
But, greatly pitying whom the world calls happy,
Gently spin out the silken thread of life ;
While from her lips attentive I receive
The tenderest dictates of the purest flame,
And from her eyes (where soft complacence sits
Illumined with the radiant beams of sense)

Tranquillity beyond a monarch's reach.
Forgive me, Heaven, this only avarice
My soul indulges; I confess the crime
(If to esteem, to covet such perfection
Be criminal). Oh, grant me Delia! grant me wealth!
Wealth to alleviate, not increase my wants;
And grant me virtue, without which nor wealth
Nor Delia can avail to make me blessed.

WRITTEN IN A FIT OF ILLNESS.

R. S. S.

In these sad hours, a prey to ceaseless pain,
While feverish pulses leap in every vein,
When each faint breath the last short effort seems
Of life just parting from my feeble limbs;
How wild soe'er my wandering thoughts may be,
Still, gentle Delia, still they turn on thee!
At length if, slumbering to a short repose,
A sweet oblivion frees me from my woes,
Thy form appears, thy footsteps I pursue
Through springy vales, and meadows washed in dew;
Thy arm supports me to the fountain's brink,
Where by some secret power forbid to drink,
Gasping with thirst, I view the tempting flood
That flies my touch, or thickens into mud;
Till thine own hand immerged the goblet dips,
And bears it streaming to my burning lips.
There borne aloft on Fancy's wing we fly,
Like souls embodied to their native sky;
Now every rock, each mountain, disappears;
And the round earth an even surface wears;
When lo! the force of some resistless weight
Bears me straight down from that pernicious height;
Parting, in vain our struggling arms we close;
Abhorrèd forms, dire phantoms interpose;
With trembling voice on thy loved name I call;
And gulfs yawn ready to receive my fall.
From these fallacious visions of distress
I wake; nor are my real sorrows less.
Thy absence, Delia, heightens every ill,
And gives e'en trivial pains the power to kill.
Oh! wert thou near me; yet that wish forbear!
'Twere vain, my love,—'twere vain to wish thee near;
Thy tender heart would heave with anguish too,
And by partaking, but increase my woe.
Alone I'll grieve, till gloomy sorrow past,
Health, like the cheerful day-spring, comes at last,—
Comes fraught with bliss to banish every pain,
Hope, joy, and peace, and Delia in her train!

TO DELIA.

ME to whatever state the gods assign,
Believe, my love, whatever state be mine,
Ne'er shall my breast one anxious sorrow know,
Ne'er shall my heart confess a real woe,
If to thy share Heaven's choicest blessings fall,
As thou hast virtue to deserve them all.
Yet vain, alas! that idle hope would be
That builds on happiness remote from thee.
Oh! may thy charms, whate'er our fate decrees,
Please, as they must, but let them only please—
Not like the sun with equal influence shine,
Nor warm with transport any heart but mine.
Ye who from wealth the ill-grounded title boast
To claim whatever beauty charms you most;
Ye sons of fortune, who consult alone
Her parents' will, regardless of her own,
Know that a love like ours, a generous flame,
No wealth can purchase, and no power reclaim.
The soul's affection can be only given
Free, unextorted, as the grace of Heaven.

Is there whose faithful bosom can endure
Pangs fierce as mine, nor ever hope a cure?
Who sighs in absence of the dear-loved maid,
Nor summons once Indifference to his aid?
Who can, like me, the nice resentment prove,
The thousand soft disquietudes of love;
The trivial strifes that cause a real pain;
The real bliss when reconciled again?
Let him alone dispute the real prize,
And read his sentence in my Delia's eyes;
There shall he read all gentleness and truth,
But not himself, the dear distinguished youth;
Pity for him perhaps they may express—
Pity, that will but heighten his distress.
But, wretched rival! he must sigh to see
The sprightlier rays of love directed all to me.

And thou, dear Antidote of every pain
Which fortune can inflict, or love ordain,
Since early love has taught thee to despise
What the world's worthless votaries only prize,
Believe, my love! no less the generous god
Rules in my breast, his ever blest abode;
There has he driven each gross desire away,
Directing every wish and every thought to thee
Then can I ever leave my Delia's arms,
A slave, devoted to inferior charms?
Can e'er my soul her reason so disgrace?
For what blest minister of heavenly race
Would quit that heaven to find a happier place?

HOPE, like the short-lived ray that gleams awhile
    Through wintry skies, upon the frozen waste,
Cheers e'en the face of Misery to a smile;
    But soon the momentary pleasure's past.

How oft, my Delia, since our last farewell
    (Years that have rolled since that distressful hour),
Grieved I have said, when most our hopes prevail,
    Our promised happiness is least secure.

Oft I have thought the scene of troubles closed,
    And hoped once more to gaze upon your charms;
As oft some dire mischance has interposed,
    And snatched the expected blessing from my arms.

The seaman thus, his shattered vessel lost,
    Still vainly strives to shun the threatening death;
And while he thinks to gain the friendly coast,
    And drops his feet, and feels the sands beneath,

Borne by the wave steep-sloping from the shore,
    Back to the inclement deep, again he beats
The surge aside, and seems to tread secure;
    And now the refluent wave his baffled toil defeats.

Had you, my love, forbade me to pursue
    My fond attempt; disdainfully retired,
And with proud scorn compelled me to subdue
    The ill-fated passion by yourself inspired;

Then haply to some distant spot removed,
    Hopeless to gain, unwilling to molest
With fond entreaties whom I dearly loved,
    Despair or absence had redeemed my rest.

But now, sole partner in my Delia's heart,
    Yet doomed far off in exile to complain,
Eternal absence cannot ease my smart,
    And Hope subsists but to prolong my pain.

Oh then, kind Heaven, be this my latest breath!
    Here end my life, or make it worth my care;
Absence from whom we love is worse than death,
    And frustrate hope severer than despair.

ON THE DEATH OF SIR W. RUSSELL.

DOOMED, as I am, in solitude to waste
    The present moments, and regret the past;
Deprived of every joy I valued most,
    My friend torn from me, and my mistress lost,

Call not this gloom I wear, this anxious mien,
The dull effect of humour, or of spleen!
Still, still I mourn, with each returning day,
Him snatched by fate in early youth away,
And her, through tedious years of doubt and pain,
Fixed in her choice, and faithful, but in vain!
O prone to pity, generous, and sincere,
Whose eye ne'er yet refused the wretch a tear;
Whose heart the real claim of friendship knows,
Nor thinks a lover's are but fancied woes;
See me—ere yet my destined course half done,
Cast forth a wanderer on a world unknown!
See me neglected on the world's rude coast,
Each dear companion of my voyage lost!
Nor ask why clouds of sorrow shade my brow,
And ready tears wait only leave to flow!
Why all that soothes a heart from anguish free,
All that delights the happy—palls with me!

THE FIFTH SATIRE OF THE FIRST BOOK OF HORACE.

A HUMOROUS DESCRIPTION OF THE AUTHOR'S JOURNEY FROM ROME TO BRUNDUSIUM.

'I WAS a long journey lay before us,
When I and honest Heliodorus,
Who far in point of rhetoric
Surpasses every living Greek,
Each leaving our respective home,
Together sallied forth from Rome.
    First at Aricia we alight,
And there refresh and pass the night,
Our entertainment rather coarse
Than sumptuous, but I've met with
        worse.
Thence o'er the causeway soft and fair
To Appii Forum we repair.
But as this road is well supplied
(Temptation strong!) on either side
With inns commodious, snug, and warm,
We split the journey, and perform
In two days' time what's often done
By brisker travellers in one.
Here rather choosing not to sup
Than with bad water mix my cup,
After a warm debate in spite
Of a provoking appetite,
I sturdily resolve at last
To balk it, and pronounce a fast,

And in a moody humour wait,
While my less dainty comrades bait.
    Now o'er the spangled hemisphere
Diffused the starry train appear,
When there arose a desperate brawl;
The slaves and bargemen, one and all,
Rending their throats (have mercy on
        us!)
As if they were resolved to stun us.
"Steer the barge this way to the shore!
I tell you we'll admit no more!
Plague! will you never be content?"
Thus a whole hour at least is spent,
While they receive the several fares,
And kick the mule into his gears.
Happy, these difficulties past,
Could we have fallen asleep at last!
But, what with humming, croaking,
        biting,
Gnats, frogs, and all their plagues
        uniting,
These tuneful natives of the lake
Conspired to keep us broad awake.
Besides, to make the concert full,
Two maudlin wights, exceeding dull,

The bargeman and a passenger,
Each in his turn, essayed an air
In honour of his absent fair.
At length the passenger, oppressed
With wine, left off, and snored the rest.
The weary bargeman too gave o'er,
And hearing his companion snore,
Seized the occasion, fixed the barge,
Turned out his mule to graze at large,
And slept forgetful of his charge.

And now the sun o'er eastern hill
Discovered that our barge stood still ;
When one, whose anger vexed him sore,
With malice fraught, leaps quick on
    shore,
Plucks up a stake, with many a thwack
Assails the mule and driver's back.

Then slowly moving on with pain,
At ten Feronia's stream we gain,
And in her pure and glassy wave
Our hands and faces gladly lave.
Climbing three miles, fair Anxur's height
We reach, with stony quarries white.

While here, as was agreed, we wait,
Till, charged with business of the state,
Mæcenas and Cocceius come
(The messengers of peace) from Rome,
My eyes, by watery humours blear
And sore, I with black balsam smear.

At length they join us, and with them
Our worthy friend Fonteius came ;
A man of such complete desert,
Antony loved him at his heart.
At Fundi we refused to bait,
And laughed at vain Aufidius' state,
A prætor now, a scribe before,
The purple-bordered robe he wore,
His slave the smoking censer bore.
Tired, at Muræna's we repose,
At Formia sup at Capito's.

With smiles the rising morn we greet,
At Sinuessa pleased to meet
With Plotius, Varius, and the bard
Whom Mantua first with wonder heard.
The world no purer spirits knows,
For none my heart more warmly glows.
Oh ! what embraces we bestowed,
And with what joy our breasts o'erflowed !
Sure while my sense is sound and clear,
Long as I live, I shall prefer
A gay, good-natured, easy friend,
To every blessing Heaven can send.

At a small village, the next night,
Near the Vulturnus, we alight ;
Where, as employed on state affairs,
We were supplied by the purveyors
Frankly at once, and without hire,
With food for man and horse, and fire.
Capua next day betimes we reach,
Where Virgil and myself, who each
Laboured with different maladies,
His such a stomach, mine such eyes,
As would not bear strong exercise,
In drowsy mood to sleep resort ;
Mæcenas to the tennis-court.
Next at Cocceius' farm we're treated,
Above the Caudian tavern seated ;
His kind and hospitable board
With choice of wholesome food was
    stored.

Now, O ye Nine, inspire my lays !
To nobler themes my fancy raise !
Two combatants, who scorn to yield
The noisy, tongue-disputed field,
Sarmentus and Cicirrus, claim
A poet's tribute to their fame ;
Cicirrus of true Oscian breed,
Sarmentus, who was never freed,
But ran away. We won't defame him ;
His lady lives, and still may claim him.
Thus dignified, in harder fray
These champions their keen wit display,
And first Sarmentus led the way.
"Thy locks," quoth he, "so rough and
    coarse,
Look like the mane of some wild horse."
We laugh : Cicirrus undismayed,
"Have at you !" cries, and shakes his
    head.
"'Tis well," Sarmentus says, "you've
    lost
That horn your forehead once could
    boast ;
Since maimed and mangled as you are,
You seem to butt." A hideous scar
Improved ('tis true) with double grace
The native horrors of his face.
Well ; after much jocosely said
Of his grim front, so fiery red,
(For carbuncles had blotched it o'er,
As usual on Campania's shore,)
"Give us," he cried, "since you're so
    big,
A sample of the Cyclops' jig !

c

Your shanks methinks no buskins ask,
Nor does your phiz require a mask."
To this Cicirrus : " In return
Of you, sir, now I fain would learn,
When 'twas, no longer deemed a slave,
Your chains you to the Lares gave.
For though a scrivener's right you claim,
Your lady's title is the same.
But what could make you run away,
Since, pigmy as you are, each day
A single pound of bread would quite
O'erpower your puny appetite?"
Thus joked the champions, while we laughed,
And many a cheerful bumper quaffed.

To Beneventum next we steer;
Where our good host by over care
In roasting thrushes lean as mice
Had almost fallen a sacrifice.
The kitchen soon was all on fire,
And to the roof the flames aspire.
There might you see each man and master
Striving, amidst this sad disaster,
To save the supper.   Then they came
With speed enough to quench the flame.
From hence we first at distance see
The Apulian hills, well known to me,
Parched by the sultry western blast;
And which we never should have past,
Had not Trivicus by the way
Received us at the close of day.
But each was forced at entering here
To pay the tribute of a tear,
For more of smoke than fire was seen,
The hearth was piled with logs so green.

From hence in chaises we were carried
Miles twenty-four, and gladly tarried
At a small town, whose name my verse
(So barbarous is it) can't rehearse.
Know it you may by many a sign,
Water is dearer far than wine.
There bread is deemed such dainty fare,
That every prudent traveller
His wallet loads with many a crust;
For at Canusium, you might just
As well attempt to gnaw a stone
As think to get a morsel down.
That too with scanty streams is fed;
Its founder was brave Diomed.
Good Varius (ah, that friends must part!)
Here left us all with aching heart.
At Rubi we arrived that day,
Well jaded by the length of way,
And sure poor mortals ne'er were wetter.
Next day no weather could be better;
No roads so bad ; we scarce could crawl
Along to fishy Barium's wall.
The Egnatians next, who by the rules
Of common sense are knaves or fools,
Made all our sides with laughter heave,
Since we with them must needs believe,
That incense in their temples burns,
And without fire to ashes turns.
To circumcision's bigots tell
Such tales ! for me, I know full well,
That in high heaven, unmoved by care,
The gods eternal quiet share:
Nor can I deem their spleen the cause
Why fickle Nature breaks her laws.
Brundusium last we reach : and there
Stop short the Muse and Traveller.

THE NINTH SATIRE OF THE FIRST BOOK OF HORACE.

THE DESCRIPTION OF AN IMPERTINENT.   ADAPTED TO THE PRESENT TIMES.

SAUNTERING along the street one day,
On trifles musing by the way,
Up steps a free familiar wight;
(I scarcely knew the man by sight.)
"Carlos," he cried, "your hand, my dear.
Gad, I rejoice to meet you here !
Pray Heaven I see you well !"—"So, so;
Even well enough, as times now go.
The same good wishes, sir, to you."

Finding he still pursued me close,
"Sir, you have business, I suppose."—
" My business, sir, is quickly done,
'Tis but to make my merit known.
Sir, I have read"—"O learnèd sir,
You and your learning I revere."
Then, sweating with anxiety,
And sadly longing to get free,
Gods ! how I scampered, scuffled for't,
Ran, halted, ran again, stopped short,

Beckoned my boy, and pulled him near,
And whispered nothing in his ear.
　Teased with his loose unjointed chat,
"What street is this? What house is
　　that?"
O Harlow! how I envied thee
Thy unabashed effrontery,
Who darest a foe with freedom blame,
And call a coxcomb by his name!
When I returned him answer none,
Obligingly the fool ran on,
"I see you're dismally distressed,
Would give the world to be released,
But, by your leave, sir, I shall still
Stick to your skirts, do what you will.
Pray which way does your journey tend?"
"Oh! 'tis a tedious way, my friend,
Across the Thames, the Lord knows
　　where:
I would not trouble you so far."—
"Well, I'm at leisure to attend you."—
"Are you?" thought I, "the De'il
　　befriend you!"
No ass with double panniers racked,
Oppressed, o'erladen, broken-backed,
E'er looked a thousandth part so dull
As I, nor half so like a fool.
"Sir, I know little of myself,"
Proceeds the pert conceited elf,
"If Gray or Mason you will deem
Than me more worthy your esteem.
Poems I write by folios,
As fast as other men write prose.
Then I can sing so loud, so clear,
That Beard cannot with me compare.
In dancing, too, I all surpass,
Not Cooke can move with such a
　　grace."
Here I made shift, with much ado,
To interpose a word or two.—
"Have you no parents, sir? No friends,
Whose welfare on your own depends?"
"Parents, relations, say you? No.
They're all disposed of long ago."—
"Happy to be no more perplexed!
My fate too threatens, I go next.
Dispatch me, sir, 'tis now too late,
Alas! to struggle with my fate!
Well, I'm convinced my time is come.
When young, a gipsy told my doom;
The beldame shook her palsied head,
As she perused my palm, and said,

'Of poison, pestilence, or war,
Gout, stone, defluxion, or catarrh,
You have no reason to beware.
Beware the coxcomb's idle prate;
Chiefly, my son, beware of that;
Be sure, when you behold him, fly
Out of all earshot, or you die!'"
　To Rufus' Hall we now drew near,
Where he was summoned to appear,
Refute the charge the plaintiff brought,
Or suffer judgment by default.
"For Heaven's sake, if you love me, wait
One moment! I'll be with you straight."
Glad of a plausible pretence—
"Sir, I must beg you to dispense
With my attendance in the court.
My legs will surely suffer for't."—
"Nay, prithee, Carlos, stop awhile!"
"Faith, sir, in law I have no skill.
Besides, I have no time to spare,
I must be going, you know where."—
"Well, I protest, I'm doubtful now,
Whether to leave my suit or you!"—
"Me, without scruple!" I reply,
"Me, by all means, sir!"—"No, not I.
Allons, Monsieur!" 'Twere vain, you
　　　　　　　　　　　　　[know,
So I reluctantly obey,
And follow where he leads the way.
　"You and Newcastle are so close;
Still hand and glove, sir, I suppose?"
"Newcastle (let me tell you, sir,)
Has not his equal everywhere."—
"Well. There indeed your fortune's
　　made!
Faith, sir, you understand your trade.
Would you but give me your good word!
Just introduce me to my lord.
I should serve charmingly by way
Of second fiddle, as they say:
What think you, sir? 'twere a good jest.
'Slife, we should quickly scout the
　　rest."—
"Sir, you mistake the matter far,
We have no second fiddles there.
Richer than I some folks may be:
More learned, but it hurts not me.
Friends though he has of different kind,
Each has his proper place assigned."
"Strange matters these, alleged by
　　you!"—　　　　　　[true."—
"Strange they may be, but they are

"Well, then, I vow, 'tis mighty clever,
Now I long ten times more than ever
To be advanced extremely near
One of his shining character."—
"Have but the will—there wants no more,
'Tis plain enough you have the power.
His easy temper (that's the worst)
He knows, and is so shy at first.
But such a cavalier as you —
Lord, sir, you'll quickly bring him to!"
"Well; if I fail in my design,
Sir, it shall be no fault of mine.
If by the saucy servile tribe
Denied, what think you of a bribe?
Shut out to-day, not die with sorrow,
But try my luck again to-morrow.
Never attempt to visit him
But at the most convenient time,
Attend him on each levee day,
And there my humble duty pay.
Labour, like this, our want supplies;
And they must stoop, who mean to rise."
      While thus he wittingly harangued,
For which you'll guess I wished him hanged,
Campley, a friend of mine, came by,
Who knew his humour more than I.
We stop, salute, and—"Why so fast,

Friend Carlos? whither all this haste?"
Fired at the thoughts of a reprieve,
I pinch him, pull him, twitch his sleeve,
Nod, beckon, bite my lips, wink, pout,
Do everything but speak plain out:
While he, sad dog, from the beginning,
Determined to mistake my meaning,
Instead of pitying my curse,
By jeering made it ten times worse.
"Campley, what secret, pray, was that
You wanted to communicate?"
"I recollect. But 'tis no matter.—
Carlos, we'll talk of that hereafter.
E'en let the secret rest. 'Twill tell
Another time, sir, just as well."
      Was ever such a dismal day?
Unlucky cur! he steals away,
And leaves me, half bereft of life,
At mercy of the butcher's knife;
When sudden, shouting from afar,
See his antagonist appear!
The bailiff seized him quick as thought.
"Ho, Mr. Scoundrel! Are you caught?
Sir, you are witness to the arrest."—
"Ay, marry, sir, I'll do my best."
The mob huzzas; away they trudge,
Culprit and all, before the judge.
Meanwhile I luckily enough
(Thanks to Apollo) got clear off.

ADDRESSED TO MISS MACARTNEY,

AFTERWARDS MRS. GREVILLE, ON READING HER "PRAYER FOR INDIFFERENCE."

AND dwells there in a female heart,
  By bounteous heaven designed
The choicest raptures to impart,
  To feel the most refined;

Dwells there a wish in such a breast
  Its nature to forego,
To smother in ignoble rest
  At once both bliss and woe?

Far be the thought, and far the strain,
  Which breathes the low desire,
How sweet soe'er the verse complain,
  Though Phœbus string the lyre.

Come then, fair maid (in nature wise),
  Who, knowing them, can tell
From generous sympathy what joys
  The glowing bosom swell;

In justice to the various powers
  Of pleasing, which you share,
Join me, amid your silent hours,
  To form the better prayer.

With lenient balm may Oberon hence
  To fairy-land be driven,
With every herb that blunts the sense
  Mankind received from heaven.

"Oh! if my Sovereign Author please,
  Far be it from my fate
To live unblest in torpid ease,
  And slumber on in state;

"Each tender tie of life defied,
  Whence social pleasures spring;
Unmoved with all the world beside,
  A solitary thing."

Some Alpine mountain wrapt in snow,
　Thus braves the whirling blast,
Eternal winter doomed to know,
　No genial spring to taste ;

In vain warm suns their influence shed,
　The zephyrs sport in vain,
He rears unchanged his barren head,
　Whilst beauty decks the plain.

What though in scaly armour dressed,
　Indifference may repel
The shafts of woe, in such a breast
　No joy can ever dwell.

'Tis woven in the world's great plan,
　And fixed by Heaven's decree,
That all the true delights of man
　Should spring from Sympathy.

'Tis Nature bids, and whilst the laws
　Of Nature we retain,
Our self-approving bosom draws
　A pleasure from its pain.

Thus grief itself has comforts dear
　The sordid never know ;
And ecstasy attends the tear,
　When virtue bids it flow.

For when it streams from that pure
　　source,
　No bribes the heart can win,
To check, or alter from its course,
　The luxury within.

Peace to the phlegm of sullen elves,
　Who, if from labour eased,
Extend no care beyond themselves,
　Unpleasing and unpleased.

Let no low thought suggest the prayer !
　Oh ! grant, kind Heaven, to me,
Long as I draw ethereal air,
　Sweet Sensibility !

Where'er the heavenly nymph is seen,
　With lustre-beaming eye,
A train, attendant on their queen,
　(Her rosy chorus) fly.

The jocund Loves in Hymen's band,
　With torches ever bright,
And generous Friendship hand in hand,
　With Pity's watery sight.

The gentler Virtues too are joined,
　In youth immortal warm,
The soft relations which combined
　Give life her every charm.

The Arts come smiling in the close,
　And lend celestial fire ;
The marble breathes, the canvas glows,
　The Muses sweep the lyre.

" Still may my melting bosom cleave
　To sufferings not my own ;
And still the sigh responsive heave,
　Where'er is heard a groan.

" So Pity shall take Virtue's part,
　Her natural ally,
And fashioning my softened heart,
　Prepare it for the sky."

This artless vow may Heaven receive,
　And you, fond maid, approve ;
So may your guiding angel give
　Whate'er you wish or love.

So may the rosy-fingered hours
　Lead on the various year,
And every joy, which now is yours,
　Extend a larger sphere.

And suns to come, as round they wheel,
　Your golden moments bless,
With all a tender heart can feel,
　Or lively fancy guess.

AN ODE,

SECUNDUM ARTEM.

I.

SHALL I begin with *Ah*, or *Oh?*
Be sad? *Oh!* yes.　Be glad? *Ah!* no.
Light subjects suit not grave Pindaric ode,
Which walks in metre down the Strophic road.

But let the sober matron wear
Her own mechanic sober air :
Ah me! ill suits, *alas!* the sprightly jig,
Long robes of ermine, or Sir Cloudesley's wig.
　Come, placid Dulness, gently come,
　And all my faculties benumb ;
Let thought turn exile, while the vacant mind
To trickie words and pretty phrase confined,
　Pumping for trim description's art,
　To win the ear, neglects the heart.
So shall thy sister Taste's peculiar sons,
Lineal descendants from the Goths and Huns,
　Struck with the true and grand sublime
　Of *rhythm* converted into *rime*,
Court the quaint Muse, and con her lessons o'er,
When sleep the sluggish waves by Granta's shore :
　There shall each poet share and trim,
　Stretch, cramp, or lop the verse's limb,
While rebel Wit beholds them with disdain,
And Fancy flies aloft, nor heeds their servile chain.

2.

O Fancy, bright aërial maid !
Where have thy vagrant footsteps strayed?
For, *Ah!* I miss thee 'midst thy wonted haunt,
Since silent now the enthusiastic chaunt,
　Which erst like frenzy rolled along,
　Driven by the impetuous tide of song ;
Rushing secure where native genius bore,
Not cautious coasting by the shelving shore.
　Hail to the sons of modern Rime,
　Mechanic dealers in sublime,
Whose lady Muse full wantonly is drest,
In light expression quaint, and tinsel vest,
　Where swelling epithets are laid
　(Art's ineffectual parade)
As varnish on the cheek of harlot light ;
The rest, thin sown with profit or delight,
　But ill compares with ancient song,
　Where Genius poured its flood along ;
Yet such is Art's presumptuous idle claim,
She marshals out the way to modern fame ;
　From Grecian fable's pompous lore
　Description's studied, glittering store,
Smooth, soothing sounds, and sweet alternate rime,
Clinking, like change of bells, in tingle tangle chime.

3.

The lark shall soar in every Ode,
　With flowers of light description strewed ;
And sweetly, warbling Philomel, shall flow
Thy soothing sadness in mechanic woe.

Trim epithets shall spread their gloss,
  While every cell's o'ergrown with moss:
Here oaks shall rise in chains of ivy bound,
There mouldering stones o'erspread the rugged ground.
  Here forests brown, and azure hills,
  There babbling fonts, and prattling rills;
Here some gay river floats in crispèd streams,
While the bright sun now gilds his morning beams,
  Or sinking on his Thetis' breast,
  Drives in description down the west.
Oh let me boast, with pride-becoming skill,
I crown the summit of Parnassus' hill:
  While Taste and Genius shall dispense,
  And sound shall triumph over sense;
O'er the gay mead with curious steps I'll stray;
And, like the bee, steal all the sweets away;
  Extract its beauty, and its power,
  From every new poetic flower,
And sweets collected may a wreath compose,
To bind the poet's brow, or please the critic's nose.

LINES WRITTEN UNDER THE INFLUENCE OF DELIRIUM.

HATRED and vengeance,—my eternal portion
Scarce can endure delay of execution,—
Wait with impatient readiness to seize my
                Soul in a moment.

Damned below Judas; more abhorred than he was,
Who for a few pence sold his holy Master!
Twice-betrayed Jesus me, the last delinquent,
                Deems the profanest.

Man disavows, and Deity disowns me,
Hell might afford my miseries a shelter;
Therefore, Hell keeps her ever-hungry mouths all
                Bolted against me.

Hard lot! encompassed with a thousand dangers;
Weary, faint, trembling with a thousand terrors,
I'm called, if vanquished! to receive a sentence
                Worse than Abiram's.

Him the vindictive rod of angry Justice
Sent quick and howling to the centre headlong;
I, fed with judgment, in a fleshly tomb, am
                Buried above ground.

OLNEY HYMNS.

I. WALKING WITH GOD.

Gen. v. 24.

OH for a closer walk with God !
　A calm and heavenly frame ;
A light to shine upon the road
　That leads me to the Lamb !

Where is the blessedness I knew
　When first I saw the Lord?
Where is the soul-refreshing view
　Of Jesus and his word ?

What peaceful hours I once enjoyed !
　How sweet their memory still !
But they have left an aching void
　The world can never fill.

Return, O holy Dove, return,
　Sweet messenger of rest !
I hate the sins that made thee mourn,
　And drove thee from my breast.

The dearest idol I have known,
　Whate'er that idol be,
Help me to tear it from thy throne,
　And worship only thee.

So shall my walk be close with God,
　Calm and serene my frame ;
So purer light shall mark the road
　That leads me to the Lamb.

II. JEHOVAH-JIREH.—THE LORD WILL PROVIDE. *Gen.* xxii. 14.

THE saints should never be dismayed,
　Nor sink in hopeless fear ;
For when they least expect his aid,
　The Saviour will appear.

This Abraham found : he raised the
　knife ;
　God saw, and said, " Forbear !
Yon ram shall yield his meaner life ;
　Behold the victim there."

Once David seemed Saul's certain prey;
　But hark ! the foe's at hand ;
Saul turns his arms another way,
　To save the invaded land.

When Jonah sunk beneath the wave,
　He thought to rise no more ;
But God prepared a fish to save,
　And bear him to the shore.

Blest proofs of power and grace divine,
　That meet us in his word !
May every deep-felt care of mine
　Be trusted with the Lord.

Wait for his seasonable aid,
　And though it tarry, wait :
The promise may be long delayed,
　But cannot come too late.

III. JEHOVAH-ROPHI.—I AM THE LORD THAT HEALETH THEE.

Exod. xv. 26.

HEAL us, Emmanuel ! here we are,
　Waiting to feel thy touch :
Deep-wounded souls to thee repair,
　And, Saviour, we are such.

Our faith is feeble, we confess,
　We faintly trust thy word ;
But wilt thou pity us the less ?
　Be that far from thee, Lord !

Remember him who once applied,
　With trembling, for relief ;
" Lord, I believe," with tears he cried,
　" Oh, help my unbelief ! "

She too, who touched thee in the press,
　And healing virtue stole,
Was answered, " Daughter, go in peace,
　Thy faith hath made thee whole."

Concealed amid the gathering throng,
　She would have shunned thy view ;
And if her faith was firm and strong,
　Had strong misgivings too.

Like her, with hopes and fears we come,
　To touch thee, if we may ;
Oh ! send us not despairing home !
　Send none unhealed away !

IV. JEHOVAH-NISSI.—The Lord my Banner. *Exod.* xvii. 15.

By whom was David taught
    To aim the deadly blow,
When he Goliath fought,
    And laid the Gittite low?
Nor sword nor spear the stripling took,
But chose a pebble from the brook.

'Twas Israel's God and King
    Who sent him to the fight;
Who gave him strength to sling,
    And skill to aim aright.
Ye feeble saints, your strength endures,
Because young David's God is yours.

Who ordered Gideon forth
    To storm the invaders' camp,
With arms of little worth,
    A pitcher and a lamp?
The trumpets made his coming known,
And all the host was overthrown.

Oh! I have seen the day,
    When with a single word,
God helping me to say,
    "My trust is in the Lord,"
My soul hath quelled a thousand foes,
Fearless of all that could oppose.

But unbelief, self-will,
    Self-righteousness, and pride,
How often do they steal
    My weapon from my side!
Yet David's Lord, and Gideon's friend,
Will help his servant to the end.

V. JEHOVAH-SHALOM.—The Lord send Peace. *Judges* vi. 24.

Jesus! whose blood so freely streamed
    To satisfy the law's demand;
By thee from guilt and wrath redeemed,
    Before the Father's face I stand.

To reconcile offending man,
    Make Justice drop her angry rod;
What creature could have formed the plan,
    Or who fulfil it but a God?

No drop remains of all the curse,
    For wretches who deserved the whole;
No arrows dipt in wrath to pierce
    The guilty, but returning soul.

Peace by such means so dearly bought,
    What rebel could have hoped to see?
Peace, by his injured Sovereign wrought,
    His Sovereign fastened to a tree.

Now, Lord, thy feeble worm prepare!
    For strife with earth and hell begins;
Confirm and gird me for the war;
    They hate the soul that hates his sins.

Let them in horrid league agree!
    They may assault, they may distress;
But cannot quench thy love to me,
    Nor rob me of the Lord my peace.

VI. WISDOM. *Prov.* viii. 22—31.

"Ere God had built the mountains,
    Or raised the fruitful hills;
Before he filled the fountains
    That feed the running rills;
In me, from everlasting,
    The wonderful I am,
Found pleasures never wasting
    And Wisdom is my name.

"When, like a tent to dwell in,
    He spread the skies abroad,
And swathed about the swelling
    Of Ocean's mighty flood;
He wrought by weight and measure,
    And I was with him then;
Myself the Father's pleasure,
    And mine the sons of men."

Thus Wisdom's words discover
    Thy glory and thy grace,
Thou everlasting Lover
    Of our unworthy race!
Thy gracious eye surveyed us
    Ere stars were seen above;
In wisdom thou hast made us,
    And died for us in love.

And couldst thou be delighted
    With creatures such as we,
Who, when we saw thee, slighted,
    And nailed thee to a tree?

Unfathomable wonder,
  And mystery divine !
The Voice that speaks in thunder,
  Says, " Sinner, I am thine !"

VII. VANITY OF THE WORLD.

God gives his mercies to be spent ;
  Your hoard will do your soul no good ;
Gold is a blessing only lent,
  Repaid by giving others food.

The world's esteem is but a bribe,
  To buy their peace you sell your own ;
The slave of a vain-glorious tribe,
  Who hate you while they make you
      known.

The joy that vain amusements give,
  Oh ! sad conclusion that it brings !
The honey of a crowded hive,
  Defended by a thousand stings.

'Tis thus the world rewards the fools
  That live upon her treacherous smiles ;
She leads them blindfold by her rules,
  And ruins all whom she beguiles.

God knows the thousands who go down
  From pleasure into endless woe :
And with a long despairing groan
  Blaspheme their Maker as they go.

O fearful thought ! be timely wise ;
  Delight but in a Saviour's charms,
And God shall take you to the skies,
  Embraced in everlasting arms.

VIII. O LORD, I WILL PRAISE
THEE.   *Isaiah* xii. 1.

I will praise thee every day
Now thine anger's turned away ;
Comfortable thoughts arise
From the bleeding sacrifice.

Here, in the fair Gospel-field,
Wells of free salvation yield
Streams of life, a plenteous store,
And my soul shall thirst no more.

Jesus is become at length
My salvation and my strength ;
And his praises shall prolong,
While I live, my pleasant song.

Praise ye, then, his glorious name,
Publish his exalted fame !
Still his worth your praise exceeds ;
Excellent are all his deeds.

Raise again the joyful sound,
Let the nations roll it round !
Zion, shout ! for this is he ;
God the Saviour dwells in thee !

IX. THE CONTRITE HEART.
Isaiah lvii. 15.

The Lord will happiness divine
  On contrite hearts bestow ;
Then tell me, gracious God, is mine
  A contrite heart, or no ?

I hear, but seem to hear in vain,
  Insensible as steel ;
If aught is felt, 'tis only pain,
  To find I cannot feel.

I sometimes think myself inclined
  To love thee, if I could ;
But often feel another mind,
  Averse to all that's good.

My best desires are faint and few,
  I fain would strive for more ;
But when I cry, " My strength renew !"
  Seem weaker than before.

Thy saints are comforted, I know,
  And love thy house of prayer ;
I therefore go where others go,
  But find no comfort there.

Oh make this heart rejoice or ache ;
  Decide this doubt for me ;
And if it be not broken, break,—
  And heal it if it be.

X. THE FUTURE PEACE AND
GLORY OF THE CHURCH.
Isaiah lx. 15—20.

Hear what God the Lord hath spoken
  " O my people, faint and few,
Comfortless, afflicted, broken,
  Fair abodes I build for you.
Thorns of heartfelt tribulation
  Shall no more perplex your ways :
You shall name your walls Salvation,
  And your gates shall all be Praise.

'There, like streams that feed the garden,
  Pleasures without end shall flow ;
For the Lord, your faith rewarding,
  All his bounty shall bestow ;
Still in undisturbed possession
  Peace and righteousness shall reign ;
Never shall you feel oppression,
  Hear the voice of war again.

' Ye no more your suns descending,
  Waning moons no more shall see ;
But, your griefs for ever ending,
  Find eternal noon in me :
God shall rise, and shining o'er ye,
  Change to day the gloom of night ;
He, the Lord, shall be your glory,
  God your everlasting light."

XI. JEHOVAH OUR RIGHT-EOUSNESS. *Jer.* xxiii. 6.

My God, how perfect are thy ways !
  But mine polluted are ;
Sin twines itself about my praise,
  And slides into my prayer.

When I would speak what thou hast done
  To save me from my sin,
I cannot make thy mercies known,
  But self-applause creeps in.

Divine desire, that holy flame
  Thy grace creates in me ;
Alas ! impatience is its name,
  When it returns to thee.

This heart, a fountain of vile thoughts,
  How does it overflow,
While self upon the surface floats,
  Still bubbling from below !

Let others in the gaudy dress
  Of fancied merit shine ;
The Lord shall be my righteousness,
  The Lord for ever mine.

XII. EPHRAIM REPENTING. *Jer.* xxxi. 18—20.

My God, till I received thy stroke,
  How like a beast was I !
So unaccustomed to the yoke,
  So backward to comply.

With grief my just reproach I bear ;
  Shame fills me at the thought,
How frequent my rebellions were,
  What wickedness I wrought.

Thy merciful restraint I scorned,
  And left the pleasant road ;
Yet turn me, and I shall be turned !
  Thou art the Lord my God.

" Is Ephraim banished from my thoughts,
  Or vile in my esteem ?
" No," saith the Lord, " with all his faults,
  I still remember him."

" Is he a dear and pleasant child ?"
  " Yes, dear and pleasant still ;
Though sin his foolish heart beguiled,
  And he withstood my will.

" My sharp rebuke has laid him low,
  He seeks my face again ;
My pity kindles at his woe,
  He shall not seek in vain."

XIII. THE COVENANT. *Ezek.* xxxvi. 25—28.

The Lord proclaims his grace abroad !
  " Behold, I change your hearts of stone;
Each shall renounce his idol-god,
  And serve, henceforth, the Lord alone.

" My grace, a flowing stream, proceeds
  To wash your filthiness away ;
Ye shall abhor your former deeds,
  And learn my statutes to obey.

" My truth the great design ensures,
  I give myself away to you ;
You shall be mine, I will be yours,
  Your God unalterably true.

" Yet not unsought, or unimplored,
  The plenteous grace shall I confer ;
No—your whole hearts shall seek the
  Lord,
  I'll put a praying spirit there.

" From the first breath of life divine,
  Down to the last expiring hour,
The gracious work shall all be mine,
  Begun and ended in my power."

XIV. JEHOVAH-SHAMMAH.

Ezek. xlviii. 35.

"As birds their infant brood protect,
  And spread their wings to shelter them,
(Thus saith the Lord to his elect,)
  So will I guard Jerusalem."

And what then is Jerusalem,
  This darling object of his care?
Where is its worth in God's esteem?
  Who built it? who inhabits there?

Jehovah founded it in blood,
  The blood of his incarnate Son;
There dwell the saints, once foes to God,
  The sinners whom he calls his own.

There, though besieged on every side,
  Yet much beloved, and guarded well,
From age to age they have defied
  The utmost force of earth and hell.

Let earth repent, and hell despair,
  This city has a sure defence;
Her name is called "The Lord is there,"
  And who has power to drive him
    thence?

XV. PRAISE FOR THE
FOUNTAIN OPENED.—*Zech.* xiii. 1.

THERE is a fountain filled with blood
  Drawn from Emmanuel's veins;
And sinners, plunged beneath that flood,
  Lose all their guilty stains.

The dying thief rejoiced to see
  That fountain in his day;
And there have I, as vile as he,
  Washed all my sins away.

Dear dying Lamb, thy precious blood
  Shall never lose its power,
Till all the ransomed church of God
  Be saved, to sin no more.

E'er since, by faith, I saw the stream
  Thy flowing wounds supply,
Redeeming love has been my theme,
  And shall be till I die.

Then in a nobler, sweeter song,
  I'll sing thy power to save;
When this poor lisping, stammering
    tongue
  Lies silent in the grave.

Lord, I believe thou hast prepared
  (Unworthy though I be)
For me a blood-bought free reward,
  A golden harp for me!

'Tis strung and tuned for endless years
  And formed by power divine,
To sound in God the Father's ears
  No other name but thine.

XVI. THE SOWER. *Matt.* xiii. 3.

YE sons of earth, prepare the plough,
  Break up your fallow-ground;
The sower is gone forth to sow,
  And scatter blessings round.

The seed that finds a stony soil
  Shoots forth a hasty blade;
But ill repays the sower's toil,
  Soon withered, scorched, and dead.

The thorny ground is sure to balk
  All hopes of harvest there;
We find a tall and sickly stalk,
  But not the fruitful ear.

The beaten path and highway side
  Receive the trust in vain;
The watchful birds the spoil divide,
  And pick up all the grain.

But where the Lord of grace and power
  Has blessed the happy field,
How plenteous is the golden store
  The deep-wrought furrows yield!

Father of mercies, we have need
  Of thy preparing grace;
Let the same hand that gives the seed
  Provide a fruitful place!

XVII. THE HOUSE OF PRAYER
Mark xi. 17.

THY mansion is the Christian's heart,
  O Lord, thy dwelling-place secure!
Bid the unruly throng depart,
  And leave the consecrated door.

evoted as it is to thee,
A thievish swarm frequents the place;
hey steal away my joys from me,
And rob my Saviour of his praise.

ere, too, a sharp designing trade
Sin, Satan, and the World maintain;
or cease to press me, and persuade
To part with ease, and purchase pain.

now them, and I hate their din;
Am weary of the bustling crowd;
t while their voice is heard within,
I cannot serve thee as I would.

h for the joy thy presence gives,
What peace shall reign when thou art
here!
hy presence makes this den of thieves
A calm delightful house of prayer.

nd if thou make thy temple shine,
Yet, self-abased, will I adore;
he gold and silver are not mine;
I give thee what was thine before.

XVIII. LOVEST THOU ME?
John xxi. 16.

ARK, my soul! it is the Lord;
is thy Saviour, hear his word;
sus speaks, and speaks to thee,
Say, poor sinner, lovest thou me?

I delivered thee when bound,
nd when bleeding, healed thy wound;
ught thee wandering, set thee right;
urned thy darkness into light.

Can a woman's tender care
ease towards the child she bare?
es, she may forgetful be,
et will I remember thee.

Mine is an unchanging love,
igher than the heights above,
eeper than the depths beneath,
ree and faithful, strong as death.

Thou shalt see my glory soon,
hen the work of grace is done;
rtner of my throne shalt be;—
y, poor sinner, lovest thou me?"

Lord, it is my chief complaint,
That my love is weak and faint;
Yet I love thee and adore,—
Oh! for grace to love thee more!

XIX. CONTENTMENT. *Phil.* iv. 11.

FIERCE passions discompose the mind,
As tempests vex the sea;
But calm content and peace we find,
When, Lord, we turn to thee.

In vain by reason and by rule
We try to bend the will;
For none but in the Saviour's school
Can learn the heavenly skill.

Since at his feet my soul has sate,
His gracious words to hear,
Contented with my present state,
I cast on him my care.

"Art thou a sinner, soul?" he said,
"Then how canst thou complain?
How light thy troubles here, if weighed
With everlasting pain!

"If thou of murmuring wouldst be cured,
Compare thy griefs with mine;
Think what my love for thee endured,
And thou wilt not repine.

" 'Tis I appoint thy daily lot,
And I do all things well;
Thou soon shalt leave this wretched
spot,
And rise with me to dwell.

"In life my grace shall strength supply,
Proportioned to thy day;
At death thou still shalt find me nigh,
To wipe thy tears away."

Thus I, who once my wretched days
In vain repinings spent,
Taught in my Saviour's school of grace,
Have learned to be content.

XX. OLD TESTAMENT GOSPEL.
Heb. iv. 2.

ISRAEL in ancient days
Not only had a view
Of Sinai in a blaze,
But learned the Gospel too;
The types and figures were a glass,
In which they saw a Saviour's face,

The paschal sacrifice
   And blood-besprinkled door,
Seen with enlightened eyes,
   And once applied with power,
Would teach the need of other blood,
To reconcile an angry God.

The Lamb, the Dove, set forth
   His perfect innocence,
Whose blood of matchless worth
   Should be the soul's defence;
For he who can for sin atone
Must have no failings of his own.

The scape-goat on his head
   The people's trespass bore,
And to the desert led,
   Was to be seen no more :
In him our Surety seemed to say,
"Behold, I bear your sins away."

Dipt in his fellow's blood,
   The living bird went free ;
The type, well understood,
   Expressed the sinner's plea ;
Described a guilty soul enlarged,
And by a Saviour's death discharged.

Jesus, I love to trace,
   Throughout the sacred page,
The footsteps of thy grace,
   The same in every age !
Oh grant that I may faithful be
To clearer light vouchsafed to me !

XXI. SARDIS. *Rev.* iii. 1—6.

"Write to Sardis," saith the Lord,
   "And write what he declares,
He whose Spirit, and whose word,
   Upholds the seven stars :—
All thy works and ways I search,
   Find thy zeal and love decayed ;
Thou art called a living church,
   But thou art cold and dead.

"Watch, remember, seek, and strive,
   Exert thy former pains ;
Let thy timely care revive,
   And strengthen what remains ;
Cleanse thine heart, thy works amend,
   Former times to mind recall,
Lest my sudden stroke descend,
   And smite thee once for all.

"Yet I number now in thee
   A few that are upright ;
These my Father's face shall see,
   And walk with me in white.
When in judgment I appear,
   They for mine shall be confessed ;
Let my faithful servants hear,—
   And woe be to the rest !"

XXII. PRAYER FOR A BLESSING ON THE YOUNG.

Bestow, dear Lord, upon our youth,
   The gift of saving grace ;
And let the seed of sacred truth
   Fall in a fruitful place.

Grace is a plant, where'er it grows,
   Of pure and heavenly root ;
But fairest in the youngest shows,
   And yields the sweetest fruit.

Ye careless ones, oh hear betimes
   The voice of sovereign love !
Your youth is stained with many crimes
   But Mercy reigns above.

True, you are young, but there's a stone
   Within the youngest breast ;
Or half the crimes which you have done
   Would rob you of your rest.

For you the public prayer is made ;
   Oh join the public prayer !
For you the secret tear is shed ;
   Oh shed yourselves a tear !

We pray that you may early prove
   The Spirit's power to teach ;
You cannot be too young to love
   That Jesus whom we preach.

XXIII. PLEADING FOR AND WITH YOUTH.

Sin has undone our wretched race;
   But Jesus has restored,
And brought the sinner face to face
   With his forgiving Lord.

This we repeat from year to year,
   And press upon our youth ;
Lord, give them an attentive ear,
   Lord, save them by thy truth !

Blessings upon the rising race!
　Make this a happy hour,
According to thy richest grace,
　And thine Almighty power.

We feel for your unhappy state,
　(May you regard it too,)
And would awhile ourselves forget
　To pour out prayer for you.

We see, though you perceive it not,
　The approaching awful doom;
Oh tremble at the solemn thought,
　And flee the wrath to come!

Dear Saviour, let this new-born year
　Spread an alarm abroad;
And cry in every careless ear,
　"Prepare to meet thy God!"

XXIV. PRAYER FOR CHILDREN.

GRACIOUS Lord, our children see,
By thy mercy we are free;
But shall these, alas! remain
Subjects still of Satan's reign?
Israel's young ones, when of old
Pharaoh threatened to withhold,
Then thy messenger said, "No;
Let the children also go!"

When the angel of the Lord,
Drawing forth his dreadful sword,
Slew with an avenging hand,
All the first-born of the land;
Then thy people's doors he passed,
Where the bloody sign was placed;
Hear us, now, upon our knees
Plead the blood of Christ for these!

Lord, we tremble, for we know
How the fierce malicious foe,
Wheeling round his watchful flight,
Keeps them ever in his sight:
Spread thy pinions, King of kings!
Hide them safe beneath thy wings;
Lest the ravenous bird of prey
Stoop, and bear the brood away.

XXV. JEHOVAH JESUS.

MY song shall bless the Lord of all,
　My praise shall climb to his abode;
Thee, Saviour, by that name I call,
　The great Supreme, the Mighty God.

Without beginning or decline,
　Object of faith and not of sense;
Eternal ages saw him shine,
　He shines eternal ages hence.

As much, when in the manger laid,
　Almighty ruler of the sky,
As when the six days' work he made
　Filled all the morning stars with joy.

Of all the crowns Jehovah bears,
　Salvation is his dearest claim;
That gracious sound well pleased he hears,
　And owns Emmanuel for his name.

A cheerful confidence I feel,
　My well-placed hopes with joy I see;
My bosom glows with heavenly zeal,
　To worship him who died for me.

As man, he pities my complaint,
　His power and truth are all divine;
He will not fail, he cannot faint;
　Salvation's sure, and must be mine.

XXVI. ON OPENING A PLACE
FOR SOCIAL PRAYER.

JESUS! where'er thy people meet,
There they behold thy mercy-seat;
Where'er they seek thee, thou art found,
And every place is hallowed ground.

For thou, within no walls confined,
Inhabitest the humble mind;
Such ever bring thee where they come,
And going, take thee to their home.

Dear Shepherd of thy chosen few!
Thy former mercies here renew;
Here to our waiting hearts proclaim
The sweetness of thy saving name.

Here may we prove the power of prayer,
To strengthen faith, and sweeten care;
To teach our faint desires to rise,
And bring all heaven before our eyes.

Behold, at thy commanding word
We stretch the curtain and the cord;
Come thou, and fill this wider space,
And bless us with a large increase.

Lord, we are few, but thou art near,
Nor short thine arm, nor deaf thine ear;
Oh rend the heavens, come quickly down,
And make a thousand hearts thine own.

XXVII. WELCOME TO THE TABLE.

This is the feast of heavenly wine,
  And God invites to sup;
The juices of the living Vine
  Were pressed to fill the cup.

Oh! bless the Saviour, ye that eat,
  With royal dainties fed;
Not heaven affords a costlier treat,
  For Jesus is the bread.

The vile, the lost, he calls to them;
  Ye trembling souls, appear!
The righteous in their own esteem
  Have no acceptance here.

Approach, ye poor, nor dare refuse
  The banquet spread for you;
Dear Saviour, this is welcome news,
  Then I may venture too.

If guilt and sin afford a plea,
  And may obtain a place,
Surely the Lord will welcome me,
  And I shall see his face!

XXVIII. JESUS HASTENING TO SUFFER.

The Saviour, what a noble flame
  Was kindled in his breast,
When hasting to Jerusalem,
  He marched before the rest!

Good will to men, and zeal for God,
  His every thought engross;
He longs to be baptized with blood,
  He pants to reach the cross!

With all his sufferings full in view,
  And woes to us unknown,
Forth to the task his spirit flew;
  'Twas love that urged him on.

Lord, we return thee what we can:
  Our hearts shall sound abroad
Salvation to the dying Man,
  And to the rising God!

And while thy bleeding glories here
  Engage our wondering eyes,
We learn our lighter cross to bear,
  And hasten to the skies.

XXIX. EXHORTATION TO PRAYER.

What various hindrances we meet
In coming to a mercy-seat!
Yet who that knows the worth of prayer
But wishes to be often there?

Prayer makes the darkened cloud withdraw,
Prayer climbs the ladder Jacob saw,
Gives exercise to faith and love,
Brings every blessing from above.

Restraining prayer, we cease to fight;
Prayer makes the Christian's armour bright;
And Satan trembles when he sees
The weakest saint upon his knees.

While Moses stood with arms spread wide,
Success was found on Israel's side;
But when through weariness they failed,
That moment Amalek prevailed.

Have you no words? Ah! think again,
Words flow apace when you complain,
And fill your fellow-creature's ear
With the sad tale of all your care.

Were half the breath thus vainly spent
To Heaven in supplication sent,
Your cheerful song would oftener be,
" Hear what the Lord has done for me."

XXX. THE LIGHT AND GLORY OF THE WORD.

The Spirit breathes upon the Word,
  And brings the truth to sight;
Precepts and promises afford
  A sanctifying light.

A glory gilds the sacred page,
  Majestic like the sun;
It gives a light to every age,
  It gives, but borrows none.

The hand that gave it still supplies
  The gracious light and heat;
His truths upon the nations rise,
  They rise, but never set.

Let everlasting thanks be thine,
  For such a bright display,
As makes a world of darkness shine
  With beams of heavenly day.

My soul rejoices to pursue
  The steps of him I love,
Till glory break upon my view
  In brighter worlds above.

XXXI. ON THE DEATH OF A MINISTER.

His master taken from his head,
  Elisha saw him go;
And in desponding accents said,
  "Ah, what must Israel do?"

But he forgot the Lord, who lifts
  The beggar to the throne;
Nor knew that all Elijah's gifts
  Would soon be made his own.

What! when a Paul has run his course,
  Or when Apollos dies,
Is Israel left without resource?
  And have we no supplies?

Yes, while the dear Redeemer lives,
  We have a boundless store,
And shall be fed with what he gives,
  Who lives for evermore.

XXXII. THE SHINING LIGHT.

My former hopes are fled,
  My terror now begins;
I feel, alas! that I am dead
  In trespasses and sins.

Ah, whither shall I fly?
  I hear the thunder roar;
The law proclaims destruction nigh,
  And vengeance at the door.

When I review my ways,
  I dread impending doom:
But sure a friendly whisper says,
  "Flee from the wrath to come."

C

I see, or think I see,
  A glimmering from afar;
A beam of day, that shines for me,
  To save me from despair.

Forerunner of the sun,
  It marks the pilgrim's way;
I'll gaze upon it while I run,
  And watch the rising day.

XXXIII. THE WAITING SOUL.

Breathe from the gentle south, O Lord,
  And cheer me from the north;
Blow on the treasures of thy word,
  And call the spices forth!

I wish, thou know'st, to be resigned,
  And wait with patient hope;
But hope delayed fatigues the mind,
  And drinks the spirit up.

Help me to reach the distant goal;
  Confirm my feeble knee;
Pity the sickness of a soul
  That faints for love of thee!

Cold as I feel this heart of mine,
  Yet, since I feel it so,
It yields some hope of life divine
  Within, however low:

I seem forsaken and alone,
  I hear the lion roar;
And every door is shut but one,
  And that is Mercy's door.

There, till the dear Deliverer come,
  I'll wait with humble prayer;
And when he calls his exile home,
  The Lord shall find him there.

XXXIV. SEEKING THE BELOVED.

To those who know the Lord I speak;
  Is my Beloved near?
The Bridegroom of my soul I seek,
  Oh! when will he appear?

Though once a man of grief and shame,
  Yet now he fills a throne,
And bears the greatest, sweetest name
  That earth or heaven has known

D

Grace flies before, and love attends
 His steps where'er he goes;
Though none can see him but his friends,
 And they were once his foes.

He speaks;—obedient to his call
 Our warm affections move:
Did he but shine alike on all,
 Then all alike would love.

Then love in every heart would reign,
 And war would cease to roar;
And cruel and bloodthirsty men
 Would thirst for blood no more.

Such Jesus is, and such his grace;
 Oh, may he shine on you!
And tell him, when you see his face,
 I long to see him too.

XXXV. LIGHT SHINING OUT OF DARKNESS.

GOD moves in a mysterious way
 His wonders to perform;
He plants his footsteps in the sea,
 And rides upon the storm.

Deep in unfathomable mines
 Of never-failing skill,
He treasures up his bright designs,
 And works his sovereign will.

Ye fearful saints, fresh courage take,
 The clouds ye so much dread
Are big with mercy, and shall break
 In blessings on your head.

Judge not the Lord by feeble sense,
 But trust him for his grace;
Behind a frowning providence
 He hides a smiling face.

His purposes will ripen fast,
 Unfolding every hour;
The bud may have a bitter taste,
 But sweet will be the flower.

Blind unbelief is sure to err,
 And scan his work in vain:
God is his own interpreter,
 And He will make it plain.

XXXVI. WELCOME CROSS.

'TIS my happiness below
 Not to live without the cross,
But the Saviour's power to know,
 Sanctifying every loss:
Trials must and will befall;
 But with humble faith to see
Love inscribed upon them all,
 This is happiness to me.

God in Israel sows the seeds
 Of affliction, pain, and toil;
These spring up and choke the weeds
 Which would else o'erspread the soil:
Trials make the promise sweet,
 Trials give new life to prayer;
Trials bring me to his feet,
 Lay me low, and keep me there.

Did I meet no trials here,
 No chastisement by the way,
Might I not with reason fear
 I should prove a castaway?
Bastards may escape the rod,
 Sunk in earthly vain delight;
But the true-born child of God
 Must not,—would not, if he might.

XXXVII. AFFLICTIONS SANCTIFIED BY THE WORD.

OH, how I love thy holy word,
 Thy gracious covenant, O Lord!
It guides me in the peaceful way;
 I think upon it all the day.

What are the mines of shining wealth,
 The strength of youth, the bloom of health!
What are all joys compared with those
 Thine everlasting Word bestows!

Long unafflicted, undismayed,
 In pleasure's path secure I strayed;
Thou madest me feel thy chastening rod,
 And straight I turned unto my God.

What though it pierced my fainting heart,
 I blessed thine hand that caused the smart;
It taught my tears awhile to flow,
 But saved me from eternal woe.

Oh ! hadst thou left me unchastised,
Thy precepts I had still despised ;
And still the snare in secret laid
Had my unwary feet betrayed.

I love thee, therefore, O my God,
And breathe towards thy dear abode ;
Where, in thy presence fully blest,
Thy chosen saints for ever rest.

XXXVIII. TEMPTATION.

THE billows swell, the winds are high,
Clouds overcast my wintry sky ;
Out of the depths to thee I call,—
My fears are great, my strength is small.

O Lord, the pilot's part perform,
And guard and guide me through the
    storm ;
Defend me from each threatening ill,
Control the waves,—say, "Peace ! be
    still."

Amidst the roaring of the sea
My soul still hangs her hope on thee ;
Thy constant love, thy faithful care,
Is all that saves me from despair.

Dangers of every shape and name
Attend the followers of the Lamb,
Who leave the world's deceitful shore,
And leave it to return no more.

Though tempest-tost and half a wreck,
My Saviour through the floods I seek ;
Let neither winds nor stormy main
Force back my shattered bark again.

XXXIX. LOOKING UPWARDS
IN A STORM.

GOD of my life, to thee I call,
Afflicted at thy feet I fall ;
When the great water-floods prevail,
Leave not my trembling heart to fail !

Friend of the friendless and the faint,
Where should I lodge my deep complaint?
Where but with thee, whose open door
Invites the helpless and the poor !

Did ever mourner plead with thee,
And thou refuse that mourner's plea?
Does not the word still fixed remain,
That none shall seek thy face in vain?

That were a grief I could not bear,
Didst thou not hear and answer prayer ;
But a prayer-hearing, answering God
Supports me under every load.

Fair is the lot that's cast for me ;
I have an Advocate with thee ;
They whom the world caresses most
Have no such privilege to boast.

Poor though I am, despised, forgot,
Yet God, my God, forgets me not :
And he is safe, and must succeed,
For whom the Lord vouchsafes to plead.

XL. THE VALLEY OF THE
SHADOW OF DEATH.

MY soul is sad, and much dismayed ;
    See, Lord, what legions of my foes,
With fierce Apollyon at their head,
    My heavenly pilgrimage oppose !

See, from the ever-burning lake,
    How like a smoky cloud they rise !
With horrid blasts my soul they shake,
    With storms of blasphemies and lies.

Their fiery arrows reach the mark,
    My throbbing heart with anguish tear ;
Each lights upon a kindred spark,
    And finds abundant fuel there.

I hate the thought that wrongs the Lord ;
    Oh ! I would drive it from my breast,
With thy own sharp two-edgèd sword,
    Far as the east is from the west.

Come, then, and chase the cruel host,
    Heal the deep wounds I have received !
Nor let the powers of darkness boast
    That I am foiled, and thou art grieved !

XLI. PEACE AFTER A STORM.

WHEN darkness long has veiled my mind,
    And smiling day once more appears,
Then, my Redeemer, then I find
    The folly of my doubts and fears.

Straight I upbraid my wandering heart,
    And blush that I should ever be
Thus prone to act so base a part,
    Or harbour one hard thought of thee.

Oh! let me then at length be taught
  What I am still so slow to learn;
That God is Love, and changes not,
  Nor knows the shadow of a turn.

Sweet truth, and easy to repeat!
  But when my faith is sharply tried,
I find myself a learner yet,
  Unskilful, weak, and apt to slide.

But, O my Lord, one look from thee
  Subdues the disobedient will,
Drives doubt and discontent away,
  And thy rebellious worm is still.

Thou art as ready to forgive
  As I am ready to repine;
Thou, therefore, all the praise receive;
  Be shame and self-abhorrence mine.

XLII. MOURNING AND LONGING.

The Saviour hides his face!
  My spirit thirsts to prove
Renewed supplies of pardoning grace,
  And never-fading love.

The favoured souls who know
  What glories shine in him,
Pant for his presence as the roe
  Pants for the living stream.

What trifles tease me now!
  They swarm like summer flies;
They cleave to everything I do,
  And swim before my eyes.

How dull the Sabbath day
  Without the Sabbath's Lord!
How toilsome then to sing and pray,
  And wait upon the word!

Of all the truths I hear,
  How few delight my taste!
I glean a berry here and there,
  But mourn the vintage past.

Yet let me (as I ought)
  Still hope to be supplied;
No pleasure else is worth a thought,
  Nor shall I be denied.

Though I am but a worm,
  Unworthy of his care,
The Lord will my desire perform,
  And grant me all my prayer.

XLIII. SELF-ACQUAINTANCE.

Dear Lord! accept a sinful heart,
  Which of itself complains,
And mourns, with much and frequent smart,
  The evil it contains.

There fiery seeds of anger lurk,
  Which often hurt my frame;
And wait but for the tempter's work
  To fan them to a flame.

Legality holds out a bribe
  To purchase life from thee;
And Discontent would fain prescribe
  How thou shalt deal with me.

While Unbelief withstands thy grace,
  And puts the mercy by;
Presumption, with a brow of brass,
  Says, "Give me, or I die!"

How eager are my thoughts to roam
  In quest of what they love!
But ah! when Duty calls them home,
  How heavily they move!

Oh, cleanse me in a Saviour's blood,
  Transform me by thy power,
And make me thy beloved abode,
  And let me roam no more.

XLIV. PRAYER FOR PATIENCE.

Lord, who hast suffered all for me,
  My peace and pardon to procure,
The lighter cross I bear for thee
  Help me with patience to endure.

The storm of loud repining hush;
  I would in humble silence mourn;
Why should the unburnt, though burning bush,
  Be angry as the crackling thorn?

Man should not faint at thy rebuke,
  Like Joshua falling on his face,
When the cursed thing that Achan took
  Brought Israel into just disgrace.

Perhaps some golden wedge suppressed,
    Some secret sin offends my God;
Perhaps that Babylonish vest,
    Self-righteousness, provokes the rod.

Ah! were I buffeted all day,
    Mocked, crowned with thorns, and
        spit upon,
I yet should have no right to say,
    My great distress is mine alone.

Let me not angrily declare
    No pain was ever sharp like mine,
Nor murmur at the cross I bear,
    But rather weep, remembering thine.

XLV. SUBMISSION.

O Lord, my best desire fulfil,
    And help me to resign
Life, health, and comfort to thy will,
    And make thy pleasure mine.

Why should I shrink at thy command,
    Whose love forbids my fears?
Or tremble at the gracious hand
    That wipes away my tears?

No, rather let me freely yield
    What most I prize to thee;
Who never hast a good withheld,
    Or wilt withhold, from me.

Thy favour, all my journey through,
    Thou art engaged to grant;
What else I want, or think I do,
    'Tis better still to want.

Wisdom and mercy guide my way,
    Shall I resist them both?
A poor blind creature of a day,
    And crushed before the moth!

But ah! my inward spirit cries,
    Still bind me to thy sway;
Else the next cloud that veils the skies
    Drives all these thoughts away.

XLVI. THE HAPPY CHANGE.

How blessed thy creature is, O God,
    When, with a single eye,
He views the lustre of thy word,
    The dayspring from on high!

Through all the storms that veil the skies
    And frown on earthly things,
The Sun of Righteousness he eyes,
    With healing on his wings.

Struck by that light, the human heart,
    A barren soil no more,
Sends the sweet smell of grace abroad,
    Where serpents lurked before.

The soul, a dreary province once
    Of Satan's dark domain,
Feels a new empire formed within,
    And owns a heavenly reign.

The glorious orb whose golden beams
    The fruitful year control,
Since first, obedient to thy word,
    He started from the goal,

Has cheered the nations with the joys
    His orient rays impart;
But, Jesus, 'tis thy light alone
    Can shine upon the heart.

XLVII. RETIREMENT.

Far from the world, O Lord, I flee,
    From strife and tumult far;
From scenes where Satan wages still
    His most successful war.

The calm retreat, the silent shade,
    With prayer and praise agree;
And seem by thy sweet bounty made
    For those who follow thee.

There, if thy Spirit touch the soul,
    And grace her mean abode,
Oh! with what peace, and joy, and love,
    She communes with her God!

There like the nightingale she pours
    Her solitary lays;
Nor asks a witness of her song,
    Nor thirsts for human praise.

Author and guardian of my life,
    Sweet source of light divine,
And—all harmonious names in one—
    My Saviour! thou art mine!

What thanks I owe thee, and what love,
    A boundless, endless store,
Shall echo through the realms above,
    When time shall be no more.

XLVIII. THE HIDDEN LIFE.

To tell the Saviour all my wants,
  How pleasing is the task !
Nor less to praise him when he grants
  Beyond what I can ask.

My labouring spirit vainly seeks
  To tell but half the joy ;
With how much tenderness he speaks,
  And helps me to reply.

Nor were it wise, nor should I choose,
  Such secrets to declare ;
Like precious wines their taste they
    lose,
  Exposed to open air.

But this with boldness I proclaim,
  Nor care if thousands hear,
Sweet is the ointment of his name,
  Not life is half so dear.

And can you frown, my former friends,
  Who knew what once I was ;
And blame the song that thus commends
  The Man who bore the cross?

Trust me, I draw the likeness true,
  And not as fancy paints ;
Such honour may he give to you,
  For such have all his saints.

XLIX. JOY AND PEACE IN BELIEVING.

SOMETIMES a light surprises
  The Christian while he sings ;
It is the Lord who rises
  With healing in his wings :
When comforts are declining,
  He grants the soul again
A season of clear shining,
  To cheer it after rain.

In holy contemplation,
  We sweetly then pursue
The theme of God's salvation,
  And find it ever new :
Set free from present sorrow,
  We cheerfully can say,
E'en let the unknown to-morrow
  Bring with it what it may !

It can bring with it nothing
  But he will bear us through ;
Who gives the lilies clothing
  Will clothe his people too ;
Beneath the spreading heavens
  No creature but is fed ;
And he who feeds the ravens
  Will give his children bread.

Though vine nor fig-tree neither
  Their wonted fruit shall bear,
Though all the field should wither,
  Nor flocks nor herds be there :
Yet God the same abiding,
  His praise shall tune my voice ;
For, while in him confiding,
  I cannot but rejoice.

L. TRUE PLEASURES.

LORD, my soul with pleasure springs
  When Jesus' name I hear ;
And when God the Spirit brings
  The word of promise near :
Beauties too, in holiness,
  Still delighted I perceive ;
Nor have words that can express
  The joys thy precepts give.

Clothed in sanctity and grace,
  How sweet it is to see
Those who love thee as they pass,
  Or when they wait on thee !
Pleasant too, to sit and tell
  What we owe to love divine ;
Till our bosoms grateful swell,
  And eyes begin to shine.

Those the comforts I possess,
  Which God shall still increase,
All his ways are pleasantness,
  And all his paths are peace.
Nothing Jesus did or spoke,
  Henceforth let me ever slight ;
For I love his easy yoke,
  And find his burden light.

LI. THE CHRISTIAN.

HONOUR and happiness unite
  To make the Christian's name a praise ;
How fair the scene, how clear the light,
  That fills the remnant of his days !

A kingly character he bears,
  No change his priestly office knows;
Unfading is the crown he wears,
  His joys can never reach a close.

Adorned with glory from on high,
  Salvation shines upon his face ;
His robe is of the ethereal dye,
  His steps are dignity and grace.

Inferior honours he disdains,
  Nor stoops to take applause from earth;
The King of kings himself maintains
  The expenses of his heavenly birth.

The noblest creature seen below,
  Ordained to fill a throne above ;
God gives him all he can bestow,
  His kingdom of eternal love !

My soul is ravished at the thought !
  Methinks from earth I see him rise !
Angels congratulate his lot,
  And shout him welcome to the skies !

LII. LIVELY HOPE AND GRACIOUS FEAR.

I WAS a grovelling creature once,
  And basely cleaved to earth ;
I wanted spirit to renounce
  The clod that gave me birth.

But God has breathed upon a worm,
  And sent me from above
Wings such as clothe an angel's form,
  The wings of joy and love.

With these to Pisgah's top I fly,
  And there delighted stand,
To view beneath a shining sky
  The spacious promised land.

The Lord of all the vast domain
  Has promised it to me,
The length and breadth of all the plain
  As far as faith can see.

How glorious is my privilege !
  To thee for help I call ;
I stand upon a mountain's edge,
  Oh save me, lest I fall !

Though much exalted in the Lord,
  My strength is not my own ;
Then let me tremble at his word,
  And none shall cast me down.

LIII. FOR THE POOR.

WHEN Hagar found the bottle spent,
  And wept o'er Ishmael,
A message from the Lord was sent
  To guide her to a well.

Should not Elijah's cake and cruse
  Convince us at this day,
A gracious God will not refuse
  Provisions by the way?

His saints and servants shall be fed,
  The promise is secure ;
" Bread shall be given them," as he said,
  " Their water shall be sure."

Repasts far richer they shall prove,
  Than all earth's dainties are ;
'Tis sweet to taste a Saviour's love,
  Though in the meanest fare.

To Jesus then your trouble bring,
  Nor murmur at your lot ;
While you are poor and He is King,
  You shall not be forgot.

LIV. MY SOUL THIRSTETH FOR GOD.

I THIRST, but not as once I did,
  The vain delights of earth to share ;
Thy wounds, Emmanuel, all forbid
  That I should seek my pleasures there.

It was the sight of thy dear cross
  First weaned my soul from earthly
    things ;
And taught me to esteem as dross
  The mirth of fools and pomp of kings.

I want that grace that springs from thee,
  That quickens all things where it flows,
And makes a wretched thorn like me
  Bloom as the myrtle, or the rose.

Dear fountain of delight unknown !
  No longer sink below the brim ;
But overflow, and pour me down
  A living and life-giving stream ;

For sure of all the plants that share
　The notice of thy Father's eye,
None proves less grateful to his care,
　Or yields him meaner fruit than I.

LV. LOVE CONSTRAINING TO OBEDIENCE.

No strength of Nature can suffice
　To serve the Lord aright :
And what she has she misapplies,
　For want of clearer light.

How long beneath the law I lay
　In bondage and distress ;
I toiled the precept to obey,
　But toiled without success.

Then to abstain from outward sin
　Was more than I could do ;
Now, if I feel its power within,
　I feel I hate it too.

Then all my servile works were done
　A righteousness to raise ;
Now, freely chosen in the Son,
　I freely chuse his ways.

"What shall I do," was then the word,
　"That I may worthier grow ?"
"What shall I render to the Lord ?"
　Is my inquiry now.

To see the law by Christ fulfilled,
　And hear his pardoning voice,
Changes a slave into a child,
　And duty into choice.

LVI. THE HEART HEALED AND CHANGED BY MERCY.

Sin enslaved me many years,
　And led me bound and blind ;
Till at length a thousand fears
　Came swarming o'er my mind.
"Where," said I, in deep distress,
　"Will these sinful pleasures end ?
How shall I secure my peace,
　And make the Lord my friend ?"

Friends and ministers said much
　The Gospel to enforce ;
But my blindness still was such,
　I chose a legal course :

Much I fasted, watched, and strove,
　Scarce would show my face abroad,
Feared almost to speak or move,
　A stranger still to God.

Thus afraid to trust his grace,
　Long time did I rebel ;
Till despairing of my case,
　Down at his feet I fell :
Then my stubborn heart he broke,
　And subdued me to his sway ;
By a simple word he spoke,
　"Thy sins are done away."

LVII. HATRED OF SIN.

Holy Lord God ! I love thy truth,
　Nor dare thy least commandment
　　slight ;
Yet pierced by sin, the serpent's tooth,
　I mourn the anguish of the bite.

But though the poison lurks within,
　Hope bids me still with patience wait ;
Till death shall set me free from sin,
　Free from the only thing I hate.

Had I a throne above the rest,
　Where angels and archangels dwell,
One sin, unslain, within my breast,
　Would make that heaven as dark as
　　hell.

The prisoner sent to breathe fresh air,
　And blessed with liberty again,
Would mourn were he condemned to wear
　One link of all his former chain.

But, oh ! no foe invades the bliss,
　When glory crowns the Christian's
　　head ;
One view of Jesus as he is
　Will strike all sin for ever dead.

LVIII. THE NEW CONVERT.

The new-born child of Gospel grace,
　Like some fair tree when summer's
　　nigh,
Beneath Emmanuel's shining face
　Lifts up his blooming branch on high.

No fears he feels, he sees no foes,
    No conflict yet his faith employs,
Nor has he learnt to whom he owes
    The strength and peace his soul enjoys.

But sin soon darts its cruel sting,
    And comforts sinking day by day,
What seemed his own, a self-fed spring,
    Proves but a brook that glides away.

When Gideon armed his numerous host,
    The Lord soon made his numbers less;
And said, "Lest Israel vainly boast,
    'My arm procured me this success.'"

Thus will he bring our spirits down,
    And draw our ebbing comforts low,
That saved by grace, but not our own,
    We may not claim the praise we owe.

LIX. TRUE AND FALSE COMFORTS.

O GOD, whose favourable eye
    The sin-sick soul revives,
Holy and heavenly is the joy
    Thy shining presence gives.

Not such as hypocrites suppose,
    Who with a graceless heart
Taste not of thee, but drink a dose
    Prepared by Satan's art.

Intoxicating joys are theirs,
    Who while they boast their light,
And seem to soar above the stars,
    Are plunging into night.

Lulled in a soft and fatal sleep,
    They sin and yet rejoice;
Were they indeed the Saviour's sheep,
    Would they not hear his voice?

Be mine the comforts that reclaim
    The soul from Satan's power;
That make me blush for what I am,
    And hate my sin the more.

'Tis joy enough, my All in All,
    At thy dear feet to lie;
Thou wilt not let me lower fall,
    And none can higher fly.

LX. A LIVING AND A DEAD FAITH.

THE Lord receives his highest praise
    From humble minds and hearts sincere;
While all the loud professor says
    Offends the righteous Judge's ear.

To walk as children of the day,
    To mark the precepts' holy light,
To wage the warfare, watch, and pray,
    Show who are pleasing in his sight.

Not words alone it cost the Lord
    To purchase pardon for his own;
Nor will a soul by grace restored
    Return the Saviour words alone.

With golden bells, the priestly vest,
    And rich pomegranates bordered round,
The need of holiness expressed,
    And called for fruit as well as sound.

Easy indeed it were to reach
    A mansion in the courts above,
If swelling words and fluent speech
    Might serve instead of faith and love.

But none shall gain the blissful place,
    Or God's unclouded glory see,
Who talks of free and sovereign grace,
    Unless that grace has made him free!

LXI. ABUSE OF THE GOSPEL.

TOO many, Lord, abuse thy grace
    In this licentious day,
And while they boast they see thy face
    They turn their own away.

Thy book displays a gracious light
    That can the blind restore;
But these are dazzled by the sight,
    And blinded still the more.

The pardon such presume upon,
    They do not beg, but steal;
And when they plead it at thy throne,
    Oh! where's the Spirit's seal?

Was it for this, ye lawless tribe,
  The dear Redeemer bled?
Is this the grace the saints imbibe
  From Christ the living head?

Ah, Lord, we know thy chosen few
  Are fed with heavenly fare;
But these,—the wretched husks they
      chew
  Proclaim them what they are.

The liberty our hearts implore
  Is not to live in sin;
But still to wait at Wisdom's door,
  Till Mercy calls us in.

LXII. THE NARROW WAY.

WHAT thousands never knew the road!
  What thousands hate it when 'tis
      known!
None but the chosen tribes of God
  Will seek or choose it for their own.

A thousand ways in ruin end,
  One only leads to joys on high;
By that my willing steps ascend,
  Pleased with a journey to the sky.

No more I ask or hope to find
  Delight or happiness below;
Sorrow may well possess the mind
  That feeds where thorns and thistles
      grow.

The joy that fades is not for me,
  I seek immortal joys above;
There glory without end shall be
  The bright reward of faith and love.

Cleave to the world, ye sordid worms,
  Contented lick your native dust!
But God shall fight with all his storms
  Against the idol of your trust.

LXIII. DEPENDENCE.

To keep the lamp alive,
  With oil we fill the bowl;
'Tis water makes the willow thrive,
  And grace that feeds the soul.

The Lord's unsparing hand
  Supplies the living stream;
It is not at our own command,
  But still derived from him.

Beware of Peter's word,
  Nor confidently say,
"I never will deny thee, Lord,"—
  But,—"Grant I never may."

Man's wisdom is to seek
  His strength in God alone;
And even an angel would be weak
  Who trusted in his own.

Retreat beneath his wings,
  And in his grace confide!
This more exalts the King of kings
  Than all your works beside.

In Jesus is our store,
  Grace issues from his throne;
Whoever says, "I want no more,"
  Confesses he has none.

LXIV. NOT OF WORKS.

GRACE, triumphant in the throne,
Scorns a rival, reigns alone;
Come and bow beneath her sway,
Cast your idol works away!
Works of man, when made his plea,
Never shall accepted be;
Fruits of pride (vain-glorious worm!)
Are the best he can perform.

Self, the god his soul adores,
Influences all his powers;
Jesus is a slighted name, ·
Self-advancement all his aim:
But when God the Judge shall come
To pronounce the final doom,
Then for rocks and hills to hide
All his works and all his pride!

Still the boasting heart replies,
"What! the worthy and the wise,
Friends to temperance and peace,
Have not these a righteousness?"
Banish every vain pretence
Built on human excellence;
Perish everything in man,
But the grace that never can.

LXV. PRAISE FOR FAITH.

OF all the gifts thine hand bestows,
  Thou Giver of all good !
Not heaven itself a richer knows
  Than my Redeemer's blood.

Faith too, the blood-receiving grace,
  From the same hand we gain ;
Else, sweetly as it suits our case,
  That gift had been in vain.

Till thou thy teaching power apply,
  Our hearts refuse to see,
And weak, as a distempered eye.
  Shut out the view of thee.

Blind to the merits of thy Son,
  What misery we endure !
Yet fly that hand from which alone
  We could expect a cure.

We praise thee, and would praise thee
  To thee our all we owe ;   [more,
The precious Saviour, and the power
  That makes him precious too.

LXVI. GRACE AND PRO-VIDENCE.

ALMIGHTY King! whose wondrous hand
Supports the weight of sea and land ;
Whose grace is such a boundless store,
No heart shall break that sighs for more ;

Thy providence supplies my food,
And 'tis thy blessing makes it good ;
My soul is nourished by thy word :
Let soul and body praise the Lord !

My streams of outward comfort came
From him who built this earthly frame ;
Whate'er I want his bounty gives,
By whom my soul for ever lives.

Either his hand preserves from pain,
Or, if I feel it, heals again ;
From Satan's malice shields my breast,
Or overrules it for the best.

Forgive the song that falls so low
Beneath the gratitude I owe !
It means thy praise, however poor,
An angel's song can do no more.

LXVII. I WILL PRAISE THE LORD AT ALL TIMES.

WINTER has a joy for me,
  While the Saviour's charms I read,
Lowly, meek, from blemish free,
  In the snowdrop's pensive head.

Spring returns, and brings along
  Life-invigorating suns :
Hark ! the turtle's plaintive song
  Seems to speak his dying groans !

Summer has a thousand charms,
  All expressive of his worth ;
'Tis his sun that lights and warms,
  His the air that cools the earth.

What ! has Autumn left to say
  Nothing of a Saviour's grace?
Yes, the beams of milder day
  Tell me of his smiling face.

Light appears with early dawn,
  While the sun makes haste to rise ;
See his bleeding beauties drawn
  On the blushes of the skies.

Evening with a silent pace,
  Slowly moving in the west,
Shows an emblem of his grace,
  Points to an eternal rest.

LXVIII. LONGING TO BE WITH CHRIST.

TO Jesus, the Crown of my Hope,
  My soul is in haste to be gone ;
Oh bear me, ye cherubim, up,
  And waft me away to his throne !

My Saviour, whom absent I love,
  Whom, not having seen, I adore ;
Whose name is exalted above
  All glory, dominion, and power ;

Dissolve thou these bonds, that detain
  My soul from her portion in thee,
Ah ! strike off this adamant chain,
  And make me eternally free.

When that happy era begins,
  When arrayed in thy glories I shine,
Nor grieve any more, by my sins,
  The bosom on which I recline ;

Oh then shall the veil be removed,
  And round me thy brightness be
    poured,
I shall meet Him whom absent I loved,
  Shall see him whom unseen I
    adored.

And then, never more shall the fears,
  The trials, temptations, and woes,
Which darken this valley of tears,
  Intrude on my blissful repose.

Or, if yet remembered above,
  Remembrance no sadness shall raise,
They will be but new signs of thy love,
  New themes for my wonder and praise.

Thus the strokes which from sin and
    from pain
  Shall set me eternally free,
Will but strengthen and rivet the chain
  Which binds me, my Saviour! to
    thee.

P O E M S

B Y

WILLIAM COWPER,

Of the INNER TEMPLE, Esq.

Sicut aquæ tremulum labris ubi lumen ahenis
Sole repercussum, aut radiantis imagine lunæ,
Omnia pervolitat laté loca ; jamque sub auras
Erigitur, summique ferit laquearia tecti. VIRG. ÆN. VIII.

So water trembling in a polished vase,
Reflects the beam that plays upon its face,
The sportive light, uncertain where it falls,
Now strikes the roof, now flashes on the walls.

Nous sommes nés pour la vérité, et nous ne pouvons souffrir son
abord. les figures, les paraboles, les emblémes. sont toujours
des ornements nécessaires pour qu'elle puisse s'annoncer. et soit
quon craigne qu'elle ne découvre trop brusquement le défaut
qu'on voudroit cacher, ou qu'enfin elle n'instruise avec trop
peu de ménagement, ou veut, en la recevant, qu'elle soit
déguisée.

CARACCIOLI.

L O N D O N :

Printed for J. JOHNSON, No. 72, St. Paul's Church Yard.

1782.

PREFACE, BY THE REV. JOHN NEWTON.

WHEN an author, by appearing in print, requests an audience of the public, and is upon the point of speaking for himself, whoever presumes to step before him with a Preface, and to say, " Nay, but hear me first ! " should have something worthy of attention to offer, or he will be justly deemed officious and impertinent. The judicious reader has, probably, upon other occasions, been beforehand with me in this reflection : and I am not very willing it should now be applied to me, however I may seem to expose myself to the danger of it. But the thought of having my own name perpetuated in connexion with the name in the title-page is so pleasing and flattering to the feelings of my heart, that I am content to risk something for the gratification.

This Preface is not designed to commend the Poems to which it is prefixed. My testimony would be insufficient for those who are not qualified to judge properly for themselves, and unnecessary to those who are. Besides, the reasons which render it improper and unseemly for a man to celebrate his own performances, or those of his nearest relatives, will have some influence in suppressing much of what he might otherwise wish to say in favour of a friend, when that friend is indeed an *alter idem*, and excites almost the same emotions of sensibility and affection as he feels for himself.

It is very probable these Poems may come into the hands of some persons, in whom the sight of the author's name will awaken a recollection of incidents and scenes, which through length of time they had almost forgotten. They will be reminded of one, who was once the companion of their chosen hours, and who set out with them in early life in the paths which lead to literary honours, to influence and affluence, with equal prospects of success. But he was suddenly and power-fully withdrawn from those pursuits, and he left them without regret ; yet not till he had sufficient opportunity of counting the cost, and of knowing the value of what he gave up. If happiness could have been found in classical attainments, in an elegant taste, in the exertions of wit, fancy, and genius, and in the esteem and converse of such persons as in these respects were most congenial with himself, he would have been happy. But he was not.—He wondered (as thousands in a similar situation still do) that he should continue dissatisfied, with all the means apparently conducive to satisfaction within his reach.—But in due time the cause of his disappointment was discovered to him :—He had lived without God in the world. In a memorable hour, the wisdom which is from above visited his heart. Then he felt himself a wanderer, and then he found a guide. Upon this change of views, a change of plan and conduct followed of course. When he saw the busy and the gay world in its true light, he left it with as little reluctance as a prisoner, when called to liberty, leaves his dungeon. Not that he became a cynic or an ascetic :—a heart filled with love to God will assuredly breathe benevolence to men. But the turn of his temper inclining him to rural life, he indulged it, and the providence of God evidently preparing his way and marking out his retreat, he retired into the country. By these steps the good hand of God, unknown to me, was providing for me one of the principal blessings of my life ; a friend and a counsellor, in whose company for almost seven years, though we were seldom seven successive waking hours separated, I always found new pleasure : a friend who was not only a comfort to myself, but a blessing to the affectionate poor people among whom I then lived.

Some time after inclination had thus removed him from the hurry and bustle of life, he was still more secluded by a long indisposition, and my pleasure was succeeded by a proportionable degree of anxiety and concern. But a hope that the God whom he served would support him under his affliction, and at length vouchsafe him a happy deliverance, never forsook me. The desirable crisis, I trust, is now nearly approaching. The dawn, the presage of returning day, is already arrived. He is again enabled to resume his pen, and some of the first fruits of his recovery are here presented to the public. In his principal subjects, the same acumen which distinguished him in the early period of life is happily employed in illustrating and enforcing the truths, of which he received such deep and unalterable impressions in his maturer years. His satire, if it may be called so, is benevolent, (like the operations of the skilful and humane surgeon, who wounds only to heal,) dictated by a just regard for the honour of God, and indignant grief excited by the profligacy of the age, and a tender compassion for the souls of men.

His favourite topics are least insisted on in the piece entitled " Table Talk ; " which, therefore, with some regard to the prevailing taste, and that those who are governed by it may not be discouraged at the very threshold from proceeding farther, is placed first. In most of the large Poems which follow, his leading design is more explicitly avowed and pursued. He aims to communicate his own perceptions of the truth, beauty, and influence of the religion of the Bible,—a religion, which, however discredited by the misconduct of many who have not renounced the Christian name, proves itself, when rightly understood, and cordially embraced, to be the grand desideratum which alone can relieve the mind of man from painful and unavoidable anxieties, inspire it with stable peace and solid hope, and furnish those motives and prospects which, in the present state of things, are absolutely necessary to produce a conduct worthy of a rational creature, distinguished by a vastness of capacity, which no assemblage of earthly good can satisfy, and by a principle and pre-intimation of immortality.

At a time when hypothesis and conjecture in philosophy are so justly exploded, and little is considered as deserving the name of knowledge which will not stand the test of experiment, the very use of the term *experimental*, in religious concernments, is by too many unhappily rejected with disgust. But we well know, that they who affect to despise the inward feelings which religious persons speak of, and to treat them as enthusiasm and folly, have inward feelings of their own, which, though they would, they cannot suppress. We have been too long in the secret ourselves, to account the proud, the ambitious, or the voluptuous, happy. We must lose the remembrance of what we once were, before we can believe that a man is satisfied with himself, merely because he endeavours to appear so. A smile upon the face is often but a mask worn occasionally and in company, to prevent, if possible, a suspicion of what at the same time is passing in the heart. We know that there are people, who seldom smile when they are alone, who therefore are glad to hide themselves in a throng from the violence of their own reflections ; and who, while by their looks and their language they wish to persuade us they are happy, would be glad to change conditions with a dog. But in defiance of all their efforts, they continue to think, forebode, and tremble. This we know, for it has been our own state, and therefore we know how to commiserate it in others. From this state the Bible relieved us. When we were led to read it with attention, we found ourselves described,—we learnt the causes of our inquietude,—we were directed to a method of relief,—we found, and we were not disappointed.

Deus nobis hæc otia fecit.

We are now certain that the Gospel of Christ is the power of God unto salvation to every one that believeth. It has reconciled us to God, and to ourselves, to our

luty, and our situation. It is the balm and cordial of the present life, and a
sovereign antidote against the fear of death.

Sed hactenus hæc.—Some smaller pieces, upon less important subjects, close the
volume. Not one of them, I believe, was written with a view to publication, but
I was unwilling they should be omitted.

JOHN NEWTON.

CHARLES SQUARE, HOXTON,
February 18, 1782.

TABLE TALK.

Si te fortè meæ gravis uret sarcina chartæ,
Abjicito.—HOR. lib. i. ep. 13.

A. YOU told me, I remember, glory, built
On selfish principles, is shame and guilt;
The deeds that men admire as half divine,
Stark naught, because corrupt in their design.
Strange doctrine this! that without scruple tears
The laurel that the very lightning spares;
Brings down the warrior's trophy to the dust,
And eats into his bloody sword like rust.
 B. I grant that, men continuing what they are,
Fierce, avaricious, proud, there must be war;   10
And never meant the rule should be applied
To him that fights with justice on his side.
 Let laurels, drenched in pure Parnassian dews,
Reward his memory, dear to every muse,
Who, with a courage of unshaken root,
In honour's field advancing his firm foot,
Plants it upon the line that justice draws,
And will prevail or perish in her cause.
'Tis to the virtues of such men, man owes
His portion in the good that Heaven bestows;   20
And when recording History displays
Feats of renown, though wrought in ancient days,
Tells of a few stout hearts that fought and died
Where duty placed them, at their country's side,—
The man that is not moved with what he reads,
That takes not fire at their heroic deeds,
Unworthy of the blessings of the brave,
Is base in kind, and born to be a slave.
 But let eternal infamy pursue
The wretch to nought but his ambition true,   30
Who, for the sake of filling with one blast
The post-horns of all Europe, lays her waste.
Think yourself stationed on a towering rock,
To see a people scattered like a flock,
Some royal mastiff panting at their heels,
With all the savage thirst a tiger feels,

Ç

Then view him self-proclaimed in a gazette
Chief monster that has plagued the nations yet !
The globe and sceptre in such hands misplaced,
Those ensigns of dominion, how disgraced !   40
The glass that bids man mark the fleeting hour,
And Death's own scythe, would better speak his power.
Then grace the bony phantom in their stead
With the king's shoulder-knot and gay cockade ;
Clothe the twin brethren in each other's dress,
The same their occupation and success.
 A. 'Tis your belief the world was made for man ;
Kings do but reason on the self-same plan :
Maintaining yours, you cannot theirs condemn,
Who think, or seem to think, man made for them. 50
 B. Seldom, alas ! the power of logic reigns
With much sufficiency in royal brains ;
Such reasoning falls like an inverted cone,
Wanting its proper base to stand upon.
Man made for kings ! those optics are but dim
That tell you so ;—say, rather, they for him.
That were indeed a king-ennobling thought,
Could they, or would they, reason as they ought.
The diadem with mighty projects lined,
To catch renown by ruining mankind,   60
Is worth, with all its gold and glittering store,
Just what the toy will sell for, and no more.
 Oh ! bright occasions of dispensing good,
How seldom used, how little understood !
To pour in Virtue's lap her just reward ;
Keep Vice restrained behind a double guard ;
To quell the faction that affronts the throne,
By silent magnanimity alone ;
To nurse with tender care the thriving Arts,
Watch every beam Philosophy imparts ; 70
To give Religion her unbridled scope,
Nor judge by statute a believer's hope ;
With close fidelity and love unfeigned
To keep the matrimonial bond unstained ;
Covetous only of a virtuous praise,
His life a lesson to the land he sways ;
To touch the sword with conscientious awe,
Nor draw it but when duty bids him draw ;
To sheath it in the peace-restoring close
With joy beyond what victory bestows,— 80
Blest country ! where these kingly glories shine,
Blest England ! if this happiness be thine.
 A. Guard what you say : the patriotic tribe
Will sneer, and charge you with a bribe.—*B.* A bribe ?
The worth of his three kingdoms I defy
To lure me to the baseness of a lie ;
And, of all lies (be that one poet's boast),
The lie that flatters I abhor the most.

Those arts be theirs that hate his gentle reign,
But he that loves him has no need to feign. 90
    A. Your smooth eulogium, to one crown addressed,
Seems to imply a censure on the rest.
    B. Quevedo, as he tells his sober tale,
Asked, when in hell, to see the royal jail,
Approved their method in all other things,
"But where, good sir, do you confine your kings?"
"There," said his guide, "the group is full in view."
"Indeed!" replied the Don; "there are but few."
His black interpreter the charge disdained ;—
"Few, fellow? There are all that ever reigned." 100
    Wit, undistinguishing, is apt to strike
The guilty and not guilty, both alike.
I grant the sarcasm is too severe,
And we can readily refute it here,
While Alfred's name, the father of his age,
And the Sixth Edward's, grace the historic page.
    A. Kings then at last have but the lot of all ;
By their own conduct they must stand or fall.
    B. True. While they live, the courtly laureate pays
His quit-rent ode, his pepper-corn of praise, 110
And many a dunce whose fingers itch to write,
Adds, as he can, his tributary mite ;
A subject's faults a subject may proclaim,
A monarch's errors are forbidden game.
Thus free from censure, (overawed by fear,)
And praised for virtues that they scorn to wear,
The fleeting forms of majesty engage
Respect, while stalking o'er life's narrow stage,
Then leave their crimes for History to scan,
And ask, with busy scorn, Was this the man? 120
    I pity kings whom worship waits upon
Obsequious, from the cradle to the throne ;
Before whose infant eyes the flatterer bows,
And binds a wreath about their baby brows ;
Whom education stiffens into state,
And death awakens from that dream too late.
Oh ! if servility, with supple knees,
Whose trade it is to smile, to crouch, to please,—
If smooth dissimulation, skilled to grace
A devil's purpose with an angel's face,— 130
If smiling peeresses and simpering peers,
Encompassing his throne a few short years,—
If the gilt carriage and the pampered steed,
That wants no driving and disdains the lead,—
If guards, mechanically formed in ranks,
Playing, at beat of drum, their martial pranks,
Shouldering and standing, as if struck to stone,
While condescending majesty looks on ;
If monarchy consist in such base things,
Sighing, I say again, I pity kings ! 140

To be suspected, thwarted, and withstood,
Even when he labours for his country's good,—
To see a band called patriot for no cause
But that they catch at popular applause,
Careless of all the anxiety he feels,
Hook disappointment on the public wheels,
With all their flippant fluency of tongue,
Most confident, when palpably most wrong,—
If this be kingly, then farewell for me
All kingship, and may I be poor and free !   150
    To be the Table Talk of clubs up stairs,
To which the unwashed artificer repairs,
To indulge his genius after long fatigue
By diving into cabinet intrigue,
(For what kings deem a toil, as well they may,
To him is relaxation and mere play ;)—
To win no praise when well-wrought plans prevail,
But to be rudely censured when they fail,—
To doubt the love his favourites may pretend,
And in reality to find no friend,—   160
If he indulge a cultivated taste,
His galleries with the works of art well graced,
To hear it called extravagance and waste ;
If these attendants, and if such as these,
Must follow royalty, then welcome ease !
However humble and confined the sphere,
Happy the state that has not these to fear.
    A. Thus men, whose thoughts contemplative have
        dwelt
On situations that they never felt,
Start up sagacious, covered with the dust   170
Of dreaming study and pedantic rust,
And prate and preach about what others prove,
As if the world and they were hand and glove.
Leave kingly backs to cope with kingly cares,
They have their weight to carry, subjects theirs ;
Poets, of all men, ever least regret
Increasing taxes and the nation's debt.
Could you contrive the payment, and rehearse
The mighty plan, oracular, in verse,
No bard, howe'er majestic, old or new,   180
Should claim my fixed attention more than you.
    B. Not Brindley nor Bridgewater would essay
To turn the course of Helicon that way ;
Nor would the Nine consent the sacred tide
Should purl amidst the traffic of Cheapside,
Or tinkle in 'Change Alley, to amuse
The leathern ears of stock-jobbers and Jews.
    A. Vouchsafe, at least, to pitch the key of rhyme
To themes more pertinent, if less sublime.
When ministers and ministerial arts,—   190
Patriots who love good places at their hearts,—

When admirals extolled for standing still,
Or doing nothing with a deal of skill,
Generals who will not conquer when they may,
Firm friends to peace, to pleasure, and good pay, —
When freedom wounded almost to despair,
Though discontent alone can find out where, —
When themes like these employ the poet's tongue,
I hear, — as mute as if a syren sung.
Or tell me, if you can, what power maintains   200
A Briton's scorn of arbitrary chains?
That were a theme might animate the dead,
And move the lips of poets cast in lead.
   B. The cause, though worth the search, may yet elude
Conjecture and remark, however shrewd.
They take, perhaps, a well-directed aim,
Who seek it in his climate and his frame.
Liberal in all things else, yet Nature here
With stern severity deals out the year.
Winter invades the spring, and often pours   210
A chilling flood on summer's drooping flowers ;
Unwelcome vapours quench autumnal beams,
Ungenial blasts attending, curl the streams ;
The peasants urge their harvest, ply the fork
With double toil, and shiver at their work.
Thus with a rigour, for his good designed,
She rears her favourite man of all mankind.
His form robust and of elastic tone,
Proportioned well, half muscle and half bone,
Supplies with warm activity and force   220
A mind well lodged, and masculine of course.
Hence Liberty, sweet Liberty, inspires
And keeps alive his fierce but noble fires.
Patient of constitutional control,
He-bears it with meek manliness of soul ;
But if authority grow wanton, woe
To him that treads upon his free-born toe !
One step beyond the boundary of the laws
Fires him at once in Freedom's glorious cause.
Thus proud Prerogative, not much revered,   230
Is seldom felt, though sometimes seen and heard ;
And in his cage, like parrot fine and gay,
Is kept to strut, look big, and talk away.
   Born in a climate softer far than ours,
Not formed like us, with such Herculean powers,
The Frenchman, easy, debonair, and brisk,
Give him his lass, his fiddle, and his frisk,
Is always happy, reign whoever may,
And laughs the sense of misery far away.
He drinks his simple beverage with a gust,   240
And feasting on an onion and a crust,
We never feel the alacrity and joy
With which he shouts and carols, *"Vive le Roy !"*

Filled with as much true merriment and glee
As if he heard his king say, " Slave, be free ! "
   Thus happiness depends, as nature shows,
Less on exterior things than most suppose.
Vigilant over all that He has made,
Kind Providence attends with gracious aid,
Bids equity throughout His works prevail,   250
And weighs the nations in an even scale ;
He can encourage Slavery to a smile,
And fill with discontent a British isle.
   A. Freeman and slave then, if the case be such,
Stand on a level,—and you prove too much.
If all men indiscriminately share
His fostering power and tutelary care,
As well be yoked by Despotism's hand,
As dwell at large in Britain's chartered land.
   B. No. Freedom has a thousand charms to show,   260
That slaves, howe'er contented, never know.
The mind attains beneath her happy reign
The growth that Nature meant she should attain ;
The varied fields of science, ever new,
Opening and wider opening on her view,
She ventures onward with a prosperous force,
While no base fear impedes her in her course.
Religion, richest favour of the skies,
Stands most revealed before the freeman's eyes ;
No shades of superstition blot the day,   270
Liberty chases all that gloom away ;
The soul, emancipated, unoppressed,
Free to prove all things, and hold fast the best,
Learns much, and to a thousand listening minds
Communicates with joy the good she finds ;
Courage in arms, and ever prompt to show
His manly forehead to the fiercest foe ;
Glorious in war, but for the sake of peace,
His spirits rising as his toils increase,
Guards well what arts and industry have won,   280
And Freedom claims him for her first-born son.
Slaves fight for what were better cast away,
The chain that binds them, and a tyrant's sway ,
But they that fight for freedom, undertake
The noblest cause mankind can have at stake,
Religion, virtue, truth, whate'er we call
A blessing, freedom is the pledge of all.
O Liberty ! the prisoner's pleasing dream,
The poet's muse, his passion and his theme,
Genius is thine, and thou art Fancy's nurse,   290
Lost without thee the ennobling powers of verse ;
Heroic song from thy free touch acquires
Its clearest tone, the rapture it inspires.
Place me where Winter breathes his keenest air,
And I will sing if Liberty be there ;

And I will sing at Liberty's dear feet
In Afric's torrid clime or India's fiercest heat.
   A. Sing where you please ; in such a cause I grant
An English poet's privilege to rant.
But is not Freedom, at least is not ou̇rs,   300
Too apt to play the wanton with her powers,
Grow freakish, and o'erleaping every mound,
Spread anarchy and terror all around ?
   B. Agreed. But would you sell or slay your horse
For bounding and curvetting in his course ;
Or if, when ridden with a careless rein,
He break away, and seek the distant plain ?
No. His high mettle, under good control,
Gives him Olympic speed, and shoots him to the goal.
   Let Discipline employ her wholesome arts ;   310
Let magistrates alert perform their parts,
Not skulk, or put on a prudential mask,
As if their duty were a desperate task ;
Let active laws apply the needful curb
To guard the peace that riot would disturb,
And liberty, preserved from wild excess,
Shall raise no feuds for armies to suppress.
When Tumult lately burst his prison door,
And set plebeian thousands in a roar,
When he usurped Authority's just place,   320
And dared to look his master in the face,
When the rude rabble's watchword was, " Destroy ! "
And blazing London seemed a second Troy,
Liberty blushed, and hung her drooping head,
Beheld their progress with the deepest dread,
Blushed that effects like these she should produce,
Worse than the deeds of galley-slaves broke loose.
She loses in such storms her very name,
And fierce Licentiousness should bear the blame.
   Incomparable gem ! thy worth untold,   330
Cheap, though blood-bought, and thrown away when sold ;
May no foes ravish thee, and no false friend
Betray thee, while professing to defend :
Prize it, ye ministers ; ye monarchs, spare ;
Ye patriots, guard it with a miser's care !
   A. Patriots, alas ! the few that have been found
Where most they flourish, upon English ground,
The country's need have scantily supplied ;
And the last left the scene when Chatham died.
   B. Not so—the virtue still adorns our age,   340
Though the chief actor died upon the stage.
In him, Demosthenes was heard again,
Liberty taught him her Athenian strain ;
She clothed him with authority and awe,
Spoke from his lips, and in his looks gave law.
His speech, his form, his action, full of grace,
And all his country beaming in his face,

He stood, as some inimitable hand
Would strive to make a Paul or Tully stand.
No sycophant or slave that dared oppose   350
Her sacred cause, but trembled when he rose,
And every venal stickler for the yoke
Felt himself crushed at the first word he spoke.
  Such men are raised to station and command,
When Providence means mercy to a land.
He speaks, and they appear ; to Him they owe
Skill to direct, and strength to strike the blow,
To manage with address, to seize with power
The crisis of a dark decisive hour.
So Gideon earned a victory not his own,   360
Subserviency his praise, and that alone.
  Poor England ! thou art a devoted deer,
Beset with every ill but that of fear.
The nations hunt ; all mark thee for a prey,
They swarm around thee, and thou stand'st at bay,
Undaunted still, though wearied and perplexed ;
Once Chatham saved thee, but who saves thee next ?
Alas ! the tide of pleasure sweeps along
All that should be the boast of British song.
'Tis not the wreath that once adorned thy brow,   370
The prize of happier times, will serve thee now.
Our ancestry, a gallant Christian race,
Patterns of every virtue, every grace,
Confessed a God ; they kneeled before they fought,
And praised Him in the victories He wrought.
Now from the dust of ancient days bring forth
Their sober zeal, integrity, and worth ;
Courage, ungraced by these, affronts the skies,
Is but the fire without the sacrifice.
The stream that feeds the well-spring of the heart   380
Not more invigorates life's noblest part,
Than virtue quickens with a warmth divine
The powers that sin has brought to a decline.
  A. The inestimable estimate of Brown
Rose like a paper-kite, and charmed the town ,
But measures, planned and executed well,
Shifted the wind that raised it, and it fell.
He trod the very self-same ground you tread,
And victory refuted all he said.
  B. And yet his judgment was not framed amiss,   390
Its error, if it erred, was merely this,—
He thought the dying hour already come,
And a complete recovery struck him dumb.
  But that effeminacy, folly, lust,
Enervate and enfeeble, and needs must,—
And that a nation shamefully debased
Will be despised and trampled on at last,
Unless sweet penitence her powers renew,—
Is truth, if history itself be true.

There is a time, and justice marks the date,   400
For long-forbearing clemency to wait ;
That hour elapsed, the incurable revolt
Is punished, and down comes the thunderbolt.
If Mercy *then* put by the threatening blow,
Must she perform the same kind office *now* ?
May she ! and if offended Heaven be still
Accessible, and prayer prevail, she will.
'Tis not however insolence and noise,
The tempest of tumultuary joys,
Nor is it yet despondence and dismay,   410
Will win her visits, or engage her stay ;
Prayer only, and the penitential tear,
Can call her smiling down, and fix her here.
   But when a country (one that I could name)
In prostitution sinks the sense of shame ;
When infamous Venality, grown bold,
Writes on his bosom, *"To be let or sold ;"*
When Perjury, that heaven-defying vice,
Sells oaths by tale, and at the lowest price,
Stamps God's own name upon a lie just made,   420
To turn a penny in the way of trade ;
When Avarice starves, and never hides his face,
Two or three millions of the human race,
And not a tongue inquires how, where, or when,
Though conscience will have twinges now and then ;
When profanation of the sacred cause
In all its parts, times, ministry, and laws,
Bespeaks a land, once Christian, fallen and lost
In all that wars against that title most ;
What follows next, let cities of great name,   430
And regions long since desolate, proclaim :
Nineveh, Babylon, and ancient Rome
Speak to the present times and times to come,
They cry aloud in every careless ear,
" Stop, while ye may, suspend your mad career !
Oh learn from our example and our fate,
Learn wisdom and repentance ere too late !"
   Not only Vice disposes and prepares
The mind that slumbers sweetly in her snares,
To stoop to tyranny's usurped command,   440
And bend her polished neck beneath his hand,
(A dire effect, by one of nature's laws
Unchangeably connected with its cause ;)
But Providence himself will intervene
To throw His dark displeasure o'er the scene.
All are His instruments ; each form of war,
What burns at home, or threatens from afar,
Nature in arms, her elements at strife,
The storms that overset the joys of life,
Are but His rods to scourge a guilty land,   450
And waste it at the bidding of His hand.

He gives the word, and Mutiny soon roars
In all her gates, and shakes her distant shores ;
The standards of all nations are unfurled,
She has one foe, and that one foe, the world.
And if He doom that people with a frown,
And mark them with the seal of wrath, pressed down,
Obduracy takes place ; callous and tough,
The reprobated race grows judgment-proof ;
Earth shakes beneath them, and heaven roars above,   460
But nothing scares them from the course they love ;
To the lascivious pipe and wanton song,
That charm down fear, they frolic it along,
With mad rapidity and unconcern,
Down to the gulf from which is no return.
They trust in navies, and their navies fail,
God's curse can cast away ten thousand sail ;
They trust in armies, and their courage dies ;
In wisdom, wealth, in fortune, and in lies ;
But all they trust in withers, as it must,   470
When He commands, in whom they place no trust.
Vengeance at last pours down upon their coast,
A long despised, but now victorious host ;
Tyranny sends the chain that must abridge
The noble sweep of all their privilege,
Gives liberty the last, the mortal shock,
Slips the slave's collar on, and snaps the lock.
    A. Such lofty strains embellish what you teach ;
Mean you to prophesy, or but to preach ?
    B. I know the mind that feels indeed the fire   480
The Muse imparts, and can command the lyre,
Acts with a force, and kindles with a zeal,
Whate'er the theme, that others never feel.
If human woes her soft attention claim,
A tender sympathy pervades the frame,
She pours a sensibility divine
Along the nerve of every feeling line.
But if a deed not tamely to be borne,
Fire indignation and a sense of scorn,
The strings are swept with such a power, so loud,   490
The storm of music shakes the astonished crowd.
So when remote futurity is brought
Before the keen inquiry of her thought,
A terrible sagacity informs
The poet's heart, he looks to distant storms,
He hears the thunder ere the tempest lowers,
And, armed with strength surpassing human powers,
Seizes events as yet unknown to man,
And darts his soul into the dawning plan.
Hence, in a Roman mouth, the graceful name   500
Of prophet and of poet was the same ;
Hence British poets too the priesthood shared,
And every hallowed Druid was a bard.

But no prophetic fires to me belong,
I play with syllables, and sport in song.
   A. At Westminster, where little poets strive
To set a distich upon six and five,
Where Discipline helps opening buds of sense,
And makes his pupils proud with silver pence,
I was a poet too ;—but modern taste   510
Is so refined and delicate and chaste,
That verse, whatever fire the fancy warms,
Without a creamy smoothness has no charms.
Thus, all success depending on an ear,
And thinking I might purchase it too dear,
If sentiment were sacrificed to sound,
And truth cut short to make a period round,
I judged a man of sense could scarce do worse
Than caper in the morris-dance of verse.
   B. Thus reputation is a spur to wit,   520
And some wits flag through fear of losing it.
Give me the line that ploughs its stately course
Like a proud swan, conquering the stream by force :
That like some cottage beauty strikes the heart,
Quite unindebted to the tricks of art.
When labour and when dulness, club in hand,
Like the two figures at St. Dunstan's stand,
Beating alternately, in measured time,
The clock-work tintinnabulum of rhyme,
Exact and regular the sounds will be,   530
But such mere quarter-strokes are not for me.
   From him who rears a poem lank and long,
To him who strains his all into a song,
Perhaps some bonny Caledonian air,
All birks and braes, though he was never there ;
Or having whelped a prologue with great pains,
Feels himself spent, and fumbles for his brains ;
A prologue interdashed with many a stroke,
An art contrived to advertise a joke,
So that the jest is clearly to be seen,   540
Not in the words— but in the gap between ;
Manner is all in all, whate'er is writ,
The substitute for genius, sense, and wit.
   To dally much with subjects mean and low
Proves that the mind is weak, or makes it so.
Neglected talents rust into decay,
And every effort ends in push-pin play.
The man that means success should soar above
A soldier's feather, or a lady's glove,
Else summoning the Muse to such a theme,   550
The fruit of all her labour is whipt-cream.
As if an eagle flew aloft, and then—
Stooped from his highest pitch to pounce a wren.
As if the poet, purposing to wed,
Should carve himself a wife in gingerbread.

Ages elasped ere Homer's lamp appeared,
And ages ere the Mantuan Swan was heard;
To carry nature lengths unknown before,
To give a Milton birth, asked ages more.
Thus Genius rose and set at ordered times,   560
And shot a day-spring into distant climes;
Ennobling every region that he chose,
He sunk in Greece, in Italy he rose,
And, tedious years of Gothic darkness past,
Emerged all splendour in our isle at last.
Thus lovely halcyons dive into the main,
Then show far off their shining plumes again.
   A. Is genius only found in epic lays?
Prove this, and forfeit all pretence to praise.
Make their heroic powers your own at once,   570
Or candidly confess yourself a dunce.
   B. These were the chief; each interval of night
Was graced with many an undulating light;
In less illustrious bards his beauty shone
A meteor or a star; in these, the sun.
   The nightingale may claim the topmost bough,
While the poor grasshopper must chirp below.
Like him unnoticed, I, and such as I,
Spread little wings, and rather skip than fly;
Perched on the meagre produce of the land,   580
An ell or two of prospect we command,
But never peep beyond the thorny bound,
Or oaken fence, that hems the paddock round.
   In Eden, ere yet innocence of heart
Had faded, poetry was not an art;
Language above all teaching, or if taught,
Only by gratitude and glowing thought,—
Elegant as simplicity, and warm
As ecstasy, unmanacled by form,—
Not prompted, as in our degenerate days,   590
By low ambition and the thirst of praise,
Was natural as is the flowing stream,
And yet magnificent, a God the theme.
That theme on earth exhausted, though above
'Tis found as everlasting as His love,
Man lavished all his thoughts on human things,
The feats of heroes and the wrath of kings,
But still while virtue kindled his delight,
The song was moral, and so far was right.
'Twas thus till luxury seduced the mind   600
To joys less innocent, as less refined,
Then genius danced a bacchanal, he crowned
The brimming goblet, seized the thyrsus, bound
His brows with ivy, rushed into the field
Of wild imagination, and there reeled
The victim of his own lascivious fires,
And, dizzy with delight, profaned the sacred wires.

Anacreon, Horace, played in Greece and Rome
This Bedlam part; and, others nearer home.
When Cromwell fought for power, and while he reigned 610
The proud Protector of the power he gained,
Religion harsh, intolerant, austere,
Parent of manners like herself severe,
Drew a rough copy of the Christian face
Without the smile, the sweetness, or the grace;
The dark and sullen humour of the time
Judged every effort of the Muse a crime;
Verse in the finest mould of fancy cast,
Was lumber in an age so void of taste:
But when the second Charles assumed the way, 620
And arts revived beneath a softer day,
Then like a bow long forced into a curve,
The mind, released from too constrained a nerve,
Flew to its first position with a spring
That made the vaulted roofs of pleasure ring.
His court, the dissolute and hateful school
Of wantonness, where vice was taught by rule,
Swarmed with a scribbling herd as deep inlaid
With brutal lust as ever Circe made.
From these a long succession in the rage 630
Of rank obscenity debauched their age,
Nor ceased, till ever anxious to redress
The abuses of her sacred charge, the press,
The Muse instructed a well-nurtured train
Of abler votaries to cleanse the stain,
And claim the palm for purity of song,
That lewdness had usurped and worn so long.
Then decent pleasantry and sterling sense,
That neither gave nor would endure offence,
Whipped out of sight, with satire just and keen, 640
The puppy pack that had defiled the scene.
   In front of these came Addison.   In him
Humour, in holiday and sightly trim,
Sublimity and Attic taste combined,
To polish, furnish, and delight the mind.
Then Pope, as harmony itself exact,
In verse well-disciplined, complete, compact,
Gave virtue and morality a grace
That, quite eclipsing pleasure's painted face,
Levied a tax of wonder and applause, 650
Even on the fools that trampled on their laws.
But he (his musical finesse was such,
So nice his ear, so delicate his touch)
Made poetry a mere mechanic art,
And every warbler has his tune by heart.
Nature imparting her satiric gift,
Her serious mirth, to Arbuthnot and Swift,
With droll sobriety they raised a smile
At folly's cost, themselves unmoved the while.

That constellation set, the world in vain   660
Must hope to look upon their like again.
  A. Are we then left—*B*. Not wholly in the dark:
Wit now and then, struck smartly, shows a spark,
Sufficient to redeem the modern race
From total night and absolute disgrace.
While servile trick and imitative knack
Confine the million in the beaten track,
Perhaps some courser who disdains the road
Snuffs up the wind and flings himself abroad.
  Contemporaries all surpassed, see one,   670
Short his career, indeed, but ably run.
Churchill, himself unconscious of his powers,
In penury consumed his idle hours,
And, like a scattered seed at random sown,
Was left to spring by vigour of his own.
Lifted at length, by dignity of thought
And dint of genius, to an affluent lot,
He laid his head in luxury's soft lap,
And took too often there his easy nap.
If brighter beams than all he threw not forth,   680
'Twas negligence in him, not want of worth.
Surly and slovenly, and bold and coarse,
Too proud for art, and trusting in mere force,
Spendthrift alike of money and of wit,
Always at speed, and never drawing bit,
He struck the lyre in such a careless mood,
And so disdained the rules he understood,
The laurel seemed to wait on his command,
He snatched it rudely from the Muses' hand.
  Nature, exerting an unwearied power,   690
Forms, opens, and gives scent to every flower,
Spreads the fresh verdure of the field, and leads
The dancing Naiads through the dewy meads ;
She fills profuse ten thousand little throats
With music, modulating all their notes,
And charms the woodland scenes and wilds unknown
With artless airs and concerts of her own ;
But seldom (as if fearful of expense)
Vouchsafes to man a poet's just pretence.
Fervency, freedom, fluency of thought,   700
Harmony, strength, words exquisitely sought,
Fancy that from the bow that spans the sky
Brings colours dipt in heaven that never die,
A soul exalted above earth, a mind
Skilled in the characters that form mankind,—
And as the sun, in rising beauty dressed,
Looks to the westward from the dappled east,
And marks, whatever clouds may interpose,
Ere yet his race begins, its glorious close,
An eye like his to catch the distant goal,   710
Or ere the wheels of verse begin to roll,

Like his to shed illuminating rays
On every scene and subject it surveys,—
Thus graced, the man asserts a poet's name,
And the world cheerfully admits the claim.
　　Pity Religion has so seldom found
A skilful guide into poetic ground !
The flowers would spring where'er she deigned to stray,
And every muse attend her in her way.
Virtue indeed meets many a rhyming friend,　　　720
And many a compliment politely penned,
But unattired in that becoming vest
Religion weaves for her, and half undressed,
Stands in the desert shivering and forlorn,
A wintry figure, like a withered thorn.
The shelves are full, all other themes are sped,
Hackneyed and worn to the last flimsy thread ;
Satire has long since done his best, and curst
And loathsome Ribaldry has done his worst ;
Fancy has sported all her powers away　　　730
In tales, in trifles, and in children's play ;
And 'tis the sad complaint, and almost true,
Whate'er we write, we bring forth nothing new.
'Twere new indeed to see a bard all fire,
Touched with a coal from heaven, assume the lyre,
And tell the world, still kindling as he sung,
With more than mortal music on his tongue,
That He who died below, and reigns above,
Inspires the song, and that his name is Love.
　　For, after all, if merely to beguile　　　740
By flowing numbers and a flowery style
The tædium that the lazy rich endure,
Which now and then sweet poetry may cure,—
Or if to see the name of idol self
Stamped on the well-bound quarto, grace the shelf,
To float a bubble on the breath of fame,—
Prompt his endeavour and engage his aim,
Debased to servile purposes of pride,
How are the powers of genius misapplied !
The gift whose office is the Giver's praise,　　　750
To trace Him in His word, His works, His ways,
Then spread the rich discovery, and invite
Mankind to share in the divine delight,
Distorted from its use and just design,
To make the pitiful possessor shine,
To purchase at the fool-frequented fair
Of Vanity, a wreath for self to wear,
Is profanation of the basest kind,
Proof of a trifling and a worthless mind.
　　A. Hail Sternhold then, and Hopkins hail !　*B.* Amen.
If flattery, folly, lust employ the pen,　　　761
If acrimony, slander and abuse,
Give it a charge to blacken and traduce ;

Though Butler's wit, Pope's numbers, Prior's ease,
With all that fancy can invent to please,
Adorn the polished periods as they fall,
One madrigal of theirs is worth them all.
   A. 'Twould thin the ranks of the poetic tribe,
To dash the pen through all that you proscribe.
   B. No matter;—we could shift when they were not;   770
And should, no doubt, if they were all forgot.

THE PROGRESS OF ERROR.

Si quid loquar audiendum.—Hor. lib. iv. od. 2.

Sing, Muse (if such a theme, so dark, so long,
May find a Muse to grace it with a song),
By what unseen and unsuspected arts
The serpent Error twines round human hearts;
Tell where she lurks, beneath what flowery shades
That not a glimpse of genuine light pervades,
The poisonous, black, insinuating worm
Successfully conceals her loathsome form.
Take, if ye can, ye careless and supine,
Counsel and caution from a voice like mine!   10
Truths that the theorist could never reach,
And observation taught me, I would teach.
   Not all, whose eloquence the fancy fills,
Musical as the chime of tinkling rills,
Weak to perform, though mighty to pretend,
Can trace her mazy windings to their end,
Discern the fraud beneath the specious lure,
Prevent the danger, or prescribe the cure.
The clear harangue, and cold as it is clear,
Falls soporific on the listless ear;   20
Like quicksilver, the rhetoric they display
Shines as it runs, but, grasped at, slips away.
   Placed for his trial on this bustling stage,
From thoughtless youth to ruminating age,
Free in his will to choose or to refuse,
Man may improve the crisis, or abuse;
Else, on the fatalist's unrighteous plan,
Say, to what bar amenable were man?
With nought in charge, he could betray no trust,
And, if he fell, would fall because he must;   30
If love reward him, or if vengeance strike,
His recompense in both unjust alike.
Divine authority within his breast
Brings every thought, word, action, to the test;
Warns him or prompts, approves him or restrains,
As Reason, or as Passion, takes the reins.
Heaven from above, and Conscience from within,
Cry in his startled ear "Abstain from sin!"

The world around solicits his desire,
And kindles in his soul a treacherous fire;
While, all his purposes and steps to guard, 40
Peace follows Virtue as its sure reward,
And Pleasure brings as surely in her train
Remorse and Sorrow and vindictive Pain.

Man, thus endued with an elective voice,
Must be supplied with objects of his choice;
Where'er he turns, enjoyment and delight,
Or present or in prospect, meet his sight:
These open on the spot their honeyed store;
Those call him loudly to pursuit of more. 50
His unexhausted mine, the sordid vice
Avarice shows, and virtue is the price.
Here various motives his ambition raise—
Power, Pomp, and Splendour, and the thirst of praise
There Beauty woos him with expanded arms;
Ev'n Bacchanalian madness has its charms.

Nor these alone, whose pleasures less refined
Might well alarm the most unguarded mind,
Seek to supplant his inexperienced youth,
Or lead him devious from the path of truth; 60
Hourly allurements on his passions press,
Safe in themselves, but dangerous in the excess.

Hark! how it floats upon the dewy air!
Oh what a dying, dying close was there!
'Tis harmony from yon sequestered bower,
Sweet harmony, that soothes the midnight hour!
Long ere the charioteer of day had run
His morning course, the enchantment was begun;
And he shall gild yon mountain's height again,
Ere yet the pleasing toil becomes a pain. 70

Is this the rugged path, the steep ascent
That Virtue points to?   Can a life thus spent
Lead to the bliss she promises the wise,
Detach the soul from earth, and speed her to the skies?
Ye devotees to your adored employ,
Enthusiasts, drunk with an unreal joy,
Love makes the music of the blest above,
Heaven's harmony is universal love;
And earthly sounds, though sweet and well combined,
And lenient as soft opiates to the mind, 80
Leave vice and folly unsubdued behind.

Grey dawn appears; the sportsman and his train
Speckle the bosom of the distant plain;
'Tis he, the Nimrod of the neighbouring lairs,—
Save that his scent is less acute than theirs,
For persevering chase, and headlong leaps,
True beagle as the staunchest hound he keeps.
Charged with the folly of his life's mad scene,
He takes offence, and wonders what you mean;
The joy, the danger, and the toil o'erpays— 90

'Tis exercise, and health, and length of days.
Again impetuous to the field he flies;
Leaps every fence but one, there falls and dies;
Like a slain deer, the tumbrel brings him home,
Unmissed but by his dogs and by his groom.
    Ye clergy, while your orbit is your place,
Lights of the world, and stars of human race;
But if eccentric ye forsake your sphere,
Prodigies ominous, and viewed with fear;
The comet's baneful influence is a dream;   100
Yours real and pernicious in the extreme.
What then!—are appetites and lusts laid down
With the same ease the man puts on his gown?
Will Avarice and Concupiscence give place,
Charmed by the sounds—"Your reverence," or "Your grace?"
No.   But his own engagement binds him fast;
Or, if it does not, brands him to the last
What atheists call him—a designing knave,
A mere church juggler, hypocrite, and slave.
Oh laugh, or mourn with me, the rueful jest,   110
A cassocked huntsman, and a fiddling priest!
He from Italian songsters takes his cue;
Set Paul to music, he shall quote him too.
He takes the field, the master of the pack
Cries—"Well done, saint!" and claps him on the back.
Is this the path of sanctity?   Is this
To stand a way-mark in the road to bliss?
Himself a wanderer from the narrow way,
His silly sheep, what wonder if they stray?
Go, cast your orders at your bishop's feet,   120
Send your dishonoured gown to Monmouth Street;
The sacred function in your hands is made—
Sad sacrilege!—no function, but a trade!
    Occiduus is a pastor of renown;
When he has prayed and preached the sabbath down,
With wire and catgut he concludes the day,
Quavering and semiquavering care away.
The full concerto swells upon your ear;
All elbows shake.   Look in, and you would swear
The Babylonian tyrant with a nod   130
Had summoned them to serve his golden god;
So well that thought the employment seems to suit,
Psaltery and sackbut, dulcimer and flute.
Oh fie! 'Tis evangelical and pure:
Observe each face, how sober and demure!
Ecstasy sets her stamp on every mien;
Chins fallen, and not an eye-ball to be seen.
Still I insist, though music heretofore
Has charmed me much, (not even Occiduus more,)
Love, joy, and peace make harmony more meet   140
For Sabbath evenings, and perhaps as sweet.
    Will not the sickliest sheep of every flock

Resort to this example as a rock ;
There stand and justify the foul abuse
Of Sabbath hours, with plausible excuse?
If apostolic gravity be free
To play the fool on Sundays, why not we?
If he the tinkling harpsichord regards
As inoffensive, what offence in cards?
Strike up the fiddles ! let us all be gay !   150
Laymen have leave to dance, if parsons play.
    O Italy ! thy Sabbaths will be soon
Our Sabbaths, closed with mummery and buffoon.
Preaching and pranks will share the motley scene,
Ours parcelled out, as thine have ever been,
God's worship and the mountebank between.
What says the prophet?   Let that day be blest
With holiness and consecrated rest.
Pastime and business both it should exclude,
And bar the door the moment they intrude ;   160
Nobly distinguished above all the six
By deeds in which the world must never mix.
Hear him again.   He calls it a delight,
A day of luxury, observed aright,
When the glad soul is made heaven's welcome guest,
Sits banqueting, and God provides the feast.
But triflers are engaged and cannot come ;
Their answer to the call is—*Not at home.*
    Oh the dear pleasures of the velvet plain !
The painted tablets, dealt and dealt again !   170
Cards with what rapture, and the polished die,
The yawning chasm of indolence supply !
Then to the dance, and make the sober moon
Witness of joys that shun the sight of noon.
Blame, cynic, if you can, quadrille or ball,
The snug close party, or the splendid hall,
Where Night, down-stooping from her ebon throne,
Views constellations brighter than her own.
'Tis innocent and harmless, and refined,
The balm of care, elysium of the mind.   180
Innocent !   Oh, if venerable Time
Slain at the foot of Pleasure be no crime,
Then, with his silver beard and magic wand,
Let Comus rise Archbishop of the land ;
Let him your rubric and your feasts prescribe,
Grand Metropolitan of all the tribe.
    Of manners rough, and coarse athletic cast,
The rank debauch suits Clodio's filthy taste.
Rufillus, exquisitely formed by rule,
Not of the moral but the dancing school,   190
Wonders at Clodio's follies, in a tone
As tragical as others at his own.
He cannot drink five bottles, bilk the score,
Then kill a constable, and drink five more ;

But he can draw a pattern, make a tart,
And has the Ladies' Etiquette by heart.
Go, fool; and, arm in arm with Clodio, plead
Your cause before a bar you little dread;
But know, the law that bids the drunkard die
Is far too just to pass the trifler by.   200
Both baby-featured and of infant size,
Viewed from a distance, and with heedless eyes,
Folly and Innocence are so alike,
The difference, though essential, fails to strike.
Yet Folly ever has a vacant stare,
A simpering countenance, and a trifling air;
But Innocence, sedate, serene, erect,
Delights us by engaging our respect.
    Man, Nature's guest by invitation sweet,
Receives from her both appetite and treat;   210
But, if he play the glutton and exceed,
His benefactress blushes at the deed,
For Nature, nice, as liberal to dispense,
Made nothing but a brute the slave of sense.
Daniel ate pulse by choice—example rare!
Heaven blessed the youth, and made him fresh and fair.
Gorgonius sits abdominous and wan,
Like a fat squab upon a Chinese fan;
He snuffs far off the anticipated joy,
Turtle and venison all his thoughts employ;   220
Prepares for meals as jockeys take a sweat,
Oh nauseous!—an emetic for a whet!
Will Providence o'erlook the wasted good?
Temperance were no virtue if He could.
    That pleasures, therefore, or what such we call,
Are hurtful, is a truth confessed by all;
And some, that seem to threaten virtue less,
Still hurtful in the abuse, or by the excess.
    Is man then only for his torment placed
The centre of delights he may not taste?   230
Like fabled Tantalus, condemned to hear
The precious stream still purling in his ear,
Lip-deep in what he longs for, and yet curst
With prohibition, and perpetual thirst?
No, wrangler,—destitute of shame and sense,
The precept that enjoins him abstinence
Forbids him none but the licentious joy,
Whose fruit, though fair, tempts only to destroy.
Remorse, the fatal egg by Pleasure laid
In every bosom where her nest is made,   240
Hatched by the beams of truth, denies him rest,
And proves a raging scorpion in his breast.
No pleasure? Are domestic comforts dead?
Are all the nameless sweets of friendship fled?
Has time worn out, or fashion put to shame
Good sense, good health, good conscience, and good fame?

All these belong to virtue, and all prove
That virtue has a title to your love.
Have you no touch of pity, that the poor
Stand starved at your inhospitable door? 250
Or if yourself, too scantily supplied,
Need help, let honest industry provide.
Earn, if you want ; if you abound, impart ;
These both are pleasures to the feeling heart.
No pleasure ?   Has some sickly Eastern waste
Sent us a wind to parch us at a blast?
Can British paradise no scenes afford
To please her sated and indifferent lord?
Are sweet philosophy's enjoyments run
Quite to the lees?   And has religion none? 260
Brutes capable would tell you 'tis a lie,
And judge you from the kennel and the sty.
Delights like these, ye sensual and profane,
Ye are bid, begged, besought to entertain ;
Called to these crystal streams, do ye turn off
Obscene, to swill and swallow at a trough?
Envy the beast then, on whom Heaven bestows
Your pleasures, with no curses in the close !
　　Pleasure, admitted in undue degree,
Enslaves the will, nor leaves the judgment free. 270
'Tis not alone the grape's enticing juice
Unnerves the moral powers, and mars their use ;
Ambition, avarice, and the lust of fame,
And woman, lovely woman, does the same.
The heart, surrendered to the ruling power
Of some ungoverned passion every hour,
Finds, by degrees, the truths that once bore sway,
And all their deep impressions wear away.
So coin grows smooth, in traffic current passed
Till Cæsar's image is effaced at last. 280
　　The breach, though small at first, soon opening wide,
In rushes folly with a full-moon tide :
Then welcome errors, of whatever size,
To justify it by a thousand lies.
As creeping ivy clings to wood or stone,
And hides the ruin that it feeds upon,
So sophistry cleaves close to and protects
Sin's rotten trunk, concealing its defects.
Mortals whose pleasures are their only care,
First wish to be imposed on, and then are ; 290
And lest the fulsome artifice should fail,
Themselves will hide its coarseness with a veil.
Not more industrious are the just and true
To give to virtue what is virtue's due,
The praise of wisdom, comeliness, and worth,
And call her charms to public notice forth,
Than vice's mean and disingenuous race
To hide the shocking features of her face :

Her form with dress and lotion they repair,
Then kiss their idol, and pronounce her fair.   300
   The sacred implement I now employ
Might prove a mischief, or at best a toy,
A trifle if it move but to amuse,
But if to wrong the judgment and abuse,
Worse than a poniard in the basest hand,
It stabs at once the morals of a land.
   Ye writers of what none with safety reads,
Footing it in the dance that fancy leads,
Ye novelists, who mar what ye would mend,
Snivelling and drivelling folly without end,   310
Whose corresponding misses fill the ream
With sentimental frippery and dream,
Caught in a delicate soft silken net
By some lewd earl or rake-hell baronet;
Ye pimps, who, under Virtue's fair pretence,
Steal to the closet of young Innocence,
And teach her, inexperienced yet and green,
To scribble as you scribbled at fifteen;
Who, kindling a combustion of desire,
With some cold moral think to quench the fire;   320
Though all your engineering proves in vain,
The dribbling stream ne'er puts it out again;
Oh that a verse had power, and could command
Far, far away these flesh-flies of the land !
Who fasten without mercy on the fair,
And suck, and leave a craving maggot there.
Howe'er disguised the inflammatory tale,
And covered with a fine-spun specious veil,
Such writers and such readers owe the gust
And relish of their pleasure all to lust.   330
   But the Muse, eagle-pinioned, has in view
A quarry more important still than you;
Down, down the wind she swims and sails away,
Now stoops upon it, and now grasps the prey.
   Petronius! all the Muses weep for thee,
But every tear shall scald thy memory.
The Graces too, while Virtue at their shrine
Lay bleeding under that soft hand of thine,
Felt each a mortal stab in her own breast,
Abhorred the sacrifice, and cursed the priest: 340
Thou polished and high-finished foe to truth,
Grey-beard corrupter of our listening youth,
To purge and skim away the filth of vice,
That so refined it might the more entice,
Then pour it on the morals of thy son
To taint *his* heart, was worthy of *thine own.*
Now while the poison all high life pervades,
Write if thou canst one letter from the shades,
One, and one only, charged with deep regret,
That thy worst part, thy principles, live yet;   350

One sad epistle thence may cure mankind
Of the plague spread by bundles left behind.
   'Tis granted, and no plainer truth appears,
Our most important are our earliest years.
The mind impressible and soft, with ease
Imbibes and copies what she hears and sees,
And through life's labyrinth holds fast the clue
That education gives her, false or true.
Plants raised with tenderness are seldom strong.
Man's coltish disposition asks the thong,   360
And without discipline the favourite child,
Like a neglected forester, runs wild.
But we, as if good qualities would grow
Spontaneous, take but little pains to sow;
We give some Latin, and a smatch of Greek,
Teach him to fence and figure twice a week,
And having done, we think, the best we can,
Praise his proficiency and dub him man.
   From school to Cam or Isis, and thence home,
And thence with all convenient speed to Rome,   370
With reverend tutor clad in habit lay,
To tease for cash, and quarrel with all day;
With memorandum-book for every town,
And every post, and where the chaise broke down
His stock a few French phrases got by heart,
With much to learn but nothing to impart,
The youth, obedient to his sire's commands,
Sets off a wanderer into foreign lands:
Surprised at all they meet, the gosling pair
With awkward gait, stretched neck, and silly stare,   380
Discover huge cathedrals built with stone,
And steeples towering high much like our own,
But show peculiar light by many a grin
At Popish practices observed within.
   Ere long, some bowing, smirking, smart Abbé
Remarks two loiterers that have lost their way,
And being always primed with *politesse*
For men of their appearance and address,
With much compassion undertakes the task,
To tell them more than they have wit to ask;   390
Points to inscriptions wheresoe'er they tread,
Such as when legible were never read,
But being cankered now, and half worn out,
Craze antiquarian brains with endless doubt;
Some headless hero or some Cæsar shows,
Defective only in his Roman nose;
Exhibits elevations, drawings, plans,
Models of Herculanean pots and pans,
And sells them medals, which, if neither rare
Nor ancient, will be so, preserved with care.   400
   Strange the recital! from whatever cause
His great improvement and new lights he draws,

The squire once bashful is shamefaced no more,
But teems with powers he never felt before :
Whether increased momentum, and the force
With which from clime to clime he sped his course,
As axles sometimes kindle as they go,
Chafed him and brought dull nature to a glow ;
Or whether clearer skies and softer air,
That make Italian flowers so sweet and fair,   410
Freshening his lazy spirits as he ran,
Unfolded genially and spread the man ;
Returning, he proclaims by many a grace,
By shrugs and strange contortions of his face,
How much a dunce that has been sent to roam
Excels a dunce that has been kept at home.
    Accomplishments have taken virtue's place,
And wisdom falls before exterior grace ;
We slight the precious kernel of the stone,
And toil to polish its rough coat alone.   420
A just deportment, manners graced with ease,
Elegant phrase, and figure formed to please,
Are qualities that seem to comprehend
Whatever parents, guardians, schools intend.
Hence an unfurnished and a listless mind,
Though busy, trifling ; empty, though refined ;
Hence all that interferes, and dares to clash
With indolence and luxury, is trash ;
While learning, once the man's exclusive pride,
Seems verging fast towards the female side.   430
    Learning itself, received into a mind
By nature weak, or viciously inclined,
Serves but to lead philosophers astray
Where children would with ease discern the way.
And of all arts sagacious dupes invent
To cheat themselves and gain the world's assent,
The worst is—Scripture warped from its intent.
    The carriage bowls along, and all are pleased
If Tom be sober, and the wheels well greased ;
But if the rogue have gone a cup too far,   440
Left out his linch-pin or forgot his tar,
It suffers interruption and delay,
And meets with hindrance in the smoothest way.
When some hypothesis absurd and vain
Has filled with all its fumes a critic's brain,
The text that sorts not with his darling whim,
Though plain to others, is obscure to him.
The Will made subject to a lawless force,
All is irregular and out of course,
And Judgment drunk, and bribed to lose his way,   450
Winks hard, and talks of darkness at noon-day.
    A critic on the sacred book should be
Candid and learned, dispassionate and free ;
Free from the wayward bias bigots feel,

From fancy's influence, and intemperate zeal,
But above all (or let the wretch refrain,
Nor touch the page he cannot but profane)
Free from the domineering power of lust ;
A lewd interpreter is never just.
    How shall I speak thee, or thy power address,   460
Thou god of our idolatry, the Press ?
By thee, religion, liberty, and laws
Exert their influence, and advance their cause ;
By thee, worse plagues than Pharaoh's land befell,
Diffused, make earth the vestibule of hell :
Thou fountain, at which drink the good and wise,
Thou ever-bubbling spring of endless lies,
Like Eden's dread probationary tree,
Knowledge of good and evil is from thee.
    No wild enthusiast ever yet could rest,   470
Till half mankind were like himself possessed.
Philosophers, who darken and put out
Eternal truth by everlasting doubt,
Church quacks, with passions under no command,
Who fill the world with doctrines contraband,
Discoverers of they know not what, confined
Within no bounds, the blind that lead the blind,
To streams of popular opinion drawn,
Deposit in those shallows all their spawn.
The wriggling fry soon fill the creeks around,   480
Poisoning the waters where their swarms abound ;
Scorned by the nobler tenants of the flood,
Minnows and gudgeons gorge the unwholesome food.
The propagated myriads spread so fast,
Even Leuwenhoek himself would stand aghast,
Employed to calculate the enormous sum,
And own his crab-computing powers o'ercome.
Is this hyperbole ? The world well known,
Your sober thoughts will hardly find it one.
    Fresh confidence the speculatist takes   490
From every hare-brained proselyte he makes,
And therefore prints :—himself but half deceived,
Till others have the soothing tale believed.
Hence comment after comment, spun as fine
As bloated spiders draw the flimsy line ;
Hence the same word that bids our lusts obey,
Is misapplied to sanctify their sway.
If stubborn Greek refuse to be his friend,
Hebrew or Syriac shall be forced to bend ;
If languages and copies all cry "No !"   500
Somebody proved it centuries ago.
Like trout pursued, the critic in despair
Darts to the mud and finds his safety there.
Women, whom custom has forbid to fly
The scholar's pitch (the scholar best knows why),
With all the simple and unlettered poor,

Admire his learning, and almost adore.
Whoever errs, the priest can ne'er be wrong,
With such fine words familiar to his tongue.
    Ye ladies ! (for, indifferent in your cause,   510
I should deserve to forfeit all applause,)
Whatever shocks, or gives the least offence
To virtue, delicacy, truth, or sense
(Try the criterion, 'tis a faithful guide),
Nor has, nor can have, Scripture on its side.
    None but an author knows an author's cares,
Or fancy's fondness for the child she bears.
Committed once into the public arms,
The baby seems to smile with added charms :
Like something precious ventured far from shore,   520
'Tis valued for the danger's sake the more.
He views it with complacency supreme,
Solicits kind attention to his dream,
And daily, more enamoured of the cheat,
Kneels, and asks Heaven to bless the dear deceit.
So one, whose story serves at least to show
Men loved their own productions long ago,
Wooed an unfeeling statue for his wife,
Nor rested till the gods had given it life.
If some mere driveller suck the sugared fib,   530
One that still needs his leading-string and bib,
And praise his genius, he is soon repaid
In praise applied to the same part, his head :
For 'tis a rule that holds for ever true,
Grant me discernment, and I grant it you.
    Patient of contradiction as a child,
Affable, humble, diffident, and mild,
Such was Sir Isaac, and such Boyle and Locke ;
Your blunderer is as sturdy as a rock :
The creature is so sure to kick and bite,   540
A muleteer's the man to set him right.
First appetite enlists him truth's sworn foe,
Then obstinate self-will confirms him so.
Tell him he wanders, that his error leads
To fatal ills, that though the path he treads
Be flowery, and he see no cause of fear,
Death and the pains of hell attend him there ;
In vain : the slave of arrogance and pride,
He has no hearing on the prudent side.
His still refuted quirks he still repeats,   550
New raised objections with new quibbles meets,
Till sinking in the quicksand he defends,
He dies disputing, and the contest ends ;
But not the mischiefs : they, still left behind,
Like thistle-seeds are sown by every wind.
    Thus men go wrong with an ingenious skill,
Bend the straight rule to their own crooked will,
And with a clear and shining lamp supplied,

First put it out, then take it for a guide.
Halting on crutches of unequal size,   560
One leg by truth supported, one by lies,
They sidle to the goal with awkward pace,
Secure of nothing, but to lose the race.
 Faults in the life breed errors in the brain,
And these, reciprocally, those again.
The mind and conduct mutually imprint
And stamp their image in each other's mint ;
Each sire and dam of an infernal race
Begetting and conceiving all that's base.
 None sends his arrow to the mark in view,   570
Whose hand is feeble, or his aim untrue ;
For though ere yet the shaft is on the wing,
Or when it first forsakes the elastic string,
It err but little from the intended line,
It falls at last far wide of his design :
So he who seeks a mansion in the sky
Must watch his purpose with a steadfast eye ;
That prize belongs to none but the sincere,
The least obliquity is fatal here.
 With caution taste the sweet Circæan cup :   580
He that sips often, at last drinks it up.
Habits are soon assumed, but when we strive
To strip them off, 'tis being flayed alive.
Called to the temple of impure delight,
He that abstains, and he alone, does right.
If a wish wander that way, call it home,
He cannot long be safe whose wishes roam.
But if you pass the threshold, you are caught ;
Die then, if power Almighty save you not !
There hardening by degrees, till double steeled,   590
Take leave of nature's God, and God revealed ;
Then laugh at all you trembled at before,
And joining the freethinkers' brutal roar,
Swallow the two grand nostrums they dispense,
That Scripture lies, and blasphemy is sense ;
If clemency revolted by abuse
Be damnable, then damned without excuse.
 Some dream that they can silence when they will
The storm of passion, and say, *"Peace, be still ;"*
But " *Thus far and no farther*," when addressed   600
To the wild wave, or wilder human breast,
Implies authority that never can,
That never ought, to be the lot of man.
 But, Muse, forbear ! long flights forebode a fall,
Strike on the deep-toned chord the sum of all.
Hear the just law, the judgment of the skies :
He that hates truth shall be the dupe of lies ;
And he that *will* be cheated to the last,
Delusions strong as hell, shall bind him fast.
But if the wanderer his mistake discern,   610

Judge his own ways, and sigh for a return,
Bewildered once, must he bewail his loss
For ever and for ever?   No—the Cross!
There and there only (though the deist rave,
And atheist, if earth bear so base a slave),
There, and there only, is the power to save;
There no delusive hope invites despair,
No mockery meets you, no deception there:
The spells and charms that blinded you before,
All vanish there, and fascinate no more.   620
  I am no preacher; let this hint suffice,
The Cross once seen is death to every vice:
Else He that hung there suffered all His pain,
Bled, groaned and agonized, and died, in vain.

TRUTH.

Pensantur trutinâ.—Hor. lib. ii. ep. i.

Man, on the dubious waves of error tossed,
His ship half foundered, and his compass lost,
Sees, far as human optics may command,
A sleeping fog, and fancies it dry land:
Spreads all his canvas, every sinew plies;
Pants for it, aims at it, enters it, and dies.
Then farewell all self-satisfying schemes,
His well-built systems, philosophic dreams,
Deceitful views of future bliss, farewell!
He reads his sentence at the flames of Hell.   10
  Hard lot of man! to toil for the reward
Of virtue, and yet lose it!—Wherefore hard?
He that would win the race, must guide his horse
Obedient to the customs of the course;
Else, though unequalled to the goal he flies,
A meaner than himself shall gain the prize.
Grace leads the right way,—if you choose the wrong,
Take it and perish, but restrain your tongue;
Charge not, with light sufficient, and left free,
Your wilful suicide on God's decree.   20
  Oh how unlike the complex works of man,
Heaven's easy, artless, unencumbered plan!
No meretricious graces to beguile,
No clustering ornaments to clog the pile;
From ostentation as from weakness free,
It stands like the cærulean arch we see,
Majestic in its own simplicity.
Inscribed above the portal, from afar
Conspicuous as the brightness of a star,
Legible only by the light they give,   30

Stand the soul-quickening words—BELIEVE AND LIVE.
Too many, shocked at what should charm them most,
Despise the plain direction and are lost.
Heaven on such terms ! they cry with proud disdain,
Incredible, impossible, and vain !—
Rebel because 'tis easy to obey,
And scorn, for its own sake, the gracious way.
These are the sober, in whose cooler brains
Some thought of immortality remains ;
The rest too busy, or too gay, to wait   40
On the sad theme, their everlasting state,
Sport for a day and perish in a night,
The foam upon the waters not so light.
　　Who judged the Pharisee? What odious cause
Exposed him to the vengeance of the laws?
Had he seduced a virgin, wronged a friend,
Or stabbed a man to serve some private end ?
Was blasphemy his sin? Or did he stray
From the strict duties of the sacred day?
Sit long and late at the carousing board ?   50
(Such were the sins with which he charged his Lord.)
No—the man's morals were exact ; what then?
'Twas his ambition to be seen of men ;
His virtues were his pride ! and that one vice
Made all his virtues gewgaws of no price ;
He wore them as fine trappings for a show,
A praying, synagogue-frequenting beau.
　　The self-applauding bird, the peacock see,—
Mark what a sumptuous Pharisee is he !
Meridian sunbeams tempt him to unfold   60
His radiant glories, azure, green, and gold :
He treads as if, some solemn music near,
His measured step were governed by his ear,
And seems to say, "Ye meaner fowl, give place !
I am all splendour, dignity, and grace ! "
　　Not so the pheasant on his charms presumes,
Though he too has a glory in his plumes.
He, Christian-like, retreats with modest mien
To the close copse or far sequestered green,
And shines without desiring to be seen.   70
The plea of works, as arrogant and vain,
Heaven turns from with abhorrence and disdain ;
Not more affronted by avowed neglect
Than by the mere dissembler's feigned respect.
What is all righteousness that men devise,
What, but a sordid bargain for the skies?
But Christ as soon would abdicate His own
As stoop from heaven to sell the proud a throne.
　　His dwelling a recess in some rude rock,
Book, beads, and maple dish his meagre stock,   80
In shirt of hair, and weeds of canvas dressed,
Girt with a bell-rope that the Pope has blessed,

Adust with stripes told out for every crime,
And sore tormented long before his time;
His prayer preferred to saints that cannot aid,
His praise postponed, and never to be paid;
See the sage hermit by mankind admired,
With all that bigotry adopts, inspired,
Wearing out life in his religious whim,
Till his religious whimsy wears out him.   90
His works, his abstinence, his zeal allowed,
You think him humble—God accounts him proud;
High in demand, though lowly in pretence,
Of all his conduct this the genuine sense—
My penitential stripes, my streaming blood,
Have purchased heaven and prove my title good.
    Turn Eastward now, and Fancy shall apply
To your weak sight her telescopic eye.
The Bramin kindles on his own bare head
The sacred fire, self-torturing his trade;   100
His voluntary pains, severe and long,
Would give a barbarous air to British song;
No grand inquisitor could worse invent
Than he contrives to suffer well content.
    Which is the saintlier worthy of the two?
" Past all dispute, yon anchorite," say you.
Your sentence and mine differ.   What's a name?
I say the Bramin has the fairer claim.
If sufferings Scripture nowhere recommends,
Devised by self to answer selfish ends,   110
Give saintship, then all Europe must agree,
Ten starveling hermits suffer less than he.
    The truth is (if the truth may suit your ear,
And prejudice have left a passage clear)
Pride has attained its most luxuriant growth,
And poisoned every virtue in them both.
Pride may be pampered while the flesh grows lean,
Humility may clothe an English dean;
That grace was Cowper's—his confessed by all—
Though placed in golden Durham's second stall.   120
Not all the plenty of a bishop's board,
His palace, and his lacqueys, and " my lord,"
More nourish pride, that condescending vice,
Than abstinence, and beggary, and lice:
It thrives in misery, and abundant grows:
In misery fools upon themselves impose.
    But why before us Protestants produce
An Indian mystic or a French recluse?
Their sin is plain; but what have we to fear,
Reformed and well-instructed?   You shall hear.   130
    Yon ancient prude, whose withered features show
She might be young some forty years ago,
Her elbows pinioned close upon her hips,
Her head erect, her fan upon her lips,

Her eyebrows arched, her eyes both gone astray
To watch yon amorous couple in their play,
With bony and unkerchiefed neck defies
The rude inclemency of wintry skies,
And sails with lappet-head and mincing airs,
Duly at clink of bell, to morning prayers.   140
To thrift and parsimony much inclined,
She yet allows herself that boy behind ;
The shivering urchin, bending as he goes,
With slipshod heels, and dew-drop at his nose,
His predecessor's coat advanced to wear,
Which future pages are yet doomed to share,
Carries her Bible tucked beneath his arm,
And hides his hands to keep his fingers warm.
    She, half an angel in her own account,
Doubts not hereafter with the saints to mount,   150
Though not a grace appears on strictest search,
But that she fasts, and, *item*, goes to church.
Conscious of age, she recollects her youth,
And tells, not always with an eye to truth,
Who spanned her waist, and who, where'er he came,
Scrawled upon glass Miss Bridget's lovely name,
Who stole her slipper, filled it with Tokay,
And drank the little bumper every day.
Of temper as envenomed as an asp,
Censorious, and her every word a wasp ;   160
In faithful memory she records the crimes,
Or real or fictitious, of the times ;
Laughs at the reputations she has torn,
And holds them dangling at arm's length in scorn.
    Such are the fruits of sanctimonious pride,
Of malice fed while flesh is mortified :
Take, madam, the reward of all your prayers,
Where hermits and where Bramins meet with theirs !
Your portion is with them,—nay, never frown,
But, if you please, some fathoms lower down.   170
    Artist, attend !—your brushes and your paint—
Produce them—take a chair,—now draw a Saint.
Oh sorrowful and sad ! the streaming tears
Channel her cheeks,—a Niobe appears.
Is this a saint ? Throw tints and all away !
True piety is cheerful as the day,
Will weep indeed, and heave a pitying groan
For others' woes, but smiles upon her own.
    What purpose has the King of Saints in view?
Why falls the Gospel like a gracious dew?   180
To call up plenty from the teeming earth,
Or curse the desert with a tenfold dearth?
Is it that Adam's offspring may be saved
From servile fear, or be the more enslaved?
To loose the links that galled mankind before,
Or bind them faster on, and add still more?

The freeborn Christian has no chains to prove,
Or, if a chain, the golden one of love :
No fear attends to quench his glowing fires,
What fear he feels his gratitude inspires.   190
Shall he, for such deliverance freely wrought,
Recompense ill? He trembles at the thought.
His Master's interest and his own combined
Prompt every movement of his heart and mind;
Thought, word, and deed, his liberty evince,
His freedom is the freedom of a prince.
  Man's obligations infinite, of course
His life should prove that he perceives their force;
His utmost he can render is but small—
The principle and motive all in all.   200
You have two servants—Tom, an arch sly rogue,
From top to toe the Geta now in vogue;
Genteel in figure, easy in address,
Moves without noise, and swift as an express,
Reports a message with a pleasing grace,
Expert in all the duties of his place :
Say, on what hinge does his obedience move?
Has he a world of gratitude and love?
No, not a spark—'tis all mere sharper's play ;
He likes your house, your housemaid, and your pay ;   210
Reduce his wages, or get rid of her,
Tom quits you, with " Your most obedient, sir."
  The dinner served, Charles takes his usual stand,
Watches your eye, anticipates command ;
Sighs if perhaps your appetite should fail ;
And if he but suspects a frown, turns pale ;
Consults all day your interest and your ease,
Richly rewarded if he can but please;
And proud to make his firm attachment known,
To save your life would nobly risk his own.   220
Now, which stands highest in your serious thought?
" Charles, without doubt," say you,—and so he ought ;
One act, that from a thankful heart proceeds,
Excels ten thousand mercenary deeds.
Thus Heaven approves as honest and sincere,
The work of generous love and filial fear;
But with averted eyes the omniscient Judge
Scorns the base hireling and the slavish drudge.
  " Where dwell these matchless saints?" old Curio cries.
Even at your side, sir, and before your eyes,   230
The favoured few, the enthusiasts you despise.
And pleased at heart because on holy ground
Sometimes a canting hypocrite is found,
Reproach a people with his single fall,
And cast his filthy raiment at them all.
Attend !—an apt similitude shall show
Whence springs the conduct that offends you so.
  See where it smokes along the sounding plain,

Blown all aslant, a driving, dashing rain,
Peal upon peal redoubling all around,   240
Shakes it again, and faster, to the ground;
Now flashing wide, now glancing as in play,
Swift beyond thought the lightnings dart away.
Ere yet it came, the traveller urged his steed,
And hurried, but with unsuccessful speed;
Now drenched throughout, and hopeless of his case,
He drops the rein, and leaves him to his pace.
Suppose, unlooked for in a scene so rude,
Long hid by interposing hill or wood,
Some mansion neat and elegantly dressed,   250
By some kind hospitable heart possessed,
Offer him warmth, security, and rest;
Think with what pleasure, safe and at his ease,
He hears the tempest howling in the trees;
What glowing thanks his lips and heart employ,
While danger past is turned to present joy.
So fares it with the sinner, when he feels
A growing dread of vengeance at his heels:
His conscience, like a glassy lake before,
Lashed into foaming waves begins to roar;   260
The law grown clamorous, though silent long,
Arraigns him—charges him with every wrong—
Asserts the rights of his offended Lord,
And death or restitution is the word:
The last impossible, he fears the first,
And, having well deserved, expects the worst.
Then welcome refuge, and a peaceful home;
Oh for a shelter from the wrath to come!
Crush me, ye rocks; ye falling mountains, hide,
Or bury me in ocean's angry tide—   270
The scrutiny of those all-seeing eyes
I dare not—"And you need not," God replies;
"The remedy you want I freely give:
The book shall teach you; read, believe, and live!"
'Tis done—the raging storm is heard no more,
Mercy receives him on her peaceful shore:
And Justice, guardian of the dread command,
Drops the red vengeance from his willing hand.
A soul redeemed demands a life of praise;
Hence the complexion of his future days,   280
Hence a demeanour holy and unspecked,
And the world's hatred, as its sure effect.
   Some lead a life unblameable and just,
Their own dear virtue their unshaken trust:
They never sin—or if (as all offend)
Some trivial slips their daily walk attend,
The poor are near at hand, the charge is small,
A slight gratuity atones for all.
For though the Pope has lost his interest here,
And pardons are not sold as once they were,   290

No papist more desirous to compound
Than some grave sinners upon English ground.
That plea refuted, other quirks they seek—
Mercy is infinite, and man is weak ;
The future shall obliterate the past,
And Heaven no doubt shall be their home at last.
  Come then—a still small whisper in your ear—
He has no hope who never had a fear ;
And he that never doubted of his state,
He may perhaps—perhaps he may—too late.   300
  The path to bliss abounds with many a snare ;
Learning is one, and wit, however rare.
The Frenchman first in literary fame,
(" Mention him, if you please—Voltaire ? "—The same,)
With spirit, genius, eloquence supplied,
Lived long, wrote much, laughed heartily, and died :
The Scripture was his jest-book, whence he drew
Bon mots to gall the Christian and the Jew ;
An infidel in health, but what when sick ?
Oh—then a text would touch him at the quick :   310
View him at Paris in his last career ;
Surrounding throngs the demigod revere,
Exalted on his pedestal of pride,
And fumed with frankincense on every side,
He begs their flattery with his latest breath,
And smothered in't at last, is praised to death.
  Yon cottager, who weaves at her own door,
Pillow and bobbins all her little store ;
Content though mean, and cheerful if not gay,
Shuffling her threads about the live-long day,   320
Just earns a scanty pittance, and at night
Lies down secure, her heart and pocket light.
She, for her humble sphere by nature fit,
Has little understanding, and no wit,
Receives no praise ; but though her lot be such
(Toilsome and indigent), she renders much ;
Just knows, and knows no more, her Bible true—
A truth the brilliant Frenchman never knew ;
And in that charter reads with sparkling eyes
Her title to a treasure in the skies.   330
  O happy peasant ! O unhappy bard !
His the mere tinsel, hers the rich reward ;
He praised perhaps for ages yet to come,
She never heard of half a mile from home :
He lost in errors his vain heart prefers,
She safe in the simplicity of hers.
  Not many wise, rich, noble, or profound
In science, win one inch of heavenly ground.
And is it not a mortifying thought
The poor should gain it, and the rich should not ?   340
No ;—the voluptuaries, who ne'er forget
One pleasure lost, lose Heaven without regret ;

Regret would rouse them, and give birth to prayer,
Prayer would add faith, and faith would fix them there.
  Not that the Former of us all in this,
Or aught He does, is governed by caprice ;
The supposition is replete with sin,
And bears the brand of blasphemy burnt in.
Not so—the silver trumpet's heavenly call
Sounds for the poor, but sounds alike for all :   350
Kings are invited, and would kings obey,
No slaves on earth more welcome were than they :
But royalty, nobility, and state
Are such a dead preponderating weight,
That endless bliss (how strange soe'er it seem),
In counterpoise, flies up and kicks the beam.
'Tis open, and ye cannot enter—why ?
" Because ye will not," Conyers would reply—
And he says much that many may dispute
And cavil at with ease, but none refute.   360
Oh blessed effect of penury and want,
The seed sown there, how vigorous is the plant !
No soil like poverty for growth divine,
As leanest land supplies the richest wine.
Earth gives too little, giving only bread,
To nourish pride or turn the weakest head :
To them the sounding jargon of the schools
Seems what it is, a cap-and-bells for fools :
The light they walk by, kindled from above,
Shows them the shortest way to life and love :   370
They, strangers to the controversial field,
Where deists always foiled, yet scorn to yield,
And never checked by what impedes the wise,
Believe, rush forward, and possess the prize.
  Envy, ye great, the dull unlettered small :
Ye have much cause for envy—but not all.
We boast some rich ones whom the Gospel sways,
And one who wears a coronet and prays ;
Like gleanings of an olive-tree they show,
Here and there one upon the topmost bough.   380
  How readily upon the Gospel plan
That question has its answer—What is man ?
Sinful and weak, in every sense a wretch ;
An instrument whose chords, upon the stretch,
And strained to the last screw that he can bear,
Yield only discord in his Maker's ear :
Once the blessed residence of truth divine,
Glorious as Solyma's interior shrine,
Where, in his own oracular abode,
Dwelt visibly the light-creating God ;   390
But made long since, like Babylon of old,
A den of mischiefs never to be told :
And she, once mistress of the realms around,
Now scattered wide and nowhere to be found,

As soon shall rise and re-ascend the throne,
By native power and energy her own,
As Nature, at her own peculiar cost,
Restore to man the glories he has lost.
Go—bid the winter cease to chill the year,
Replace the wandering comet in his sphere,   400
Then boast (but wait for that unhoped-for hour)
The self-restoring arm of human power.
But what is man in his own proud esteem?
Hear him—himself the poet and the theme :
A monarch clothed with majesty and awe,
His mind his kingdom, and his will his law,
Grace in his mien and glory in his eyes,
Supreme on earth, and worthy of the skies,
Strength in his heart, dominion in his nod,
And, thunderbolts excepted, quite a god!   410
  So sings he, charmed with his own mind and form,
The song magnificent—the theme a worm!
Himself so much the source of his delight,
His Maker has no beauty in his sight.
See where he sits contemplative and fixed,
Pleasure and wonder in his features mixed,
His passions tamed and all at his control,
How perfect the composure of his soul!
Complacency has breathed a gentle gale
O'er all his thoughts, and swelled his easy sail :   420
His books well trimmed, and in the gayest style,
Like regimented coxcombs rank and file,
Adorn his intellects as well as shelves,
And teach him notions splendid as themselves :
The Bible only stands neglected there,
Though that of all most worthy of his care ;
And, like an infant troublesome awake,
Is left to sleep for peace and quiet sake.
  What shall the man deserve of humankind,
Whose happy skill and industry combined   430
Shall prove (what argument could never yet)
The Bible an imposture and a cheat?
The praises of the libertine professed,
The worst of men, and curses of the best.
Where should the living, weeping o'er his woes,—
The dying, trembling at the awful close,—
Where the betrayed, forsaken, and oppressed,
The thousands whom the world forbids to rest,—
Where should they find (those comforts at an end
The Scripture yields), or hope to find, a friend?   440
Sorrow might muse herself to madness then,
And, seeking exile from the sight of men,
Bury herself in solitude profound,
Grow frantic with her pangs, and bite the ground.
Thus often Unbelief, grown sick of life,
Flies to the tempting pool, or felon knife.

The jury meet, the coroner is short,
And lunacy the verdict of the court :
Reverse the sentence, let the truth be known,
Such lunacy is ignorance alone ;   450
They knew not, what some bishops may not know,
That Scripture is the only cure of woe ;
That field of promise, how it flings abroad
Its odour o'er the Christian's thorny road !
The soul, reposing on assured relief,
Feels herself happy amidst all her grief,
Forgets her labour as she toils along,
Weeps tears of joy, and bursts into a song.
   But the same word, that, like the polished share,
Ploughs up the roots of a believer's care,   460
Kills too the flowery weeds, where'er they grow,
That bind the sinner's bacchanalian brow.
Oh that unwelcome voice of heavenly love,
Sad messenger of mercy from above !
How does it grate upon his thankless ear,
Crippling his pleasures with the cramp of fear !
His will and judgment at continual strife,
That civil war embitters all his life :
In vain he points his powers against the skies,
In vain he closes or averts his eyes,   470
Truth will intrude—she bids him yet beware ;
And shakes the sceptic in the scorner's chair.
   Though various foes against the Truth combine,
Pride above all opposes her design ;
Pride, of a growth superior to the rest,
The subtlest serpent with the loftiest crest,
Swells at the thought, and, kindling into rage,
Would hiss the cherub Mercy from the stage.
   " And is the soul indeed so lost ! "—she cries,
" Fallen from her glory and too weak to rise !   480
Torpid and dull beneath a frozen zone,
Has she no spark that may be deemed her own ?
Grant her indebted to what zealots call
Grace undeserved, yet surely not for all—
Some beams of rectitude she yet displays,
Some love of virtue, and some power to praise ;
Can lift herself above corporeal things,
And, soaring on her own unborrowed wings,
Possess herself of all that's good or true,
Assert the skies, and vindicate her due.   490
Past indiscretion is a venial crime,
And if the youth, unmellowed yet by time,
Bore on his branch luxuriant then and rude
Fruits of a blighted size, austere and crude,
Maturer years shall happier stores produce,
And meliorate the well-concocted juice.
Then, conscious of her meritorious zeal,
To Justice she may make her bold appeal,

And leave to Mercy, with a tranquil mind,
The worthless and unfruitful of mankind."   500
Hear then how Mercy, slighted and defied,
Retorts the affront against the crown of Pride.
  "Perish the virtue, as it ought, abhorred,
And the fool with it, that insults his Lord.
The atonement a Redeemer's love has wrought,
Is not for you,—the righteous need it not.
Seest thou yon harlot wooing all she meets,
The worn-out nuisance of the public streets,
Herself from morn to night, from night to morn,
Her own abhorrence, and as much your scorn :   510
The gracious shower, unlimited and free,
Shall fall on her, when Heaven denies it thee.
Of all that wisdom dictates this the drift,
That man is dead in sin, and life a gift."
  "Is virtue then, unless of Christian growth,
Mere fallacy, or foolishness, or both?
Ten thousand sages lost in endless woe,
For ignorance of what they could not know?"
That speech betrays at once a bigot's tongue,
Charge not a God with such outrageous wrong!   520
Truly not I—The partial light men have,
My creed persuades me, well employed, may save ;
While he that scorns the noonday beam, perverse,
Shall find the blessing unimproved a curse.
Let heathen worthies, whose exalted mind
Left sensuality and dross behind,
Possess for me their undisputed lot,
And take unenvied the reward they sought,
But still in virtue of a Saviour's plea ;
Not blind by choice, but destined not to see.   530
Their fortitude and wisdom were a flame
Celestial, though they knew not whence it came,
Derived from the same source of light and grace
That guides the Christian in his swifter race :
Their judge was Conscience, and her rule their law,
That rule, pursued with reverence and with awe,
Led them, however faltering, faint, and slow,
From what they knew, to what they wished to know.
But let not him that shares a brighter day
Traduce the splendour of a noontide ray,   540
Prefer the twilight of a darker time,
And deem his base stupidity no crime;
The wretch who slights the bounty of the skies,
And sinks, while favoured with the means to rise,
Shall find them rated at their full amount,
The good he scorned all carried to account.
  Marshalling all his terrors as he came,
Thunder and earthquake, and devouring flame,
From Sinai's top Jehovah gave the law,
Life for obedience, death for every flaw.   550

When the great Sovereign would His will express,
He gives a perfect rule; what can He less?
And guards it with a sanction as severe
As vengeance can inflict, or sinners fear:
Else his own glorious rights he would disclaim,
And man might safely trifle with his name.
He bids him glow with unremitting love
To all on earth, and to Himself above;
Condemns the injurious deed, the slanderous tongue,
The thought that meditates a brother's wrong: 560
Brings not alone the more conspicuous part,
His conduct, to the test, but tries his heart.

   Hark! universal Nature shook and groaned,
'Twas the last trumpet—see the Judge enthroned:
Rouse all your courage at your utmost need,
Now summon every virtue, stand and plead.
What! silent? Is your boasting heard no more?
That self-renouncing wisdom, learned before,
Had shed immortal glories on your brow,
That all your virtues cannot purchase now.   570

   All joy to the believer! he can speak—
Trembling yet happy, confident yet meek,—
"Since the dear hour that brought me to thy foot,
And cut up all my follies by the root,
I never trusted in an arm but thine,
Nor hoped, but in thy righteousness divine:
My prayers and alms, imperfect and defiled,
Were but the feeble efforts of a child;
Howe'er performed, it was their brightest part,
That they proceeded from a grateful heart: 580
Cleansed in thine own all-purifying blood,
Forgive their evil, and accept their good;
I cast them at thy feet—my only plea
Is what it was, dependence upon Thee,
While struggling in the vale of tears below,
That never failed, nor shall it fail me now."

   Angelic gratulations rend the skies,
Pride falls unpitied, never more to rise,
Humility is crowned, and Faith receives the prize.

EXPOSTULATION.

*Tantane, tam patiens, nullo certamine tolli
Dona sines?*—Virgil.

Why weeps the Muse for England? What appears
In England's case to move the Muse to tears?
From side to side of her delightful isle
Is she not clothed with a perpetual smile?
Can Nature add a charm, or art confer
A new-found luxury not seen in her?

Where under heaven is pleasure more pursued,
Or where does cold reflection less intrude?
Her fields a rich expanse of wavy corn,
Poured out from Plenty's overflowing horn;   10
Ambrosial gardens, in which Art supplies
The fervour and the force of Indian skies;
Her peaceful shores, where busy Commerce waits
To pour his golden tide through all her gates;
Whom fiery suns, that scorch the russet spice
Of Eastern groves, and oceans floored with ice,
Forbid in vain to push his daring way
To darker climes, or climes of brighter day;
Whom the winds waft where'er the billows roll,
From the world's girdle to the frozen pole;   20
The chariots bounding in her wheel-worn streets,
Her vaults below, where every vintage meets;
Her theatres, her revels, and her sports;
The scenes to which not youth alone resorts,
But age, in spite of weakness and of pain,
Still haunts, in hope to dream of youth again;
All speak her happy: let the Muse look round
From East to West, no sorrow can be found;
Or only what, in cottages confined,
Sighs unregarded to the passing wind.   30
Then wherefore weep for England?   What appears
In England's case to move the Muse to tears?
   The prophet wept for Israel; wished his eyes
Were fountains fed with infinite supplies:
For Israel dealt in robbery and wrong;
There were the scorner's and the slanderer's tongue,
Oaths, used as playthings or convenient tools,
As interest biassed knaves, or fashion fools;
Adultery neighing at his neighbour's door;
Oppression labouring hard to grind the poor,   40
The partial balance, and deceitful weight;
The treacherous smile, a mask for secret hate,
Hypocrisy, formality in prayer,
And the dull service of the lip, were there.
Her women insolent and self-caressed,
By Vanity's unwearied finger dressed,
Forgot the blush, that virgin fears impart
To modest cheeks, and borrowed one from art;
Were just such trifles without worth or use,
As silly pride and idleness produce;   50
Curled, scented, furbelowed and flounced around,
With feet too delicate to touch the ground,
They stretched the neck, and rolled the wanton eye,
And sighed for every fool that fluttered by.
   He saw his people slaves to every lust,
Lewd, avaricious, arrogant, unjust;
He heard the wheels of an avenging God
Groan heavily along the distant road;

Saw Babylon set wide her two-leaved brass
To let the military deluge pass ;   60
Jerusalem a prey, her glory soiled,
Her princes captive, and her treasures spoiled ;
Wept till all Israel heard his bitter cry,
Stamped with his foot, and smote upon his thigh :
But wept, and stamped, and smote his thigh in vain,
Pleasure is deaf when told of future pain,
And sounds prophetic are too rough to suit
Ears long accustomed to the pleasing lute :
They scorned his inspiration and his theme,
Pronounced him frantic, and his fears a dream ;   70
With self-indulgence winged the fleeting hours,
Till the foe found them, and down fell the towers.
　　Long time Assyria bound them in her chain,
Till penitence had purged the public stain,
And Cyrus, with relenting pity moved,
Returned them happy to the land they loved ;
There, proof against prosperity, awhile
They stood the test of her ensnaring smile,
And had the grace in scenes of peace to show
The virtue they had learned in scenes of woe.   80
But man is frail, and can but ill sustain
A long immunity from grief and pain,
And after all the joys that plenty leads
With tiptoe step vice silently succeeds.
　　When he that ruled them with a shepherd's rod,
In form a man, in dignity a God,
Came, not expected in that humble guise,
To sift, and search them with unerring eyes,
He found, concealed beneath a fair outside,
The filth of rottenness and worm of pride ;   90
Their piety a system of deceit,
Scripture employed to sanctify the cheat ;
The pharisee the dupe of his own art,
Self-idolized, and yet a knave at heart.
　　When nations are to perish in their sins,
'Tis in the church the leprosy begins ;
The priest, whose office is with zeal sincere
To watch the fountain, and preserve it clear,
Carelessly nods and sleeps upon the brink,
While others poison what the flock must drink ;   100
Or, waking at the call of lust alone,
Infuses lies and errors of his own ;
His unsuspecting sheep believe it pure,
And, tainted by the very means of cure,
Catch from each other a contagious spot,
The foul forerunner of a general rot.
Then Truth is hushed, that Heresy may preach ;
And all is trash that Reason cannot reach :
Then God's own image on the soul impressed
Becomes a mockery and a standing jest ;   110

And faith, the root whence only can arise
The graces of a life that wins the skies,
Loses at once all value and esteem,
Pronounced by greybeards a pernicious dream :
Then ceremony leads her bigots forth,
Prepared to fight for shadows of no worth ;
While truths, on which eternal things depend,
Find not, or hardly find, a single friend :
As soldiers watch the signal of command,
They learn to bow, to kneel, to sit, to stand ;   120
Happy to fill religion's vacant place
With hollow form, and gesture, and grimace.
  Such, when the Teacher of his church was there,
People and priest, the sons of Israel were ;
Stiff in the letter, lax in the design
And import of their oracles divine ;
Their learning legendary, false, absurd,
And yet exalted above God's own word ;
They drew a curse from an intended good,
Puffed up with gifts they never understood.   130
He judged them with as terrible a frown,
As if not love, but wrath, had brought him down :
Yet he was gentle as soft summer airs,
Had grace for others' sins, but none for theirs ;
Through all he spoke a noble plainness ran—
Rhetoric is artifice, the work of man ;
And tricks and turns, that fancy may devise,
Are far too mean for Him that rules the skies.
The astonished vulgar trembled while he tore
The mask from faces never seen before ;   140
He stripped the impostors in the noonday sun,
Showed that they followed all they seemed to shun ;
Their prayers made public, their excesses kept
As private as the chambers where they slept ;
The temple and its holy rites profaned
By mummeries he that dwelt in it disdained ;
Uplifted hands, that at convenient times
Could act extortion and the worst of crimes,
Washed with a neatness scrupulously nice,
And free from every taint but that of vice.   150
Judgment, however tardy, mends her pace
When Obstinacy once has conquered Grace.
They saw distemper healed, and life restored,
In answer to the fiat of his word ;
Confessed the wonder, and with daring tongue
Blasphemed the authority from which it sprung,
They knew, by sure prognostics seen on high,
The future tone and temper of the sky,
But, grave dissemblers ! could not understand
That sin let loose speaks punishment at hand.   160
  Ask now of history's authentic page,
And call up evidence from every age ;

Display with busy and laborious hand
The blessings of the most indebted land ;
What nation will you find, whose annals prove
So rich an interest in Almighty love?
Where dwell they now ? Where dwelt in ancient day
A people planted, watered, blest as they?
Let Egypt's plagues and Canaan's woes proclaim
The favours poured upon the Jewish name ;   170
Their freedom purchased for them at the cost
Of all their hard oppressors valued most ;
Their title to a country not their own
Made sure by prodigies till then unknown ;
For them the state they left made waste and void ;
For them the states to which they went destroyed ;
A cloud to measure out their march by day,
By night a fire to cheer the gloomy way ;
That moving signal summoning, when best,
Their host to move, and when it stayed, to rest.   180
For them the rocks dissolved into a flood,
The dews condensed into angelic food,
Their very garments sacred, old yet new,
And Time forbid to touch them as he flew ;
Streams, swelled above the bank, enjoined to stand,
While they passed through to their appointed land ;
Their leader armed with meekness, zeal, and love,
And graced with clear credentials from above ;
Themselves secured beneath the Almighty wing ;
Their God their captain, lawgiver, and king ;   190
Crowned with a thousand victories, and at last
Lords of the conquered soil, there rooted fast,
In peace possessing what they won by war,
Their name far published, and revered as far ;
Where will you find a race like theirs, endowed
With all that man e'er wished, or heaven bestowed ?
    They, and they only, amongst all mankind
Received the transcript of the eternal mind ;
Were trusted with his own engraven laws,
And constituted guardians of his cause ;   200
Theirs were the prophets, theirs the priestly call,
And theirs by birth the Saviour of us all.
In vain the nations, that had seen them rise
With fierce and envious yet admiring eyes,
Had sought to crush them, guarded as they were
By power divine, and skill that could not err.
Had they maintained allegiance firm and sure,
And kept the faith immaculate and pure,
Then the proud eagles of all-conquering Rome
Had found one city not to be o'ercome ;   210
And the twelve standards of the tribes unfurled
Had bid defiance to the warring world.
But grace abused brings forth the foulest deeds,
As richest soil the most luxuriant weeds.

Cured of the golden calves, their fathers' sin,
They set up self, that idol-god within ;
Viewed a Deliverer with disdain and hate
Who left them still a tributary state ;
Seized fast his hand, held out to set them free
From a worse yoke, and nailed it to the tree :　　　　220
There was the consummation and the crown,
The flower of Israel's infamy full blown ;
Thence date their sad declension and their fall,
Their woes not yet repealed ; thence date them all.
　　Thus fell the best instructed in her day,
And the most favoured land, look where we may.
Philosophy indeed on Grecian eyes
Had poured the day, and cleared the Roman skies ;
In other climes perhaps creative art,
With power surpassing theirs, performed her part,　　230
Might give more life to marble, or might fill
The glowing tablets with a juster skill,
Might shine in fable, and grace idle themes
With all the embroidery of poetic dreams ;
'Twas theirs alone to dive into the plan
That truth and mercy had revealed to man ;
And while the world beside, that plan unknown,
Deified useless wood, or senseless stone,
They breathed in faith their well-directed prayers,
And the true God, the God of truth, was theirs.　　240
　　Their glory faded, and their race dispersed,
The last of rations now, though once the first ;
They warn and teach the proudest, would they learn,
" Keep wisdom, or meet vengeance in your turn :
If we escaped not, if heaven spared not us,
Peeled, scattered, and exterminated thus ;
If vice received her retribution due,
When we were visited, what hope for you ?
When God arises with an awful frown
To punish lust, or pluck presumption down ;　　250
When gifts perverted, or not duly prized,
Pleasure o'ervalued, and his grace despised,
Provoke the vengeance of his righteous hand
To pour down wrath upon a thankless land ;
He will be found impartially severe,
Too just to wink, or speak the guilty clear."
　　O Israel, of all nations most undone !
Thy diadem displaced, thy sceptre gone ;
Thy temple, once thy glory, fallen and rased,
And thou a worshipper e'en where thou mayst ;　　260
Thy services, once holy without spot,
Mere shadows now, their ancient pomp forgot ;
Thy Levites, once a consecrated host,
No longer Levites, and their lineage lost ;
And thou thyself o'er every country sown,
With none on earth that thou canst call thine own ;

Cry aloud, thou that sittest in the dust,
Cry to the proud, the cruel, and unjust ;
Knock at the gates of nations, rouse their fears ;
Say wrath is coming, and the storm appears ;   270
But raise the shrillest cry in British ears.
    What ails thee, restless as the waves that roar
And fling their foam against thy chalky shore ?
Mistress, at least while Providence shall please,
And trident-bearing queen of the wide seas—
Why, having kept good faith, and often shown
Friendship and truth to others, findest thou none ?
Thou that hast set the persecuted free,
None interposes now to succour thee ;
Countries indebted to thy power, that shine   280
With light derived from thee, would smother thine :
Thy very children watch for thy disgrace—
A lawless brood,—and curse thee to thy face.
Thy rulers load thy credit, year by year,
With sums Peruvian mines could never clear ;
As if, like arches built with skilful hand,
The more 'twere pressed the firmer it would stand.
The cry in all thy ships is still the same,
" Speed us away to battle and to fame."
Thy mariners explore the wild expanse,   290
Impatient to descry the flags of France ;
But, though they fight as thine have ever fought,
Return ashamed without the wreaths they sought.
Thy senate is a scene of civil jar,
Chaos of contrarieties at war ;
Where sharp and solid, phlegmatic and light,
Discordant atoms meet, ferment, and fight ;
Where Obstinacy takes his sturdy stand,
To disconcert what Policy has planned ;
Where Policy is busied all night long   300
In setting right what Faction has set wrong ;
Where flails of oratory thresh the floor,
That yields them chaff and dust, and nothing more.
Thy racked inhabitants repine, complain,
Taxed till the brow of Labour sweats in vain ;
War lays a burden on the reeling state,
And Peace does nothing to relieve the weight ;
Successive loads succeeding broils impose,
And sighing millions prophesy the close.
    Is adverse Providence, when pondered well,   310
So dimly writ, or difficult to spell,
Thou canst not read with readiness and ease
Providence adverse in events like these ?
Know, then, that heavenly wisdom on this ball
Creates, gives birth to, guides, consummates all ;
That, while laborious and quick-thoughted man
Snuffs up the praise of what he seems to plan,
He first conceives, then perfects his design,

As a mere instrument in hands divine :
Blind to the working of that secret power,   320
That balances the wings of every hour,
The busy trifler dreams himself alone,
Frames many a purpose, and God works his own.
States thrive or wither as moons wax and wane,
E'en as His will and His decrees ordain ;
While honour, virtue, piety bear sway,
They flourish ; and as these decline, decay :
In just resentment of his injured laws,
He pours contempt on them and on their cause ;
Strikes the rough thread of error right athwart   330
The web of every scheme they have at heart ;
Bids rottenness invade and bring to dust
The pillars of support in which they trust,
And do his errand of disgrace and shame
On the chief strength and glory of the frame.
None ever yet impeded what He wrought,
None bars Him out from his most secret thought :
Darkness itself before His eye is light,
And hell's close mischief naked in His sight.
    Stand now and judge thyself—Hast thou incurred   340
His anger, who can waste thee with a word,
Who poises and proportions sea and land,
Weighing them in the hollow of his hand,
And in whose awful sight all nations seem
As grasshoppers, as dust, a drop, a dream ?
Hast thou (a sacrilege his soul abhors)
Claimed all the glory of thy prosperous wars,
Proud of thy fleets and armies, stolen the gem
Of his just praise, to lavish it on them ?
Hast thou not learned, what thou art often told,   350
A truth still sacred, and believed of old,
That no success attends on spears and swords
Unblessed, and that the battle is the Lord's ?
That Courage is his creature, and Dismay
The post, that at his bidding speeds away,
Ghastly in feature, and his stammering tongue
With doleful rumour and sad presage hung,
To quell the valour of the stoutest heart,
And teach the combatant a woman's part ?
That he bids thousands fly when none pursue,   360
Saves as he will by many or by few,
And claims for ever, as his royal right,
The event and sure decision of the fight ?
    Hast thou, though suckled at fair Freedom's breast,
Exported slavery to the conquered East ?
Pulled down the tyrants India served with dread,
And raised thyself, a greater, in their stead ?
Gone thither armed and hungry, returned full,
Fed from the richest veins of the Mogul,
A despot big with power obtained by wealth,   370

And that obtained by rapine and by stealth?
With Asiatic vices stored thy mind,
But left their virtues and thine own behind;
And, having trucked thy soul, brought home the fee,
To tempt the poor to sell himself to thee?
   Hast thou by statute shoved from its design
The Saviour's feast, his own blest bread and wine,
And made the symbols of atoning grace
An office key, a picklock to a place,
That infidels may prove their title good   380
By an oath dipped in sacramental blood?
A blot that will be still a blot, in spite
Of all that grave apologists may write;
And though a bishop toil to cleanse the stain,
He wipes and scours the silver cup in vain.
And hast thou sworn on every slight pretence,
Till perjuries are common as bad pence,
While thousands, careless of the damning sin,
Kiss the book's outside, who ne'er look within?
   Hast thou, when heaven has clothed thee with disgrace,
And, long provoked, repaid thee to thy face,   391
(For thou hast known eclipses, and endured
Dimness and anguish, all thy beams obscured,
When sin has shed dishonour on thy brow;
And never of a sabler hue than now;)
Hast thou with heart perverse and conscience seared,
Despising all rebuke, still persevered,
And having chosen evil, scorned the voice
That cried, "Repent!"—and gloried in thy choice?
Thy fastings, when calamity at last   400
Suggests the expedient of a yearly fast,
What mean they?   Canst thou dream there is a power
In lighter diet at a later hour,
To charm to sleep the threatenings of the skies,
And hide past folly from all-seeing eyes?
The fast that wins deliverance, and suspends
The stroke that a vindictive God intends,
Is to renounce hypocrisy; to draw
Thy life upon the pattern of the law;
To war with pleasures idolized before;   410
To vanquish lust, and wear its yoke no more.
All fasting else, whate'er be the pretence,
Is wooing mercy by renewed offence.
   Hast thou within thee sin, that in old time
Brought fire from heaven, the sex-abusing crime,
Whose horrid perpetration stamps disgrace
Baboons are free from upon human race?
Think on the fruitful and well-watered spot
That fed the flocks and herds of wealthy Lot,
Where Paradise seemed still vouchsafed on earth,   420
Burning and scorched into perpetual dearth,
Or, in his words who damned the base desire,

Suffering the vengeance of eternal fire:
Then Nature injured, scandalized, defiled,
Unveiled her blushing cheek, looked on, and smiled;
Beheld with joy the lovely scene defaced,
And praised the wrath that laid her beauties waste.
   Far be the thought from any verse of mine,
And farther still the formed and fixed design,
To thrust the charge of deeds that I detest   430
Against an innocent, unconscious breast:
The man that dares traduce, because he can
With safety to himself, is not a man:
An individual is a sacred mark,
Not to be pierced in play or in the dark;
But public censure speaks a public foe,
Unless a zeal for virtue guide the blow.
   The priestly brotherhood, devout, sincere,
From mean self-interest and ambition clear,
Their hope in heaven, servility their scorn,   440
Prompt to persuade, expostulate, and warn,
Their wisdom pure, and given them from above,
Their usefulness ensured by zeal and love,
As meek as the man Moses, and withal
As bold as in Agrippa's presence Paul,
Should fly the world's contaminating touch,
Holy and unpolluted :—are thine such?
Except a few with Eli's spirit blest,
Hophni and Phineas may describe the rest.
   Where shall a teacher look, in days like these,   450
For ears and hearts that he can hope to please?
Look to the poor—the simple and the plain
Will hear perhaps thy salutary strain :
Humility is gentle, apt to learn,
Speak but the word, will listen and return.
Alas, not so ! the poorest of the flock
Are proud, and set their faces as a rock ;
Denied that earthly opulence they choose,
God's better gift they scoff at and refuse.
The rich, the produce of a nobler stem,   460
Are more intelligent at least,—try them.
O vain inquiry ! they without remorse
Are altogether gone a devious course ;
Where beckoning Pleasure leads them, wildly stray ;
Have burst the bands, and cast the yoke away.
   Now borne upon the wings of truth sublime,
Review thy dim original and prime.
This island, spot of unreclaimed rude earth,
The cradle that received thee at thy birth,
Was rocked by many a rough Norwegian blast,   470
And Danish howlings scared thee as they passed ;
For thou wast born amid the din of arms,
And sucked a breast that panted with alarms.
While yet thou wast a grovelling puling chit,

Thy bones not fashioned, and thy joints not knit,
The Roman taught thy stubborn knee to bow,
Though twice a Cæsar could not bend thee now :
His victory was that of orient light,
When the sun's shafts disperse the gloom of night :
Thy language at this distant moment shows   480
How much the country to the conqueror owes :
Expressive, energetic, and refined,
It sparkles with the gems he left behind :
He brought thy land a blessing when he came,
He found thee savage, and he left thee tame ;
Taught thee to clothe thy pinked and painted hide,
And grace thy figure with a soldier's pride ;
He sowed the seeds of order where he went,
Improved thee far beyond his own intent,
And, while he ruled thee by the sword alone,   490
Made thee at last a warrior like his own.
Religion, if in heavenly truths attired,
Needs only to be seen to be admired ;
But thine, as dark as witcheries of the night,
Was formed to harden hearts and shock the sight ;
Thy Druids struck the well-strung harps they bore
With fingers deeply dyed in human gore ;
And, while the victim slowly bled to death,
Upon the tolling chords rung out his dying breath.
  Who brought the lamp that with awaking beams   500
Dispelled thy gloom, and broke away thy dreams,
Tradition, now decrepit and worn out,
Babbler of ancient fables, leaves a doubt :
But still light reached thee ; and those gods of thine,
Woden and Thor, each tottering in his shrine,
Fell broken and defaced at his own door,
As Dagon in Philistia long before.
But Rome with sorceries and magic wand
Soon raised a cloud that darkened every land ;
And thine was smothered in the stench and fog   510
Of Tiber's marshes and the papal bog.
Then priests with bulls and briefs and shaven crowns,
And griping fists, and unrelenting frowns,
Legates and delegates with powers from hell,
Though heavenly in pretension, fleeced thee well ;
And to this hour, to keep it fresh in mind,
Some twigs of that old scourge are left behind.
Thy soldiery, the Pope's well-managed pack,
Were trained beneath his lash, and knew the smack,
And, when he laid them on the scent of blood,   520
Would hunt a Saracen through fire and flood.
Lavish of life to win an empty tomb,
That proved a mint of wealth, a mine to Rome,
They left their bones beneath unfriendly skies,
His worthless absolution all the prize.
Thou wast the veriest slave in days of yore

C   H

That ever dragged a chain or tugged an oar ;
Thy monarchs arbitrary, fierce, unjust,
Themselves the slaves of bigotry or lust,
Disdained thy counsels, only in distress　　　　530
Found thee a goodly sponge for Power to press.
Thy chiefs, the lords of many a petty fee,
Provoked and harassed, in return plagued thee ;
Called thee away from peaceable employ,
Domestic happiness and rural joy,
To waste thy life in arms, or lay it down
In causeless feuds and bickerings of their own.
Thy parliaments adored on bended knees
The sovereignty they were convened to please ;
Whate'er was asked, too timid to resist,　　　　540
Complied with, and were graciously dismissed ;
And if some Spartan soul a doubt expressed,
And, blushing at the tameness of the rest,
Dared to suppose the subject had a choice,
He was a traitor by the general voice.
O slave ! with powers thou didst not dare exert,
Verse cannot stoop so low as thy desert ;
It shakes the sides of splenetic Disdain,
Thou self-entitled ruler of the main,
To trace thee to the date when yon fair sea,　　　550
That clips thy shores, had no such charms for thee ;
When other nations flew from coast to coast,
And thou hadst neither fleet nor flag to boast.
　　Kneel now, and lay thy forehead in the dust ;
Blush if thou canst,—not petrified, thou must ;
Act but an honest and a faithful part ;
Compare what then thou wast with what thou art ;
And God's disposing providence confessed,
Obduracy itself must yield the rest.—
Then art thou bound to serve him, and to prove,　　560
Hour after hour, thy gratitude and love.
　　Has he not hid thee, and thy favoured land,
For ages safe beneath his sheltering hand,
Given thee his blessing on the clearest proof,
Bid nations leagued against thee stand aloof,
And charged hostility and hate to roar
Where else they would, but not upon thy shore ?
His power secured thee, when presumptuous Spain
Baptized her fleet Invincible in vain ;
Her gloomy monarch, doubtful and resigned　　　570
To every pang that racks an anxious mind,
Asked of the waves that broke upon his coast,
" What tidings ?" and the surge replied—"All lost."
And when the Stuart leaning on the Scot,
Then too much feared, and now too much forgot,
Pierced to the very centre of the realm,
And hoped to seize his abdicated helm,
'Twas but to prove how quickly with a frown

He that had raised thee could have plucked thee down.
Peculiar is the grace by thee possessed,   580
Thy foes implacable, thy land at rest;
Thy thunders travel over earth and seas,
And all at home is pleasure, wealth, and ease.
'Tis thus, extending his tempestuous arm,
Thy Maker fills the nations with alarm,
While his own heaven surveys the troubled scene,
And feels no change, unshaken and serene.
Freedom, in other lands scarce known to shine,
Pours out a flood of splendour upon thine ;
Thou hast as bright an interest in her rays,   590
As ever Roman had in Rome's best days.
True freedom is where no restraint is known
That Scripture, justice, and good sense disown,
Where only vice and injury are tied,
And all from shore to shore is free beside.
Such freedom is—and Windsor's hoary towers
Stood trembling at the boldness of thy powers,
That won a nymph on that immortal plain,
Like her the fabled Phœbus wooed in vain :
He found the laurel only—happier you,   600
The unfading laurel, and the virgin too !
    Now think, if Pleasure have a thought to spare ;
If God himself be not beneath her care ;
If business, constant as the wheels of time,
Can pause an hour to read a serious rhyme ;
If the new mail thy merchants now receive,
Or expectation of the next, give leave ;
Oh think, if chargeable with deep arrears
For such indulgence gilding all thy years,
How much, though long neglected, shining yet,   610
The beams of heavenly truth have swelled the debt.
When persecuting zeal made royal sport
With tortured innocence in Mary's court,
And Bonner, blithe as shepherd at a wake,
Enjoyed the show, and danced about the stake ;
The Sacred Book, its value understood,
Received the seal of martyrdom in blood.
Those holy men, so full of truth and grace,
Seem to reflection of a different race,
Meek, modest, venerable, wise, sincere,   620
In such a cause they could not dare to fear ;
They could not purchase Earth with such a prize,
Nor spare a life too short to reach the skies.
From them to thee conveyed along the tide,
Their streaming hearts poured freely, when they died,
Those truths, which neither use nor years impair,
Invite thee, woo thee, to the bliss they share.
What dotage will not Vanity maintain ?
What web too weak to catch a modern brain ?
The moles and bats in full assembly find,   630

On special search, the keen-eyed eagle blind.
And did they dream, and art thou wiser now?
Prove it—if better, I submit and bow.
Wisdom and Goodness are twin born, one heart
Must hold both sisters, never seen apart.
    So then—as darkness overspread the deep,
Ere Nature rose from her eternal sleep,
And this delightful earth, and that fair sky,
Leaped out of nothing, called by the Most High:
By such a change thy darkness is made light,   640
Thy chaos order, and thy weakness might;
And He, whose power mere nullity obeys,
Who found thee nothing, formed thee for his praise.
To praise him is to serve him, and fulfil,
Doing and suffering, his unquestioned will;
'Tis to believe what men inspired of old,
Faithful, and faithfully informed, unfold:
Candid and just, with no false aim in view,
To take for truth what cannot but be true;
To learn in God's own school the Christian part,   650
And bind the task assigned thee to thine heart:
Happy the man there seeking and there found,
Happy the nation where such men abound!
    How shall a verse impress thee?   By what name
Shall I adjure thee not to court thy shame?
By theirs, whose bright example unimpeached
Directs thee to that eminence they reached,
Heroes and worthies of days past, thy sires?
Or His, who touched their heart with hallowed fires?
Their names, alas! in vain reproach an age   660
Whom all the vanities they scorned engage!
And His, that seraphs trembled at, is hung
Disgracefully on every trifler's tongue,
Or serves the champion in forensic war
To flourish and parade with at the bar.
Pleasure herself perhaps suggests a plea,
If interest move thee, to persuade even thee;
By every charm, that smiles upon her face,
By joys possessed, and joys still held in chase,
If dear society be worth a thought,   670
And if the feast of freedom cloy thee not,
Reflect that these, and all that seems thine own,
Held by the tenure of His will alone,
Like angels in the service of their Lord,
Remain with thee, or leave thee at His word;
That gratitude and temperance in our use
Of what he gives, unsparing and profuse,
Secure the favour, and enhance the joy,
That thankless waste and wild abuse destroy.
    But above all reflect,—how cheap soe'er   680
Those rights that millions envy thee appear,
And, though resolved to risk them, and swim down

The tide of pleasure, heedless of His frown,—
That blessings truly sacred, and, when given,
Marked with the signature and stamp of Heaven,
The word of prophecy, those truths divine,
Which make that heaven, if thou desire it, thine,
(Awful alternative ! believed, beloved,
Thy glory,—and thy shame if unimproved,)
Are never long vouchsafed, if pushed aside   690
With cold disgust or philosophic pride ;
And that, judicially withdrawn, disgrace,
Error, and darkness occupy their place.
    A world is up in arms, and thou, a spot
Not quickly found, if negligently sought,
Thy soul as ample as thy bounds are small,
Endurest the brunt, and darest defy them all :
And wilt thou join to this bold enterprise
A bolder still, a contest with the skies?
Remember, if He guard thee and secure,   700
Whoe'er assails thee, thy success is sure ;
But if He leave thee, though the skill and power
Of nations sworn to spoil thee and devour
Were all collected in thy single arm,
And thou couldst laugh away the fear of harm,
That strength would fail, opposed against the push
And feeble pigmy onset of a pigmy rush.
Say not (and if the thought of such defence
Should spring within thy bosom, drive it thence,)
" What nation amongst all my foes is free   710
From crimes as base as any charged on me?"
Their measure filled, they too shall pay the debt,
Which God, though long forborn, will not forget.
But know that Wrath divine, when most severe,
Makes justice still the guide of his career,
And will not punish, in one mingled crowd,
Them without light, and thee without a cloud.
    Muse, hang this harp upon yon aged beech,
Still murmuring with the solemn truths I teach;
And while at intervals a cold blast sings   720
Through the dry leaves, and pants upon the strings,
My soul shall sigh in secret, and lament
A nation scourged, yet tardy to repent.
I know the warning song is sung in vain,
That few will hear and fewer heed the strain ;
But if a sweeter voice, and one designed
A blessing to my country and mankind,
Reclaim the wandering thousands, and bring home
A flock so scattered and so wont to roam,
Then place it once again between my knees ;   730
The sound of truth will then be sure to please :
And truth alone, where'er my life be cast,
In scenes of plenty, or the pining waste,
Shall be my chosen theme, my glory to the last.

HOPE.

—— doceas iter, et sacra ostia pandas.

VIRG. Æn. vi.

ASK what is human life—the sage replies,
With disappointment lowering in his eyes,
A painful passage o'er a restless flood,
A vain pursuit of fugitive false good,
A scene of fancied bliss and heartfelt care,
Closing at last in darkness and despair.
The poor, inured to drudgery and distress,
Act without aim, think little, and feel less,
And nowhere, but in feigned Arcadian scenes,
Taste happiness, or know what pleasure means.   10
Riches are passed away from hand to hand,
As fortune, vice, or folly may command;
As in a dance the pair that take the lead
Turn downward, and the lowest pair succeed,
So shifting and so various is the plan
By which Heaven rules the mixt affairs of man;
Vicissitude wheels round the motley crowd,
The rich grow poor, the poor become purse-proud;
Business is labour, and man's weakness such,
Pleasure is labour too, and tires as much,   20
The very sense of it foregoes its use,
By repetition palled, by age obtuse.
Youth lost in dissipation we deplore,
Through life's sad remnant, what no sighs restore;
Our years, a fruitless race without a prize,
Too many, yet too few to make us wise.
    Dangling his cane about, and taking snuff,
Lothario cries, "What philosophic stuff—
O querulous and weak!—whose useless brain
Once thought of nothing, and now thinks in vain: 30
Whose eye reverted weeps o'er all the past,
Whose prospect shows thee a disheartening waste;
Would age in thee resign his wintry reign,
And youth invigorate that frame again,
Renewed desire would grace with other speech
Joys always prized, when placed within our reach.
For lift thy palsied head, shake off the gloom
That overhangs the borders of thy tomb,
See Nature gay as when she first began,
With smiles alluring her admirer, man;   40
She spreads the morning over eastern hills,
Earth glitters with the drops the night distils;
The sun obedient at her call appears,
To fling his glories o'er the robe she wears;

Banks clothed with flowers, groves filled with sprightly sounds,
The yellow tilth, green meads, rocks, rising grounds,
Streams edged with osiers, fattening every field
Where'er they flow, now seen and now concealed;
From the blue rim, where skies and mountains meet,
Down to the very turf beneath thy feet,   50
Ten thousand charms, that only fools despise,
Or pride can look at with indifferent eyes,
All speak one language, all with one sweet voice
Cry to her universal realm, Rejoice!
Man feels the spur of passions and desires,
And she gives largely more than he requires;
Not that, his hours devoted all to care,
Hollow-eyed abstinence, and lean despair,
The wretch may pine, while to his smell, taste, sight,
She holds a paradise of rich delight;   60
But gently to rebuke his awkward fear,
To prove that what she gives, she gives sincere,
To banish hesitation, and proclaim
His happiness her dear, her only aim.
'Tis grave philosophy's absurdest dream,
That heaven's intentions are not what they seem,
That only shadows are dispensed below,
And earth has no reality but woe.
    Thus things terrestrial wear a different hue,
As youth or age persuades; and neither true.   70
So Flora's wreath through coloured crystal seen,
The rose or lily appears blue or green,
But still the imputed tints are those alone
The medium represents, and not their own.
    To rise at noon, sit slipshod and undressed,
To read the news, or fiddle, as seems best,
Till half the world comes rattling at his door,
To fill the dull vacuity till four;
And, just when evening turns the blue vault grey,
To spend two hours in dressing for the day;   80
To make the sun a bauble without use,
Save for the fruits his heavenly beams produce;
Quite to forget, or deem it worth no thought
Who bids him shine, or if he shine or not;
Through mere necessity to close his eyes
Just when the larks and when the shepherds rise;
Is such a life, so tediously the same,
So void of all utility or aim,
That poor Jonquil, with almost every breath,
Sighs for his exit, vulgarly called death;   90
For he, with all his follies, has a mind
Not yet so blank, or fashionably blind,
But now and then perhaps a feeble ray
Of distant wisdom shoots across his way,
By which he reads, that life without a plan,
As useless as the moment it began,

Serves merely as a soil for discontent
To thrive in ; an incumbrance ere half spent.
Oh weariness beyond what asses feel,
That tread the circuit of the cistern wheel ;　　　　100
A dull rotation, never at a stay,
Yesterday's face twin image of to-day ;
While conversation, an exhausted stock,
Grows drowsy as the clicking of a clock.
"No need," he cries, " of gravity stuffed out
With academic dignity devout,
To read wise lectures, vanity the text :
Proclaim the remedy, ye learned, next ;
For truth self-evident, with pomp impressed,
Is vanity surpassing all the rest."　　　　110
　　That remedy, not hid in deeps profound,
Yet seldom sought where only to be found,
While Passion turns aside from its due scope
The inquirer's aim, that remedy is Hope.
Life is His gift, from whom whate'er life needs,
And every good and perfect gift, proceeds ;
Bestowed on man, like all that we partake,
Royally, freely, for his bounty's sake ;
Transient indeed, as is the fleeting hour,
And yet the seed of an immortal flower ;　　　　120
Designed in honour of his endless love,
To fill with fragrance his abode above ;
No trifle, howsoever short it seem,
And, howsoever shadowy, no dream ;
Its value, what no thought can ascertain,
Nor all an angel's eloquence explain.
　　Men deal with life as children with their play,
Who first misuse, then cast their toys away ;
Live to no sober purpose, and contend
That their Creator had no serious end.　　　　130
When God and man stand opposite in view,
Man's disappointment must of course ensue.
The just Creator condescends to write,
In beams of inextinguishable light,
His names of wisdom, goodness, power, and love,
On all that blooms below, or shines above,
To catch the wandering notice of mankind,
And teach the world, if not perversely blind,
His gracious attributes, and prove the share
His offspring hold in his paternal care.　　　　140
If, led from earthly things to things divine,
His creature thwart not his august design,
Then praise is heard instead of reasoning pride,
And captious cavil and complaint subside.
Nature, employed in her allotted place,
Is handmaid to the purposes of Grace ;
By good vouchsafed makes known superior good,
And bliss not seen by blessings understood :

That bliss, revealed in Scripture, with a glow
Bright as the covenant-ensuring bow,   150
Fires all his feelings with a noble scorn
Of sensual evil ; and thus Hope is born.
    Hope sets the stamp of vanity on all
That men have deemed substantial since the fall,
Yet has the wondrous virtue to educe
From emptiness itself a real use ;
And while she takes, as at a father's hand,
What health and sober appetite demand,
From fading good derives, with chymic art,
That lasting happiness, a thankful heart.   160
Hope, with uplifted foot, set free from earth,
Pants for the place of her ethereal birth,
On steady wing sails through the immense abyss,
Plucks amaranthine joys from bowers of bliss,
And crowns the soul, while yet a mourner here,
With wreaths like those triumphant spirits wear.
Hope, as an anchor firm and sure, holds fast
The Christian vessel, and defies the blast.
Hope ! nothing else can nourish and secure
His newborn virtues, and preserve him pure.   170
Hope ! let the wretch once conscious of the joy,
Whom now despairing agonies destroy,
Speak, for he can, and none so well as he,
What treasures centre, what delights, in thee.
Had he the gems, the spices, and the land
That boasts the treasure, all at his command,
The fragrant grove, the inestimable mine,
Were light, when weighed against one smile of thine.
    Though, clasped and cradled in his nurse's arms,
He shine with all a cherub's artless charms,   180
Man is the genuine offspring of revolt,
Stubborn and sturdy, a wild ass's colt ;
His passions, like the watery stores that sleep
Beneath the smiling surface of the deep,
Wait but the lashes of a wintry storm
To frown and roar, and shake his feeble form.
From infancy through childhood's giddy maze,
Froward at school, and fretful in his plays,
The puny tyrant burns to subjugate
The free republic of the whip-gig state.   190
If one, his equal in athletic frame,
Or, more provoking still, of nobler name,
Dare step across his arbitrary views,
An Iliad, only not in verse, ensues ;
The little Greeks look trembling at the scales,
Till the best tongue or heaviest hand prevails.
    Now see him launched into the world at large :
If priest, supinely droning o'er his charge,
Their fleece his pillow, and his weekly drawl,
Though short, too long, the price he pays for all ;   200

If lawyer, loud whatever cause he plead,
But proudest of the worst, if that succeed ;
Perhaps a grave physician, gathering fees,
Punctually paid for lengthening out disease ;
No COTTON, whose humanity sheds rays,
That make superior skill his second praise ;
If arms engage him, he devotes to sport
His date of life, so likely to be short,
A soldier may be anything, if brave ;
So may a tradesman, if not quite a knave.   210
Such stuff the world is made of ; and mankind
To passion, interest, pleasure, whim, resigned,
Insist on, as if each were his own Pope,
Forgiveness, and the privilege of hope ;
But Conscience, in some awful silent hour,
When captivating lusts have lost their power,
Perhaps when sickness, or some fearful dream,
Reminds him of religion, hated theme !
Starts from the down, on which she lately slept,
And tells of laws despised, at least not kept :   220
Shows with a pointing finger, and no noise,
A pale procession of past sinful joys,
All witnesses of blessings foully scorned,
And life abused, and not to be suborned.
" Mark these," she says ; " these, summoned from afar
Begin their march to meet thee at the bar ;
There find a Judge inexorably just,
And perish there, as all presumption must."
    Peace be to those (such peace as earth can give)
Who live in pleasure, dead even while they live ;   230
Born capable indeed of heavenly truth ;
But down to latest age, from earliest youth,
Their mind a wilderness through want of care,
The plough of wisdom never entering there.
Peace (if insensibility may claim
A right to the meek honours of her name)
To men of pedigree, their noble race,
Emulous always of the nearest place
To any throne, except the throne of grace.
Let cottagers and unenlightened swains   240
Revere the laws they dream that heaven ordains ;
Resort on Sundays to the house of prayer,
And ask, and fancy they find, blessings there ;
Themselves, perhaps, when weary they retreat
To enjoy cool nature in a country seat,
To exchange the centre of a thousand trades
For clumps, and lawns, and temples, and cascades,
May now and then their velvet cushions take,
And seem to pray, for good example' sake ;
Judging, in charity no doubt, the town   250
Pious enough, and having need of none.
Kind souls ! to teach their tenantry to prize

What they themselves, without remorse, despise :
Nor hope have they, nor fear, of aught to come,
As well for them had prophecy been dumb ;
They could have held the conduct they pursue,
Had Paul of Tarsus lived and died a Jew ;
And truth, proposed to reasoners wise as they,
Is a pearl cast—completely cast, away.
    They die.—Death lends them, pleased, and as in sport, 260
All the grim honours of his ghastly court.
Far other paintings grace the chamber now,
Where late we saw the mimic landscape glow :
The busy heralds hang the sable scene
With mournful scutcheons, and dim lamps between ;
Proclaim their titles to the crowd around,
But they that wore them move not at the sound ;
The coronet placed idly at their head
Adds nothing now to the degraded dead ;
And even the star that glitters on the bier   270
Can only say—" Nobility lies here."
Peace to all such—'twere pity to offend,
By useless censure, whom we cannot mend ;
Life without hope can close but in despair ;
'Twas there we found them, and must leave them there.
    As when two pilgrims in a forest stray,
Both may be lost, yet each in his own way ;
So fares it with the multitudes beguiled
In vain opinion's waste and dangerous wild ;
Ten thousand rove the brakes and thorns among,   280
Some eastward, and some westward, and all wrong.
But here, alas ! the fatal difference lies,
Each man's belief is right in his own eyes ;
And he that blames what they have blindly chose,
Incurs resentment for the love he shows.
    Say, botanist, within whose province fall
The cedar and the hyssop on the wall,
Of all that deck the lanes, the fields, the bowers,
What parts the kindred tribes of weeds and flowers ?
Sweet scent, or lovely form, or both combined,   290
Distinguish every cultivated kind ;
The want of both denotes a meaner breed,
And Chloe from her garland picks the weed.
Thus hopes of every sort, whatever sect
Esteem them, sow them, rear them, and protect,
If wild in nature, and not duly found,
Gethsemane ! in thy dear hallowed ground,—
That cannot bear the blaze of Scripture light,
Nor cheer the spirit, nor refresh the sight,
Nor animate the soul to Christian deeds,—   300
(Oh cast them from thee !) are weeds, arrant weeds,
    Ethelred's house, the centre of six ways,
Diverging each from each, like equal rays,
Himself as bountiful as April rains,

Lord paramount of the surrounding plains,
Would give relief of bed and board to none
But guests that sought it in the appointed ONE :
And they might enter at his open door,
Even till his spacious hall would hold no more.
He sent a servant forth by every road,　　　　　　　310
To sound his horn, and publish it abroad,
That all might mark—knight, menial, high, and low—
An ordinance it concerned them much to know.
If after all some headstrong hardy lout
Would disobey, though sure to be shut out,
Could he with reason murmur at his case,
Himself sole author of his own disgrace ?
No ! the decree was just and without flaw ;
And he that made had right to make the law ;
His sovereign power and pleasure unrestrained,　　320
The wrong was his who wrongfully complained.
　　Yet half mankind maintain a churlish strife
With Him, the Donor of eternal life,
Because the deed by which his love confirms
The largess he bestows, prescribes the terms.
Compliance with his will your lot ensures ;
Accept it only, and the boon is yours.
And sure it is as kind to smile and give,
As with a frown to say, " Do this, and live."
Love is not pedler's trumpery, bought and sold :　　330
He *will* give freely, or he *will* withhold ;
His soul abhors a mercenary thought,
And him as deeply who abhors it not :
He stipulates indeed, but merely this,
That man will freely take an unbought bliss,
Will trust him for a faithful generous part,
Nor set a price upon a willing heart.
Of all the ways that seem to promise fair,
To place you where his saints his presence share,
This only can ; for this plain cause, expressed　　340
In terms as plain, Himself has shut the rest.
But oh the strife, the bickering, and debate,
The tidings of unpurchased heaven create !
The flirted fan, the bridle, and the toss,
All speakers, yet all language at a loss.
From stuccoed walls smart arguments rebound ;
And beaus, adepts in every thing profound,
Die of disdain, or whistle off the sound.
Such is the clamour of rooks, daws, and kites,
The explosion of the levelled tube excites,　　　　350
Where mouldering abbey walls o'erhang the glade,
And oaks coeval spread a mournful shade ;
The screaming nations, hovering in mid air,
Loudly resent the stranger's freedom there,
And seem to warn him never to repeat
His bold intrusion on their dark retreat.

"Adieu," Vinosa cries, ere yet he sips
The purple bumper trembling at his lips,
"Adieu to all morality, if Grace
Make works a vain ingredient in the case.   360
The Christian hope is—Waiter, draw the cork—
If I mistake not—Blockhead! with a fork!
Without good works, whatever some may boast,
Mere folly and delusion—Sir, your toast.
My firm persuasion is, at least sometimes,
That Heaven will weigh man's virtues and his crimes
With nice attention, in a righteous scale,
And save or damn as these or those prevail.
I plant my foot upon this ground of trust,
And silence every fear with—God is just.   370
But if perchance on some dull drizzling day
A thought intrude, that says, or seems to say,
If thus the important cause is to be tried,
Suppose the beam should dip on the wrong side;
I soon recover from these needless frights,
And God is merciful—sets all to rights.
Thus between justice, as my prime support,
And mercy, fled to as the last resort,
I glide and steal along with heaven in view,
And,—pardon me, the bottle stands with you."   380
"I never will believe," the colonel cries,
"The sanguinary schemes that some devise,
Who make the good Creator on their plan
A being of less equity than man.
If appetite, or what divines call lust,
Which men comply with, even because they must,
Be punished with perdition, who is pure?
Then theirs, no doubt, as well as mine is sure.
If sentence of eternal pain belong
To every sudden slip and transient wrong,   390
Then Heaven enjoins the fallible and frail
A hopeless task, and damns them if they fail.
My creed (whatever some creed-makers mean
By Athanasian nonsense, or Nicene),
My creed is, He is safe that does his best,
And death's a doom sufficient for the rest."
"Right," says an ensign, "and for aught I see,
Your faith and mine substantially agree;
The best of every man's performance here
Is to discharge the duties of his sphere.   400
A lawyer's dealing should be just and fair,
Honesty shines with great advantage there.
Fasting and prayer sit well upon a priest,
A decent caution and reserve at least.
A soldier's best is courage in the field,
With nothing here that wants to be concealed:
Manly deportment, gallant, easy, gay;
A hand as liberal as the light of day.

The soldier thus endowed, who never shrinks
Nor closets up his thought, whate'er he thinks,　　410
Who scorns to do an injury by stealth,
Must go to heaven—and I must drink his health.
Sir Smug," he cries (for lowest at the board,
Just made fifth chaplain of his patron lord,
His shoulders witnessing by many a shrug
How much his feelings suffered, sat Sir Smug),
" Your office is to winnow false from true ;
Come, prophet, drink, and tell us, what think you ?"
　　Sighing and smiling as he takes his glass,
Which they that woo preferment rarely pass,　　420
" Fallible man," the church-bred youth replies,
" Is still found fallible, however wise ;
And differing judgments serve but to declare,
That truth lies somewhere, if we knew but where.
Of all it ever was my lot to read,
Of critics now alive, or long since dead,
The book of all the world that charmed me most
Was—well-a-day, the title-page was lost ;
The writer well remarks, a heart that knows
To take with gratitude what Heaven bestows,　　430
With prudence always ready at our call,
To guide our use of it, is all in all.
Doubtless it is.—To which, of my own store,
I superadd a few essentials more ;
But these, excuse the liberty I take,
I waive just now, for conversation sake."—
" Spoke like an oracle !" they all exclaim,
And add Right Reverend to Smug's honoured name.
　　And yet our lot is given us in a land,
Where busy arts are never at a stand ;　　440
Where Science points her telescopic eye,
Familiar with the wonders of the sky ;
Where bold Inquiry, diving out of sight,
Brings many a precious pearl of truth to light ;
Where nought eludes the persevering quest,
That fashion, taste, or luxury suggest.
　　But above all, in her own light arrayed,
See Mercy's grand apocalypse displayed !
The Sacred Book no longer suffers wron,
Bound in the fetters of an unknown tongue ;　　450
But speaks, with plainness art could never mend,
What simplest minds can soonest comprehend.
God gives the word, the preachers throng around,
Live from his lips, and spread the glorious sound :
That sound bespeaks Salvation on her way,
The trumpet of a life-restoring day ;
'Tis heard where England's Eastern glory shines,
And in the gulfs of her Cornubian mines.
And still it spreads.　See Germany send forth
Her sons to pour it on the farthest north :　　460

Fired with a zeal peculiar, they defy
The rage and rigour of a polar sky,
And plant successfully sweet Sharon's Rose
On icy plains, and in eternal snows.
  O blessed within the inclosure of your rocks,
Nor herds have ye to boast, nor bleating flocks,
No fertilizing streams your fields divide,
That show, reversed, the villas on their side ;
No groves have ye ; no cheerful sound of bird,
Or voice of turtle, in your land is heard ;   470
Nor grateful eglantine regales the smell
Of those that walk at evening where ye dwell :
But Winter, armed with terrors here unknown,
Sits absolute on his unshaken throne ;
Piles up his stores amidst the frozen waste,
And bids the mountains he has built stand fast ;
Beckons the legions of his storms away
From happier scenes, to make your land a prey ;
Proclaims the soil a conquest he has won,
And scorns to share it with the distant sun.   480
—Yet Truth is yours, remote, unenvied isle !
And Peace, the genuine offspring of her smile ;
The pride of lettered ignorance, that binds
In chains of error our accomplished minds,
That decks, with all the splendour of the true,
A false religion, is unknown to you.
Nature indeed vouchsafes for our delight
The sweet vicissitudes of day and night ;
Soft airs and genial moisture feed and cheer
Field, fruit, and flower, and every creature here;   490
But brighter beams than his who fires the skies
Have risen at length on your admiring eyes,
That shoot into your darkest caves the day,
From which our nicer optics turn away.
    Here see the encouragement Grace gives to vice,
The dire effect of mercy without price !
What were they? What some fools are made by art
They were by nature, atheists, head and heart.
The gross idolatry blind heathens teach
Was too refined for them, beyond their reach.   500
Not even the glorious sun, though men revere
The monarch most that seldom will appear,
And though his beams, that quicken where they shine,
May claim some right to be esteemed divine,
Not even the sun, desirable as rare,
Could bend one knee, engage one votary there ;
They were, what base credulity believes
True Christians are, dissemblers, drunkards, thieves.
The full-gorged savage, at his nauseous feast
Spent half the darkness, and snored out the rest,   510
Was one whom Justice, on an equal plan
Denouncing death upon the sins of man,

Might almost have indulged with an escape,
Chargeable only with a human shape.
    What are they now?—Morality may spare
Her grave concern, her kind suspicions there:
The wretch who once sang wildly, danced, and laughed,
And sucked in dizzy madness with his draught,
Has wept a silent flood, reversed his ways,
Is sober, meek, benevolent, and prays,   520
Feeds sparingly, communicates his store,
Abhors the craft he boasted of before,
And he that stole has learned to steal no more.
Well spake the prophet, " Let the desert sing:
Where sprang the thorn, the spiry fir shall spring ;
And where unsightly and rank thistles grew,
Shall grow the myrtle and luxuriant yew."
    Go now, and with important tone demand
On what foundation virtue is to stand,
If self-exalting claims be turned adrift,   530
And grace be grace indeed, and life a gift ;
The poor reclaimed inhabitant, his eyes
Glistening at once with pity and surprise,
Amazed that shadows should obscure the sight
Of one whose birth was in the land of light,
Shall answer, " Hope, sweet Hope, has set me free,
And made all pleasures else mere dross to me."
    These, amidst scenes as waste as if denied
The common care that waits on all beside,
Wild as if Nature there, void of all good,   540
Played only gambols in a frantic mood,
(Yet charge not heavenly skill with having planned
A plaything world, unworthy of his hand;)
Can see his love, though secret evil lurks
In all we touch, stamped plainly on his works;
Deem life a blessing with its numerous woes,
Nor spurn away a gift a God bestows.
    Hard task indeed o'er Arctic seas to roam !
Is hope exotic ? grows it not at home ?
Yes ; but an object, bright as orient morn,   550
May press the eye too closely to be borne :
A distant virtue we can all confess ;
It hurts our pride, and moves our envy, less.
    Leuconomus (beneath well-sounding Greek
I slur a name a poet must not speak)
Stood pilloried on infamy's high stage,
And bore the pelting scorn of half an age;
The very butt of slander, and the blot
For every dart that malice ever shot.
The man that mentioned *him* at once dismissed   560
All mercy from his lips, and sneered, and hissed ;
His crimes were such as Sodom never knew,
And Perjury stood up to swear all true ;
His aim was mischief, and his zeal pretence,

His speech rebellion against common sense;
A knave, when tried on honesty's plain rule,
And when by that of reason, a mere fool;
The world's best comfort was, his doom was passed,
Die when he might, he must be damned at last.
    Now, Truth, perform thine office; waft aside   570
The curtain drawn by prejudice and pride,
Reveal (the man is dead) to wondering eyes
This more than monster in his proper guise.
    He loved the world that hated him: the tear
That dropped upon his Bible was sincere:
Assailed by scandal and the tongue of strife,
His only answer was a blameless life;
And he that forged, and he that threw the dart,
Had each a brother's interest in his heart.
Paul's love of Christ, and steadiness unbribed,   580
Were copied close in him, and well transcribed.
He followed Paul; his zeal a kindred flame,
His apostolic charity the same.
Like him, crossed cheerfully tempestuous seas,
Forsaking country, kindred, friends, and ease;
Like him he laboured, and like him content
To bear it, suffered shame where'er he went.
    Blush, Calumny; and write upon his tomb,
If honest eulogy can spare thee room,
Thy deep repentance of thy thousand lies,   590
Which, aimed at him, have pierced the offended skies!
And say, " Blot out my sin, confessed, deplored,
Against thine image in thy saint, O Lord!"
    No blinder bigot, I maintain it still,
Than he who must have pleasure, come what will:
He laughs, whatever weapon Truth may draw,
And deems her sharp artillery mere straw.
Scripture indeed is plain; but God and he
On Scripture ground are sure to disagree;
Some wiser rule must teach him how to live   600
Than that his Maker has seen fit to give;
Supple and flexible as Indian cane,
To take the bend his appetites ordain;
Contrived to suit frail nature's crazy case,
And reconcile his lusts with saving grace.
By this, with nice precision of design,
He draws upon life's map a zigzag line,
That shows how far 'tis safe to follow sin,
And where his danger and God's wrath begin.
By this he forms, as pleased he sports along,   610
His well-poised estimate of right and wrong;
And finds the modish manners of the day,
Though loose, as harmless as an infant's play.
    Build by whatever plan caprice decrees,
With what materials, on what ground you please;
Your hope shall stand unblamed, perhaps admired,

3   I

If not that hope the Scripture has required.
The strange conceits, vain projects, and wild dreams,
With which hypocrisy for ever teems,
(Though other follies strike the public eye, 620
And raise a laugh) pass unmolested by;
But if, unblameable in word and thought,
A *man* arise, a man whom God has taught,
With all Elijah's dignity of tone,
And all the love of the beloved John,
To storm the citadels they build in air,
And smite the untempered wall 'tis death to spare ;
To sweep away all refuges of lies,
And place, instead of quirks themselves devise,
LAMA SABACHTHANI before their eyes ; 630
To prove, that without Christ all gain is loss,
All hope despair, that stands not on his cross ;
Except the few his God may have impressed,
A tenfold frenzy seizes all the rest.
  Throughout mankind, the Christian kind at least,
There dwells a consciousness in every breast,
That folly ends where genuine hope begins,
And he that finds his heaven must lose his sins.
Nature opposes with her utmost force
This riving stroke, this ultimate divorce ; 640
And, while religion seems to be her view,
Hates with a deep sincerity *the true :*
For this, of all that ever influenced man,
Since Abel worshipped, or the world began,
This only spares no lust, admits no plea,
But makes him, if at all, completely free ;
Sounds forth the signal, as she mounts her car,
Of an eternal, universal war ;
Rejects all treaty, penetrates all wiles,
Scorns with the same indifference frowns and smiles ; 650
Drives through the realms of Sin, where Riot reels,
And grinds his crown beneath her burning wheels !
Hence all that is in man, pride, passion, art,
Powers of the mind, and feelings of the heart,
Insensible of Truth's almighty charms,
Starts at her first approach, and sounds to arms !
While Bigotry, with well-dissembled fears,
His eyes shut fast, his fingers in his ears,
Mighty to parry and push by God's word
With senseless noise, his argument the sword, 660
Pretends a zeal for godliness and grace,
And spits abhorrence in the Christian's face.
  Parent of Hope, immortal Truth ! make known
Thy deathless wreaths and triumphs all thine own :
The silent progress of thy power is such,
Thy means so feeble, and despised so much,
That few believe the wonders thou hast wrought,
And none can teach them, but whom thou hast taught.

O see me sworn to serve thee, and command
A painter's skill into a poet's hand,   670
That, while I trembling trace a work divine,
Fancy may stand aloof from the design,
And light, and shade, and every stroke be thine.
  If ever thou hast felt another's pain,
If ever when he sighed hast sighed again,
If ever on thine eyelid stood the tear
That pity had engendered, drop one here.
This man was happy—had the world's good word,
And with it every joy it can afford ;
Friendship and love seemed tenderly at strife,   680
Which most should sweeten his untroubled life ;
Politely learned, and of a gentle race,
Good breeding and good sense gave all a grace,
And whether at the toilet of the fair
He laughed and trifled, made him welcome there,—
Or if in masculine debate he shared,
Ensured him mute attention and regard.
Alas, how changed ! expressive of his mind,
His eyes are sunk, arms folded, head reclined ;
Those awful syllables, Hell, Death, and Sin,   690
Though whispered, plainly tell what works within,
That conscience there performs her proper part,
And writes a doomsday sentence on his heart ;
Forsaking and forsaken of all friends,
He now perceives where earthly pleasure ends ;
Hard task ! for one who lately knew no care,
And harder still as learnt beneath despair ;
His hours no longer pass unmarked away,
A dark importance saddens every day ;
He hears the notice of the clock perplexed,   700
And cries, " Perhaps eternity strikes next ;"
Sweet music is no longer music here,
And laughter sounds like madness in his ear :
His grief the world of all her power disarms,
Wine has no taste, and beauty has no charms :
God's holy word, once trivial in his view,
Now by the voice of his experience true,
Seems, as it is, the fountain whence alone
Must spring that hope he pants to make his own.
  Now let the bright reverse be known abroad ;   710
Say man's a worm, and power belongs to God.
As when a felon, whom his country's laws
Have justly doomed for some atrocious cause,
Expects in darkness and heart-chilling fears,
The shameful close of all his misspent years ;
If chance, on heavy pinions slowly borne,
A tempest usher in the dreaded morn,
Upon his dungeon walls the lightnings play,
The thunder seems to summon him away,
The warder at the door his key applies,   720

Shoots back the bolt, and all his courage dies ;
If then, just then, all thoughts of mercy lost,
When hope, long lingering, at last yields the ghost,
The sound of pardon pierce his startled ear,
He drops at once his fetters and his fear ;
A transport glows in all he looks and speaks,
And the first thankful tears bedew his cheeks.
Joy, far superior joy, that much outweighs
The comfort of a few poor added days,
Invades, possesses, and o'erwhelms the soul   730
Of him whom hope has with a touch made whole.
'Tis heaven, all heaven descending on the wings
Of the glad legions of the King of kings ;
'Tis more—'tis God diffused through every part,
'Tis God himself triumphant in his heart.
O, welcome now the sun's once hated light,
His noonday beams were never half so bright.
Not kindred minds alone are called to employ
Their hours, their days, in listening to his joy ;
Unconscious nature, all that he surveys,   740
Rocks, groves, and streams, must join him in his praise.
     These are thy glorious works, eternal Truth,
The scoff of withered age and beardless youth ;
These move the censure and illiberal grin
Of fools that hate thee and delight in sin :
But these shall last when night has quenched the pole,
And heaven is all departed as a scroll.
And when, as Justice has long since decreed,
This earth shall blaze, and a new world succeed,
Then these thy glorious works, and they who share   750
That Hope, which can alone exclude despair,
Shall live exempt from weakness and decay,
The brightest wonders of an endless day.
     Happy the bard (if that fair name belong
To him that blends no fable with his song)
Whose lines uniting, by an honest art,
The faithful monitor's and poet's part,
Seek to delight, that they may mend, mankind,
And, while they captivate, inform the mind ;
Still happier, if he till a thankful soil,   760
And fruit reward his honourable toil :
But happier far, who comfort those that wait
To hear plain truth at Judah's hallowed gate :
Their language simple, as their manners meek,
No shining ornaments have they to seek ;
Nor labour they, nor time nor talents waste,
In sorting flowers to suit a fickle taste ;
But while they speak the wisdom of the skies,
Which art can only darken and disguise,
The abundant harvest, recompense divine,   770
Repays their work—the gleaning only mine.

CHARITY.

Quo nihil majus meliusve terris
Fata donavere, bonique divi;
Nec dabunt, quamvis redeant in aurum
    Tempora priscum.—HOR. lib. iv. ode 2

FAIREST and foremost of the train that wait
On man's most dignified and happiest state,
Whether we name thee Charity or Love,
Chief grace below, and all in all above,
Prosper (I press thee with a powerful plea)
A task I venture on, impelled by thee:
Oh never seen but in thy blest effects,
Nor felt but in the soul that Heaven selects;
Who seeks to praise thee, and to make thee known
To other hearts, must have thee in his own.   10
Come, prompt me with benevolent desires,
Teach me to kindle at thy gentle fires,
And though disgraced and slighted, to redeem
A poet's name, by making thee the theme.
   God, working ever on a social plan,
By various ties attaches man to man:
He made at first, though free and unconfined,
One man the common father of the kind;
That every tribe, though placed as he sees best,
Where seas or deserts part them from the rest,   20
Differing in language, manners, or in face,
Might feel themselves allied to all the race.
When Cook—lamented, and with tears as just
As ever mingled with heroic dust—
Steered Britain's oak into a world unknown,
And in his country's glory sought his own,
Wherever he found man, to nature true,
The rights of man were sacred in his view;
He soothed with gifts, and greeted with a smile,
The simple native of the new-found isle;   30
He spurned the wretch that slighted or withstood
The tender argument of kindred blood,
Nor would endure that any should control
His freeborn brethren of the southern pole.
   But though some nobler minds a law respect,
That none shall with impunity neglect,
In baser souls unnumbered evils meet,
To thwart its influence, and its end defeat.
While Cook is loved for savage lives he saved,
See Cortez odious for a world enslaved!   40
Where wast thou then, sweet Charity! where then,
Thou tutelary friend of helpless men?

Wast thou in monkish cells and nunneries found,
Or building hospitals on English ground?
No.—Mammon makes the world his legatee
Through fear, not love; and Heaven abhors the fee.
Wherever found (and all men need thy care),
Nor age nor infancy could find thee there.
The hand, that slew till it could slay no more,
Was glued to the sword-hilt with Indian gore.   50
Their prince, as justly seated on his throne
As vain imperial Philip in his own,
Tricked out of all his royalty by art,
That stripped him bare, and broke his honest heart,
Died by the sentence of a shaven priest,
For scorning what they taught him to detest.
How dark the veil that intercepts the blaze
Of Heaven's mysterious purposes and ways;
God stood not, though he seemed to stand, aloof;
And at this hour the conqueror feels the proof: 60
The wreath he won drew down an instant curse,
The fretting plague is in the public purse,
The cankered spoil corrodes the pining state,
Starved by that indolence their mines create.
    Oh could their ancient Incas rise again,
How would they take up Israel's taunting strain!
" Art thou too fallen, Iberia? Do we see
The robber and the murderer weak as we?
Thou that hast wasted earth, and dared despise
Alike the wrath and mercy of the skies,   70
Thy pomp is in the grave, thy glory laid
Low in the pits thine avarice has made.
We come with joy from our eternal rest,
To see the oppressor in his turn oppressed.
Art thou the god, the thunder of whose hand
Rolled over all our desolated land,
Shook principalities and kingdoms down,
And made the mountains tremble at his frown?
The sword shall light upon thy boasted powers,
And waste them, as thy sword has wasted ours."   80
'Tis thus Omnipotence his law fulfils,
And vengeance executes what justice wills.
    Again—the band of commerce was designed
To associate all the branches of mankind;
And if a boundless plenty be the robe,
Trade is the golden girdle of the globe.
Wise to promote whatever end he means,
God opens fruitful Nature's various scenes:
Each climate needs what other climes produce,
And offers something to the general use;   90
No land but listens to the common call,
And in return receives supply from all.
This genial intercourse, and mutual aid,
Cheers what were else a universal shade,

Calls Nature from her ivy-mantled den,
And softens human rockwork into men.
Ingenious Art, with her expressive face,
Steps forth to fashion and refine the race,
Not only fills necessity's demand,
But overcharges her capacious hand :   100
Capricious taste itself can crave no more,
Than she supplies from her abounding store ;
She strikes out all that luxury can ask,
And gains new vigour at her endless task.
Hers is the spacious arch, the shapely spire,
The painter's pencil, and the poet's lyre ;
From her the canvas borrows light and shade,
And verse, more lasting, hues that never fade.
She guides the finger o'er the dancing keys,
Gives difficulty all the grace of ease,   110
And pours a torrent of sweet notes around,
Fast as the thirsting ear can drink the sound.
   These are the gifts of Art, and Art thrives most
Where commerce has enriched the busy coast ;
He catches all improvements in his flight,
Spreads foreign wonders in his country's sight,
Imports what others have invented well,
And stirs his own to match them or excel.
'Tis thus reciprocating, each with each,
Alternately the nations learn and teach ;   120
While Providence enjoins to every soul
A union with the vast terraqueous whole.
   Heaven speed the canvas, gallantly unfurled
To furnish and accommodate a world,
To give the pole the produce of the sun,
And knit the unsocial climates into one. —
Soft airs and gentle heavings of the wave
Impel the fleet, whose errand is to save,
To succour wasted regions, and replace
The smile of opulence in sorrow's face. —   130
Let nothing adverse, nothing unforeseen,
Impede the bark that ploughs the deep serene,
Charged with a freight transcending in its worth
The gems of India, nature's rarest birth,
That flies, like Gabriel on his Lord's commands,
A herald of God's love to pagan lands.
But ah ! what wish can prosper, or what prayer,
For merchants rich in cargoes of despair,
Who drive a loathsome traffic, gauge and span,
And buy the muscles and the bones of man ?   140
The tender ties of father, husband, friend,
All bonds of nature in that moment end ;
And each endures, while yet he draws his breath,
A stroke as fatal as the scythe of death.
The sable warrior, frantic with regret
Of her he loves, and never can forget,

Loses in tears the far receding shore,
But not the thought that they must meet no more ;
Deprived of her and freedom at a blow,
What has he left, that he can yet forego ?   150
Yes, to deep sadness sullenly resigned,
He feels his body's bondage in his mind ;
Puts off his generous nature; and, to suit
His manners with his fate, puts on the brute.
    O most degrading of all ills, that wait
On man, a mourner in his best estate !
All other sorrows virtue may endure,
And find submission more than half a cure ;
Grief is itself a medicine, and bestowed
To improve the fortitude that bears the load,   160
To teach the wanderer, as his woes increase,
The path of Wisdom, all whose paths are peace ;
But slavery !—Virtue dreads it as her grave :
Patience itself is meanness in a slave ;
Or if the will and sovereignty of God
Bid suffer it awhile, and kiss the rod,
Wait for the dawning of a brighter day,
And snap the chain the moment when you may.
Nature imprints upon whate'er we see
That has a heart and life in it, " Be free ! "   170
The beasts are chartered—neither age nor force
Can quell the love of freedom in a horse :
He breaks the cord that held him at the rack ;
And, conscious of an unencumbered back,
Snuffs up the morning air, forgets the rein ;
Loose fly his forelock and his ample mane;
Responsive to the distant neigh, he neighs ;
Nor stops till, overleaping all delays,
He finds the pasture where his fellows graze.
    Canst thou, and honoured with a Christian name, 180
Buy what is woman-born, and feel no shame ?
Trade in the blood of innocence, and plead
Expedience as a warrant for the deed ?
So may the wolf, whom famine has made bold
To quit the forest and invade the fold ;
So may the ruffian, who with ghostly glide,
Dagger in hand, steals close to your bedside ;
Not he, but his emergence forced the door,
He found it inconvenient to be poor.
Has God then given its sweetness to the cane,   190
Unless his laws be trampled on—in vain ?
Built a brave world, which cannot yet subsist,
Unless his right to rule it be dismissed ?
Impudent blasphemy ! So Folly pleads,
And, Avarice being judge, with ease succeeds.
    But grant the plea, and let it stand for just,
That man make man his prey, because he *must :*
Still there is room for pity to abate,

And soothe the sorrows of so sad a state.
A Briton knows, or if he knows it not,   200
The Scripture placed within his reach, he ought,
That souls have no discriminating hue,
Alike important in their Maker's view ;
That none are free from blemish since the fall,
And love divine has paid one price for all.
The wretch that works and weeps without relief,
Has one that notices his silent grief.
He, from whose hands alone all power proceeds,
Ranks its abuse among the foulest deeds,
Considers *all* injustice with a frown ;   210
But *marks* the man, that treads his fellow down.
Begone—the whip and bell in that hard hand
Are hateful ensigns of usurped command.
Not Mexico could purchase kings a claim
To scourge him, weariness his only blame.
Remember, Heaven has an avenging rod,—
To smite the poor is treason against God.

Trouble is grudgingly and hardly brooked,
While life's sublimest joys are overlooked :
We wander o'er a sunburnt thirsty soil,   220
Murmuring and weary of our daily toil,
Forget to enjoy the palm-tree's offered shade,
Or taste the fountain in the neighbouring glade ;
Else who would lose, that had the power to improve,
The occasion of transmuting fear to love ?
Oh, 'tis a godlike privilege to save,
And he that scorns it is himself a slave.
Inform his mind ; one flash of heavenly day
Would heal his heart, and melt his chains away.
"Beauty for ashes" is a gift indeed,   230
And slaves, by truth enlarged, are doubly freed.
Then would he say, submissive at thy feet,
While gratitude and love made service sweet,
" My dear deliverer out of hopeless night,
Whose bounty bought me but to give me light,
I was a bondman on my native plain,
Sin forged, and ignorance made fast, the chain ;
Thy lips have shed instruction as the dew,
Taught me what path to shun, and what pursue :
Farewell my former joys ! I sigh no more   240
For Africa's once loved, benighted shore ;
Serving a benefactor I am free ;
At my best home, if not exiled from thee."
Some men make gain a fountain, whence proceeds
A stream of liberal and heroic deeds ;
The swell of pity, not to be confined
Within the scanty limits of the mind,
Disdains the bank, and throws the golden sands,
A rich deposit, on the bordering lands :
These have an ear for His paternal call,   250

Who makes some rich for the supply of all;
God's gift with pleasure in His praise employ;
And THORNTON is familiar with the joy.
    Oh, could I worship aught beneath the skies,
That earth has seen, or fancy can devise,
Thine altar, sacred Liberty, should stand,
Built by no mercenary vulgar hand,
With fragrant turf, and flowers as wild and fair
As ever dressed a bank, or scented summer air.
Duly, as ever on the mountain's height   260
The peep of Morning shed a dawning light,
Again, when Evening in her sober vest
Drew the grey curtain of the fading west,
My soul should yield thee willing thanks and praise,
For the chief blessings of my fairest days:
But that were sacrilege—praise is not thine,
But His who gave thee, and preserves thee mine:
Else I would say, and as I spake bid fly
A captive bird into the boundless sky,
"This triple realm adores thee—thou art come   270
From Sparta hither, and art here at home.
We feel thy force still active, at this hour
Enjoy immunity from priestly power,
While Conscience, happier than in ancient years,
Owns no superior but the God she fears.
Propitious spirit! yet expunge a wrong
Thy rights have suffered, and our land, too long.
Teach mercy to ten thousand hearts, that share
The fears and hopes of a commercial care;
Prisons expect the wicked, and were built   280
To bind the lawless, and to punish guilt;
But shipwreck, earthquake, battle, fire, and flood,
Are mighty mischiefs, not to be withstood;
And honest merit stands on slippery ground,
Where covert guile and artifice abound.
Let just restraint, for public peace designed,
Chain up the wolves and tigers of mankind;
The foe of virtue has no claim to thee,
But let insolvent innocence go free."
    Patron of else the most despised of men,   290
Accept the tribute of a stranger's pen;
Verse, like the laurel, its immortal meed,
Should be the guerdon of a noble deed;
I may alarm thee, but I fear the shame
(Charity chosen as my theme and aim)
I must incur, forgetting HOWARD's name.
Blest with all wealth can give thee, to resign
Joys doubly sweet to feelings quick as thine,
To quit the bliss thy rural scenes bestow,
To seek a nobler amidst scenes of woe,   300
To traverse seas, range kingdoms, and bring home
Not the proud monuments of Greece or Rome,

But knowledge such as only dungeons teach,
And only sympathy like thine could reach;
That grief, sequestered from the public stage,
Might smooth her feathers, and enjoy her cage;
Speaks a divine ambition, and a zeal,
The boldest patriot might be proud to feel.
Oh that the voice of clamour and debate,
That pleads for peace till it disturbs the state,   310
Were hushed in favour of thy generous plea,
The poor thy clients, and Heaven's smile thy fee!
   Philosophy, that does not dream or stray,
Walks arm in arm with Nature all his way,
Compasses Earth, dives into it, ascends
Whatever steep Enquiry recommends,
Sees planetary wonders smoothly roll
Round other systems under her control,
Drinks wisdom at the milky stream of light,
That cheers the silent journey of the night,   320
And brings at his return a bosom charged
With rich instruction, and a soul enlarged.
The treasured sweets of the capacious plan
That Heaven spreads wide before the view of man,
All prompt his pleased pursuit, and to pursue
Still prompt him, with a pleasure always new;
He too has a connecting power, and draws
Man to the centre of the common cause,
Aiding a dubious and deficient sight
With a new medium and a purer light.   330
All truth is precious, if not all divine;
And what dilates the powers must needs refine.
He reads the skies, and watching every change,
Provides the faculties an ampler range;
And wins mankind, as his attempts prevail,
A prouder station on the general scale.
But Reason still, unless divinely taught,
Whate'er she learns, learns nothing as she ought;
The lamp of revelation only shows,
What human wisdom cannot but oppose,   340
That man, in nature's richest mantle clad,
And graced with all philosophy can add,
Though fair without, and luminous within,
Is still the progeny and heir of sin.
Thus taught, down falls the plumage of his pride;
He feels his need of an unerring guide,
And knows, that falling he shall rise no more,
Unless the power that bade him stand restore.
This is indeed philosophy; this known,
Makes wisdom, worthy of the name, his own: 350
And without this, whatever he discuss,—
Whether the space between the stars and us;
Whether he measure Earth, compute the sea,
Weigh sunbeams, carve a fly, or spit a flea;

The solemn trifler with his boasted skill
Toils much, and is a solemn trifler still:
Blind was he born, and, his misguided eyes
Grown dim in trifling studies, blind he dies.
Self-knowledge truly learned, of course implies
The rich possession of a nobler prize: 360
For self to self, and God to man revealed
(Two themes to Nature's eye for ever sealed),
Are taught by rays, that fly with equal pace
From the same centre of enlightening grace.
Here stay thy foot; how copious, and how clear,
The o'erflowing well of Charity springs here!
Hark! 'tis the music of a thousand rills,
Some through the groves, some down the sloping hills,
Winding a secret or an open course,
And all supplied from an eternal source.   370
The ties of Nature do but feebly bind;
And Commerce partially reclaims mankind;
Philosophy, without his heavenly guide,
May blow up self-conceit, and nourish pride,
But, while his province is the reasoning part,
Has still a veil of midnight on his heart:
'Tis Truth divine exhibited on earth,
Gives Charity her being and her birth.
    Suppose (when thought is warm and fancy flows,
What will not argument sometimes suppose?)   380
An isle possessed by creatures of our kind,
Endued with reason, yet by nature blind.
Let Supposition lend her aid once more,
And land some grave optician on the shore:
He claps his lens, if haply they may see,
Close to the part where vision ought to be;
But finds, that, though his tubes assist the sight,
They cannot give it, or make darkness light.
He reads wise lectures, and describes aloud
A sense they know not, to the wondering crowd;   390
He talks of light, and the prismatic hues,
As men of depth in erudition use;
But all he gains for his harangue is—"Well!
What monstrous lies some travellers will tell!"
    The soul, whose sight all-quickening grace renews,
Takes the resemblance of the good she views,
As diamonds, stripped of their opaque disguise,
Reflect the noonday glory of the skies.
She speaks of Him, her Author, Guardian, Friend,
Whose love knew no beginning, knows no end,   400
In language warm as all that love inspires,
And in the glow of her intense desires,
Pants to communicate her noble fires.
She sees a world stark blind to what employs
Her eager thought, and feeds her flowing joys;
Though Wisdom hail them, heedless of her call,

Flies to save some, and feels a pang for all :
Herself as weak as her support is strong,
She feels that frailty she denied so long ;
And, from a knowledge of her own disease,   410
Learns to compassionate the sick she sees.
Here see, acquitted of all vain pretence,
The reign of genuine Charity commence ;
Though scorn repay her sympathetic tears,
She still is kind, and still she perseveres ;
The truth she loves a sightless world blaspheme,
'Tis childish dotage, a delirious dream.
The danger they discern not, they deny ;
Laugh at their only remedy, and die.
But still a soul thus touched can never cease,   420
Whoever threatens war, to speak of peace.
Pure in her aim, and in her temper mild,
Her wisdom seems the weakness of a child :
She makes excuses where she might condemn,
Reviled by those that hate her, prays for them ;
Suspicion lurks not in her artless breast,
The worst suggested, she believes the best ;
Not soon provoked, however stung and teased,
And, if perhaps made angry, soon appeased ;
She rather waives than will dispute her right,   430
And, injured, makes forgiveness her delight.
    Such was the portrait an apostle drew,
The bright original was one he knew ;
Heaven held his hand, the likeness must be true.
    When one, that holds communion with the skies,
Has filled his urn where these pure waters rise,
And once more mingles with us meaner things,
'Tis even as if an Angel shook his wings ;
Immortal fragrance fills the circuit wide,
That tells us whence his treasures are supplied.   440
So when a ship, well freighted with the stores
The sun matures on India's spicy shores,
Has dropped her anchor, and her canvas furled,
In some safe haven of our western world,
'Twere vain enquiry to what port she went,
The gale informs us, laden with the scent.
    Some seek, when queasy conscience has its qualms,
To lull the painful malady with alms ;
But charity not feigned intends alone
Another's good—theirs centres in their own ;   450
And, too short-lived to reach the realms of peace,
Must cease for ever when the poor shall cease.
Flavia, most tender of her own good name,
Is rather careless of her sister's fame :
Her superfluity the poor supplies,
But, if she touch a character, it dies.
The seeming virtue weighed against the vice,
She deems all safe, for she has paid the price :

No charity but alms aught values she,
Except in porcelain on her mantel-tree.   460
How many deeds with which the world has rung,
From pride in league with ignorance have sprung !
But God o'errules all human follies still,
And bends the tough materials to His will.
A conflagration, or a wintry flood,
Has left some hundreds without home or food ;
Extravagance and Avarice shall subscribe,
While fame and self-complacence are the bribe.
The brief proclaimed, it visits every pew,
But first the Squire's, a compliment but due :   470
With slow deliberation he unties
His glittering purse, that envy of all eyes,
And while the clerk just puzzles out the psalm,
Slides guinea behind guinea in his palm ;
Till finding, what he might have found before,
A smaller piece amidst the precious store,
Pinched close between his finger and his thumb,
He half exhibits, and then drops the sum.
Gold to be sure !—Throughout the town 'tis told,
How the good Squire gives never less than gold.   480
From motives such as his, though not the best,
Springs in due time supply for the distressed ;
Not less effectual than what love bestows,
Except that Office clips it as it goes.
    But lest I seem to sin against a friend,
And wound the grace I mean to recommend,
(Though vice derided with a just design
Implies no trespass against love divine,)
Once more I would adopt the graver style ;
A teacher should be sparing of his smile.   490
    Unless a love of virtue light the flame,
Satire is, more than those he brands, to blame ;
He hides behind a magisterial air
His own offences, and strips others bare ;
Affects indeed a most humane concern,
That men, if gently tutored, will not learn ;
That mulish folly, not to be reclaimed
By softer methods, must be made ashamed ;
But (I might instance in St. Patrick's dean)
Too often rails to gratify his spleen.   500
Most satirists are indeed a public scourge ;
Their mildest physic is a farrier's purge ;
Their acrid temper turns, as soon as stirred,
The milk of their good purpose all to curd.
Their zeal begotten, as their works rehearse,
By lean despair upon an empty purse,
The wild assassins start into the street,
Prepared to poniard whomsoe'er they meet.
No skill in swordsmanship, however just,
Can be secure against a madman's thrust !   510

And even Virtue so unfairly matched,
Although immortal, may be pricked or scratched.
When Scandal has new-minted an old lie,
Or taxed invention for a fresh supply,
'Tis called a Satire, and the world appears
Gathering around it with erected ears :
A thousand names are tossed into the crowd ;
Some whispered softly, and some twanged aloud ;
Just as the sapience of an author's brain
Suggests it safe or dangerous to be plain.   520
Strange ! how the frequent interjected dash
Quickens a market, and helps off the trash ;
The important letters that include the rest
Serve as a key to those that are suppressed ;
Conjecture gripes the victims in his paw,
The world is charmed, and Scrib escapes the law.
So, when the cold damp shades of night prevail,
Worms may be caught by either head or tail ;
Forcibly drawn from many a close recess,
They meet with little pity, no redress ;   530
Plunged in the stream, they lodge upon the mud,
Food for the famished rovers of the flood.

All zeal for a reform that gives offence
To peace and charity, is mere pretence :
A bold remark, but which, if well applied,
Would humble many a towering poet's pride.
Perhaps the man was in a sportive fit,
And had no other play-place for his wit ;
Perhaps, enchanted with the love of fame,
He sought the jewel in his neighbour's shame ;   540
Perhaps—whatever end he might pursue,
The cause of virtue could not be his view.
At every stroke wit flashes in our eyes ;
The turns are quick, the polished points surprise,
But shine with cruel and tremendous charms,
That, while they please, possess us with alarms :
So have I seen, (and hastened to the sight
On all the wings of holiday delight,)
Where stands that monument of ancient power,
Named with emphatic dignity, the Tower,   550
Guns, halberts, swords, and pistols, great and small,
In starry forms disposed upon the wall ;
We wonder, as we gazing stand below,
That brass and steel should make so fine a show ;
But though we praise the exact designer's skill,
Account them implements of mischief still.

No works shall find acceptance in that day
When all disguises shall be rent away,
That square not truly with the Scripture plan,
Nor spring from love to God, or love to man.   560
As He ordains things sordid in their birth
To be resolved into their parent earth ;

And, though the soul shall seek superior orbs,
Whate'er this world produces, it absorbs ;
So self starts nothing, but what tends apace,
Home to the goal, where it began the race.
Such as our motive is, our aim must be ;
If this be servile, that can ne'er be free :
If self employ us, whatsoe'er is wrought,
We glorify that self, not Him we ought ;   570
Such virtues had need prove their own reward,
The Judge of all men owes them no regard.
True Charity, a plant divinely nursed,
Fed by the love from which it rose at first,
Thrives against hope, and in the rudest scene
Storms but enliven its unfading green ;
Exuberant is the shadow it supplies,
Its fruit on earth, its growth above the skies.
To look at Him, who formed us and redeemed,
So glorious now, though once so disesteemed,   580
To see a God stretch forth His human hand,
To uphold the boundless scenes of His command ;
To recollect, that, in a form like ours,
He bruised beneath His feet the infernal powers,
Captivity led captive, rose to claim
The wreath He won so dearly in our name ;
That, throned above all height, He condescends
To call the few that trust in Him His friends ;
That in the heaven of heavens, that space He deems
Too scanty for the exertion of His beams,   590
And shines, as if impatient to bestow
Life and a kingdom upon worms below ;
That sight imparts a never-dying flame,
Though feeble in degree, in kind the same.
Like Him, the soul thus kindled from above
Spreads wide her arms of universal love ;
And, still enlarged as she receives the grace,
Includes creation in her close embrace.
Behold a Christian !—and without the fires
The Founder of that name alone inspires,   600
Though all accomplishments, all knowledge meet,
To make the shining prodigy complete,
Whoever boasts that name—behold a cheat !
  Were love, in these the world's last doting years,
As frequent as the want of it appears,
The churches warmed, they would no longer hold
Such frozen figures, stiff as they are cold ;
Relenting forms would lose their power, or cease ;
And even the dipped and sprinkled live in peace :
Each heart would quit its prison in the breast,   610
And flow in free communion with the rest.
The statesman, skilled in projects dark and deep,
Might burn his useless Machiavel, and sleep ;
His budget, often filled, yet always poor,

Might swing at ease behind his study door,
No longer prey upon our annual rents,
Nor scare the nation with its big contents :
Disbanded legions freely might depart,
And slaying man would cease to be an art.
No learned disputants would take the field,   620
Sure not to conquer, and sure not to yield ;
Both sides deceived, if rightly understood,
Pelting each other for the public good.
Did Charity prevail, the press would prove
A vehicle of virtue, truth, and love ;
And I might spare myself the pains to show
What few can learn, and all suppose they know.
Thus have I sought to grace a serious lay
With many a wild, indeed, but flowery spray,
In hopes to gain, what else I must have lost,   630
The attention Pleasure has so much engrossed.
But if, unhappily deceived, I dream,
And prove too weak for so divine a theme,
Let Charity forgive me a mistake,
That zeal, not vanity, has chanced to make,
And spare the poet for his subject sake.

CONVERSATION.

Nam neque me tantum venientis sibilus austri,
Nec percussa juvant fluctû tam litora, nec quæ
Saxosas inter decurrunt flumina valles.
                                   VIRG. *Ecl.* v.

THOUGH Nature weigh our talents, and dispense
To every man his modicum of sense,
And Conversation in its better part
May be esteemed a gift, and not an art,
Yet much depends, as in the tiller's toil,
On culture, and the sowing of the soil.
Words learned by rote a parrot may rehearse,
But talking is not always to converse ;
Not more distinct from harmony divine
The constant creaking of a country sign.   10
As alphabets in ivory employ,
Hour after hour, the yet unlettered boy,
Sorting and puzzling with a deal of glee
Those seeds of science called his A B C,
So language in the mouths of the adult,
Witness its insignificant result,
Too often proves an implement of play,
A toy to sport with, and pass time away.
Collect at evening what the day brought forth,
Compress the sum into its solid worth,   20

C   K

And if it weigh the importance of a fly,
The scales are false, or algebra a lie.
Sacred interpreter of human thought,
How few respect or use thee as they ought!
But all shall give account of every wrong,
Who dare dishonour or defile the tongue,
Who prostitute it in the cause of vice,
Or sell their glory at a market-price,
Who vote for hire, or point it with lampoon,
The dear-bought placeman, and the cheap buffoon.   30
    There is a prurience in the speech of some,
Wrath stays Him, or else God would strike them dumb:
His wise forbearance has their end in view,
They fill their measure, and receive their due.
The heathen lawgivers of ancient days,
Names almost worthy of a Christian's praise,
Would drive them forth from the resort of men,
And shut up every satyr in his den.
Oh come not ye near innocence and truth,
Ye worms that eat into the bud of youth!   40
Infectious as impure, your blighting power
Taints in its rudiments the promised flower;
Its odour perished and its charming hue,
Thenceforth 'tis hateful, for it smells of you.
Not even the vigorous and headlong rage
Of adolescence, or a firmer age,
Affords a plea allowable or just
For making speech the pamperer of lust;
But when the breath of age commits the fault,
'Tis nauseous as the vapour of a vault.   50
So withered stumps disgrace the sylvan scene,
No longer fruitful, and no longer green;
The sapless wood, divested of the bark,
Grows fungous, and takes fire at every spark.
    Oaths terminate, as Paul observes, all strife—
Some men have surely then a peaceful life;
Whatever subject occupy discourse,
The feats of Vestris, or the naval force,
Asseveration blustering in your face
Makes contradiction such a hopeless case.   60
In every tale they tell, or false or true,
Well known, or such as no man ever knew,
They fix attention, heedless of your pain,
With oaths like rivets forced into the brain;
And even when sober truth prevails throughout,
They swear it, till affirmance breeds a doubt.
A Persian, humble servant of the sun,
Who though devout, yet bigotry had none,
Hearing a lawyer, grave in his address,
With adjurations every word impress,   70
Supposed the man a bishop, or at least,
God's name so much upon his lips, a priest;

Bowed at the close with all his graceful airs,
And begged an interest in his frequent prayers.
  Go, quit the rank to which ye stood preferred,
Henceforth associate in one common herd ;
Religion, virtue, reason, common sense,
Pronounce your human form a false pretence,
A mere disguise in which a devil lurks,
Who yet betrays his secret by his works.   80
  Ye powers who rule the tongue, if such there are,
And make colloquial happiness your care,
Preserve me from the thing I dread and hate,
A duel in the form of a debate.
The clash of arguments and jar of words,
Worse than the mortal brunt of rival swords,
Decide no question with their tedious length,
(For opposition gives opinion strength,)
Divert the champions prodigal of breath,
And put the peaceably-disposed to death.   90
Oh thwart me not, Sir Soph, at every turn,
Nor carp at every flaw you may discern ;
Though syllogisms hang not on my tongue,
I am not surely always in the wrong ;
'Tis hard if all is false that I advance,
A fool must now and then be right by chance.
Not that all freedom of dissent I blame ;
No,—there I grant the privilege I claim.
A disputable point is no man's ground,
Rove where you please, 'tis common all around.   100
Discourse may want an animated No,
To brush the surface, and to make it flow ;
But still remember, if you mean to please,
To press your point with modesty and ease.
The mark at which my juster aim I take,
Is contradiction for its own dear sake.
Set your opinion at whatever pitch,
Knots and impediments make something hitch ;
Adopt his own, 'tis equally in vain,
Your thread of argument is snapped again ;   110
The wrangler, rather than accord with you,
Will judge himself deceived,—and prove it too.
Vociferated logic kills me quite,
A noisy man is always in the right ;
I twirl my thumbs, fall back into my chair,
Fix on the wainscot a distressful stare,
And when I hope his blunders are all out,
Reply discreetly, " To be sure—no doubt."
  Dubius is such a scrupulous good man,—
Yes, you may catch him tripping if you can.   120
He would not with a peremptory tone
Assert the nose upon his face his own ;
With hesitation admirably slow,
He humbly hopes—presumes—it may be so.

His evidence, if he were called by law
To swear to some enormity he saw,
For want of prominence and just relief,
Would hang an honest man, and save a thief.
Through constant dread of giving truth offence,
He ties up all his hearers in suspense;   130
Knows what he knows, as if he knew it not;
What he remembers seems to have forgot;
His sole opinion, whatsoe'er befall,
Centering at last in having none at all.
Yet though he tease and baulk your listening ear,
He makes one useful point exceeding clear;
Howe'er ingenious on his darling theme
A sceptic in philosophy may seem,
Reduced to practice, his beloved rule
Would only prove him a consummate fool;   140
Useless in him alike both brain and speech,
Fate having placed all truth above his reach ;
His ambiguities his total sum,
He might as well be blind and deaf and dumb.
    Where men of judgment creep and feel their way,
The positive pronounce without dismay,
Their want of light and intellect supplied
By sparks absurdity strikes out of pride :
Without the means of knowing right from wrong,
They always are decisive, clear, and strong;   150
Where others toil with philosophic force,
Their nimble nonsense takes a shorter course,
Flings at your head conviction in the lump,
And gains remote conclusions at a jump ;
Their own defect, invisible to them,
Seen in another, they at once condemn,
And, though self-idolized in every case,
Hate their own likeness in a brother's face.
The cause is plain and not to be denied,
The proud are always most provoked by pride ;   160
Few competitions but engender spite,
And those the most where neither has a right.
    The Point of Honour has been deemed of use,
To teach good manners and to curb abuse ;
Admit it true, the consequence is clear,
Our polished manners are a mask we wear,
And at the bottom, barbarous still and rude,
We are restrained indeed, but not subdued.
The very remedy, however sure,
Springs from the mischief it intends to cure,   170
And savage in its principle appears,
Tried, as it should be, by the fruit it bears.
'Tis hard indeed, if nothing will defend
Mankind from quarrels but their fatal end ;
That now and then a hero must decease,
That the surviving world may live in peace.

Perhaps at last close scrutiny may show
The practice dastardly, and mean, and low,
That men engage in it compelled by force,
And fear, not courage, is its proper source :   180
The fear of tyrant custom, and the fear
Lest fops should censure us, and fools should sneer.
At least to trample on our Maker's laws,
And hazard life for any or no cause,
To rush into a fixed eternal state
Out of the very flames of rage and hate,
Or send another shivering to the bar
With all the guilt of such unnatural war,
Whatever use may urge, or honour plead,
On reason's verdict is a madman's deed.   190
Am I to set my life upon a throw,
Because a bear is rude and surly?   No.
A moral, sensible, and well-bred man
Will not affront me,—and no other can.
Were I empowered to regulate the lists,
They should encounter with well-loaded fists ;
A Trojan combat would be something new,
Let DARES beat ENTELLUS black and blue ;
Then each might show to his admiring friends
In honourable bumps his rich amends,   200
And carry in contusions of his skull
A satisfactory receipt in full.
   A story in which native humour reigns
Is often useful, always entertains ;
A graver fact enlisted on your side
May furnish illustration, well applied ;
But sedentary weavers of long tales
Give me the fidgets, and my patience fails.
'Tis the most asinine employ on earth,
To hear them tell of parentage and birth,   210
And echo conversations dull and dry,
Embellished with—*he said*, and *so said I*.
At every interview their route the same,
The repetition makes attention lame ;
We bustle up with unsuccessful speed,
And in the saddest part cry—" Droll indeed !"
The path of narrative with care pursue,
Still making probability your clue,
On all the vestiges of truth attend,
And let them guide you to a decent end.   220
Of all ambitions man may entertain,
The worst that can invade a sickly brain
Is that which angles hourly for surprise,
And baits its hook with prodigies and lies.
Credulous infancy or age as weak
Are fittest auditors for such to seek,
Who to please others will themselves disgrace,
Yet please not, but affront you to your face.

A great retailer of this curious ware,
Having unloaded, and made many stare,   230
" Can this be true ?" an arch observer cries :
" Yes" (rather moved), " I saw it with these eyes."
" Sir! I believe it on that ground alone;
I could not had I seen it with my own."
    A tale should be judicious, clear, succinct,
The language plain, and incidents well linked.
Tell not as new what everybody knows,
And, new or old, still hasten to a close ;
There, centering in a focus round and neat,
Let all your rays of information meet.   240
What neither yields us profit nor delight,
Is like a nurse's lullaby at night ;
Guy Earl of Warwick and fair Eleanore,
Or giant-killing Jack, would please me more.
    The pipe, with solemn interposing puff,
Makes half a sentence at a time enough ;
The dozing sages drop the drowsy strain,
Then pause, and puff—and speak, and pause again.
Such often, like the tube they so admire,
Important triflers! have more smoke than fire.   250
Pernicious weed ! whose scent the fair annoys,
Unfriendly to society's chief joys,
Thy worst effect is banishing for hours
The sex whose presence civilizes ours.
Thou art indeed the drug a gardener wants,
To poison vermin that infest his plants ;
But are we so to wit and beauty blind
As to despise the glory of our kind,
And show the softest minds and fairest forms
As little mercy as he grubs and worms ?   260
They dare not wait the riotous abuse
Thy thirst-creating steams at length produce,
When wine has given indecent language birth,
And forced the flood-gates of licentious mirth !
For sea-born Venus her attachment shows
Still to that element from which she rose,
And with a quiet which no fumes disturb,
Sips meek infusions of a milder herb.
    The emphatic speaker dearly loves to oppose
In contact inconvenient, nose to nose ;   270
As if the gnomon on his neighbour's phiz,
Touched with the magnet, had attracted his.
His whispered theme, dilated and at large,
Proves after all a wind-gun's airy charge,
An extract of his diary—no more,
A tasteless journal of the day before.
He walked abroad, o'ertaken in the rain
Called on a friend, drank tea, stepped home again ;
Resumed his purpose, had a world of talk
With one he stumbled on, and lost his walk.   280

I interrupt him with a sudden bow,
" Adieu, dear Sir! lest you should lose it now."
    I cannot talk with civet in the room,
A fine puss-gentleman that's all perfume;
The sight's enough—no need to smell a beau—
Who thrusts his nose into a raree show?
His odoriferous attempts to please
Perhaps might prosper with a swarm of bees;
But we that make no honey, though we sting,
Poets, are sometimes apt to maul the thing.   290
'Tis wrong to bring into a mixed resort
What makes some sick, and others *à-la-mort*,
An argument of cogence, we may say,
Why such a one should keep himself away.
    A graver coxcomb we may sometimes see,
Quite as absurd, though not so light as he:
A shallow brain behind a serious mask,
An oracle within an empty cask,
The solemn fop; significant and budge;
A fool with judges, amongst fools a judge;   300
He says but little, and that little said
Owes all its weight, like loaded dice, to lead.
His wit invites you by his looks to come,
But when you knock it never is at home:
'Tis like a parcel sent you by the stage,
Some handsome present, as your hopes presage;
'Tis heavy, bulky, and bids fair to prove
An absent friend's fidelity and love;
But when unpacked, your disappointment groans
To find it stuffed with brickbats, earth, and stones.   310
    Some men employ their health, an ugly trick,
In making known how oft they have been sick,
And give us in recitals of disease
A doctor's trouble, but without the fees;
Relate how many weeks they kept their bed,
How an emetic or cathartic sped;
Nothing is slightly touched, much less forgot,
Nose, ears, and eyes seem present on the spot.
Now the distemper, spite of draught or pill,
Victorious seemed, and now the doctor's skill;   320
And now—alas for unforeseen mishaps!
They put on a damp nightcap and relapse;
They thought they must have died, they were so bad;
Their peevish hearers almost wish they had.
    Some fretful tempers wince at every touch,
You always do too little or too much:
You speak with life, in hopes to entertain,—
Your elevated voice goes through the brain;
You fall at once into a lower key,—
That's worse, the drone-pipe of an humble-bee.   330
The southern sash admits too strong a light,
You rise and drop the curtain—now 'tis night;

He shakes with cold ;—you stir the fire and strive
To make a blaze—that's roasting him alive.
Serve him with venison, and he chooses fish ;
With sole—that's just the sort he would not wish :
He takes what he at first professed to loathe,
And in due time feeds heartily on both ;
Yet still, o'erclouded with a constant frown,
He does not swallow, but he gulps it down.   340
Your hope to please him vain on every plan,
Himself should work that wonder, if he can—
Alas ! his efforts double his distress,
He likes yours little, and his own still less.
Thus always teasing others, always teased,
His only pleasure is— to be displeased.
  I pity bashful men, who feel the pain
Of fancied scorn and undeserved disdain,
And bear the marks upon a blushing face
Of needless shame, and self-imposed disgrace.   350
Our sensibilities are so acute,
The fear of being silent makes us mute.
We sometimes think we could a speech produce
Much to the purpose, if our tongues were loose ;
But being tied, it dies upon the lip,
Faint as a chicken's note that has the pip :
Our wasted oil unprofitably burns,
Like hidden lamps in old sepulchral urns.
Few Frenchmen of this evil have complained ;
It seems as if we Britons were ordained,   360
By way of wholesome curb upon our pride,
To fear each other, fearing none beside.
The cause perhaps inquiry may descry,
Self-searching with an introverted eye,
Concealed within an unsuspected part,
The vainest corner of our own vain heart :
For ever aiming at the World's esteem,
Our self-importance ruins its own scheme ;
In other eyes our talents rarely shown,
Become at length so splendid in our own,   370
We dare not risk them into public view,
Lest they miscarry of what seems their due.
True modesty is a discerning grace,
And only blushes in the proper place ;
But counterfeit is blind, and skulks through fear,
Where 'tis a shame to be ashamed to appear :
Humility the parent of the first,
The last by Vanity produced and nursed.
The circle formed, we sit in silent state,
Like figures drawn upon a dial-plate ;   380
" Yes, Ma'am," and " No, Ma'am," uttered softly, show
Every five minutes how the minutes go ;
Each individual, suffering a constraint
Poetry may, but colours cannot paint,

As if in close committee on the sky,
Reports it hot or cold, or wet or dry;
And finds a changing clime a happy source
Of wise reflection, and well-timed discourse.
We next inquire, but softly and by stealth,
Like conservators of the public health,   390
Of epidemic throats, if such there are,
And coughs, and rheums, and phthisic, and catarrh.
That theme exhausted, a wide chasm ensues,
Filled up at last with interesting news,
Who danced with whom, and who are like to wed,
And who is hanged, and who is brought to bed;
But fear to call a more important cause,
As if 'twere treason against English laws.
The visit paid, with ecstasy we come,
As from a seven years' transportation, home,   400
And there resume an unembarrassed brow,
Recovering what we lost we know not how,
The faculties that seemed reduced to nought,
Expression and the privilege of thought.
   The reeking, roaring hero of the chase,
I give him over as a desperate case.
Physicians write in hopes to work a cure,
Never, if honest ones, when death is sure;
And though the fox he follows may be tamed,
A mere fox-follower never is reclaimed.   410
Some farrier should prescribe his proper course,
Whose only fit companion is his horse,
Or if, deserving of a better doom,
The noble beast judge otherwise, his groom.
Yet even the rogue that serves him, though he stand,
To take his honour's orders, cap in hand,
Prefers his fellow-grooms, with much good sense;
Their skill a truth, his master's a pretence.
If neither horse nor groom affect the squire,
Where can at last his jockeyship retire?   420
Oh to the club, the scene of savage joys,
The school of coarse good fellowship and noise;
There, in the sweet society of those
Whose friendship from his boyish years he chose,
Let him improve his talent if he can,
Till none but beasts acknowledge him a man.
   Man's heart had been impenetrably sealed,
Like theirs that cleave the flood or graze the field,
Had not his Maker's all-bestowing hand
Given him a soul, and bade him understand;   430
The reasoning power vouchsafed of course inferred
The power to clothe that reason with his word;
For all is perfect that God works on earth,
And He that gives conception aids the birth.
If this be plain, 'tis plainly understood,
What uses of his boon the Giver would.

The Mind, despatched upon her busy toil,
Should range where Providence has blessed the soil;
Visiting every flower with labour meet,
And gathering all her treasures sweet by sweet,   440
She should imbue the tongue with what she sips,
And shed the balmy blessing on the lips,
That good diffused may more abundant grow,
And speech may praise the power that bids it flow.
Will the sweet warbler of the livelong night,
That fills the listening lover with delight,
Forget his harmony, with rapture heard,
To learn the twittering of a meaner bird?
Or make the parrot's mimicry his choice,
That odious libel on a human voice?   450
No—Nature, unsophisticate by man,
Starts not aside from her Creator's plan;
The melody that was at first designed
To cheer the rude forefathers of mankind,
Is note for note delivered in our ears,
In the last scene of her six thousand years.
Yet Fashion, leader of a chattering train,
Whom man for his own hurt permits to reign,
Who shifts and changes all things but his shape,
And would degrade her votary to an ape,   460
The fruitful parent of abuse and wrong,
Holds a usurped dominion o'er his tongue;
There sits and prompts him with his own disgrace,
Prescribes the theme, the tone, and the grimace,
And, when accomplished in her wayward school,
Calls gentleman whom she has made a fool.
'Tis an unalterable fixed decree,
That none could frame or ratify but she,
That Heaven and Hell, and righteousness and sin,
Snares in his path, and foes that lurk within,   470
God and His attributes (a field of day
Where 'tis an angel's happiness to stray),
Fruits of his love and wonders of his might,
Be never named in ears esteemed polite.
That he who dares, when she forbids, be grave,
Shall stand proscribed a madman or a knave,
A close designer not to be believed,
Or, if excused that charge, at least deceived.
Oh folly worthy of the nurse's lap,
Give it the breast, or stop its mouth with pap!   480
Is it incredible, or can it seem
A dream to any, except those that dream,
That man should love his Maker, and *that* fire,
Warming his heart, should at his lips transpire?
Know then, and modestly let fall your eyes,
And veil your daring crest that braves the skies,
That air of insolence affronts your God,
You need his pardon, and provoke his rod:

Now, in a posture that becomes you more
Than that heroic strut assumed before,   490
Know, your arrears with every hour accrue
For mercy shown, while wrath is justly due.
The time is short, and there are souls on earth,
Though future pain may serve for present mirth,
Acquainted with the woes that fear or shame,
By Fashion taught, forbade them once to name,
And, having felt the pangs you deem a jest,
Have proved them truths too big to be expressed.
Go seek on Revelation's hallowed ground,
Sure to succeed, the remedy they found ;   500
Touched by that power that you have dared to mock,
That makes seas stable, and dissolves the rock,
Your heart shall yield a life-renewing stream,
That fools, as you have done, shall call a dream.
　　It happened on a solemn eventide,
Soon after He that was our surety died,
Two bosom friends, each pensively inclined,
The scene of all those sorrows left behind,
Sought their own village, busied as they went
In musings worthy of the great event: 510
They spake of him they loved, of him whose life,
Though blameless, had incurred perpetual strife,
Whose deeds had left, in spite of hostile arts,
A deep memorial graven on their hearts.
The recollection, like a vein of ore,
The farther traced, enriched them still the more ;
They thought him, and they justly thought him, one
Sent to do more than he appeared to have done,
To exalt a people, and to place them high
Above all else, and wondered he should die.   520
Ere yet they brought their journey to an end,
A stranger joined them, courteous as a friend,
And asked them with a kind engaging air
What their affliction was, and begged a share.
Informed, he gathered up the broken thread,
And, truth and wisdom gracing all he said,
Explained, illustrated, and searched so well
The tender theme, on which they chose to dwell,
That reaching home, " The night," they said, " is near,
We must not now be parted, sojourn here."   530
The new acquaintance soon became a guest,
And, made so welcome at their simple feast,
He blessed the bread, but vanished at the word,
And left them both exclaiming, " 'Twas the Lord !
Did not our hearts feel all he deigned to say,
Did they not burn within us by the way ? "
　　Now theirs was converse such as it behoves
Man to maintain, and such as God approves :
Their views indeed were indistinct and dim,
But yet successful, being aimed at him.   540

Christ and his character their only scope,
Their object, and their subject, and their hope,
They felt what it became them much to feel,
And wanting him to loose the sacred seal,
Found him as prompt, as their desire was true,
To spread the newborn glories in their view.
   Well—what are ages and the lapse of time
Matched against truths as lasting as sublime?
Can length of years on God himself exact?
Or make that fiction, which was once a fact?   550
No—marble and recording brass decay,
And like the graver's memory pass away;
The works of man inherit, as is just,
Their author's frailty, and return to dust:
But truth divine for ever stands secure,
Its head as guarded as its base is sure;
Fixed in the rolling flood of endless years
The pillar of the eternal plan appears,
The raving storm and dashing wave defies,
Built by that Architect who built the skies.   560
Hearts may be found, that harbour at this hour
That love of Christ in all its quickening power,
And lips unstained by folly or by strife,
Whose wisdom, drawn from the deep well of life,
Tastes of its healthful origin, and flows
A Jordan for the ablution of our woes.
O days of heaven, and nights of equal praise,
Serene and peaceful as those heavenly days,
When souls drawn upwards, in communion sweet,
Enjoy the stillness of some close retreat,   570
Discourse, as if released and safe at home,
Of dangers past, and wonders yet to come,
And spread the sacred treasures of the breast
Upon the lap of covenanted rest.
   "What, always dreaming over heavenly things,
Like angel-heads in stone with pigeon-wings?
Canting and whining out all day the word,
And half the night? fanatic and absurd!
Mine be the friend less frequent in his prayers,
Who makes no bustle with his soul's affairs,   580
Whose wit can brighten up a wintry day,
And chase the splenetic dull hours away;
Content on earth in earthly things to shine,
Who waits for heaven ere he becomes divine,
Leaves saints to enjoy those altitudes they teach,
And plucks the fruit placed more within his reach."
   Well spoken, advocate of sin and shame,
Known by thy bleating, Ignorance thy name.
Is sparkling wit the world's exclusive right?
The fixed fee-simple of the vain and light?   590
Can hopes of heaven, bright prospects of an hour
That comes to waft us out of sorrow's power,

Obscure or quench a faculty, that finds
Its happiest soil in the serenest minds?
Religion curbs indeed its wanton play,
And brings the trifler under rigorous sway,
But gives it usefulness unknown before,
And purifying, makes it shine the more.
A Christian's wit is inoffensive light,
A beam that aids but never grieves the sight;   600
Vigorous in age as in the flush of youth,
'Tis always active on the side of truth;
Temperance and peace insure its healthful state,
And make it brightest at its latest date.
Oh I have seen (nor hope perhaps in vain,
Ere life go down, to see such sights again)
A veteran warrior in the Christian field,
Who never saw the sword he could not wield;
Grave without dulness, learned without pride,
Exact, yet not precise, though meek, keen-eyed;   610
A man that would have foiled at their own play
A dozen would-be's of the modern day;
Who, when occasion justified its use,
Had wit as bright as ready to produce,
Could fetch from records of an earlier age,
Or from philosophy's enlightened page,
His rich materials, and regale your ear
With strains it was a privilege to hear!
Yet above all his luxury supreme,
And his chief glory, was the gospel theme;   620
There he was copious as old Greece or Rome,
His happy eloquence seemed there at home,
Ambitious not to shine or to excel,
But to treat justly what he loved so well.
   It moves me more perhaps than folly ought,
When some green heads, as void of wit as thought,
Suppose themselves monopolists of sense,
And wiser men's ability pretence.
Though time will wear us, and we must grow old,
Such men are not forgot as soon as cold,   630
Their fragrant memory will outlast their tomb,
Embalmed for ever in its own perfume.
And to say truth, though in its early prime,
And when unstained with any grosser crime,
Youth has a sprightliness and fire to boast,
That in the valley of decline are lost,
And Virtue with peculiar charms appears,
Crowned with the garland of life's blooming years;
Yet Age, by long experience well informed,
Well read, well tempered, with religion warmed,   640
That fire abated, which impels rash youth,
Proud of his speed, to overshoot the truth,
As time improves the grape's authentic juice,
Mellows and makes the speech more fit for use,

And claims a reverence in its shortening day,
That 'tis an honour and a joy to pay.
The fruits of age, less fair, are yet more sound
Than those a brighter season pours around ;
And, like the stores autumnal suns mature,
Through wintry rigours unimpaired endure.   650
  What is fanatic frenzy, scorned so much,
And dreaded more than a contagious touch ?
I grant it dangerous, and approve your fear,
That fire is catching if you draw too near ;
But sage observers oft mistake the flame,
And give true piety that odious name.
To tremble (as the creature of an hour
Ought at the view of an Almighty power)
Before His presence, at whose awful throne
All tremble in all worlds, except our own ;   660
To supplicate his mercy, love his ways,
And prize them above pleasure, wealth, or praise,
Though common sense, allowed a casting voice,
And free from bias, must approve the choice,
Convicts a man fanatic in the extreme,
And wild as madness in the world's esteem.
But that disease, when soberly defined,
Is the false fire of an o'erheated mind ;
It views the truth with a distorted eye,
And either warps or lays it useless by ;   670
'Tis narrow, selfish, arrogant, and draws
Its sordid nourishment from man's applause ;
And while at heart sin unrelinquished lies,
Presumes itself chief favourite of the skies.
'Tis such a light as putrefaction breeds
In fly-blown flesh, whereon the maggot feeds,
Shines in the dark, but, ushered into day,
The stench remains, the lustre dies away.
  True bliss, if man may reach it, is composed
Of hearts in union mutually disclosed ;   680
And, farewell else all hope of pure delight,
Those hearts should be reclaimed, renewed, upright.
Bad men, profaning friendship's hallowed name,
Form, in its stead, a covenant of shame,
A dark confederacy against the laws
Of virtue, and religion's glorious cause :
They build each other up with dreadful skill,
As bastions set point blank against God's will ;
Enlarge and fortify the dread redoubt,
Deeply resolved to shut a Saviour out :   690
Call legions up from hell to back the deed ;
And, curst with conquest, finally succeed.
But souls that carry on a blest exchange
Of joys they meet with in their heavenly range,
And with a fearless confidence make known
The sorrows sympathy esteems its own,

Daily derive increasing light and force
From such communion in their pleasant course,
Feel less the journey's roughness and its length,
Meet their opposers with united strength,   700
And, one in heart, in interest, and design,
Gird up each other to the race divine.
   But Conversation, choose what theme we may,
And chiefly when religion leads the way,
Should flow, like waters after summer showers,
Not as if raised by mere mechanic powers.
The Christian in whose soul, though now distressed,
Lives the dear thought of joys he once possessed,
When all his glowing language issued forth
With God's deep stamp upon its current worth,   710
Will speak without disguise, and must impart,
Sad as it is, his undissembling heart,
Abhors constraint, and dares not feign a zeal,
Or seem to boast a fire he does not feel.
The song of Sion is a tasteless thing,
Unless, when rising on a joyful wing,
The soul can mix with the celestial bands,
And give the strain the compass it demands.
   Strange tidings these to tell a world, who treat
All but their own experience as deceit !   720
Will they believe, though credulous enough
To swallow much upon much weaker proof,
That there are blest inhabitants of earth,
Partakers of a new ethereal birth,
Their hopes, desires, and purposes estranged
From things terrestrial, and divinely changed,
Their very language of a kind that speaks
The soul's sure interest in the good she seeks,
Who deal with Scripture, its importance felt,
As Tully with philosophy once dealt,   730
And in the silent watches of the night,
And through the scenes of toil-renewing light,
The social walk, or solitary ride,
Keep still the dear companion at their side ?
No—shame upon a self-disgracing age,
God's work may serve an ape upon a stage
With such a jest as filled with hellish glee
Certain invisibles as shrewd as he ;
But veneration or respect finds none,
Save from the subjects of that work alone.   740
The world grown old her deep discernment shows,
Claps spectacles on her sagacious nose,
Peruses closely the true Christian's face,
And finds it a mere mask of sly grimace ;
Usurps God's office, lays his bosom bare,
And finds hypocrisy close-lurking there ;
And, serving God herself through mere constraint,
Concludes his unfeigned love of him a feint.

And yet, God knows, look human nature through,
(And in due time the world shall know it too)   750
That since the flowers of Eden felt the blast,
That after man's defection laid all waste,
Sincerity towards the heart-searching God
Has made the new-born creature her abode,
Nor shall be found in unregenerate souls,
Till the last fire burn all between the poles.
Sincerity !   Why 'tis his only pride;
Weak and imperfect in all grace beside,
He knows that God demands his heart entire,
And gives him all his just demands require.   760
Without it, his pretensions were as vain,
As, having it, he deems the world's disdain;
That great defect would cost him not alone
Man's favourable judgment, but his own;
His birthright shaken, and no longer clear,
Than while his conduct proves his heart sincere.
Retort the charge, and let the world be told
She boasts a confidence she does not hold ;
That, conscious of her crimes, she feels instead
A cold misgiving, and a killing dread :   770
That while in health the ground of her support
Is madly to forget that life is short ;
That sick she trembles, knowing she must die,
Her hope presumption, and her faith a lie ;
That while she dotes, and dreams that she believes,
She mocks her Maker, and herself deceives,
Her utmost reach, historical assent,
The docrines warped to what they never meant;
That truth itself is in her head as dull
And useless as a candle in a skull,   780
And all her love of God a groundless claim,
A trick upon the canvas, painted flame.
Tell her again, the sneer upon her face,
And all her censures of the work of grace,
Are insincere, meant only to conceal
A dread she would not, yet is forced to feel ;
That in her heart the Christian she reveres,
And while she seems to scorn him, only fears.
    A poet does not work by square or line,
As smiths and joiners perfect a design ;   790
At least we moderns, our attention less,
Beyond the example of our sires digress,
And claim a right to scamper and run wide,
Wherever chance, caprice, or fancy guide.
The world and I fortuitously met ;
I owed a trifle and have paid the debt ;
She did me wrong, I recompensed the deed,
And, having struck the balance, now proceed.
Perhaps however as some years have passed
Since she and I conversed together last,   800

And I have lived recluse in rural shades,
Which seldom a distinct report pervades ;
Great changes and new manners have occurred,
And blest reforms, that I have never heard,
And she may now be as discreet and wise,
As once absurd in all discerning eyes.
Sobriety perhaps may now be found,
Where once intoxication pressed the ground ;
The subtle and injurious may be just,
And he grown chaste that was the slave of lust ;   810
Arts once esteemed may be with shame dismissed,
Charity may relax the miser's fist,
The gamester may have cast his cards away,
Forgot to curse, and only kneel to pray.
It has indeed been told me (with what weight,
How credibly, 'tis hard for me to state)
That fables old, that seemed for ever mute,
Revived are hastening into fresh repute,
And gods and goddesses discarded long
Like useless lumber, or a stroller's song,   820
Are bringing into vogue their heathen train,
And Jupiter bids fair to rule again ;
That certain feasts are instituted now,
Where Venus hears the lover's tender vow ;
That all Olympus through the country roves,
To consecrate our few remaining groves,
And echo learns politely to repeat
The praise of names for ages obsolete ;
That having proved the weakness, it should seem,
Of Revelation's ineffectual beam,   830
To bring the passions under sober sway,
And give the moral springs their proper play,
They mean to try what may at last be done
By stout substantial gods of wood and stone,
And whether Roman rites may not produce
The virtues of old Rome for English use.
May much success attend the pious plan,
May Mercury once more embellish man,
Grace him again with long forgotten arts,
Reclaim his taste, and brighten up his parts,   840
Make him athletic as in days of old,
Learned at the bar, in the palæstra bold,
Divest the rougher sex of female airs,
And teach the softer not to copy theirs :
The change shall please, nor shall it matter aught
Who works the wonder, if it be but wrought.
'Tis time, however, if the case stand thus,
For us plain folks, and all who side with us,
To build our altar, confident and bold,
And say as stern Elijah said of old,   850
" The strife now stands upon a fair award,
If Israel's Lord be God, then serve the Lord :

C   L

If He be silent, faith is all a whim ;
Then Baal is the God, and worship him."
   Digression is so much in modern use,
Thought is so rare, and fancy so profuse,
Some never seem so wide of their intent,
As when returning to the theme they meant ;
As mendicants, whose business is to roam,
Make every parish but their own their home.   860
Though such continual zigzags in a book,
Such drunken reelings, have an awkward look,
And I had rather creep to what is true
Than rove and stagger with no mark in view ;
Yet to consult a little seemed no crime,
The freakish humour of the present time :
But now, to gather up what seems dispersed,
And touch the subject I designed at first,
May prove, though much beside the rules of art,
Best for the public, and my wisest part.   870
And first, let no man charge me, that I mean
To clothe in sables every social scene,
And give good company a face severe,
As if they met around a father's bier ;
For tell some men that pleasure all their bent,
And laughter all their work, is life misspent,
Their wisdom bursts into this sage reply,
" Then mirth is sin, and we should always cry."
To find the medium asks some share of wit,
And therefore 'tis a mark fools never hit.   880
But though life's valley be a vale of tears,
A brighter scene beyond that vale appears,
Whose glory, with a light that never fades,
Shoots between scattered rocks and opening shades,
And, while it shows the land the soul desires,
The language of the land she seeks inspires.
Thus touched, the tongue receives a sacred cure
Of all that was absurd, profane, impure ;
Held within modest bounds, the tide of speech
Pursues the course that truth and nature teach,   890
No longer labours merely to produce
The pomp of sound, or tinkle without use :
Where'er it winds, the salutary stream,
Sprightly and fresh, enriches every theme,
While all the happy man possessed before,
The gift of nature, or the classic store,
Is made subservient to the grand design
For which Heaven formed the faculty divine.
So should an idiot, while at large he strays,
Find the sweet lyre on which an artist plays,   900
With rash and awkward force the chords he shakes,
And grins with wonder at the jar he makes ;
But let the wise and well-instructed hand
Once take the shell beneath its just command,

In gentle sounds it seems as it complained
Of the rude injuries it late sustained,
Till tuned at length to some immortal song,
It sounds Jehovah's name, and pours his praise along.

RETIREMENT.

. . . . . studiis florens ignobilis oti.
VIRG. *Georg.* lib. iv.

HACKNEYED in business, wearied at that oar
Which thousands, once fast chained to, quit no more,
But which, when life at ebb runs weak and low,
All wish, or seem to wish, they could forego ;
The statesman, lawyer, merchant, man of trade,
Pants for the refuge of some rural shade,
Where, all his long anxieties forgot
Amid the charms of a sequestered spot,
Or recollected only to gild o'er
And add a smile to what was sweet before,   10
He may possess the joys he thinks he sees,
Lay his old age upon the lap of Ease,
Improve the remnant of his wasted span,
And, having lived a trifler, die a man.
Thus Conscience pleads her cause within the breast,
Though long rebelled against, not yet suppressed,
And calls a creature formed for God alone,
For heaven's high purposes, and not his own,
Calls him away from selfish ends and aims,
From what debilitates and what inflames,   20
From cities humming with a restless crowd,
Sordid as active, ignorant as loud,
Whose highest praise is that they live in vain,
The dupes of pleasure, or the slaves of gain,
Where works of man are clustered close around,
And works of God are hardly to be found,
To regions where, in spite of sin and woe,
Traces of Eden are still seen below,
Where mountain, river, forest, field and grove,
Remind him of his Maker's power and love.   30
'Tis well if, looked for at so late a day,
In the last scene of such a senseless play,
True wisdom will attend his feeble call,
And grace his action ere the curtain fall.
Souls that have long despised their heavenly birth,
Their wishes all impregnated with Earth,
For threescore years employed with ceaseless care
In catching smoke and feeding upon air,
Conversant only with the ways of men,
Rarely redeem the short remaining ten,   40

Inveterate habits choke the unfruitful heart,
Their fibres penetrate its tenderest part,
And, draining its nutritious powers to feed
Their noxious growth, starve every better seed.
    Happy, if full of days—but happier far,
If, ere we yet discern life's evening star,
Sick of the service of a world that feeds
Its patient drudges with dry chaff and weeds,
We can escape from Custom's idiot sway,
To serve the Sovereign we were born to obey.   50
Then sweet to muse upon his skill displayed
(Infinite skill) in all that He has made !
To trace in Nature's most minute design
The signature and stamp of power divine,
Contrivance intricate, expressed with ease,
Where unassisted sight no beauty sees,
The shapely limb and lubricated joint,
Within the small dimensions of a point,
Muscle and nerve miraculously spun,
His mighty work who speaks and it is done,   60
The Invisible in things scarce seen revealed,
To whom an atom is an ample field ;
To wonder at a thousand insect forms,
These hatched, and those resuscitated worms,
New life ordained and brighter scenes to share,
Once prone on earth, now buoyant upon air,
Whose shape would make them, had they bulk and size,
More hideous foes than fancy can devise ;
With helmet heads, and dragon scales adorned,
The mighty myriads, now securely scorned,   70
Would mock the majesty of man's high birth,
Despise his bulwarks, and unpeople earth :
Then with a glance of fancy to survey,
Far as the faculty can stretch away,
Ten thousand rivers poured at his command
From urns, that never fail, through every land ;
These like a deluge with impetuous force,
Those winding modestly a silent course ;
The cloud-surmounting Alps, the fruitful vales ;
Seas, on which every nation spreads her sails ;   80
The sun, a world whence other worlds drink light,
The crescent moon, the diadem of night ;
Stars countless, each in his appointed place,
Fast anchored in the deep abyss of space—
At such a sight to catch the poet's flame,
And with a rapture like his own exclaim,
" These are thy glorious works, thou Source of good,
How dimly seen, how faintly understood !
Thine, and upheld by thy paternal care,
This universal frame, thus wondrous fair ;   90
Thy power divine, and bounty beyond thought,
Adored and praised in all that thou hast wrought.

Absorbed in that immensity I see,
I shrink abased, and yet aspire to thee ;
Instruct me, guide me to that heavenly day
Thy words, more clearly than thy works, display,
That, while thy truths my grosser thoughts refine,
I may resemble thee, and call thee mine."
   O blest proficiency ! surpassing all
That men erroneously their glory call,   100
The recompense that arts or arms can yield,
The bar, the senate, or the tented field.
Compared with this sublimest life below,
Ye kings and rulers, what have courts to show ?
Thus studied, used and consecrated thus,
On earth what is, seems formed indeed for us :
Not as the plaything of a froward child,
Fretful unless diverted and beguiled,
Much less to feed and fan the fatal fires
Of pride, ambition, or impure desires,   110
But as a scale, by which the soul ascends
From mighty means to more important ends,
Securely, though by steps but rarely trod,
Mounts from inferior beings up to God,
And sees, by no fallacious light or dim,
Earth made for man, and man himself for Him.
   Not that I mean to approve, or would enforce,
A superstitious and monastic course :
Truth is not local, God alike pervades
And fills the world of traffic and the shades,   120
And may be feared amid the busiest scenes,
Or scorned where business never intervenes.
But 'tis not easy with a mind like ours,
Conscious of weakness in its noblest powers,
And in a world where, other ills apart,
The roving eye misleads the careless heart,
To limit Thought, by nature prone to stray
Wherever freakish Fancy points the way ;
To bid the pleadings of Self-love be still,
Resign our own, and seek our Maker's will ;   130
To spread the page of Scripture, and compare
Our conduct with the laws engraven there ;
To measure all that passes in the breast,
Faithfully, fairly, by that sacred test ;
To dive into the secret deeps within,
To spare no passion and no favourite sin,
And search the themes, important above all,
Ourselves, and our recovery from our fall.
But leisure, silence, and a mind released
From anxious thoughts how wealth may be increased,   140
How to secure, in some propitious hour,
The point of interest or the post of power,
A soul serene, and equally retired
From objects too much dreaded or desired,

Safe from the clamours of perverse dispute,
At least are friendly to the great pursuit.
   Opening the map of God's extensive plan,
We find a little isle, this life of man ;
Eternity's unknown expanse appears
Circling around and limiting his years.   150
The busy race examine and explore
Each creek and cavern of the dangerous shore,
With care collect what in their eyes excels,
Some shining pebbles, and some weeds and shells ;
Thus laden, dream that they are rich and great,
And happiest he that groans beneath his weight :
The waves o'ertake them in their serious play,
And every hour sweeps multitudes away ;
They shriek and sink, survivors start and weep,
Pursue their sport, and follow to the deep.   160
A few forsake the throng ; with lifted eyes
Ask wealth of Heaven, and gain a real prize,
Truth, wisdom, grace, and peace like that above,
Sealed with His signet whom they serve and love ;
Scorned by the rest, with patient hope they wait
A kind release from their imperfect state,
And unregretted are soon snatched away
From scenes of sorrow into glorious day.
   Nor these alone prefer a life recluse,
Who seek retirement for its proper use ;   170
The love of change that lives in every breast,
Genius, and temper, and desire of rest,
Discordant motives in one centre meet,
And each inclines its votary to retreat.
Some minds by nature are averse to noise,
And hate the tumult half the world enjoys,
The lure of avarice, or the pompous prize,
That courts display before ambitious eyes ;
The fruits that hang on pleasure's flowery stem,
Whate'er enchants them, are no snares to them.   180
To them the deep recess of dusky groves,
Or forest where the deer securely roves,
The fall of waters and the song of birds,
And hills that echo to the distant herds,
Are luxuries excelling all the glare
The world can boast, and her chief favourites share.
With eager step, and carelessly arrayed,
For such a cause the poet seeks the shade :
From all he sees he catches new delight,
Pleased fancy claps her pinions at the sight ;   190
The rising or the setting orb of day,
The clouds that flit, or slowly float away,
Nature in all the various shapes she wears,
Frowning in storms, or breathing gentle airs,
The snowy robe her wintry state assumes,
Her summer heats, her fruits, and her perfumes,

All, all alike, transport the glowing bard,
Success in rhyme his glory and reward.
O Nature ! whose Elysian scenes disclose
His bright perfections, at whose word they rose,   200
Next to that Power, who formed thee and sustains,
Be thou the great inspirer of my strains,
Still, as I touch the lyre, do thou expand
Thy genuine charms, and guide an artless hand,
That I may catch a fire but rarely known,
Give useful light, though I should miss renown,
And, poring on thy page, whose every line
Bears proof of an intelligence divine,
May feel a heart enriched by what it pays,
That builds its glory on its Maker's praise.   210
Woe to the man whose wit disclaims its use,
Glittering in vain, or only to seduce,
Who studies nature with a wanton eye,
Admires the work, but slips the lesson by ;
His hours of leisure and recess employs
In drawing pictures of forbidden joys,
Retires to blazon his own worthless name,
Or shoot the careless with a surer aim.
     The lover too shuns business and alarms,
Tender idolater of absent charms.   220
Saints offer nothing in their warmest prayers
That he devotes not with a zeal like theirs ;
'Tis consecration of his heart, soul, time,
And every thought that wanders is a crime.
In sighs he worships his supremely fair,
And weeps a sad libation in despair,
Adores a creature, and, devout in vain,
Wins in return an answer of disdain.
As woodbine weds the plants within her reach,
Rough elm, or smooth-grained ash, or glossy beech,   230
In spiral rings ascends the trunk, and lays
Her golden tassels on the leafy sprays,
But does a mischief while she lends a grace,
Straitening its growth by such a strict embrace ;
So Love, that clings around the noblest minds,
Forbids the advancement of the soul he binds ;
The suitor's air indeed he soon improves,
And forms it to the taste of her he loves,
Teaches his eyes a language, and no less
Refines his speech, and fashions his address ;   240
But farewell promises of happier fruits,
Manly designs, and learning's grave pursuits ;
Girt with a chain he cannot wish to break,
His only bliss is sorrow for her sake ;
Who will may pant for glory and excel,
Her smile his aim, all higher aims farewell !
Thyrsis, Alexis, or whatever name
May least offend against so pure a flame,

Though sage advice of friends the most sincere
Sound harshly in so delicate an ear,   250
And lovers, of all creatures, tame or wild,
Can least brook management, however mild,
Yet let a poet (poetry disarms
The fiercest animals with magic charms)
Risk an intrusion on thy pensive mood,
And woo and win thee to thy proper good.
Pastoral images and still retreats,
Umbrageous walks and solitary seats,
Sweet birds in concert with harmonious streams,
Soft airs, nocturnal vigils, and day dreams,   260
Are all enchantments in a case like thine,
Conspire against thy peace with one design,
Soothe thee to make thee but a surer prey,
And feed the fire that wastes thy powers away.
Up—God has formed thee with a wiser view,
Not to be led in chains, but to subdue ;
Calls thee to cope with enemies, and first
Points out a conflict with thyself, the worst.
Woman indeed, a gift he would bestow
When he designed a paradise below,   270
The richest earthly boon his hands afford,
Deserves to be beloved, but not adored.
Post away swiftly to more active scenes,
Collect the scattered truths that study gleans,
Mix with the world, but with its wiser part,
No longer give an image all thine heart ;
Its empire is not hers, nor is it thine,
'Tis God's just claim, prerogative divine.
    Virtuous and faithful HEBERDEN, whose skill
Attempts no task it cannot well fulfil,   280
Gives melancholy up to nature's care,
And sends the patient into purer air.
Look where he comes—in this embowered alcove,
Stand close concealed, and see a statue move :
Lips busy, and eyes fixed, foot falling slow,
Arms hanging idly down, hands clasped below,
Interpret to the marking eye distress,
Such as its symptoms can alone express.
That tongue is silent now ; that silent tongue
Could argue once, could jest or join the song,   290
Could give advice, could censure or commend,
Or charm the sorrows of a drooping friend.
Renounced alike its office and its sport,
Its brisker and its graver strains fall short ;
Both fail beneath a fever's secret sway,
And like a summer brook are past away.
This is a sight for Pity to peruse,
Till she resemble faintly what she views,
Till Sympathy contract a kindred pain,
Pierced with the woes that she laments in vain.   300

This, of all maladies that man infest,
Claims most compassion, and receives the least :
Job felt it, when he groaned beneath the rod
And the barbed arrows of a frowning God ;
And such emollients as his friends could spare,
Friends such as his for modern Jobs prepare.
Blest, rather curst, with hearts that never feel,
Kept snug in caskets of close hammered steel,
With mouths made only to grin wide and eat,
And minds that deem derided pain a treat ;   310
With limbs of British oak, and nerves of wire,
And wit, that puppet-prompters might inspire,
Their sovereign nostrum is a clumsy joke
On pangs enforced with God's severest stroke.
But with a soul, that ever felt the sting
Of sorrow, sorrow is a sacred thing :
Not to molest, or irritate, or raise
A laugh at its expense, is slender praise ;
He, that has not usurped the name of man,
Does all, and deems too little all, he can   320
To assuage the throbbings of the festered part,
And stanch the bleedings of a broken heart.
'Tis not, as heads that never ache suppose,
Forgery of fancy, and a dream of woes ;
Man is a harp whose chords elude the sight,
Each yielding harmony, disposed aright ;
The screws reversed (a task which if He please
God in a moment executes with ease)
Ten thousand thousand strings at once go loose,
Lost, till He tune them, all their power and use.   330
Then neither heathy wilds, nor scenes as fair
As ever recompensed the peasant's care,
Nor soft declivities with tufted hills,
Nor view of waters turning busy mills,
Parks in which Art preceptress Nature weds,
Nor gardens interspersed with flowery beds,
Nor gales, that catch the scent of blooming groves,
And waft it to the mourner as he roves,
Can call up life into his faded eye
That passes all he sees unheeded by :   340
No wounds like those a wounded spirit feels ;
No cure for such, till God, who makes them, heals.
And thou, sad sufferer under nameless ill,
That yields not to the touch of human skill,
Improve the kind occasion, understand
A Father's frown, and kiss his chastening hand.
To thee the day-spring, and the blaze of noon,
The purple evening and resplendent moon,
The stars, that, sprinkled o'er the vault of night,
Seem drops descending in a shower of light,   350
Shine not, or undesired and hated shine,
Seen through the medium of a cloud like thine :

Yet seek Him, in his favour life is found ;
All bliss beside, a shadow or a sound :
Then Heaven, eclipsed so long, and this dull Earth,
Shall seem to start into a second birth ;
Nature, assuming a more lovely face,
Borrowing a beauty from the works of grace,
Shall be despised and overlooked no more,
Shall fill thee with delights unfelt before,   360
Impart to things inanimate a voice,
And bid her mountains and her hills rejoice ;
The sound shall run along the winding vales,
And thou enjoy an Eden ere it fails.
  " Ye groves," the statesman at his desk exclaims,
Sick of a thousand disappointed aims,
" My patrimonial treasure and my pride,
Beneath your shades your grey possessor hide,
Receive me languishing for that repose
The servant of the public never knows.   370
Ye saw me once (ah those regretted days,
When boyish innocence was all my praise !)
Hour after hour delightfully allot
To studies then familiar, since forgot,
And cultivate a taste for ancient song,
Catching its ardour as I mused along ;
Nor seldom, as propitious heaven might send,
What once I valued and could boast, a friend,
Were witnesses how cordially I pressed
His undissembling virtue to my breast ;   380
Receive me now, not uncorrupt as then,
Nor guiltless of corrupting other men,
But versed in arts, that, while they seem to stay
A fallen empire, hasten its decay.
To the fair haven of my native home,
The wreck of what I was, fatigued I come ;
For once I can approve the patriot's voice,
And make the course he recommends my choice :
We meet at last in one sincere desire,
His wish and mine both prompt me to retire."   390
'Tis done—he steps into the welcome chaise,
Lolls at his ease behind four handsome bays,
That whirl away from business and debate
The disencumbered Atlas of the state.
Ask not the boy, who, when the breeze of morn
First shakes the glittering drops from every thorn,
Unfolds his flock, then under bank or bush
Sits linking cherry-stones, or platting rush,
How fair is freedom?—he was always free :
To carve his rustic name upon a tree,   400
To snare the mole, or with ill-fashioned hook
To draw the incautious minnow from the brook,
Are life's prime pleasures in his simple view,
His flock the chief concern he ever knew ;

She shines but little in his heedless eyes,
The good we never miss we rarely prize :
But ask the noble drudge in state affairs,
Escaped from office and its constant cares,
What charms he sees in freedom's smile expressed,
In freedom lost so long, now repossessed ;   410
The tongue, whose strains were cogent as commands,
Revered at home, and felt in foreign lands,
Shall own itself a stammerer in that cause,
Or plead its silence as its best applause.
He knows indeed that, whether dressed or rude,
Wild without art, or artfully subdued,
Nature in every form inspires delight,
But never marked her with so just a sight.
Her hedge-row shrubs, a variegated store,
With woodbine and wild roses mantled o'er,   420
Green balks and furrowed lands, the stream that spreads
Its cooling vapour o'er the dewy meads,
Downs, that almost escape the inquiring eye,
That melt and fade into the distant sky,
Beauties he lately slighted as he passed,
Seem all created since he travelled last.
Master of all the enjoyments he designed,
No rough annoyance rankling in his mind,
What early philosophic hours he keeps,
How regular his meals, how sound he sleeps !   430
Not sounder he that on the mainmast head,
While morning kindles with a windy red,
Begins a long look-out for distant land,
Nor quits till evening-watch his giddy stand,
Then swift descending with a seaman's haste,
Slips to his hammock, and forgets the blast.
He chooses company, but not the squire's,
Whose wit is rudeness, whose good breeding tires ;
Nor yet the parson's, who would gladly come,
Obsequious when abroad, though proud at home ;   440
Nor can he much affect the neighbouring peer,
Whose toe of emulation treads too near;
But wisely seeks a more convenient friend,
With whom, dismissing forms, he may unbend :
A man whom marks of condescending grace
Teach, while they flatter him, his proper place :
Who comes when called, and at a word withdraws,
Speaks with reserve, and listens with applause ;
Some plain mechanic, who, without pretence
To birth or wit, nor gives nor takes offence,   450
On whom he rests well pleased his weary powers,
And talks and laughs away his vacant hours.
  The tide of life, swift always in its course,
May run in cities with a brisker force,
But nowhere with a current so serene,
Or half so clear, as in the rural scene.

Yet how fallacious is all earthly bliss,
What obvious truths the wisest heads may miss ;
Some pleasures live a month, and some a year,
But short the date of all we gather here ;   460
No happiness is felt, except the true,
That does not charm the more for being new.
This observation, as it chanced, not made,
Or, if the thought occurred, not duly weighed,
He sighs—for, after all, by slow degrees
The spot he loved has lost the power to please ;
To cross his ambling pony day by day
Seems at the best but dreaming life away ;
The prospect, such as might enchant despair,
He views it not, or sees no beauty there ;   470
With aching heart, and discontented looks,
Returns at noon to billiards or to books,
But feels, while grasping at his faded joys,
A secret thirst of his renounced employs.
He chides the tardiness of every post,
Pants to be told of battles won or lost,
Blames his own indolence, observes, though late,
'Tis criminal to leave a sinking state,
Flies to the levee, and received with grace,
Kneels, kisses hands, and shines again in place.   480
    Suburban villas, highway-side retreats,
That dread the encroachment of our growing streets,
Tight boxes, neatly sashed, and in a blaze
With all a July sun's collected rays,
Delight the citizen, who, gasping there,
Breathes clouds of dust, and calls it country air.
O sweet retirement, who would balk the thought,
That could afford retirement, or could not ?
'Tis such an easy walk, so smooth and straight,
The second milestone fronts the garden gate ;   490
A step if fair, and, if a shower approach,
You find safe shelter in the next stage-coach.
There prisoned in a parlour snug and small,
Like bottled wasps upon a southern wall,
The man of business and his friends compressed
Forget their labours, and yet find no rest ;
But still 'tis rural—trees are to be seen
From every window, and the fields are green ;
Ducks paddle in the pond before the door,
And what could a remoter scene show more ?   500
A sense of elegance we rarely find
The portion of a mean or vulgar mind,
And ignorance of better things makes man,
Who cannot much, rejoice in what he can ;
And he, that deems his leisure well bestowed
In contemplation of a turnpike road,
Is occupied as well, employs his hours
As wisely, and as much improves his powers,

As he that slumbers in pavilions graced
With all the charms of an accomplished taste.   510
Yet hence, alas ! insolvencies ; and hence
The unpitied victim of ill-judged expense,
From all his wearisome engagements freed,
Shakes hands with business, and retires indeed.
    Your prudent grandmammas, ye modern belles,
Content with Bristol, Bath, and Tunbridge Wells,
When health required it, would consent to roam,
Else more attached to pleasures found at home.
But now alike, gay widow, virgin, wife,
Ingenious to diversify dull life,   520
In coaches, chaises, caravans, and hoys,
Fly to the coast for daily, nightly joys,
And all, impatient of dry land, agree
With one consent to rush into the sea.⌐
Ocean exhibits, fathomless and broad,
Much of the power and majesty of God.
He swathes about the swelling of the deep,
That shines, and rests, as infants smile and sleep ;
Vast as it is, it answers as it flows
The breathings of the lightest air that blows ;   530
Curling and whitening over all the waste,
The rising waves obey the increasing blast,
Abrupt and horrid as the tempest roars,
Thunder and flash upon the steadfast shores,
Till He that rides the whirlwind checks the rein,
Then all the world of waters sleeps again.—
Nereids or Dryads, as the fashion leads,
Now in the floods, now panting in the meads,
Votaries of Pleasure still, where'er she dwells,
Near barren rocks, in palaces, or cells,   540
O grant a poet leave to recommend
(A poet fond of Nature, and your friend)
Her slighted works to your admiring view,
Her works must needs excel who fashioned you.
Would ye, when rambling in your morning ride,
With some unmeaning, coxcomb at your side,
Condemn the prattler for his idle pains,
To waste unheard the music of his strains,
And, deaf to all the impertinence of tongue,
That, while it courts, affronts and does you wrong,—   550
Mark well the finished plan without a fault,
The seas globose and huge, the o'erarching vault,
Earth's millions daily fed, a world employed
In gathering plenty yet to be enjoyed,
Till gratitude grew vocal in the praise
Of God, beneficent in all His ways ;
Graced with such wisdom, how would beauty shine !
Ye want but that to seem indeed divine.
    Anticipated rents and bills unpaid
Force many a shining youth into the shade,   560

Not to redeem his time, but his estate,
And play the fool, but at a cheaper rate :
There, hid in loathed obscurity, removed
From pleasures left, but never more beloved,
He just endures, and with a sickly spleen
Sighs o'er the beauties of the charming scene.
Nature indeed looks prettily in rhyme ;
Streams tinkle sweetly in poetic chime :
The warblings of the blackbird, clear and strong,
Are musical enough in Thomson's song ;   570
And Cobham's groves, and Windsor's green retreats,
When Pope describes them, have a thousand sweets ;
He likes the country, but in truth must own,
Most likes it when he studies it in town.

    Poor Jack—no matter who—for when I blame,
I pity, and must therefore sink the name —
Lived in his saddle, loved the chase, the course,
And always, ere he mounted, kissed his horse.
The estate his sires had owned in ancient years
Was quickly distanced, matched against a peer's.   580
Jack vanished, was regretted and forgot ;
'Tis wild good-nature's never-failing lot.
At length, when all had long supposed him dead,
By cold submersion, razor, rope, or lead,
My lord, alighting at his usual place,
The Crown, took notice of an ostler's face.
Jack knew his friend, but hoped in that disguise
He might escape the most observing eyes,
And whistling, as if unconcerned and gay,
Curried his nag and looked another way.   590
Convinced at last, upon a nearer view,
'Twas he, the same, the very Jack he knew,
O'erwhelmed at once with wonder, grief, and joy,
He pressed him much to quit his base employ ;
His countenance, his purse, his heart, his hand,
Influence and power, were all at his command :
Peers are not always generous as well-bred,
But Granby was, meant truly what he said.
Jack bowed, and was obliged—confessed 'twas strange,
That so retired he should not wish a change,   600
But knew no medium between guzzling beer
And his old stint—three thousand pounds a year.

    Thus some retire to nourish hopeless woe ;
Some seeking happiness not found below ;
Some to comply with humour, and a mind
To social scenes by nature disinclined ;
Some swayed by fashion, some by deep disgust ;
Some self-impoverished, and because they must ;
But few, that court Retirement, are aware
Of half the toils they must encounter there.   610

    Lucrative offices are seldom lost
For want of powers proportioned to the post :

Give even a dunce the employment he desires,
And he soon finds the talents it requires ;
A business with an income at its heels
Furnishes always oil for its own wheels.
But in his arduous enterprise to close
His active years with indolent repose,
He finds the labours of that state exceed
His utmost faculties, severe indeed. 620
'Tis easy to resign a toilsome place,
But not to manage leisure with a grace ;
Absence of occupation is not rest,
A mind quite vacant is a mind distressed.
The veteran steed, excused his task at length,
In kind compassion of his failing strength,
And turned into the park or mead to graze,
Exempt from future service all his days,
There feels a pleasure perfect in its kind,
Ranges at liberty, and snuffs the wind. 630
But when his lord would quit the busy road,
To taste a joy like that he has bestowed,
He proves, less happy than his favoured brute,
A life of ease a difficult pursuit.
Thought, to the man that never thinks, may seem
As natural as when asleep to dream ;
But reveries (for human minds will act)
Specious in show, impossible in fact,
Those flimsy webs, that break as soon as wrought,
Attain not to the dignity of thought : 640
Nor yet the swarms that occupy the brain,
Where dreams of dress, intrigue, and pleasure reign ;
Nor such as useless conversation breeds,
Or lust engenders, and indulgence feeds.
Whence and what are we? to what end ordained?
What means the drama by the world sustained?
Business or vain amusement, care, or mirth,
Divide the frail inhabitants of earth.
Is duty a mere sport, or an employ?
Life an intrusted talent, or a toy? 650
Is there, as reason, conscience, scripture, say,
Cause to provide for a great future day,
When, earth's assigned duration at an end,
Man shall be summoned, and the dead attend?
The trumpet—will it sound? the curtain rise?
And show the august tribunal of the skies,
Where no prevarication shall avail,
Where eloquence and artifice shall fail,
The pride of arrogant distinctions fall,
And conscience and our conduct judge us all ? 660
Pardon me, ye that give the midnight oil
To learned cares or philosophic toil,
Though I revere your honourable names,
Your useful labours and important aims,

And hold the world indebted to your aid,
Enriched with the discoveries ye have made ;
Yet let me stand excused, if I esteem
A mind employed on so sublime a theme,
Pushing her bold inquiry to the date
And outline of the present transient state,   670
And, after poising her adventurous wings,
Settling at last upon eternal things,
Far more intelligent, and better taught
The strenuous use of profitable thought,
Than ye, when happiest, and enlightened most
And highest in renown, can justly boast.
   A mind unnerved, or indisposed to bear
The weight of subjects worthiest of her care,
Whatever hopes a change of scene inspires,
Must change her nature, or in vain retires.   680
An idler is a watch that wants both hands,
As useless if it goes as when it stands.
Books therefore, not the scandal of the shelves,
In which lewd sensualists print out themselves ;
Nor those in which the stage gives vice a blow,
With what success let modern manners show ;
Nor his who, for the bane of thousands born,
Built God a church, and laughed his word to scorn,
Skilful alike to seem devout and just,
And stab religion with a sly side-thrust ;   690
Nor those of learned philologists, who chase
A panting syllable through time and space,
Start it at home, and hunt it in the dark,
To Gaul, to Greece, and into Noah's ark ;
But such as learning without false pretence,
The friend of truth, the associate of sound sense,
And such as, in the zeal of good design,
Strong judgment labouring in the scripture mine,
All such as manly and great souls produce,
Worthy to live, and of eternal use ;   700
Behold in these what leisure hours demand,
Amusement and true knowledge hand in hand.
Luxury gives the mind a childish cast,
And, while she polishes, perverts the taste ;
Habits of close attention, thinking heads,
Become more rare as dissipation spreads,
Till authors hear at length one general cry,
Tickle and entertain us, or we die.
The loud demand, from year to year the same,
Beggars Invention, and makes Fancy lame ;   710
Till farce itself, most mournfully *jejune,*
Calls for the kind assistance of a tune,
And novels (witness every month's Review)
Belie their name, and offer nothing new.
The mind relaxing into needful sport,
Should turn to writers of an abler sort,

Whose wit well managed, and whose classic style,
Give truth a lustre, and make wisdom smile.
   Friends, (for I cannot stint, as some have done,
Too rigid in my view, that name to one ;   720
Though one, I grant it, in the generous breast,
Will stand advanced a step above the rest :
Flowers by that name promiscuously we call,
But one, the rose, the regent of them all)—
Friends, not adopted with a schoolboy's haste,
But chosen with a nice discerning taste,
Well born, well disciplined, who, placed apart
From vulgar minds, have honour much at heart,
And, though the world may think the ingredients odd,
The love of virtue, and the fear of God !   730
Such friends prevent what else would soon succeed,
A temper rustic as the life we lead,
And keep the polish of the manners clean,
As theirs who bustle in the busiest scene ;
For solitude, however some may rave,
Seeming a sanctuary, proves a grave,
A sepulchre, in which the living lie,
Where all good qualities grow sick and die.
I praise the Frenchman,* his remark was shrewd—
How sweet, how passing sweet, is solitude !   740
But grant me still a friend in my retreat,
Whom I may whisper, solitude is sweet."
Yet neither these delights, nor aught beside
That appetite can ask, or wealth provide,
Can save us always from a tedious day,
Or shine the dulness of still life away ;
Divine communion, carefully enjoyed,
Or sought with energy, must fill the void.
O sacred art, to which alone life owes
Its happiest seasons, and a peaceful close,   750
Scorned in a world, indebted to that scorn
For evils daily felt, and hardly borne,—
Not knowing thee, we reap with bleeding hands
Flowers of rank odour upon thorny lands,
And, while experience cautions us in vain,
Grasp seeming happiness, and find it pain.
Despondence, self-deserted in her grief,
Lost by abandoning her own relief ;
Murmuring and ungrateful Discontent,
That scorns afflictions mercifully meant,   760
Those humours tart as wines upon the fret,
Which idleness and weariness beget ;
These and a thousand plagues that haunt the breast,
Fond of the phantom of an earthly rest,
Divine communion chases, as the day
Drives to their dens the obedient beasts of prey.
See Judah's promised king, bereft of all,

* Bruyère.
M

Driven out an exile from the face of Saul.
To distant caves the lonely wanderer flies,
To seek that peace a tyrant's frown denies.   770
Hear the sweet accents of his tuneful voice,
Hear him, o'erwhelmed with sorrow, yet rejoice ;
No womanish or wailing grief has part,
No, not a moment, in his royal heart ;
'Tis manly music, such as martyrs make,
Suffering with gladness for a Saviour's sake :
His soul exults, hope animates his lays,
The sense of mercy kindles into praise,
And wilds, familiar with the lion's roar,
Ring with ecstatic sounds unheard before :   780
'Tis love like his that can alone defeat
The foes of man, or make a desert sweet.
    Religion does not censure or exclude
Unnumbered pleasures harmlessly pursued ;
To study culture, and with artful toil
To meliorate and tame the stubborn soil ;
To give dissimilar yet fruitful lands
The grain, or herb, or plant, that each demands ;
To cherish virtue in an humble state,
And share the joys your bounty may create ;   790
To mark the matchless workings of the power
That shuts within its seed the future flower,
Bids these in elegance of form excel,
In colour these, and those delight the smell,
Sends Nature forth, the daughter of the skies,
To dance on Earth, and charm all human eyes ;
To teach the canvas innocent deceit,
Or lay the landscape on the snowy sheet—
These, these are arts, pursued without a crime,
That leave no stain upon the wing of Time.   800
    Me poetry (or rather notes that aim
Feebly and faintly at poetic fame)
Employs, shut out from more important views,
Fast by the banks of the slow-winding Ouse ;
Content if thus sequestered I may raise
A monitor's, though not a poet's praise,
And while I teach an art too little known,
To close life wisely, may not waste my own.

THE DOVES.

Reasoning at every step he treads,
　　Man yet mistakes his way,
While meaner things, whom instinct leads,
　　Are rarely known to stray.

One silent eve I wandered late,
　　And heard the voice of love;
The turtle thus addressed her mate,
　　And soothed the listening dove:

"Our mutual bond of faith and truth
　　No time shall disengage,
Those blessings of our early youth
　　Shall cheer our latest age;

"While innocence without disguise,
　　And constancy sincere,
Shall fill the circles of those eyes,
　　And mine can read them there;

"Those ills, that wait on all below,
　　Shall ne'er be felt by me,
Or gently felt, and only so,
　　As being shared with thee.

"When lightnings flash among the trees,
　　Or kites are hovering near,
I fear lest thee alone they seize,
　　And know no other fear.

"'Tis then I feel myself a wife,
　　And press thy wedded side,
Resolved a union formed for life
　　Death never shall divide.

"But oh! if, fickle and unchaste,
　　(Forgive a transient thought,)
Thou couldst become unkind at last,
　　And scorn thy present lot,

"No need of lightnings from on high,
　　Or kites with cruel beak;
Denied the endearments of thine eye,
　　This widowed heart would break."

Thus sang the sweet sequestered bird,
　　Soft as the passing wind,
And I recorded what I heard,
　　A lesson for mankind.

A FABLE.

A raven, while with glossy breast
Her new-laid eggs she fondly pressed,
And, on her wicker-work high mounted,
Her chickens prematurely counted,
(A fault philosophers might blame,
If quite exempted from the same,)
Enjoyed at ease the genial day;
'Twas April, as the bumpkins say,
The legislature called it May.
But suddenly a wind, as high
As ever swept a winter sky,
Shook the young leaves about her ears,
And filled her with a thousand fears,
Lest the rude blast should snap the bough,
And spread her golden hopes below.
But just at eve the blowing weather
And all her fears were hushed together;
"And now," quoth poor unthinking Ralph,
"'Tis over, and the brood is safe;"
(For ravens, though, as birds of omen,
They teach both conjurers and old women
To tell us what is to befall,
Can't prophesy themselves at all).
The morning came, when neighbour Hodge,
Who long had marked her airy lodge,
And destined all the treasure there
A gift to his expecting fair,
Climbed like a squirrel to his dray,
And bore the worthless prize away.

MORAL.

'Tis Providence alone secures
In every change both mine and yours:
Safety consists not in escape
From dangers of a frightful shape;
An earthquake may be bid to spare
The man that's strangled by a hair.
Fate steals along with silent tread,
Found oftenest in what least we dread,
Frowns in the storm with angry brow,
But in the sunshine strikes the blow.

A COMPARISON.

THE lapse of time and rivers is the same,
Both speed their journey with a restless stream ;
The silent pace with which they steal away,
No wealth can bribe, no prayers persuade to stay;
Alike irrevocable both when past,
And a wide ocean swallows both at last.
Though each resemble each in every part,
A difference strikes at length the musing heart;
Streams never flow in vain ; where streams abound
How laughs the land with various plenty crowned !
But time, that should enrich the nobler mind,
Neglected, leaves a dreary waste behind.

ANOTHER.

ADDRESSED TO A YOUNG LADY.

SWEET stream, that winds through
    yonder glade,
Apt emblem of a virtuous maid !
Silent and chaste she steals along,
Far from the world's gay busy throng,
With gentle yet prevailing force,
Intent upon her destined course;
Graceful and useful all she does,
Blessing and blessed where'er she
    goes ;
Pure-bosomed as that watery glass,
And heaven reflected in her face!

VERSES

SUPPOSED TO BE WRITTEN BY ALEXANDER SELKIRK DURING HIS SOLITARY
ABODE ON THE ISLAND OF JUAN FERNANDEZ.

I AM monarch of all I survey,
   My right there is none to dispute,
From the centre all round to the sea,
   I am lord of the fowl and the brute.
O Solitude ! where are the charms
   That sages have seen in thy face ?
Better dwell in the midst of alarms,
   Than reign in this horrible place.

I am out of humanity's reach,
   I must finish my journey alone,
Never hear the sweet music of speech,
   I start at the sound of my own.
The beasts that roam over the plain,
   My form with indifference see ;
They are so unacquainted with man,
   Their tameness is shocking to me.

Society, friendship, and love,
   Divinely bestowed upon man,
Oh, had I the wings of a dove,
   How soon would I taste you again !
My sorrows I then might assuage
   In the ways of religion and truth,
Might learn from the wisdom of age,
   And be cheered by the sallies of youth.

Religion ! what treasure untold
   Resides in that heavenly word !
More precious than silver and gold,
   Or all that this earth can afford.
But the sound of the church-going bell
   These valleys and rocks never heard
Never sighed at the sound of a knell,
   Or smiled when a sabbath appeared.

Ye winds, that have made me your sport,
  Convey to this desolate shore
Some cordial endearing report
  Of a land I shall visit no more.
My friends,—do they now and then send
  A wish or a thought after me?
O tell me I yet have a friend,
  Though a friend I am never to see.

How fleet is a glance of the mind!
  Compared with the speed of its flight,
The tempest itself lags behind,
  And the swift-winged arrows of light.

When I think of my own native land,
  In a moment I seem to be there;
But alas! recollection at hand
  Soon hurries me back to despair.

But the sea-fowl is gone to her nest,
  The beast is laid down in his lair,
Even here is a season of rest,
  And I to my cabin repair.
There's mercy in every place,
  And mercy, encouraging thought!
Gives even affliction a grace,
  And reconciles man to his lot.

ON THE PROMOTION OF EDWARD THURLOW, ESQ.

TO THE LORD HIGH CHANCELLORSHIP OF ENGLAND.

ROUND Thurlow's head in early youth,
  And in his sportive days,
Fair Science poured the light of truth,
  And Genius shed his rays.

"See!" with united wonder cried
  The experienced and the sage,
"Ambition in a boy supplied
  With all the skill of age!

"Discernment, eloquence, and grace
  Proclaim him born to sway
The balance in the highest place.
  And bear the palm away."

The praise bestowed was just and wise;
  He sprang impetuous forth,
Secure of conquest where the prize
  Attends superior worth.

So the best courser on the plain
Ere yet he starts is known,
And does but at the goal obtain
What all had deemed his own.

ODE TO PEACE.

COME, peace of mind, delightful guest!
Return and make thy downy nest
  Once more in this sad heart:
Nor riches I, nor power pursue,
Nor hold forbidden joys in view;
  We therefore need not part.

Where wilt thou dwell, if not with me,
From avarice and ambition free,
  And pleasure's fatal wiles?
For whom, alas! dost thou prepare
The sweets that I was wont to share,
  The banquet of thy smiles?

The great, the gay, shall they partake
The heaven that thou alone canst make,
  And wilt thou quit the stream
That murmurs through the dewy mead,
The grove and the sequestered shed,
  To be a guest with them?

For thee I panted, thee I prized,
For thee I gladly sacrificed
  Whate'er I loved before,
And shall I see thee start away,
And helpless, hopeless, hear thee say,
  Farewell! we meet no more"?

HUMAN FRAILTY.

WEAK and irresolute is man;
   The purpose of to-day,
Woven with pains into his plan,
   To-morrow rends away.

The bow well bent and smart the spring,
   Vice seems already slain,
But passion rudely snaps the string,
   And it revives again.

Some foe to his upright intent
   Finds out his weaker part,
Virtue engages his assent,
   But pleasure wins his heart.

'Tis here the folly of the wise
   Through all his art we view,
And while his tongue the charge denies,
   His conscience owns it true.

Bound on a voyage of awful length
   And dangers little known,
A stranger to superior strength,
   Man vainly trusts his own.

But oars alone can ne'er prevail
   To reach the distant coast,
The breath of heaven must swell the sail,
   Or all the toil is lost.

THE MODERN PATRIOT.

REBELLION is my theme all day;
   I only wish 'twould come
(As who knows but perhaps it may?)
   A little nearer home.

Yon roaring boys, who rave and fight
   On t'other side the Atlantic,
I always held them in the right,
   But most so when most frantic.

When lawless mobs insult the court,
   That man shall be my toast,
If breaking windows be the sport,
   Who bravely breaks the most.

But oh! for him my fancy culls
   The choicest flowers she bears,
Who constitutionally pulls
   Your house about your ears.

Such civil broils are my delight,
   Though some folks can't endure 'em,
Who say the mob are mad outright,
   And that a rope must cure 'em.

A rope! I wish we patriots had
   Such strings for all who need 'em.—
What! hang a man for going mad!
   Then farewell British freedom.

ON OBSERVING SOME NAMES OF LITTLE NOTE

RECORDED IN THE "BIOGRAPHIA BRITANNICA."

OH, fond attempt to give a deathless lot
To names ignoble, born to be forgot!
In vain, recorded in historic page,
They court the notice of a future age:
Those twinkling tiny lustres of the land
Drop one by one from Fame's neglecting hand;
Lethæan gulfs receive them as they fall,
And dark oblivion soon absorbs them all.
   So when a child (as playful children use)
Has burnt to tinder a stale last-year's news,
The flame extinct, he views the roving fire—
There goes my lady, and there goes the squire,
There goes the parson, oh illustrious spark!
And there, scarce less illustrious, goes the clerk!

REPORT OF AN ADJUDGED CASE.

NOT TO BE FOUND IN ANY OF THE BOOKS.

BETWEEN Nose and Eyes a strange contest arose,
  The spectacles set them unhappily wrong;
The point in dispute was, as all the world knows,
  To which the said spectacles ought to belong.

So Tongue was the lawyer, and argued the cause
  With a great deal of skill, and a wig full of learning;
While Chief Baron Ear sat to balance the laws,
  So famed for his talent in nicely discerning.

"In behalf of the Nose it will quickly appear,
  And your lordship," he said, "will undoubtedly find,
That the Nose has had spectacles always in wear,
  Which amounts to possession time out of mind."

Then holding the spectacles up to the court—
  "Your lordship observes they are made with a straddle,
As wide as the ridge of the Nose is; in short,
  Designed to sit close to it, just like a saddle.

"Again, would your lordship a moment suppose
  ('Tis a case that has happened, and may be again,)
That the visage or countenance had not a Nose,
  Pray who would, or who could, wear spectacles then?

"On the whole it appears, and my argument shows,
  With a reasoning the court will never condemn,
That the spectacles plainly were made for the Nose,
  And the Nose was as plainly intended for them."

Then shifting his side, as a lawyer knows how,
  He pleaded again in behalf of the Eyes:
But what were his arguments few people know,
  For the court did not think they were equally wise.

So his lordship decreed with a grave solemn tone,
  Decisive and clear, without one if or but—
That, whenever the Nose put his spectacles on,
  By daylight or candlelight—Eyes should be shut!

ON THE BURNING OF LORD MANSFIELD'S LIBRARY,

TOGETHER WITH HIS MSS.,

BY THE MOB, IN THE MONTH OF JUNE 1780.

So then—the Vandals of our isle,
  Sworn foes to sense and law,
Have burnt to dust a nobler pile
  Than ever Roman saw!

And Murray sighs o'er Pope, and Swift,
  And many a treasure more,
The well-judged purchase, and the gift,
  That graced his lettered store.

Their pages mangled, burnt, and torn,
The loss was his alone;
But ages yet to come shall mourn
The burning of *his own.*

ON THE SAME.

WHEN Wit and Genius meet their doom
In all devouring flame,
They tell us of the fate of Rome,
And bid us fear the same.

O'er Murray's loss the Muses wept,
They felt the rude alarm,
Yet blessed the guardian care that kept
His sacred head from harm.

There Memory, like the bee that's fed
From Flora's balmy store,
The quintessence of all he read
Had treasured up before.

The lawless herd, with fury blind,
Have done him cruel wrong;
The flowers are gone—but still we find
The honey on his tongue.

THE LOVE OF THE WORLD REPROVED;*

OR, HYPOCRISY DETECTED.

THUS says the prophet of the Turk,
"Good Mussulman, abstain from pork;
There is a part in every swine
No friend or follower of mine
May taste, whate'er his inclination,
On pain of excommunication."
Such Mahomet's mysterious charge,
And thus he left the point at large.
Had he the sinful part expressed,
They might with safety eat the rest;
But for one piece they thought it hard
From the whole hog to be debarred,
And set their wit at work to find
What joint the prophet had in mind.
Much controversy straight arose,
These choose the back, the belly those;
By some 'tis confidently said
He meant not to forbid the head;
While others at that doctrine rail,
And piously prefer the tail.
Thus, Conscience freed from every clog,
Mahometans eat up the hog.

You laugh—'tis well—the tale applied
May make you laugh on t'other side.
"Renounce the world," the preacher cries.
"We do," a multitude replies.
While one as innocent regards
A snug and friendly game at cards;
And one, whatever you may say,
Can see no evil in a play;
Some love a concert, or a race;
And others shooting and the chase.
Reviled and loved, renounced and followed,
Thus, bit by bit, the world is swallowed;
Each thinks his neighbour makes too free,
Yet likes a slice as well as he:
With sophistry their sauce they sweeten,
Till quite from tail to snout 'tis eaten.

THE LILY AND THE ROSE.

THE nymph must lose her female friend
If more admired than she—
But where will fierce contention end,
If flowers can disagree?

Within the garden's peaceful scene
Appeared two lovely foes,
Aspiring to the rank of Queen,
The Lily and the Rose.

* It may be proper to inform the reader that this piece has already appeared in print, having found its way, though with some unnecessary additions by an unknown hand, into the "Leeds Journal," without the author's privity.—*Author's note.*

The Rose soon reddened into rage,
  And, swelling with disdain,
Appealed to many a poet's page
  To prove her right to reign.

The Lily's height bespoke command,
  A fair imperial flower;
She seemed designed for Flora's hand,
  The sceptre of her power.

This civil bickering and debate
  The goddess chanced to hear,
And flew to save, ere yet too late,
  The pride of the parterre.

Yours is, she said, the noblest hue,
  And yours the statelier mien;
And, till a third surpasses you,
  Let each be deemed a queen.

Thus soothed and reconciled, each seeks
  The fairest British fair ;
The seat of empire is her cheeks,
  They reign united there.

IDEM LATINE REDDITUM.

Heu inimicitias quoties parit æmula forma,
  Quam raro pulchræ, pulchra placere potest !
Sed fines ultrà solitos discordia tendit,
  Cum flores ipsos bilis et ira movent.

Hortus ubi dulces præbet tacitosque recessûs,
  Se rapit in partes gens animosa duas ;
Hic sibi regales Amaryllis candida cultûs,
  Illic purpureo vindicat ore Rosa.

Ira Rosam et meritis quæsita superbia tangunt,
  Multaque ferventi vix cohibenda sinû,
Dum sibi fautorum ciet undique nomina vatûm,
  Jusque suum, multo carmine fulta, probat.

Altior emicat illa, et celso vertice nutat,
  Ceu flores inter non habitura parem,
Fastiditque alios, et nata videtur in usûs
  Imperii, sceptrum, Flora quod ipsa gērat.

Nec Dea non sensit civilis murmura rixæ,
  Cui curæ est pictas pandere ruris opes,
Deliciasque suas nunquam non prompta tueri,
  Dum licet et locus est, ut tueatur, adest.

" Et tibi forma datur procerior omnibus," inquit;
  " Et tibi, principibus qui solet esse, color,
Et donec vincat quædam formosior ambas,
  Et tibi reginæ nomen, et esto tibi."

His ubi sedatus furor est, petit utraque nympham,
  Qualem inter Veneres Anglia sola parit ;
Hanc penes imperium est, nihil optant amplius, hujus
  Regnant in nitidis, et sine lite, genis.

THE NIGHTINGALE AND GLOW-WORM.

A NIGHTINGALE, that all day long
Had cheered the village with his song,
Nor yet at eve his note suspended,
Nor yet when eventide was ended,
Began to feel, as well he might,
The keen demands of appetite;
When, looking eagerly around,
He spied far off, upon the ground,
A something shining in the dark,
And knew the glow-worm by his spark;
So stooping down from hawthorn top,
He thought to put him in his crop.
The worm, aware of his intent,
Harangued him thus, right eloquent—
  "Did you admire my lamp," quoth he,
"As much as I your minstrelsy,
You would abhor to do me wrong,
As much as I to spoil your song;
For 'twas the self-same Power divine
Taught you to sing and me to shine;

That you with music, I with light,
Might beautify, and cheer the night."
  The songster heard his short oration,
And, warbling out his approbation,
Released him, as my story tells,
And found a supper somewhere else.
  Hence jarring sectaries may learn
Their real interest to discern;
That brother should not war with
        brother,
And worry and devour each other;
But sing and shine by sweet consent,
Till life's poor transient night is spent,
Respecting, in each other's case,
The gifts of nature and of grace.
  Those Christians best deserve the
        name
Who studiously make peace their aim;
Peace both the duty and the prize
Of him that creeps and him that flies.

VOTUM.

O MATUTINI rores, auræque salubres,
O nemora, et lætæ rivis felicibus herbæ,
Graminei colles, et amœnæ in vallibus umbræ!
Fata modò dederint quas olim in rure paterno
Delicias, procul arte, procul formidine novi,
Quam vellem ignotus, quod mens mea semper avebat,
Ante larem proprium placidam expectare senectam,
Tum demùm, exactis non infeliciter annis,
Sortiri tacitum lapidem, aut sub cespite condi.

ON A GOLDFINCH STARVED TO DEATH IN HIS CAGE.

TIME was when I was free as air,
The thistle's downy seed my fare,
  My drink the morning dew;
I perched at will on every spray,
My form genteel, my plumage gay,
  My strains for ever new.

But gaudy plumage, sprightly strain,
And form genteel were all in vain,
  And of a transient date;   [death,
For, caught and caged, and starved to
In dying sighs my little breath
  Soon passed the wiry grate.

Thanks, gentle swain, for all my woes,
And thanks for this effectual close
    And cure of every ill!
More cruelty could none express;
And I, if you had shown me less,
    Had been your prisoner still.

THE PINEAPPLES AND THE BEE.

THE Pineapples, in triple row,
Were basking hot, and all in blow;
A Bee of most discerning taste
Perceived the fragrance as he passed;
On eager wing the spoiler came,
And searched for crannies in the frame,
Urged his attempt on every side,
To every pane his trunk applied;
But still in vain, the frame was tight,
And only pervious to the light;
Thus having wasted half the day,
He trimmed his flight another way.
    "Methinks," I said, "in thee I find
The sin and madness of mankind.
To joys forbidden man aspires,
Consumes his soul with vain desires;
Folly the spring of his pursuit,
And disappointment all the fruit.
While Cynthio ogles, as she passes,
The nymph between two chariot glasses,
She is the Pineapple, and he
The silly unsuccessful Bee.
The maid who views with pensive air
The showglass fraught with glittering ware,
Sees watches, bracelets, rings, and lockets,
But sighs at thought of empty pockets;
Like thine, her appetite is keen,
But ah, the cruel glass between!"
    Our dear delights are often such,
Exposed to view, but not to touch;
The sight our foolish heart inflames,
We long for pineapples in frames;
With hopeless wish one looks and lingers;
One breaks the glass, and cuts his fingers;
But they whom Truth and Wisdom lead,
Can gather honey from a weed.

HORACE, BOOK II. ODE X.

RECEIVE, dear friend, the truths I teach,
So shalt thou live beyond the reach
    Of adverse fortune's power;
Not always tempt the distant deep,
Nor always timorously creep
    Along the treacherous shore.

He that holds fast the golden mean,
And lives contentedly between
    The little and the great,
Feels not the wants that pinch the poor,
Nor plagues that haunt the rich man's door,
    Imbittering all his state.

The tallest pines feel most the power
Of wintry blasts; the loftiest tower
    Comes heaviest to the ground;
The bolts that spare the mountain's side
His cloud-capt eminence divide,
    And spread the ruin round.

The well-informed philosopher
Rejoices with a wholesome fear,
    And hopes in spite of pain;
If Winter bellow from the north,
Soon the sweet Spring comes dancing forth,
    And Nature laughs again.

What if thine Heaven be overcast?
The dark appearance will not last;
    Expect a brighter sky;
The God that strings the silver bow,
Awakes sometimes the Muses too,
    And lays his arrows by.

If hindrances obstruct thy way,
Thy magnanimity display,
    And let thy strength be seen;
But O! if Fortune fill thy sail
With more than a propitious gale,
    Take half thy canvas in!

A REFLECTION ON THE FOREGOING ODE.

AND is this all? Can Reason do no more
Than bid me shun the deep and dread the shore?
Sweet moralist! afloat on life's rough sea,
The Christian has an art unknown to thee!

He holds no parley with unmanly fears ;
Where Duty bids, he confidently steers,
Faces a thousand dangers at her call,
And, trusting in his God, surmounts them all.

TRANSLATIONS FROM VINCENT BOURNE.

I. THE GLOW-WORM.

BENEATH the hedge or near the stream,
    A worm is known to stray,
That shows by night a lucid beam,
    Which disappears by day.

Disputes have been, and still prevail,
    From whence his rays proceed ;
Some give that honour to his tail,
    And others to his head.

But this is sure—the hand of might
    That kindles up the skies,
Gives *him* a modicum of light
    Proportioned to his size.

Perhaps indulgent Nature meant,
    By such a lamp bestowed,
To bid the traveller, as he went,
    Be careful where he trod ;

Nor crush a worm, whose useful light
    Might serve, however small,
To show a stumbling stone by night,
    And save him from a fall.

What'er she meant, this truth divine
    Is legible and plain,
'Tis power Almighty bids him shine,
    Nor bids him shine in vain.

Ye proud and wealthy ! let this theme
    Teach humbler thoughts to you,
Since such a reptile has its gem,
    And boasts its splendour too.

II. THE JACKDAW.

THERE is a bird who by his coat,
And by the hoarseness of his note,
    Might be supposed a crow :
A great frequenter of the church,
Where bishop-like he finds a perch,
    And dormitory too.

Above the steeple shines a plate,
That turns and turns, to indicate
    From what point blows the weather ;

Look up—your brains begin to swim,
'Tis in the clouds—that pleases him,
    He chooses it the rather.

Fond of the speculative height,
Thither he wings his airy flight,
    And thence securely sees
The bustle and the raree-show
That occupy mankind below,
    Secure and at his ease.

You think, no doubt, he sits and muses
On future broken bones and bruises,
    If he should chance to fall.
No ; not a single thought like that
Employs his philosophic pate,
    Or troubles it at all.

He sees that this great roundabout,
The world, with all its motley rout,
    Church, army, physic, law,
Its customs, and its businesses,
Are no concern at all of his,
    And says—what says he ?—" Caw."

Thrice happy bird ! I too have seen
Much of the vanities of men ;
    And sick of having seen 'em,
Would cheerfully these limbs resign
For such a pair of wings as thine,
    And such a head between 'em.

III. THE CRICKET.

LITTLE inmate, full of mirth,
Chirping on my kitchen hearth,
Wheresoe'er be thine abode,
Always harbinger of good,
Pay me for thy warm retreat
With a song more soft and sweet ;
In return thou shalt receive
Such a strain as I can give.

Thus thy praise shall be expressed,
Inoffensive, welcome guest !
While the rat is on the scout,
And the mouse with curious snout,

With what vermin else infest
Every dish, and spoil the best ;
Frisking thus before the fire,
Thou hast all thine heart's desire.

Though in voice and shape they be
Formed as if akin to thee,
Thou surpassest, happier far,
Happiest grasshoppers that are ;
Theirs is but a summer's song,
Thine endures the winter long,
Unimpaired, and shrill, and clear,
Melody throughout the year.

Neither night, nor dawn of day,
Puts a period to thy play ;
Sing then—and extend thy span
Far beyond the date of man ;
Wretched man, whose years are spent
In repining discontent,
Lives not, aged though he be,
Half a span compared with thee.

IV. THE PARROT.

In painted plumes superbly drest,
A native of the gorgeous East,
  By many a billow tost ;
Poll gains at length the British shore,
Part of the captain's precious store,
  A present to his Toast.

Belinda's maids are soon preferred
To teach him now and then a word,
  As Poll can master it ;

But 'tis her own important charge
To qualify him more at large,
  And make him quite a wit.

" Sweet Poll ! " his doting mistress cries,
" Sweet Poll ! " the mimic bird replies,
  And calls aloud for sack.
She next instructs him in the kiss ;
'Tis now a little one, like Miss,
  And now a hearty smack.

At first he aims at what he hears ;
And, listening close with both his ears,
  Just catches at the sound ;
But soon articulates aloud,
Much to the amusement of the crowd,
  And stuns the neighbours round.

A querulous old woman's voice
His humorous talent next employs,
  He scolds and gives the lie.
And now he sings, and now is sick,
" Here Sally, Susan, come, come quick,
  Poor Poll is like to die ! "

Belinda and her bird ! 'tis rare
To meet with such a well-matched pair,
  The language and the tone,
Each character in every part
Sustained with so much grace and art,
  And both in unison.

When children first begin to spell,
And stammer out a syllable,
  We think them tedious creatures ;
But difficulties soon abate,
When birds are to be taught to prate,
  And women are the teachers.

THE SHRUBBERY.
WRITTEN IN A TIME OF AFFLICTION.

O happy shades ! to me unblest !
  Friendly to peace, but not to me !
How ill the scene that offers rest,
  And heart that cannot rest, agree !

This glassy stream, that spreading pine,
  Those alders quivering to the breeze,
Might soothe a soul less hurt than mine,
  And please, if anything could please.

But fixed unalterable Care
  Foregoes not what she feels within,
Shows the same sadness everywhere,
  And slights the season and the scene.

For all that pleased in wood or lawn,
  While Peace possessed these silent
    bowers,
Her animating smile withdrawn,
  Has lost its beauties and its powers.

The saint or moralist should tread
  This moss-grown alley, musing, slow ;
They seek like me the secret shade,
  But not, like me, to nourish woe !

Me fruitful scenes and prospects waste
  Alike admonish not to roam ;
These tell me of enjoyments past,
  And those of sorrows yet to come.

THE WINTER NOSEGAY.

WHAT Nature, alas ! has denied
 To the delicate growth of our isle,
Art has in a measure supplied,
 And winter is decked with a smile.
See, Mary, what beauties I bring
 From the shelter of that sunny shed,
Where the flowers have the charms of
  the spring,
 Though abroad they are frozen and
  dead.

'Tis a bower of Arcadian sweets,
 Where Flora 'tis still in her prime,
A fortress to which she retreats
 From the cruel assaults of the clime.

While earth wears a mantle of snow,
 These pinks are as fresh and as
  gay
As the fairest and sweetest that blow
 On the beautiful bosom of May.

See how they have safely survived
 The frowns of a sky so severe ;
Such Mary's true love, that has lived
 Through many a turbulent year.
The charms of the late-blowing rose
 Seem graced with a livelier hue,
And the winter of sorrow best shows
 The truth of a friend such as you.

MUTUAL FORBEARANCE.

NECESSARY TO THE HAPPINESS OF THE MARRIED STATE.

THE lady thus addressed her spouse—
" What a mere dungeon is this house !
By no means large enough, and was it,
Yet this dull room and that dark closet,
Those hangings with their worn-out
  graces,
Long beards, long noses, and pale
  faces,
Are such an antiquated scene,
They overwhelm me with the spleen."
 Sir Humphrey, shooting in the dark,
Makes answer quite beside the mark :
" No doubt, my dear, I bade him come,
Engaged myself to be at home,
And shall expect him at the door,
Precisely when the clock strikes four."
 " You are so deaf," the lady cried,
(And raised her voice, and frowned be-
  side)
" You are so sadly deaf, my dear,
What shall I do to make you hear ? "
" Dismiss poor Harry ! " he replies,
" Some people are more nice than wise,
For one slight trespass all this stir ?
What if he did ride whip and spur ?
'Twas but a mile—your favourite horse
Will never look one hair the worse."
" Well, I protest 'tis past all bearing !"—
" Child ! I am rather hard of hearing."—
" Yes, truly ; one must scream and bawl :
I tell you you can't hear at all ! "
Then, with a voice exceeding low,
" No matter if you hear or no."

Alas ! and is domestic strife,
That sorest ill of human life,
A plague so little to be feared,
As to be wantonly incurred,
To gratify a fretful passion,
On every trivial provocation ?
The kindest and the happiest pair
Will find occasion to forbear ;
And something, every day they live,
To pity and, perhaps, forgive.
But if infirmities, that fall
In common to the lot of all,
A blemish, or a sense impaired,
Are crimes so little to be spared,
Then farewell all that must create
The comfort of the wedded state ;
Instead of harmony, 'tis jar,
And tumult and intestine war.
 The love that cheers life's latest
  stage,
Proof against sickness and old age,
Preserved by virtue from declension,
Becomes not weary of attention ;
But lives when that exterior grace
Which first inspired the flame decays.
'Tis gentle, delicate, and kind,
To faults compassionate or blind,
And will with sympathy endure
Those evils it would gladly cure ;
But angry, coarse, and harsh expression
Shows love to be a mere profession ;
Proves that the heart is none of his,
Or soon expels him if it is.

TO THE REV. MR. NEWTON.

AN INVITATION INTO THE COUNTRY.

THE swallows in their torpid state
  Compose their useless wing,
And bees in hives as idly wait
  The call of early spring.

The keenest frost that binds the stream,
  The wildest wind that blows,
Are neither felt nor feared by them,
  Secure of their repose :

But man, all feeling and awake,
  The gloomy scene surveys ;
With present ills his heart must ache,
  And pant for brighter days.

Old Winter, halting o'er the mead,
  Bids me and Mary mourn ;
But lovely Spring peeps o'er his head,
  And whispers your return.

Then April with her sister May
  Shall chase him from the bowers,
And weave fresh garlands every day,
  To crown the smiling hours.

And if a tear that speaks regret
  Of happier times appear,
A glimpse of joy that we have met
  Shall shine, and dry the tear.

TRANSLATION OF PRIOR'S CHLOE AND EUPHELIA.

MERCATOR, vigiles oculos ut fallere possit,
  Nomine sub ficto trans mare mittit opes ;
Lenè sonat liquidumque meis Euphelia chordis,
  Sed solam exoptant te, mea vota, Chlöe.

Ad speculum ornabat nitidos Euphelia crines,
  Cum dixit mea lux, heus, cane, sume lyram,
Namque lyram juxtà positam cum carmine vidit,
  Suave quidem carmen dulcisonamque lyram.

Fila lyræ vocemque paro, suspiria surgunt,
  Et miscent numeris murmura mœsta meis,
Dumque tuæ memoro laudes, Euphelia, formæ,
  Tota anima intereà pendet ab ore Chlöes.

Subrubet illa pudore, et contrahit altera frontem,
  Me torquet mea mens conscia, psallo, tremo ;
Atque Cupidineâ dixit Dea cincta coronâ,
  Heu ! fallendi artem quam didicere parum.

BOADICEA. AN ODE.

WHEN the British warrior queen,
  Bleeding from the Roman rods,
Sought, with an indignant mien,
  Counsel of her country's gods,

Sage beneath a spreading oak
  Sat the Druid, hoary chief,
Every burning word he spoke
  Full of rage and full of grief :

" Princess ! if our aged eyes
  Weep upon thy matchless wrongs,
'Tis because resentment ties
  All the terrors of our tongues.

" Rome shall perish,—write that word
  In the blood that she has spilt ;
Perish hopeless and abhorred,
  Deep in ruin as in guilt.

" Rome, for empire far renowned,
    Tramples on a thousand states ;
Soon her pride shall kiss the ground,—
    Hark ! the Gaul is at her gates.

"Other Romans shall arise,
    Heedless of a soldier's name,
Sounds, not arms, shall win the prize,
    Harmony the path to fame.

" Then the progeny that springs
    From the forests of our land,
Armed with thunder, clad with wings,
    Shall a wider world command.

" Regions Cæsar never knew
    Thy posterity shall sway,
Where his eagles never flew,
    None invincible as they."

Such the bard's prophetic words,
    Pregnant with celestial fire,
Bending as he swept the chords
    Of his sweet but awful lyre.

She, with all a monarch's pride,
    Felt them in her bosom glow,
Rushed to battle, fought and died,
    Dying, hurled them at the foe.

" Ruffians, pitiless as proud,
    Heaven awards the vengeance due ;
Empire is on us bestowed,
    Shame and ruin wait for you !"

HEROISM.

There was a time when Ætna's silent fire
Slept unperceived, the mountain yet entire ;
When, conscious of no danger from below,
She towered a cloud-capt pyramid of snow.
No thunders shook with deep intestine sound
The blooming groves that girdled her around ;
Her unctuous olives and her purple vines,
(Unfelt the fury of those bursting mines)
The peasant's hopes, and not in vain, assured,
In peace upon her sloping sides matured.
When on a day; like that of the last doom,
A conflagration labouring in her womb,
She teemed and heaved with an infernal birth,
That shook the circling seas and solid earth.
Dark and voluminous the vapours rise,
And hang their horrors in the neighbouring skies,
While through the Stygian veil that blots the day
In dazzling streaks the vivid lightnings play.
But oh ! what muse, and in what powers of song,
Can trace the torrent as it burns along ?
Havoc and devastation in the van,
It marches o'er the prostrate works of man,
Vines, olives, herbage, forests disappear,
And all the charms of a Sicilian year.

Revolving seasons, fruitless as they pass,
See it an uninformed and idle mass,
Without a soil to invite the tiller's care,
Or blade that might redeem it from despair.
Yet time at length (what will not time achieve?)
Clothes it with earth, and bids the produce live.

Once more the spiry myrtle crowns the glade,
And ruminating flocks enjoy the shade.
O bliss precarious, and unsafe retreats!
O charming paradise of short-lived sweets!
The self-same gale that wafts the fragrance round
Brings to the distant ear a sullen sound:
Again the mountain feels the imprisoned foe,
Again pours ruin on the vale below,
Ten thousand swains the wasted scene deplore,
That only future ages can restore.

Ye monarchs, whom the lure of honour draws,
Who write in blood the merits of your cause,
Who strike the blow, then plead your own defence,
Glory your aim, but Justice your pretence,
Behold in Ætna's emblematic fires
The mischiefs your ambitious pride inspires!

Fast by the stream that bounds your just domain,
And tells you where ye have a right to reign,
A nation dwells, not envious of your throne,
Studious of peace, their neighbours' and their own.
Ill-fated race! how deeply must they rue
Their only crime, vicinity to you!
The trumpet sounds, your legions swarm abroad,
Through the ripe harvest lies their destined road,
At every step beneath their feet they tread
The life of multitudes, a nation's bread!
Earth seems a garden in its loveliest dress
Before them, and behind a wilderness;
Famine, and Pestilence her first-born son,
Attend to finish what the sword begun;
And echoing praises such as fiends might earn,
And folly pays, resound at your return.
A calm succeeds;—but Plenty, with her train
Of heartfelt joys, succeeds not soon again,
And years of pining indigence must show
What scourges are the gods that rule below.

Yet man, laborious man, by slow degrees,
(Such is his thirst of opulence and ease,)
Plies all the sinews of industrious toil,
Gleans up the refuse of the general spoil,
Rebuilds the towers that smoked upon the plain,
And the sun gilds the shining spires again.

Increasing commerce and reviving art
Renew the quarrel on the conqueror's part;
And the sad lesson must be learned once more,
That wealth within is ruin at the door.

What are ye, monarchs, laurelled heroes, say,
But Ætnas of the suffering world ye sway?
Sweet Nature, stripped of her embroidered robe,
Deplores the wasted regions of her globe,

C   N

And stands a witness at Truth's awful bar,
To prove you there destroyers, as ye are.

Oh place me in some heaven-protected isle,
Where peace and equity and freedom smile,
Where no volcano pours his fiery flood,
No crested warrior dips his plume in blood,
Where power secures what industry has won,
Where to succeed is not to be undone,
A land that distant tyrants hate in vain,
In Britain's isle, beneath a George's reign.

THE POET, THE OYSTER, AND SENSITIVE PLANT.

An Oyster, cast upon the shore,
Was heard, though never heard before,
Complaining in a speech well worded,
And worthy thus to be recorded—

" Ah, hapless wretch ! condemned to
        dwell
For ever in my native shell ;
Ordained to move when others please,
Not for my own content or ease ;
But tossed and buffeted about,
Now in the water, and now out.
'Twere better to be born a stone,
Of ruder shape, and feeling none,
Than with a tenderness like mine,
And sensibilities so fine !
I envy that unfeeling shrub,
Fast-rooted against every rub."
    The plant he meant grew not far off,
And felt the sneer with scorn enough ;
Was hurt, disgusted, mortified,
And with asperity replied :—

    ("When," cry the botanists, and stare,
"Did plants called Sensitive grow there?"
No matter when—a poet's muse is
To make them grow just where she
        chooses.)

    " You shapeless nothing in a dish !
You that are but almost a fish,
I scorn your coarse insinuation,
And have most plentiful occasion
To wish myself the rock I view,
Or such another dolt as you.
For many a grave and learned clerk,
And many a gay unlettered spark,
With curious touch examines me,
If I can feel as well as he ;

And when I bend, retire, and shrink,
Says—' Well, 'tis more than one woul[d]
        think !'
Thus life is spent (oh fie upon't !)
In being touched, and crying 'Don't !'

    A poet, in his evening walk,
O'erheard and checked this idle talk.
" And your fine sense," he said, " ar[e]
        yours,
Whatever evil it endures,
Deserves not, if so soon offended,
Much to be pitied or commended.
Disputes, though short, are far too lon[g]
Where both alike are in the wrong ;
Your feelings in their full amount
Are all upon your own account.
    You, in your grotto-work enclosed,
Complain of being thus exposed ;
Yet nothing feel in that rough coat,
Save when the knife is at your throat,
Wherever driven by wind or tide,
Exempt from every ill beside.
    And as for you, my Lady Squeamis[h]
Who reckon every touch a blemish,
If all the plants that can be found
Embellishing the scene around,
Should droop and wither where the[y]
        grow,
You would not feel at all, not you.
The noblest minds their virtue prove
By pity, sympathy, and love :
These, these are feelings truly fine,
And prove their owner half divine."

His censure reached them as he dealt i[t]
And each by shrinking showed he felt i[t]

TO THE REV. WILLIAM CAWTHORNE UNWIN.

UNWIN, I should but ill repay
  The kindness of a friend,
Whose worth deserves as warm a lay
  As ever friendship penned,
Thy name omitted in a page
That would reclaim a vicious age.

A union formed, as mine with thee,
  Not rashly or in sport,
May be as fervent in degree,
  And faithful in its sort,
And may as rich in comfort prove,
As that of true fraternal love.

The bud inserted in the rind,
  The bud of peach or rose,
Adorns, though differing in its kind,
  The stock whereon it grows,
With flower as sweet or fruit as fair
As if produced by nature there.

Not rich, I render what I may,
  I seize thy name in haste,
And place it in this first assay,
  Lest this should prove the last.
'Tis where it should be—in a plan
That holds in view the good of man.

The poet's lyre, to fix his fame,
  Should be the poet's heart;
Affection lights a brighter flame
  Than ever blazed by art.
No muses on these lines attend,
I sink the poet in the friend.

THE

T A S K,

A

P O E M,

IN SIX BOOKS.

By WILLIAM COWPER,
OF THE INNER TEMPLE, ESQ.

Fit surculus arbor.
ANONYM.

To which are added,

BY THE SAME AUTHOR,

An EPISTLE to JOSEPH HILL, Esq. TIROCINIUM, or a
REVIEW of SCHOOLS, and the HISTORY of JOHN GILPIN.

―――――――

LONDON:
PRINTED FOR J. JOHNSON, No 72, ST. PAUL'S
CHURCH-YARD:
1785.

[*Copy of the title-page of Cowper's second publication.*]

ADVERTISEMENT.

THE history of the following production is briefly this : A lady, fond of blank verse, demanded a poem of that kind from the author, and gave him the SOFA for a subject. He obeyed ; and, having much leisure, connected another subject with it ; and, pursuing the train of thought to which his situation and turn of mind led him, brought forth at length, instead of the trifle which he at first intended, a serious affair—a Volume.

In the poem on the subject of Education, he would be very sorry to stand suspected of having aimed his censure at any particular school. His objections are such as naturally apply themselves to schools in general. If there were not, as for the most part there is, wilful neglect in those who manage them, and an omission even of such discipline as they are susceptible of, the objects are yet too numerous for minute attention ; and the aching hearts of ten thousand parents, mourning under the bitterest of all disappointments, attest the truth of the allegation. His quarrel, therefore, is with the mischief at large, and not with any particular instance of it.

THE TASK.

BOOK I.

THE SOFA.

I sing the Sofa.   I who lately sang
Truth, Hope, and Charity, and touched with awe
The solemn chords, and with a trembling hand
Escaped with pain from that adventurous flight,
Now seek repose upon an humbler theme ;
The theme though humble, yet august and proud
The occasion—for the Fair commands the song.
    Time was, when clothing sumptuous or for use,
Save their own painted skins, our sires had none.
As yet black breeches were not, satin smooth,   10
Or velvet soft, or plush with shaggy pile :
The hardy chief, upon the rugged rock
Washed by the sea, or on the gravelly bank
Thrown up by wintry torrents roaring loud,
Fearless of wrong, reposed his weary strength.
Those barbarous ages past, succeeded next
The birthday of Invention, weak at first,
Dull in design, and clumsy to perform.
Joint-stools were then created ; on three legs
Upborne they stood :—three legs upholding firm   20
A massy slab, in fashion square or round.
On such a Stool immortal Alfred sat,
And swayed the sceptre of his infant realms ;
And such in ancient halls and mansions drear
May still be seen, but perforated sore
And drilled in holes the solid oak is found,
By worms voracious eating through and through.

At length a generation more refined
Improved the simple plan; made three legs four,
Gave them a twisted form vermicular,   30
And o'er the seat, with plenteous wadding stuffed,
Induced a splendid cover, green and blue,
Yellow and red, of tapestry richly wrought
And woven close, or needlework sublime.
There might ye see the peony spread wide,
The full-blown rose, the shepherd and his lass,
Lap-dog and lambkin with black staring eyes,
And parrots with twin cherries in their beak.
  Now came the cane from India, smooth and bright
With Nature's varnish, severed into stripes   40
That interlaced each other, these supplied
Of texture firm a lattice-work, that braced
The new machine, and it became a CHAIR.
But restless was the chair; the back erect
Distressed the weary loins, that felt no ease;
The slippery seat betrayed the sliding part
That pressed it, and the feet hung dangling down,
Anxious in vain to find the distant floor.
These for the rich; the rest, whom fate had placed
In modest mediocrity, content   50
With base materials, sat on well-tanned hides
Obdurate and unyielding, glassy smooth,
With here and there a tuft of crimson yarn,
Or scarlet crewel in the cushion fixed:
If cushion might be called what harder seemed
Than the firm oak of which the frame was formed.
No want of timber then was felt or feared
In Albion's happy isle.   The lumber stood
Ponderous, and fixed by its own massy weight.
But elbows still were wanting; these, some say,   60
An alderman of Cripplegate contrived,
And some ascribe the invention to a priest
Burly and big, and studious of his ease.
But rude at first, and not with easy slope
Receding wide, they pressed against the ribs,
And bruised the side, and elevated high
Taught the raised shoulders to invade the ears.
Long time elapsed or e'er our rugged sires
Complained, though incommodiously pent in,
And ill at ease behind.   The ladies first   70
'Gan murmur, as became the softer sex.
Ingenious Fancy, never better pleased
Than when employed to accommodate the fair,
Heard the sweet moan with pity, and devised
The soft SETTEE; one elbow at each end,
And in the midst an elbow, it received,
United yet divided, twain at once.
So sit two kings of Brentford on one throne;
And so two citizens who take the air

Close packed and smiling, in a chaise and one.   80
But relaxation of the languid frame,
By soft recumbency of outstretched limbs,
Was bliss reserved for happier days ;—so slow
The growth of what is excellent, so hard
To attain perfection in this nether world.
Thus first Necessity invented Stools,
Convenience next suggested Elbow-chairs,
And Luxury the accomplished SOFA last.
　　The nurse sleeps sweetly, hired to watch the sick,
Whom snoring she disturbs.　As sweetly he   90
Who quits the coach-box at the midnight hour
To sleep within the carriage more secure,
His legs depending at the open door.
Sweet sleep enjoys the curate in his desk,
The tedious rector drawling o'er his head,
And sweet the clerk below : but neither sleep
Of lazy nurse, who snores the sick man dead,
Nor his who quits the box at midnight hour
To slumber in the carriage more secure,
Nor sleep enjoyed by curate in his desk,   100
Nor yet the dozings of the clerk, are sweet,
Compared with the repose the Sofa yields.
　　Oh ! may I live exempted (while I live
Guiltless of pampered appetite obscene)
From pangs arthritic that infest the toe
Of libertine excess.　The Sofa suits
The gouty limb, 'tis true ; but gouty limb,
Though on a Sofa, may I never feel :
For I have loved the rural walk through lanes
Of grassy swarth, close cropped by nibbling sheep   110
And skirted thick with intertexture firm
Of thorny boughs ; have loved the rural walk
O'er hills, through valleys, and by rivers' brink,
E'er since a truant boy I passed my bounds
To enjoy a ramble on the banks of Thames ;
And still remember, nor without regret,
Of hours that sorrow since has much endeared,
How oft, my slice of pocket store consumed,
Still hungering, penniless and far from home,
I fed on scarlet hips and stony haws,   120
Or blushing crabs, or berries that emboss
The bramble, black as jet, or sloes austere.
Hard fare ! but such as boyish appetite
Disdains not, nor the palate undepraved
By culinary arts, unsavoury deems.
No Sofa then awaited my return,
Nor Sofa then I needed.　Youth repairs
His wasted spirits quickly, by long toil
Incurring short fatigue ; and though our years,
As life declines, speed rapidly away,   130
And not a year but pilfers as he goes

Some youthful grace that age would gladly keep,
A tooth or auburn lock, and by degrees
Their length and colour from the locks they spare,
The elastic spring of an unwearied foot
That mounts the stile with ease, or leaps the fence,
That play of lungs, inhaling and again
Respiring freely the fresh air, that makes
Swift pace or steep ascent no toil to me,
Mine have not pilfered yet ; nor yet impaired   140
My relish of fair prospect : scenes that soothed
Or charmed me young, no longer young, I find
Still soothing and of power to charm me still.
And witness, dear companion of my walks,
Whose arm this twentieth winter I perceive
Fast locked in mine, with pleasure such as love,
Confirmed by long experience of thy worth
And well-tried virtues, could alone inspire,
Witness a joy that thou hast doubled long.
Thou knowest my praise of nature most sincere,   150
And that my raptures are not conjured up
To serve occasions of poetic pomp,
But genuine, and art partner of them all.
How oft upon yon eminence our pace
Has slackened to a pause, and we have borne
The ruffling wind, scarce conscious that it blew,
While admiration feeding at the eye,
And still unsated, dwelt upon the scene.
Thence with what pleasure have we just discerned
The distant plough slow moving, and beside   160
His labouring team, that swerved not from the track,
The sturdy swain diminished to a boy.
Here Ouse, slow winding through a level plain
Of spacious meads with cattle sprinkled o'er,
Conducts the eye along his sinuous course
Delighted.   There, fast rooted in their bank,
Stand, never overlooked, our favourite elms,
That screen the herdsman's solitary hut ;
While far beyond, and overthwart the stream,
That, as with molten glass, inlays the vale,   170
The sloping land recedes into the clouds ;
Displaying on its varied side the grace
Of hedge-row beauties numberless, square tower,
Tall spire, from which the sound of cheerful bells
Just undulates upon the listening ear ;
Groves, heaths, and smoking villages remote.
Scenes must be beautiful which, daily viewed,
Please daily, and whose novelty survives
Long knowledge and the scrutiny of years :
Praise justly due to those that I describe.   180
   Nor rural sights alone, but rural sounds
Exhilarate the spirit, and restore
The tone of languid nature.   Mighty winds,

That sweep the skirt of some far-spreading wood
Of ancient growth, make music not unlike
The dash of Ocean on his winding shore,
And lull the spirit while they fill the mind;
Unnumbered branches waving in the blast,
And all their leaves fast fluttering, all at once.
Nor less composure waits upon the roar   190
Of distant floods, or on the softer voice
Of neighbouring fountain, or of rills that slip
Through the cleft rock, and chiming as they fall
Upon loose pebbles, lose themselves at length
In matted grass, that with a livelier green
Betrays the secret of their silent course.
Nature inanimate employs sweet sounds,
But animated nature sweeter still,
To soothe and satisfy the human ear.
Ten thousand warblers cheer the day, and one   200
The livelong night: nor these alone, whose notes
Nice-fingered art must emulate in vain,
But cawing rooks, and kites that swim sublime
In still repeated circles, screaming loud;
The jay, the pie, and even the boding owl
That hails the rising moon, have charms for me.
Sounds inharmonious in themselves and harsh,
Yet heard in scenes where peace for ever reigns,
And only there, please highly for their sake.
    Peace to the artist, whose ingenious thought   210
Devised the weather-house, that useful toy!
Fearless of humid air and gathering rains
Forth steps the man,—an emblem of myself,—
More delicate, his timorous mate retires.
When Winter soaks the fields, and female feet,
Too weak to struggle with tenacious clay,
Or ford the rivulets, are best at home,
The task of new discoveries falls on me.
At such a season, and with such a charge,
Once went I forth, and found, till then unknown,   220
A cottage, whither oft we since repair:
'Tis perched upon the green-hill top, but close
Environed with a ring of branching elms
That overhang the thatch, itself unseen,
Peeps at the vale below; so thick beset
With foliage of such dark redundant growth,
I called the low-roofed lodge the *Peasant's Nest.*
And hidden as it is, and far remote
From such unpleasing sounds as haunt the ear
In village or in town, the bay of curs   230
Incessant, clinking hammers, grinding wheels,
And infants clamorous whether pleased or pained,
Oft have I wished the peaceful covert mine.
Here, I have said, at least I should possess
The poet's treasure, silence, and indulge

The dreams of fancy, tranquil and secure.
Vain thought! the dweller in that still retreat
Dearly obtains the refuge it affords.
Its elevated site forbids the wretch
To drink sweet waters of the crystal well;   240
He dips his bowl into the weedy ditch,
And heavy-laden brings his beverage home,
Far-fetched and little worth : nor seldom waits,
Dependent on the baker's punctual call,
To hear his creaking panniers at the door,
Angry and sad, and his last crust consumed.
So farewell envy of the *Peasant's Nest.*
If solitude make scant the means of life,
Society for me!—Thou seeming sweet,
Be still a pleasing object in my view,   250
My visit still, but never mine abode.
    Not distant far, a length of colonnade
Invites us : monument of ancient taste,
Now scorned, but worthy of a better fate.
Our fathers knew the value of a screen
From sultry suns, and in their shaded walks
And long protracted bowers enjoyed at noon
The gloom and coolness of declining day.
We bear our shades about us; self-deprived
Of other screen, the thin umbrella spread,   260
And range an Indian waste without a tree.
Thanks to Benevolus*—he spares me yet
These chestnuts ranged in corresponding lines,
And, though himself so polished, still reprieves
The obsolete prolixity of shade.
    Descending now (but cautious, lest too fast)
A sudden steep, upon a rustic bridge,
We pass a gulf, in which the willows dip
Their pendent boughs, stooping as if to drink.
Hence, ankle-deep in moss and flowery thyme,   270
We mount again, and feel at every step
Our foot half sunk in hillocks green and soft,
Raised by the mole, the miner of the soil.
He, not unlike the great ones of mankind,
Disfigures earth, and, plotting in the dark,
Toils much to earn a monumental pile,
That may record the mischiefs he has done.
    The summit gained, behold the proud alcove
That crowns it ! yet not all its pride secures
The grand retreat from injuries impressed   280
By rural carvers, who with knives deface
The panels, leaving an obscure, rude name,
In characters uncouth, and spelt amiss.
So strong the zeal to immortalize himself
Beats in the breast of man, that even a few,

---

* John Courtenay Throckmorton, Esq., of Weston Underwood.

Few transient years, won from the abyss abhorred
Of blank oblivion, seem a glorious prize,
And even to a clown.   Now roves the eye,
And posted on this speculative height
Exults in its command.   The sheepfold here   290
Pours out its fleecy tenants o'er the glebe.
At first, progressive as a stream, they seek
The middle field ; but scattered by degrees,
Each to his choice, soon whiten all the land.
There from the sunburnt hayfield, homeward creeps
The loaded wain, while, lightened of its charge,
The wain that meets it passes swiftly by,
The boorish driver leaning o'er his team
Vociferous, and impatient of delay.
Nor less attractive is the woodland scene,   300
Diversified with trees of every growth,
Alike yet various.   Here the grey smooth trunks
Of ash, or lime, or beech, distinctly shine,
Within the twilight of their distant shades ;
There lost behind a rising ground, the wood
Seems sunk, and shortened to its topmost boughs.
No tree in all the grove but has its charms,
Though each its hue peculiar : paler some,
And of a wannish grey ; the willow such,
And poplar that with silver lines his leaf,   310
And ash far stretching his umbrageous arm ;
Of deeper green the elm ; and deeper still,
Lord of the woods, the long-surviving oak.
Some glossy-leaved, and shining in the sun,
The maple, and the beech of oily nuts
Prolific, and the lime at dewy eve
Diffusing odours : nor unnoted pass
The sycamore, capricious in attire,
Now green, now tawny, and ere autumn yet
Have changed the woods, in scarlet honours bright.   320
O'er these, but far beyond (a spacious map
Of hill and valley interposed between),
The Ouse, dividing the well-watered land,
Now glitters in the sun, and now retires,
As bashful, yet impatient to be seen.
   Hence the declivity is sharp and short,
And such the re-ascent ; between them weeps
A little naiad her impoverished urn
All summer long, which winter fills again.
The folded gates would bar my progress now,   330
But that the lord of this enclosed demesne,
Communicative of the good he owns,
Admits me to a share : the guiltless eye
Commits no wrong, nor wastes what it enjoys.
Refreshing change ! where how the blazing sun ?
By short transition we have lost his glare,
And stepped at once into a cooler clime.

Ye fallen avenues ! once more I mourn
Your fate unmerited, once more rejoice
That yet a remnant of your race survives.   340
How airy and how light the graceful arch,
Yet awful as the consecrated roof
Re-echoing pious anthems ! while beneath
The chequered earth seems restless as a flood
Brushed by the wind.   So sportive is the light
Shot through the boughs, it dances as they dance,
Shadow and sunshine intermingling quick,
And darkening and enlightening, as the leaves
Play wanton, every moment, every spot.
    And now, with nerves new-braced and spirits cheered, 350
We tread the Wilderness, whose well-rolled walks,
With curvature of slow and easy sweep—
Deception innocent—give ample space
To narrow bounds.   The Grove receives us next ;
Between the upright shafts of whose tall elms
We may discern the thresher at his task.
Thump after thump resounds the constant flail,
That seems to swing uncertain, and yet falls
Full on the destined ear.   Wide flies the chaff ;
The rustling straw sends up a frequent mist   360
Of atoms, sparkling in the noonday beam.
Come hither, ye that press your beds of down
And sleep not ; see him sweating o'er his bread
Before he eats it.—'Tis the primal curse,
But softened into mercy ; made the pledge
Of cheerful days, and nights without a groan.
    By ceaseless action all that is subsists.
Constant rotation of the unwearied wheel
That Nature rides upon, maintains her health,
Her beauty, her fertility.   She dreads   370
An instant's pause, and lives but while she moves.
Its own revolvency upholds the world.
Winds from all quarters agitate the air,
And fit the limpid element for use,
Else noxious : oceans, rivers, lakes, and streams,
All feel the freshening impulse, and are cleansed
By restless undulation.   Even the oak
Thrives by the rude concussion of the storm :
He seems indeed indignant, and to feel
The impression of the blast with proud disdain,   380
Frowning as if in his unconscious arm
He held the thunder.   But the monarch owes
His firm stability to what he scorns,
More fixed below, the more disturbed above.
The law by which all creatures else are bound,
Binds man, the lord of all.   Himself derives
No mean advantage from a kindred cause,
From strenuous toil his hours of sweetest ease.
The sedentary stretch their lazy length

When custom bids, but no refreshment find,   390
For none they need : the languid eye, the cheek
Deserted of its bloom, the flaccid, shrunk,
And withered muscle, and the vapid soul,
Reproach their owner with that love of rest
To which he forfeits even the rest he loves.
Not such the alert and active.   Measure life
By its true worth, the comforts it affords,
And theirs alone seems worthy of the name.
Good health, and its associate in the most,
Good temper ; spirits prompt to undertake,   400
And not soon spent, though in an arduous task ;
The powers of fancy and strong thought, are theirs ;
Even age itself seems privileged in them
With clear exemption from its own defects.
A sparkling eye beneath a wrinkled front
The veteran shows, and gracing a grey beard
With youthful smiles, descends toward the grave
Sprightly, and old almost without decay.
    Like a coy maiden, Ease, when courted most,
Farthest retires—an idol, at whose shrine   410
Who oftenest sacrifice are favoured least.
The love of Nature, and the scenes she draws,
Is Nature's dictate.   Strange there should be found
Who, self-imprisoned in their proud saloons,
Renounce the odours of the open field
For the unscented fictions of the loom ;
Who, satisfied with only pencilled scenes,
Prefer to the performance of a God
The inferior wonders of an artist's hand.
Lovely indeed the mimic works of Art,   420
But Nature's works far lovelier.   I admire,
None more admires, the painter's magic skill,
Who shows me that which I shall never see,
Conveys a distant country into mine,
And throws Italian light on English walls :
But imitative strokes can do no more
Than please the eye—sweet Nature every sense.
The air salubrious of her lofty hills,
The cheering fragrance of her dewy vales,
And music of her woods—no works of man   430
May rival these ; these all bespeak a power
Peculiar, and exclusively her own.
Beneath the open sky she spreads the feast ;
'Tis free to all—'tis every day renewed ;
Who scorns it, starves deservedly at home.
He does not scorn it, who, imprisoned long
In some unwholesome dungeon, and a prey
To sallow sickness, which the vapours dank
And clammy of his dark abode have bred,
Escapes at last to liberty and light :   440
His cheek recovers soon its healthful hue,

His eye relumines its extinguished fires,
He walks, he leaps, he runs—is winged with joy,
And riots in the sweets of every breeze.
He does not scorn it, who has long endured
A fever's agonies, and fed on drugs.
Nor yet the mariner, his blood inflamed
With acrid salts; his very heart athirst
To gaze at Nature in her green array,
Upon the ship's tall side he stands, possessed   450
With visions prompted by intense desire :
Fair fields appear below, such as he left
Far distant, such as he would die to find,—
He seeks them headlong, and is seen no more.
　　The spleen is seldom felt where Flora reigns ;
The lowering eye, the petulance, the frown,
And sullen sadness, that o'ershade, distort,
And mar the face of beauty, when no cause
For such immeasurable woe appears,
These Flora banishes, and gives the fair   460
Sweet smiles, and bloom less transient than her own.
It is the constant revolution, stale
And tasteless, of the same repeated joys,
That palls and satiates, and makes languid life
A pedler's pack, that bows the bearer down.
Health suffers, and the spirits ebb ; the heart
Recoils from its own choice—at the full feast
Is famished—finds no music in the song,
No smartness in the jest, and wonders why.
Yet thousands still desire to journey on,   470
Though halt, and weary of the path they tread.
The paralytic who can hold her cards
But cannot play them, borrows a friend's hand
To deal and shuffle, to divide and sort
Her mingled suits and sequences, and sits
Spectatress both and spectacle, a sad
And silent cipher, while her proxy plays.
Others are dragged into the crowded room
Between supporters ; and, once seated, sit
Through downright inability to rise,   480
Till the stout bearers lift the corpse again.
These speak a loud memento.   Yet even these
Themselves love life, and cling to it, as he
That overhangs a torrent, to a twig.
They love it, and yet loathe it ; fear to die,
Yet scorn the purposes for which they live.
Then wherefore not renounce them ? No—the dread,
The slavish dread of solitude, that breeds
Reflection and remorse, the fear of shame,
And their inveterate habits, all forbid.   490
　　Whom call we gay ?   That honour has been long
The boast of mere pretenders to the name.
The innocent are gay—the lark is gay,

That dries his feathers saturate with dew
Beneath the rosy cloud, while yet the beams
Of dayspring overshoot his humble nest.
The peasant too, a witness of his song,
Himself a songster, is as gay as he.
But save me from the gaiety of those
Whose headaches nail them to a noonday bed :   500
And save me too from theirs whose haggard eyes
Flash desperation, and betray their pangs
For property stripped off by cruel chance ;
From gaiety that fills the bones with pain.
The mouth with blasphemy, the heart with woe.
    The earth was made so various, that the mind
Of desultory man, studious of change,
And pleased with novelty, might be indulged.
Prospects, however lovely, may be seen
Till half their beauties fade ; the weary sight,   510
Too well acquainted with their smiles, slides off
Fastidious, seeking less familiar scenes.
Then snug enclosures in the sheltered vale,
Where frequent hedges intercept the eye,
Delight us, happy to renounce awhile,
Not senseless of its charms, what still we love,
That such short absence may endear it more.
Then forests, or the savage rock, may please,
That hides the sea-mew in his hollow clefts
Above the reach of man : his hoary head,   520
Conspicuous many a league, the mariner
Bound homeward, and in hope already there,
Greets with three cheers exulting.   At his waist
A girdle of half-withered shrubs he shows,
And at his feet the baffled billows die.
The common, overgrown with fern, and rough
With prickly gorse, that, shapeless and deformed,
And dangerous to the touch, has yet its bloom,
And decks itself with ornaments of gold,
Yields no unpleasing ramble ; there the turf   530
Smells fresh, and, rich in odoriferous herbs
And fungous fruits of earth, regales the sense
With luxury of unexpected sweets.
    There often wanders one, whom better days
Saw better clad, in cloak of satin trimmed
With lace, and hat with splendid riband bound.
A serving-maid was she, and fell in love
With one who left her, went to sea, and died.
Her fancy followed him through foaming waves
To distant shores, and she would sit and weep   540
At what a sailor suffers ; fancy too,
Delusive most where warmest wishes are,
Would oft anticipate his glad return,
And dream of transports she was not to know.
She heard the doleful tidings of his death,

And never smiled again.   And now she roams
The dreary waste ; there spends the livelong day,
And there, unless when charity forbids,
The livelong night.   A tattered apron hides,
Worn as a cloak, and hardly hides, a gown   550
More tattered still ; and both but ill conceal
A bosom heaved with never-ceasing sighs.
She begs an idle pin of all she meets,
And hoards them in her sleeve ; but needful food,
Though pressed with hunger oft, or comelier clothes,
Though pinched with cold, asks never.—Kate is crazed.
    I see a column of slow-rising smoke
O'ertop the lofty wood that skirts the wild.
A vagabond and useless tribe there eat
Their miserable meal.   A kettle, slung   560
Between two poles upon a stick transverse,
Receives the morsel ; flesh obscene of dog,
Or vermin, or, at best, of cock purloined
From his accustomed perch.   Hard-faring race !
They pick their fuel out of every hedge,
Which, kindled with dry leaves, just saves unquenched
The spark of life.   The sportive wind blows wide
Their fluttering rags, and shows a tawny skin,
The vellum of the pedigree they claim.
Great skill have they in palmistry, and more   570
To conjure clean away the gold they touch,
Conveying worthless dross into its place ;
Loud when they beg, dumb only when they steal.
Strange ! that a creature rational, and cast
In human mould, should brutalize by choice
His nature, and, though capable of arts
By which the world might profit and himself,
Self banished from society, prefer
Such squalid sloth to honourable toil !
Yet even these, though, feigning sickness oft,   580
They swathe the forehead, drag the limping limb,
And vex their flesh with artificial sores,
Can change their whine into a mirthful note
When safe occasion offers ; and with dance,
And music of the bladder and the bag,
Beguile their woes, and make the woods resound.
Such health and gaiety of heart enjoy
The houseless rovers of the sylvan world ;
And breathing wholesome air, and wandering much,
Need other physic none to heal the effects   590
Of loathsome diet, penury, and cold.
    Blest he, though undistinguished from the crowd
By wealth or dignity, who dwells secure
Where man, by nature fierce, has laid aside
His fierceness, having learnt, though slow to learn
The manners and the arts of civil life.
His wants, indeed, are many ; but supply

Is obvious; placed within the easy reach
Of temperate wishes and industrious hands.
Here Virtue thrives as in her proper soil;　　　600
Not rude and surly, and beset with thorns,
And terrible to sight, as when she springs
(If e'er she spring spontaneous) in remote
And barbarous climes, where violence prevails,
And strength is lord of all; but gentle, kind,
By culture tamed, by liberty refreshed,
And all her fruits by radiant truth matured.
War and the chase engross the savage whole:
War followed for revenge, or to supplant
The envied tenants of some happier spot;　　　610
The chase for sustenance, precarious trust!
His hard condition with severe constraint
Binds all his faculties, forbids all growth
Of wisdom, proves a school in which he learns
Sly circumvention, unrelenting hate,
Mean self-attachment, and scarce aught beside.
Thus fare the shivering natives of the north,
And thus the rangers of the western world,
Where it advances far into the deep,
Towards the Antarctic.　Even the favoured isles,　620
So lately found, although the constant sun
Cheer all their seasons with a grateful smile,
Can boast but little virtue: and, inert
Through plenty, lose in morals what they gain
In manners—victims of luxurious ease.
These therefore I can pity, placed remote
From all that science traces, art invents,
Or inspiration teaches; and enclosed
In boundless oceans, never to be passed
By navigators uninformed as they,　　　630
Or ploughed perhaps by British bark again.
But far beyond the rest, and with most cause,
Thee, gentle savage!* whom no love of thee
Or thine, but curiosity, perhaps,
Or else vain-glory, prompted us to draw
Forth from thy native bowers, to show thee here
With what superior skill we can abuse
The gifts of Providence, and squander life.
The dream is past; and thou hast found again
Thy cocoas and bananas, palms and yams,　　　640
And homestall thatched with leaves. But hast thou found
Their former charms? And having seen our state,
Our palaces, our ladies, and our pomp
Of equipage, our gardens, and our sports,
And heard our music; are thy simple friends,
Thy simple fare, and all thy plain delights
As dear to thee as once? And have thy joys

* Omai.

o 2

Lost nothing by comparison with ours?
Rude as thou art (for we returned thee rude
And ignorant, except of outward show),   650
I cannot think thee yet so dull of heart
And spiritless, as never to regret
Sweets tasted here, and left as soon as known.
Methinks I see thee straying on the beach,
And asking of the surge that bathes thy foot
If ever it has washed our distant shore.
I see thee weep, and thine are honest tears,
A patriot's for his country : thou art sad
At thought of her forlorn and abject state,
From which no power of thine can raise her up.   660
Thus fancy paints thee, and, though apt to err,
Perhaps errs little when she paints thee thus.
She tells me too, that duly every morn
Thou climb'st the mountain top, with eager eye
Exploring far and wide the watery waste
For sight of ship from England. Every speck
Seen in the dim horizon turns thee pale
With conflict of contending hopes and fears.
But comes at last the dull and dusky eve,
And sends thee to thy cabin, well prepared   670
To dream all night of what the day denied.
Alas! expect it not. We found no bait
To tempt us in thy country. Doing good,
Disinterested good, is not our trade.
We travel far, 'tis true, but not for nought ;
And must be bribed to compass earth again
By other hopes and richer fruits than yours.
     But though true worth and virtue, in the mild
And genial soil of cultivated life,
Thrive most, and may perhaps thrive only there,   680
Yet not in cities oft: in proud and gay
And gain-devoted cities. Thither flow,
As to a common and most noisome sewer,
The dregs and feculence of every land.
In cities foul example on most minds
Begets its likeness. Rank abundance breeds
In gross and pampered cities sloth and lust,
And wantonness and gluttonous excess.
In cities vice is hidden with most ease,
Or seen with least reproach ; and virtue, taught   690
By frequent lapse, can hope no triumph there
Beyond the achievement of successful flight.
I do confess them nurseries of the arts,
In which they flourish most ; where, in the beams
Of warm encouragement, and in the eye
Of public note, they reach their perfect size.
Such London is, by taste and wealth proclaimed
The fairest capital of all the world,
By riot and incontinence the worst.

There, touched by Reynolds, a dull blank becomes   700
A lucid mirror, in which Nature sees
All her reflected features.   Bacon there
Gives more than female beauty to a stone,
And Chatham's eloquence to marble lips.
Nor does the chisel occupy alone
The powers of Sculpture, but the style as much ;
Each province of her art her equal care.
With nice incision of her guided steel
She ploughs a brazen field, and clothes a soil
So sterile with what charms soe'er she will,   710
The richest scenery and the loveliest forms.
Where finds Philosophy her eagle eye,
With which she gazes at yon burning disk
Undazzled, and detects and counts his spots?
In London.   Where her implements exact,
With which she calculates, computes, and scans
All distance, motion, magnitude, and now
Measures an atom, and now girds a world ?
In London.   Where has commerce such a mart,
So rich, so thronged, so drained, and so supplied,   720
As London, opulent, enlarged, and still
Increasing London?   Babylon of old
Not more the glory of the earth than she,
A more accomplished world's chief glory now.
    She has her praise.   Now mark a spot or two
That so much beauty would do well to purge ;
And show this queen of cities, that so fair
May yet be foul, so witty yet not wise.
It is not seemly, nor of good report,
That she is slack in discipline ; more prompt   730
To avenge than to prevent the breach of law ;
That she is rigid in denouncing death
On petty robbers, and indulges life
And liberty, and ofttimes honour too,
To peculators of the public gold ;
That thieves at home must hang, but he that puts
Into his overgorged and bloated purse
The wealth of Indian provinces, escapes.
Nor is it well, nor can it come to good,
That, through profane and infidel contempt   740
Of Holy Writ, she has presumed to annul
And abrogate, as roundly as she may,
The total ordinance and will of God ;
Advancing Fashion to the post of Truth,
And centering all authority in modes
And customs of her own, till Sabbath rites
Have dwindled into unrespected forms,
And knees and hassocks are well-nigh divorced.
    God made the country, and man made the town :
What wonder then that health and virtue, gifts   750
That can alone make sweet the bitter draught

That life holds out to all, should most abound
And least be threatened in the fields and groves?
Possess ye therefore, ye who, borne about
In chariots and sedans, know no fatigue
But that of idleness, and taste no scenes
But such as art contrives, possess ye still
Your element; there only ye can shine,
There only minds like yours can do no harm.
Our groves were planted to console at noon   760
The pensive wanderer in their shades.   At eve
The moonbeam, sliding softly in between
The sleeping leaves, is all the light they wish,
Birds warbling all the music.   We can spare
The splendour of your lamps, they but eclipse
Our softer satellite.   Your songs confound
Our more harmonious notes: the thrush departs
Scared, and the offended nightingale is mute.
There is a public mischief in your mirth,
It plagues your country.   Folly such as yours   770
Graced with a sword, and worthier of a fan,
Has made, what enemies could ne'er have done,
Our arch of empire, steadfast but for you,
A mutilated structure, soon to fall.

BOOK II.

THE TIME-PIECE.

ARGUMENT.—Reflections suggested by the conclusion of the former book—Peace among the nations recommended on the ground of their common fellowship in sorrow—Prodigies enumerated—Sicilian earthquakes—Man rendered obnoxious to these calamities by sin—God the agent in them—The philosophy that stops at secondary causes reproved—Our own late miscarriages accounted for—Satirical notice taken of our trips to Fontainbleau—But the pulpit, not satire, the proper engine of reformation—The reverend advertiser of engraved sermons—Petit-maître parson—The good preacher—Picture of a theatrical clerical coxcomb—Story-tellers and jesters in the pulpit reproved—Apostrophe to popular applause—Retailers of ancient philosophy expostulated with—Sum of the whole matter—Effects of sacerdotal mismanagement on the laity —Their folly and extravagance—The mischiefs of profusion—Profusion itself, with all its consequent evils, ascribed, as to its principal cause, to the want of discipline in the universities.

Oh for a lodge in some vast wilderness,
Some boundless contiguity of shade,
Where rumour of oppression and deceit,
Of unsuccessful or successful war,
Might never reach me more !   My ear is pained,
My soul is sick with every day's report
Of wrong and outrage with which earth is filled.
There is no flesh in man's obdurate heart,
It does not feel for man ; the natural bond

Of brotherhood is severed as the flax   10
That falls asunder at the touch of fire.
He finds his fellow guilty of a skin
Not coloured like his own, and having power
To enforce the wrong, for such a worthy cause
Dooms and devotes him as his lawful prey.
Lands intersected by a narrow frith
Abhor each other.   Mountains interposed
Make enemies of nations who had else
Like kindred drops been mingled into one.
Thus man devotes his brother, and destroys;   20
And worse than all, and most to be deplored,
As human nature's broadest, foulest blot,
Chains him, and tasks him, and exacts his sweat
With stripes that Mercy, with a bleeding heart,
Weeps when she sees inflicted on a beast.
Then what is man?   And what man seeing this,
And having human feelings, does not blush
And hang his head, to think himself a man?
I would not have a slave to till my ground,
To carry me, to fan me while I sleep,   30
And tremble when I wake, for all the wealth
That sinews bought and sold have ever earned.
No: dear as freedom is, and in my heart's
Just estimation prized above all price,
I had much rather be myself the slave
And wear the bonds, than fasten them on him.
We have no slaves at home.—Then why abroad?
And they themselves once ferried o'er the wave
That parts us, are emancipate and loosed.
Slaves cannot breathe in England; if their lungs   40
Receive our air, that moment they are free,
They touch our country, and their shackles fall.
That's noble, and bespeaks a nation proud
And jealous of the blessing.   Spread it then,
And let it circulate through every vein
Of all your empire; that where Britain's power
Is felt, mankind may feel her mercy too.
    Sure there is need of social intercourse,
Benevolence, and peace, and mutual aid,
Between the nations, in a world that seems   50
To toll the death-bell of its own decease,
And by the voice of all its element,
To preach the general doom.*   When were the winds
Let slip with such a warrant to destroy?
When did the waves so haughtily o'erleap
Their ancient barriers, deluging the dry?
Fires from beneath, and meteors† from above,
Portentous, unexampled, unexplained,

* Alluding to the late calamities in Jamaica.
† Aug. 18, 1783.

Have kindled beacons in the skies, and the old
And crazy earth has had her shaking fits   60
More frequent, and foregone her usual rest.
Is it a time to wrangle, when the props
And pillars of our planet seem to fail,
And Nature* with a dim and sickly eye
To wait the close of all? But grant her end
More distant, and that prophecy demands
A longer respite, unaccomplished yet;
Still they are frowning signals, and bespeak
Displeasure in His breast who smites the earth
Or heals it, makes it languish or rejoice.   70
And 'tis but seemly that, where all deserve
And stand exposed by common peccancy
To what no few have felt, there should be peace,
And brethren in calamity should love.
    Alas for Sicily! rude fragments now
Lie scattered where the shapely column stood.
Her palaces are dust.   In all her streets
The voice of singing and the sprightly chord
Are silent.   Revelry and dance and show
Suffer a syncope and solemn pause,   80
While God performs upon the trembling stage
Of His own works His dreadful part alone.
How does the earth receive Him?—with what signs
Of gratulation and delight, her King?
Pours she not all her choicest fruits abroad,
Her sweetest flowers, her aromatic gums,
Disclosing Paradise where'er He treads?
She quakes at His approach.   Her hollow womb
Conceiving thunders, through a thousand deeps
And fiery caverns, roars beneath His foot.   90
The hills move lightly, and the mountains smoke,
For He has touched them.   From the extremest point
Of elevation down into the abyss,
His wrath is busy and His frown is felt.
The rocks fall headlong, and the valleys rise,
The rivers die into offensive pools,
And, charged with putrid verdure, breathe a gross
And mortal nuisance into all the air.
What solid was, by transformation strange
Grows fluid, and the fixed and rooted earth,   100
Tormented into billows, heaves and swells,
Or with vortiginous and hideous whirl
Sucks down its prey insatiable.   Immense
The tumult and the overthrow, the pangs
And agonies of human and of brute
Multitudes, fugitive on every side,
And fugitive in vain.   The sylvan scene
Migrates uplifted, and with all its soil

* Alluding to the fog that covered both Europe and Asia during the whole summer of 1783.

Alighting in far distant fields, finds out
A new possessor, and survives the change.   110
Ocean has caught the frenzy, and upwrought
To an enormous and o'erbearing height,
Not by a mighty wind, but by that voice
Which winds and waves obey, invades the shore
Resistless. Never such a sudden flood,
Upridged so high, and sent on such a charge,
Possessed an inland scene. Where now the throng
That pressed the beach, and hasty to depart
Looked to the sea for safety? They are gone,
Gone with the refluent wave into the deep—   120
A prince with half his people! Ancient towers,
And roofs embattled high, the gloomy scenes
Where beauty oft and lettered worth consume
Life in the unproductive shades of death,
Fall prone ; the pale inhabitants come forth,
And, happy in their unforeseen release
From all the rigours of restraint, enjoy
The terrors of the day that sets them free.
Who then that has thee would not hold thee fast,
Freedom ! whom they that lose thee, so regret,   130
That even a judgment making way for thee
Seems in their eyes a mercy, for thy sake.
    Such evil sin hath wrought ; and such a flame
Kindled in heaven, that it burns down to earth,
And in the furious inquest that it makes
On God's behalf, lays waste His fairest works.
The very elements, though each be meant
The minister of man, to serve his wants,
Conspire against him. With his breath he draws
A plague into his blood ; and cannot use   140
Life's necessary means, but he must die.
Storms rise to o'erwhelm him : or if stormy winds
Rise not, the waters of the deep shall rise,
And needing none assistance of the storm,
Shall roll themselves ashore, and reach him there.
The earth shall shake him out of all his holds,
Or make his house his grave : nor so content,
Shall counterfeit the motions of the flood,
And drown him in her dry and dusty gulfs.
What then?—were they the wicked above all,   150
And we the righteous, whose fast-anchored isle
Moved not, while theirs was rocked like a light skiff,
The sport of every wave? No : none are clear,
And none than we more guilty. But where all
Stand chargeable with guilt, and to the shafts
Of wrath obnoxious, God may choose His mark,
May punish, if He please, the less, to warn
The more malignant. If He spared not them,
Tremble and be amazed at thine escape,
Far guiltier England ! lest He spare not thee,   160

Happy the man who sees a God employed
In all the good and ill that chequer life !
Resolving all events, with their effects
And manifold results, into the will
And arbitration wise of the Supreme.
Did not His eye rule all things, and intend
The least of our concerns, (since from the least
The greatest oft originate,) could chance
Find place in His dominion, or dispose
One lawless particle to thwart His plan,   170
Then God might be surprised, and unforeseen
Contingence might alarm Him, and disturb
The smooth and equal course of His affairs.
This truth Philosophy, though eagle-eyed
In nature's tendencies, oft overlooks,
And, having found His instrument, forgets
Or disregards, or, more presumptuous still,
Denies the power that wills it.   God proclaims
His hot displeasure against foolish men
That live an atheist life : involves the heaven   180
In tempests ; quits His grasp upon the winds,
And gives them all their fury ; bids a plague
Kindle a fiery boil upon the skin,
And putrefy the breath of blooming health.
He calls for Famine, and the meagre fiend
Blows mildew from between his shrivelled lips,
And taints the golden ear.   He springs His mines,
And desolates a nation at a blast.
Forth steps the spruce philosopher, and tells
Of homogeneal and discordant springs   190
And principles ; of causes, how they work
By necessary laws their sure effects ;
Of action and reaction.   He has found
The source of the disease that nature feels,
And bids the world take heart and banish fear.
Thou fool ! will thy discovery of the cause
Suspend the effect, or heal it ?   Has not God
Still wrought by means since first He made the world,
And did He not of old employ His means
To drown it ?   What is His creation less   200
Than a capacious reservoir of means
Formed for His use, and ready at His will ?
Go, dress thine eyes with eye-salve, ask of Him,
Or ask of whomsoever He has taught,
And learn, though late, the genuine cause of all.
  England, with all thy faults, I love thee still,
My country ! and, while yet a nook is left
Where English minds and manners may be found,
Shall be constrained to love thee.   Though thy clime
Be fickle, and thy year, most part, deformed   210
With dripping rains, or withered by a frost,
I would not yet exchange thy sullen skies

And fields without a flower, for warmer France
With all her vines ; nor for Ausonia's groves
Of golden fruitage, and her myrtle bowers.
To shake thy senate, and from heights sublime
Of patriot eloquence to flash down fire
Upon thy foes, was never meant my task ;
But I can feel thy fortunes, and partake
Thy joys and sorrows with as true a heart   220
As any thunderer there.   And I can feel
Thy follies too, and with a just disdain
Frown at effeminates, whose very looks
Reflect dishonour on the land I love.
How, in the name of soldiership and sense,
Should England prosper, when such things, as smooth
And tender as a girl, all-essenced o'er
With odours, and as profligate as sweet,
Who sell their laurel for a myrtle wreath,
And love when they should fight,—when such as these   230
Presume to lay their hand upon the ark
Of her magnificent and awful cause ?
Time was when it was praise and boast enough
In every clime, and travel where we might,
That we were born her children ; praise enough
To fill the ambition of a private man,
That Chatham's language was his mother tongue,
And Wolfe's great name compatriot with his own.
Farewell those honours, and farewell with them
The hope of such hereafter !   They have fallen   240
Each in his field of glory : one in arms,
And one in council—Wolfe upon the lap
Of smiling Victory that moment won,
And Chatham, heart-sick of his country's shame !
They made us many soldiers.   Chatham still
Consulting England's happiness at home,
Secured it by an unforgiving frown
If any wronged her.   Wolfe, where'er he fought,
Put so much of his heart into his act,
That his example had a magnet's force,   250
And all were swift to follow whom all loved.
Those suns are set.   Oh rise some other such !
Or all that we have left is empty talk
Of old achievements, and despair of new.
   Now hoist the sail, and let the streamers float
Upon the wanton breezes.   Strew the deck
With lavender, and sprinkle liquid sweets,
That no rude savour maritime invade
The nose of nice nobility.   Breathe soft,
Ye clarionets, and softer still, ye flutes,   260
That winds and waters lulled by magic sounds
May bear us smoothly to the Gallic shore.
True, we have lost an empire—let it pass.
True, we may thank the perfidy of France

That picked the jewel out of England's crown,
With all the cunning of an envious shrew.
And let that pass,—'twas but a trick of state.
A brave man knows no malice, but at once
Forgets in peace, the injuries of war,
And gives his direst foe a friend's embrace.   270
And shamed as we have been, to the very beard
Braved and defied, and in our own sea proved
Too weak for those decisive blows that once
Ensured us mastery there, we yet retain
Some small pre-eminence; we justly boast
At least superior jockeyship, and claim
The honours of the turf as all our own.
Go then, well worthy of the praise ye seek,
And show the shame ye might conceal at home,
In foreign eyes!—be grooms, and win the plate,   280
Where once your nobler fathers won a crown!—
'Tis generous to communicate your skill
To those that need it.   Folly is soon learned:
And under such preceptors who can fail!
   There is a pleasure in poetic pains
Which only poets know.   The shifts and turns,
The expedients and inventions multiform
To which the mind resorts, in chase of terms
Though apt, yet coy, and difficult to win,—
To arrest the fleeting images that fill   290
The mirror of the mind, and hold them fast,
And force them sit, till he has pencilled off
A faithful likeness of the forms he views;
Then to dispose his copies with such art
That each may find its most propitious light,
And shine by situation, hardly less
Than by the labour and the skill it cost,
Are occupations of the poet's mind
So pleasing, and that steal away the thought
With such address from themes of sad import,   300
That, lost in his own musings, happy man!
He feels the anxieties of life, denied
Their wonted entertainment, all retire.
Such joys has he that sings.   But ah! not such,
Or seldom such, the hearers of his song.
Fastidious, or else listless, or perhaps
Aware of nothing arduous in a task
They never undertook, they little note
His dangers or escapes, and haply find
Their least amusement where he found the most.   310
But is amusement all?   Studious of song,
And yet ambitious not to sing in vain,
I would not trifle merely, though the world
Be loudest in their praise who do no more.
Yet what can satire, whether grave or gay?
It may correct a foible, may chastise

The freaks of fashion, regulate the dress,
Retrench a sword-blade, or displace a patch;
But where are its sublimer trophies found?
What vice has it subdued? whose heart reclaimed   320
By rigour, or whom laughed into reform?
Alas! Leviathan is not so tamed:
Laughed at, he laughs again; and, stricken hard,
Turns to the stroke his adamantine scales,
That fear no discipline of human hands.
   The pulpit, therefore (and I name it filled
With solemn awe, that bids me well beware
With what intent I touch that holy thing)—
The pulpit (when the satirist has at last,   330
Strutting and vapouring in an empty school,
Spent all his force, and made no proselyte)—
I say the pulpit (in the sober use
Of its legitimate, peculiar powers)
Must stand acknowledged, while the world shall stand,
The most important and effectual guard,
Support, and ornament of virtue's cause.
There stands the messenger of truth.   There stands
The legate of the skies; his theme divine,
His office sacred, his credentials clear.
By him, the violated law speaks out   340
Its thunders, and by him, in strains as sweet
As angels use, the Gospel whispers peace.
He 'stablishes the strong, restores the weak,
Reclaims the wanderer, binds the broken heart,
And, armed himself in panoply complete
Of heavenly temper, furnishes with arms
Bright as his own, and trains by every rule
Of holy discipline, to glorious war,
The sacramental host of God's elect.
Are all such teachers?   Would to Heaven all were!   350
But hark,—the Doctor's voice!—fast wedged between
Two empirics he stands, and with swollen cheeks
Inspires the news, his trumpet.   Keener far
Than all invective is his bold harangue,
While through that public organ of report
He hails the clergy; and, defying shame,
Announces to the world his own and theirs.
He teaches those to read, whom schools dismissed,
And colleges, untaught; sells accent, tone,
And emphasis in score, and gives to prayer   360
The *adagio* and *andante* it demands.
He grinds divinity of other days
Down into modern use; transforms old print
To zigzag manuscript, and cheats the eyes
Of gallery critics by a thousand arts.
Are there who purchase of the Doctor's ware?
Oh name it not in Gath!—it cannot be
That grave and learned Clerks should need such aid.

He doubtless is in sport, and does but droll,
Assuming thus a rank unknown before—
Grand caterer and dry-nurse of the church.   370
    I venerate the man whose heart is warm,
Whose hands are pure, whose doctrine and whose life
Coincident, exhibit lucid proof
That he is honest in the sacred cause.
To such I render more than mere respect,
Whose actions say that they respect themselves.
But loose in morals, and in manners vain,
In conversation frivolous, in dress
Extreme, at once rapacious and profuse,   380
Frequent in park, with lady at his side,
Ambling and prattling scandal as he goes,
But rare at home, and never at his books,
Or with his pen, save when he scrawls a card ;
Constant at routs, familiar with a round
Of ladyships, a stranger to the poor ;
Ambitious of preferment for its gold,
And well prepared by ignorance and sloth
By infidelity and love o' the world,
To make God's work a sinecure ; a slave   390
To his own pleasures and his patron's pride :—
From such apostles, O ye mitred heads,
Preserve the church ! and lay not careless hands
On skulls that cannot teach, and will not learn.
    Would I describe a preacher, such as Paul,
Were he on earth, would hear, approve, and own,
Paul should himself direct me.   I would trace
His master-strokes, and draw from his design.
I would express him simple, grave, sincere ;
In doctrine uncorrupt ; in language plain,   400
And plain in manner ; decent, solemn, chaste,
And natural in gesture ; much impressed
Himself, as conscious of his awful charge,
And anxious mainly that the flock he feeds
May feel it too ; affectionate in look,
And tender in address, as well becomes
A messenger of grace to guilty men.
Behold the picture !   Is it like ?—Like whom ?
The things that mount the rostrum with a skip,
And then skip down again ; pronounce a text,   410
Cry-hem ! and reading what they never wrote,
Just fifteen minutes, huddle up their work,
And with a well-bred whisper close the scene !
    In man or woman, but far most in man,
And most of all in man that ministers
And serves the altar, in my soul I loathe
All affectation.   'Tis my perfect scorn ;
Object of my implacable disgust.
What !—will a man play tricks, will he indulge
A silly fond conceit of his fair form   420

And just proportion, fashionable mien,
And pretty face, in presence of his God?
Or will he seek to dazzle me with tropes,
As with the diamond on his lily hand,
And play his brilliant parts before my eyes
When I am hungry for the bread of life?
He mocks his Maker, prostitutes and shames
His noble office, and, instead of truth,
Displaying his own beauty, starves his flock.
Therefore, avaunt all attitude and stare,   430
And start theatric, practised at the glass.
I seek divine simplicity in him
Who handles things divine; and all besides,
Though learned with labour, and though much admired
By curious eyes and judgments ill informed,
To me is odious as the nasal twang
Heard at conventicle, where worthy men,
Misled by custom, strain celestial themes
Through the pressed nostril, spectacle-bestrid.
Some, decent in demeanour while they preach,   440
That task performed, relapse into themselves,
And having spoken wisely, at the close
Grow wanton, and give proof to every eye—
Whoe'er was edified, themselves were not.
Forth comes the pocket mirror.   First we stroke
An eyebrow; next, compose a straggling lock;
Then with an air, most gracefully performed,
Fall back into our seat, extend an arm,
And lay it at its ease with gentle care,
With handkerchief in hand, depending low.   450
The better hand, more busy, gives the nose
Its bergamot, or aids the indebted eye
With opera-glass to watch the moving scene,
And recognise the slow-retiring fair.
Now this is fulsome, and offends me more
Than in a churchman slovenly neglect
And rustic coarseness would.   A heavenly mind
May be indifferent to her house of clay,
And slight the hovel as beneath her care;
But how a body so fantastic, trim,   460
And quaint in its deportment and attire,
Can lodge a heavenly mind—demands a doubt.
    He that negotiates between God and man,
As God's ambassador, the grand concerns
Of judgment and of mercy, should beware
Of lightness in his speech.   'Tis pitiful
To court a grin, when you should woo a soul;
To break a jest, when pity would inspire
Pathetic exhortation; and to address
The skittish fancy with facetious tales,   470
When sent with God's commission to the heart.
So did not Paul.   Direct me to a quip

Or merry turn in all he ever wrote,
And I consent you take it for your text,
Your only one, till sides and benches fail.
No: he was serious in a serious cause,
And understood too well the weighty terms
That he had ta'en in charge.   He would not stoop
To conquer those by jocular exploits,
Whom truth and soberness assailed in vain.   480
    Oh, popular applause! what heart of man
Is proof against thy sweet seducing charms?
The wisest and the best feel urgent need
Of all their caution in thy gentlest gales;
But swelled into a gust—who then, alas!
With all his canvas set, and inexpert,
And therefore heedless, can withstand thy power?
Praise from the rivelled lips of toothless, bald
Decrepitude, and in the looks of lean
And craving poverty, and in the bow   490
Respectful of the smutched artificer,
Is oft too welcome, and may much disturb
The bias of the purpose.   How much more
Poured forth by beauty splendid and polite,
In language soft as adoration breathes?
Ah, spare your idol! think him human still;
Charms he may have, but he has frailties too;
Dote not too much, nor spoil what ye admire.
    All truth is from the sempiternal source
Of Light Divine.   But Egypt, Greece, and Rome   500
Drew from the stream below.   More favoured, we
Drink, when we choose it, at the fountain-head.
To them it flowed much mingled and defiled
With hurtful error, prejudice, and dreams
Illusive of philosophy, so called,
But falsely.   Sages after sages strove
In vain to filter off a crystal draught
Pure from the lees, which often more enhanced
The thirst than slaked it, and not seldom bred
Intoxication and delirium wild.   510
In vain they pushed inquiry to the birth
And spring-time of the world; asked, Whence is man?
Why formed at all?   And wherefore as he is?
Where must he find his Maker?   With what rites
Adore Him?   Will He hear, accept, and bless?
Or does He sit regardless of His works?
Has man within him an immortal seed?
Or does the tomb take all?   If he survive
His ashes, where? and in what weal or woe?
Knots worthy of solution, which alone   520
A Deity could solve.   Their answers vague,
And all at random, fabulous and dark,
Left them as dark themselves.   Their rules of life
Defective and unsanctioned, proved too weak

To bind the roving appetite, and lead
Blind Nature to a God not yet revealed.
'Tis Revelation satisfies all doubts,
Explains all mysteries, except her own,
And so illuminates the path of life,
That fools discover it, and stray no more.   530
Now tell me, dignified and sapient sir,
My man of morals, nurtured in the shades
Of Academus, is this false or true?
Is Christ the abler teacher, or the schools?
If Christ, then why resort at every turn
To Athens or to Rome, for wisdom short
Of man's occasions, when in Him reside
Grace, knowledge, comfort,—an unfathomed store?
How oft, when Paul has served us with a text,
Has Epictetus, Plato, Tully, preached!   540
Men that, if now alive, would sit content
And humble learners of a Saviour's worth,
Preach it who might.   Such was their love of truth,
Their thirst of knowledge, and their candour too.
    And thus it is.   The pastor, either vain
By nature, or by flattery made so, taught
To gaze at his own splendour, and to exalt
Absurdly, not his office, but himself,—
Or unenlightened, and too proud to learn,—
Or vicious, and not therefore apt to teach,—   550
Perverting often by the stress of lewd
And loose example, whom he should instruct,—
Exposes and holds up to broad disgrace
The noblest function, and discredits much
The brightest truths that man has ever seen.
For ghostly counsel, if it either fall
Below the exigence, or be not backed
With show of love, at least with hopeful proof
Of some sincerity on the giver's part;
Or be dishonoured in the exterior form   560
And mode of its conveyance, by such tricks
As move derision, or by foppish airs
And histrionic mummery, that let down
The pulpit to the level of the stage,
Drops from the lips a disregarded thing.
The weak perhaps are moved, but are not taught,
While prejudice in men of stronger minds
Takes deeper root, confirmed by what they see.
A relaxation of religion's hold
Upon the roving and untutored heart   570
Soon follows, and the curb of conscience snapped,
The laity run wild.—But do they now?
Note their extravagance, and be convinced.
    As nations, ignorant of God, contrive
A wooden one, so we, no longer taught
By monitors that mother church supplies,

Now make our own.   Posterity will ask
(If e'er posterity see verse of mine),
Some fifty or a hundred lustrums hence,
What was a monitor in George's days?   580
My very gentle reader yet unborn,
Of whom I needs must augur better things,
Since Heaven would sure grow weary of a world
Productive only of a race like ours,
A monitor is wood.   Plank shaven thin.
We wear it at our backs.   There closely braced
And neatly fitted, it compresses hard
The prominent and most unsightly bones,
And binds the shoulders flat.   We prove its use
Sovereign and most effectual to secure   590
A form not now gymnastic as of yore,
From rickets and distortion, else our lot.
But thus admonished we can walk erect,
One proof at least of manhood ; while the friend
Sticks close, a Mentor worthy of his charge.
Our habits, costlier than Lucullus wore,
And by caprice as multiplied as his,
Just please us while the fashion is at full,
But change with every moon.   The sycophant
Who waits to dress us, arbitrates their date ;   600
Surveys his fair reversion with keen eye ;
Finds one ill made, another obsolete,
This fits not nicely, that is ill conceived ;
And, making prize of all that he condemns
With our expenditure defrays his own.
Variety's the very spice of life,
That gives it all its flavour.   We have run
Through every change that fancy at the loom
Exhausted, has had genius to supply ;
And, studious of mutation still, discard   610
A real elegance, a little used,
For monstrous novelty and strange disguise.
We sacrifice to dress, till household joys
And comforts cease.   Dress drains our cellar dry,
And keeps our larder lean ; puts out our fires,
And introduces hunger, frost, and woe,
Where peace and hospitality might reign.
What man that lives, and that knows how to live,
Would fail to exhibit at the public shows
A form as splendid as the proudest there,   620
Though appetite raise outcries at the cost ?
A man o' the town dines late, but soon enough,
With reasonable forecast and dispatch,
To ensure a side-box station at half-price.
You think, perhaps, so delicate his dress,
His daily fare as delicate.   Alas !
He picks clean teeth, and, busy as he seems
With an old tavern quill, is hungry yet.

The Rout is Folly's circle, which she draws
With magic wand.   So potent is the spell,   630
That none decoyed into that fatal ring,
Unless by Heaven's peculiar grace, escape.
There we grow early grey, but never wise ;
There form connexions, but acquire no friend ;
Solicit pleasure, hopeless of success ;
Waste youth in occupations only fit
For second childhood ; and devote old age
To sports which only childhood could excuse.
There they are happiest who dissemble best
Their weariness ; and they the most polite   640
Who squander time and treasure with a smile,
Though at their own destruction.   She that asks
Her dear five hundred friends, contemns them all,
And hates their coming.   They (what can they less ?)
Make just reprisals, and with cringe and shrug,
And bow obsequious, hide their hate of her.
All catch the frenzy, downward from her Grace,
Whose flambeaux flash against the morning skies
And gild our chamber ceilings as they pass,
To her who, frugal only that her thrift   650
May feed excesses she can ill afford,
Is hackneyed home unlackeyed ; who in haste
Alighting, turns the key in her own door,
And at the watchman's lantern borrowing light,
Finds a cold bed her only comfort left.
Wives beggar husbands, husbands starve their wives,
On Fortune's velvet altar offering up
Their last poor pittance—Fortune, most severe
Of goddesses yet known, and costlier far
Than all that held their routs in Juno's heaven !   660
So fare we in this prison-house the world.
And 'tis a fearful spectacle to see
So many maniacs dancing in their chains.
They gaze upon the links that hold them fast,
With eyes of anguish, execrate their lot,
Then shake them in despair, and dance again.
   Now basket up the family of plagues
That waste our vitals ; peculation, sale
Of honour, perjury, corruption, frauds
By forgery, by subterfuge of law,   670
By tricks and lies as numerous and as keen
As the necessities their authors feel ;
Then cast them, closely bundled, every brat
At the right door.   Profusion is the sire.
Profusion unrestrained, with all that's base
In character, has littered all the land,
And bred, within the memory of no few,
A priesthood such as Baal's was of old,
A people such as never was till now.
It is a hungry vice :—it eats up all   680

That gives society its beauty, strength,
Convenience, and security, and use:
Makes men mere vermin, worthy to be trapped
And gibbeted as fast as catchpole-claws
Can seize the slippery prey: unties the knot
Of union, and converts the sacred band
That holds mankind together, to a scourge.
Profusion deluging a state with lusts
Of grossest nature and of worst effects,
Prepares it for its ruin: hardens, blinds,   690
And warps the consciences of public men
Till they can laugh at virtue; mock the fools
That trust them; and, in the end, disclose a face
That would have shocked credulity herself
Unmasked, vouchsafing this their sole excuse;
Since all alike are selfish—why not they?
This does Profusion, and the accursèd cause
Of such deep mischief has itself a cause.
    In colleges and halls, in ancient days,
When learning, virtue, piety, and truth   700
Were precious, and inculcated with care,
There dwelt a sage called Discipline.   His head
Not yet by time completely silvered o'er,
Bespoke him past the bounds of freakish youth,
But strong for service still, and unimpaired.
His eye was meek and gentle, and a smile
Played on his lips, and in his speech was heard
Paternal sweetness, dignity, and love.
The occupation dearest to his heart
Was to encourage goodness.   He would stroke   710
The head of modest and ingenuous worth
That blushed at its own praise; and press the youth
Close to his side that pleased him.   Learning grew
Beneath his care, a thriving vigorous plant;
The mind was well informed, the passions held
Subordinate, and diligence was choice.
If e'er it chanced, as sometimes chance it must,
That one among so many overleaped
The limits of control, his gentle eye
Grew stern, and darted a severe rebuke;   720
His frown was full of terror, and his voice
Shook the delinquent with such fits of awe
As left him not, till penitence had won
Lost favour back again, and closed the breach.
But Discipline, a faithful servant long,
Declined at length into the vale of years;
A palsy struck his arm, his sparkling eye
Was quenched in rheums of age, his voice unstrung
Grew tremulous, and moved derision more
Than reverence, in perverse rebellious youth.   730
So colleges and halls neglected much
Their good old friend, and Discipline at length

O'erlooked and unemployed, fell sick, and died.
Then Study languished, Emulation slept,
And Virtue fled.   The schools became a scene
Of solemn farce, where Ignorance in stilts,
His cap well lined with logic not his own,
With parrot-tongue performed the scholar's part,
Proceeding soon a graduated dunce.
Then compromise had place, and scrutiny   740
Became stone blind, precedence went in truck,
And he was competent whose purse was so.
A dissolution of all bonds ensued ;
The curbs invented for the mulish mouth
Of headstrong youth were broken ; bars and bolts
Grew rusty by disuse, and massy gates
Forgot their office, opening with a touch ;
Till gowns at length are found mere masquerade ;
The tasselled cap and the spruce band a jest,
A mockery of the world.   What need of these   750
For gamesters, jockeys, brothellers impure,
Spendthrifts and booted sportsmen, oftener seen
With belted waist and pointers at their heels
Than in the bounds of duty?   What was learned,
If aught was learned in childhood, is forgot,
And such expense as pinches parents blue,
And mortifies the liberal hand of love,
Is squandered in pursuit of idle sports
And vicious pleasures ; buys the boy a name,
That sits a stigma on his father's house,   760
And cleaves through life inseparably close
To him that wears it.   What can after-games
Of riper joys, and commerce with the world,
The lewd vain world that must receive him soon,
Add to such erudition thus acquired,
Where science and where virtue are professed ?
They may confirm his habits, rivet fast
His folly, but to spoil him is a task
That bids defiance to the united powers
Of fashion, dissipation, taverns, stews.   770
Now, blame we most the nurslings or the nurse?
The children crooked and twisted and deformed
Through want of care, or her whose winking eye
And slumbering oscitancy mars the brood ?
The nurse no doubt.   Regardless of her charge,
She needs herself correction ; needs to learn
That it is dangerous sporting with the world,
With things so sacred as a nation's trust,
The nurture of her youth, her dearest pledge.
   All are not such.   I had a brother once—   780
Peace to the memory of a man of worth,
A man of letters, and of manners too ;
Of manners sweet as virtue always wears
When gay good-nature dresses her in smiles.

He graced a college,* in which order yet
Was sacred; and was honoured, loved, and wept
By more than one, themselves conspicuous there.
Some minds are tempered happily, and mixed
With such ingredients of good sense and taste
Of what is excellent in man, they thirst   790
With such a zeal to be what they approve,
That no restraints can circumscribe them more
Than they themselves by choice, for wisdom's sake.
Nor can example hurt them; what they see
Of vice in others but enhancing more
The charms of virtue in their just esteem.
If such escape contagion, and emerge
Pure, from so foul a pool, to shine abroad,
And give the world their talents and themselves,
Small thanks to those whose negligence or sloth   800
Exposed their inexperience to the snare,
And left them to an undirected choice.
    See then the quiver broken and decayed,
In which are kept our arrows.   Rusting there
In wild disorder, and unfit for use,
What wonder, if discharged into the world,
They shame their shooters with a random flight,
Their points obtuse, and feathers drunk with wine.
Well may the church wage unsucessful war,
With such artillery armed.   Vice parries wide   810
The undreaded volley with a sword of straw,
And stands an impudent and fearless mark.
    Have we not tracked the felon home, and found
His birthplace and his dam?   The country mourns,
Mourns, because every plague that can infest
Society, and that saps and worms the base
Of the edifice that Policy has raised,
Swarms in all quarters; meets the eye, the ear,
And suffocates the breath at every turn.
Profusion breeds them; and the cause itself   820
Of that calamitous mischief has been found:
Found too where most offensive, in the skirts
Of the robed pedagogue.   Else, let the arraigned
Stand up unconscious, and refute the charge.
So when the Jewish leader stretched his arm,
And waved his rod divine, a race obscene,
Spawned in the muddy beds of Nile, came forth,
Polluting Egypt.   Gardens, fields, and plains
Were covered with the pest.   The streets were filled:
The croaking nuisance lurked in every nook,   830
Nor palaces nor even chambers 'scaped,
And the land stank, so numerous was the fry.

* Benet College, Cambridge.

BOOK III.

THE GARDEN.

As one, who, long in thickets and in brakes
Entangled, winds now this way and now that
His devious course uncertain, seeking home ;
Or having long in miry ways been foiled
And sore discomfited, from slough to slough
Plunging, and half despairing of escape,
If chance at length he finds a greensward smooth
And faithful to the foot, his spirits rise,
He cherups brisk his ear-erecting steed,
And winds his way with pleasure and with ease ;   10
So I, designing other themes, and called
To adorn the Sofa with eulogium due,
To tell its slumbers and to paint its dreams,
Have rambled wide : in country, city, seat
Of academic fame (howe'er deserved),
Long held and scarcely disengaged at last.
But now with pleasant pace a cleanlier road
I mean to tread.   I feel myself at large,
Courageous, and refreshed for future toil,
If toil awaits me, or if dangers new.   20
    Since pulpits fail, and sounding-boards reflect
Most part an empty ineffectual sound,
What chance that I, to fame so little known,
Nor conversant with men or manners much,
Should speak to purpose, or with better hope
Crack the satiric thong ?   'Twere wiser far
For me, enamoured of sequestered scenes,
And charmed with rural beauty, to repose
Where chance may throw me, beneath elm or vine,
My languid limbs when summer sears the plains,   30
Or when rough winter rages, on the soft
And sheltered Sofa, while the nitrous air
Feeds a blue flame, and makes a cheerful hearth ;
There, undisturbed by Folly, and apprised
How great the danger of disturbing her,
To muse in silence, or at least confine
Remarks that gall so many, to the few

My partners in retreat.   Disgust concealed
Is ofttimes proof of wisdom, when the fault
Is obstinate, and cure beyond our reach.   40
    Domestic happiness, thou only bliss
Of Paradise that has survived the fall!
Though few now taste thee unimpaired and pure,
Or tasting long enjoy thee, too infirm
Or too incautious to preserve thy sweets
Unmixed with drops of bitter, which neglect
Or temper sheds into thy crystal cup.
Thou art the nurse of Virtue.   In thine arms
She smiles, appearing, as in truth she is,
Heaven-born, and destined to the skies again.   50
Thou art not known where Pleasure is adored,
That reeling goddess with the zoneless waist
And wandering eyes, still leaning on the arm
Of Novelty, her fickle frail support;
For thou art meek and constant, hating change,
And finding in the calm of truth-tried love
Joys that her stormy raptures never yield.
Forsaking thee, what shipwreck have we made
Of honour, dignity, and fair renown,
Till prostitution elbows us aside   60
In all our crowded streets, and senates seem
Convened for purposes of empire less,
Than to release the adultress from her bond.
The adultress! what a theme for angry verse!
What provocation to the indignant heart
That feels for injured love! but I disdain
The nauseous task to paint her as she is,
Cruel, abandoned, glorying in her shame.
No.   Let her pass, and charioted along
In guilty splendour, shake the public ways;   70
The frequency of crimes has washed them white;
And verse of mine shall never brand the wretch,
Whom matrons now, of character unsmirched,
And chaste themselves, are not ashamed to own.
Virtue and vice had boundaries in old time,
Not to be passed; and she that had renounced
Her sex's honour, was renounced herself
By all that prized it; not for prudery's sake,
But dignity's, resentful of the wrong.
'Twas hard perhaps on here and there a waif,   80
Desirous to return, and not received;
But was a wholesome rigour in the main,
And taught the unblemished to preserve with care
That purity, whose loss was loss of all.
Men too were nice in honour in those days,
And judged offenders well.   Then he that sharped,
And pocketed a prize by fraud obtained,
Was marked and shunned as odious.   He that sold
His country, or was slack when she required

His every nerve in action and at stretch,   90
Paid with the blood that he had basely spared
The price of his default.   But now—yes, now,
We are become so candid and so fair,
So liberal in construction, and so rich
In Christian charity, (good-natured age !)
That they are safe, sinners of either sex,
Transgress what laws they may.   Well dressed, well bred,
Well equipaged, is ticket good enough
To pass us readily through every door.
Hypocrisy, detest her as we may,   100
(And no man's hatred ever wronged her yet,)
May claim this merit still—that she admits
The worth of what she mimics with such care,
And thus gives Virtue indirect applause;
But she has burned her mask, not needed here,
Where Vice has such allowance, that her shifts
And specious semblances have lost their use.
   I was a stricken deer that left the herd
Long since; with many an arrow deep infixed
My panting side was charged, when I withdrew   110
To seek a tranquil death in distant shades.
There was I found by One who had Himself
Been hurt by the archers.   In His side He bore,
And in His hands and feet, the cruel scars.
With gentle force soliciting the darts,
He drew them forth, and healed and bade me live.
Since then, with few associates, in remote
And silent woods I wander, far from those
My former partners of the peopled scene;
With few associates, and not wishing more.   120
Here much I ruminate, as much I may,
With other views of men and manners now
Than once, and others of a life to come.
I see that all are wanderers, gone astray
Each in his own delusions; they are lost
In chase of fancied happiness, still wooed
And never won.   Dream after dream ensues,
And still they dream that they shall still succeed,
And still are disappointed.   Rings the world
With the vain stir.   I sum up half mankind,   130
And add two-thirds of the remaining half,
And find the total of their hopes and fears
Dreams, empty dreams.   The million flit as gay
As if created only like the fly
That spreads his motley wings in the eye of noon,
To sport their season, and be seen no more.
The rest are sober dreamers, grave and wise,
And pregnant with discoveries new and rare.
Some write a narrative of wars, and feats
Of heroes little known, and call the rant   140
A history : describe the man, of whom

His own coevals took but little note,
And paint his person, character, and views,
As they had known him from his mother's womb.
They disentangle from the puzzled skein
In which obscurity has wrapped them up,
The threads of politic and shrewd design
That ran through all his purposes, and charge
His mind with meanings that he never had,
Or having, kept concealed.   Some drill and bore   150
The solid earth, and from the strata there
Extract a register, by which we learn
That He who made it, and revealed its date
To Moses, was mistaken in its age.
Some, more acute and more industrious still,
Contrive creation; travel Nature up
To the sharp peak of her sublimest height,
And tell us whence the stars; why some are fixed,
And planetary some; what gave them first
Rotation, from what fountain flowed their light.   160
Great contest follows, and much learned dust
Involves the combatants, each claiming truth,
And truth disclaiming both: and thus they spend
The little wick of life's poor shallow lamp
In playing tricks with nature, giving laws
To distant worlds, and trifling in their own.
Is't not a pity now, that tickling rheums
Should ever tease the lungs and blear the sight
Of oracles like these?   Great pity too,
That having wielded the elements, and built   170
A thousand systems, each in his own way,
They should go out in fume and be forgot?
Ah! what is life thus spent? and what are they
But frantic who thus spend it all for smoke?
Eternity for bubbles proves at last
A senseless bargain.   When I see such games
Played by the creatures of a Power who swears
That He will judge the earth, and call the fool
To a sharp reckoning that has lived in vain;
And when I weigh this seeming wisdom well,   180
And prove it in the infallible result
So hollow and so false—I feel my heart
Dissolve in pity, and account the learned,
If this be learning, most of all deceived.
Great crimes alarm the conscience, but it sleeps
While thoughtful man is plausibly amused.
"Defend me therefore, common sense," say I,
"From reveries so airy, from the toil
Of dropping buckets into empty wells,
And growing old in drawing nothing up!"   190
    "'Twere well," says one sage erudite, profound,
Terribly arched and aquiline his nose,
And overbuilt with most impending brows—

" 'Twere well, could you permit the world to live
As the world pleases. What's the world to you?"
Much.   I was born of woman, and drew milk,
As sweet as charity, from human breasts.
I think, articulate, I laugh and weep,
And exercise all functions of a man.
How then should I and any man that lives   200
Be strangers to each other?   Pierce my vein,
Take of the crimson stream meandering there,
And catechise it well.   Apply thy glass,
Search it, and prove now if it be not blood
Congenial with thine own: and if it be,
What edge of subtlety canst thou suppose
Keen enough, wise and skilful as thou art,
To cut the link of brotherhood, by which
One common Maker bound me to the kind?
True; I am no proficient, I confess,   210
In arts like yours.   I cannot call the swift
And perilous lightnings from the angry clouds,
And bid them hide themselves in earth beneath;
I cannot analyse the air, nor catch
The parallax of yonder luminous point
That seems half quenched in the immense abyss;
Such powers I boast not—neither can I rest
A silent witness of the headlong rage
Or heedless folly by which thousands die,
Bone of my bone, and kindred souls to mine.   220
   God never meant that man should scale the heavens
By strides of human wisdom.   In His works,
Though wondrous, He commands us in His word
To seek Him rather where His mercy shines.
The mind indeed, enlightened from above,
Views Him in all; ascribes to the grand cause
The grand effect; acknowledges with joy
His manner, and with rapture tastes His style.
But never yet did philosophic tube,
That brings the planets home into the eye   230
Of observation, and discovers, else
Not visible, His family of worlds,
Discover Him that rules them; such a veil
Hangs over mortal eyes, blind from the birth,
And dark in things divine.   Full often too
Our wayward intellect, the more we learn
Of nature, overlooks her Author more,
From instrumental causes proud to draw
Conclusions retrograde, and mad mistake.
But if His word once teach us, shoot a ray   240
Through all the heart's dark chambers, and reveal
Truths undiscerned but by that holy light,
Then all is plain.   Philosophy baptized
In the pure fountain of eternal love
Has eyes indeed; and viewing all she sees

As meant to indicate a God to man,
Gives Him His praise, and forfeits not her own.
Learning has borne such fruit in other days
On all her branches : piety has found
Friends in the friends of science, and true prayer   250
Has flowed from lips wet with Castalian dews.
Such was thy wisdom, Newton, childlike sage !
Sagacious reader of the works of God,
And in His word sagacious.   Such too thine,
Milton, whose genius had angelic wings,
And fed on manna.   And such thine, in whom
Our British Themis gloried with just cause,
Immortal Hale ! for deep discernment praised
And sound integrity, not more than famed
For sanctity of manners undefiled.   260

   All flesh is grass, and all its glory fades
Like the fair flower dishevelled in the wind ;
Riches have wings, and grandeur is a dream ;
The man we celebrate must find a tomb,
And we that worship him, ignoble graves.
Nothing is proof against the general curse
Of vanity, that seizes all below.
The only amaranthine flower on earth
Is virtue ; the only lasting treasure, truth.
But what is truth?   'Twas Pilate's question put   270
To Truth itself, that deigned him no reply.
And wherefore? will not God impart His light
To them that ask it?—Freely—'tis His joy,
His glory and His nature, to impart.
But to the proud, uncandid, insincere,
Or negligent inquirer, not a spark.
What's that which brings contempt upon a book,
And him who writes it, though the style be neat,
The method clear, and argument exact?
That makes a minister in holy things   280
The joy of many, and the dread of more,
His name a theme for praise and for reproach?
That while it gives us worth in God's account,
Depreciates and undoes us in our own?
What pearl is it that rich men cannot buy,
That learning is too proud to gather up,
But which the poor and the despised of all
Seek and obtain, and often find unsought?
Tell me, and I will tell thee what is truth.

   Oh friendly to the best pursuits of man,   290
Friendly to thought, to virtue, and to peace,
Domestic life in rural leisure passed !
Few know thy value, and few taste thy sweets,
Though many boast thy favours, and affect
To understand and choose thee for their own.
But foolish man foregoes his proper bliss,
Even as his first progenitor, and quits,

Though placed in Paradise, (for earth has still
Some traces of her youthful beauty left,)
Substantial happiness for transient joy.   300
Scenes formed for contemplation, and to nurse
The growing seeds of wisdom—that suggest,
By every pleasing image they present,
Reflections such as meliorate the heart,
Compose the passions, and exalt the mind—
Scenes such as these, 'tis his supreme delight
To fill with riot, and defile with blood.
Should some contagion, kind to the poor brutes
We persecute, annihilate the tribes
That draw the sportsman over hill and dale   310
Fearless, and rapt away from all his cares;
Should never game-fowl hatch her eggs again,
Nor baited hook deceive the fish's eye;
Could pageantry and dance, and feast and song,
Be quelled in all our summer-months' retreats;
How many self-deluded nymphs and swains,
Who dream they have a taste for fields and groves,
Would find them hideous nurseries of the spleen,
And crowd the roads, impatient for the town!
They love the country, and none else, who seek   320
For their own sake its silence and its shade;
Delights which who would leave, that has a heart
Susceptible of pity, or a mind
Cultured and capable of sober thought,
For all the savage din of the swift pack,
And clamours of the field? Detested sport,
That owes its pleasures to another's pain,
That feeds upon the sobs and dying shrieks
Of harmless nature, dumb, but yet endued
With eloquence that agonies inspire,   330
Of silent tears and heart-distending sighs!
Vain tears, alas! and sighs that never find
A corresponding tone in jovial souls.
Well,—one at least is safe. One sheltered hare
Has never heard the sanguinary yell
Of cruel man, exulting in her woes.
Innocent partner of my peaceful home,
Whom ten long years' experience of my care
Has made at last familiar, she has lost
Much of her vigilant instinctive dread,   340
Not needful here, beneath a roof like mine.
Yes,—thou mayst eat thy bread, and lick the hand
That feeds thee; thou mayst frolic on the floor
At evening, and at night retire secure
To thy straw couch, and slumber unalarmed:
For I have gained thy confidence, have pledged
All that is human in me to protect
Thine unsuspecting gratitude and love.
If I survive thee I will dig thy grave;

And when I place thee in it, sighing say,   350
I knew at least one hare that had a friend.
  How various his employments whom the world
Calls idle, and who justly in return
Esteems that busy world an idler too !
Friends, books, a garden, and perhaps his pen,
Delightful industry enjoyed at home,
And Nature in her cultivated trim
Dressed to his taste, inviting him abroad—
Can he want occupation who has these ?
Will he be idle who has much to enjoy ?   360
Me, therefore, studious of laborious ease,
Not slothful, happy to deceive the time
Not waste it, and aware that human life
Is but a loan to be repaid with use,
When He shall call His debtors to account,
From whom are all our blessings, business finds
Even here ; while sedulous I seek to improve,
At least neglect not, or leave unemployed,
The mind He gave me ; driving it, though slack
Too oft, and much impeded in its work   370
By causes not to be divulged in vain,
To its just point—the service of mankind.
He that attends to his interior self,—
That has a heart and keeps it,—has a mind
That hungers and supplies it,—and who seeks
A social, not a dissipated life,—
Has business ; feels himself engaged to achieve
No unimportant, though a silent task.
A life all turbulence and noise may seem
To him that leads it, wise and to be praised ;   380
But wisdom is a pearl with most success
Sought in still water, and beneath clear skies.
He that is ever occupied in storms
Or dives not for it, or brings up instead,
Vainly industrious, a disgraceful prize.
  The morning finds the self-sequestered man
Fresh for his task, intend what task he may.
Whether inclement seasons recommend
His warm but simple home, where he enjoys,
With her who shares his pleasures and his heart,   390
Sweet converse, sipping calm the fragrant lymph
Which neatly she prepares ; then to his book
Well chosen, and not sullenly perused
In selfish silence, but imparted oft
As aught occurs that she may smile to hear,
Or turn to nourishment digested well.
Or if the garden with its many cares,
All well repaid, demand him, he attends
The welcome call, conscious how much the hand
Of lubbard Labour needs his watchful eye,   400
Oft loitering lazily if not o'erseen,

Or misapplying his unskilful strength.
Nor does he govern only or direct,
But much performs himself.   No works indeed
That ask robust tough sinews bred to toil,
Servile employ; but such as may amuse,
Not tire, demanding rather skill than force.
Proud of his well-spread walls, he views his trees
That meet, no barren interval between,
With pleasure more than even their fruits afford,   410
Which, save himself who trains them, none can feel :
These therefore are his own peculiar charge,
No meaner hand may discipline the shoots,
None but his steel approach them.   What is weak,
Distempered, or has lost prolific powers,
Impaired by age, his unrelenting hand
Dooms to the knife : nor does he spare the soft
And succulent, that feeds its giant growth
But barren, at the expense of neighbouring twigs
Less ostentatious, and yet studded thick   420
With hopeful gems.   The rest, no portion left
That may disgrace his art, or disappoint
Large expectation, he disposes neat
At measured distances, that air and sun,
Admitted freely, may afford their aid,
And ventilate and warm the swelling buds.
Hence Summer has her riches, Autumn hence,
And hence even Winter fills his withered hand
With blushing fruits, and plenty not his own.*
Fair recompense of labour well bestowed,   430
And wise precaution, which a clime so rude
Makes needful still, whose Spring is but the child
Of churlish Winter, in her froward moods
Discovering much the temper of her sire.
For oft, as if in her the stream of mild
Maternal nature had reversed its course,
She brings her infants forth with many smiles,
But once delivered, kills them with a frown.
He therefore, timely warned, himself supplies
Her want of care, screening and keeping warm   440
The plenteous bloom, that no rough blast may sweep
His garlands from the boughs.   Again, as oft
As the sun peeps and vernal airs breathe mild,
The fence withdrawn, he gives them every beam,
And spreads his hopes before the blaze of day.
   To raise the prickly and green-coated gourd,
So grateful to the palate, and when rare
So coveted, else base and disesteemed,—
Food for the vulgar merely,—is an art
That toiling ages have but just matured,   450
And at this moment unassayed in song.

---

* " Miraturque novos fructus et non sua poma."—Virg.

Yet gnats have had, and frogs and mice, long since
Their eulogy ; those sang the Mantuan bard,
And these the Grecian, in ennobling strains ;
And in thy numbers, Philips, shines for aye
The solitary Shilling.   Pardon then,
Ye sage dispensers of poetic fame,
The ambition of one meaner far, whose powers,
Presuming an attempt not less sublime,
Pant for the praise of dressing to the taste   460
Of critic appetite, no sordid fare,
A cucumber, while costly yet and scarce.
    The stable yields a stercoraceous heap,
Impregnated with quick fermenting salts,
And potent to resist the freezing blast :
For ere the beech and elm have cast their leaf
Deciduous, when now November dark
Checks vegetation in the torpid plant
Exposed to his cold breath, the task begins.
Warily therefore, and with prudent heed,   470
He seeks a favoured spot ; that where he builds
The agglomerated pile, his frame may front
The sun's meridian disk, and at the back
Enjoy close shelter, wall, or reeds, or hedge
Impervious to the wind.   First he bids spread
Dry fern or littered hay, that may imbibe
The ascending damps ; then leisurely impose,
And lightly, shaking it with agile hand
From the full fork, the saturated straw.
What longest binds the closest, forms secure   480
The shapely side, that as it rises takes,
By just degrees, an overhanging breadth,
Sheltering the base with its projected eaves.
The uplifted frame, compact at every joint,
And overlaid with clear translucent glass,
He settles next upon the sloping mount,
Whose sharp declivity shoots off secure
From the dashed pane the deluge as it falls :
He shuts it close, and the first labour ends.
Thrice must the voluble and restless earth   490
Spin round upon her axle, ere the warmth,
Slow gathering in the midst, through the square mass
Diffused, attain the surface : when, behold !
A pestilent and most corrosive steam,
Like a gross fog Bœotian, rising fast,
And fast condensed upon the dewy sash,
Asks egress ; which obtained, the overcharged
And drenched conservatory breathes abroad,
In volumes wheeling slow, the vapour dank,
And purified, rejoices to have lost   500
Its foul inhabitant.   But to assuage
The impatient fervour which it first conceives
Within its reeking bosom, threatening death

To his young hopes, requires discreet delay.
Experience, slow preceptress ; teaching oft
The way to glory by miscarriage foul,
Must prompt him, and admonish how to catch
The auspicious moment, when the tempered heat,
Friendly to vital motion, may afford
Soft fermentation, and invite the seed. 510
The seed, selected wisely, plump, and smooth,
And glossy, he commits to pots of size
Diminutive, well filled with well-prepared
And fruitful soil, that has been treasured long,
And drunk no moisture from the dripping clouds :
These on the warm and genial earth that hides
The smoking manure, and o'erspreads it all,
He places lightly, and as time subdues
The rage of fermentation, plunges deep
In the soft medium, till they stand immersed. 520
Then rise the tender germs, upstarting quick
And spreading wide their spongy lobes, at first
Pale, wan, and livid, but assuming soon,
If fanned by balmy and nutritious air,
Strained through the friendly mats, a vivid green.
Two leaves produced, two rough indented leaves,
Cautious he pinches from the second stalk
A pimple, that portends a future sprout,
And interdicts its growth. Thence straight succeed
The branches, sturdy to his utmost wish, 530
Prolific all, and harbingers of more.
The crowded roots demand enlargement now,
And transplantation in an ampler space.
Indulged in what they wish, they soon supply
Large foliage, overshadowing golden flowers,
Blown on the summit of the apparent fruit.
These have their sexes, and when summer shines,
The bee transports the fertilizing meal
From flower to flower, and even the breathing air
Wafts the rich prize to its appointed use. 540
Not so when Winter scowls. Assistant art
Then acts in Nature's office, brings to pass
The glad espousals, and ensures the crop.
    Grudge not, ye rich, (since luxury must have
His dainties, and the world's more numerous half
Lives by contriving delicates for you,)
Grudge not the cost. Ye little know the cares,
The vigilance, the labour, and the skill
That day and night are exercised, and hang
Upon the ticklish balance of suspense, 550
That ye may garnish your profuse regales
With summer fruits brought forth by wintry suns.
Ten thousand dangers lie in wait to thwart
The process. Heat and cold, and wind and steam,
Moisture and drought, mice, worms, and swarming flies,

c

Minute as dust and numberless, oft work
Dire disappointment that admits no cure,
And which no care can obviate. It were long,
Too long to tell the expedients and the shifts
Which he that fights a season so severe   560
Devises, while he guards his tender trust,
And oft at last in vain. The learned and wise,
Sarcastic, would exclaim, and judge the song
Cold as its theme, and, like its theme, the fruit
Of too much labour, worthless when produced.
    Who loves a garden, loves a greenhouse too.
Unconscious of a less propitious clime,
There blooms exotic beauty, warm and snug,
While the winds whistle and the snows descend.
The spiry myrtle with unwithering leaf   570
Shines there and flourishes. The golden boast
Of Portugal and western India there,
The ruddier orange and the paler lime,
Peep through their polished foliage at the storm,
And seem to smile at what they need not fear.
The amomum there with intermingling flowers
And cherries hangs her twigs. Geranium boasts
Her crimson honours, and the spangled beau,
Ficoides, glitters bright the winter long.
All plants, of every leaf that can endure   580
The winter's frown, if screened from his shrewd bite,
Live there and prosper. Those Ausonia claims,
Levantine regions these; the Azores send
Their jessamine, her jessamine remote
Caffraria: foreigners from many lands,
They form one social shade, as if convened
By magic summons of the Orphean lyre.
Yet just arrangement, rarely brought to pass
But by a master's hand, disposing well
The gay diversities of leaf and flower,   590
Must lend its aid to illustrate all their charms,
And dress the regular yet various scene.
Plant behind plant aspiring, in the van
The dwarfish, in the rear retired, but still
Sublime above the rest, the statelier stand.
So once were ranged the sons of ancient Rome,
A noble show! while Roscius trod the stage;
And so, while Garrick as renowned as he,
The sons of Albion, fearing each to lose
Some note of Nature's music from his lips,   600
And covetous of Shakspeare's beauty seen
In every flash of his far-beaming eye.
Nor taste alone and well-contrived display
Suffice to give the marshalled ranks the grace
Of their complete effect. Much yet remains
Unsung, and many cares are yet behind,
And more laborious; cares on which depends

Their vigour, injured soon, not soon restored.
The soil must be renewed, which, often washed,
Loses its treasure of salubrious salts,   610
And disappoints the roots ; the slender roots
Close interwoven, where they meet the vase
Must smooth be shorn away ; the sapless branch
Must fly before the knife ; the withered leaf
Must be detached, and where it strews the floor
Swept with a woman's neatness, breeding else
Contagion, and disseminating death.
Discharge but these kind offices, (and who
Would spare, that loves them, offices like these?)
Well they reward the toil.   The sight is pleased,   620
The scent regaled, each odoriferous leaf,
Each opening blossom, freely breathes abroad
Its gratitude, and thanks him with its sweets.
    So manifold, all pleasing in their kind,
All healthful, are the employs of rural life,
Reiterated as the wheel of time
Runs round ; still ending, and beginning still.
Nor are these all.   To deck the shapely knoll,
That, softly swelled and gaily dressed, appears
A flowery island, from the dark green lawn   630
Emerging, must be deemed a labour due
To no mean hand, and asks the touch of taste.
Here also grateful mixture of well-matched
And sorted hues (each giving each relief,
And by contrasted beauty shining more)
Is needful.   Strength may wield the ponderous spade,
May turn the clod, and wheel the compost home,
But elegance, chief grace the garden shows,
And most attractive, is the fair result
Of thought, the creature of a polished mind.   640
Without it, all is gothic as the scene
To which the insipid citizen resorts
Near yonder heath ; where industry misspent,
But proud of his uncouth ill-chosen task,
Has made a heaven on earth ; with suns and moons
Of close-rammed stones has charged the encumbered soil
And fairly laid the zodiac in the dust.
He therefore who would see his flowers disposed
Sightly and in just order, ere he gives
The beds the trusted treasure of their seeds,   650
Forecasts the future whole ; that when the scene
Shall break into its preconceived display,
Each for itself, and all as with one voice
Conspiring, may attest his bright design.
Nor even then, dismissing as performed
His pleasant work, may he suppose it done.
Few self-supported flowers endure the wind
Uninjured, but expect the upholding aid
Of the smooth shaven prop, and neatly tied,
Q 2

Are wedded thus, like beauty to old age,   660
For interest sake, the living to the dead.
Some clothe the soil that feeds them, far diffused
And lowly creeping, modest and yet fair,
Like virtue, thriving most where little seen;
Some, more aspiring, catch the neighbour shrub
With clasping tendrils, and invest his branch,
Else unadorned, with many a gay festoon
And fragrant chaplet, recompensing well
The strength they borrow with the grace they lend.
All hate the rank society of weeds,   670
Noisome, and ever greedy to exhaust
The impoverished earth; an overbearing race,
That, like the multitude made faction-mad,
Disturb good order, and degrade true worth.
   O blest seclusion from a jarring world,
Which he, thus occupied, enjoys!   Retreat
Cannot indeed to guilty man restore
Lost innocence, or cancel follies past;
But it has peace, and much secures the mind
From all assaults of evil, proving still   680
A faithful barrier, not o'erleaped with ease
By vicious custom, raging uncontrolled
Abroad, and desolating public life.
When fierce temptation, seconded within
By traitor appetite, and armed with darts
Tempered in Hell, invades the throbbing breast,
To combat may be glorious, and success
Perhaps may crown us, but to fly is safe.
Had I the choice of sublunary good,
What could I wish that I possess not here?   690
Health, leisure, means to improve it, friendship, peace,
No loose or wanton, though a wandering muse,
And constant occupation without care.
Thus blest, I draw a picture of that bliss;
Hopeless indeed that dissipated minds,
And profligate abusers of a world
Created fair so much in vain for them,
Should seek the guiltless joys that I describe,
Allured by my report: but sure no less
That, self condemned, they must neglect the prize,   700
And what they will not taste must yet approve.
What we admire we praise; and when we praise,
Advance it into notice, that its worth
Acknowledged, others may admire it too.
I therefore recommend, though at the risk
Of popular disgust, yet boldly still,
The cause of piety, and sacred truth,
And virtue, and those scenes which God ordained
Should best secure them and promote them most;
Scenes that I love, and with regret perceive   710
Forsaken, or through folly not enjoyed.

Pure is the nymph, though liberal of her smiles,
And chaste, though unconfined, whom I extol;
Not as the prince in Shushan, when he called,
Vainglorious of her charms, his Vashti forth
To grace the full pavilion. His design
Was but to boast his own peculiar good,
Which all might view with envy, none partake.
My charmer is not mine alone; my sweets,
And she that sweetens all my bitters too,   720
Nature, enchanting Nature, in whose form
And lineaments divine I trace a hand
That errs not, and find raptures still renewed,
Is free to all men—universal prize.
Strange that so fair a creature should yet want
Admirers, and be destined to divide
With meaner objects even the few she finds.
Stripped of her ornaments, her leaves, and flowers,
She loses all her influence. Cities then
Attract us, and neglected nature pines,   730
Abandoned, as unworthy of our love.
But are not wholesome airs, though unperfumed
By roses, and clear suns though scarcely felt,
And groves, if unharmonious, yet secure
From clamour, and whose very silence charms,
To be preferred to smoke, to the eclipse
That metropolitan volcanoes make,
Whose Stygian throats breathe darkness all day long,
And to the stir of Commerce, driving slow,
And thundering loud, with his ten thousand wheels?   740
They would be, were not madness in the head,
And folly in the heart; were England now
What England was, plain, hospitable, kind,
And undebauched. But we have bid farewell
To all the virtues of those better days,
And all their honest pleasures. Mansions once
Knew their own masters, and laborious hinds
Who had survived the father, served the son.
Now the legitimate and rightful lord
Is but a transient guest, newly arrived,   750
And soon to be supplanted. He that saw
His patrimonial timber cast its leaf
Sells the last scantling, and transfers the price
To some shrewd sharper, ere it buds again.
Estates are landscapes, gazed upon awhile,
Then advertised, and auctioneered away.
The country starves, and they that feed the o'ercharged
And surfeited lewd town with her fair dues,
By a just judgment strip and starve themselves.
The wings that waft our riches out of sight   760
Grow on the gamester's elbows, and the alert
And nimble motion of those restless joints,
That never tire, soon fans them all away.

Improvement too, the idol of the age,
Is fed with many a victim.   Lo ! he comes,—
The omnipotent magician, Brown, appears.
Down falls the venerable pile, the abode
Of our forefathers, a grave whiskered race,
But tasteless.   Springs a palace in its stead,
But in a distant spot, where more exposed,   770
It may enjoy the advantage of the north,
And aguish east, till time shall have transformed
Those naked acres to a sheltering grove.
He speaks.   The lake in front becomes a lawn,
Woods vanish, hills subside, and valleys rise,
And streams, as if created for his use,
Pursue the track of his directing wand,
Sinuous or straight, now rapid and now slow,
Now murmuring soft, now roaring in cascades,
Even as he bids.   The enraptured owner smiles.   780
'Tis finished ! and yet, finished as it seems,
Still wants a grace, the loveliest it could show,
A mine to satisfy the enormous cost.
Drained to the last poor item of his wealth,
He sighs, departs, and leaves the accomplished plan
That he has touched, retouched, many a long day
Laboured, and many a night pursued in dreams,
Just when it meets his hopes, and proves the heaven
He wanted, for a wealthier to enjoy.
And now perhaps the glorious hour is come,   790
When having no stake left, no pledge to endear
Her interests, or that gives her sacred cause
A moment's operation on his love,
He burns with most intense and flagrant zeal
To serve his country.   Ministerial grace
Deals him out money from the public chest ;
Or if that mine be shut, some private purse
Supplies his need with a usurious loan,
To be refunded duly, when his vote,
Well managed, shall have earned its worthy price.   800
Oh innocent, compared with arts like these,
Crape and cocked pistol, and the whistling ball
Sent through the traveller's temples !   He that finds
One drop of Heaven's sweet mercy in his cup,
Can dig, beg, rot, and perish, well content
So he may wrap himself in honest rags
At his last gasp ; but could not for a world
Fish up his dirty and dependent bread
From pools and ditches of the commonwealth,
Sordid and sickening at his own success.   810
   Ambition, avarice, penury incurred
By endless riot, vanity, the lust
Of pleasure and variety, despatch,
As duly as the swallows disappear,
The world of wandering knights and squires to town.

London ingulfs them all.   The shark is there,
And the shark's prey ; the spendthrift and the leech
That sucks him.   There the sycophant, and he
Who, with bareheaded and obsequious bows,
Begs a warm office, doomed to a cold jail,   820
And groat per diem, if his patron frown.
The levee swarms, as if, in golden pomp,
Were charactered on every statesman's door,
" Battered and bankrupt fortunes mended here."
These are the charms that sully and eclipse
The charms of nature.   'Tis the cruel gripe
That lean hard-handed Poverty inflicts,
The hope of better things, the chance to win,
The wish to shine, the thirst to be amused,
That at the sound of Winter's hoary wing   830
Unpeople all our counties of such herds
Of fluttering, loitering, cringing, begging, loose
And wanton vagrants, as make London, vast
And boundless as it is, a crowded coop.
 Oh thou, resort and mart of all the earth,
Chequered with all complexions of mankind,
And spotted with all crimes ; in whom I see
Much that I love, and more that I admire,
And all that I abhor ; thou freckled fair,
That pleasest and yet shockest me, I can laugh 840
And I can weep, can hope and can despond,
Feel wrath and pity, when I think on thee !
Ten righteous would have saved a city once,
And thou hast many righteous.—Well for thee !
That salt preserves thee ; more corrupted else,
And therefore more obnoxious at this hour,
Than Sodom in her day had power to be,
For whom God heard His Abraham plead in vain.

BOOK IV.

THE WINTER EVENING.

Argument.—The post comes in—The newspaper is read—The world contemplated at a distance—
Address to winter—The rural amusements of a winter evening compared with the fashionable
ones—Address to evening—A brown study—Fall of snow in the evening—The waggoner—A
poor family piece—The rural thief—Public-houses—The multitude of them censured—The
farmer's daughter ; what she was ; what she is—The simplicity of country manners almost
lost—Causes of the change—Desertion of the country by the rich—Neglect of magistrates—
The militia principally in fault—The new recruit and his transformation—Reflection on bodies
corporate—The love of rural objects natural to all, and never to be totally extinguished.

Hark ! 'tis the twanging horn !   O'er yonder bridge,
That with its wearisome but needful length

Bestrides the wintry flood, in which the moon
Sees her unwrinkled face reflected bright,
He comes, the herald of a noisy world,
With spattered boots, strapped waist, and frozen locks,
News from all nations lumbering at his back.
True to his charge, the close-packed load behind,
Yet careless what he brings, his one concern
Is to conduct it to the destined inn,   10
And having dropped the expected bag—pass on.
He whistles as he goes, light-hearted wretch,
Cold and yet cheerful : messenger of grief
Perhaps to thousands, and of joy to some,
To him indifferent whether grief or joy.
Houses in ashes, and the fall of stocks,
Births, deaths, and marriages, epistles wet
With tears that trickled down the writer's cheeks
Fast as the periods from his fluent quill,
Or charged with amorous sighs of absent swains,   20
Or nymphs responsive, equally affect
His horse and him, unconscious of them all.
But oh the important budget ! ushered in
With such heart-shaking music, who can say
What are its tidings ? have our troops awaked ?
Or do they still, as if with opium drugged,
Snore to the murmurs of the Atlantic wave?
Is India free? and does she wear her plumed
And jewelled turban with a smile of peace,
Or do we grind her still ?   The grand debate,   30
The popular harangue, the tart reply,
The logic, and the wisdom, and the wit,
And the loud laugh—I long to know them all ;
I burn to set the imprisoned wranglers free,
And give them voice and utterance once again.
   Now stir the fire, and close the shutters fast,
Let fall the curtains, wheel the sofa round,
And while the bubbling and loud hissing urn
Throws up a steamy column, and the cups
That cheer but not inebriate, wait on each,   40
So let us welcome peaceful evening in.
Not such his evening, who with shining face
Sweats in the crowded theatre, and squeezed
And bored with elbow-points through both his sides,
Outscolds the ranting actor on the stage ;
Nor his, who patient stands till his feet throb,
And his head thumps, to feed upon the breath
Of patriots bursting with heroic rage,
Or placemen all tranquillity and smiles.
This folio of four pages, happy work !   50
Which not even critics criticise ; that holds
Inquisitive attention, while I read,
Fast bound in chains of silence, which the fair,
Though eloquent themselves, yet fear to break ;

What is it but a map of busy life,
Its fluctuations, and its vast concerns?
Here runs the mountainous and craggy ridge
That tempts ambition. On the summit, see,
The seals of office glitter in his eyes;
He climbs, he pants, he grasps them. At his heels,   60
Close at his heels, a demagogue ascends,
And with a dexterous jerk soon twists him down,
And wins them, but to lose them in his turn.
Here rills of oily eloquence in soft
Meanders lubricate the course they take;
The modest speaker is ashamed and grieved
To engross a moment's notice, and yet begs,
Begs a propitious ear for his poor thoughts,
However trivial all that he conceives.
Sweet bashfulness! it claims, at least, this praise   70
The dearth of information and good sense
That it foretells us, always comes to pass.
Cataracts of declamation thunder here,
There forests of no meaning spread the page
In which all comprehension wanders lost;
While fields of pleasantry amuse us there
With merry descants on a nation's woes.
The rest appears a wilderness of strange
But gay confusion; roses for the cheeks
And lilies for the brows of faded age,   80
Teeth for the toothless, ringlets for the bald,
Heaven, earth, and ocean plundered of their sweets,
Nectareous essences, Olympian dews,
Sermons and city feasts, and favourite airs,
Æthereal journeys, submarine exploits,
And Katerfelto, with his hair on end
At his own wonders, wondering for his bread.
  'Tis pleasant through the loopholes of retreat
To peep at such a world; to see the stir
Of the great Babel, and not feel the crowd;   90
To hear the roar she sends through all her gates
At a safe distance, where the dying sound
Falls a soft murmur on the uninjured ear.
Thus sitting, and surveying thus at ease
The globe and its concerns, I seem advanced
To some secure and more than mortal height,
That liberates and exempts me from them all.
It turns submitted to my view, turns round
With all its generations; I behold
The tumult, and am still. The sound of war   100
Has lost its terrors ere it reaches me;
Grieves, but alarms me not. I mourn the pride
And avarice that make man a wolf to man,
Hear the faint echo of those brazen throats,
By which he speaks the language of his heart,
And sigh, but never tremble at the sound.

He travels and expatiates, as the bee
From flower to flower, so he from land to land ;
The manners, customs, policy of all
Pay contribution to the store he gleans ;   110
He sucks intelligence in every clime,
And spreads the honey of his deep research
At his return, a rich repast for me.
He travels, and I too.   I tread his deck,
Ascend his topmast, through his peering eyes
Discover countries, with a kindred heart
Suffer his woes, and share in his escapes ;
While fancy, like the finger of a clock,
Runs the great circuit, and is still at home.
    O Winter ! ruler of the inverted year,   120
Thy scattered hair with sleet like ashes filled,
Thy breath congealed upon thy lips, thy cheeks
Fringed with a beard made white with other snows
Than those of age, thy forehead wrapt in clouds,
A leafless branch thy sceptre, and thy throne
A sliding car, indebted to no wheels,
But urged by storms along its slippery way ;
I love thee, all unlovely as thou seemest,
And dreaded as thou art.   Thou holdest the sun
A prisoner in the yet undawning east,   130
Shortening his journey between morn and noon,
And hurrying him, impatient of his stay,
Down to the rosy west ; but kindly still
Compensating his loss with added hours
Of social converse and instructive ease,
And gathering, at short notice, in one group
The family dispersed, and fixing thought,
Not less dispersed by daylight and its cares.
I crown thee King of intimate delights,
Fireside enjoyments, homeborn happiness,   140
And all the comforts that the lowly roof
Of undisturbed retirement, and the hours
Of long uninterrupted evening know.
No rattling wheels stop short before these gates ;
No powdered pert, proficient in the art
Of sounding an alarm, assaults these doors
Till the street rings ; no stationary steeds
Cough their own knell, while, heedless of the sound,
The silent circle fan themselves, and quake :
But here the needle plies its busy task,   150
The pattern grows, the well-depicted flower,
Wrought patiently into the snowy lawn,
Unfolds its bosom ; buds, and leaves, and sprigs,
And curling tendrils, gracefully disposed,
Follow the nimble finger of the fair ;
A wreath that cannot fade, of flowers that blow
With most success when all besides decay.
The poet's or historian's page, by one

Made vocal for the amusement of the rest;
The sprightly lyre, whose treasure of sweet sounds   160
The touch from many a trembling chord shakes out;
And the clear voice symphonious, yet distinct,
And in the charming strife triumphant still;
Beguile the night, and set a keener edge
On female industry: the threaded steel
Flies swiftly, and unfelt the task proceeds.
The volume closed, the customary rites
Of the last meal commence. A Roman meal,
Such as the mistress of the world once found
Delicious, when her patriots of high note,   170
Perhaps by moonlight, at their humble doors,
And under an old oak's domestic shade,
Enjoyed, spare feast! a radish and an egg.
Discourse ensues, not trivial, yet not dull,
Nor such as with a frown forbids the play
Of fancy, or proscribes the sound of mirth;
Nor do we madly, like an impious world,
Who deem religion frenzy, and the God
That made them an intruder on their joys,
Start at His awful name, or deem His praise   180
A jarring note. Themes of a graver tone,
Exciting oft our gratitude and love,
While we retrace with memory's pointing wand,
That calls the past to our exact review,
The dangers we have 'scaped, the broken snare,
The disappointed foe, deliverance found
Unlooked for, life preserved and peace restored,
Fruits of omnipotent eternal love.
" Oh evenings worthy of the gods!" exclaimed
The Sabine bard. Oh evenings, I reply,   190
More to be prized and coveted than yours,
As more illumined, and with nobler truths,
That I and mine, and those we love, enjoy.
   Is Winter hideous in a garb like this?
Needs he the tragic fur, the smoke of lamps,
The pent-up breath of an unsavoury throng,
To thaw him into feeling, or the smart
And snappish dialogue that flippant wits
Call comedy, to prompt him with a smile?
The self-complacent actor, when he views   200
(Stealing a sidelong glance at a full house)
The slope of faces from the floor to the roof
(As if one master spring controlled them all)
Relaxed into an universal grin,
Sees not a countenance there that speaks of joy
Half so refined or so sincere as ours.
Cards were superfluous here, with all the tricks
That idleness has ever yet contrived
To fill the void of an unfurnished brain,
To palliate dulness, and give time a shove.   210

Time as he passes us, has a dove's wing,
Unsoiled and swift, and of a silken sound;
But the world's Time is Time in masquerade.
Theirs, should I paint him, has his pinions fledged
With motley plumes; and where the peacock shows
His azure eyes, is tinctured black and red
With spots quadrangular of diamond form,
Ensanguined hearts, clubs typical of strife,
And spades, the emblems of untimely graves.
What should be, and what was an hour-glass once,   220
Becomes a dice-box, and a billiard mace
Well does the work of his destructive scythe.
Thus decked, he charms a world whom fashion blinds
To his true worth, most pleased when idle most,
Whose only happy are their wasted hours.
Even misses, at whose age their mothers wore
The backstring and the bib, assume the dress
Of womanhood, sit pupils in the school
Of card-devoted Time, and night by night
Placed at some vacant corner of the board,   230
Learn every trick, and soon play all the game.
But truce with censure.   Roving as I rove,
Where shall I find an end, or how proceed?
As he that travels far, oft turns aside
To view some rugged rock or mouldering tower,
Which seen, delights him not; then coming home,
Describes and prints it, that the world may know
How far he went for what was nothing worth;
So I, with brush in hand and pallet spread,
With colours mixed for a far different use,   240
Paint cards and dolls, and every idle thing
That fancy finds in her excursive flights.

   Come, Evening, once again, season of peace;
Return, sweet Evening, and continue long!
Methinks I see thee in the streaky west,
With matron step slow moving, while the Night
Treads on thy sweeping train; one hand employed
In letting fall the curtain of repose
On bird and beast, the other charged for man
With sweet oblivion of the cares of day;   250
Not sumptuously adorned, nor needing aid,
Like homely-featured Night, of clustering gems;
A star or two just twinkling on thy brow
Suffices thee; save that the moon is thine
No less than hers, not worn indeed on high
With ostentatious pageantry, but set
With modest grandeur in thy purple zone,
Resplendent less, but of an ampler round.
Come then, and thou shalt find thy votary calm,
Or make me so.   Composure is thy gift: 260
And whether I devote thy gentler hours
To books, to music, or the poet's toil;

To weaving nets for bird-alluring fruit;
Or twining silken threads round ivory reels,
When they command whom man was born to please;
I slight thee not, but make thee welcome still.
  Just when our drawing-rooms begin to blaze
With lights, by clear reflexion multiplied
From many a mirror, in which he of Gath,
Goliath, might have seen his giant bulk   270
Whole without stooping, towering crest and all,
My pleasures too begin.   But me perhaps
The glowing hearth may satisfy awhile
With faint illumination, that uplifts
The shadow to the ceiling, there by fits
Dancing uncouthly to the quivering flame.
Not undelightful is an hour to me
So spent in parlour twilight; such a gloom
Suits well the thoughtful or unthinking mind,
The mind contemplative, with some new theme   280
Pregnant, or indisposed alike to all.
Laugh ye, who boast your more mercurial powers,
That never feel a stupor, know no pause,
Nor need one; I am conscious, and confess,
Fearless, a soul that does not always think.
Me oft has fancy, ludicrous and wild,
Soothed with a waking dream of houses, towers,
Trees, churches, and strange visages expressed
In the red cinders, while with poring eye
I gazed, myself creating what I saw.   290
Nor less amused have I quiescent watched
The sooty films that play upon the bars
Pendulous, and foreboding, in the view
Of superstition, prophesying still,
Though still deceived, some stranger's near approach.
'Tis thus the understanding takes repose
In indolent vacuity of thought,
And sleeps and is refreshed.   Meanwhile the face
Conceals the mood lethargic with a mask
Of deep deliberation, as the man   300
Were tasked to his full strength, absorbed and lost.
Thus oft, reclined at ease, I lose an hour
At evening, till at length the freezing blast,
That sweeps the bolted shutter, summons home
The recollected powers, and snapping short
The glassy threads with which the fancy weaves
Her brittle toils, restores me to myself.
How calm is my recess, and how the frost,
Raging abroad, and the rough wind, endear
The silence and the warmth enjoyed within!   310
I saw the woods and fields at close of day
A variegated show; the meadows green,
Though faded; and the lands, where lately waved
The golden harvest, of a mellow brown,

Upturned so lately by the forceful share :
I saw far off the weedy fallows smile
With verdure not unprofitable, grazed
By flocks, fast feeding, and selecting each
His favourite herb ; while all the leafless groves
That skirt the horizon, wore a sable hue,   320
Scarce noticed in the kindred dusk of eve.
To-morrow brings a change, a total change !
Which even now, though silently performed
And slowly, and by most unfelt, the face
Of universal nature undergoes.
Fast falls a fleecy shower : the downy flakes
Descending, and, with never-ceasing lapse,
Softly alighting upon all below,
Assimilate all objects.   Earth receives
Gladly the thickening mantle, and the green   330
And tender blade that feared the chilling blast
Escapes unhurt beneath so warm a veil.
    In such a world, so thorny, and where none
Finds happiness unblighted, or, if found,
Without some thistly sorrow at its side,
It seems the part of wisdom, and no sin
Against the law of love, to measure lots
With less distinguished than ourselves, that thus
We may with patience bear our moderate ills,
And sympathise with others, suffering more.   340
Ill fares the traveller now, and he that stalks
In ponderous boots beside his reeking team.
The wain goes heavily, impeded sore
By congregrated loads adhering close
To the clogged wheels ; and in its sluggish pace
Noiseless appears a moving hill of snow.
The toiling steeds expand the nostril wide,
While every breath, by respiration strong
Forced downward, is consolidated soon
Upon their jutting chests.   He, formed to bear   35c
The pelting brunt of the tempestuous night,
With half-shut eyes and puckered cheeks, and teeth
Presented bare against the storm, plods on.
One hand secures his hat, save when with both
He brandishes his pliant length of whip,
Resounding oft, and never heard in vain.
Oh happy ! and in my account, denied
That sensibility of pain with which
Refinement is endued, thrice happy thou.
Thy frame, robust and hardy, feels indeed   360
The piercing cold, but feels it unimpaired
The learnèd finger never need explore
Thy vigorous pulse ; and the unhealthful east,
That breathes the spleen, and searches every bone
Of the infirm, is wholesome air to thee.
Thy days roll on exempt from household care ;

The waggon is thy wife ; and the poor beasts
That drag the dull companion to and fro,
Thine helpless charge, dependent on thy care.
Ah, treat them kindly ! rude as thou appearest,   370
Yet show that thou hast mercy, which the great,
With needless hurry whirled from place to place,
Humane as they would seem, not always show.
    Poor, yet industrious, modest, quiet, neat,
Such claim compassion in a night like this,
And have a friend in every feeling heart.
Warmed, while it lasts, by labour, all day long
They brave the season, and yet find at eve,
Ill clad and fed but sparely, time to cool.
The frugal housewife trembles when she lights   380
Her scanty stock of brushwood, blazing clear,
But dying soon, like all terrestrial joys.
The few small embers left she nurses well,
And while her infant race, with outspread hands,
And crowded knees, sit cowering o'er the sparks,
Retires, content to quake, so they be warmed.
The man feels least, as more inured than she
To winter, and the current in his veins
More briskly moved by his severer toil ;
Yet he too finds his own distress in theirs.   390
The taper soon extinguished, which I saw
Dangled along at the cold finger's end
Just when the day declined, and the brown loaf
Lodged on the shelf, half eaten without sauce
Of savoury cheese, or butter costlier still,
Sleep seems their only refuge : for, alas !
Where penury is felt the thought is chained,
And sweet colloquial pleasures are but few.
With all this thrift they thrive not.   All the care,
Ingenious parsimony takes, but just   400
Saves the small inventory, bed and stool,
Skillet and old carved chest, from public sale.
They live, and live without extorted alms
From grudging hands, but other boast have none
To soothe their honest pride, that scorns to beg ;
Nor comfort else, but in their mutual love.
I praise you much, ye meek and patient pair,
For ye are worthy ; choosing rather far
A dry but independent crust, hard earned,
And eaten with a sigh, than to endure   410
The rugged frowns and insolent rebuffs
Of knaves in office, partial in the work
Of distribution ; liberal of their aid
To clamorous importunity in rags,
But ofttimes deaf to suppliants who would blush
To wear a tattered garb however coarse,
Whom famine cannot reconcile to filth ;
These ask with painful shyness, and refused

Because deserving, silently retire.
But be ye of good courage.   Time itself   420
Shall much befriend you.   Time shall give increase,
And all your numerous progeny, well trained
But helpless, in few years shall find their hands,
And labour too.   Meanwhile ye shall not want
What, conscious of your virtues, we can spare,
Nor what a wealthier than ourselves may send.
I mean the man who, when the distant poor
Need help, denies them nothing but his name.
    But poverty, with most who whimper forth
Their long complaints, is self-inflicted woe ;   430
The effect of laziness or sottish waste.
Now goes the nightly thief prowling abroad
For plunder ; much solicitous how best
He may compensate for a day of sloth,
By works of darkness and nocturnal wrong.
Woe to the gardener's pale, the farmer's hedge
Plashed neatly, and secured with driven stakes
Deep in the loamy bank.   Uptorn by strength,
Resistless in so bad a cause, but lame
To better deeds, he bundles up the spoil,   440
An ass's burden, and when laden most
And heaviest, light of foot steals fast away.
Nor does the boarded hovel better guard
The well-stacked pile of riven logs and roots
From his pernicious force.   Nor will he leave
Unwrenched the door, however well secured,
Where chanticleer amidst his harem sleeps
In unsuspecting pomp.   Twitched from the perch,
He gives the princely bird, with all his wives,
To his voracious bag, struggling in vain,   450
And loudly wondering at the sudden change.
Nor this to feed his own.   'Twere some excuse
Did pity of their sufferings warp aside
His principle, and tempt him into sin
For their support, so destitute.   But they
Neglected pine at home, themselves, as more
Exposed than others, with less scruple made
His victims, robbed of their defenceless all.
Cruel is all he does.   'Tis quenchless thirst
Of ruinous ebriety that prompts   460
His every action, and imbrutes the man.
Oh for a law to noose the villain's neck
Who starves his own : who persecutes the blood
He gave them in his children's veins, and hates
And wrongs the woman he has sworn to love !
    Pass where we may, through city or through town,
Village or hamlet, of this merry land,
Though lean and beggared, every twentieth pace
Conducts the unguarded nose to such a whiff
Of stale debauch, forth issuing from the styes   470

That law has licensed, as makes temperance reel.
There sit, involved and lost in curling clouds
Of Indian fume, and guzzling deep, the boor,
The lackey, and the groom ; the craftsman there
Takes a Lethean leave of all his toil ;
Smith, cobbler, joiner, he that plies the shears,
And he that kneads the dough ; all loud alike,
All learnèd, and all drunk.   The fiddle screams
Plaintive and piteous, as it wept and wailed
Its wasted tones and harmony unheard ;   480
Fierce the dispute, whate'er the theme ; while she,
Fell Discord, arbitress of such debate,
Perched on the sign-post, holds with even hand
Her undecisive scales.   In this she lays
A weight of ignorance ; in that, of pride ;
And smiles delighted with the eternal poise.
Dire is the frequent curse, and its twin sound
The cheek-distending oath, not to be praised
As ornamental, musical, polite,
Like those which modern senators employ,   490
Whose oath is rhetoric, and who swear for fame.
Behold the schools in which plebeian minds,
Once simple, are initiated in arts
Which some may practise with politer grace,
But none with readier skill !   'Tis here they learn
The road that leads from competence and peace
To indigence and rapine ; till at last
Society, grown weary of the load,
Shakes her encumbered lap, and casts them out.
But censure profits little : vain the attempt   500
To advertise in verse a public pest,
That like the filth with which the peasant feeds
His hungry acres, stinks, and is of use.
The Excise is fattened with the rich result
Of all this riot ; and ten thousand casks,
For ever dribbling out their base contents,
Touched by the Midas finger of the State,
Bleed gold for ministers to sport away.
Drink and be mad then : 'tis your country bids
Gloriously drunk, obey the important call !   510
Her cause demands the assistance of your throats ;
Ye all can swallow, and she asks no more.
   Would I had fallen upon those happier days
That poets celebrate ; those golden times
And those Arcadian scenes that Maro sings,
And Sidney, warbler of poetic prose.
Nymphs were Dianas then, and swains had hearts
That felt their virtues : Innocence, it seems,
From courts dismissed, found shelter in the groves.
The footsteps of simplicity, impressed   520
Upon the yielding herbage (so they sing),
Then were not all effaced : then speech profane,

R

And manners profligate, were rarely found,
Observed as prodigies, and soon reclaimed.
Vain wish ! those days were never : airy dreams
Sat for the picture ; and the poet's hand,
Imparting substance to an empty shade,
Imposed a gay delirium for a truth.
Grant it : I still must envy them an age
That favoured such a dream, in days like these   530
Impossible, when Virtue is so scarce,
That to suppose a scene where she presides
Is tramontane, and stumbles all belief.
No : we are polished now.   The rural lass,
Whom once her virgin modesty and grace,
Her artless manner, and her neat attire,
So dignified,that she was hardly less
Than the fair shepherdess of old romance,
Is seen no more.   The character is lost.
Her head, adorned with lappets pinned aloft,   540
And ribands streaming gay, superbly raised,
And magnified beyond all human size,
Indebted to some smart wig-weaver's hand
For more than half the tresses it sustains ;
Her elbows ruffled, and her tottering form
Ill propped upon French heels ; she might be deemed
(But that the basket dangling on her arm
Interprets her more truly) of a rank
Too proud for dairy work or sale of eggs.
Expect her soon with footboy at her heels,   550
No longer blushing for her awkward load,
Her train and her umbrella all her care.
   The town has tinged the country ; and the stain
Appears a spot upon a vestal's robe,
The worse for what it soils.   The fashion runs
Down into scenes still rural ; but, alas !
Scenes rarely graced with rural manners now
Time was when in the pastoral retreat
The unguarded door was safe ; men did not watch
To invade another's right, or guard their own.   560
Then sleep was undisturbed by fear, unscared
By drunken howlings ; and the chilling tale
Of midnight murder was a wonder heard
With doubtful credit, told to frighten babes.
But farewell now to unsuspicious nights,
And slumbers unalarmed.   Now, ere you sleep,
See that your polished arms be primed with care,
And drop the nightbolt ; ruffians are abroad ;
And the first 'larum of the cock's shrill throat
May prove a trumpet, summoning your ear   570
To horrid sounds of hostile feet within.
Even daylight has its dangers ; and the walk
Through pathless wastes and woods, unconscious once
Of other tenants than melodious birds

Or harmless flocks, is hazardous and bold.
Lamented change ! to which full many a cause
Inveterate, hopeless of a cure, conspires.
The course of human things from good to ill,
From ill to worse, is fatal, never fails.
Increase of power begets increase of wealth ;   580
Wealth luxury, and luxury excess ;
Excess, the scrofulous and itchy plague
That seizes first the opulent, descends
To the next rank contagious, and in time
Taints downward all the graduated scale
Of order, from the chariot to the plough.
The rich, and they that have an arm to check
The licence of the lowest in degree,
Desert their office ; and themselves intent
On pleasure, haunt the capital, and thus   590
To all the violence of lawless hands
Resign the scenes their presence might protect
Authority herself not seldom sleeps,
Though resident, and witness of the wrong.
The plump convivial parson often bears
The magisterial sword in vain, and lays
His reverence and his worship both to rest
On the same cushion of habitual sloth.
Perhaps timidity restrains his arm ;
When he should strike, he trembles, and sets free,   600
Himself enslaved by terror of the band,
The audacious convict, whom he dares not bind.
Perhaps, though by profession ghostly pure,
He too may have his vice, and sometimes prove
Less dainty than becomes his grave outside
In lucrative concerns.   Examine well
His milk-white hand ; the palm is hardly clean, —
But here and there an ugly smutch appears.
Foh ! 'twas a bribe that left it : he has touched
Corruption.   Whoso seeks an audit here   610
Propitious, pays his tribute, game or fish,
Wildfowl or venison, and his errand speeds.
    But faster far, and more than all the rest,
A noble cause, which none who bears a spark
Of public virtue ever wished removed,
Works the deplored and mischievous effect.
'Tis universal soldiership has stabbed
The heart of merit in the meaner class.
Arms, through the vanity and brainless rage
Of those that bear them, in whatever cause,   620
Seem most at variance with all moral good,
And incompatible with serious thought.
The clown, the child of nature, without guile,
Blest with an infant's ignorance of all
But his own simple pleasures, now and then
A wrestling-match, a foot-race, or a fair,

R 2

Is balloted, and trembles at the news :
Sheepish he doffs his hat, aud mumbling swears
A Bible-oath to be whate'er they please,
To do he knows not what.   The task performed,   630
That instant he becomes the serjeant's care,
His pupil, and his torment, and his jest.
His awkward gait, his introverted toes,
Bent knees, round shoulders, and dejected looks,
Procure him many a curse.   By slow degrees,
Unapt to learn, and formed of stubborn stuff,
He yet by slow degrees puts off himself,
Grows conscious of a change, and likes it well ;
He stands erect ; his slouch becomes a walk ;
He steps right onward, martial in his air,   640
His form, and movement ; is as smart above
As meal and larded locks can make him ; wears
His hat, or his plumed helmet, with a grace ;
And, his three years of heroship expired,
Returns indignant to the slighted plough.
He hates the field, in which no fife or drum
Attends him, drives his cattle to a march,
And sighs for the smart comrades he has left.
'Twere well if his exterior change were all—
But with his clumsy port the wretch has lost   650
His ignorance and harmless manners too.
To swear, to game, to drink, to show at home
By lewdness, idleness, and Sabbath breach,
The great proficiency he made abroad,
To astonish and to grieve his gazing friends,
To break some maiden's and his mother's heart,
To be a pest where he was useful once,
Are his sole aim, and all his glory now.
    Man in society is like a flower
Blown in its native bed : 'tis there alone   660
His faculties, expanded in full bloom,
Shine out ; there only reach their proper use.
But man associated and leagued with man
By regal warrant, or self-joined by bond
For interest sake, or swarming into clans
Beneath one head for purposes of war,
Like flowers selected from the rest, and bound
And bundled close to fill some crowded vase,
Fades rapidly, and by compression marred,
Contracts defilement not to be endured.   670
Hence chartered boroughs are such public plagues ;
And burghers, men immaculate perhaps
In all their private functions, once combined,
Become a loathsome body, only fit
For dissolution, hurtful to the main.
Hence merchants, unimpeachable of sin
Against the charities of domestic life,
Incorporated, seem at once to lose

Their nature, and disclaiming all regard
For mercy and the common rights of man,   680
Build factories with blood, conducting trade
At the sword's point, and dyeing the white robe
Of innocent commercial justice red.
Hence too the field of glory, as the world
Misdeems it, dazzled by its bright array,
With all its majesty of thundering pomp,
Enchanting music, and immortal wreaths,
Is but a school where thoughtlessness is taught
On principle, where foppery atones
For folly, gallantry for every vice.   690
   But slighted as it is, and by the great
Abandoned, and, which still I more regret,
Infected with the manners and the modes
It knew not once, the country wins me still.
I never framed a wish, or formed a plan,
That flattered me with hopes of earthly bliss,
But there I laid the scene.   There early strayed
My fancy, ere yet liberty of choice
Had found me, or the hope of being free.
My very dreams were rural, rural too   700
The firstborn efforts of my youthful muse,
Sportive, and jingling her poetic bells
Ere yet her ear was mistress of their powers.
No bard could please me but whose lyre was tuned
To Nature's praises.   Heroes and their feats
Fatigued me, never weary of the pipe
Of Tityrus, assembling, as he sang,
The rustic throng beneath his favourite beech.
Then MILTON had indeed a poet's charms :
New to my taste, his Paradise surpassed   710
The struggling efforts of my boyish tongue
To speak its excellence ; I danced for joy.
I marvelled much that, at so ripe an age
As twice seven years, his beauties had then first
Engaged my wonder, and admiring still,
And still admiring, with regret supposed
The joy half lost because not sooner found.
Thee too, enamoured of the life I loved,
Pathetic in its praise, in its pursuit
Determined, and possessing it at last   720
With transports such as favoured lovers feel,
I studied, prized, and wished that I had known,
Ingenious Cowley ! and though now reclaimed
By modern lights from an erroneous taste,
I cannot but lament thy splendid wit
Entangled in the cobwebs of the schools ;
I still revere thee, courtly though retired,
Though stretched at ease in Chertsey's silent bowers,
Not unemployed, and finding rich amends
For a lost world in solitude and verse.   730

'Tis born with all : the love of Nature's works
Is an ingredient in the compound, man,
Infused at the creation of the kind.
And though the Almighty Maker has throughout
Discriminated each from each, by strokes
And touches of His hand, with so much art
Diversified, that two were never found
Twins at all points—yet this obtains in all,
That all discern a beauty in His works,
And all can taste them : minds that have been formed   740
And tutored with a relish more exact,
But none without some relish, none unmoved.
It is a flame that dies not even there
Where nothing feeds it : neither business, crowds,
Nor habits of luxurious city life,
Whatever else they smother of true worth
In human bosoms, quench it or abate.
The villas with which London stands begirt,
Like a swarth Indian with his belt of beads,
Prove it.   A breath of unadulterate air,   750
The glimpse of a green pasture, how they cheer
The citizen, and brace his languid frame !
Even in the stifling bosom of the town,
A garden in which nothing thrives has charms
That soothe the rich possessor ; much consoled
That here and there some sprigs of mournful mint,
Of nightshade, or valerian, grace the well
He cultivates.   These serve him with a hint
That Nature lives ; that sight-refreshing green
Is still the livery she delights to wear,   760
Though sickly samples of the exuberant whole.
What are the casements lined with creeping herbs,
The prouder sashes fronted with a range
Of orange, myrtle, or the fragrant weed,
The Frenchman's darling ? *   Are they not all proofs
That man, immured in cities, still retains
His inborn inextinguishable thirst
Of rural scenes, compensating his loss
By supplemental shifts, the best he may ?
The most unfurnished with the means of life,   770
And they that never pass their brick-wall bounds
To range the fields and treat their lungs with air,
Yet feel the burning instinct ; over-head
Suspend their crazy boxes, planted thick,
And watered duly.   There the pitcher stands
A fragment, and the spoutless teapot there ;
Sad witnesses how close-pent man regrets
The country, with what ardour he contrives
A peep at nature, when he can no more.
   Hail, therefore, patroness of health and ease   780

---

* Mignonette.

And contemplation, heart-consoling joys
And harmless pleasures, in the thronged abode
Of multitudes unknown ! hail, rural life !
Address himself who will to the pursuit
Of honours, or emolument, or fame,
I shall not add myself to such a chase,
Thwart his attempts, or envy his success.
Some must be great.   Great offices will have
Great talents : and God gives to every man
The virtue, temper, understanding, taste,   790
That lifts him into life, and lets him fall
Just in the niche he was ordained to fill.
To the deliverer of an injured land
He gives a tongue to enlarge upon, a heart
To feel, and courage to redress her wrongs ;
To monarchs dignity ; to judges sense ;
To artists ingenuity and skill ;
To me an unambitious mind, content
In the low vale of life, that early felt
A wish for ease and leisure, and ere long   800
Found here that leisure and that ease I wished.

BOOK V.

THE WINTER MORNING WALK.

ARGUMENT.—A frosty morning—The foddering of cattle—The woodman and his dog—The poultry
—Whimsical effects of frost at a waterfall—The Empress of Russia's palace of ice—Amusements
of monarchs—War, one of them—Wars, whence—And whence monarchy—The evils of it—
English and French loyalty contrasted—The Bastile, and a prisoner there—Liberty the chief
recommendation of this country—Modern patriotism questionable, and why—The perishable
nature of the best human institutions—Spiritual liberty not perishable—The slavish state of
man by nature—Deliver him, Deist, if you can—Grace must do it—The respective merits of
patriots and martyrs stated—Their different treatment—Happy freedom of the man whom
grace makes free—His relish of the works of God—Address to the Creator.

'TIS morning ; and the sun with ruddy orb
Ascending, fires the horizon : while the clouds
That crowd away before the driving wind,
More ardent as the disk emerges more,
Resemble most some city in a blaze,
Seen through the leafless wood.   His slanting ray
Slides ineffectual down the snowy vale,
And tinging all with his own rosy hue,
From every herb and every spiry blade
Stretches a length of shadow o'er the field.   10
Mine, spindling into longitude immense,
In spite of gravity, and sage remark

That I myself am but a fleeting shade,
Provokes me to a smile.   With eye askance
I view the muscular proportioned limb
Transformed to a lean shank.   The shapeless pair,
As they designed to mock me, at my side
Take step for step ; and as I near approach
The cottage, walk along the plastered wall,
Preposterous sight ! the legs without the man.   20
The verdure of the plain lies buried deep
Beneath the dazzling deluge ; and the bents
And coarser grass, upspearing o'er the rest,
Of late unsightly and unseen, now shine
Conspicuous, and in bright apparel clad,
And fledged with icy feathers, nod superb.
The cattle mourn in corners where the fence
Screens them, and seem half-petrified to sleep
In unrecumbent sadness.   There they wait
Their wonted fodder, not like hungering man,   30
Fretful if unsupplied, but silent, meek,
And patient of the slow-paced swain's delay.
He from the stack carves out the accustomed load,
Deep-plunging, and again deep-plunging oft,
His broad keen knife into the solid mass ;
Smooth as a wall the upright remnant stands,
With such undeviating and even force
He severs it away : no needless care
Lest storms should overset the leaning pile
Deciduous, or its own unbalanced weight.   40
Forth goes the woodman, leaving unconcerned
The cheerful haunts of man, to wield the axe
And drive the wedge in yonder forest drear,
From morn to eve his solitary task.
Shaggy, and lean, and shrewd, with pointed ears
And tail cropped short, half lurcher and half cur,
His dog attends him.   Close behind his heel
Now creeps he slow ; and now with many a frisk
Wide scampering, snatches up the drifted snow
With ivory teeth, or ploughs it with his snout ;   50
Then shakes his powdered coat, and barks for joy.
Heedless of all his pranks, the sturdy churl
Moves right toward the mark ; nor stops for aught,
But now and then with pressure of his thumb
To adjust the fragrant charge of a short tube
That fumes beneath his nose : the trailing cloud
Streams far behind him, scenting all the air.
Now from the roost, or from the neighbouring pale,
Where, diligent to catch the first faint gleam
Of smiling day, they gossiped side by side,   60
Come trooping at the housewife's well-known call
The feathered tribes domestic.   Half on wing,
And half on foot, they brush the fleecy flood,
Conscious, and fearful of too deep a plunge.

The sparrows peep, and quit the sheltering eaves
To seize the fair occasion. Well they eye
The scattered grain, and thievishly resolved
To escape the impending famine, often scared
As oft return, a pert voracious kind.
Clean riddance quickly made, one only care   70
Remains to each, the search of sunny nook,
Or shed impervious to the blast.   Resigned
To sad necessity, the cock foregoes
His wonted strut, and wading at their head
With well-considered steps, seems to resent
His altered gait and stateliness retrenched.
How find the myriads that in summer cheer
The hills and valleys with their ceaseless songs
Due sustenance, or where subsist they now?
Earth yields them nought : the imprisoned worm is safe   80
Beneath the frozen clod ; all seeds of herbs
Lie covered close ; and berry-bearing thorns
That feed the thrush (whatever some suppose)
Afford the smaller minstrels no supply.
The long-protracted rigour of the year
Thins all their numerous flocks.   In chinks and holes
Ten thousand seek an unmolested end,
As instinct prompts, self-buried ere they die.
The very rooks and daws forsake the fields,
Where neither grub nor root nor earth-nut now   90
Repays their labour more ; and perched aloft
By the wayside, or stalking in the path,
Lean pensioners upon the traveller's track,
Pick up their nauseous dole, though sweet to them,
Of voided pulse or half-digested grain.
The streams are lost amid the splendid blank,
O'erwhelming all distinction.   On the flood,
Indurated and fixed, the snowy weight
Lies undissolved ; while silently beneath,
And unperceived, the current steals away.   100
Not so, where scornful of a check it leaps
The mill-dam, dashes on the restless wheel,
And wantons in the pebbly gulf below :
No frost can bind it there ; its utmost force
Can but arrest the light and smoky mist
That in its fall the liquid sheet throws wide.
And see where it has hung the embroidered banks
With forms so various, that no powers of art,
The pencil or the pen, may trace the scene !
Here glittering turrets rise, upbearing high   110
(Fantastic misarrangement !) on the roof
Large growth of what may seem the sparkling trees
And shrubs of fairy land.   The crystal drops
That trickle down the branches, fast congealed,
Shoot into pillars of pellucid length,
And prop the pile they but adorned before

Here grotto within grotto safe defies
The sunbeam ; there embossed and fretted wild,
The growing wonder takes a thousand shapes
Capricious, in which fancy seeks in vain   120
The likeness of some object seen before.
Thus Nature works as if to mock at Art,
And in defiance of her rival powers ;
By these fortuitous and random strokes
Performing such inimitable feats,
As she with all her rules can never reach.
Less worthy of applause, though more admired,
Because a novelty, the work of man,
Imperial mistress of the fur-clad Russ !
Thy most magnificent and mighty freak,   130
The wonder of the North.   No forest fell
When thou wouldst build ; no quarry sent its stores
To enrich thy walls ; but thou didst hew the floods,
And make thy marble of the glassy wave.
In such a palace Aristæus found
Cyrene, when he bore the plaintive tale
Of his lost bees to her maternal ear :
In such a palace poetry might place
The armoury of Winter ; where his troops,
The gloomy clouds, find weapons, arrowy sleet,   140
Skin-piercing volley, blossom-bruising hail,
And snow that often blinds the traveller's course,
And wraps him in an unexpected tomb.
Silently as a dream the fabric rose ;
No sound of hammer or of saw was there.
Ice upon ice, the well-adjusted parts
Were soon conjoined, nor other cement asked
Than water interfused to make them one.
Lamps gracefully disposed, and of all hues,
Illumined every side ; a watery light   150
Gleamed through the clear transparency, that seemed
Another moon new risen, or meteor fallen
From heaven to earth, of lambent flame serene.
So stood the brittle prodigy ; though smooth
And slippery the materials, yet frostbound
Firm as a rock.   Nor wanted aught within,
That royal residence might well befit,
For grandeur or for use.   Long wavy wreaths
Of flowers, that feared no enemy but warmth,
Blushed on the panels.   Mirror needed none   160
Where all was vitreous ; but in order due
Convivial table and commodious seat
(What seemed at least commodious seat) were there,
Sofa and couch and high-built throne august.
The same lubricity was found in all,
And all was moist to the warm touch ; a scene
Of evanescent glory, once a stream,
And soon to slide into a stream again.

Alas! 'twas but a mortifying stroke
Of undesigned severity, that glanced   170
(Made by a monarch) on her own estate,
On human grandeur and the courts of kings.
'Twas transient in its nature, as in show
'Twas durable; as worthless as it seemed
Intrinsically precious; to the foot
Treacherous and false; it smiled, and it was cold.
   Great princes have great playthings. Some have played
At hewing mountains into men, and some
At building human wonders mountain high.
Some have amused the dull sad years of life,   180
Life spent in indolence, and therefore sad,
With schemes of monumental fame; and sought
By pyramids and mausolean pomp,
Short-lived themselves, to immortalize their bones.
Some seek diversion in the tented field,
And make the sorrows of mankind their sport.
But war's a game, which, were their subjects wise,
Kings would not play at. Nations would do well
To extort their truncheons from the puny hands
Of heroes, whose infirm and baby minds   190
Are gratified with mischief, and who spoil,
Because men suffer it, their toy the world.
   When Babel was confounded, and the great
Confederacy of projectors wild and vain
Was split into diversity of tongues,
Then, as a shepherd separates his flock,
These to the upland, to the valley those,
God drave asunder, and assigned their lot
To all the nations. Ample was the boon
He gave them, in its distribution fair   200
And equal, and he bade them dwell in peace.
Peace was awhile their care: they ploughed and sowed,
And reaped their plenty without grudge or strife.
But violence can never longer sleep
Than human passions please. In every heart
Are sown the sparks that kindle fiery war;
Occasion needs but fan them, and they blaze.
Cain had already shed a brother's blood;
The Deluge washed it out, but left unquenched
The seeds of murder in the breast of man.   210
Soon, by a righteous judgment, in the line
Of his descending progeny was found
The first artificer of death; the shrewd
Contriver who first sweated at the forge,
And forced the blunt and yet unbloodied steel
To a keen edge, and made it bright for war.
Him, Tubal named, the Vulcan of old times,
The sword and falchion their inventor claim,
And the first smith was the first murderer's son.
His art survived the waters; and ere long,   220

When man was multiplied and spread abroad
In tribes and clans, and had begun to call
These meadows and that range of hills his own,
The tasted sweets of property begat
Desire of more ; and industry in some,
To improve and cultivate their just demesne,
Made others covet what they saw so fair.
Thus war began on earth ; these fought for spoil,
And those in self-defence.   Savage at first
The onset, and irregular.   At length   230
One eminent above the rest, for strength,
For stratagem, or courage, or for all,
Was chosen leader ; him they served in war,
And him in peace, for sake of warlike deeds
Reverenced no less.   Who could with him compare ?
Or who so worthy to control themselves
As he whose prowess had subdued their foes ?
Thus war affording field for the display
Of virtue, made one chief, whom times of peace,
Which have their exigencies too, and call   240
For skill in government, at length made king.
King was a name too proud for man to wear
With modesty and meekness ; and the crown,
So dazzling in their eyes who set it on,
Was sure to intoxicate the brows it bound,
It is the abject property of most,
That being parcel of the common mass,
And destitute of means to raise themselves,
They sink and settle lower than they need.
They know not what it is to feel within   250
A comprehensive faculty that grasps
Great purposes with ease, that turns and wields,
Almost without an effort, plans too vast
For their conception, which they cannot move.
Conscious of impotence, they soon grow drunk
With gazing, when they see an able man
Step forth to notice ; and besotted thus,
Build him a pedestal, and say, "Stand there,
And be our admiration and our praise."
They roll themselves before him in the dust,   260
Then most deserving in their own account
When most extravagant in his applause,
As if exalting him they raised themselves.
Thus by degrees, self-cheated of their sound
And sober judgment, that he is but man,
They demi-deify and fume him so,
That in due season he forgets it too.
Inflated and astrut with self-conceit,
He gulps the windy diet, and ere long,
Adopting their mistake, profoundly thinks   270
The world was made in vain, if not for him.
Thenceforth they are his cattle : drudges born

To bear his burdens ; drawing in his gears
And sweating in his service; his caprice
Becomes the soul that animates them all.
He deems a thousand, or ten thousand lives,
Spent in the purchase of renown for him,
An easy reckoning, and they think the same.
Thus kings were first invented, and thus kings
Were burnished into heroes, and became   280
The arbiters of this terraqueous swamp,
Storks among frogs, that have but croaked and died.
Strange, that such folly as lifts bloated man
To eminence fit only for a god
Should ever drivel out of human lips,
Even in the cradled weakness of the world !
Still stranger much, that when at length mankind
Had reached the sinewy firmness of their youth,
And could discriminate and argue well
On subjects more mysterious, they were yet   290
Babes in the cause of freedom, and should fear
And quake before the gods themselves had made !
But above measure strange, that neither proof
Of sad experience, nor examples set
By some whose patriot virtue has prevailed,
Can even now, when they are grown mature
In wisdom, and with philosophic deeds
Familiar, serve to emancipate the rest !
Such dupes are men to custom, and so prone
To reverence what is ancient, and can plead   300
A course of long observance for its use,
That even servitude, the worst of ills,
Because delivered down from sire to son,
Is kept and guarded as a sacred thing.
But is it fit, or can it bear the shock
Of rational discussion, that a man,
Compounded and made up like other men
Of elements tumultuous, in whom lust
And folly in as ample measure meet
As in the bosoms of the slaves he rules,   310
Should be a despot absolute, and boast
Himself the only freeman of his land ?
Should, when he pleases, and on whom he will,
Wage war, with any or with no pretence
Of provocation given or wrong sustained,
And force the beggarly last doit, by means
That his own humour dictates, from the clutch
Of poverty, that thus he may procure
His thousands, weary of penurious life,
A splendid opportunity to die ?   320
Say ye, who (with less prudence than of old
Jotham ascribed to his assembled trees
In politic convention) put your trust
In the shadow of a bramble, and reclined

In fancied peace beneath his dangerous branch,
Rejoice in him, and celebrate his sway,
Where find ye passive fortitude ?   Whence springs
Your self-denying zeal that holds it good
To stroke the prickly grievance, and to hang
His thorns with streamers of continual praise ?
We too are friends to loyalty.   We love   330
The king who loves the law, respects his bounds,
And reigns content within them : him we serve
Freely and with delight, who leaves us free :
But recollecting still that he is man,
We trust him not too far.   King though he be,
And king in England too, he may be weak,
And vain enough to be ambitious still,
May exercise amiss his proper powers,
Or covet more than freemen choose to grant :   340
Beyond that mark is treason.   He is ours,
To administer, to guard, to adorn the State,
But not to warp or change it.   We are his,
To serve him nobly in the common cause,
True to the death, but not to be his slaves.
Mark now the difference, ye that boast your love
Of kings, between your loyalty and ours :
We love the man, the paltry pageant you ;
We the chief patron of the commonwealth,
You the regardless author of its woes ;   350
We, for the sake of liberty, a king,
You chains and bondage for a tyrant's sake.
Our love is principle, and has its root
In reason, is judicious, manly, free ;
Yours, a blind instinct, crouches to the rod,
And licks the foot that treads it in the dust.
Were kingship as true treasure as it seems,
Sterling, and worthy of a wise man's wish,
I would not be a king to be beloved
Causeless, and daubed with undiscerning praise,   360
Where love is mere attachment to the throne,
Not to the man who fills it as he ought.
   Whose freedom is by sufferance, and at will
Of a superior, he is never free.
Who lives, and is not weary of a life
Exposed to manacles, deserves them well.
The State that strives for liberty, though foiled,
And forced to abandon what she bravely sought,
Deserves at least applause for her attempt,
And pity for her loss.   But that's a cause   370
Not often unsuccessful ; power usurped
Is weakness when opposed ; conscious of wrong,
'Tis pusillanimous and prone to flight.
But slaves that once conceive the glowing thought
Of freedom, in that hope itself possess
All that the contest calls for ; spirit, strength,

The scorn of danger, and united hearts,
The surest presage of the good they seek.*
　　Then shame to manhood, and opprobrious more
To France than all her losses and defeats,　　　　380
Old or of later date, by sea or land,
Her house of bondage, worse than that of old
Which God avenged on Pharaoh—the Bastille.
Ye horrid towers, the abode of broken hearts,
Ye dungeons, and ye cages of despair,
That monarchs have supplied from age to age
With music such as suits their sovereign ears,
The sighs and groans of miserable men !
There's not an English heart that would not leap
To hear that ye were fallen at last ; to know　　390
That even our enemies, so oft employed
In forging chains for us, themselves were free.
For he who values liberty confines
His zeal for her predominance within
No narrow bounds ; her cause engages him
Wherever pleaded. 'Tis the cause of man.
There dwell the most forlorn of human kind,
Immured though unaccused, condemned untried,
Cruelly spared, and hopeless of escape.
There, like the visionary emblem seen　　　　400
By him of Babylon, life stands a stump,
And, filleted about with hoops of brass,
Still lives, though all its pleasant boughs are gone.
To count the hour-bell, and expect no change ;
And ever as the sullen sound is heard,
Still to reflect, that though a joyless note
To him whose moments all have one dull pace,
Ten thousand rovers in the world at large
Account it music ; that it summons some
To theatre or jocund feast or ball ;　　　　410
The wearied hireling finds it a release
From labour ; and the lover, who has chid
Its long delay, feels every welcome stroke
Upon his heart-strings, trembling with delight—
To fly for refuge from distracting thought
To such amusements as ingenious woe
Contrives, hard shifting and without her tools—
To read engraven on the mouldy walls,
In staggering types, his predecessor's tale,
A sad memorial, and subjoin his own—　　　　420
To turn purveyor to an overgorged
And bloated spider, till the pampered pest
Is made familiar, watches his approach,
Comes at his call, and serves him for a friend—

---

* The author hopes that he shall not be censured for unnecessary warmth upon so interesting a
ιbject. He is aware that it is become almost fashionable to stigmatize such sentiments as no
etter than empty declamation ; but it is an ill symptom, and peculiar to modern times.

To wear out time in numbering to and fro
The studs that thick emboss his iron door,
Then downward, and then upward, then aslant,
And then alternate, with a sickly hope
By dint of change to give his tasteless task
Some relish, till the sum exactly found   430
In all directions, he begins again :—
Oh comfortless existence ! hemmed around
With woes, which who that suffers would not kneel
And beg for exile, or the pangs of death?
That man should thus encroach on fellow-man,
Abridge him of his just and native rights,
Eradicate him, tear him from his hold
Upon the endearments of domestic life
And social, nip his fruitfulness and use,
And doom him for perhaps a heedless word   440
To barrenness, and solitude, and tears,
Moves indignation, makes the name of king
(Of king whom such prerogative can please)
As dreadful as the Manichean God,
Adored through fear, strong only to destroy.
   'Tis liberty alone that gives the flower
Of fleeting life its lustre and perfume,
And we are weeds without it.   All constraint,
Except what wisdom lays on evil men,
Is evil ; hurts the faculties, impedes   450
Their progress in the road of science ; blinds
The eyesight of discovery, and begets,
In those that suffer it, a sordid mind
Bestial, a meagre intellect, unfit
To be the tenant of man's noble form.
Thee therefore still, blameworthy as thou art,
With all thy loss of empire, and though squeezed
By public exigence till annual food
Fails for the craving hunger of the State,
Thee I account still happy, and the chief   460
Among the nations, seeing thou art free,
My native nook of earth !   Thy clime is rude,
Replete with vapours, and disposes much
All hearts to sadness, and none more than mine ;
Thine unadulterate manners are less soft
And plausible than social life requires,
And thou hast need of discipline and art
To give thee what politer France receives
From nature's bounty—that humane address
And sweetness, without which no pleasure is   470
In converse, either starved by cold reserve,
Or flushed with fierce dispute, a senseless brawl ;
Yet being free I love thee : for the sake
Of that one feature can be well content,
Disgraced as thou hast been, poor as thou art,
To seek no sublunary rest beside.

But once enslaved, farewell ! I could endure
Chains nowhere patiently, and chains at home,
Where I am free by birthright, not at all.
Then what were left of roughness in the grain   480
Of British natures, wanting its excuse
That it belongs to freemen, would disgust
And shock me. I should then with double pain
Feel all the rigour of thy fickle clime ;
And if I must bewail the blessing lost
For which our Hampdens and our Sidneys bled,
I would at least bewail it under skies
Milder, among a people less austere,
In scenes which, having never known me free,
Would not reproach me with the loss I felt.   490
Do I forebode impossible events,
And tremble at vain dreams? Heaven grant I may !
But the age of virtuous politics is past,
And we are deep in that of cold pretence.
Patriots are grown too shrewd to be sincere,
And we too wise to trust them. He that takes
Deep in his soft credulity the stamp
Designed by loud declaimers on the part
Of liberty, themselves the slaves of lust,
Incurs derision for his easy faith   500
And lack of knowledge, and with cause enough :
For when was public virtue to be found
Where private was not? Can he love the whole
Who loves no part? He be a nation's friend
Who is, in truth, the friend of no man there ?
Can he be strenuous in his country's cause
Who slights the charities for whose dear sake
That country, if at all, must be beloved?
  'Tis therefore sober and good men are sad
For England's glory, seeing it wax pale   510
And sickly, while her champions wear their hearts
So loose to private duty, that no brain,
Healthful and undisturbed by factious fumes,
Can dream them trusty to the general weal.
Such were not they of old, whose tempered blades
Dispersed the shackles of usurped control,
And hewed them link from link. Then Albion's sons
Were sons indeed ; they felt a filial heart
Beat high within them at a mother's wrongs,
And shining each in his domestic sphere,   520
Shone brighter still, once called to public view.
'Tis therefore many, whose sequestered lot
Forbids their interference, looking on,
Anticipate perforce some dire event ;
And seeing the old castle of the State,
That promised once more firmness, so assailed
That all its tempest-beaten turrets shake,
Stand motionless, expectants of its fall.

s

All has its date below ; the fatal hour
Was registered in heaven ere time began.   530
We turn to dust, and all our mightiest works
.Die too : the deep foundations that we lay,
Time ploughs them up, and not a trace remains.
We build with what we deem eternal rock ;
A distant age asks where the fabric stood ;
And in the dust, sifted and searched in vain,
The indiscoverable secret sleeps.
    But there is yet a liberty unsung
By poets, and by senators unpraised,
Which monarchs cannot grant, nor all the powers   540
Of earth and hell confederate take away ;
A liberty which persecution, fraud,
Oppression, prisons, have no power to bind ;
Which whoso tastes can be enslaved no more.
'Tis liberty of heart, derived from Heaven,
Bought with His blood who gave it to mankind,
And sealed with the same token.   It is held
By charter, and that charter sanctioned sure
By the unimpeachable and awful oath
And promise of a God.   His other gifts   550
All bear the royal stamp that speaks them His,
And are august, but this transcends them all.
His other works, the visible display
Of all-creating energy and might,
Are grand, no doubt, and worthy of the Word
That, finding an interminable space
Unoccupied, has filled the void so well,
And made so sparkling what was dark before.
But these are not his glory.   Man, 'tis true,
Smit with the beauty of so fair a scene,   560
Might well suppose the artificer divine
Meant it eternal, had He not Himself
Pronounced it transient, glorious as it is,
And still designing a more glorious far,
Doomed it as insufficient for His praise.
These therefore are occasional, and pass ;
Formed for the confutation of the fool,
Whose lying heart disputes against a God ;
That office served, they must be swept away.
Not so the labours of His love : they shine   570
In other heavens than these that we behold,
And fade not.   There is paradise that fears
No forfeiture, and of its fruits He sends
Large prelibation oft to saints below.
Of these the first in order, and the pledge
And confident assurance of the rest,
Is liberty ; a flight into His arms,
Ere yet mortality's fine threads give way,
A clear escape from tyrannizing lust,
And full immunity from penal woe.   580

Chains are the portion of revolted man,
Stripes, and a dungeon ; and his body serves
The triple purpose.   In that sickly, foul,
Opprobrious residence he finds them all.
Propense his heart to idols, he is held
In silly dotage on created things,
Careless of their Creator.   And that low
And sordid gravitation of his powers
To a vile clod so draws him, with such force
Resistless, from the centre he should seek,   590
That he at last forgets it.   All his hopes
Tend downwards ; his ambition is to sink,
To reach a depth profounder still, and still
Profounder, in the fathomless abyss
Of folly, plunging in pursuit of death.
But ere he gain the comfortless repose
He seeks, and acquiescence of his soul
In heaven-renouncing exile, he endures—
What does he not ? from lusts opposed in vain,
And self-reproaching conscience.   He foresees   600
The fatal issue to his health, fame, peace,
Fortune and dignity ; the loss of all
That can ennoble man, and make frail life,
Short as it is, supportable.   Still worse,
Far worse than all the plagues with which his sins
Infect his happiest moments, he forebodes
Ages of hopeless misery ; future death,
And death still future : not an hasty stroke
Like that which sends him to the dusty grave,
But unrepealable enduring death.   610
Scripture is still a trumpet to his fears :
What none can prove a forgery, may be true ;
What none but bad men wish exploded, must.
That scruple checks him.   Riot is not loud
Nor drunk enough to drown it.   In the midst
Of laughter his compunctions are sincere,
And he abhors the jest by which he shines.
Remorse begets reform.   His master-lust
Falls first before his resolute rebuke,
And seems dethroned and vanquished.   Peace ensues,   620
But spurious and short-lived, the puny child
Of self-congratulating Pride, begot
On fancied Innocence.   Again he falls,
And fights again ; but finds his best essay
A presage ominous, portending still.
Its own dishonour by a worse relapse,
Till Nature, unavailing Nature, foiled
So oft, and wearied in the vain attempt,
Scoffs at her own performance.   Reason now
Takes part with Appetite, and pleads the cause   630
Perversely, which of late she so condemned ;
With shallow shifts and old devices, worn

And tattered in the service of debauch,
Covering his shame from his offended sight.
  " Hath God indeed given appetites to man,
And stored the earth so plenteously with means
To gratify the hunger of his wish,
And doth He reprobate, and will He damn,
The use of His own bounty? making first
So frail a kind, and then enacting laws   640
So strict, that less than perfect must despair ?
Falsehood ! which whoso but suspects of truth
Dishonours God, and makes a slave of man.
Do they themselves, who undertake for hire
The teacher's office, and dispense at large
Their weekly dole of edifying strains,
Attend to their own music? Have they faith
In what, with such solemnity of tone
And gesture, they propound to our belief ?
Nay,—conduct hath the loudest tongue.   The voice   650
Is but an instrument on which the priest
May play what tune he pleases.   In the deed,
The unequivocal authentic deed,
We find sound argument, we read the heart."
  Such reasonings (if that name must needs belong
To excuses in which reason has no part)
Serve to compose a spirit well inclined
To live on terms of amity with vice,
And sin without disturbance.   Often urged,
(As often as, libidinous discourse   660
Exhausted, he resorts to solemn themes
Of theological and grave import,)
They gain at last his unreserved assent ;
Till hardened his heart's temper in the forge
Of lust, and on the anvil of despair,
He slights the strokes of conscience.   Nothing moves,
Or nothing much, his constancy in ill ;
Vain tampering has but fostered his disease ;
'Tis desperate, and he sleeps the sleep of death.
Haste now, philosopher, and set him free.   670
Charm the deaf serpent wisely.   Make him hear
Of rectitude and fitness ; moral truth
How lovely, and the moral sense how sure,
Consulted and obeyed, to guide his steps
Directly to THE FIRST AND ONLY FAIR.
Spare not in such a cause.   Spend all the powers
Of rant and rhapsody in virtue's praise ;
Be most sublimely good, verbosely grand,
And with poetic trappings grace thy prose,
Till it outmantle all the pride of verse.—   680
Ah, tinkling cymbal and high-sounding brass,
Smitten in vain ! such music cannot charm
The eclipse that intercepts truth's heavenly beam,
And chills and darkens a wide wandering soul.

The *still small voice* is wanted.   He must speak,
Whose word leaps forth at once to its effect,
Who calls for things that are not, and they come.
  Grace makes the slave a freeman.   'Tis a change
That turns to ridicule the turgid speech
And stately tone of moralists, who boast,   690
As if, like him of fabulous renown,
They had indeed ability to smooth
The shag of savage nature, and were each
An Orpheus, and omnipotent in song.
But transformation of apostate man
From fool to wise, from earthly to divine,
Is work for Him that made him.   He alone,
And He by means in philosophic eyes
Trivial and worthy of disdain, achieves
The wonder; humanizing what is brute   700
In the lost kind, extracting from the lips
Of asps their venom, overpowering strength
By weakness, and hostility by love.
  Patriots have toiled, and in their country's cause
Bled nobly ; and their deeds, as they deserve,
Receive proud recompense.   We give in charge
Their names to the sweet lyre.   The historic Muse,
Proud of the treasure, marches with it down
To latest times ; and Sculpture, in her turn,
Gives bond in stone and ever-during brass   710
To guard them, and to immortalize her trust.
But fairer wreaths are due, though never paid,
To those who, posted at the shrine of truth,
Have fallen in her defence.   A patriot's blood,
Well spent in such a strife, may earn indeed,
And for a time ensure to his loved land,
The sweets of liberty and equal laws ;
But martyrs struggle for a brighter prize,
And win it with more pain.   Their blood is shed
In confirmation of the noblest claim,   720
Our claim to feed upon immortal truth,
To walk with God, to be divinely free,
To soar, and to anticipate the skies.
Yet few remember them.   They lived unknown
Till Persecution dragged them into fame,
And chased them up to heaven.   Their ashes flew—
No marble tells us whither.   With their names
No bard embalms and sanctifies his song ;
And history, so warm on meaner themes,
Is cold on this.   She execrates indeed   730
The tyranny that doomed them to the fire,
But gives the glorious sufferers little praise.*
  He is the freeman whom the truth makes free,
And all are slaves beside.   There's not a chain

* See Hume.

That hellish foes confederate for his harm
Can wind around him, but he casts it off
With as much ease as Samson his green withes.
He looks abroad into the varied field
Of nature, and though poor perhaps compared
With those whose mansions glitter in his sight,   740
Calls the delightful scenery all his own.
His are the mountains, and the valleys his,
And the resplendent rivers.   His to enjoy
With a propriety that none can feel,
But who, with filial confidence inspired,
Can lift to heaven an unpresumptuous eye,
And smiling say—"My Father made them all!"
Are they not his by a peculiar right,
And by an emphasis of interest his,
Whose eye they fill with tears of holy joy,   750
Whose heart with praise, and whose exalted mind
With worthy thoughts of that unwearied love
That planned, and built, and still upholds a world
So clothed with beauty, for rebellious man?
Yes—ye may fill your garners, ye that reap
The loaded soil, and ye may waste much good
In senseless riot; but ye will not find
In feast or in the chase, in song or dance,
A liberty like his, who unimpeached
Of usurpation, and to no man's wrong,   760
Appropriates nature as his Father's work,
And has a richer use of yours than you.
He is indeed a freeman.   Free by birth
Of no mean city, planned or ere the hills
Were built, the fountains opened, or the sea
With all his roaring multitude of waves.
His freedom is the same in every State,
And no condition of this changeful life,
So manifold in cares, whose every day
Brings its own evil with it, makes it less: 770
For he has wings that neither sickness, pain,
Nor penury, can cripple or confine.
No nook so narrow but he spreads them there
With ease, and is at large.   The oppressor holds
His body bound, but knows not what a range
His spirit takes, unconscious of a chain,
And that to bind him is a vain attempt
Whom God delights in, and in whom He dwells.
     Acquaint thyself with God, if thou wouldst taste
His works.   Admitted once to His embrace,   780
Thou shalt perceive that thou wast blind before;
Thine eye shall be instructed, and thine heart,
Made pure, shall relish with divine delight,
Till then unfelt, what hands divine have wrought.
Brutes graze the mountain-top with faces prone
And eyes intent upon the scanty herb

It yields them; or, recumbent on its brow,
Ruminate heedless of the scene outspread
Beneath, beyond, and stretching far away
From inland regions to the distant main.   790
Man views it and admires, but rests content
With what he views.   The landscape has his praise,
But not its Author.   Unconcerned who formed
The paradise he sees, he finds it such ;
And such well-pleased to find it, asks no more.
Not so the mind that has been touched from Heaven,
And in the school of sacred wisdom taught
To read His wonders, in whose thought the world,
Fair as it is, existed ere it was.
Not for its own sake merely, but for His   800
Much more who fashioned it, he gives it praise ;
Praise that from earth resulting, as it ought,
To earth's acknowledged Sovereign, finds at once
Its only just proprietor in Him.
The soul that sees Him, or receives sublimed
New faculties, or learns at least to employ
More worthily the powers she owned before,
Discerns in all things what, with stupid gaze
Of ignorance, till then she overlooked,
A ray of heavenly light gilding all forms   810
Terrestrial, in the vast and the minute,
The unambiguous footsteps of the God
Who gives its lustre to an insect's wing,
And wheels His throne upon the rolling worlds.
Much conversant with Heaven, she often holds
With those fair ministers of light to man
That fill the skies nightly with silent pomp,
Sweet conference ; enquires what strains were they
With which heaven rang, when every star, in haste
To gratulate the new-created earth,   820
Sent forth a voice, and all the sons of God
Shouted for joy.—"Tell me, ye shining hosts
That navigate a sea that knows no storms,
Beneath a vault unsullied with a cloud,
If from your elevation, whence ye view
Distinctly scenes invisible to man,
And systems of whose birth no tidings yet
Have reached this nether world, ye spy a race
Favoured as ours, transgressors from the womb,
And hasting to a grave, yet doomed to rise,   830
And to possess a brighter heaven than yours ?
As one who long detained on foreign shores
Pants to return, and when he sees afar
His country's weather-bleached and battered rocks
From the green wave emerging, darts an eye
Radiant with joy towards the happy land,
So I with animated hopes behold,
And many an aching wish, your beamy fires,

That show like beacons in the blue abyss,
Ordained to guide the embodied spirit home,　　　840
From toilsome life to never-ending rest.
Love kindles as I gaze.　I feel desires
That give assurance of their own success,
And that, infused from Heaven, must thither tend."
　　So reads he nature whom the lamp of truth
Illuminates.　Thy lamp, mysterious Word!
Which whoso sees, no longer wanders lost,
With intellects bemazed in endless doubt,
But runs the road of wisdom.　Thou hast built,
With means that were not till by thee employed,　850
Worlds that had never been hadst Thou in strength
Been less, or less benevolent than strong.
They are thy witnesses, who speak thy power
And goodness infinite, but speak in ears
That hear not or receive not their report.
In vain thy creatures testify of thee
Till Thou proclaim thyself.　Theirs is indeed
A teaching voice; but 'tis the praise of thine
That whom it teaches it makes prompt to learn,
And with the boon gives talents for its use.　860
Till Thou art heard, imaginations vain
Possess the heart, and fables false as hell,
Yet deemed oracular, lure down to death
The uninformed and heedless souls of men.
We give to Chance, blind Chance, ourselves as blind,
The glory of thy work, which yet appears
Perfect and unimpeachable of blame,
Challenging human scrutiny, and proved
Then skilful most when most severely judged.
But Chance is not; or is not where Thou reignest:　870
Thy Providence forbids that fickle power
(If power she be that works but to confound)
To mix the wild vagaries with thy laws.
Yet thus we dote, refusing, while we can
Instruction, and inventing to ourselves
Gods such as guilt makes welcome; gods that sleep,
Or disregard our follies, or that sit
Amused spectators of this bustling stage.
Thee we reject, unable to abide
Thy purity, till pure as Thou art pure,　　　880
Made such by thee, we love thee for that cause
For which we shunned and hated thee before.
Then we are free: then liberty like day
Breaks on the soul, and by a flash from heaven
Fires all the faculties with glorious joy.
A voice is heard that mortal ears hear not
Till Thou hast touched them; 'tis the voice of song,
A loud Hosanna sent from all thy works,
Which he that hears it with a shout repeats,
And adds his rapture to the general praise.　　890

In that blest moment, Nature throwing wide
Her veil opaque, discloses with a smile
The Author of her beauties, who, retired
Behind his own creation, works unseen
By the impure, and hears his power denied.
Thou art the source and centre of all minds,
Their only point of rest, Eternal Word!
From thee departing, they are lost and rove
At random without honour, hope, or peace.
From thee is all that soothes the life of man,   900
His high endeavour, and his glad success,
His strength to suffer, and his will to serve.
But oh, Thou bounteous Giver of all good!
Thou art of all thy gifts thyself the crown!
Give what Thou canst, without Thee we are poor;
And with Thee rich, take what Thou wilt away.

BOOK VI.

THE WINTER WALK AT NOON.

ARGUMENT — Bells at a distance—Their effect—A fine noon in winter—A sheltered walk—
Meditation better than books—Our familiarity with the course of nature makes it appear less
wonderful than it is—The transformation that spring effects in a shrubbery described—A
mistake concerning the course of nature corrected—God maintains it by an unremitted act—
The amusements fashionable at this hour of the day reproved—Animals happy, a delightful
sight—Origin of cruelty to animals—That it is a great crime proved from Scripture—That
proof illustrated by a tale—A line drawn between the lawful and unlawful destruction of them
—Their good and useful properties insisted on—Apology for the encomiums bestowed by the
author upon animals—Instances of man's extravagant praise of man—The groans of the
creation shall have an end—View taken of the restoration of all things—An invocation and
an invitation of Him who shall bring it to pass—The retired man vindicated from the charge
of uselessness—Conclusion.

THERE is in souls a sympathy with sounds,
And as the mind is pitched the ear is pleased
With melting airs or martial, brisk or grave :
Some chord in unison with what we hear
Is touched within us, and the heart replies.
How soft the music of those village bells
Falling at intervals upon the ear
In cadence sweet! now dying all away,
Now pealing loud again, and louder still,
Clear and sonorous, as the gale comes on.   10
With easy force it opens all the cells
Where memory slept.   Wherever I have heard
A kindred melody, the scene recurs,
And with it all its pleasures and its pains.

Such comprehensive views the spirit takes,
That in a few short moments I retrace
(As in a map the voyager his course)
The windings of my way through many years.
Short as in retrospect the journey seems,
It seemed not always short; the rugged path,　　　20
And prospect oft so dreary and forlorn,
Moved many a sigh at its disheartening length.
Yet feeling present evils, while the past
Faintly impress the mind, or not at all,
How readily we wish time spent revoked,
That we might try the ground again, where once
(Through inexperience as we now perceive)
We missed that happiness we might have found!
Some friend is gone, perhaps his son's best friend,
A father, whose authority, in show　　　30
When most severe, and mustering all its force,
Was but the graver countenance of love;
Whose favour, like the clouds of spring, might lower,
And utter now and then an awful voice,
But had a blessing in its darkest frown,
Threatening at once and nourishing the plant.
We loved, but not enough, the gentle hand
That reared us.　At a thoughtless age allured
By every gilded folly, we renounced
His sheltering side, and wilfully forewent　　　40
That converse which we now in vain regret.
How gladly would the man recall to life
The boy's neglected sire! a mother too,
That softer friend, perhaps more gladly still,
Might he demand them at the gates of death.
Sorrow has, since they went, subdued and tamed
The playful humour; he could now endure
(Himself grown sober in the vale of tears)
And feel a parent's presence no restraint.
But not to understand a treasure's worth　　　50
Till time has stolen away the slighted good,
Is cause of half the poverty we feel,
And makes the world the wilderness it is.
The few that pray at all pray oft amiss,
And, seeking grace to improve the prize they hold,
Would urge a wiser suit than asking more.
　The night was winter in his roughest mood,
The morning sharp and clear.　But now at noon,
Upon the southern side of the slant hills,
And where the woods fence off the northern blast,　　　60
The season smiles, resigning all its rage,
And has the warmth of May.　The vault is blue
Without a cloud, and white without a speck
The dazzling splendour of the scene below.
Again the harmony comes o'er the vale,
And through the trees I view the embattled tower

Whence all the music.   I again perceive
The soothing influence of the wafted strains,
And settle in soft musings as I tread
The walk, still verdant, under oaks and elms,   70
Whose outspread branches overarch the glade.
The roof, though moveable through all its length
As the wind sways it, has yet well sufficed,
And intercepting in their silent fall
The frequent flakes, has kept a path for me.
No noise is here, or none that hinders thought.
The redbreast warbles still, but is content
With slender notes, and more than half suppressed :
Pleased with his solitude, and flitting light
From spray to spray, where'er he rests he shakes   80
From many a twig the pendent drops of ice,
That tinkle in the withered leaves below.
Stillness, accompanied with sounds so soft,
Charms more than silence.   Meditation here
May think down hours to moments.   Here the heart
May give a useful lesson to the head,
And learning wiser grow without his books.
Knowledge and wisdom, far from being one,
Have ofttimes no connexion.   Knowledge dwells
In heads replete with thoughts of other men,   90
Wisdom in minds attentive to their own.
Knowledge, a rude unprofitable mass,
The mere materials with which wisdom builds,
Till smoothed and squared and fitted to its place,
Does but encumber whom it seems to enrich.
Knowledge is proud that he has learned so much ;
Wisdom is humble that he knows no more.
Books are not seldom talismans and spells,
By which the magic art of shrewder wits
Holds an unthinking multitude enthralled.   100
Some to the fascination of a name
Surrender judgment hoodwinked.   Some the style
Infatuates, and through labyrinths and wilds
Of error leads them, by a tune entranced.
While sloth seduces more, too weak to bear
The insupportable fatigue of thought,
And swallowing therefore, without pause or choice,
The total grist unsifted, husks and all.
But trees, and rivulets whose rapid course
Defies the check of winter, haunts of deer,   110
And sheepwalks populous with bleating lambs,
And lanes in which the primrose ere her time
Peeps through the moss that clothes the hawthorn root,
Deceive no student.   Wisdom there, and Truth,
Not shy as in the world, and to be won
By slow solicitation, seize at once
The roving thought, and fix it on themselves.
    What prodigies can power divine perform

More grand than it produces year by year,
And all in sight of inattentive man?   120
Familiar with the effect we slight the cause,
And in the constancy of nature's course,
The regular return of genial months,
And renovation of a faded world,
See nought to wonder at.   Should God again,
As once in Gibeon, interrupt the race
Of the undeviating and punctual sun,
How would the world admire!   But speaks it less
An agency divine, to make him know
His moment when to sink and when to rise,   130
Age after age, than to arrest his course?
All we behold is miracle, but seen
So duly, all is miracle in vain.
Where now the vital energy that moved,
While summer was, the pure and subtle lymph
Through the imperceptible meandering veins
Of leaf and flower?   It sleeps: and the icy touch
Of unprolific winter has impressed
A cold stagnation on the intestine tide.
But let the months go round, a few short months,   140
And all shall be restored.   These naked shoots,
Barren as lances, among which the wind
Makes wintry music, sighing as it goes,
Shall put their graceful foliage on again,
And more aspiring, and with ampler spread,
Shall boast new charms, and more than they have lost.
Then each, in its peculiar honours clad,
Shall publish, even to the distant eye,
Its family and tribe.   Laburnum rich
In streaming gold; Syringa ivory pure;   150
The scentless and the scented Rose, this red
And of an humbler growth, the other tall,*
And throwing up into the darkest gloom
Of neighbouring Cypress, or more sable Yew,
Her silver globes, light as the foamy surf
That the wind severs from the broken wave ;
The Lilac various in array, now white,
Now sanguine, and her beauteous head now set
With purple spikes pyramidal, as if
Studious of ornament, yet unresolved   160
Which hue she most approved, she chose them all ;
Copious of flowers the Woodbine, pale and wan,
But well compensating her sickly looks
With never cloying odours, early and late ;
Hypericum all bloom, so thick a swarm
Of flowers like flies clothing her slender rods
That scarce a leaf appears ; Mezereon too,
Though leafless, well attired, and thick beset

* The Guelder Rose.

With blushing wreaths investing every spray ;
Althæa with the purple eye ; the Broom,   170
Yellow and bright as bullion unalloyed
Her blossoms ; and luxuriant above all
The Jasmine, throwing wide her elegant sweets,
The deep dark green of whose unvarnished leaf
Makes more conspicuous and illumines more
The bright profusion of her scattered stars.—
These have been, and these shall be in their day ;
And all this uniform uncóloured scene
Shall be dismantled of its fleecy load,
And flush into variety again.   180
From dearth to plenty, and from death to life,
Is Nature's progress when she lectures man
In heavenly truth ; evincing, as she makes
The grand transition, that there lives and works
A soul in all things, and that soul is God.
The beauties of the wilderness are His,
That make so gay the solitary place
Where no eye sees them. And the fairer forms,
That cultivation glories in, are His.
He sets the bright procession on its way,   190
And marshals all the order of the year ;
He marks the bounds which winter may not pass,
And blunts his pointed fury ; in its case,
Russet and rude, folds up the tender germ
Uninjured, with inimitable art ;
And, ere one flowery season fades and dies,
Designs the blooming wonders of the next.
 Some say that in the origin of things,
When all creation started into birth,
The infant elements received a law   200
From which they swerve not since. That under force
Of that controlling ordinance they move,
And need not His immediate hand who first
Prescribed their course, to regulate it now.
Thus dream they, and contrive to save a God
The encumbrance of His own concerns, and spare
The great Artificer of all that moves
The stress of a continual act, the pain
Of unremitted vigilance and care,
As too laborious and severe a task.   210
So man, the moth, is not afraid, it seems,
To span Omnipotence, and measure might
That knows no measure by the scanty rule
And standard of his own, that is to-day,
And is not ere to-morrow's sun go down.
But how should matter occupy a charge,
Dull as it is, and satisfy a law
So vast in its demands, unless impelled
To ceaseless service by a ceaseless force,
And under pressure of some conscious cause ? 220

The Lord of all, Himself through all diffused,
Sustains and is the life of all that lives.
Nature is but a name for an effect
Whose cause is God.   He feeds the secret fire
By which the mighty process is maintained,
Who sleeps not, is not weary ; in whose sight
Slow-circling ages are as transient days ;
Whose work is without labour ; whose designs
No flaw deforms, no difficulty thwarts ;
And whose beneficence no charge exhausts.   230
Him blind antiquity profaned, not served,
With self-taught rites, and under various names,
Female and male, Pomona, Pales, Pan,
And Flora and Vertumnus ; peopling earth
With tutelary goddesses and gods
That were not ; and commending as they would
To each some province, garden, field or grove.
But all are under One.   One spirit—His
Who wore the plaited thorns with bleeding brows—
Rules universal nature.   Not a flower   240
But shows some touch in freckle, streak or stain,
Of His unrivalled pencil.   He inspires
Their balmy odours and imparts their hues,
And bathes their eyes with nectar, and includes,
In grains as countless as the seaside sands,
The forms with which He sprinkles all the earth.
Happy who walks with Him ! whom what he finds
Of flavour or of scent in fruit or flower,
Or what he views of beautiful or grand
In nature, from the broad majestic oak   250
To the green blade that twinkles in the sun,
Prompts with remembrance of a present God.
His presence, who made all so fair, perceived,
Makes all still fairer.   As with him no scene
Is dreary, so with him all seasons please.
Though winter had been none, had man been true,
And earth be punished for its tenant's sake,
Yet not in vengeance ; as this smiling sky,
So soon succeeding such an angry night,
And these dissolving snows, and this clear stream   260
Recovering fast its liquid music, prove.
   Who then that has a mind well strung and tuned
To contemplation, and within his reach
A scene so friendly to his favourite task,
Would waste attention at the chequered board,
His host of wooden warriors to and fro
Marching and countermarching, with an eye
As fixed as marble, with a forehead ridged
And furrowed into storms, and with a hand
Trembling, as if eternity were hung   270
In balance on his conduct of a pin ?
Nor envies he aught more their idle sport

Who pant with application misapplied
To trivial toys, and, pushing ivory balls
Across a velvet level, feel a joy
Akin to rapture, when the bauble finds
Its destined goal of difficult access.
Nor deems he wiser him who gives his noon
To miss, the mercer's plague, from shop to shop
Wandering, and littering with unfolded silks   280
The polished counter, and approving none,
Or promising with smiles to call again.
Nor him who, by his vanity seduced,
And soothed into a dream that he discerns
The difference of a Guido from a daub,
Frequents the crowded auction.   Stationed there
As duly as the Langford of the show,
With glass at eye, and catalogue in hand,
And tongue accomplished in the fulsome cant
And pedantry that coxcombs learn with ease,   290
Oft as the price-deciding hammer falls,
He notes it in his book, then raps his box,
Swears 'tis a bargain, rails at his hard fate
That he has let it pass—but never bids.
    Here unmolested, through whatever sign
The sun proceeds, I wander ; neither mist,
Nor freezing sky nor sultry, checking me,
Nor stranger intermeddling with my joy.
Even in the spring and playtime of the year,
That calls the unwonted villager abroad   300
With all her little ones, a sportive train,
To gather kingcups in the yellow mead,
And prink their hair with daisies, or to pick
A cheap but wholesome salad from the brook,
These shades are all my own.   The timorous hare,
Grown so familiar with her frequent guest,
Scarce shuns me ; and the stockdove unalarmed
Sits cooing in the pine-tree, nor suspends
His long love-ditty for my near approach.
Drawn from his refuge in some lonely elm   310
That age or injury has hollowed deep,
Where on his bed of wool and matted leaves
He has outslept the winter, ventures forth
To frisk awhile, and bask in the warm sun,
The squirrel, flippant, pert, and full of play.
He sees me, and at once, swift as a bird,
Ascends the neighbouring beech ; there whisks his brush,
And perks his ears, and stamps and scolds aloud,
With all the prettiness of feigned alarm,
And anger insignificantly fierce.   320
    The heart is hard in nature, and unfit
For human fellowship, as being void
Of sympathy, and therefore dead alike
To love and friendship both, that is not pleased

With sight of animals enjoying life,
Nor feels their happiness augment his own.
The bounding fawn that darts across the glade
When none pursues, through mere delight of heart,
And spirits buoyant with excess of glee ;
The horse, as wanton and almost as fleet, 330
That skims the spacious meadow at full speed,
Then stops and snorts, and throwing high his heels,
Starts to the voluntary race again ;
The very kine that gambol at high noon,
The total herd receiving first from one
That leads the dance a summons to be gay,
Though wild their strange vagaries, and uncouth
Their efforts, yet resolved with one consent
To give such act and utterance as they may
To ecstasy too big to be suppressed ;— 340
These, and a thousand images of bliss,
With which kind Nature graces every scene
Where cruel man defeats not her design,
Impart to the benevolent, who wish
All that are capable of pleasure pleased,
A far superior happiness to theirs,
The comfort of a reasonable joy.
 Man scarce had risen, obedient to His call
Who formed him from the dust, his future grave,
When he was crowned as never king was since. 350
God set the diadem upon his head,
And angel choirs attended. Wondering stood
The new-made monarch, while before him passed,
All happy, and all perfect in their kind,
The creatures, summoned from their various haunts
To see their sovereign, and confess his sway.
Vast was his empire, absolute his power,
Or bounded only by a law whose force
'Twas his sublimest privilege to feel
And own, the law of universal love. 360
He ruled with meekness, they obeyed with joy;
No cruel purpose lurked within his heart,
And no distrust of his intent in theirs.
So Eden was a scene of harmless sport,
Where kindness on his part who ruled the whole
Begat a tranquil confidence in all,
And fear as yet was not, nor cause for fear.
But sin marred all ; and the revolt of man,
That source of evils not exhausted yet,
Was punished with revolt of his from him. 370
Garden of God, how terrible the change
Thy groves and lawns then witnessed ! Every heart,
Each animal of every name, conceived
A jealousy and an instinctive fear,
And, conscious of some danger, either fled
Precipitate the loathed abode of man,

Or growled defiance in such angry sort,
As taught him too to tremble in his turn.
Thus harmony and family accord
Were driven from Paradise ; and in that hour   380
The seeds of cruelty, that since have swelled
To such gigantic and enormous growth,
Were sown in human nature's fruitful soil.
Hence date the persecution and the pain
That man inflicts on all inferior kinds,
Regardless of their plaints.   To make him sport,
To gratify the frenzy of his wrath,
Or his base gluttony, are causes good
And just in his account, why bird and beast
Should suffer torture, and the streams be dyed   390
With blood of their inhabitants impaled.
Earth groans beneath the burden of a war
Waged with defenceless innocence, while he,
Not satisfied to prey on all around,
Adds tenfold bitterness to death by pangs
Needless, and first torments ere he devours.
Now happiest they that occupy the scenes
The most remote from his abhorred resort,
Whom once, as delegate of God on earth,
They feared, and as His perfect image loved.   400
The wilderness is theirs, with all its caves,
Its hollow glens, its thickets, and its plains
Unvisited by man.   There they are free,
And howl and roar as likes them, uncontrolled,
Nor ask his leave to slumber or to play.
Woe to the tyrant, if he dare intrude
Within the confines of their wild domain :
The lion tells him, " I am monarch here ! "
And if he spare him, spares him on the terms
Of royal mercy, and through generous scorn   410
To rend a victim trembling at his foot.
In measure, as by force of instinct drawn,
Or by necessity constrained, they live
Dependent upon man, those in his fields,
These at his crib, and some beneath his roof.
They prove too often at how dear a rate
He sells protection.   Witness, at his foot,
The spaniel dying for some venial fault,
Under dissection of the knotted scourge ;
Witness, the patient ox, with stripes and yells   420
Driven to the slaughter, goaded, as he runs,
To madness, while the savage at his heels
Laughs at the frantic sufferer's fury spent
Upon the guiltless passenger o'erthrown.
He too is witness, noblest of the train
That wait on man, the flight-performing horse :
With unsuspecting readiness he takes
His murderer on his back, and pushed all day,

Ç   T

With bleeding sides and flanks that heave for life,
To the far-distant goal, arrives and dies.   450
So little mercy shows who needs so much !
Does law, so jealous in the cause of man,
Denounce no doom on the delinquent?   None.
He lives, and o'er his brimming beaker boasts
(As if barbarity were high desert)
The inglorious feat, and clamorous in praise
Of the poor brute, seems wisely to suppose
The honours of his matchless horse his own.
But many a crime deemed innocent on earth
Is registered in heaven ; and these, no doubt,   440
Have each their record, with a curse annexed.
Man may dismiss compassion from his heart,
But God will never.   When He charged the Jew
To assist his foe's down-fallen beast to rise ;
And when the bush-exploring boy that seized
The young, to let the parent bird go free ;
Proved He not plainly that His meaner works
Are yet His care, and have an interest all,
All, in the universal Father's love?
On Noah, and in him on all mankind,   450
The charter was conferred, by which we hold
The flesh of animals in fee, and claim
O'er all we feed on, power of life and death.
But read the instrument, and mark it well :
The oppression of a tyrannous control
Can find no warrant there.   Feed then, and yield
Thanks for thy food.   Carnivorous through sin,
Feed on the slain, but spare the living brute.
    The Governor of all, Himself to all
So bountiful, in whose attentive ear   460
The unfledged raven and the lion's whelp
Plead not in vain for pity on the pangs
Of hunger unassuaged, has interposed,
Not seldom, His avenging arm, to smite
The injurious trampler upon nature's law,
That claims forbearance even for a brute.
He hates the hardness of a Balaam's heart ;
And prophet as he was, he might not strike
The blameless animal, without rebuke,
On which he rode.   Her opportune offence   470
Saved him, or the unrelenting seer had died.
He sees that human equity is slack
To interfere, though in so just a cause,
And makes the task His own : inspiring dumb
And helpless victims with a sense so keen
Of injury, with such knowledge of their strength
And such sagacity to take revenge,
That oft the beast has seemed to judge the man.
An ancient, not a legendary tale,
By one of sound intelligence rehearsed,   480

(If such who plead for Providence may seem
In modern eyes,) shall make the doctrine clear.
   Where England, stretched towards the setting sun,
Narrow and long, o'erlooks the western wave,
Dwelt young Misagathus; a scorner he
Of God and goodness, atheist in ostent,
Vicious in act, in temper savage-fierce.
He journeyed; and his chance was as he went
To join a traveller, of far different note,
Evander, famed for piety, for years   490
Deserving honour, but for wisdom more.
Fame had not left the venerable man
A stranger to the manners of the youth,
Whose face too was familiar to his view.
Their way was on the margin of the land,
O'er the green summit of the rocks whose base
Beats back the roaring surge, scarce heard so high.
The charity that warmed his heart was moved
At sight of the man-monster.   With a smile
Gentle, and affable, and full of grace,   500
As fearful of offending whom he wished
Much to persuade, he plied his ear with truths
Not harshly thundered forth, or rudely pressed,
But, like his purpose, gracious, kind, and sweet.
"And dost thou dream," the impenetrable man
Exclaimed, "that me the lullabies of age,
And fantasies of dotards such as thou,
Can cheat, or move a moment's fear in me?
Mark now the proof I give thee, that the brave
Need no such aids as superstition lends,   510
To steel their hearts against the dread of death."
He spoke, and to the precipice at hand
Pushed with a madman's fury. Fancy shrinks,
And the blood thrills and curdles at the thought
Of such a gulf as he designed his grave.
But though the felon on his back could dare
The dreadful leap, more rational his steed
Declined the death, and wheeling swiftly round,
Or e'er his hoof had pressed the crumbling verge,
Baffled his rider, saved against his will.   520
The frenzy of the brain may be redressed
By medicine well applied, but without grace
The heart's insanity admits no cure.
Enraged the more by what might have reformed
His horrible intent, again he sought
Destruction, with a zeal to be destroyed,
With sounding whip, and rowels died in blood.
But still in vain. The Providence that meant
A longer date to the far nobler beast,
Spared yet again the ignobler for his sake.   530
And now, his prowess proved, and his sincere
Incurable obduracy evinced,

His rage grew cool; and pleased perhaps to have earned
So cheaply the renown of that attempt,
With looks of some complacence he resumed
His road, deriding much the blank amaze
Of good Evander, still where he was left
Fixed motionless, and petrified with dread.
So on they fared; discourse on other themes
Ensuing, seemed to obliterate the past,   540
And tamer far for so much fury shown,
(As is the course of rash and fiery men,)
The rude companion smiled, as if transformed.
But 'twas a transient calm.   A storm was near,
An unsuspected storm.   His hour was come.
The impious challenger of power divine
Was now to learn that Heaven, though slow to wrath,
Is never with impunity defied.
His horse, as he had caught his master's mood,
Snorting, and starting into sudden rage,   550
Unbidden, and not now to be controlled,
Rushed to the cliff, and having reached it, stood.
At once the shock unseated him: he flew
Sheer o'er the craggy barrier, and immersed
Deep in the flood, found, when he sought it not,
The death he had deserved, and died alone.
So God wrought double justice; made the fool
The victim of his own tremendous choice,
And taught a brute the way to safe revenge.
    I would not enter on my list of friends   560
(Though graced with polished manners and fine sense,
Yet wanting sensibility) the man
Who needlessly sets foot upon a worm.
An inadvertent step may crush the snail
That crawls at evening in the public path;
But he that has humanity, forewarned,
Will tread aside, and let the reptile live.
The creeping vermin, loathsome to the sight,
And charged perhaps with venom, that intrudes,
A visitor unwelcome, into scenes   570
Sacred to neatness and repose, the alcove,
The chamber, or refectory, may die:
A necessary act incurs no blame.
Not so when, held within their proper bounds,
And guiltless of offence, they range the air,
Or take their pastime in the spacious field:
There they are privileged; and he that hunts
Or harms them there is guilty of a wrong,
Disturbs the economy of Nature's realm,
Who, when she formed, designed them an abode.   580
The sum is this: if man's convenience, health,
Or safety interfere, his rights and claims
Are paramount, and must extinguish theirs.
Else they are all—the meanest things that are—

As free to live, and to enjoy that life,
As God was free to form them at the first,
Who in His sovereign wisdom made them all.
Ye therefore who love mercy, teach your sons
To love it too.   The spring-time of our years
Is soon dishonoured and defiled in most   590
By budding ills, that ask a prudent hand
To check them.   But, alas! none sooner shoots,
If unrestrained, into luxuriant growth,
Than cruelty, most devilish of them all.
Mercy to him that shows it, is the rule
And righteous limitation of its act,
By which Heaven moves in pardoning guilty man
And he that shows none, being ripe in years,
And conscious of the outrage he commits,
Shall seek it and not find it in his turn.   600
    Distinguished much by reason, and still more
By our capacity of grace divine,
From creatures that exist but for our sake,
Which, having served us, perish, we are held
Accountable, and God, some future day,
Will reckon with us roundly for the abuse
Of what He deems no mean or trivial trust.
Superior as we are, they yet depend
Not more on human help than we on theirs.
Their strength, or speed, or vigilance, were given   610
In aid of our defects.   In some are found
Such teachable and apprehensive parts,
That man's attainments in his own concerns,
Matched with the expertness of the brutes in theirs,
Are ofttimes vanquished and thrown far behind.
Some show that nice sagacity of smell,
And read with such discernment, in the port
And figure of the man, his secret aim,
That oft we owe our safety to a skill
We could not teach, and must despair to learn.   620
But learn we might, if not too proud to stoop
To quadruped instructors, many a good
And useful quality, and virtue too,
Rarely exemplified among ourselves:
Attachment never to be weaned or changed
By any change of fortune, proof alike
Against unkindness, absence, and neglect;
Fidelity that neither bribe nor threat
Can move or warp; and gratitude for small
And trivial favours, lasting as the life,   630
And glistening even in the dying eye.
    Man praises man.   Desert in arts or arms
Wins public honour; and ten thousand sit
Patiently present at a sacred song,
Commemoration-mad; content to hear
(O wonderful effect of music's power!)

Messiah's eulogy for Handel's sake.
But less, methinks, than sacrilege might serve—
(For was it less? what heathen would have dared
To strip Jove's statue of his oaken wreath,   640
And hang it up in honour of a man?)
Much less might serve, when all that we design
Is but to gratify an itching ear,
And give the day to a musician's praise.
Remember Handel? Who that was not born
Deaf as the dead to harmony, forgets,
Or can, the more than Homer of his age?
Yes—we remember him; and while we praise
A talent so divine, remember too
That His most holy book from whom it came   650
Was never meant, was never used before,
To buckram out the memory of a man.
But hush!—the Muse perhaps is too severe,
And, with a gravity beyond the size
And measure of the offence, rebukes a deed
Less impious than absurd, and owing more
To want of judgment than to wrong design.
So in the chapel of old Ely House,
When wandering Charles, who meant to be the third,
Had fled from William, and the news was fresh,   660
The simple clerk, but loyal, did announce,
And eke did rear right merrily, two staves,
Sung to the praise and glory of King George.
   Man praises man; and Garrick's memory next,
When time hath somewhat mellowed it, and made
The idol of our worship while he lived
The god of our idolatry once more,
Shall have its altar; and the world shall go
In pilgrimage to bow before his shrine.
The theatre too small shall suffocate   670
Its squeezed contents, and more than it admits
Shall sigh at their exclusion, and return
Ungratified. For there some noble lord
Shall stuff his shoulders with King Richard's bunch,
Or wrap himself in Hamlet's inky cloak,
And strut, and storm, and straddle, stamp and stare,
To show the world how Garrick did not act.
For Garrick was a worshipper himself;
He drew the liturgy, and framed the rites
And solemn ceremonial of the day,   680
And called the world to worship on the banks
Of Avon, famed in song. Ah, pleasant proof
That piety has still in human hearts
Some place, a spark or two not yet extinct!
The mulberry-tree was hung with blooming wreaths;
The mulberry-tree stood centre of the dance;
The mulberry-tree was hymned with dulcet airs;
And from his touchwood trunk the mulberry-tree

Supplied such relics as devotion holds
Still sacred, and preserves with pious care. 690
So 'twas a hallowed time : decorum reigned,
And mirth without offence. No few returned,
Doubtless, much edified, and all refreshed.
Man praises man. The rabble all alive
From tippling benches, cellars, stalls, and styes,
Swarm in the streets. The statesman of the day,
A pompous and slow-moving pageant, comes.
Some shout him, and some hang upon his car,
To gaze in his eyes, and bless him. Maidens wave
Their kerchiefs, and old women weep for joy; 700
While others, not so satisfied, unhorse
The gilded equipage, and turning loose
His steeds, usurp a place they well deserve.
Why? what has charmed them? Hath he saved the State?
No. Doth he purpose its salvation? No.
Enchanting novelty, that moon at full,
That finds out every crevice of the head
That is not sound and perfect, hath in theirs
Wrought this disturbance. But the wane is near,
And his own cattle must suffice him soon. 710
Thus idly do we waste the breath of praise,
And dedicate a tribute, in its use
And just direction sacred, to a thing
Doomed to the dust, or lodged already there.
Encomium in old time was poet's work ;
But poets having lavishly long since
Exhausted all materials of the art,
The task now falls into the public hand ;
And I, contented with an humble theme,
Have poured my stream of panegyric down 720
The vale of nature, where it creeps and winds
Among her lovely works with a secure
And unambitious course, reflecting clear,
If not the virtues, yet the worth, of brutes.
And I am recompensed, and deem the toils
Of poetry not lost, if verse of mine
May stand between an animal and woe,
And teach one tyrant pity for his drudge.
　The groans of nature in this nether world,
Which Heaven has heard for ages, have an end. 730
Foretold by prophets, and by poets sung,
Whose fire was kindled at the prophet's lamp,
The time of rest, the promised Sabbath, comes.
Six thousand years of sorrow have well nigh
Fulfilled their tardy and disastrous course
Over a sinful world ; and what remains
Of this tempestuous state of human things
Is merely as the working of a sea
Before a calm, that rocks itself to rest :
For He, whose car the winds are, and the clouds 740

The dust that waits upon His sultry march,
When sin hath moved Him, and His wrath is hot,
Shall visit earth in mercy ; shall descend
Propitious in His chariot paved with love ;
And what His storms have blasted and defaced
For man's revolt, shall with a smile repair.
  Sweet is the harp of prophecy ; too sweet
Not to be wronged by a mere mortal touch ;
Nor can the wonders it records be sung
To meaner music, and not suffer loss.   750
But when a poet, or when one like me,
Happy to rove among poetic flowers,
Though poor in skill to rear them, lights at last
On some fair theme, some theme divinely fair,
Such is the impulse and the spur he feels
To give it praise proportioned to its worth,
That not to attempt it, arduous as he deems
The labour, were a task more arduous still.
  O scenes surpassing fable, and yet true,
Scenes of accomplished bliss ! which who can see,   760
Though but in distant prospect, and not feel
His soul refreshed with foretaste of the joy ?
Rivers of gladness water all the earth,
And clothe all climes with beauty. The reproach
Of barrenness is past. The fruitful field
Laughs with abundance ; and the land once lean,
Or fertile only in its own disgrace,
Exults to see its thistly curse repealed.
The various seasons woven into one,
And that one season an eternal spring,   770
The garden fears no blight, and needs no fence,
For there is none to covet, all are full.
The lion, and the libbard, and the bear
Graze with the fearless flocks ; all bask at noon
Together, or all gambol in the shade
Of the same grove, and drink one common stream,
Antipathies are none. No foe to man
Lurks in the serpent now : the mother sees,
And smiles to see, her infant's playful hand
Stretched forth to dally with the crested worm,   780
To stroke his azure neck, or to receive
The lambent homage of his arrowy tongue.
All creatures worship man, and all mankind
One Lord, one Father. Error has no place :
That creeping pestilence is driven away :
The breath of heaven has chased it. In the heart
No passion touches a discordant string,
But all is harmony and love. Disease
Is not : the pure and uncontaminate blood
Holds its due course, nor fears the frost of age.   790
One song employs all nations, and all cry,
" Worthy the Lamb, for He was slain for us ! "

The dwellers in the vales and on the rocks
Shout to each other, and the mountain-tops
From distant mountains catch the flying joy,
Till, nation after nation taught the strain,
Earth rolls the rapturous Hosanna round.
Behold the measure of the promise filled ;
See Salem built, the labour of a God !
Bright as a sun the sacred city shines ;   800
All kingdoms and all princes of the earth
Flock to that light ; the glory of all lands
Flows into her ; unbounded is her joy,
And endless her increase.   Thy rams are there,
Nebaioth, and the flocks of Kedar there ;*
The looms of Ormus, and the mines of Ind,
And Saba's spicy groves, pay tribute there.
Praise is in all her gates ; upon her walls,
And in her streets, and in her spacious courts,
Is heard salvation.   Eastern Java there   810
Kneels with the native of the farthest West,
And Æthiopia spreads abroad the hand,
And worships.   Her report has travelled forth
Into all lands.   From every clime they come
To see thy beauty, and to share thy joy,
O Sion ! an assembly such as earth
Saw never, such as Heaven stoops down to see.
    Thus heavenward all things tend.   For all were once
Perfect, and all must be at length restored.
So God has greatly purposed ; who would else   820
In His dishonoured works Himself endure
Dishonour, and be wronged without redress.
Haste then, and wheel away a shattered world,
Ye slow-revolving seasons ! we would see
(A sight to which our eyes are strangers yet)
A world that does not dread and hate His laws,
And suffer for its crime ; would learn how fair
The creature is that God pronounces good,
How pleasant in itself what pleases Him.
Here every drop of honey hides a sting,   830
Worms wind themselves into our sweetest flowers,
And even the joy that haply some poor heart
Derives from Heaven, pure as the fountain is,
Is sullied in the stream ; taking a taint
From touch of human lips, at best impure.
Oh for a world in principle as chaste
As this is gross and selfish ! over which
Custom and prejudice shall bear no sway,
That govern all things here, shouldering aside
The meek and modest Truth, and forcing her   840

---

* Nebaioth and Kedar, the sons of Ishmael, and progenitors of the Arabs, in the prophetic
Scripture here alluded to, may be reasonably considered as representatives of the Gentiles
at large.

To seek a refuge from the tongue of strife
In nooks obscure, far from the ways of men;
Where violence shall never lift the sword,
Nor cunning justify the proud man's wrong,
Leaving the poor no remedy but tears;
Where he that fills an office, shall esteem
The occasion it presents of doing good
More than the perquisite; where law shall speak
Seldom, and never but as wisdom prompts
And equity; not jealous more to guard   850
A worthless form than to decide aright;
Where fashion shall not sanctify abuse,
Nor smooth good-breeding (supplemental grace)
With lean performance ape the work of love.
　　Come then, and added to Thy many crowns,
Receive yet one, the crown of all the earth,
Thou who alone art worthy! It was Thine
By ancient covenant ere nature's birth,
And Thou hast made it Thine by purchase since,
And overpaid its value with Thy blood.   860
Thy saints proclaim Thee King; and in their hearts
Thy title is engraven with a pen
Dipped in the fountain of eternal love.
Thy saints proclaim Thee King; and Thy delay
Gives courage to their foes, who, could they see
The dawn of Thy last advent, long-desired,
Would creep into the bowels of the hills,
And flee for safety to the falling rocks.
The very spirit of the world is tired
Of its own taunting question, asked so long,   870
" Where is the promise of your Lord's approach?"
The infidel has shot his bolts away,
Till his exhausted quiver yielding none,
He gleans the blunted shafts that have recoiled,
And aims them at the shield of Truth again.
The veil is rent, rent too by priestly hands,
That hides divinity from mortal eyes;
And all the mysteries to faith proposed,
Insulted and traduced, are cast aside
As useless, to the moles and to the bats.   880
They now are deemed the faithful, and are praised,
Who, constant only in rejecting Thee,
Deny Thy Godhead with a martyr's zeal,
And quit their office for their error's sake.
Blind, and in love with darkness! yet even these
Worthy, compared with sycophants, who knee
Thy name, adoring, and then preach Thee man!
So fares Thy church. But how Thy church may fare
The world takes little thought. Who will may preach,
And what they will. All pastors are alike   890
To wandering sheep, resolved to follow none.
Two gods divide them all, Pleasure and Gain:

For these they live, they sacrifice to these,
And in their service wage perpetual war
With conscience and with Thee.   Lust in their hearts,
And mischief in their hands, they roam the earth
To prey upon each other : stubborn, fierce,
High-minded, foaming out their own disgrace.
Thy prophets speak of such ; and, noting down
The features of the last degenerate times,   900
Exhibit every lineament of these.
Come then, and added to Thy many crowns,
Receive yet one, as radiant as the rest,
Due to Thy last and most effectual work,
Thy word fulfilled, the conquest of a world.
    He is the happy man, whose life even now
Shows somewhat of that happier life to come ;
Who, doomed to an obscure but tranquil state,
Is pleased with it, and, were he free to choose,
Would make his fate his choice ; whom peace, the fruit   910
Of virtue, and whom virtue, fruit of faith,
Prepare for happiness ; bespeak him one
Content indeed to sojourn while he must
Below the skies, but having there his home.
The world o'erlooks him in her busy search
Of objects more illustrious in her view ;
And occupied as earnestly as she,
Though more sublimely, he o'erlooks the world.
She scorns his pleasures, for she knows them not ;
He seeks not hers, for he has proved them vain.   920
He cannot skim the ground like summer birds
Pursuing gilded flies, and such he deems
Her honours, her emoluments, her joys.
Therefore in contemplation is his bliss,
Whose power is such, that whom she lifts from earth
She makes familiar with a heaven unseen,
And shows him glories yet to be revealed.
Not slothful he, though seeming unemployed,
And censured oft as useless.   Stillest streams
Oft water fairest meadows, and the bird   930
That flutters least is longest on the wing.
Ask him, indeed, what trophies he has raised,
Or what achievements of immortal fame
He purposes, and he shall answer—None.
His warfare is within.   There unfatigued
His fervent spirit labours.   There he fights,
And there obtains fresh triumphs o'er himself,
And never-withering wreaths, compared with which
The laurels that a Cæsar reaps are weeds.
Perhaps the self-approving haughty world,   940
That as she sweeps him with her whistling silks
Scarce deigns to notice him, or, if she see,
Deems him a cipher in the works of God,
Receives advantage from his noiseless hours,

Of which she little dreams.   Perhaps she owes
Her sunshine and her rain, her blooming spring
And plenteous harvest, to the prayer he makes,
When, Isaac-like, the solitary saint
Walks forth to meditate at eventide,
And think on her, who thinks not for herself.   950
Forgive him then, thou bustler in concerns
Of little worth, and idler in the best,
If, author of no mischief and some good,
He seeks his proper happiness by means
That may advance, but cannot hinder, thine.
Nor though he tread the secret path of life,
Engage no notice, and enjoy much ease,
Account him an encumbrance on the state,
Receiving benefits, and rendering none.
His sphere though humble, if that humble sphere   960
Shine with his fair example, and though small
His influence, if that influence all be spent
In soothing sorrow and in quenching strife,
In aiding helpless indigence, in works
From which at least a grateful few derive
Some taste of comfort in a world of woe,
Then let the supercilious great confess
He serves his country, recompenses well
The state beneath the shadow of whose vine
He sits secure, and in the scale of life   970
Holds no ignoble, though a slighted, place.
The man whose virtues are more felt than seen
Must drop indeed the hope of public praise ;
But he may boast what few that win it can,
That if his country stand not by his skill,
At least his follies have not wrought her fall.
Polite refinement offers him in vain
Her golden tube, through which a sensual world
Draws gross impurity, and likes it well,
The neat conveyance hiding all the offence.   980
Not that he peevishly rejects a mode
Because that world adopts it.   If it bear
The stamp and clear impression of good sense,
And be not costly more than of true worth,
He puts it on, and for decorum sake
Can wear it even as gracefully as she.
She judges of refinement by the eye,
He by the test of conscience, and a heart
Not soon deceived ; aware that what is base
No polish can make sterling, and that vice,   990
Though well perfumed and elegantly dressed,
Like an unburied carcase tricked with flowers,
Is but a garnished nuisance, fitter far
For cleanly riddance than for fair attire.
So life glides smoothly and by stealth away,
More golden than that age of fabled gold

Renowned in ancient song ; not vexed with care
Or stained with guilt, beneficent, approved
Of God and man, and peaceful in its end.
So glide my life away ! and so at last,   1000
My share of duties decently fulfilled,
May some disease, not tardy to perform
Its destined office, yet with gentle stroke
Dismiss me weary to a safe retreat,
Beneath the turf that I have often trod.
It shall not grieve me, then, that once, when called
To dress a Sofa with the flowers of verse,
I played awhile, obedient to the fair,
With that light task ; but soon, to please her more,
Whom flowers alone I knew would little please,   1010
Let fall the unfinished wreath, and roved for fruit ;
Roved far, and gathered much : some harsh, 'tis true,
Picked from the thorns and briars of reproof,
But wholesome, well digested ; grateful some
To palates that can taste immortal truth,
Insipid else, and sure to be despised.
But all is in His hand whose praise I seek.
In vain the poet sings, and the world hears,
If He regard not, though divine the theme.
'Tis not in artful measures, in the chime   1020
And idle tinkling of a minstrel's lyre,
To charm His ear, whose eye is on the heart ;
Whose frown can disappoint the proudest strain,
Whose approbation prosper—even mine.

AN EPISTLE TO JOSEPH HILL, Esq.

DEAR JOSEPH,—Five and twenty years ago—
Alas, how time escapes !—'tis even so—
With frequent intercourse, and always sweet,
And always friendly, we were wont to cheat
A tedious hour, and now we never meet !
As some grave gentleman in Terence says
('Twas therefore much the same in ancient days),
Good lack, we know not what to-morrow brings—
Strange fluctuation of all human things !
True.   Changes will befall, and friends may part,   10
But distance only cannot change the heart :
And were I called to prove the assertion true,
One proof should serve—a reference to you.
      Whence comes it, then, that in the wane of life,
Though nothing have occurred to kindle strife,
We find the friends we fancied we had won,
Though numerous once, reduced to few or none ?
Can gold grow worthless, that has stood the touch ?
No ; gold they seemed, but they were never such.
      Horatio's servant once, with bow and cringe,   20
Swinging the parlour door upon its hinge,
Dreading a negative, and overawed
Lest he should trespass, begged to go abroad.
" Go, fellow !—whither ? "—turning short about—
" Nay.   Stay at home—you're always going out."—
" 'Tis but a step, sir ; just at the street's end."—
" For what ?"—"An please you, sir, to see a friend."—
" A friend !" Horatio cried, and seemed to start—
" Yea marry shalt thou, and with all my heart.
And fetch my cloak ; for, though the night be raw,   30
I'll see him too—the first I ever saw."
      I knew the man, and knew his nature mild,
And was his plaything often when a child ;
But somewhat at that moment pinched him close,
Else he was seldom bitter or morose.
Perhaps, his confidence just then betrayed,
His grief might prompt him with the speech he made ;
Perhaps 'twas mere good humour gave it birth,
The harmless play of pleasantry and mirth.
Howe'er it was, his language, in my mind,   40
Bespoke at least a man that knew mankind.
      But not to moralize too much, and strain
To prove an evil of which all complain,

(I hate long arguments verbosely spun,) ·
One story more, dear Hill, and I have done.
Once on a time, an emperor, a wise man,
No matter where, in China or Japan,
Decreed, that whosoever should offend
Against the well-known duties of a friend,
Convicted once, should ever after wear   50
But half a coat, and show his bosom bare:
The punishment importing this, no doubt,
That all was naught within, and all found out.
   O happy Britain ! we have not to fear
Such hard and arbitrary measure here ;
Else, could a law like that which I relate
Once have the sanction of our triple state,
Some few that I have known in days of old,
Would run most dreadful risk of catching cold ;
While you, my friend, whatever wind should blow,   60
Might traverse England safely to and fro,
An honest man, close buttoned to the chin,
Broadcloth without, and a warm heart within.

TIROCINIUM;

OR,

A REVIEW OF SCHOOLS,

Κεφαλαιον δη παιδειας ορθη τροφη.—PLATO.

Αρχη πολιτειας απασης νεων τροφα.—DIOG. LAERT.

TO THE REV. WILLIAM CAWTHORNE UNWIN,

Rector of Stock, in Essex.

THE TUTOR OF HIS TWO SONS,

The following POEM, *recommending Private Tuition in preference to an Education at School,*

IS INSCRIBED, BY HIS AFFECTIONATE FRIEND,

WILLIAM COWPER.

OLNEY, *Nov.* 6, 1784.

It is not from his form, in which we trace
Strength joined with beauty, dignity with grace,
That man, the master of this globe, derives
His right of empire over all that lives.
That form indeed, the associate of a mind
Vast in its powers, ethereal in its kind,—
That form, the labour of Almighty skill,
Framed for the service of a free-born will,
Asserts precedence, and bespeaks control,
But borrows all its grandeur from the soul.   10
Hers is the state, the splendour, and the throne,
An intellectual kingdom all her own.
For her the Memory fills her ample page
With truths poured down from every distant age;
For her amasses an unbounded store,
The wisdom of great nations, now no more;
Though laden, not encumbered with her spoil;
Laborious, yet unconscious of her toil;
When copiously supplied, then most enlarged;
Still to be fed, and not to be surcharged.   20
For her the Fancy, roving unconfined,
The present muse of every pensive mind,
Works magic wonders, adds a brighter hue
To Nature's scenes than Nature ever knew.
At her command winds rise and waters roar,
Again she lays them slumbering on the shore;

With flower and fruit the wilderness supplies,
Or bids the rocks in ruder pomp arise.
For her the Judgment, umpire in the strife
That Grace and Nature have to wage through life, 30
Quick-sighted arbiter of good and ill,
Appointed sage preceptor to the Will,
Condemns, approves, and with a faithful voice
Guides the decision of a doubtful choice.
   Why did the fiat of a God give birth
To yon fair Sun, and his attendant Earth?
And when descending he resigns the skies,
Why takes the gentler Moon her turn to rise,
Whom Ocean feels through all his countless waves,
And owns her power on every shore he laves? 40
Why do the seasons still enrich the year,
Fruitful and young as in their first career?
Spring hangs her infant blossoms on the trees,
Rocked in the cradle of the western breeze ;
Summer in haste the thriving charge receives
Beneath the shade of her expanded leaves,
Till Autumn's fiercer heats and plenteous dews
Dye them at last in all their glowing hues. —
'Twere wild profusion all, and bootless waste,
Power misemployed, munificence misplaced, 50
Had not its Author dignified the plan,
And crowned it with the majesty of man.
Thus formed, thus placed, intelligent, and taught,
Look where he will, the wonders God has wrought,
The wildest scorner of his Maker's laws
Finds in a sober moment time to pause,
To press the important question on his heart,
" Why formed at all, and wherefore as thou art ? "
If man be what he seems, this hour a slave,
The next mere dust and ashes in the grave, 60
Endued with reason only to descry
His crimes and follies with an aching eye ;
With passions, just that he may prove with pain,
The force he spends against their fury vain ;
And if, soon after having burned, by turns,
With every lust with which frail nature burns,
His being end where death dissolves the bond,
The tomb take all, and all be blank beyond ;
That he, of all that nature has brought forth,
Stands self-impeached the creature of least worth 70
And useless while he lives, and when he dies,
Brings into doubt the wisdom of the skies.
   Truths that the learned pursue with eager thought
Are not important always as dear-bought,
Proving at last, though told in pompous strains,
A childish waste of philosophic pains ;
But truths on which depend our main concern,
That 'tis our shame and misery not to learn,

C   U

Shine by the side of every path we tread
With such a lustre, he that runs may read. 80
'Tis true that, if to trifle life away
Down to the sunset of their latest day,
Then perish on futurity's wide shore
Like fleeting exhalations found no more,
Were all that Heaven required of humankind,
And all the plan their destiny designed,
What none could reverence all might justly blame,
And man would breathe but for his Maker's shame.
But reason heard, and nature well perused,
At once the dreaming mind is disabused. 90
If all we find possessing earth, sea, air,
Reflect His attributes who placed them there,
Fulfil the purpose, and appear designed
Proofs of the wisdom of the all-seeing mind,
'Tis plain the creature whom He chose to invest
With kingship and dominion o'er the rest,
Received his nobler nature, and was made
Fit for the power in which he stands arrayed ;
That first or last, hereafter if not here,
He too might make his Author's wisdom clear, 100
Praise Him on earth, or obstinately dumb,
Suffer His justice in a world to come.
This once believed, 'twere logic misapplied
To prove a consequence by none denied,
That we are bound to cast the minds of youth
Betimes into the mould of heavenly truth,
That taught of God they may indeed be wise,
Nor ignorantly wandering miss the skies.
    In early days the conscience has in most
A quickness, which in later life is lost : 110
Preserved from guilt by salutary fears,
Or guilty, soon relenting into tears.
Too careless often, as our years proceed,
What friends we sort with, or what books we read,
Our parents yet exert a prudent care,
To feed our infant minds with proper fare ;
And wisely store the nursery by degrees
With wholesome learning, yet acquired with ease.
Neatly secured from being soiled or torn
Beneath a pane of thin translucent horn, 120
A book (to please us at a tender age
'Tis called a book, though but a single page)
Presents the prayer the Saviour deigned to teach,
Which children use, and parsons—when they preach.
Lisping our syllables, we scramble next
Through moral narrative, or sacred text ;
And learn with wonder how this world began,
Who made, who marred, and who has ransomed man,—
Points, which, unless the Scripture made them plain,
The wisest heads might agitate in vain. 130

O thou, whom, borne on fancy's eager wing
Back to the season of life's happy spring,
I pleased remember, and, while Memory yet
Holds fast her office here, can ne'er forget ;
Ingenious dreamer, in whose well-told tale
Sweet fiction and sweet truth alike prevail ;
Whose humorous vein, strong sense, and simple style
May teach the gayest, make the gravest smile ;
Witty, and well employed, and, like thy Lord,
Speaking in parables His slighted word ;   140
I name thee not, lest so despised a name
Should move a sneer at thy deservèd fame,
Yet e'en in transitory life's late day,
That mingles all my brown with sober gray,
Revere the man whose PILGRIM marks the road,
And guides the PROGRESS of the soul to God.
'Twere well with most, if books that could engage
Their childhood, pleased them at a riper age ;
The man, approving what had charmed the boy,
Would die at last in comfort, peace, and joy ;   150
And not with curses on his art who stole
The gem of truth from his unguarded soul.
The stamp of artless piety impressed
By kind tuition on his yielding breast,
The youth now bearded, and yet pert and raw,
Regards with scorn, though once received with awe,
And warped into the labyrinth of lies,
That babblers, called philosophers, devise,
Blasphemes his creed, as founded on a plan
Replete with dreams, unworthy of a man.   160
Touch but his nature in its ailing part,
Assert the native evil of his heart,
His pride resents the charge, although the proof *
Rise in his forehead, and seem rank enough :
Point to the cure, describe a Saviour's cross
As God's expedient to retrieve his loss,
The young apostate sickens at the view,
And hates it with the malice of a Jew.
    How weak the barrier of mere Nature proves,
Opposed against the pleasures Nature loves !   170
While self-betrayed, and wilfully undone,
She longs to yield, no sooner wooed than won.
Try now the merits of this blest exchange
Of modest truth for wit's eccentric range.
Time was he closed as he began the day,
With decent duty, not ashamed to pray :
The practice was a bond upon his heart,
A pledge he gave for a consistent part ;
Nor could he dare presumptuously displease
A Power, confessed so lately on his knees.   180

* See 2 Chron. xxvi. 19.
U 2

But now farewell all legendary tales,
The shadows fly, philosophy prevails ;
Prayer to the winds, and caution to the waves ;
Religion makes the free by nature slaves ;
Priests have invented, and the world admired
What knavish priests promulgate as inspired !
Till Reason, now no longer overawed,
Resumes her powers, and spurns the clumsy fraud,
And, common-sense diffusing real day,
The meteor of the Gospel dies away.   190
Such rhapsodies our shrewd discerning youth
Learn from expert inquirers after truth ;
Whose only care, might truth presume to speak,
Is not to find what they profess to seek.
And thus, well-tutored only while we share
A mother's lectures and a nurse's care ;
And taught at schools much mythologic stuff,*
But sound religion sparingly enough ;
Our early notices of truth, disgraced,
Soon lose their credit, and are all effaced.   200

Would you your son should be a sot or dunce,
Lascivious, headstrong, or all these at once ;
That in good time the stripling's finished taste
For loose expense, and fashionable waste,
Should prove your ruin, and his own at last ;
Train him in public with a mob of boys,
Childish in mischief only and in noise,
Else of a mannish growth, and five in ten
In infidelity and lewdness men.
There shall he learn, ere sixteen winters old,   210
That authors are most useful pawned or sold ;
That pedantry is all that schools impart,
But taverns teach the knowledge of the heart ;
There waiter Dick, with bacchanalian lays,
Shall win his heart, and have his drunken praise,
His counsellor and bosom friend shall prove,
And some street-pacing harlot his first love.
Schools, unless discipline were doubly strong,
Detain their adolescent charge too long ;
The management of tyros of eighteen   220
Is difficult ; their punishment obscene.
The stout tall captain, whose superior size
The minor heroes view with envious eyes,
Becomes their pattern, upon whom they fix
Their whole attention, and ape all his tricks.
His pride, that scorns to obey or to submit,
With them is courage ; his effrontery wit ;

---

* The author begs leave to explain.—Sensible that, without such knowledge, neither the ancient poets nor historians can be tasted, or indeed understood, he does not mean to censure the pains that are taken to instruct a schoolboy in the religion of the heathen, but merely that neglect of Christian culture which leaves him shamefully ignorant of his own.

His wild excursions, window-breaking feats,
Robbery of gardens, quarrels in the streets,
His hairbreadth 'scapes, and all his daring schemes,   230
Transport them, and are made their favourite themes.
In little bosoms such achievements strike
A kindred spark: they burn to do the like.
Thus half-accomplished ere he yet begin
To show the peeping down upon his chin;
And, as maturity of years comes on,
Made just the adept that you designed your son;
To ensure the perseverance of his course,
And give your monstrous project all its force,
Send him to college. If he there be tamed,   240
Or in one article of vice reclaimed,
Where no regard of ord'nances is shown
Or looked for now, the fault must be his own.
Some sneaking virtue lurks in him, no doubt,
Where neither strumpets' charms, nor drinking bout,
Nor gambling practices, can find it out.
Such youths of spirit, and that spirit too,
Ye nurseries of our boys, we owe to you:
Though from ourselves the mischief more proceeds,
For public schools 'tis public folly feeds.   250
The slaves of custom and established mode,
With packhorse constancy we keep the road,
Crooked or straight, through quags or thorny dells,
True to the jingling of our leader's bells.
To follow foolish precedents, and wink
With both our eyes, is easier than to think;
And such an age as ours balks no expense,
Except of caution, and of common-sense:
Else sure, notorious fact and proof so plain
Would turn our steps into a wiser train.   260
I blame not those who, with what care they can,
O'erwatch the numerous and unruly clan:
Or, if I blame, 'tis only that they dare
Promise a work, of which they must despair.
Have ye, ye sage intendants of the whole,
A ubiquarian presence and control,
Elisha's eye, that, when Gehazi strayed,
Went with him and saw all the game he played?
Yes—ye are conscious; and on all the shelves
Your pupils strike upon, have struck yourselves.   270
Or if, by nature sober, ye had then,
Boys as ye were, the gravity of men;
Ye knew at least, by constant proofs addressed
To ears and eyes, the vices of the rest.
But ye connive at what ye cannot cure,
And evils not to be endured, endure,
Lest power exerted but without success,
Should make the little ye retain still less.
Ye once were justly famed for bringing forth

Undoubted scholarship and genuine worth: 280
And in the firmament of fame still shines
A glory, bright as that of all the signs,
Of poets raised by you, and statesmen, and divines.
Peace to them all! those brilliant times are fled,
And no such lights are kindling in their stead.
Our striplings shine indeed, but with such rays
As set the midnight riot in a blaze;
And seem, if judged by their expressive looks,
Deeper in none than in their surgeons' books.
  Say, Muse (for, education made the song,   290
No Muse can hesitate, or linger long),
What causes move us, knowing as we must,
That these *menageries* all fail their trust,
To send our sons to scout and scamper there,
While colts and puppies cost us so much care?
  Be it a weakness, it deserves some praise,
We love the play-place of our early days.
The scene is touching, and the heart is stone
That feels not at that sight, and feels at none.
The wall on which we tried our graving skill,   300
The very name we carved subsisting still;
The bench on which we sat while deep employed,
Though mangled, hacked, and hewed, not yet destroyed:
The little ones, unbuttoned, glowing hot,
Playing our games, and on the very spot;
As happy as we once, to kneel and draw
The chalky ring, and knuckle down at taw;
To pitch the ball into the grounded hat,
Or drive it devious with a dexterous pat;
The pleasing spectacle at once excites   310
Such recollection of our own delights,
That, viewing it, we seem almost to obtain
Our innocent sweet simple years again.
This fond attachment to the well-known place
Whence first we started into life's long race,
Maintains its hold with such unfailing sway,
We feel it e'en in age, and at our latest day.
Hark! how the sire of chits, whose future share
Of classic food begins to be his care,
With his own likeness placed on either knee,   320
Indulges all a father's heartfelt glee;
And tells them, as he strokes their silver locks,
That they must soon learn Latin, and to box:
Then turning, he regales his listening wife
With all the adventures of his early life;
His skill in coachmanship, or driving chaise,
In bilking tavern bills, and spouting plays;
What shifts he used, detected in a scrape,
How he was flogged, or had the luck to escape;
What sums he lost at play, and how he sold   330
Watch, seals, and all—till all his pranks are told.

Retracing thus his *frolics* ('tis a name
That palliates deeds of folly and of shame),
He gives the local bias all its sway;
Resolves that where he played his sons shall play,
And destines their bright genius to be shown
Just in the scene where he displayed his own.
The meek and bashful boy will soon be taught
To be as bold and forward as he ought;
The rude will scuffle through with ease enough,   340
Great schools suit best the sturdy and the rough.
Ah, happy designation, prudent choice,
The event is sure; expect it, and rejoice!
Soon see your wish fulfilled in either child,
The pert made perter, and the tame made wild.
The great, indeed, by titles, riches, birth,
Excused the incumbrance of more solid worth,
Are best disposed of where with most success
They may acquire that confident address,
Those habits of profuse and lewd expense,   350
That scorn of all delights but those of sense,
Which though in plain plebeians we condemn,
With so much reason all expect from them.
But families of less illustrious fame,
Whose chief distinction is their spotless name,
Whose heirs, their honours none, their income small,
Must shine by true desert, or not at all,
What dream they of, that with so little care
They risk their hopes, their dearest treasure, there?
They dream of little Charles or William graced   360
With wig prolix, down flowing to his waist;
They see the attentive crowds his talents draw,
They hear him speak—the oracle of law.
The father who designs his babe a priest,
Dreams him episcopally such at least;
And, while the playful jockey scours the room
Briskly, astride upon the parlour broom,
In fancy sees him more superbly ride
In coach with purple lined, and mitres on its side.
Events improbable and strange as these,   370
Which only a parental eye foresees,
A public school shall bring to pass with ease.
But how? resides such virtue in that air,
As must create an appetite for prayer?
And will it breathe into him all the zeal,
That candidates for such a prize should feel;
To take the lead, and be the foremost still
In all true worth and literary skill?
  " Ah, blind to bright futurity, untaught
  " The knowledge of the world, and dull of thought!   380
  " Church-ladders are not always mounted best
  " By learned clerks, and Latinists professed.
  " The exalted prize demands an upward look,

" Not to be found by poring on a book.
" Small skill in Latin, and still less in Greek,
" Is more than adequate to all I seek.
" Let erudition grace him, or not grace,
" I give the bauble but the second place ;
" His wealth, fame, honours, all that I intend,
" Subsist and centre in one point—a friend.   390
" A friend, whate'er he studies or neglects,
" Shall give him consequence, heal all defects.
" His intercourse with peers and sons of peers—
" There dawns the splendour of his future years ;
" In that bright quarter his propitious skies
" Shall blush betimes, and there his glory rise.
" *Your Lordship*, and *Your Grace!* what school can teach
" A rhetoric equal to those parts of speech ?
" What need of Homer's verse, or Tully's prose,
" Sweet interjections ! if he learn but those ?   400
" Let reverend churls his ignorance rebuke,
" Who starve upon a dog's-eared Pentateuch,
" The parson knows enough who knows a duke."
Egregious purpose ! worthily begun
In barbarous prostitution of your son ;
Pressed on his part by means that would disgrace
A scrivener's clerk, or footman out of place,
And ending, if at last its end be gained,
In sacrilege, in God's own house profaned.
It may succeed ; and, if his sins should call   410
For more than common punishment, it shall ;
The wretch shall rise, and be the thing on earth
Least qualified in honour, learning, worth,
To occupy a sacred, awful post,
In which the best and worthiest tremble most.
The *royal letters* are a thing of course,
A king that would, might recommend his horse ;
And Deans, no doubt, and Chapters, with one voice
As bound in duty, would confirm the choice.
Behold your Bishop ; well he plays his part,   420
Christian in name, and infidel in heart,
Ghostly in office, earthly in his plan,
A slave at court, elsewhere a lady's man.
Dumb as a senator, and as a priest
A piece of mere church furniture at best ;
To live estranged from God his total scope,
And his end sure, without one glimpse of hope.
But fair although and feasible it seem,
Depend not much upon your golden dream ;
For Providence, that seems concerned to exempt   430
The hallowed bench from absolute contempt,
In spite of all the wrigglers into place,
Still keeps a seat or two for worth and grace ;
And therefore 'tis that, though the sight be rare,
We sometimes see a Lowth or Bagot there.

Besides, school friendships are not always found,
Though fair in promise, permanent and sound ;
The most disinterested and virtuous minds,
In early years connected, time unbinds ;
New situations give a different cast   440
Of habit, inclination, temper, taste ;
And he that seemed our counterpart at first
Soon shows the strong similitude reversed.
Young heads are giddy, and young hearts are warm,
And make mistakes for manhood to reform.
Boys are at best but pretty buds unblown,
Whose scent and hues are rather guessed than known ;
Each dreams that each is just what he appears,
But learns his error in maturer years,
When disposition, like a sail unfurled,   450
Shows all its rents and patches to the world.
If, therefore, e'en when honest in design,
A boyish friendship may so soon decline,
'Twere wiser sure to inspire a little heart
With just abhorrence of so mean a part,
Than set your son to work at a vile trade
For wages so unlikely to be paid.
   Our public hives of puerile resort,
That are of chief and most approved report,
To such base hopes, in many a sordid soul,   460
Owe their repute in part, but not the whole.
A principle whose proud pretensions pass
Unquestioned, though the jewel be but glass,
That with a world not often over-nice
Ranks as a virtue, and is yet a vice ;
Or rather a gross compound, justly tried,
Of envy, hatred, jealousy, and pride—
Contributes most perhaps to enhance their fame,
And emulation is its specious name.
Boys, once on fire with that contentious zeal,   470
Feel all the rage that female rivals feel :
The prize of beauty in a woman's eyes
Not brighter than in theirs the scholar's prize.
The spirit of that competition burns
With all varieties of ills by turns ;
Each vainly magnifies his own success,
Resents his fellow's, wishes it were less,
Exults in his miscarriage if he fail,
Deems his reward too great if he prevail,
And labours to surpass him day and night,   480
Less for improvement than to tickle spite.
The spur is powerful, and I grant its force ;
It pricks the genius forward in its course,
Allows short time for play, and none for sloth :
And, felt alike by each, advances both :
But judge, where so much evil intervenes,
The end, though plausible, not worth the means.

Weigh, for a moment, classical desert
Against a heart depraved and temper hurt ;
Hurt too perhaps for life ; for early wrong,   490
Done to the nobler part, affects it long ;
And you are staunch indeed in learning's cause
If you can crown a discipline, that draws
Such mischiefs after it, with much applause.
  Connexion formed for interest, and endeared
By selfish views, thus censured and cashiered ;
And emulation, as engendering hate,
Doomed to a no less ignominious fate :
The props of such proud seminaries fall,
The Jachin and the Boaz of them all.   500
Great schools rejected then, as those that swell
Beyond a size that can be managed well,
Shall royal institutions miss the bays,
And small academies win all the praise ?
Force not my drift beyond its just intent ;
I praise a school as Pope a government :
So take my judgment in his language dressed,
'Whate'er is best administered is best.'
Few boys are born with talents that excel,
But are all capable of living well ;   510
Then ask not, Whether limited or large ?
But, Watch they strictly, or neglect the charge ?
If anxious only that their boys may *learn*,
While *morals* languish, a despised concern,
The great and small deserve one common blame,
Different in size, but in effect the same.
Much zeal in virtue's cause all teachers boast,
Though motives of mere lucre sway the most :
Therefore in towns and cities they abound,
For there the game they seek is easiest found ;   520
Though there, in spite of all that care can do,
Traps to catch youth are most abundant too.
If shrewd, and of a well-constructed brain,
Keen in pursuit, and vigorous to retain,
Your son come forth a prodigy of skill ;
As, wheresoever taught, so formed he will ;
The pedagogue, with self-complacent air,
Claims more than half the praise as his due share.
But if, with all his genius, he betray,
Not more intelligent than loose and gay,   530
Such vicious habits as disgrace his name,
Threaten his health, his fortune, and his fame ;
Though want of due restraint alone have bred
The symptoms that you see with so much dread ;
Unenvied there, he may sustain alone
The whole reproach, the fault was all his own.
  Oh 'tis a sight to be with joy perused,
By all whom sentiment has not abused ;
New-fangled sentiment, the boasted grace

Of those who never feel in the right place ;   540
A sight surpassed by none that we can show,
Though Vestris on one leg still shine below ;
A father blest with an ingenuous son,
Father, and friend, and tutor, all in one.
How !—turn again to tales long since forgot,
Æsop, and Phædrus, and the rest ?—Why not ?
He will not blush, that has a father's heart,
To take in childish plays a childish part ;
But bends his sturdy back to any toy
That youth takes pleasure in, to please his boy ;   550
Then why resign into a stranger's hand
A task as much within your own command,
That God and Nature, and your interest too,
Seem with one voice to delegate to you ?
Why hire a lodging in a house unknown
For one whose tenderest thoughts all hover round your own ?
This second weaning, needless as it is,
How does it lacerate both your heart and his !
The indented stick, that loses day by day
Notch after notch, till all are smoothed away,   560
Bears witness, long ere his dismission come,
With what intense desire he wants his home.
But though the joys he hopes beneath your roof
Bid fair enough to answer in the proof,
Harmless and safe, and natural, as they are,
A disappointment waits him even there :
Arrived, he feels an unexpected change,
He blushes, hangs his head, is shy and strange ;
No longer takes, as once with fearless ease,
His favourite stand between his father's knees,   570
But seeks the corner of some distant seat,
And eyes the door, and watches a retreat ;
And least familiar where he should be most,
Feels all his happiest privileges lost.
Alas, poor boy !—the natural effect
Of love by absence chilled into respect.
Say, what accomplishments at school acquired,
Brings he, to sweeten fruits so undesired ?
Thou well deservest an alienated son,
Unless thy conscious heart acknowledge—none ;   580
None that, in thy domestic snug recess,
He had not made his own with more address,
Though some perhaps that shock thy feeling mind,
And better never learned, or left behind.
Add too, that thus estranged, thou canst obtain
By no kind arts his confidence again ;
That here begins with most that long complaint
Of filial frankness lost, and love grown faint,
Which, oft neglected, in life's waning years
A parent pours into regardless ears.   590
  Like caterpillars dangling under trees

By slender threads, and swinging in the breeze,
Which filthily bewray and sore disgrace
The boughs in which are bred th' unseemly race ;
While every worm industriously weaves
And winds his web about the rivelled leaves ;
So numerous are the follies that annoy
The mind and heart of every sprightly boy ;
Imaginations noxious and perverse,
Which admonition can alone disperse.   600
Th' encroaching nuisance asks a faithful hand,
Patient, affectionate, of high command,
To check the procreation of a breed
Sure to exhaust the plant on which they feed.
'Tis not enough that Greek or Roman page,
At stated hours, his freakish thoughts engage ;
E'en in his pastimes he requires a friend,
To warn and teach him safely to unbend ;
O'er all his pleasures gently to preside,
Watch his emotions, and control their tide ;   610
And levying thus, and with an easy sway,
A tax of profit from his very play,
To impress a value, not to be erased,
On moments squandered else, and running all to waste.
And seems it nothing in a father's eye,
That unimproved those many moments fly ?
And is he well content his son should find
No nourishment to feed his growing mind,
But conjugated verbs, and nouns declined ?
For such is all the mental food purveyed   620
By public hackneys in the schooling trade ;
Who feed a pupil's intellect with store
Of syntax, truly, but with little more ;
Dismiss their cares when they dismiss their flock,
Machines themselves, and governed by a clock.
Perhaps a father, blessed with any brains,
Would deem it no abuse, or waste of pains,
To improve this diet, at no great expense,
With savoury truth and wholesome common sense :
To lead his son, for prospects of delight,   630
To some not steep, though philosophic height,
Thence to exhibit to his wondering eyes
Yon circling worlds, their distance, and their size ;
The moons of Jove, and Saturn's belted ball,
And the harmonious order of them all ;
To show him in an insect or a flower
Such microscopic proof of skill and power,
As, hid from ages past, God now displays,
To combat atheists with in modern days ;
To spread the earth before him, and commend   640
With designation of the finger's end,
Its various parts to his attentive note,
Thus bringing home to him the most remote ;

To teach his heart to glow with generous flame,
Caught from the deeds of men of ancient fame :
And, more than all, with commendation due,
To set some living worthy in his view,
Whose fair example may at once inspire
A wish to copy what he must admire.
Such knowledge, gained betimes, and which appears,   650
Though solid, not too weighty for his years,
Sweet in itself, and not forbidding sport,
When health demands it, of athletic sort,
Would make him—what some lovely boys have been,
And more than one perhaps that I have seen—
An evidence and reprehension both
Of the mere schoolboy's lean and tardy growth.
    Art thou a man professionally tied,
With all thy faculties elsewhere applied,
Too busy to intend a meaner care   660
Than how to enrich thyself, and next, thine heir ;
Or art thou (as, though rich, perhaps thou art)
But poor in knowledge, having none to impart :
Behold that figure, neat, though plainly clad ;
His sprightly mingled with a shade of sad ;
Not of a nimble tongue, though now and then
Heard to articulate like other men ;
No jester, and yet lively in discourse ;
His phrase well-chosen, clear, and full of force ;
And his address, if not quite French in ease,   670
Not English stiff, but frank, and formed to please ;
Low in the world, because he scorns its arts ;
A man of letters, manners, morals, parts ;
Unpatronized, and therefore little known ;
Wise for himself and his few friends alone—
In him thy well-appointed proxy see,
Armed for a work too difficult for thee ;
Prepared by taste, by learning, and true worth,
To form thy son, to strike his genius forth ;
Beneath thy roof, beneath thine eye, to prove   680
The force of discipline when backed by love ;
To double all thy pleasure in thy child,
His mind informed, his morals undefiled.
Safe under such a wing, the boy shall show
No spots contracted among grooms below,
Nor taint his speech with meannesses, designed
By footman Tom for witty and refined.
There, in his commerce with the liveried herd,
Lurks the contagion chiefly to be feared ;
For since (so fashion dictates) all, who claim   690
A higher than a mere plebeian fame,
Find it expedient, come what mischief may,
To entertain a thief or two in pay,
(And they that can afford the expense of more,
Some half a dozen, and some half a score,)

Great cause occurs to save him from a band
So sure to spoil him, and so near at hand ;
A point secured, if once he be supplied
With some such Mentor always at his side.
Are such men rare?   Perhaps they would abound   700
Were occupation easier to be found,
Were education, else so sure to fail,
Conducted on a manageable scale,
And schools, that have outlived all just esteem,
Exchanged for the secure domestic scheme.—
But having found him, be thou duke or earl,
Show thou hast sense enough to prize the pearl,
And, as thou wouldst the advancement of thine heir
In all good faculties beneath his care,
Respect, as is but rational and just,   710
A man deemed worthy of so dear a trust.
Despised by thee, what more can he expect
From youthful folly than the same neglect?
A flat and fatal negative obtains
That instant, upon all his future pains ;
His lessons tire, his mild rebukes offend,
And all the instructions of thy son's best friend
Are a stream choked, or trickling to no end.
Doom him not then to solitary meals ;
But recollect that he has sense, and feels ;   720
And that, possessor of a soul refined,
An upright heart, and cultivated mind,
His post not mean, his talents not unknown,
He deems it hard to vegetate alone.
And if admitted at thy board he sit,
Account him no just mark for idle wit ;
Offend not him, whom modesty restrains
From repartee, with jokes that he disdains ;
Much less transfix his feelings with an oath ;
Nor frown, unless he vanish with the cloth.—   730
And, trust me, his utility may reach
To more than he is hired or bound to teach,
Much trash unuttered, and some ills undone,
Through reverence of the censor of thy son.
    But, if thy table be indeed unclean,
Foul with excess, and with discourse obscene,
And thou a wretch, whom, following her old plan,
The world accounts an honourable man,
Because forsooth thy courage has been tried,
And stood the test, perhaps on the wrong side ;   740
Though thou hadst never grace enough to prove
That anything but vice could win thy love ;—
Or hast thou a polite, card-playing wife,
Chained to the routs that she frequents for life ;
Who, just when industry begins to snore,
Flies, winged with joy, to some coach-crowded door ;
And thrice in every winter throngs thine own

With half the chariots and sedans in town,
Thyself meanwhile e'en shifting as thou mayst;
Not very sober though, nor very chaste ;—   750
Or is thine house, though less superb thy rank,
If not a scene of pleasure, a mere blank,
And thou at best, and in thy soberest mood,
A trifler vain, and empty of all good?
Though mercy for thyself thou canst have none,
Hear Nature plead, show mercy to thy son.
Saved from his home, where every day brings forth
Some mischief fatal to his future worth,
Find him a better in a distant spot,
Within some pious pastor's humble cot,   760
Where vile example (yours I chiefly mean,
The most seducing, and the oftenest seen)
May never more be stamped upon his breast,
Not yet perhaps incurably impressed.
Where early rest makes early rising sure,
Disease or comes not, or finds easy cure,
Prevented much by diet neat and plain ;
Or, if it enter, soon starved out again.
Where all the attention of his faithful host,
Discreetly limited to two at most,   770
May raise such fruits as shall reward his care,
And not at last evaporate in air :
Where, stillness aiding study, and his mind
Serene, and to his duties much inclined ;
Not occupied in day-dreams, as at home,
Of pleasures past, or follies yet to come ;
His virtuous toil may terminate at last
In settled habit and decided taste.—
But whom do I advise? the fashion-led,
The incorrigibly wrong, the deaf, the dead !   780
Whom care and cool deliberation suit
Not better much than spectacles a brute ;
Who, if their sons some slight tuition share,
Deem it of no great moment whose, or where ;
Too proud to adopt the thoughts of one unknown,
And much too gay to have any of their own.
' But, courage, man !' methought the Muse replied,
' Mankind are various, and the world is wide :
The ostrich, silliest of the feathered kind,
And formed of God without a parent's mind,   790
Commits her eggs, incautious, to the dust,
Forgetful that the foot may crush the trust ;
And while on public nurseries they rely,
Not knowing, and too oft not caring, why,
Irrational in what they thus prefer,
No few, that would seem wise, resemble her.
But all are not alike.   Thy warning voice
May here and there prevent erroneous choice ;
And some perhaps, who, busy as they are,

Yet make their progeny their dearest care   800
(Whose hearts will ache, once told what ills may reach
Their offspring, left upon so wild a beach),
Will need no stress of argument to enforce
The expedience of a less adventurous course :
The rest will slight thy counsel, or condemn :
But *they* have human feelings ; turn to *them.*'
   To you, then, tenants of life's middle state,
Securely placed between the small and great,
Whose character, yet undebauched, retains
Two-thirds of all the virtue that remains :   810
Who, wise yourselves, desire your sons should learn
Your wisdom and your ways—to you I turn.
Look round you on a world perversely blind ;
See what contempt has fallen on human kind ;
See wealth abused, and dignities misplaced,
Great titles, offices, and trusts disgraced,
Long lines of ancestry, renowned of old,
Their noble qualities all quenched and cold ;
See Bedlam's closeted and handcuffed charge
Surpassed in frenzy by the mad at large ;   820
See great commanders making war a trade,
Great lawyers, lawyers without study made ;
Churchmen, in whose esteem their blessed employ
Is odious, and their wages all their joy ;
Who, far enough from furnishing their shelves
With Gospel lore, turn infidels themselves ;
See womanhood despised, and manhood shamed
With infamy too nauseous to be named,
Fops at all corners, lady-like in mien,
Civeted fellows, smelt ere they are seen ;   830
Else coarse and rude in manners, and their tongue
On fire with curses, and with nonsense hung ;
Now flushed with drunkenness, now with whoredom pale,
Their breath a sample of last night's regale :
See volunteers in all the vilest arts,
Men well endowed, of honourable parts,
Designed by Nature wise, but self-made fools ;
All these, and more like these, were bred at schools.
And if it chance, as sometimes chance it will,
That though school-bred, the boy be virtuous still,   840
Such rare exceptions, shining in the dark,
Prove, rather than impeach, the just remark,
As here and there a twinkling star descried
Serves but to show how black is all beside.
Now look on him, whose very voice in tone
Just echoes thine, whose features are thine own,
And stroke his polished cheek of purest red,
And lay thine hand upon his flaxen head,
And say, "My boy, the unwelcome hour is come,
" When thou, transplanted from thy genial home,   850
" Must find a colder soil and bleaker air,

" And trust for safety to a stranger's care ;
" What character, what turn, thou wilt assume
" From constant converse with I know not whom ;
" Who there will court thy friendship, with what views,
" And, artless as thou art, whom thou wilt choose ;
" Though much depends on what thy choice shall be,
" Is all chance-medley, and unknown to me."
Canst thou, the tear just trembling on thy lids,
And while the dreadful risk foreseen forbids;   860
Free too, and under no constraining force,
Unless the sway of custom warp thy course ;
Lay such a stake upon the losing side,
Merely to gratify so blind a guide?
Thou canst not ! Nature, pulling at thine heart,
Condemns the unfatherly, the imprudent part.
Thou wouldst not, deaf to Nature's tenderest plea,
Turn him adrift upon a rolling sea,
Nor say, " Go thither," conscious that there lay
A brood of asps, or quicksands in his way ;   870
Then, only governed by the self-same rule
Of natural pity, send him not to school.
No—guard him better. Is he not thine own,
Thyself in miniature, thy flesh, thy bone?
And hopest thou not ('tis every father's hope)
That since thy strength must with thy years elope,
And thou wilt need some comfort to assuage
Health's last farewell, a staff of thine old age,
That then, in recompense of all thy cares,
Thy child shall show respect to thy gray hairs,   880
Befriend thee, of all other friends bereft,
And give thy life its only cordial left ?
Aware then how much danger intervenes,
To compass that good end, forecast the means.
His heart, now passive, yields to thy command ;
Secure it thine, its key is in thine hand.
If thou desert thy charge, and throw it wide,
Nor heed what guests there enter and abide,
Complain not if attachments lewd and base
Supplant thee in it, and usurp thy place.   890
But if thou guard its sacred chambers sure
From vicious inmates, and delights impure,
Either his gratitude shall hold him fast,
And keep him warm and filial to the last :
Or, if he prove unkind, (as who can say
But being man, and therefore frail, he may)
One comfort yet shall cheer thine aged heart ;
Howe'er he slight thee, thou hast done thy part.
    " Oh, barbarous ! wouldst thou with a Gothic hand
" Pull down the schools—what!—all the schools i' the land ;
" Or throw them up to livery-nags and grooms,   901
" Or turn them into shops and auction-rooms ?"—
" A captious question, sir, (and yours is one)

Deserves an answer similar, or none.
Wouldst thou, possessor of a flock, employ
(Apprised that he is such) a careless boy,
And feed him well, and give him handsome pay,
Merely to sleep, and let them run astray?
Survey our schools and colleges, and see
A sight not much unlike my simile.   910
From education, as the leading cause,
The public character its colour draws;
Thence the prevailing manners take their cast,
Extravagant or sober, loose or chaste.
And though I would not advertise them yet,
Nor write on each—"*This building to be let,*"
Unless the world were all prepared to embrace
A plan well worthy to supply their place;
Yet, backward as they are, and long have been,
To cultivate and keep the MORALS clean,   920
(Forgive the crime) I wish them, I confess,
Or better managed, or encouraged less.

THE DIVERTING HISTORY

OF

JOHN GILPIN:

SHOWING HOW HE WENT FARTHER THAN HE INTENDED AND CAME SAFE HOME AGAIN.

JOHN GILPIN was a citizen
  Of credit and renown,
A train-band captain eke was he
  Of famous London town.

John Gilpin's spouse said to her dear,
  "Though wedded we have been
These twice ten tedious years, yet we
  No holiday have seen.

"To-morrow is our wedding-day,
  And we will then repair
Unto the Bell at Edmonton,
  All in a chaise and pair.

"My sister, and my sister's child,
  Myself, and children three,
Will fill the chaise; so you must ride
  On horseback after we."

He soon replied, "I do admire
  Of womankind but one,
And you are she, my dearest dear,
  Therefore it shall be done.

"I am a linen-draper bold,
  As all the world doth know,
And my good friend the calender
  Will lend his horse to go."

Quoth Mrs. Gilpin, "That's well said;
  And for that wine is dear,
We will be furnished with our own,
  Which is both bright and clear."

John Gilpin kissed his loving wife;
  O'erjoyed was he to find,
That though on pleasure she was bent,
  She had a frugal mind.

The morning came, the chaise was brought,
    But yet was not allowed
To drive up to the door, lest all
    Should say that she was proud.

So three doors off the chaise was stayed,
    Where they did all get in ;
Six precious souls, and all agog
    To dash through thick and thin.

Smack went the whip, round went the wheels,
    Were never folk so glad,
The stones did rattle underneath,
    As if Cheapside were mad.

John Gilpin at his horse's side
    Seized fast the flowing mane,
And up he got, in haste to ride,
    But soon came down again ;

For saddle-tree scarce reached had he,
    His journey to begin,
When, turning round his head, he saw
    Three customers come in.

So down he came ; for loss of time,
    Although it grieved him sore,
Yet loss of pence, full well he knew,
    Would trouble him much more.

'Twas long before the customers
    Were suited to their mind,
When Betty screaming came down stairs,
    " The wine is left behind !"

' Good lack !' quoth he—" yet bring it me,
    My leathern belt likewise,
In which I bear my trusty sword,
    When I do exercise."

Now Mistress Gilpin (careful soul !)
    Had two stone bottles found,
To hold the liquor that she loved,
    And keep it safe and sound.

Each bottle had a curling ear,
    Through which the belt he drew,
And hung a bottle on each side,
    To make his balance true.

Then over all, that he might be
    Equipped from top to toe,
His long red cloak, well brushed and neat,
    He manfully did throw.

Now see him mounted once again
    Upon his nimble steed,
Full slowly pacing o'er the stones,
    With caution and good heed.

But finding soon a smoother road
    Beneath his well-shod feet,
The snorting beast began to trot,
    Which galled him in his seat.

So, " Fair and softly," John he cried,
    But John he cried in vain ;
That trot became a gallop soon,
    In spite of curb and rein.

So stooping down, as needs he must
    Who cannot sit upright,
He grasped the mane with both his hands,
    And eke with all his might.

His horse, who never in that sort
    Had handled been before,
What thing upon his back had got
    Did wonder more and more.

Away went Gilpin, neck or nought ;
    Away went hat and wig ;
He little dreamt, when he set out,
    Of running such a rig.

The wind did blow, the cloak did fly,
    Like streamer long and gay,
Till, loop and button failing both,
    At last it flew away.

Then might all people well discern
    The bottles he had slung ;
A bottle swinging at each side,
    As hath been said or sung.

The dogs did bark, the children screamed,
    Up flew the windows all ;
And every soul cried out, " Well done !"
    As loud as he could bawl.

Away went Gilpin—who but he?
    His fame soon spread around ;
" He carries weight ! "   " He rides a
        race ! "
    " 'Tis for a thousand pound ! "

And still, as fast as he drew near,
    'Twas wonderful to view,
How in a trice the turnpike-men
    Their gates wide open threw.

And now, as he went bowing down
    His reeking head full low,
The bottles twain behind his back
    Were shattered at a blow.

Down ran the wine into the road,
    Most piteous to be seen,
Which made his horse's flanks to
        smoke
    As they had basted been.

But still he seemed to carry weight,
    With leathern girdle braced ;
For all might see the bottle-necks
    Still dangling at his waist.

Thus all through merry Islington
    These gambols he did play,
Until he came unto the Wash
    Of Edmonton so gay ;

And there he threw the Wash about
    On both sides of the way,
Just like unto a trundling mop,
    Or a wild goose at play.

At Edmonton his loving wife
    From the balcony spied
Her tender husband, wondering much
    To see how he did ride.

" Stop, stop, John Gilpin !—Here's the
        house ! "
    They all at once did cry ;
" The dinner waits, and we are tired ; "—
    Said Gilpin—" So am I ! "

But yet his horse was not a whit
    Inclined to tarry there !
For why ?—his owner had a house
    Full ten miles off, at Ware

So like an arrow swift he flew,
    Shot by an archer strong ;
So did he fly—which brings me to
    The middle of my song.

Away went Gilpin, out of breath,
    And sore against his will,
Till at his friend the calender's
    His horse at last stood still.

The calender, amazed to see
    His neighbour in such trim,
Laid down his pipe, flew to the gate,
    And thus accosted him :

" What news? what news? your tidings
        tell ;
    Tell me you must and shall—
Say why bareheaded you are come,
    " Or why you come at all ? "

Now Gilpin had a pleasant wit,
    And loved a timely joke ;
And thus unto the calender
    In merry guise he spoke :

" I came because your horse would come,
    And, if I well forebode,
My hat and wig will soon be here,—
    They are upon the road. "

The calender, right glad to find
    His friend in merry pin,
Returned him not a single word,
    But to the house went in ;

Whence straight he came with hat and
        wig ;
    A wig that flowed behind,
A hat not much the worse for wear,
    Each comely in its kind.

He held them up, and in his turn
    Thus showed his ready wit,
" My head is twice as big as yours,
    They therefore needs must fit.

" But let me scrape the dirt away
    That hangs upon your face ;
And stop and eat, for well you may
    Be in a hungry case. "

Said John, "It is my wedding-day,
  And all the world would stare,
If wife should dine at Edmonton,
  And I should dine at Ware."

So turning to his horse, he said,
  "I am in haste to dine;
'Twas for your pleasure you came here,
  You shall go back for mine."

Ah, luckless speech, and bootless boast!
  For which he paid full dear;
For, while he spake, a braying ass
  Did sing most loud and clear;

Whereat his horse did snort, as he
  Had heard a lion roar,
And galloped off with all his might,
  As he had done before.

Away went Gilpin, and away
  Went Gilpin's hat and wig:
He lost them sooner than at first;
  For why?—they were too big.

Now Mistress Gilpin, when she saw
  Her husband posting down
Into the country far away,
  She pulled out half-a-crown;

And thus unto the youth she said
  That drove them to the Bell,
"This shall be yours, when you bring back
  My husband safe and well."

The youth did ride, and soon did meet
  John coming back amain:
Whom in a trice he tried to stop,
  By catching at his rein;

But not performing what he meant,
  And gladly would have done,
The frighted steed he frighted more,
  And made him faster run.

Away went Gilpin, and away
  Went postboy at his heels,
The postboy's horse right glad to miss
  The lumbering of the wheels.

Six gentlemen upon the road,
  Thus seeing Gilpin fly,
With postboy scampering in the rear,
  They raised the hue and cry:

"Stop thief! stop thief!—a highway-
      man!"
  Not one of them was mute;
And all and each that passed that way
  Did join in the pursuit.

And now the turnpike gates again
  Flew open in short space;
The toll-men thinking, as before,
  That Gilpin rode a race.

And so he did, and won it too,
  For he got first to town;
Nor stopped till where he had got up
  He did again get down.

Now let us sing, Long live the king!
  And Gilpin, long live he!
And when he next doth ride abroad
  May I be there to see!

POEMS

ADDED BY THE AUTHOR IN SUBSEQUENT EDITIONS OF HIS WORKS.

ON THE DEATH OF
MRS. THROCKMORTON'S BULLFINCH.

YE Nymphs, if e'er your eyes were red
With tears o'er hapless favourites shed,
    Oh share Maria's grief!
Her favourite, even in his cage
(What will not hunger's cruel rage?)
    Assassined by a thief.

Where Rhenus strays his vines among
The egg was laid from which he sprung;
    And though by nature mute,
Or only with a whistle blessed,
Well-taught, he all the sounds expressed
    Of flageolet or flute.

The honours of his ebon poll
Were brighter than the sleekest mole,
    His bosom of the hue
With which Aurora decks the skies,
When piping winds shall soon arise
    To sweep away the dew.

Above, below, in all the house,
Dire foe alike of bird and mouse,
    No cat had leave to dwell;
And Bully's cage supported stood
On props of smoothest-shaven wood,
    Large built and latticed well.

Well latticed,—but the grate, alas!
Not rough with wire of steel or brass,
    For Bully's plumage sake,
But smooth with wands from Ouse's side,
With which, when neatly peeled and
     dried,
    The swains their baskets make.

Night veiled the pole; all seemed secure;
When, led by instinct sharp and sure,
    Subsistence to provide,

A beast forth sallied on the scout,
Long backed, long tailed, with whiskered
     snout,
    And badger-coloured hide.

He, entering at the study door,
Its ample area 'gan explore;
    And something in the wind
Conjectured, sniffing round and round,
Better than all the books he found,
    Food chiefly for the mind.

Just then, by adverse fate impressed,
A dream disturbed poor Bully's rest;
    In sleep he seemed to view
A rat fast clinging to the cage,
And screaming at the sad presage,
    Awoke and found it true.

For, aided both by ear and scent,
Right to his mark the monster went,—
    Ah, Muse! forbear to speak
Minute the horrors that ensued;
His teeth were strong, the cage was
     wood,—
    He left poor Bully's beak.

Oh, had he made that too his prey!
That beak, whence issued many a lay
    Of such mellifluous tone,
Might have repaid him well, I wote,
For silencing so sweet a throat,
    Fast stuck within his own.

Maria weeps,—the Muses mourn;—
So, when by Bacchanalians torn,
    On Thracian Hebrus' side
The tree-enchanter Orpheus fell,
His head alone remained to tell
    The cruel death he died.

THE ROSE.

The rose had been washed, just washed in a shower,
  Which Mary to Anna conveyed,
The plentiful moisture encumbered the flower,
  And weighed down its beautiful head.

The cup was all filled, and the leaves were all wet,
  And it seemed, to a fanciful view,
To weep for the buds it had left with regret
  On the flourishing bush where it grew.

I hastily seized it, unfit as it was
  For a nosegay, so dripping and drowned ;
And swinging it rudely, too rudely, alas !
  I snapped it—it fell to the ground.

"And such," I exclaimed, "is the pitiless part
  Some act by the delicate mind,
Regardless of wringing and breaking a heart
  Already to sorrow resigned !

"This elegant rose, had I shaken it less,
  Might have bloomed with its owner awhile ;
And the tear that is wiped with a little address
  May be followed perhaps by a smile."

ODE TO APOLLO.

ON AN INK-GLASS ALMOST DRIED IN THE SUN.

Patron of all those luckless brains
  That, to the wrong side leaning,
Indite much metre with much pains,
  And little or no meaning :

Ah why, since oceans, rivers, streams,
  That water all the nations,
Pay tribute to thy glorious beams,
  In constant exhalations ;

Why, stooping from the noon of day,
  Too covetous of drink,
Apollo, hast thou stolen away
  A poet's drop of ink ?

Upborne into the viewless air,
  It floats a vapour now,

Impelled through regions dense and rare
  By all the winds that blow.

Ordained, perhaps, ere summer flies,
  Combined with millions more,
To form an Iris in the skies,
  Though black and foul before.

Illustrious drop ! and happy then
  Beyond the happiest lot,
Of all that ever passed my pen,
  So soon to be forgot !

Phœbus, if such be thy design,
  To place it in thy bow,
Give wit, that what is left may shine
  With equal grace below.

THE POET'S NEW-YEAR'S GIFT.

TO MRS. (AFTERWARDS LADY) THROCKMORTON.

MARIA! I have every good
　For thee wished many a time,
Both sad and in a cheerful mood,
　But never yet in rhyme.

To wish thee fairer is no need,
　More prudent, or more sprightly,
Or more ingenious, or more freed
　From temper-flaws unsightly.

What favour then not yet possessed
　Can I for thee require,

In wedded love already blessed
　To thy whole heart's desire?

None here is happy but in part ;
　Full bliss is bliss divine ;
There dwells some wish in every heart,
　And doubtless one in thine.

That wish, on some fair future day
　Which Fate shall brightly gild,
('Tis blameless, be it what it may)
　I wish it all fulfilled.

PAIRING TIME ANTICIPATED.*

A FABLE.

I SHALL not ask Jean Jacques Rousseau
If birds confabulate or no ;
'Tis clear that they were always able
To hold discourse, at least in fable ;
And even the child who knows no better
Than to interpret by the letter
A story of a cock and bull,
Must have a most uncommon skull.
　It chanced then on a winter's day,
But warm and bright and calm as May,
The birds, conceiving a design
To forestall sweet St. Valentine,
In many an orchard, copse, and grove,
Assembled on affairs of love,
And with much twitter and much chatter
Began to agitate the matter.
At length a Bullfinch, who could boast
More years and wisdom than the most,
Entreated, opening wide his beak,
A moment's liberty to speak ;
And, silence publicly enjoined,
Delivered briefly thus his mind :

---

* It was one of the whimsical speculations of this philosopher, that all fables which ascribe reason and speech to animals should be withheld from children, as being only vehicles of deception. But what child was ever deceived by them, or can be, against the evidence of his senses ?

"My friends ! be cautious how ye treat
The subject upon which we meet ;
I fear we shall have winter yet."
　A Finch, whose tongue knew no control,
With golden wing and satin poll,
A last year's bird, who ne'er had tried
What marriage means, thus pert replied :
　"Methinks the gentleman," quoth she,
"Opposite in the apple tree,
By his good will would keep us single
Till yonder heaven and earth shall mingle ;
Or (which is likelier to befall)
Till death exterminate us all.
I marry without more ado ;
My dear Dick Redcap, what say you ?"
　Dick heard, and tweedling, ogling, bridling,
Turning short round, strutting, and sidling,
Attested, glad, his approbation
Of an immediate conjugation.
Their sentiments so well expressed
Influenced mightily the rest ;
All paired, and each pair built a nest.
　But though the birds were thus in haste,
The leaves came on not quite so fast,
And Destiny, that sometimes bears
An aspect stern on man's affairs,
Not altogether smiled on theirs.
The wind, of late breathed gently forth,
Now shifted east, and east by north ;
Bare trees and shrubs but ill, you know,
Could shelter them from rain or snow :
Stepping into their nests, they paddled,
Themselves were chilled, their eggs were addled :
Soon every father-bird and mother
Grew quarrelsome, and pecked each other,
Parted without the least regret,
Except that they had ever met,
And learnt in future to be wiser
Than to neglect a good adviser.

MORAL.

Misses ! the tale that I relate
This lesson seems to carry—
Choose not alone a proper mate,
But proper time to marry.

THE DOG AND THE WATER-LILY.

NO FABLE.

THE noon was shady, and soft airs
   Swept Ouse's silent tide,
When, 'scaped from literary cares,
   I wandered on his side.

My spaniel, prettiest of his race,
   And high in pedigree,
(Two nymphs* adorned with every grace
   That spaniel found for me)

Now wantoned, lost in flags and reeds,
   Now starting into sight,
Pursued the swallow o'er the meads
   With scarce a slower flight.

It was the time when Ouse displayed
   His lilies newly blown ;
Their beauties I intent surveyed
   And one I wished my own.

With cane extended far, I sought
   To steer it close to land ;
But still the prize, though nearly caught,
   Escaped my eager hand.

Beau marked my unsuccessful pains
   With fixed considerate face,
And puzzling set his puppy brains
   To comprehend the case.

But with a cherup clear and strong
   Dispersing all his dream,
I thence withdrew, and followed long
   The windings of the stream.

My ramble ended, I returned ;
   Beau, trotting far before,
The floating wreath again discerned,
   And plunging left the shore.

I saw him with that lily cropped
   Impatient swim to meet
My quick approach, and soon he dropped
   The treasure at my feet.

Charmed with the sight, " The world,"
     I cried,
   " Shall hear of this thy deed :
My dog shall mortify the pride
   Of man's superior breed :

But chief myself I will enjoin,
   Awake at duty's call,
To show a love as prompt as thine
   To Him who gives me all."

CATHARINA.

ADDRESSED TO MISS STAPLETON (AFTERWARDS MRS. COURTENAY).

SHE came—she is gone—we have met—
   And meet perhaps never again ;
The sun of that moment is set,
   And seems to have risen in vain.
Catharina has fled like a dream—
   (So vanishes pleasure, alas !)
But has left a regret and esteem
   That will not so suddenly pass.

The last evening ramble we made,—
   Catharina, Maria, and I,—
Our progress was often delayed
   By the nightingale warbling nigh.
We paused under many a tree,
   And much she was charmed with a tone
Less sweet to Maria and me,
   Who so lately had witnessed her own.

* Sir Robert Gunning's daughters.

My numbers that day she had sung,
  And gave them a grace so divine,
As only her musical tongue
  Could infuse into numbers of mine.
The longer I heard, I esteemed
  The work of my fancy the more,
And e'en to myself never seemed
  So tuneful a poet before.

Though the pleasures of London exceed
  In number the days of the year,
Catharina, did nothing impede,
  Would feel herself happier here:
For the close-woven arches of limes
  On the banks of our river, I know,
Are sweeter to her many times
  Than all that the city can show.

So it is, when the mind is endued
  With a well-judging taste from above,
Then, whether embellished or rude,
  'Tis nature alone that we love.

The achievements of art may amuse,
  May even our wonder excite;
But groves, hills, and valleys, diffuse
  A lasting, a sacred delight.

Since then in the rural recess
  Catharina alone can rejoice,
May it still be her lot to possess
  The scene of her sensible choice!
To inhabit a mansion remote
  From the clatter of street-pacing steeds,
And by Philomel's annual note
  To measure the life that she leads.

With her book, and her voice, and her lyre,
  To wing all her moments at home;
And with scenes that new rapture inspire,
  As oft as it suits her to roam;
She will have just the life she prefers,
  With little to hope or to fear,
And ours would be pleasant as hers,
  Might we view her enjoying it here.

THE MORALIZER CORRECTED.

A TALE.

A HERMIT (or if 'chance you hold
That title now too trite and old),
A man once young, who lived retired
As hermit could have well desired,
His hours of study closed at last,
And finished his concise repast,
Stoppled his cruse, replaced his book
Within its customary nook,
And, staff in hand, set forth to share
The sober cordial of sweet air,
Like Isaac, with a mind applied
To serious thought at evening tide.
Autumnal rains had made it chill,
And from the trees that fringed his hill
Shades slanting at the close of day
Chilled more his else delightful way.
Distant a little mile he spied
A western bank's still sunny side,
And right toward the favoured place
Proceeding with his nimblest pace,
In hope to bask a little yet,
Just reached it when the sun was set.

Your hermit, young and jovial sirs!
Learns something from whate'er occurs,
And "Hence," he said, "my mind computes
The real worth of man's pursuits.
His object chosen, wealth or fame,
Or other sublunary game,
Imagination to his view
Presents it decked with every hue
That can seduce him not to spare
His powers of best exertion there,
But youth, health, vigour to expend
On so desirable an end.
Ere long approach life's evening shades,
The glow that fancy gave it fades;
And, earned too late, it wants the grace
That first engaged him in the chase."
  "True," answered an angelic guide,
Attendant at the senior's side,—
"But whether all the time it cost
To urge the fruitless chase be lost,

Must be decided by the worth
Of that which called his ardour forth.
Trifles pursued, whate'er the event,
Must cause him shame or discontent;
A vicious object still is worse,
Successful there, he wins a curse;
But he whom, e'en in life's last stage,
Endeavours laudable engage,

Is paid at least in peace of mind,
And sense of having well designed;
And if, ere he attain his end,
His sun precipitate descend,
A brighter prize than that he meant
Shall recompense his mere intent.
No virtuous wish can bear a date
Either too early or too late."

THE FAITHFUL BIRD.

THE greenhouse is my summer seat;
My shrubs displaced from that retreat
Enjoyed the open air;
Two goldfinches, whose sprightly song
Had been their mutual solace long,
Lived happy prisoners there.

They sang as blithe as finches sing
That flutter loose on golden wing,
And frolic where they list;
Strangers to liberty, 'tis true,
But that delight they never knew,
And therefore never missed.

But nature works in every breast,
With force not easily suppressed;
And Dick felt some desires,
That, after many an effort vain,
Instructed him at length to gain
A pass between his wires.

The open windows seemed to invite
The freeman to a farewell flight;
But Tom was still confined;
And Dick, although his way was clear,
Was much too generous and sincere
To leave his friend behind.

So settling on his cage, by play,
And chirp, and kiss, he seemed to say,
" You must not live alone;"—
Nor would he quit that chosen stand
Till I, with slow and cautious hand,
Returned him to his own.

O ye, who never taste the joys
Of friendship, satisfied with noise,
Fandango, ball, and rout!
Blush when I tell you how a bird
A prison with a friend preferred
To liberty without.

THE NEEDLESS ALARM.

A TALE.

THERE is a field through which I often pass,
Thick overspread with moss and silky grass,
Adjoining close to Kilwick's echoing wood,
Where oft the bitch-fox hides her hapless brood,
Reserved to solace many a neighbouring squire,
That he may follow them through brake and brier,
Contusion hazarding of neck or spine,
Which rural gentlemen call sport divine.
A narrow brook, by rushy banks concealed,
Runs in a bottom, and divides the field;
Oaks intersperse it, that had once a head,
But now wear crests of oven-wood instead;

And where the land slopes to its watery bourn
Wide yawns a gulf beside a ragged thorn ;
Bricks line the sides, but shivered long ago,
And horrid brambles intertwine below ;
A hollow scooped, I judge, in ancient time,
For baking earth, or burning rock to lime.
　　Not yet the hawthorn bore her berries red,
With which the fieldfare, wintry guest, is fed ;
Nor Autumn yet had brushed from every spray,
With her chill hand, the mellow leaves away ;
But corn was housed, and beans were in the stack ;
Now therefore issued forth the spotted pack,
With tails high mounted, ears hung low, and throats
With a whole gamut filled of heavenly notes,
For which, alas ! my destiny severe,
Though ears she gave me two, gave me no ear.
　　The sun, accomplishing his early march,
His lamp now planted on heaven's topmost arch,
When, exercise and air my only aim,
And heedless whither, to that field I came,
Ere yet with ruthless joy the happy hound
Told hill and dale that Reynard's track was found,
Or with the high-raised horn's melodious clang
All Kilwick* and all Dinglederry* rang.
　　Sheep grazed the field ; some with soft bosom pressed
The herb as soft, while nibbling strayed the rest ;
Nor noise was heard but of the hasty brook,
Struggling, detained in many a petty nook.
All seemed so peaceful, that from them conveyed,
To me their peace by kind contagion spread.
　　But when the huntsman, with distended cheek,
'Gan make his instrument of music speak,
And from within the wood that crash was heard,
Though not a hound from whom it burst appeared,
The sheep recumbent and the sheep that grazed,
All huddling into phalanx, stood and gazed,
Admiring, terrified, the novel strain,
Then coursed the field around, and coursed it round again ;
But recollecting, with a sudden thought,
That flight in circles urged advanced them nought,
They gathered close around the old pit's brink,
And thought again—but knew not what to think.
　　The man to solitude accustomed long
Perceives in every thing that lives a tongue ;
Not animals alone, but shrubs and trees
Have speech for him, and understood with ease ;
After long drought, when rains abundant fall,
He hears the herbs and flowers rejoicing all ;
Knows what the freshness of their hue implies,
How glad they catch the largess of the skies ;

* Two woods belonging to John Throckmorton, Esq.

But, with precision nicer still, the mind
He scans of every locomotive kind ;
Birds of all feather, beasts of every name,
That serve mankind or shun them, wild or tame ;
The looks and gestures of their griefs and fears
Have all articulation in his ears ;
He spells them true by intuition's light,
And needs no glossary to set him right.

    This truth premised was needful as a text,
To win due credence to what follows next.

    Awhile they mused ; surveying every face,
Thou hadst supposed them of superior race ;
Their periwigs of wool and fears combined
Stamped on each countenance such marks of mind,
That sage they seemed, as lawyers o'er a doubt,
Which, puzzling long, at last they puzzle out ;
Or academic tutors, teaching youths,
Sure ne'er to want them, mathematic truths ;
When thus a mutton statelier than the rest,
A Ram, the ewes and wethers sad addressed :
    " Friends ! we have lived too long. I never heard
Sounds such as these, so worthy to be feared.
Could I believe, that winds for ages pent
In earth's dark womb have found at last a vent,
And from their prison-house below arise,
With all these hideous howlings to the skies,
I could be much composed, nor should appear,
For such a cause, to feel the slightest fear.
Yourselves have seen, what time the thunders rolled
All night, me resting quiet in the fold.
Or heard we that tremendous bray alone,
I could expound the melancholy tone ;
Should deem it by our old companion made,
The Ass ; for he, we know, has lately strayed,
And being lost, perhaps, and wandering wide,
Might be supposed to clamour for a guide.
But ah ! those dreadful yells what soul can hear
That owns a carcass, and not quake for fear ?
Demons produce them doubtless, brazen-clawed,
And fanged with brass, the demons are abroad ;
I hold it therefore wisest and most fit
That, life to save, we leap into the pit."

    Him answered then his loving mate and true,
But more discreet than he, a Cambrian Ewe :
    "How ! leap into the pit our life to save?
To save our life leap all into the grave ?
For can we find it less ? Contemplate first
The depth how awful ! falling there, we burst :
Or should the brambles interposed our fall
In part abate, that happiness were small ;
For with a race like theirs no chance I see
Of peace or ease to creatures clad as we.

Meantime, noise kills not.   Be it Dapple's bray,
Or be it not, or be it whose it may,
And rush those other sounds, that seem by tongues
Of demons uttered, from whatever lungs,
Sounds are but sounds, and, till the cause appear,
We have at least commodious standing here.
Come fiend, come fury, giant, monster, blast
From earth or hell, we can but plunge at last."
    While thus she spake, I fainter heard the peals,
For Reynard, close attended at his heels
By panting dog, tired man, and spattered horse,
Through mere good fortune took a different course.
The flock grew calm again, and I, the road
Following, that led me to my own abode,
Much wondered that the silly sheep had found
Such cause of terror in an empty sound,
So sweet to huntsman, gentleman, and hound.

MORAL.

Beware of desperate steps.   The darkest day,
Live till to-morrow, will have passed away.

ON THE RECEIPT OF MY MOTHER'S PICTURE
OUT OF NORFOLK;

THE GIFT OF MY COUSIN, ANN BODHAM.

OH THAT those lips had language !   Life has passed
With me but roughly since I heard thee last.
Those lips are thine—thy own sweet smile I see,
The same that oft in childhood solaced me ;
Voice only fails, else how distinct they say,
" Grieve not, my child, chase all thy fears away !"
The meek intelligence of those dear eyes
(Blessed be the art that can immortalize,
The art that baffles Time's tyrannic claim
To quench it) here shines on me still the same.
    Faithful remembrancer of one so dear,
O welcome guest, though unexpected here !
Who bidst me honour with an artless song,
Affectionate, a mother lost so long,
I will obey, not willingly alone,
But gladly, as the precept were her own :
And, while that face renews my filial grief,
Fancy shall weave a charm for my relief,
Shall steep me in Elysian reverie,
A momentary dream that thou art she.
    My mother ! when I learnt that thou wast dead,
Say, wast thou conscious of the tears I shed ?

Hovered thy spirit o'er thy sorrowing son,
Wretch even then, life's journey just begun?
Perhaps thou gavest me, though unfelt, a kiss :
Perhaps a tear, if souls can weep in bliss—
Ah, that maternal smile ! It answers—Yes.
I heard the bell tolled on thy burial day,
I saw the hearse that bore thee slow away,
And, turning from my nursery window, drew
A long, long sigh, and wept a last adieu !
But was it such ?—It was.—Where thou art gone
Adieus and farewells are a sound unknown.
May I but meet thee on that peaceful shore,
The parting word shall pass my lips no more !
Thy maidens, grieved themselves at my concern,
Oft gave me promise of thy quick return.
What ardently I wished I long believed,
And, disappointed still, was still deceived.
By expectation every day beguiled,
Dupe of *to-morrow* even from a child.
Thus many a sad to-morrow came and went,
Till, all my stock of infant sorrow spent,
I learnt at last submission to my lot ;
But, though I less deplored thee, ne'er forgot.
    Where once we dwelt our name is heard no more,
Children not thine have trod my nursery floor ;
And where the gardener Robin, day by day,
Drew me to school along the public way,
Delighted with my bauble coach, and wrapped
In scarlet mantle warm, and velvet capped,
'Tis now become a history little known,
That once we called the pastoral house our own.
Short-lived possession ! but the record fair
That memory keeps, of all thy kindness there,
Still outlives many a storm that has effaced
A thousand other themes less deeply traced.
Thy nightly visits to my chamber made,
That thou mightst know me safe and warmly laid ;
Thy morning bounties ere I left my home,
The biscuit, or confectionary plum ;
The fragrant waters on my cheek bestowed
By thy own hand, till fresh they shone and glowed ;
All this, and more endearing still than all,
Thy constant flow of love, that knew no fall,
Ne'er roughened by those cataracts and brakes
That humour interposed too often makes ;
All this still legible in memory's page,
And still to be so to my latest age,
Adds joy to duty, makes me glad to pay
Such honours to thee as my numbers may ;
Perhaps a frail memorial, but sincere,
Not scorned in heaven, though little noticed here.
    Could Time, his flight reversed, restore the hours,

When, playing with thy vesture's tissued flowers,
The violet, the pink, and jessamine,
I pricked them into paper with a pin
(And thou wast happier than myself the while,
Wouldst softly speak, and stroke my head and smile),
Could those few pleasant days again appear,
Might one wish bring them, would I wish them here?
I would not trust my heart—the dear delight
Seems so to be desired, perhaps I might.—
But no—what here we call our life is such
So little to be loved, and thou so much,
That I should ill requite thee to constrain
Thy unbound spirit into bonds again.
    Thou, as a gallant bark from Albion's coast
(The storms all weathered and the ocean crossed)
Shoots into port at some well-havened isle,
Where spices breathe, and brighter seasons smile,
There sits quiescent on the floods that show
Her beauteous form reflected clear below,
While airs impregnated with incense play
Around her, fanning light her streamers gay;
So thou, with sails how swift! hast reached the shore,
"Where tempests never beat nor billows roar,"*
And thy loved consort on the dangerous tide
Of life long since has anchored by thy side.
But me, scarce hoping to attain that rest,
Always from port withheld, always distressed—
Me howling blasts drive devious, tempest tost,
Sails ripped, seams opening wide, and compass lost,
And day by day some current's thwarting force
Sets me more distant from a prosperous course.
Yet, oh, the thought that thou art safe, and he!
That thought is joy, arrive what may to me.
My boast is not, that I deduce my birth
From loins enthroned and rulers of the earth;
But higher far my proud pretensions rise—
The son of parents passed into the skies!
And now, farewell—Time unrevoked has run
His wonted course, yet what I wished is done.
By contemplation's help, not sought in vain,
I seem to have lived my childhood o'er again;
To have renewed the joys that once were mine,
Without the sin of violating thine:
And, while the wings of Fancy still are free,
And I can view this mimic show of thee,
Time has but half succeeded in his theft—
Thyself removed, thy power to soothe me left.

* Garth.

THE POPLAR FIELD.

The poplars are felled ; farewell to the shade,
And the whispering sound of the cool colonnade
The winds play no longer and sing in the leaves,
Nor Ouse on his bosom their image receives.

Twelve years have elapsed since I first took a view
Of my favourite field, and the bank where they grew ;
And now in the grass behold they are laid,
And the tree is my seat that once lent me a shade !

The blackbird has fled to another retreat,
Where the hazels afford him a screen from the heat,
And the scene where his melody charmed me before
Resounds with his sweet-flowing ditty no more.

My fugitive years are all hasting away,
And I must ere long lie as lowly as they,
With a turf on my breast, and a stone at my head,
Ere another such grove shall arise in its stead.

'Tis a sight to engage me, if anything can,
To muse on the perishing pleasures of man ;
Though his life be a dream, his enjoyments, I see,
Have a being less durable even than he.*

IDEM LATINE REDDITUM.

Populeæ cecidit gratissima copia silvæ,
Conticuêre susurri, omnisque evanuit umbra.
Nullæ jam levibus se miscent frondibus auræ,
Et nulla in fluvio ramorum ludit imago.

Hei mihi.! bis senos dum luctu torqueor annos,
His cogor silvis suetoque carere recessu,
Cum serò rediens, stratasque in gramine cernens,
Insedi arboribus, sub queîs errare solebam.

Ah ubi nunc merulæ cantus ?   Felicior illum
Silva tegit, duræ nondum permissa bipenni ;
Scilicet exustos colles camposque patentes
Odit, et indignans et non rediturus abivit.

Sed qui succisas doleo succidar et ipse,
Et priùs huic parilis quàm creverit altera silva
Flebor, et, exequiis parvis donatus, habebo
Defixum lapidem tumulique cubantis acervum.

ote to Ed. of 1803. Mr. Cowper afterwards altered this last stanza in the following manner :
The change both my heart and my fancy employs,
I reflect on the frailty of man and his joys :
Short-lived as we are, yet our pleasures, we see,
Have a still shorter date, and die sooner than we:
y 2

Tam subitò periisse videns tam digna manere,
Agnosco humanas sortes et tristia fata—
Sit licèt ipse brevis, volucrique simillimus umbræ,
Est homini brevior citiùsque obitura voluptas.

INSCRIPTION FOR THE TOMB OF MR. HAMILTON.

PAUSE here, and think : a monitory rhyme
Demands one moment of thy fleeting time.
  Consult life's silent clock, thy bounding vein ;
Seems it to say, " Health here has long to reign " ?
Hast thou the vigour of thy youth ?—an eye
That beams delight ?—a heart untaught to sigh ?
Yet fear. Youth, ofttimes healthful and at ease,
Anticipates a day it never sees ;
And many a tomb, like HAMILTON'S, aloud
Exclaims, " Prepare thee for an early shroud."

EPITAPH ON A HARE.

HERE lies, whom hound did ne'er pursue,
  Nor swifter greyhound follow,
Whose foot ne'er tainted morning dew,
  Nor ear heard huntsman's halloo ;

Old Tiney, surliest of his kind,
  Who, nursed with tender care,
And to domestic bounds confined,
  Was still a wild Jack hare.

Though duly from my hand he took
  His pittance every night,
He did it with a jealous look,
  And, when he could, would bite.

His diet was of wheaten bread,
  And milk, and oats, and straw ;
Thistles, or lettuces instead,
  With sand to scour his maw.

On twigs of hawthorn he regaled,
  On pippins' russet peel,
And, when his juicy salads failed,
  Sliced carrot pleased him well.

A Turkey carpet was his lawn,
  Whereon he loved to bound,

To skip and gambol like a fawn,
  And swing his rump around.

His frisking was at evening hours,
  For then he lost his fear,
But most before approaching shower
  Or when a storm drew near.

Eight years and five round-rolling mo
  He thus saw steal away,
Dozing out all his idle noons,
  And every night at play.

I kept him for his humour's sake,
  For he would oft beguile
My heart of thoughts that made it a
  And force me to a smile.

But now beneath this walnut shade
  He finds his long last home,
And waits, in snug concealment lai
  Till gentler Puss shall come.

He, still more agèd, feels the shock
  From which no care can save,
And, partner once of Tiney's box,
  Must soon partake his grave.

EPITAPHIUM ALTERUM.

Hic etiam jacet,
Qui totum novennium vixit,
Puss.
Siste paulisper,
Qui præteriturus es,
Et tecum sic reputa—
Hunc neque canis venaticus,
Nec plumbum missile,
Nec laqueus,
Nec imbres nimii,
Confecêre :
Tamen mortuus est—
Et moriar ego.

POSTHUMOUS POEMS

OF

MIDDLE AND LATER LIFE.

(This division includes some pieces published anonymously during the Author's lifetime.)

A TALE, FOUNDED ON A FACT

WHICH HAPPENED IN JANUARY 1779.

WHERE Humber pours his rich commercial stream
There dwelt a wretch, who breathed but to blaspheme;
In subterraneous caves his life he led,
Black as the mine in which he wrought for bread.
When on a day, emerging from the deep,
A Sabbath-day, (such sabbaths thousands keep!)
The wages of his weekly toil he bore
To buy a cock—whose blood might win him more;
As if the noblest of the feathered kind
Were but for battle and for death designed;
As if the consecrated hours were meant
For sport to minds on cruelty intent;
It chanced (such chances Providence obey)
He met a fellow-labourer on the way,
Whose heart the same desires had once inflamed;
But now the savage temper was reclaimed,
Persuasion on his lips had taken place;
For all plead well who plead the cause of grace.
His iron heart with Scripture he assailed,
Wooed him to hear a sermon, and prevailed.
His faithful bow the mighty preacher drew;
Swift as the lightning-glimpse the arrow flew.
He wept; he trembled; cast his eyes around,
To find a worse than he; but none he found.
He felt his sins, and wondered he should feel;
Grace made the wound, and grace alone could heal.
Now farewell oaths, and blasphemies, and lies!
He quits the sinner's for the martyr's prize.
That holy day was washed with many a tear,
Gilded with hope, yet shaded, too, by fear.

The next, his swarthy brethren of the mine
Learned, by his altered speech, the change divine!
Laughed when they should have wept, and swore the **day**
Was nigh when he would swear as fast as they.
" No," said the penitent,—" such words shall share
" This breath no more ; devoted now to prayer.
" O ! if Thou seest (Thine eye the future sees)
" That I shall yet again blaspheme, like these,
" Now strike me to the ground on which I kneel,
" Ere yet this heart relapses into steel :
" Now take me to that heaven I once defied,
" Thy presence, Thy embrace ! "—He spoke, and died !

TO THE REV. MR. NEWTON,

ON HIS RETURN FROM RAMSGATE.

THAT ocean you of late surveyed,
　Those rocks, I too have seen,
But I afflicted and dismayed,
　You tranquil and serene.

To me the waves that ceaseless broke
　Upon the dangerous coast,
Hoarsely and ominously spoke
　Of all my treasure lost.

You from the flood-controlling steep
　Saw stretched before your view,
With conscious joy, the threatening deep,
　No longer such to you.

Your sea of troubles you have past,
　And found the peaceful shore ;
I, tempest-tossed, and wrecked at last,
　Come home to port no more.

　　　October, 1780.

MONUMENTAL INSCRIPTION TO WILLIAM NORTHCOT.

HIC sepultus est
Inter suorum lacrymas
GULIELMUS NORTHCOT,
GULIELMI et MARIÆ filius
Unicus, unicè dilectus,
Qui floris ritu succisus est semihiantis,
Aprilis die septimo,
1780, Æt. 10.

Care, vale ! Sed non æternùm, care, valeto !
　Namque iterùm tecum, sim modò dignus, ero.
Tum nihil amplexus poterit divellere nostros,
　Nec tu marcesces, nec lacrymabor ego.

TRANSLATION.

FAREWELL ! " But not for ever," Hope replies ;
Trace but his steps and meet him in the skies !
There nothing shall renew our parting pain ;
Thou shalt not wither, nor I weep, again.

RIDDLE.

I AM just two and two, I am warm, I am cold,
And the parent of numbers that cannot be told,
I am lawful, unlawful—a duty, a fault,—
I am often sold dear, good for nothing when bought ;
An extraordinary boon, and a matter of course,
And yielded with pleasure when taken by force.

July, 1780.

TO SIR JOSHUA REYNOLDS.

DEAR President, whose art sublime
Gives perpetuity to Time,
And bids transactions of a day,
That fleeting hours would waft away
To dark futurity, survive,
And in unfading beauty live,—
You cannot with a grace decline
A special mandate of the Nine—
Yourself, whatever task you choose,
So much indebted to the Muse.
    Thus say the sisterhood :—We come-
Fix well your pallet on your thumb,
Prepare the pencil and the tints—
We come to furnish you with hints.
French disappointment, British glory,
Must be the subject of the story.
    First strike a curve, a graceful bow,
Then slope it to a point below ;
Your outline easy, airy, light,
Filled up becomes a paper kite.
Let Independence, sanguine, horrid,
Blaze, like a meteor in the forehead :
Beneath (but lay aside your graces)
Draw six-and-twenty rueful faces,
Each with a staring, steadfast eye,
Fixed on his great and good ally.
France flies the kite—'tis on the wing—
Britannia's lightning cuts the string.
The wind that raised it, ere it ceases,
Just rends it into thirteen pieces,
Takes charge of every fluttering sheet,
And lays them all at George's feet.
    Iberia, trembling from afar,
Renounces the confederate war ;
Her efforts and her arts o'ercome,
France calls her shattered navies home ;

Repenting Holland learns to mourn
The sacred treaties she has torn ;
Astonishment and awe profound
Are stamped upon the nations round ;
Without one friend, above all foes,
Britannia gives the world repose.

1781.

IMPROMPTU ON READING THE CHAPTER ON POLYGAMY, IN MR. MADAN'S THELYPHTHORA.

IF John marries Mary, and Mary alone,
'Tis a very good match between Mary and John.
Should John wed a score, oh, the claws and the scratches !
It can't be a match—'tis a bundle of matches.

1780.

ON A REVIEW CONDEMNING THELYPHTHORA.

I HAVE read the Review ; it is learned and wise,
Clear, candid, and witty—Thelyphthora dies.

ON MADAN'S ANSWER TO NEWTON'S COMMENTS ON THELYPHTHORA.

M. quarrels with N., because M. wrote a book
And N. did not like it, which M. could not brook ;
So he called him a bigot, a wrangler, a monk,
With as many hard names as would line a good trunk,
And set up his back, and clawed like a cat ;
But N. liked it never the better for that.
　Now N. had a wife, and he wanted but one,
Which stuck in M.'s stomach as cross as a bone :
It has always been reckoned a just cause of strife
For a man to make free with another man's wife ;
But the strife is the strangest that ever was known,
If a man must be scolded for loving his own.

ANTI-THELYPHTHORA.

A TALE, IN VERSE.

Ah miser,
Quantâ laboras in Charybdi !
HOR. *Od.* i. 27

AIRY DEL CASTRO was as bold a knight
As ever earned a lady's love in fight.
Many he sought, but one above the rest
His tender heart victoriously impressed.

In fairy-land was born the matchless dame,
The land of dreams, Hypothesis her name.
There Fancy nursed her in ideal bowers,
And laid her soft in amaranthine flowers ;
Delighted with her babe, the enchantress smiled,
And graced with all her gifts the favourite child.
Her wooed Sir Airy, by meandering streams,
In daily musings and in nightly dreams ;
With all the flowers he found, he wove in haste
Wreaths for her brow, and girdles for her waist ;
His time, his talents, and his ceaseless care,
All consecrated to adorn the fair ;
No pastime but with her he deigned to take,
And if he studied, studied for her sake.
And, for Hypothesis was somewhat long,
Nor soft enough to suit a lover's tongue,
He called her Posy, with an amorous art,
And graved it on a gem, and wore it next his heart.
  But she, inconstant as the beams that play
On rippling waters in an April day,
With many a freakish trick deceived his pains,
To pathless wilds and unfrequented plains
Enticed him from his oaths of knighthood far,
Forgetful of the glorious toils of war.
'Tis thus the tenderness that Love inspires
Too oft betrays the votaries of his fires ;
Borné far away on elevated wings,
They sport like wanton doves in airy rings,
And laws and duties are neglected things.
  Nor he alone addressed the wayward fair,
Full many a knight had been entangled there ;
But still, whoever wooed her or embraced,
On every mind some mighty spell she cast.
Some she would teach (for she was wondrous wise,
And made her dupes see all things with her eyes)
That forms material, whatsoe'er we dream,
Are not at all, or are not what they seem ;
That substances and modes of every kind
Are mere impressions on the passive mind ;
And he that splits his cranium, breaks at most
A fancied head against a fancied post :
Others, that earth, ere sin had drowned it all,
Was smooth and even as an ivory ball ;
That all the various beauties we survey,
Hills, valleys, rivers, and the boundless sea,
Are but departures from the first design,
Effects of punishment and wrath divine.
She tutored some in Dædalus's art,
And promised they should act his wildgoose part,
On waxen pinions soar without a fall,
Swift as the proudest gander of them all.
  But fate reserved Sir Airy to maintain

The wildest project of her teeming brain ; —
That wedlock is not rigorous, as supposed,
But man, within a wider pale enclosed,
May rove at will, where appetite shall lead,
Free as the lordly bull that ranges o'er the mead;
That forms and rites are tricks of human law,
As idle as the chattering of a daw ;
That lewd incontinence, and lawless rape,
Are marriage in its true and proper shape ;
That man by faith and truth is made a slave,
The ring a bauble, and the priest a knave.
    " Fair fall the deed !" the knight exulting cried,
" Now is the time to make the maid a bride !"
    'T'was on the noon of an autumnal day,
October hight, but mild and fair as May ;
When scarlet fruits the russet hedge adorn,
And floating films envelop every thorn ;
When gently as in June the rivers glide,
And only miss the flowers that graced their side ;
The linnet twittered out his parting song,
With many a chorister the woods among ;
On southern banks the ruminating sheep
Lay snug and warm ;—'twas Summer's farewell peep.
Propitious to his fond intent there grew
An arbour near at hand of thickest yew,
With many a boxen bush close clipt between,
And phillyrea of a gilded green.
    But what old Chaucer's merry page befits,
The chaster muse of modern days omits.
Suffice it then in decent terms to say,
She saw,—and turned her rosy cheek away.
Small need of prayer-book or of priest, I ween,
Where parties are agreed, retired the scene,
Occasion prompt, and appetite so keen.
Hypothesis (for with such magic power
Fancy endued her in her natal hour)
From many a steaming lake and reeking bog,
Bade rise in haste a dank and drizzling fog,
That curtained round the scene where they reposed,
And wood and lawn in dusky folds enclosed.
    Fear seized the trembling sex ; in every grove
They wept the wrongs of honourable love :
" In vain," they cried, " are hymeneal rites,
" Vain our delusive hope of constant knights ;
" The marriage bond has lost its power to bind,
" And flutters loose, the sport of every wind.
" The bride, while yet her bride's attire is on,
" Shall mourn her absent lord, for he is gone,
" Satiate of her, and weary of the same,
" To distant wilds, in quest of other game.
" Ye fair Circassians ! all your lutes employ,
" Seraglios sing, and harems dance for joy !

" For British nymphs whose lords were lately true,
" Nymphs quite as fair, and happier once than you,
" Honour, esteem, and confidence forgot,
" Feel all the meanness of your slavish lot.
" O curst Hypothesis ! your hellish arts
" Seduce our husbands, and estrange their hearts.
" Will none arise ? no knight who still retains
" The blood of ancient worthies in his veins,
" To assert the charter of the chaste and fair,
" Find out her treacherous heart, and plant a dagger there?
" A knight (can he that serves the fair do less?)
" Starts at the call of beauty in distress ;
" And he that does not, whatsoe'er occurs,
" Is recreant, and unworthy of his spurs." *
 Full many a champion, bent on hardy deed,
Called for his arms and for his princely steed.
So swarmed the Sabine youth, and grasped the shield,
When Roman rapine, by no laws withheld,
Lest Rome should end with her first founders' lives,
Made half their maids, *sans* ceremony, wives.
But not the mitred few ; the soul their charge,
They left these bodily concerns at large ;
Forms or no forms, pluralities or pairs,
Right reverend sirs ! was no concern of theirs.
The rest, alert and active as became
A courteous knighthood, caught the generous flame ;
One was accoutred when the cry began,
Knight of the Silver Moon, Sir Marmadan.†
 Oft as his patroness, who rules the night,
Hangs out her lamp in yon cærulean height,
His vow was (and he well performed his vow),
Armed at all points, with terror on his brow,
To judge the land, to purge atrocious crimes,
And quell the shapeless monsters of the times.
For cedars famed, fair Lebanon supplied
The well-poised lance that quivered at his side ;
Truth armed it with a point so keen, so just,
No spell or charm was proof against the thrust.
He couched it firm upon his puissant thigh,
And darting through his helm an eagle's eye,
On all the wings of chivalry advanced
To where the fond Sir Airy lay entranced.
 He dreamt not of a foe, or if his fear
Foretold one, dreamt not of a foe so near.
Far other dreams his feverish mind employed,
Of rights restored, variety enjoyed ;
Of virtue too well fenced to fear a flaw;
Vice passing current by the stamp of law;
Large population on a liberal plan,

---

* When a knight was degraded, his spurs were chopped off.
† " Monthly Review " for October [1780].

And woman trembling at the foot of man ;
How simple wedlock fornication works,
And Christians marrying may convert the Turks.
   The trumpet now spoke Marmadan at hand,
A trumpet that was heard through all the land.
His high-bred steed expands his nostrils wide,
And snorts aloud to cast the mist aside ;
But he, the virtues of his lance to show,
Struck thrice the point upon his saddle-bow;
Three sparks ensued that chased it all away,
And set the unseemly pair in open day.
" To horse !" he cried, " or, by this good right hand
" And better spear, I smite you where you stand."
   Sir Airy, not a whit dismayed or scared,
Buckled his helm, and to his steed repaired,
Whose bridle, while he cropped the grass below,
Hung not far off upon a myrtle bough.
He mounts at once,—such confidence infused
The insidious witch that had his wits abused ;
And she, regardless of her softer kind,
Seized fast the saddle and sprang up behind.
" Oh, shame to knighthood !" his assailant cried ;
" Oh, shame !" ten thousand echoing nymphs replied.
Placed with advantage at his listening ear,
She whispered still that he had nought to fear,
That he was cased in such enchanted steel,
So polished and compact from head to heel,
" Come ten, come twenty, should an army call
Thee to the field, thou shouldst withstand them all."
   " By Dian's beams !" Sir Marmadan exclaimed,
" The guiltiest still are ever least ashamed !
" But guard thee well, expect no feigned attack ;
" And guard beside the sorceress at thy back !"
   He spoke indignant, and his spurs applied,
Though little need, to his good palfrey's side :
The barb sprang forward, and his lord, whose force
Was equal to the swiftness of his horse,
Rushed with a whirlwind's fury on the foe,
And, Phineas like, transfixed them at a blow.
   Then sang the married and the maiden throng,
Love graced the theme, and harmony the song ;
The Fauns and Satyrs, a lascivious race,
Shrieked at the sight, and, conscious, fled the place :
And Hymen, trimming his dim torch anew,
His snowy mantle o'er his shoulders threw ;
He turned, and viewed it oft on every side,
And reddening with a just and generous pride,
Blessed the glad beams of that propitious day,
The spot he loathed so much for ever cleansed away.

1781.

LOVE ABUSED.

WHAT is there in the vale of life
Half so delightful as a Wife,
When friendship, love, and peace combine
To stamp the marriage-bond divine?
The stream of pure and genuine love
Derives its current from above;
And earth a second Eden shows,
Where'er the healing water flows:
But ah, if, from the dykes and drains
Of sensual nature's feverish veins,
Lust, like a lawless headstrong flood,
Impregnated with ooze and mud,
Descending fast on every side,
Once mingles with the sacred tide,
Farewell the soul-enlivening scene!
The banks that wore a smiling green,
With rank defilement overspread,
Bewail their flowery beauties dead.
The stream polluted, dark, and dull,
Diffused into a Stygian pool,
Through life's last melancholy years
Is fed with ever-flowing tears:
Complaints supply the zephyr's part,
And sighs that heave a breaking heart.

IN SEDITIONEM HORRENDAM,

CORRUPTELIS GALLICIS, UT FERTUR, LONDINI NUPER EXORTAM.

PERFIDA, crudelis, victa et lymphata furore,
  Non armis, laurum Gallia fraude petit.
Venalem pretio plebem conducit, et urit
  Undique privatas patriciasque domos.

Nequicquàm conata suâ, fœdissima sperat
  Posse tamen nostrâ nos superare manu.
Gallia, vana struis! Precibus nunc utere! Vinces
  Nam mites timidis supplicibusque sumus.

TRANSLATION.

FALSE, cruel, disappointed, stung to the heart,
France quits the warrior's for the assassin's part,
To dirty hands a dirty bribe conveys,
Bids the low street and lofty palace blaze.
Her sons too weak to vanquish us alone,
She hires the worst and basest of our own.
Kneel, France! a suppliant conquers us with ease,
We always spare a coward on his knees.

1780.

A CARD.

POOR Vestris, grieved beyond all measure,
To have incurred so much displeasure,
Although a Frenchman, disconcerted,
And though light-heeled, yet heavy-hearted,
Begs humbly to inform his friends,
Next first of April he intends
To take a boat and row right down
To Cuckold's-Point from Richmond town ;
And as he goes, alert and gay,
Leap all the bridges in his way.
The boat, borne downward with the tide,
Shall catch him safe on t'other side.
He humbly hopes by this expedient
To prove himself their most obedient,
(Which shall be always his endeavour,)
And jump into the former favour.

1781.

ON THE HIGH PRICE OF FISH.

(TO MRS. NEWTON.)

COCOA-NUT naught,
  Fish too dear,
None must be bought
  For us that are here :

No lobster on earth,
  That ever I saw,
To me would be worth
  Sixpence a claw.

So, dear Madam, wait
  Till fish can be got
At a reasonable rate,
  Whether lobster or not.

Till the French and the Dutch
  Have quitted the seas,
And then send as much
  And as oft as you please.

Aug. 1781.

TO MRS. NEWTON.

Sept. 16, 1781.

A NOBLE theme demands a noble verse ;
In such I thank you for your fine oys*ters*.
The barrel was magnificently large,
But, being sent to Olney at free charge,
Was not inserted in the driver's list,
And therefore overlooked, forgot, or missed ;
For, when the messenger whom we despatched
Inquired for oysters, Hob his noddle scratched,
Denying that his waggon or his wain
Did any such commodity contain.
In consequence of which your welcome boon
Did not arrive till yesterday at noon ;
In consequence of which some chanced to die,
And some, though very sweet, were very dry.
Now Madam says, (and what she says must still
Deserve attention, say she what she will,)

That what we call the Diligence, be-case
It goes to London with a swifter pace,
Would better suit the carriage of your gift,
Returning downward with a pace as swift ;
And therefore recommends it with this aim—
To save at least three days,—the price the same ;
For though it will not carry or convey
For less than twelve pence, send whate'er you may,
For oysters, bred upon the salt sea-shore,
Packed in a barrel, they will charge no more.
   News have I none that I can deign to write,
Save that it rained prodigiously last night,
And that ourselves were, at the seventh hour,
Caught in the first beginning of the shower ;
But walking, running, and with much ado,
Got home—just time enough to be wet through.
Yet both are well, and, wondrous to be told,
Soused as we were, we yet have caught no cold ;
And wishing just the same good hap to you,
We say, good Madam, and good Sir, Adieu !

A POETICAL EPISTLE TO LADY AUSTEN.

DEAR Anna—between friend and friend,
Prose answers every common end ;
Serves, in a plain and homely way,
To express the occurrence of the day ;
Our health, the weather, and the news,
What walks we take, what books we chuse,
And all the floating thoughts we find
Upon the surface of the mind.
   But when a poet takes the pen,
Far more alive than other men,
He feels a gentle tingling come
Down to his finger and his thumb,
Derived from nature's noblest part,
The centre of a glowing heart :
And this is what the world, who knows
No flights above the pitch of prose,
His more sublime vagaries slighting,
Denominates an itch for writing.
No wonder I, who scribble rhyme
To catch the triflers of the time,
And tell them truths divine and clear,
Which, couched in prose, they will not hear ;
Who labour hard to allure and draw
The loiterers I never saw,
Should feel that itching and that tingling
With all my purpose intermingling,
To your intrinsic merit true,
When called to address myself to you.

Mysterious are His ways, whose power
Brings forth that unexpected hour,
When minds that never met before,
Shall meet, unite, and part no more :
It is the allotment of the skies,
The hand of the Supremely Wise,
That guides and governs our affections,
And plans and orders our connexions :
Directs us in our distant road,
And marks the bounds of our abode.
Thus we were settled when you found us,
Peasants and children all around us,
Not dreaming of so dear a friend,
Deep in the abyss of Silver-End.
Thus Martha, even against her will,
Perchèd on the top of yonder hill ;
And you, though you must needs prefer
The fairer scenes of sweet Sancerre,
Are come from distant Loire to chuse
A cottage on the banks of Ouse.
This page of Providence quite new,
And now just opening to our view,
Employs our present thoughts and pains
To guess and spell what it contains :
But day by day, and year by year,
Will make the dark enigma clear ;
And furnish us, perhaps, at last,
Like other scenes already past,
With proof, that we, and our affairs,
Are part of a Jehovah's cares ;
For God unfolds by slow degrees
The purport of His deep decrees ;
Sheds every hour a clearer light
In aid of our defective sight ;
And spreads, at length, before the soul,
A beautiful and perfect whole,
Which busy man's inventive brain
Toils to anticipate, in vain.

Say, Anna, had you never known
The beauties of a rose full blown,
Could you, though luminous your eye,
By looking on the bud, descry,
Or guess, with a prophetic power,
The future splendour of the flower?
Just so the Omnipotent, who turns
The system of a world's concerns,
From mere minutiæ can educe
Events of most important use,
And bid a dawning sky display
The blaze of a meridian day.
The works of man tend, one and all,
As needs they must, from great to small ;

And vanity absorbs at length
The monuments of human strength.
But who can tell how vast the plan
Which this day's incident began?
Too small, perhaps, the slight occasion
For our dim-sighted observation;
It passed unnoticed, as the bird
That cleaves the yielding air unheard,
And yet may prove, when understood,
A harbinger of endless good.
   Not that I deem, or mean to call,
Friendship a blessing cheap or small:
But merely to remark, that ours,
Like some of Nature's sweetest flowers,
Rose from a seed of tiny size,
That seemed to promise no such prize;
A transient visit intervening,
And made almost without a meaning,
(Hardly the effect of inclination,
Much less of pleasing expectation,)
Produced a friendship, then begun,
That has cemented us in one;
And placed it in our power to prove,
By long fidelity and love,
That Solomon has wisely spoken,—
" A threefold cord is not soon broken."

17th Dec. 1781.

THE FLATTING MILL.

AN ILLUSTRATION.

WHEN a bar of pure silver or ingot of gold
  Is sent to be flatted or wrought into length,
It is passed between cylinders often, and rolled
  In an engine of utmost mechanical strength.

Thus tortured and squeezed, at last it appears
  Like a loose heap of ribbon, a glittering show,
Like music it tinkles and rings in your ears,
  And warmed by the pressure, is all in a glow.

This process achieved, it is doomed to sustain
  The thump after thump of a gold-beater's mallet,
And at last is of service in sickness or pain
  To cover a pill for a delicate palate.

Alas for the poet! who dares undertake
  To urge reformation of national ill—
His head and his heart are both likely to ache
  With the double employment of mallet and mill.

If he wish to instruct, he must learn to delight;
  Smooth, ductile, and even, his fancy must flow,
Must tinkle and glitter like gold to the sight,
  And catch in its progress a sensible glow.

After all, he must beat it as thin and as fine
  As the leaf that enfolds what an invalid swallows;
For truth is unwelcome, however divine,
  And unless you adorn it, a nausea follows.

TO THE REV. MR. NEWTON,

RECTOR OF ST. MARY WOOLNOTH.

SAYS the Pipe to the Snuff-box, "I can't understand
  What the ladies and gentlemen see in your face,
That you are in fashion all over the land,
  And I am so much fallen into disgrace.

"Do but see what a pretty contemplative air
  I give to the company,—pray do but note 'em,—
You would think that the wise men of Greece were all there,
  Or, at least, would suppose them the wise men of Gotham.

"My breath is as sweet as the breath of blown roses,
  While you are a nuisance where'er you appear;
There is nothing but snivelling and blowing of noses,
  Such a noise as turns any man's stomach to hear."

Then, lifting his lid in a delicate way,
  And opening his mouth with a smile quite engaging,
The Box in reply was heard plainly to say,
  "What a silly dispute is this we are waging!

"If you have a little of merit to claim,
  You may thank the sweet-smelling Virginian weed;
And I, if I seem to deserve any blame,
  The before-mentioned drug in apology plead.

"Thus neither the praise nor the blame is our own,
  No room for a sneer, much less a cachinnus;
We are vehicles, not of tobacco alone,
  But of any thing else they may choose to put in us."

May 28, 1782.

A SIMILE LATINISED.

SORS adversa gerit stimulum, sed tendit et alas:
Pungit api similis, sed velut ista fugit.

VERSES TO THE MEMORY OF DR. LLOYD,*

SPOKEN AT THE WESTMINSTER ELECTION NEXT AFTER HIS DECEASE.

ABIIT senex ! periit senex amabilis !
    Quo non fuit jucundior.
Lugete vos, ætas quibus maturior
    Senem colendum præstitit ;
Seu quando, viribus valentioribus
    Firmoque fretus pectore,
Florentiori vos juventute excolens
    Curâ fovebat patriâ ;
Seu quando, fractus, jamque donatus rude
    Vultu sed usque blandulo,
Miscere gaudebat suas facetias
    His annuis leporibus.
Vixit probus, puraque simplex indole,
    Blandisque comis moribus,
Et dives æquâ mente—charus omnibus,
    Unius † auctus munere.
Ite tituli ! meritis beatioribus
    Aptate laudes debitas !
Nec invidebat ille, si quibus favens
    Fortuna plus arriserat.
Placide senex ! levi quiescas cespite,
    Etsi superbum nec vivo tibi
Decus sit inditum, nec mortuo
    Lapis notatus nomine.   .

THE SAME IN ENGLISH.

OUR good old friend is gone, gone to his rest,
Whose social converse was, itself, a feast.
O ye of riper age, who recollect
How once ye loved, and eyed him with respect,
Both in the firmness of his better day,
While yet he ruled you with a father's sway,
And when, impaired by time and glad to rest,
Yet still with looks in mild complacence drest,

---

* I make no apology for the introduction of the following lines, though I have never learned who wrote them. Their elegance will sufficiently recommend them to persons of classical taste and erudition, and I shall be happy if the English version that they have received from me be found not to dishonour them. Affection for the memory of the worthy man whom they celebrate alone prompted me to this endeavour.—W. COWPER.

† He was Usher and Under-master of Westminster nearly fifty years, and retired from his occupation when he was near seventy, with a handsome pension from the king. [Hayley.]

He took his annual seat and mingled here
His sprightly vein with yours—now drop a tear.
In morals blameless as in manners meek,
He knew no wish that he might blush to speak,
But, happy in whatever state below,
And richer than the rich in being so,
Obtained the hearts of all, and such a meed
At length from one,* as made him rich indeed.
Hence, then, ye titles ; hence, not wanted here ;
Go, garnish merit in a brighter sphere,
The brows of those whose more exalted lot
He could congratulate, but envied not.
    Light lie the turf, good senior ! on thy breast,
And tranquil as thy mind was be thy rest !
Though, living, thou hadst more desert than fame,
And not a stone now chronicles thy name.

FRIENDSHIP.

WHAT Virtue, or what mental grace,
But men unqualified and base
    Will boast it their possession ?
Profusion apes the noble part
Of Liberality of heart,
    And Dulness of Discretion.

If every polished gem we find,
Illuminating heart or mind,
    Provoke to imitation,
No wonder friendship does the same,
That jewel of the purest flame,
    Or rather constellation.

No knave but boldly will pretend
The requisites that form a friend,
    A real and a sound one ;
Nor any fool he would deceive,
But prove as ready to believe,
    And dream that he had found one.

Candid, and generous, and just,
Boys care but little whom they trust,—
    An error soon corrected ;
For who but learns in riper years
That man, when smoothest he appears,
    Is most to be suspected ?

But here again a danger lies,
Lest, having misapplied our eyes,
    And taken trash for treasure,
We should unwarily conclude
Friendship a false ideal good,
    A mere Utopian pleasure.

An acquisition rather rare
Is yet no subject of despair ;
    Nor is it wise complaining,
If either on forbidden ground,
Or where it was not to be found,
    We sought without attaining.

No Friendship will abide the test
That stands on sordid interest,
    Or mean self-love erected ;
Nor such as may a while subsist
Between the sot and sensualist,
    For vicious ends connected.

Who seeks a friend should come disposed
To exhibit, in full bloom disclosed,
    The graces and the beauties
That form the character he seeks ;
For 'tis a union that bespeaks
    Reciprocated duties.

* See the note to the Latin copy.

Mutual attention is implied,
And equal truth on either side,
   And constantly supported ;
'Tis senseless arrogance to accuse
Another of sinister views,
   Our own as much distorted.

But will Sincerity suffice ?
It is indeed above all price,
   And must be made the basis ;
But every virtue of the soul
Must constitute the charming whole,
   All shining in their places.

A fretful temper will divide
The closest knot that may be tied,
   By ceaseless sharp corrosion ;
A temper passionate and fierce
May suddenly your joys disperse
   At one immense explosion.

In vain the talkative unite
In hopes of permanent delight ;
   The secret just committed,
Forgetting its important weight,
They drop through mere desire to prate,
   And by themselves outwitted.

How bright soe'er the prospect seems,
All thoughts of friendship are but
      dreams,
   If Envy chance to creep in ;
An envious man, if you succeed,
May prove a dangerous foe indeed,
   But not a friend worth keeping.

As Envy pines at good possessed,
So Jealousy looks forth distressed
   On good that seems approaching,
And if success his steps attend,
Discerns a rival in a friend,
   And hates him for encroaching.

Hence authors of illustrious name,
Unless belied by common fame,
   Are sadly prone to quarrel,
To deem the wit a friend displays
A tax upon their own just praise,
   And pluck each other's laurel.

A man renowned for repartee
Will seldom scruple to make free
   With Friendship's finest feeling ;

Will thrust a dagger at your breast,
And say he wounded you in jest,
   By way of balm for healing.

Whoever keeps an open ear
For tattlers, will be sure to hear
   The trumpet of contention ;
Aspersion is the babbler's trade,
To listen is to lend him aid
   And rush into dissension.

A Friendship that in frequent fits
Of controversial rage emits
   The sparks of disputation,
Like Hand-in-Hand insurance plates,
Most unavoidably creates
   The thought of conflagration.

Some fickle creatures boast a soul
True as a needle to the pole,
   Their humour yet so various—
They manifest their whole life through
The needle's deviations too,
   Their love is so precarious.

The great and small but rarely meet
On terms of amity complete ;
   Plebeians must surrender,
And yield so much to noble folk,
It is combining fire with smoke,
   Obscurity with splendour.

Some are so placid and serene
(As Irish bogs are always green)
   They sleep secure from waking ;
And are indeed a bog, that bears
Your unparticipated cares,
   Unmoved and without quaking.

Courtier and patriot cannot mix
Their heterogeneous politics
   Without an effervescence,
Like that of salts with lemon-juice,
Which does not yet like that produce
   A friendly coalescence.

Religion should extinguish strife,
And make a calm of human life ;
   But friends that chance to differ
On points which God has left at large,
How fiercely will they meet and charge !
   No combatants are stiffer.

To prove at last my main intent
Needs no expense of argument,
　　No cutting and contriving—
Seeking a real friend, we seem
To adopt the chymists' golden dream,
　　With still less hope of thriving.

Sometimes the fault is all our own,
Some blemish in due time made known
　　By trespass or omission :
Sometimes occasion brings to light
Our friend's defect, long hid from sight,
　　And even from suspicion.

Then judge yourself, and prove your man
As circumspectly as you can,
　　And, having made election,
Beware no negligence of yours,
Such as a friend but ill endures,
　　Enfeeble his affection.

That secrets are a sacred trust,
That friends should be sincere and just,
　　That constancy befits them,
Are observations on the case
That savour much of commonplace,
　　And all the world admits them.

But 'tis not timber, lead, and stone,
An architect requires alone
　　To finish a fine building—
The palace were but half complete,
If he could possibly forget
　　The carving and the gilding.

The man that hails you Tom or Jack,
And proves by thumps upon your back
　　How he esteems your merit,
Is such a friend that one had need
Be very much his friend indeed,
　　To pardon or to bear it.

As similarity of mind,
Or something not to be defined,
　　First fixes our attention ;

So manners decent and polite,
The same we practised at first sight,
　　Must save it from declension.

Some act upon this prudent plan,
" Say little, and hear all you can ; "
　　Safe policy, but hateful.
So barren sands imbibe the shower,
But render neither fruit nor flower,—
　　Unpleasant and ungrateful.

The man I trust, if shy to me,
Shall find me as reserved as he,
　　No subterfuge or pleading
Shall win my confidence again ;
I will by no means entertain
　　A spy on my proceeding.

These samples—for alas ! at last
These are but samples, and a taste
　　Of evils yet unmentioned—
May prove the task a task indeed,
In which 'tis much if we succeed,
　　However well-intentioned.

Pursue the search, and you will find
Good sense and knowledge of mankind
　　To be at least expedient,
And, after summing all the rest,
Religion ruling in the breast
　　A principal ingredient.

The noblest Friendship ever shown
The Saviour's history makes known,
　　Though some have turned and turned
　　　　it ;
And, whether being crazed or blind,
Or seeking with a biassed mind,
　　Have not, it seems, discerned it.

O Friendship ! if my soul forego
Thy dear delights while here below,
　　To mortify and grieve me,
May I myself at last appear
Unworthy, base, and insincere,
　　Or may my friend deceive me !

1782.

TO THE REV. WILLIAM BULL.

My dear Friend,
If reading verse be your delight,
'Tis mine as much, or more, to write;
But what we would, so weak is man,
Lies oft remote from what we can.
For instance, at this very time
I feel a wish by cheerful rhyme
To soothe my friend, and, had I power,
To cheat him of an anxious hour;
Not meaning (for I must confess,
It were but folly to suppress)
His pleasure or his good alone,
But squinting partly at my own.
But though the sun is flaming high
In the centre of yon arch, the sky,
And he had once (and who but he?)
The name for setting genius free,
Yet whether poets of past days
Yielded him undeserved praise,
And he by no uncommon lot
Was famed for virtues he had not;
Or whether, which is like enough,
His Highness may have taken huff,
So seldom sought with invocation,
Since it has been the reigning fashion
To disregard his inspiration,—
I seem no brighter in my wits
For all the radiance he emits,
Than if I saw, through midnight vapour,
The glimmering of a farthing taper.
Oh for a succedaneum, then,
To accelerate a creeping pen!
Oh for a ready succedaneum
Quod caput, cerebrum, et cranium
Pondere liberet exoso,
Et morbo jam caliginoso!
'Tis here; this oval box, well filled
With best tobacco finely milled,

June 22, 1782.

Beats all Anticyra's pretences
To disengage the encumbered senses.
Oh Nymph of transatlantic fame,
Where'er thine haunt, whate'er thy
    name,
Whether reposing on the side
Of Oroonoquo's spacious tide,
Or listening with delight not small
To Niagara's distant fall,
'Tis thine to cherish and to feed
The pungent nose-refreshing weed,
Which, whether pulverised, it gain
A speedy passage to the brain,
Or whether, touched with fire, it rise
In circling eddies to the skies,
Does thought more quicken and refine
Than all the breath of all the Nine—
Forgive the bard, if bard he be,
Who once too wantonly made free,
To touch with a satiric wipe
That symbol of thy power, the pipe;
So may no blight infest thy plains,
And no unseasonable rains,
And so may smiling peace once more
Visit America's sad shore;
And thou, secure from all alarms
Of thundering drums and glittering
    arms,
Rove unconfined beneath the shade
Thy wide expanded leaves have made;
So may thy votaries increase,
And fumigation never cease.
May Newton with renewed delights
Perform thy odoriferous rites,
While clouds of incense half divine
Involve thy disappearing shrine;
And so may smoke-inhaling Bull
Be always filling, never full.

TO LADY AUSTEN.

ON A FLOOD AT OLNEY.

To watch the storms, and hear the sky
Give all our almanacks the lie;
To shake with cold, and see the plains
In autumn drowned with wintry rains;

'Tis thus I spend my moments here,
And wish myself a Dutch mynheer ;
I then should have no need of wit,
For lumpish Hollander unfit !
Nor should I then repine at mud,
Or meadows deluged with a flood ;
But in a bog live well content,
And find it just my element :
Should be a clod, and not a man ;
Nor wish in vain for Sister Ann,
With charitable aid to drag
My mind out of its proper quag ;
Should have the genius of a boor,
And no ambition to have more.

Aug. 1782.

THE COLUBRIAD.

CLOSE by the threshold of a door nailed fast
Three kittens sat ; each kitten looked aghast.
I, passing swift and inattentive by,
At the three kittens cast a careless eye ;
Not much concerned to know what they did there ;
Not deeming kittens worth a poet's care.
But presently a loud and furious hiss
Caused me to stop, and to exclaim, " What's this ? "
When lo ! upon the threshold met my view,
With head erect, and eyes of fiery hue,
A viper, long as Count de Grasse's queue.
Forth from his head his forked tongue he throws,
Darting it full against a kitten's nose ;
Who having never seen, in field or house,
The like, sat still and silent as a mouse ;
Only projecting, with attention due,
Her whiskered face, she asked him, " Who are you ? "
On to the hall went I, with pace not slow,
But swift as lightning, for a long Dutch hoe :
With which well armed I hastened to the spot,
To find the viper, but I found him not.
And turning up the leaves and shrubs around,
Found only that he was not to be found.
But still the kittens, sitting as before,
Sat watching close the bottom of the door.
" I hope," said I, " the villain I would kill
Has slipped between the door and the door-sill ;
And if I make despatch, and follow hard,
No doubt but I shall find him in the yard : "
For long ere now it should have been rehearsed,
'Twas in the garden that I found him first.
E'en there I found him, there the full-grown cat
His head, with velvet paw, did gently pat ;

As curious as the kittens erst had been
To learn what this phenomenon might mean
Filled with heroic ardour at the sight,
And fearing every moment he would bite,
And rob our household of our only cat
That was of age to combat with a rat,
With outstretched hoe I slew him at the door,
And taught him NEVER TO COME THERE NO MORE.

Aug. 1782.

TO A YOUNG LADY,

WITH A PRESENT OF TWO COCKSCOMBS.

MADAM,—Two Cockscombs wait at your command,
And, what is strange, both dressed by Nature's hand ;
Like other fops they dread a hasty shower,
And beg a refuge in your closest bower ;
Showy like them, like them they yield no fruit,
But then, to make amends, they both are mute.

SONG ON PEACE.

AIR—" *My fond Shepherds of late.*"

No longer I follow a sound ;
    No longer a dream I pursue ;
Oh Happiness ! not to be found,
    Unattainable treasure, adieu !

I have sought thee in splendour and dress,
    In the regions of pleasure and taste ;
I have sought thee, and seemed to possess,
    But have proved thee a vision at last.

An humble ambition and hope
    The voice of true Wisdom inspires ;
'Tis sufficient, if Peace be the scope,
    And the summit of all our desires.

Peace may be the lot of the mind
    That seeks it in meekness and love ;
But rapture and bliss are confined
    To the glorified spirits above.

SONG.

AIR—" *The Lass of Pattie's Mill.*"

WHEN all within is peace,
    How Nature seems to smile !
Delights that never cease
    The livelong day beguile.
From morn to dewy eve,
    With open hand she showers
Fresh blessings, to deceive
    And soothe the silent hours.

It is content of heart
    Gives Nature power to please ;
The mind that feels no smart
    Enlivens all it sees,

Can make a wintry sky
    Seem bright as smiling May,
And evening's closing eye
    As peep of early day.

The vast majestic globe,
    So beauteously arrayed
In Nature's various robe,
    With wondrous skill displayed,
Is to a mourner's heart
    A dreary wild at best ;
It flutters to depart,
    And longs to be at rest.

ON THE LOSS OF THE ROYAL GEORGE.

WRITTEN WHEN THE NEWS ARRIVED.

To the march in " Scipio."

Toll for the brave !
　　The brave that are no more !
All sunk beneath the wave,
　　Fast by their native shore !

Eight hundred of the brave,
　　Whose courage well was tried,
Had made the vessel heel,
　　And laid her on her side.

A land-breeze shook the shrouds,
　　And she was overset ;
Down went the Royal George,
　　With all her crew complete.

Toll for the brave !
　　Brave Kempenfelt is gone ;
His last sea-fight is fought ;
　　His work of glory done.

It was not in the battle ;
　　No tempest gave the shock ;

Sept. 1782.

She sprang no fatal leak ;
　　She ran upon no rock.

His sword was in its sheath ;
　　His fingers held the pen,
When Kempenfelt went down
　　With twice four hundred men.

Weigh the vessel up,
　　Once dreaded by our foes !
And mingle with our cup
　　The tears that England owes.

Her timbers yet are sound,
　　And she may float again
Full charged with England's thunder,
　　And plough the distant main.

But Kempenfelt is gone,
　　His victories are o'er ;
And he and his eight hundred
　　Shall plough the wave no more.

IN SUBMERSIONEM NAVIGII CUI, GEORGIUS REGALE NOMEN, INDITUM.

Plangimus fortes. Periêre fortes,
Patrium propter periêre littus
Bis quatèr centum ; subitò sub alto
　　Æquore mersi.

Navis, innitens lateri, jacebat,
Malus ad summas trepidabat undas,
Cum levis, funes quatiens, ad imum
　　Depulit aura.

Plangimus fortes. Nimis, heu, caducam
Fortibus vitem voluêre parcæ,
Nec sinunt ultra tibi nos recentes
　　Nectere laurûs.

Magne, qui nomen, licet incanorum,
Traditum ex multis atavis tulisti !
At tuos olim memorabit ævum
　　Omne triumphos.

Non hyems illos furibunda mersit,
Non mari in clauso scopuli latentes,
Fissa non rimis abies, nec atrox
　　Abstulit ensis.

Navitæ sed tum nimium jocosi
Voce fallebant hilari laborem,
Et quiescebat, calamoque dextram im-
　　pleverat heros.

Vos, quibus cordi est grave opus piumque,
Humidum ex alto spolium levate,
Et putrescentes sub aquis amicos
　　Reddite amicis !

Hi quidem (sic dîs placuit) fuêre :
Sed ratis, nondum putris, ire possit
Rursus in bellum, Britonumque nomen
　　Tollere ad astra.

THE DISTRESSED TRAVELLERS;

OR, LABOUR IN VAIN.

A New Song to a Tune never sung before.

I.

I SING of a journey to Clifton
   We would have performed if we could,
Without cart or barrow to lift on
   Poor Mary and me through the mud.
      Slee sla slud,
      Stuck in the mud,
Oh it is pretty to wade through a flood!

2.

So away we went, slipping and sliding,
   Hop, hop, *à la mode de deux* frogs,
'Tis near as good walking as riding,
   When ladies are dressed in their clogs.
      Wheels, no doubt,
      Go briskly about,
But they clatter and rattle, and make such a rout!

3.

SHE.

" Well! now I protest it is charming;
   How finely the weather improves!
That cloud, though, is rather alarming,
   How slowly and stately it moves!"

HE.

   " Pshaw! never mind,
   'Tis not in the wind,
We are travelling south and shall leave it behind."

4.

SHE.

" I am glad we are come for an airing,
   For folks may be pounded and penned,
Until they grow rusty, not caring
   To stir half a mile to an end."

HE.

   " The longer we stay,
   The longer we may;
It's a folly to think about weather or way."

5.

SHE.

" But now I begin to be frighted ;
If I fall, what a way I should roll !
I am glad that the bridge was indicted,—
Stop ! stop ! I am sunk in a hole !"

HE.

" Nay, never care !
'Tis a common affair ;
You'll not be the last that will set a foot there."

6.

SHE.

" Let me breathe now a little, and ponder
On what it were better to do ;
That terrible lane I see yonder,
I think we shall never get through."

HE.

" So think I :—
But, by the bye,
We never shall know, if we never should try."

7.

SHE.

" But should we get there, how shall we get home?
What a terrible deal of bad road we have past !
Slipping and sliding ; and if we should come
To a difficult stile, I am ruined at last !
O this lane !
Now it is plain
That struggling and striving is labour in vain."

8.

HE.

" Stick fast there while I go and look—"

SHE.

" Don't go away, for fear I should fall !"

HE.

" I have examined it every nook,
And what you have here is a sample of all.
Come, wheel round,
The dirt we have found
Would be an estate at a farthing a pound."

9.

Now, sister Anne, the guitar you must take,
  Set it, and sing it, and make it a song ;
I have varied the verse for variety's sake,
  And cut it off short—because it was long.
      'Tis hobbling and lame,
      Which critics won't blame,
For the sense and the sound, they say, should be the same.

IN BREVITATEM VITÆ SPATII HOMINIBUS CONCESSI.

BY DR. JORTIN.

HEI mihi ! Lege ratâ sol occidit atque resurgit,
Lunaque mutatæ reparat dispendia formæ,
Astraque, purpurei telis extincta diei,
Rursus nocte vigent. Humiles telluris alumni,
Graminis herba virens, et florum picta propago,
Quos crudelis hyems lethali tabe peredit,
Cum Zephyri vox blanda vocat, rediitque sereni
Temperies anni, fœcundo è cespite surgunt.
Nos domini rerum, nos, magna et pulchra minati,
Cum breve ver vitæ robustaque transiit ætas,
Deficimus ; nec nos ordo revolubilis auras
Reddit in æthereas, tumuli neque claustra resolvit.

ON THE SHORTNESS OF HUMAN LIFE.

TRANSLATION OF THE FOREGOING.

SUNS that set, and moons that wane,
Rise and are restored again ;
Stars that orient day subdues,
Night at her return renews.
Herbs and flowers, the beauteous birth
Of the genial womb of earth,
Suffer but a transient death
From the winter's cruel breath.
Zephyr speaks ; serener skies
Warm the glebe, and they arise.
We, alas ! earth's haughty kings,
We, that promise mighty things,
Losing soon life's happy prime,
Droop, and fade, in little time.
Spring returns, but not our bloom ;
Still 'tis winter in the tomb.

Jan. 1784.

THE VALEDICTION.

FAREWELL, false hearts ! whose best affections fail,
Like shallow brooks which summer suns exhale !
Forgetful of the man whom once ye chose,
Cold in his cause, and careless of his woes,
I bid you both a long and last adieu,
Cold in my turn, and unconcerned like you.
   First, farewell Niger ! whom, now duly proved,
I disregard as much as once I loved.
Your brain well furnished, and your tongue well taught
To press with energy your ardent thought,
Your senatorial dignity of face,
Sound sense, intrepid spirit, manly grace,
Have raised you high as talents can ascend,
Made you a peer, but spoilt you for a friend !
Pretend to all that parts have e'er acquired ;
Be great, be feared, be envied, be admired ;
To fame as lasting as the earth pretend,
But not, hereafter, to the name of friend !
I sent you verse, and, as your lordship knows,
Backed with a modest sheet of humble prose ;
Not to recall a promise to your mind,
Fulfilled with ease had you been so inclined,
But to comply with feelings, and to give
Proof of an old affection still alive.
Your sullen silence serves at least to tell
Your altered heart ; and so, my lord, farewell !
   Next, busy actor on a meaner stage,
Amusement-monger of a trifling age,
Illustrious histrionic patentee,
Terentius, once my friend, farewell to thee !
In thee some virtuous qualities combine
To fit thee for a nobler part than thine,
Who, born a gentleman, hast stooped too low,
To live by buskin, sock, and raree-show.
Thy schoolfellow, and partner of thy plays,
Where Nichol swung the birch and twined the bays,
And having known thee bearded, and full grown,
The weekly censor of a laughing town,
I thought the volume I presumed to send,
Graced with the name of a long-absent friend,
Might prove a welcome gift, and touch thine heart,
Not hard by nature, in a feeling part.
But thou, it seems, (what cannot grandeur do,
Though but a dream !) art grown disdainful too ;
And strutting in thy school of queens and kings,
Who fret their hour and are forgotten things,
Hast caught the cold distemper of the day,
And, like his lordship, cast thy friend away.

Oh, Friendship ! cordial of the human breast !
So little felt, so fervently professed !
Thy blossoms deck our unsuspecting years ;
The promise of delicious fruit appears :
We hug the hopes of constancy and truth,
Such is the folly of our dreaming youth ;
But soon, alas ! detect the rash mistake
That sanguine inexperience loves to make ;
And view with tears the expected harvest lost,
Decayed by time, or withered by a frost.
Whoever undertakes a friend's great part
Should be renewed in nature, pure in heart,
Prepared for martyrdom, and strong to prove
A thousand ways the force of genuine love.
He may be called to give up health and gain,
To exchange content for trouble, ease for pain,
To echo sigh for sigh, and groan for groan,
And wet his cheeks with sorrows not his own.
The heart of man, for such a task too frail,
When most relied on is most sure to fail ;
And, summoned to partake its fellow's woe,
Starts from its office like a broken bow.
   Votaries of business and of pleasure prove
Faithless alike in friendship and in love.
Retired from all the circles of the gay,
And all the crowds that bustle life away,
To scenes where competition, envy, strife,
Beget no thunder-clouds to trouble life,
Let me, the charge of some good angel, find
One who has known and has escaped mankind ;
Polite, yet virtuous, who has brought away
The manners, not the morals, of the day :
With him, perhaps with *her*, (for men have known
No firmer friendships than the fair have shown,)
Let me enjoy, in some unthought-of spot,
All former friends forgiven and forgot,
Down to the close of life's fast fading scene,
Union of hearts, without a flaw between.
'Tis grace, 'tis bounty, and it calls for praise,
If God give health, that sunshine of our days !
And if He add, a blessing shared by few,
Content of heart, more praises still are due :
But if He grant a friend, that boon possessed
Indeed is treasure, and crowns all the rest ;
And giving one, whose heart is in the skies,
Born from above, and made divinely wise,
He gives, what bankrupt Nature never can,
Whose noblest coin is light and brittle man,
Gold, purer far than Ophir ever knew,
A soul, an image of Himself, and therefore true.

Nov. 1783.

TO AN AFFLICTED PROTESTANT LADY IN FRANCE.

MADAM,—A stranger's purpose in these lays
Is to congratulate and not to praise.
To give the creature the Creator's due
Were sin in me, and an offence to you.
From man to man, or even to woman paid,
Praise is the medium of a knavish trade,
A coin by craft for folly's use designed,
Spurious, and only current with the blind.
　The path of sorrow, and that path alone,
Leads to the land where sorrow is unknown ;
No traveller ever reached that blest abode,
Who found not thorns and briers in his road.
The world may dance along the flowery plain,
Cheered as they go by many a sprightly strain :
Where Nature has her mossy velvet spread,
With unshod feet they yet securely tread ;
Admonished, scorn the caution and the friend,
Bent all on pleasure, heedless of its end.
But He who knew what human hearts would prove,
How slow to learn the dictates of His love,
That, hard by nature and of stubborn will,
A life of ease would make them harder still,
In pity to the souls His grace designed
To rescue from the ruins of mankind,
Called for a cloud to darken all their years,
And said, " Go, spend them in the vale of tears."
O balmy gales of soul-reviving air !
O salutary streams that murmur there !
These flowing from the Fount of Grace above,
Those breathed from lips of everlasting love.
The flinty soil indeed their feet annoys,
Chill blasts of trouble nip their springing joys ;
An envious world will interpose its frown,
To mar delights superior to its own,
And many a pang experienced still within
Reminds them of their hated inmate, Sin ;
But ills of every shape and every name,
Transformed to blessings, miss their cruel aim ;
And every moment's calm that soothes the breast
Is given in earnest of eternal rest.
　Ah, be not sad, although thy lot be cast
Far from the flock and in a boundless waste !
No shepherds' tents within thy view appear,
But the Chief Shepherd even there is near ;
Thy tender sorrows and thy plaintive strain
Flow in a foreign land, but not in vain ;
Thy tears all issue from a source divine,
And every drop bespeaks a Saviour thine.
So once in Gideon's fleece the dews were found,
And drought on all the drooping herbs around.

TO THE IMMORTAL MEMORY OF THE HALIBUT

ON WHICH I DINED THIS DAY, MONDAY, APRIL 26, 1784.

WHERE hast thou floated? in what seas pursued
Thy pastime? When wast thou an egg new spawned,
Lost in the immensity of ocean's waste?
Roar as they might, the overbearing winds
That rocked the deep, thy cradle, thou wast safe—
And in thy minikin and embryo state,
Attached to the firm leaf of some salt weed,
Didst outlive tempests, such as wrung and racked
The joints of many a stout and gallant bark,
And whelmed them in the unexplored abyss.
Indebted to no magnet and no chart,
Nor under guidance of the polar fire,
Thou wast a voyager on many coasts,
Grazing at large in meadows submarine,
Where flat Batavia, just emerging, peeps
Above the brine,—where Caledonia's rocks
Beat back the surge,—and where Hibernia shoots
Her wondrous causeway far into the main.
Wherever thou hast fed, thou little thought'st,
And I not more, that I should feed on thee.
Peace, therefore, and good health, and much good fish,
To him who sent thee! and success, as oft
As it descends into the billowy gulf,
To the same drag that caught thee!—Fare thee well!
Thy lot thy brethren of the slimy fin
Would envy, could they know that thou wast doomed
To feed a bard, and to be praised in verse.

TO A LADY

WHO WORE A LOCK OF HIS HAIR SET WITH DIAMONDS.

THE star that beams on Anna's breast
  Conceals her William's hair,
'Twas lately severed from the rest
  To be promoted there.
The heart that beats beneath that breast
  Is William's well I know,
A nobler prize and richer far
  Than India could bestow.
She thus his favoured lot* prefers,
  To make her William shine;
The ornament indeed is hers,
  But all the honour mine.

* *Query*, lock.

A A 2

WRITTEN ON A PAGE OF "THE MONTHLY REVIEW,"

WHICH HAD SPOKEN OF MR. NEWTON'S OPINIONS AS CANT.

THESE critics, who to faith no quarter grant,
But call it mere hypocrisy and cant
To make a just acknowledgment of praise,
And thanks to God for governing our ways,
Approve Confucius more, and Zoroaster,
Than Christ's own servant, or that servant's Master.

1784.

EPITAPH ON DR. JOHNSON.

HERE Johnson lies, a sage by all allowed,
Whom to have bred may well make England proud ;
Whose prose was eloquence, by wisdom taught,
The graceful vehicle of virtuous thought ;
Whose verse may claim, grave, masculine, and strong,
Superior praise to the mere poet's song ;
Who many a noble gift from Heaven possessed,
And faith at last, alone worth all the rest.
O man, immortal by a double prize,
By fame on earth, by glory in the skies !

Jan. 1785.

ON THE AUTHOR OF "LETTERS ON LITERATURE."*

THE genius of the Augustan age
   His head among Rome's ruins reared,
And bursting with heroic rage,
   When literary Heron appeared,

" Thou hast," he cried, " like him of old
   Who set the Ephesian dome on fire,
By being scandalously bold,
   Attained the mark of thy desire ;

" And for traducing Virgil's name
   Shalt share his merited reward ;
A perpetuity of fame,
   That rots, and stinks, and is abhorred."

* Nominally by Robert Heron, but written by John Pinkerton. 8vo. 1785.

TO MISS C——, ON HER BIRTHDAY.

How many between east and west
Disgrace their parent earth,
Whose deeds constrain us to detest
The day that gave them birth !
Not so when Stella's natal morn
Revolving months restore,
We can rejoice that she was born,
And wish her born once more !

1786.

GRATITUDE.

ADDRESSED TO LADY HESKETH.

This cap, that so stately appears,
With ribbon-bound tassel on high,
Which seems by the crest that it rears
Ambitious of brushing the sky :
This cap to my cousin I owe,
She gave it, and gave me beside,
Wreathed into an elegant bow,
The ribbon with which it is tied.

This wheel-footed studying chair,
Contrived both for toil and repose,
Wide-elbowed, and wadded with hair,
In which I both scribble and doze,
Bright-studded to dazzle the eyes,
And rival in lustre of that
Which, or astronomy lies,
Fair Cassiopeïa sat :

These carpets, so soft to the foot,
Caledonia's traffic and pride !
Oh spare them, ye knights of the boot,
Escaped from a cross-country ride !
This table and mirror within,
Secure from collision and dust,
At which I oft shave cheek and chin,
And periwig nicely adjust :

This movable structure of shelves,
For its beauty admired and its use,
And charged with octavos and twelves,
The gayest I had to produce ;

1786.

Where, flaming in scarlet and gold
  My poems enchanted I view,
And hope, in due time, to behold
  My Iliad and Odyssey too :

This china, that decks the alcove,
  Which here people call a boufet,
But what the gods call it above
  Has ne'er been revealed to us yet :
These curtains, that keep the room warm
  Or cool, as the season demands :
These stoves, that for pattern and form
  Seem the labour of Mulciber's hands :

All these are not half that I owe
  To one, from our earliest youth
To me ever ready to show
  Benignity, friendship, and truth ;
For Time, the destroyer declared
  And foe of our perishing kind,
If even her face he has spared,
  Much less could he alter her mind.

Thus compassed about with the goods
  And chattels of leisure and ease,
I indulge my poetical moods
  In many such fancies as these ;
And fancies I fear they will seem—
  Poets' goods are not often so fine;
The poets will swear that I dream
  When I sing of the splendour of mine.

THE YEARLY DISTRESS;

OR, TITHING TIME AT STOCK, IN ESSEX.

Verses addressed to a country Clergyman, complaining of the disagreeableness of the day annually appointed for receiving the dues at the Parsonage.

COME, ponder well, for 'tis no jest,
  To laugh it would be wrong,
The troubles of a worthy priest,
  The burden of my song.

This priest he merry is and blithe
  Three quarters of a year,
But oh ! it cuts him like a scythe
  When tithing-time draws near.

He then is full of frights and fears,
  As one at point to die,
And long before the day appears
  He heaves up many a sigh.

For then the farmers come jog, jog,
  Along the miry road,
Each heart as heavy as a log,
  To make their payments good.

In sooth, the sorrow of such days
  Is not to be expressed,
When he that takes, and he that pays,
  Are both alike distressed.

Now, all unwelcome at his gates,
  The clumsy swains alight,
With rueful faces and bald pates—
  He trembles at the sight.

And well he may, for well he knows
  Each bumpkin of the clan,
Instead of paying what he owes,
  Will cheat him if he can.

So in they come—each makes his leg,
  And flings his head before,
And looks as if he came to beg,
  And not to quit a score.

" And how does Miss and Madam do,
  The little boy and all ? "

" All tight and well.   And how do you,
  Good Mr. What-d'ye call ? "

The dinner comes, and down they sit :
  Were e'er such hungry folk ?
There's little talking and no wit ;
  It is no time to joke.

One wipes his nose upon his sleeve,
  One spits upon the floor,
Yet, not to give offence or grieve,
  Holds up the cloth before.

The punch goes round, and they are dull
  And lumpish still as ever ;
Like barrels with their bellies full,
  They only weigh the heavier.

At length the busy time begins :
  " Come, neighbours, we must wag"—
The money chinks, down drop their chins,
  Each lugging out his bag.

One talks of mildew and of frost,
  And one of storms of hail,
And one of pigs that he has lost
  By maggots at the tail.

Quoth one, " A rarer man than you
  In pulpit none shall hear :
But yet, methinks, to tell you true,
  You sell it plaguy dear."

Oh, why are farmers made so coarse,
  Or clergy made so fine ?
A kick that scarce would move a horse,
  May kill a sound divine.

Then let the boobies stay at home ;
  'Twould cost him, I dare say,
Less trouble taking twice the sum,
  Without the clowns that pay.

LINES COMPOSED FOR A MEMORIAL OF ASHLEY COWPER, ESQ.

IMMEDIATELY AFTER HIS DEATH,

BY HIS NEPHEW WILLIAM OF WESTON.

FAREWELL ! endued with all that could engage
All hearts to love thee, both in youth and age !
In prime of life, for sprightliness enrolled
Among the gay, yet virtuous as the old ;

In life's last stage, (O blessing rarely found !)
Pleasant as youth with all its blossoms crowned ,
Through every period of this changeful state
Unchanged thyself—wise, good, affectionate !

Marble may flatter, and lest this should seem
O'ercharged with praises on so dear a theme,
Although thy worth be more than half supprest,
Love shall be satisfied, and veil the rest.

June 1788.

SONNET,

ADDRESSED TO HENRY COWPER, ESQ.

*On his emphatical and interesting delivery of the defence of Warren Hastings, Esq.
in the House of Lords.*

COWPER, whose silver voice, tasked sometimes hard,
  Legends prolix delivers in the ears
  (Attentive when thou readest) of England's peers,
Let verse at length yield thee thy just reward.

Thou wast not heard with drowsy disregard,
  Expending late on all that length of plea
  Thy generous powers ; but silence honoured thee,
Mute as e'er gazed on orator or bard.

Thou art not voice alone, but hast beside
  Both heart and head ; and couldst with music sweet
    Of Attic phrase and senatorial tone,
Like thy renowned forefathers, far and wide
  Thy fame diffuse, praised not for utterance meet
    Of *others'* speech, but magic of *thy own.*

1788.

ON MRS. MONTAGU'S FEATHER-HANGINGS.

THE birds put off their every hue,
To dress a room for Montagu :
The peacock sends his heavenly dyes,
His rainbows and his starry eyes ;
The pheasant plumes, which round infold
His mantling neck with downy gold ;
The cock his arched tail's azure show ;
And, river-blanched, the swan his snow ;
All tribes beside of Indian name,
That glossy shine, or vivid flame,
Where rises and where sets the day,
Whate'er they boast of rich and gay,
Contribute to the gorgeous plan,
Proud to advance it all they can.
This plumage neither dashing shower,
Nor blasts, that shake the dripping bower,
Shall drench again or discompose,
But, screened from every storm that blows,
It boasts a splendour ever new,
Safe with protecting Montagu.
　To the same Patroness resort,
Secure of favour at her court,
Strong Genius, from whose forge of thought
Forms rise, to quick perfection wrought,
Which, though new-born, with vigour move,
Like Pallas springing armed from Jove—
Imagination scattering round
Wild roses over furrowed ground,
Which Labour of his frown beguile,
And teach Philosophy a smile—
Wit flashing on Religion's side,
Whose fires, to sacred Truth applied,
The gem, though luminous before,
Obtrude on human notice more,
Like sunbeams on the golden height
Of some tall temple playing bright—
Well tutored Learning, from his books
Dismissed with grave, not haughty, looks,
Their order on his shelves exact,
Not more harmonious or compact
Than that, to which he keeps confined
The various treasures of his mind—
All these to Montagu's repair,
Ambitious of a shelter there.
There Genius, Learning, Fancy, Wit,
Their ruffled plumage calm refit,
(For stormy troubles loudest roar
Around their flight who highest soar,)

And in her eye, and by her aid,
Shine safe without a fear to fade.
    She thus maintains divided sway
With yon bright regent of the day ;
The plume and poet both, we know,
Their lustre to his influence owe ;
And she the works of Phœbus aiding,
Both poet saves and plume from fading.

1788.

THE NEGRO'S COMPLAINT.

FORCED from home and all its pleasures,
    Afric's coast I left forlorn,
To increase a stranger's treasures,
    O'er the raging billows borne.
Men from England bought and sold me,
    Paid my price in paltry gold ;
But, though slave they have enrolled me,
    Minds are never to be sold.

Still in thought as free as ever,
    What are England's rights, I ask,
Me from my delights to sever,
    Me to torture, me to task ?
Fleecy locks and black complexion
    Cannot forfeit Nature's claim ;
Skins may differ, but affection
    Dwells in white and black the same

Why did all-creating Nature
    Make the plant for which we toil ?
Sighs must fan it, tears must water,
    Sweat of ours must dress the soil.
Think, ye masters iron-hearted,
    Lolling at your jovial boards,
Think how many backs have smarted,
    For the sweets your cane affords.

Is there,—as ye sometimes tell us,—
    Is there One who reigns on high ?
Has He bid you buy and sell us,
    Speaking from his throne, the sky ?

1788.

Ask Him, if your knotted scourges,
    Matches, blood-extorting screws,
Are the means that duty urges
    Agents of his will to use ?

Hark ! He answers !—Wild tornadoes
    Strewing yonder sea with wrecks,
Wasting towns, plantations, meadows,
    Are the voice with which He speaks.
He, foreseeing what vexations
    Afric's sons should undergo,
Fixed their tyrants' habitations
    Where his whirlwinds answer—"No."

By our blood in Afric wasted,
    Ere our necks received the chain ;
By the miseries that we tasted,
    Crossing in your barks the main ;
By our sufferings, since ye brought us
    To the man-degrading mart,
All sustained by patience, taught us
    Only by a broken heart ;

Deem our nation brutes no longer,
    Till some reason ye shall find
Worthier of regard and stronger
    Than the colour of our kind.
Slaves of gold, whose sordid dealings
    Tarnish all your boasted powers,
Prove that you have human feelings,
    Ere you proudly question ours !

PITY FOR POOR AFRICANS.

Video meliora proboque,
Deteriora sequor. ——

I OWN I am shocked at the purchase of slaves,
And fear those who buy them and sell them are knaves;
What I hear of their hardships, their tortures, and groans
Is almost enough to draw pity from stones.

I pity them greatly, but I must be mum,
For how could we do without sugar and rum?
Especially sugar, so needful we see;
What! give up our desserts, our coffee, and tea?

Besides, if we do, the French, Dutch, and Danes,
Will heartily thank us, no doubt, for our pains:
If we do not buy the poor creatures, they will;
And tortures and groans will be multiplied still.

If foreigners likewise would give up the trade,
Much more in behalf of your wish might be said;
But while they get riches by purchasing blacks,
Pray tell me why we may not also go snacks?

Your scruples and arguments bring to my mind
A story so pat, you may think it is coined,
On purpose to answer you, out of my mint;
But I can assure you I saw it in print.

A youngster at school, more sedate than the rest,
Had once his integrity put to the test;
His comrades had plotted an orchard to rob,
And asked him to go and assist in the job.

He was shocked, sir, like you, and answered—" Oh, no!
What! rob our good neighbour? I pray you don't go;
Besides, the man's poor, his orchard's his bread:
Then think of his children, for they must be fed."

" You speak very fine, and you look very grave,
But apples we want, and apples we'll have:
If you will go with us, you shall have a share;
If not, you shall have neither apple nor pear."

They spoke, and Tom pondered—" I see they will go:
Poor man! what a pity to injure him so!
Poor man! I would save him his fruit if I could,
But staying behind will do him no good.

" If the matter depended alone upon me,
His apples might hang till they dropped from the tree;
But since they will take them, I think I'll go too;
He will lose none by me, though I get a few."

His scruples thus silenced, Tom felt more at ease,
And went with his comrades the apples to seize;
He blamed and protested, but joined in the plan;
He shared in the plunder, but pitied the man.

THE MORNING DREAM.

'TWAS in the glad season of spring,
  Asleep at the dawn of the day,
I dreamed what I cannot but sing,
  So pleasant it seemed as I lay.
I dreamed that, on ocean afloat,
  Far hence to the westward I sailed,
While the billows high-lifted the boat,
  And the fresh-blowing breeze never failed.

In the steerage a woman I saw;
  Such at least was the form that she wore,
Whose beauty impressed me with awe,
  Never taught me by woman before.
She sat, and a shield at her side
  Shed light, like a sun on the waves,
And smiling divinely, she cried—
  " I go to make freemen of slaves."

Then raising her voice to a strain
  The sweetest that ear ever heard,
She sang of the slave's broken chain
  Wherever her glory appeared.
Some clouds, which had over us hung,
  Fled, chased by her melody clear,
And methought while she liberty sung,
  'Twas liberty only to hear.

Thus swiftly dividing the flood,
  To a slave-cultured island we came,
Where a Demon, her enemy, stood—
  Oppression his terrible name.
In his hand, as the sign of his sway,
  A scourge hung with lashes he bore,
And stood looking out for his prey
  From Africa's sorrowful shore.

But soon as approaching the land,
  That goddess-like woman he viewed,
The scourge he let fall from his hand,
  With blood of his subjects imbrued.
I saw him both sicken and die,
  And, the moment the monster expired,
Heard shouts that ascended the sky,
  From thousands with rapture inspired.

Awaking, how could I but muse
  At what such a dream should betide?
But soon my ear caught the glad news,
  Which served my weak thought for a guide,—
That Britannia, renowned o'er the waves
  For the hatred she ever has shown
To the black-sceptred rulers of slaves,
  Resolves to have none of her own.

ON A MISCHIEVOUS BULL,

WHICH THE OWNER OF HIM SOLD AT THE AUTHOR'S INSTANCE.

Go! thou art all unfit to share
  The pleasures of this place
With such as its old tenants are,
  Creatures of gentler race.

The squirrel here his hoard provides,
  Aware of wintry storms,
And woodpeckers explore the sides
  Of rugged oaks for worms.

The sheep here smooths the knotted
        thorn
    With frictions of her fleece ;
And here I wander eve and morn,
    Like her, a friend to peace.

Ah ! I could pity thee exiled
    From this secure retreat—
I would not lose it to be styled
    The happiest of the great.

But thou canst taste no calm delight ;
    Thy pleasure is to show
Thy magnanimity in fight,
    Thy prowess ; therefore go !

I care not whether east or north,
    So I no more may find thee ;
The angry Muse thus sings thee forth,
    And claps the gate behind thee.

ANNUS MEMORABILIS, 1789.

WRITTEN IN COMMEMORATION OF HIS MAJESTY'S HAPPY RECOVERY.

I RANSACKED, for a theme of song,
Much ancient chronicle, and long ;
I read of bright embattled fields,
Of trophied helmets, spears, and shields,
Of chiefs, whose single arm could boast
Prowess to dissipate a host :
Through tomes of fable and of dream
I sought an eligible theme,
But none I found, or found them shared
Already by some happier bard.
    To modern times, with Truth to
        guide
My busy search, I next applied ;
Here cities won, and fleets dispersed,
Urged loud a claim to be rehearsed,
Deeds of unperishing renown,
Our fathers' triumphs and our own.
    Thus, as the bee, from bank to bower,
Assiduous sips at every flower,
But rests on none till that be found
Where most nectareous sweets abound,
So I from theme to theme displayed
In many a page historic strayed,
Siege after siege, fight after fight,
Contemplating with small delight
(For feats of sanguinary hue
Not always glitter in my view) ;
Till settling on the current year,
I found the far-sought treasure near ;
A theme for poetry divine,
A theme to ennoble even mine,
In memorable Eighty-nine.
    The spring of Eighty-nine shall be
An era cherished long by me,
Which joyful I will oft record,
And thankful, at my frugal board ;
For then the clouds of Eighty-eight,

That threatened England's trembling
        state
With loss of what she least could spare,
Her sovereign's tutelary care,
One breath of Heaven, that cried—
        " Restore ! "
Chased, never to assemble more :
And far the richest crown on earth,
If valued by its wearer's worth,
The symbol of a righteous reign,
Sat fast on George's brows again.
    Then peace and joy again possessed
Our Queen's long-agitated breast ;
Such joy and peace as can be known
By sufferers like herself alone,
Who losing, or supposing lost,
The good on earth they valued most,
For that dear sorrow's sake forego
All hope of happiness below,
Then suddenly regain the prize,
And flash thanksgivings to the skies !
    O Queen of Albion, queen of isles !
Since all thy tears were changed to smiles,
The eyes that never saw thee, shine
With joy not unallied to thine,
Transports not chargeable with art
Illume the land's remotest part,
And strangers to the air of courts,
Both in their toils and at their sports,
The happiness of answered prayers,
That gilds thy features, show in theirs.
If they who on thy state attend,
Awe-struck, before thy presence bend,
'Tis but the natural effect
Of grandeur that ensures respect ;
But she is something more than queen
Who is beloved where never seen.

EPIGRAM.

(PRINTED IN THE "NORTHAMPTON MERCURY.")

To purify their wine some people bleed
A lamb into the barrel, and succeed ;
No nostrum, planters say, is half so good
To make fine sugar as a *negro's* blood.
Now *lambs* and *negroes* both are harmless things,
And thence perhaps this wondrous virtue springs.
'Tis in the blood of innocence alone—
Good cause why planters never try their own.

HYMN,

FOR THE USE OF THE SUNDAY SCHOOL AT OLNEY.

HEAR, Lord, the song of praise and
    prayer,
  In heaven thy dwelling-place,
From infants made the public care,
  And taught to seek thy face.

Thanks for thy Word, and for thy day ;
  And grant us, we implore,
Never to waste in sinful play
  Thy holy sabbaths more.

Thanks that we hear,—but oh, impart
  To each desires sincere,
That we may listen with our heart,
  And learn as well as hear !

    1789.

For if vain thoughts the minds engage
  Of older far than we,
What hope, that, at our heedless age,
  Our minds should e'er be free ?

Much hope, if thou our spirits take
  Under thy gracious sway,
Who canst the wisest wiser make,
  And babes as wise as they.

Wisdom and bliss thy word bestows,
  A sun that ne'er declines,
And be thy mercies showered on those
  Who placed us where it shines.

STANZAS

SUBJOINED TO THE YEARLY BILL OF MORTALITY OF THE PARISH OF ALL SAINTS, NORTHAMPTON ;

FOR THE YEAR 1787.

> Pallida Mors æquo pulsat pede pauperum tabernas
>   Regumque turres.—HORACE.
> Pale Death with equal foot strikes wide the door
> Of royal halls and hovels of the poor.

WHILE thirteen moons saw smoothly run
  The Nen's barge-laden wave,
All these, life's rambling journey done,
  Have found their home, the grave.

Was man (frail always) made more frail
  Than in foregoing years ?

Did famine or did plague prevail,
  That so much death appears ?

No : these were vigorous as their sires,
  Nor plague nor famine came ;
This annual tribute Death requires,
  And never waives his claim.

Like crowded forest-trees we stand,
  And some are marked to fall ;
The axe will smite at God's command,
  And soon shall smite us all.

Green as the bay-tree, ever green,
  With its new foliage on,
The gay, the thoughtless, have I seen ;
  I passed—and they were gone.

Read, ye that run, the awful truth
  With which I charge my page ;
A worm is in the bud of youth,
  And at the root of age.

No present health can health ensure
  For yet an hour to come ;
No medicine, though it oft can cure,
  Can always balk the tomb.

And oh ! that humble as my lot,
  And scorned as is my strain,
These truths, though known, too much forgot,
  I may not teach in vain.

So prays your Clerk with all his heart,
  And ere he quits the pen,
Begs *you* for once to take *his* part,
  And answer all—" Amen ! "

ON A SIMILAR OCCASION,

FOR THE YEAR 1788.

> Quod adest, memento
> Componere æquus. Cætera fluminis
> Ritu feruntur.—HORACE.

> Improve the present hour, or all beside
> Is a mere feather on a torrent's tide.

COULD I, from heaven inspired, as sure presage
To whom the rising year shall prove his last,
As I can number in my punctual page,
And item down the victims of the past ;

How each would trembling wait the mournful sheet,
On which the press might stamp him next to die ;
And reading here his sentence, how replete
With anxious meaning, heavenward turn his eye !

Time then would seem more precious than the joys
In which he sports away the treasure now ;
And prayer more seasonable than the noise
Of drunkards, or the music-drawing bow.

Then doubtless many a trifler, on the brink
Of this world's hazardous and headlong shore,
Forced to a pause, would feel it good to think,
Told that his setting sun must rise no more.

Ah, self-deceived ! Could I, prophetic, say
Who next is fated, and who next to fall,
The rest might then seem privileged to play ;
But naming none, the Voice now speaks to ALL.

Observe the dappled foresters, how light
They bound, and airy, o'er the sunny glade—
One falls—the rest, wide-scattered with affright,
Vanish at once into the darkest shade.

Had we their wisdom, should we, often warned,
Still need repeated warnings, and at last,
A thousand awful admonitions scorned,
Die self-accused of life run all to waste?

Sad waste ! for which no after-thrift atones :
The grave admits no cure for guilt or sin ;
Dewdrops may deck the turf that hides the bones,
But tears of godly grief ne'er flow within.

Learn then, ye living ! by the mouths be taught
Of all these sepulchres, instructors true,
That, soon or late, death also is your lot,
And the next opening grave may yawn for you.

ON A SIMILAR OCCASION,

FOR THE YEAR 1789.

Placidaque ibi demum morte quievit.—VIRGIL.
There calm at length he breathed his soul away.

" O MOST delightful hour by man
  Experienced here below,
The hour that terminates his span,
  His folly, and his woe !

" Worlds should not bribe me back to
    tread
  Again life's dreary waste,
To see again my day o'erspread
  With all the gloomy past.

" My home henceforth is in the skies—
  Earth, seas, and sun adieu !
All heaven unfolded to my eyes,
  I have no sight for you."

So spake Aspasio, firm possessed
  Of faith's supporting rod,
Then breathed his soul into its rest,
  The bosom of his God.

He was a man among the few
  Sincere on virtue's side ;

And all his strength from Scripture
    drew,
  To hourly use applied.

That rule he prized, by that he feared,
  He hated, hoped, and loved ;
Nor ever frowned, or sad appeared,
  But when his heart had roved.

For he was frail as thou or I,
  And evil felt within :
But when he felt it, heaved a sigh,
  And loathed the thought of sin.

Such lived Aspasio ; and at last,
  Called up from earth to heaven,
The gulf of death triumphant passed,
  By gales of blessing driven.

"*His* joys be *mine*," each reader cries,
  " When my last hour arrives ! "
" They shall be yours," my Verse replies,
  " Such only be your lives."

ON A SIMILAR OCCASION,

FOR THE YEAR 1790.

Ne commonentem recta sperne.—BUCHANAN.
Despise not my good counsel.

He who sits from day to day
　　Where the prisoned lark is hung,
Heedless of his loudest lay,
　　Hardly knows that he has sung.

Where the watchman in his round
　　Nightly lifts his voice on high,
None, accustomed to the sound,
　　Wakes the sooner for his cry.

So your verse-man I, and clerk,
　　Yearly in my song proclaim
Death at hand—yourselves his mark—
　　And the foe's unerring aim.

Duly at my time I come,
　　Publishing to all aloud—
Soon the grave must be your home,
　　And your only suit a shroud.

But the monitory strain,
　　Oft repeated in your ears,

Seems to sound too much in vain,
　　Wins no notice, wakes no fears.

Can a truth, by all confessed
　　Of such magnitude and weight,
Grow, by being oft expressed,
　　Trivial as a parrot's prate?

Pleasure's call attention wins,
　　Hear it often as we may;
New as ever seem our sins,
　　Though committed every day.

Death and Judgment, Heaven and
　　Hell—
These alone, so often heard,
No more move us than the bell
　　When some stranger is interred.

Oh then, ere the turf or tomb
　　Cover us from every eye,
Spirit of instruction! come
　　Make us learn that we must die.

ON A SIMILAR OCCASION,

FOR THE YEAR 1792.

Felix, qui potuit rerum cognoscere causas,
Atque metus omnes et inexorabile fatum
Subjecit pedibus, strepitumque Acherontis avari!—VIRG.

Happy the mortal who has traced effects
To their first cause, cast fear beneath his feet,
And death, and roaring hell's voracious fires!

Thankless for favours from on high,
　　Man thinks he fades too soon;
Though 'tis his privilege to die,
　　Would he improve the boon.

But he, not wise enough to scan
　　His best concerns aright,
Would gladly stretch life's little span
　　To ages, if he might.

To ages in a world of pain,
　　To ages, where he goes
Galled by affliction's heavy chain,
　　And hopeless of repose.

Strange fondness of the human heart,
　　Enamoured of its harm!
Strange world, that costs it so much
　　smart,
　　And still has power to charm.

Whence has the world her magic power?
    Why deem we Death a foe?
Recoil from weary life's best hour,
    And covet longer woe?

The cause is Conscience;—Conscience oft
    Her tale of guilt renews:
Her voice is terrible, though soft,
    And dread of Death ensues.

Then, anxious to be longer spared,
    Man mourns his fleeting breath:

And evils then seem light, compared
    With the approach of Death.

'Tis judgment shakes him; there's the fear
    That prompts the wish to stay:
He has incurred a long arrear,
    And must despair to pay.

Pay!—follow Christ, and all is paid:
    His death your peace ensures;
Think on the grave where *He* was laid,
    And calm descend to *yours*.

ON A SIMILAR OCCASION,

FOR THE YEAR 1793.

De sacris autem hæc sit una sententia, ut conserventur.—Cic. *de Leg.*

But let us all concur in this one sentiment, that things sacred be inviolate.

HE lives who lives to God, alone,
    And all are dead beside;
For other source than God is none
    Whence life can be supplied.

To live to God is to requite
    His love as best we may;
To make His precepts our delight,
    His promises our stay.

But life, within a narrow ring
    Of giddy joys comprised,
Is falsely named, and no such thing,
    But rather death disguised.

Can life in them deserve the name,
    Who only live to prove
For what poor toys they can disclaim
    An endless life above?

Who, much diseased, yet nothing feel;
    Much menaced, nothing dread;
Have wounds which only God can heal,
    Yet never ask His aid?

Who deem His house a useless place,
    Faith, want of common sense,
And ardour in the Christian race
    A hypocrite's pretence?

Who trample order; and the day
    Which God asserts His own
Dishonour with unhallowed play,
    And worship Chance alone?

If scorn of God's commands, impressed
    On word and deed, imply
The better part of man unblessed
    With life that cannot die;

Such want it: and that want, uncured
    Till man resigns his breath,
Speaks him a criminal, assured
    Of everlasting death.

Sad period to a pleasant course!
    Yet so will God repay
Sabbaths profaned without remorse,
    And Mercy cast away.

C

IMPROMPTU,

ON WRITING A LETTER WITHOUT HAVING ANYTHING TO SAY.

So have I seen the maids in vain
Tumble and tease a tangled skein ;
They bite the lip and scratch the head,
And cry, " The deuce is in the thread ! "
They torture it and jerk it round,
Till the right end at last is found ;
Then wind, and wind, and wind away,
And what was work is changed to play.

ON THE QUEEN'S VISIT TO LONDON,

THE NIGHT OF THE 17TH MARCH, 1789.

WHEN, long sequestered from his throne,
    George took his seat again,
By right of worth, not blood alone,
    Entitled here to reign ;

Then Loyalty, with all her lamps
    New trimmed, a gallant show,
Chasing the darkness and the damps,
    Set London in a glow.

'Twas hard to tell of streets or squares
    Which formed the chief display ;
These most resembling clustered stars,
    Those the long milky way.

Bright shone the roofs, the domes, the spires,
    And rockets flew, self-driven,
To hang their momentary fires
    Amid the vault of heaven.

So, fire with water to compare,
    The ocean serves, on high
Up-spouted by a whale in air,
    To express unwieldy joy.

Had all the pageants of the world
    In one procession joined,
And all the banners been unfurled
    That heralds e'er designed,

For no such sight had England's Queen
    Forsaken her retreat,
Where George recovered made a scene,
    Sweet always, doubly sweet.

Yet glad she came that night to prove,
    A witness undescried,
How much the object of her love
    Was loved by all beside.

Darkness the skies had mantled o'er
    In aid of her design,—
Darkness, O Queen ! ne'er called before
    To veil a deed of thine.

On borrowed wheels away she flies,
    Resolved to be unknown,
And gratify no curious eyes
    That night, except her own.

Arrived, a night like noon she sees,
    And hears the million hum ;
As all by instinct, like the bees,
    Had known their sovereign come.

Pleased she beheld aloft portrayed,
    On many a splendid wall,
Emblems of health and heavenly aid,
    And George the theme of all :

Unlike the enigmatic line,
    So difficult to spell,
Which shook Belshazzar at his wine
    The night his city fell.

Soon, watery grew her eyes and dim,
    But with a joyful tear :
None else, except in prayer for him,
    George ever drew from her.

t was a scene in every part
  Like those in fable feigned,
And seemed by some magician's art
  Created and sustained.

But other magic there, she knew,
  Had been exerted none,
To raise such wonders in her view,
  Save love of George alone.

That cordial thought her spirits cheered,
  And through the cumbrous throng,
Not else unworthy to be feared,
  Conveyed her calm along.

So, ancient poets say, serene
  The sea-maid rides the waves,
And fearless of the billowy scene
  Her peaceful bosom laves.

With more than astronomic eyes
  She viewed the sparkling show ;
One Georgian star adorns the skies,
  She myriads found below.

Yet let the glories of a night
  Like that, once seen, suffice ;
Heaven grant us no such future sight,
  Such previous woe the price !

THE COCK-FIGHTER'S GARLAND.

MUSE, hide his name of whom I sing,
  Lest his surviving house thou bring
    For his sake into scorn ;
Nor speak the school from which he
      drew
  The much or little that he knew,
    Nor place where he was born.

That such a man once was, may seem
  Worthy of record (if the theme
    Perchance may credit win),
For proof to man what man may prove,
  Ere grace depart, and demons move
    The source of guilt within.

This man (for since the howling wild
  Disclaims him, man he must be styled)
    Wanted no good below ;
Gentle he was, if gentle birth
  Could make him such ; and he had worth,
    If wealth can worth bestow.

In social talk and ready jest
  He shone superior at the feast,
    And qualities of mind
Illustrious in the eyes of those
  Whose gay society he chose
    Possessed of every kind.

Methinks I see him powdered red,
  With bushy locks his well-dressed head
    Winged broad on either side,

The mossy rosebud not so sweet ;
His steeds superb, his carriage neat
    As luxury could provide.

Can such be cruel ? Such can be
Cruel as hell, and so was he ;
    A tyrant entertained
With barbarous sports, whose fell delight
Was to encourage mortal fight
    'Twixt birds to battle trained.

One feathered champion he possessed,
His darling far beyond the rest,
    Which never knew disgrace,
Nor e'er had fought but he made flow
The life-blood of his fiercest foe,
    The Cæsar of his race.

It chanced at last, when on a day
He pushed him to the desperate fray,
    His courage drooped, he fled.
The master stormed, the prize was lost,
And, instant, frantic at the cost,
    He doomed his favourite dead.

He seized him fast, and from the pit
Flew to the kitchen, snatched the spit,
    And " Bring me cord ! " he cried :
The cord was brought, and, at his word,
To that dire implement the bird
    Alive and struggling tied.

B B 2

The horrid sequel asks a veil,
And all the terrors of the tale
    That can be, shall be, sunk.
Led by the sufferer's screams aright,
His shocked companions view the sight
    And him with fury drunk.

All, suppliant, beg a milder fate
For the old warrior at the grate :
    He, deaf to pity's call,
Whirled round him rapid as a wheel
His culinary club of steel,
    Death menacing on all.

May, 1789.

But Vengeance hung not far remote,
For while he stretched his clamorou
    throat,
    And heaven and earth defied,
Big with the curse too closely pent
That struggled vainly for a vent,
    He tottered, reeled, and died.

'Tis not for us, with rash surmise,
To point the judgments of the skies ;
    But judgments plain as this,
That, sent for Man's instruction, bring
A written label on their wing,
    'Tis hard to read amiss.

LINES AFTER THE MANNER OF HOMER,

DESCRIPTIVE OF THE OPENING OF A HAMPER.

THE straw-stuffed hamper with his ruthless steel
He opened, cutting sheer the inserted cords
Which bound the lid and lip secure.   Forth came
The rustling package ; first, bright straw of wheat,
Or oats, or barley; next a bottle, green,
Throat-full, clear spirits the contents, distilled
Drop after drop odorous, by the art
Of the fair mother of his friend—the Rose.

Sept. 11, 1789.

ON THE

BENEFIT RECEIVED BY HIS MAJESTY FROM SEA-BATHIN(

IN THE YEAR 1789.

O SOVEREIGN of an isle renowned
    For undisputed sway,
Wherever o'er yon gulf profound
    Her navies wing their way ;

With juster claim she builds at length
    Her empire on the sea,
And well may boast the waves her strength,
    Which strength restored to thee.

TO MRS. THROCKMORTON,

ON HER BEAUTIFUL TRANSCRIPT OF HORACE'S ODE "AD LIBRUM SUUM."

MARIA, could Horace have guessed
    What honour awaited his ode
To his own little volume addressed,
    The honour which you have bestowed,
Who have traced it in characters here,
    So elegant, even, and neat,
He had laughed at the critical sneer
    Which he seems to have trembled to meet.

" And sneer, if you please," he had said,
    " Hereafter a nymph shall arise
" Who shall give me, when you are all dead,
    " The glory your malice denies ;
" Shall dignity give to my lay,
    " Although but a mere bagatelle ;
" And even a poet shall say,
    " Nothing ever was written so well."

Feb. 1790.

INSCRIPTION

FOR A STONE ERECTED AT THE SOWING OF A GROVE OF OAKS AT
CHILLINGTON, THE SEAT OF T. GIFFARD, ESQ. 1790.

OTHER stones the era tell
When some feeble mortal fell ;
I stand here to date the birth
Of these hardy sons of earth.
    Which shall longest brave the sky,
Storm and frost—these Oaks or I ?
Pass an age or two away,
I must moulder and decay ;
But the years that crumble me
Shall invigorate the tree,
Spread its branch, dilate its size,
Lift its summit to the skies.
    Cherish honour, virtue, truth,
So shalt thou prolong thy youth :
Wanting these, however fast
Man be fixed, and formed to last,
He is lifeless even now,
Stone at heart, and cannot grow.

June, 1790

*

ANOTHER,

FOR A STONE ERECTED ON A SIMILAR OCCASION AT THE SAME PLACE IN
THE FOLLOWING YEAR.

Reader ! behold a monument
That asks no sigh or tear,
Though it perpetuate the event
Of a great burial here.

Anno 1791.

TO MRS. KING,

ON HER KIND PRESENT TO THE AUTHOR, A PATCHWORK QUILT OF
HER OWN MAKING.

THE Bard, if e'er he feel at all,
Must sure be quickened by a call
　　Both on his heart and head,
To pay with tuneful thanks the care
And kindness of a lady fair
　　Who deigns to deck his bed.

A bed like this, in ancient time,
On Ida's barren top sublime,
　　(As Homer's Epic shows),
Composed of sweetest vernal flowers,
Without the aid of sun or showers,
　　For Jove and Juno rose.

Less beautiful, however gay,
Is that which in the scorching day
　　Receives the weary swain,
Who, laying his long scythe aside,
Sleeps on some bank with daisies pied,
　　Till roused to toil again.

August 14, 1790.

What labours of the loom I see !
Looms numberless have groaned for me
　　Should every maiden come
To scramble for the patch that bears
The impress of the robe she wears,
　　The bell would toll for some.

And oh, what havoc would ensue !
This bright display of every hue
　　All in a moment fled !
As if a storm should strip the bowers
Of all their tendrils, leaves, and flowers,—
　　Each pocketing a shred.

Thanks, then, to every gentle fair,
Who will not come to peck me bare
　　As bird of borrowed feather,
And thanks to one, above them all,
The gentle fair of Pertenhall,
　　Who put the whole together.

STANZAS

ON THE LATE INDECENT LIBERTIES TAKEN WITH THE REMAINS OF THE
GREAT MILTON, ANNO 1790.

" ME too, perchance, in future days,
　" The sculptured stone shall show,
" With Paphian myrtle, or with bays
　" Parnassian on my brow.

      " But I, or ere that season come,
        " Escaped from every care,
      " Shall reach my refuge in the tomb,
        " And sleep securely there." *

    So sang, in Roman tone and style,
      The youthful bard, ere long
    Ordained to grace his native isle
      With her sublimest song.

    Who then but must conceive disdain,
      Hearing the deed unblest
    Of wretches who have dared profane
      His dread sepulchral rest ?

    Ill fare the hands that heaved the stones
      Where Milton's ashes lay,
    That trembled not to grasp his bones
      And steal his dust away !

    O ill-requited bard ! neglect
      Thy living worth repaid,
    And blind idolatrous respect
      As much affronts thee dead.

August, 1790.

IN MEMORY OF THE LATE JOHN THORNTON, ESQ.

POETS attempt the noblest task they can,
Praising the Author of all good in man,
And, next, commemorating worthies lost,
The dead in whom that good abounded most.
    Thee, therefore, of commercial fame, but more
Famed for thy probity from shore to shore ;
Thee, THORNTON ! worthy in some page to shine,
As honest and more eloquent than mine,
I mourn ; or, since thrice happy thou must be,
The world no longer thy abode, not thee.
Thee to deplore were grief misspent indeed ;
It were to weep that goodness has its meed,
That there is bliss prepared in yonder sky,
And glory, for the virtuous when they die.
    What pleasure can the miser's fondled hoard
Or spendthrift's prodigal excess afford,
Sweet as the privilege of healing woe
By virtue suffered combating below ?

---

   * Forsitan et nostros ducat de marmore vultus
    Nectens aut Paphia myrti aut Parnasside lauri
    Fronde comas—At ego securâ pace quiescam.
                MILTON *in Manso.*

That privilege was thine ; Heaven gave thee means
To illumine with delight the saddest scenes,
Till thy appearance chased the gloom, forlorn
As midnight, and despairing of a morn.
Thou hadst an industry in doing good,
Restless as his who toils and sweats for food ;
Avarice in thee was the desire of wealth
By rust unperishable or by stealth ;
And if the genuine worth of gold depend
On application to its noblest end,
Thine had a value in the scales of Heaven,
Surpassing all that mine or mint had given.
And, though God made thee of a nature prone
To distribution boundless of thy own,
And still by motives of religious force
Impelled thee more to that heroic course,
Yet was thy liberality discreet,
Nice in its choice, and of a tempered heat,
And though in act unwearied, secret still,
As in some solitude the summer rill
Refreshes, where it winds, the faded green,
And cheers the drooping flowers, unheard, unseen.
  Such was thy charity; no sudden start,
After long sleep, of passion in the heart,
But steadfast principle, and, in its kind,
Of close relation to the Eternal Mind,
Traced easily to its true source above,
To Him whose works bespeak His nature Love.
  Thy bounties all were Christian, and I make
This record of thee for the Gospel's sake :
That the incredulous themselves may see
Its use and power exemplified in thee.

November, 1790.

TO REV. WALTER BAGOT.

EXCUSE FOR DELAY IN WRITING TO HIM.

IT is a maxim of much weight,
  Worth conning o'er and o'er,
He who has Homer to translate,
  Had need do nothing more.

February 26, 1791.

THE FOUR AGES ;

A BRIEF FRAGMENT OF AN EXTENSIVE PROJECTED POEM.

" I COULD be well content, allowed the use
  Of past experience, and the wisdom gleaned
From worn-out follies, now acknowledged such,
To recommence life's trial, in the hope
Of fewer errors, on a second proof ! "

Thus, while grey evening lulled the wind, and called
Fresh odours from the shrubbery at my side,
Taking my lonely winding walk, I mused,
And held accustomed conference with my heart ;
When from within it thus a voice replied :
" Couldst thou in truth ? and art thou taught at length
This wisdom, and but this, from all the past ?
Is not the pardon of thy long arrear,
Time wasted, violated laws, abuse
Of talents, judgments, mercies, better far
Than opportunity vouchsafed to err
With less excuse, and, haply, worse effect ? "
   I heard, and acquiesced : then to and fro
Oft pacing, as the mariner his deck,
My gravelly bounds, from self to human kind
I passed, and next considered, What is man ?
   Knows he his origin ? can he ascend
By reminiscence to his earliest date ?
Slept he in Adam ? and in those from him
Through numerous generations, till he found
At length his destined moment to be born ?
Or was he not, till fashioned in the womb ?
Deep mysteries both ! which schoolmen must have toiled
To unriddle, and have left them mysteries still.
   It is an evil incident to man,
And of the worst, that unexplored he leaves
Truths useful and attainable with ease,
To search forbidden deeps, where mystery lies
Not to be solved, and useless if it might.
Mysteries are food for angels ; they digest
With ease, and find them nutriment ; but man,
While yet he dwells below, must stoop to glean
His manna from the ground, or starve, and die.

*   *   *

May, 1791.

THE JUDGMENT OF THE POETS.

Two nymphs, both nearly of an age,
  Of numerous charms possessed,
A warm dispute once chanced to wage
  Whose temper was the best.

The worth of each had been complete
  Had both alike been mild ;
But one, although her smile was sweet,
  Frowned oftener than she smiled ;

And in her humour, when she frowned,
  Would raise her voice, and roar,
And shake with fury to the ground
  The garland that she wore.

The other was of gentler cast,
  From all such frenzy clear,
Her frowns were seldom known to last,
  And never proved severe.

To poets of renown in song
  The nymphs referred the cause,
Who, strange to tell, all judged it wrong,
  And gave misplaced applause.

They gentle called, and kind and soft,
  The flippant and the scold,
And though she changed her mood so oft,
  That failing left untold.

No judges, sure, were e'er so mad,
Or so resolved to err,—
In short, the charms her sister had
They lavished all on her.

Then thus the god, whom fondly they
Their great Inspirer call,
Was heard, one genial summer's day,
To reprimand them all.

May, 1791.

" Since thus ye have combined," he said,
" My favourite nymph to slight,
" Adorning May, that peevish maid,
" With June's undoubted right,

" The minx shall, for your folly's sake,
" Still prove herself a shrew,
" Shall make your scribbling fingers ache,
" And pinch your noses blue."

ON

THE REFUSAL OF THE UNIVERSITY OF OXFORD TO SUBSCRIBE
TO HIS TRANSLATION OF HOMER.

COULD Homer come himself, distressed and poor,
And tune his harp at Rhedycina's door,
The rich old vixen would exclaim (I fear)
" Begone ! no tramper gets a farthing here ! "

1791.

EPITAPH ON MRS. M. HIGGINS, OF WESTON.

LAURELS may flourish round the conqueror's tomb,
But happiest they who win the world to come :
Believers have a silent field to fight,
And their exploits are veiled from human sight.
They in some nook, where little known they dwell,
Kneel, pray in faith, and rout the hosts of hell ;
Eternal triumphs crown their toils divine,
And all those triumphs, Mary, now are thine.

1791.

THE RETIRED CAT.

A POET'S cat, sedate and grave
As poet well could wish to have,
Was much addicted to inquire
For nooks to which she might retire,
And where, secure as mouse in chink,
She might repose, or sit and think.
I know not where she caught the trick,—
Nature perhaps herself had cast her
In such a mould PHILOSOPHIQUE,
Or else she learned it of her master.

Sometimes ascending, debonair,
An apple-tree, or lofty pear,
Lodged with convenience in the fork,
She watched the gardener at his work ;
Sometimes her ease and solace sought
In an old empty watering-pot ;
There, wanting nothing save a fan
To seem some nymph in her sedan,
Apparelled in exactest sort,
And ready to be borne to court.

But love of change, it seems, has place
Not only in our wiser race ;
Cats also feel, as well as we,
That passion's force, and so did she.
Her climbing, she began to find,
Exposed her too much to the wind,
And the old utensil of tin
Was cold and comfortless within :
She therefore wished instead of those
Some place of more serene repose,
Where neither cold might come, nor air
Too rudely wanton with her hair,
And sought it in the likeliest mode
Within her master's snug abode.

A drawer, it chanced, at bottom lined
With linen of the softest kind,
With such as merchants introduce
From India, for the ladies' use—
A drawer impending o'er the rest,
Half open in the topmost chest,
Of depth enough, and none to spare,
Invited her to slumber there ;
Puss with delight beyond expression
Surveyed the scene, and took possession.
Recumbent at her ease ere long,
And lulled by her own humdrum song,
She left the cares of life behind,
And slept as she would sleep her last,
When in came, housewifely inclined,
The chambermaid, and shut it fast,
By no malignity impelled,
But all unconscious whom it held.

Awakened by the shock, cried Puss,
" Was ever cat attended thus !
" The open drawer was left, I see,
" Merely to prove a nest for me.
" For soon as I was well composed,
" Then came the maid, and it was closed.
" How smooth these 'kerchiefs, and how
        sweet !
" Oh, what a delicate retreat !
" I will resign myself to rest
" Till Sol, declining in the west,
" Shall call to supper, when, no doubt,
" Susan will come and let me out."

The evening came, the sun descended,
And puss remained still unattended.
The night rolled tardily away,
(With her indeed 'twas never day,)
The sprightly morn her course renewed,
The evening gray again ensued,

1791.

And puss came into mind no more
Than if entombed the day before.
With hunger pinched, and pinched for
        room,
She now presaged approaching doom,
Nor slept a single wink, or purred,
Conscious of jeopardy incurred.

That night, by chance, the poet
        watching,
Heard an inexplicable scratching ;
His noble heart went pit-a-pat,
And to himself he said—" What's that?"
He drew the curtain at his side,
And forth he peeped, but nothing spied ;
Yet, by his ear directed, guessed
Something imprisoned in the chest,
And, doubtful what, with prudent care
Resolved it should continue there.
At length, a voice which well he knew,
A long and melancholy mew,
Saluting his poetic ears,
Consoled him, and dispelled his fears ;
He left his bed, he trod the floor,
He 'gan in haste the drawers explore,
The lowest first, and without stop
The rest in order to the top ;
For 'tis a truth well known to most,
That whatsoever thing is lost,
We seek it, ere it come to light,
In every cranny but the right.
Forth skipped the cat, not now replete
As erst with airy self-conceit,
Nor in her own fond apprehension
A theme for all the world's attention,
But modest, sober, cured of all
Her notions hyperbolical,
And wishing for a place of rest
Anything rather than a chest.
Then stepped the poet into bed,
With this reflection in his head :

MORAL.

Beware of too sublime a sense
Of your own worth and consequence.
The man who dreams himself so great,
And his importance of such weight,
That all around in all that's done
Must move and act for him alone,
Will learn in school of tribulation
The folly of his expectation.

YARDLEY OAK.

SURVIVOR sole, and hardly such, of all
That once lived here, thy brethren !—at my birth
(Since which I number threescore winters past)
A shattered veteran, hollow-trunked perhaps,
As now, and with excoriate forks deform,
Relics of ages !—could a mind, imbued
With truth from Heaven, created thing adore,
I might with reverence kneel and worship thee.
     It seems idolatry with some excuse,
When our forefather Druids in their oaks
Imagined sanctity. The conscience, yet
Unpurified by an authentic act
Of amnesty, the meed of blood divine,
Loved not the light, but, gloomy, into gloom
Of thickest shades, like Adam after taste
Of fruit proscribed, as to a refuge, fled.
     Thou wast a bauble once ; a cup and ball,
Which babes might play with ; and the thievish jay,
Seeking her food, with ease might have purloined
The auburn nut that held thee, swallowing down
Thy yet close-folded latitude of boughs,
And all thine embryo vastness, at a gulp.
But fate thy growth decreed ; autumnal rains
Beneath thy parent tree mellowed the soil
Designed thy cradle ; and a skipping deer,
With pointed hoof dibbling the glebe, prepared
The soft receptacle, in which, secure,
Thy rudiments should sleep the winter through.
     So fancy dreams. Disprove it, if ye can,
Ye reasoners broad awake, whose busy search
Of argument, employed too oft amiss,
Sifts half the pleasures of short life away !
     Thou fell'st mature ; and in the loamy clod
Swelling with vegetative force instinct
Didst burst thine egg, as theirs the fabled Twins,
Now stars ; two lobes, protruding, paired exact ;
A leaf succeeded, and another leaf,
And, all the elements thy puny growth
Fostering propitious, thou becamest a twig.
     Who lived when thou wast such ? Oh, couldst thou speak,
As in Dodona once thy kindred trees
Oracular, I would not curious ask
The future, best unknown, but at thy mouth
Inquisitive, the less ambiguous past.
     By thee I might correct, erroneous oft,
The clock of history, facts and events
Timing more punctual, unrecorded facts
Recovering, and misstated setting right—
Desperate attempt, till trees shall speak again !

Time made thee what thou wast, king of the woods,
And Time hath made thee what thou art—a cave
For owls to roost in.   Once thy spreading boughs
O'erhung the champaign ; and the numerous flocks
That grazed it stood beneath that ample cope
Uncrowded, yet safe-sheltered from the storm.
No flock frequents thee now.   Thou hast outlived
Thy popularity, and art become
(Unless verse rescue thee awhile) a thing
Forgotten, as the foliage of thy youth.
   While thus through all the stages thou hast pushed
Of treeship—first a seedling, hid in grass ;
Then twig ; then sapling; and, as century rolled
Slow after century, a giant-bulk
Of girth enormous, with moss-cushioned root
Upheaved above the soil, and sides embossed
With prominent wens globose,—till at the last
The rottenness, which Time is charged to inflict
On other mighty ones, found also thee.
   What exhibitions various hath the world
Witnessed, of mutability in all
That we account most durable below !
Change is the diet on which all subsist,
Created changeable, and change at last
Destroys them.   Skies uncertain, now the heat
Transmitting cloudless, and the solar beam
Now quenching in a boundless sea of clouds,—
Calm and alternate storm, moisture and drought,
Invigorate by turns the springs of life
In all that live, plant, animal, and man,
And in conclusion mar them.   Nature's threads,
Fine passing thought, even in her coarsest works,
Delight in agitation, yet sustain
The force that agitates, not unimpaired ;
But, worn by frequent impulse, to the cause
Of their best tone their dissolution owe.
   Thought cannot spend itself, comparing still
The great and little of thy lot, thy growth
From almost nullity into a state
Of matchless grandeur, and declension thence,
Slow, into such magnificent decay.
Time was when, settling on thy leaf, a fly
Could shake thee to the root—and time has been
When tempests could not.   At thy firmest age
Thou hadst within thy bole solid contents,
That might have ribbed the sides and planked the deck
Of some flagged admiral ; and tortuous arms,
The shipwright's darling treasure, didst present
To the four-quartered winds, robust and bold,
Warped into tough knee-timber,* many a load !

* Knee-timber is found in the crooked arms of oak, which, by reason of their distortion, are casily adjusted to the angle formed where the deck and the ship's sides meet.

But the axe spared thee. In those thriftier days
Oaks fell not, hewn by thousands, to supply
The bottomless demands of contest waged
For senatorial honours. Thus to Time
The task was left to whittle thee away
With his sly scythe, whose ever-nibbling edge,
Noiseless, an atom, and an atom more,
Disjoining from the rest, has, unobserved,
Achieved a labour, which had, far and wide,
By man performed, made all the forest ring.
  Embowelled now, and of thy ancient self
Possessing nought but the scooped rind,— that seems
A huge throat calling to the clouds for drink,
Which it would give in rivulets to thy root,—
Thou temptest none, but rather much forbiddest
The feller's toil, which thou couldst ill requite.
Yet is thy root sincere, sound as the rock,
A quarry of stout spurs and knotted fangs,
Which, crooked into a thousand whimsies, clasp
The stubborn soil, and hold thee still erect.
  So stands a kingdom, whose foundation yet
Fails not, in virtue and in wisdom laid,
Though all the superstructure, by the tooth
Pulverized of venality, a shell
Stands now, and semblance only of itself !
  Thine arms have left thee. Winds have rent them off
Long since, and rovers of the forest wild
With bow and shaft have burnt them. Some have left
A splintered stump, bleached to a snowy white :
And some memorial none, where once they grew.
Yet life still lingers in thee, and puts forth
Proof not contemptible of what she can,
Even where death predominates. The Spring
Finds thee not less alive to her sweet force
Than yonder upstarts of the neighbouring wood,
So much thy juniors, who their birth received
Half a millennium since the date of thine.
  But since, although well qualified by age
To teach, no spirit dwells in thee, nor voice
May be expected from thee, seated here
On thy distorted root, with hearers none,
Or prompter, save the scene, I will perform
Myself the oracle, and will discourse
In my own ear such matter as I may.
  One man alone, the father of us all,
Drew not his life from woman ; never gazed,
With mute unconsciousness of what he saw,
On all around him ; learned not by degrees,
Nor owed articulation to his ear ;
But moulded by his Maker into man
At once, upstood intelligent, surveyed
All creatures, with precision understood

Their purport, uses, properties ; assigned
To each his name significant, and, filled
With love and wisdom, rendered back to Heaven
In praise harmonious the first air he drew.
He was excused the penalties of dull
Minority.   No tutor charged his hand
With the thought-tracing quill, or tasked his mind
With problems.   History, not wanted yet,
Leaned on her elbow, watching Time, whose course,
Eventful, should supply her with a theme.

     *   *   *   *

1791.

TO THE NIGHTINGALE

WHICH THE AUTHOR HEARD SING ON NEW YEAR'S DAY, 1792.

WHENCE is it, that amazed I hear
  From yonder withered spray,
This foremost morn of all the year,
  The melody of May?

And why, since thousands would be
      proud
  Of such a favour shown,
Am I selected from the crowd,
  To witness it alone?

Sing'st thou, sweet Philomel, to me,
  For that I also long
Have practised in the groves like thee,
  Though not like thee, in song?

Or sing'st thou rather, under force
  Of some divine command,
Commissioned to presage a course
  Of happier days at hand?

Thrice welcome then ! for many a long
  And joyless year have I,
As thou to-day, put forth my song
  Beneath a wintry sky.

But thee no wintry skies can harm,
  Who only need'st to sing,
To make even January charm,
  And every season Spring.

1792.

TO WARREN HASTINGS, ESQ.

BY AN OLD SCHOOLFELLOW OF HIS AT WESTMINSTER.

HASTINGS ! I knew thee young, and of a mind,
While young, humane, conversable, and kind ;
Nor can I well believe thee, gentle then,
Now grown a villain, and the worst of men ;
But rather some suspect who have oppressed
And worried thee, as not themselves the best.

1792.

LINES

WRITTEN FOR INSERTION IN A COLLECTION OF HANDWRITINGS AND
SIGNATURES, MADE BY MISS PATTY, SISTER OF HANNAH MORE.

IN vain to live from age to age
While modern bards endeavour,
I write my name in Patty's page,
And gain my point for ever.

March 6, 1792.   W. COWPER.

TO WILLIAM WILBERFORCE, ESQ.

THY country, Wilberforce, with just disdain,
Hears thee by cruel men and impious called
Fanatic, for thy zeal to loose the enthralled
From exile, public sale, and slavery's chain.
Friend of the poor, the wronged, the fetter-galled,
Fear not lest labour such as thine be vain!
Thou hast achieved a part ; hast gained the ear
Of Britain's senate to thy glorious cause.
Hope smiles, joy springs, and though cold caution pause
And weave delay, the better hour is near
That shall remunerate thy toils severe
By peace for Afric, fenced with British laws.
    Enjoy what thou hast won, esteem and love
    From all the just on earth and all the blest above.

April 16, 1792.

TO DR. AUSTEN, OF CECIL STREET, LONDON.

AUSTEN ! accept a grateful verse from me,
The poet's treasure, no inglorious fee.
Loved by the Muses, thy ingenuous mind
Pleasing requital in a verse may find ;
Verse oft has dashed the scythe of Time aside,
Immortalizing names which else had died.
And oh ! could I command the glittering wealth
With which sick kings are glad to purchase health,
Yet, if extensive fame, and sure to live,
Were in the power of verse like mine to give,
I would not recompense his heart with less,
Who, giving Mary health, heals my distress.
    Friend of my friend !* I love thee, though unknown,
    And boldly call thee, being his, my own.

May 26, 1792.   •

* Hayley.

EPITAPH ON A FREE BUT TAME REDBREAST,

A FAVOURITE OF MISS SALLY HURDIS.

THESE are not dew-drops, these are
tears,
 And tears by Sally shed
For absent Robin, who she fears,
 With too much cause, is dead.

One morn he came not to her hand
 As he was wont to come,
And, on her finger perched, to stand
 Picking his breakfast-crumb.

Alarmed she called him, and perplext
 She sought him, but in vain ;
That day he came not, nor the next,
 Nor ever came again.

March, 1792.

She therefore raised him here a tomb,
 Though where he fell, or how,
None knows, so secret was his doom,
 Nor where he moulders now.

Had half a score of coxcombs died
 In social Robin's stead,
Poor Sally's tears had soon been dried,
 Or haply never shed.

But Bob was neither rudely bold
 Nor spiritlessly tame,
Nor was, like theirs, his bosom cold,
 But always in a flame.

TRANSLATION OF A SIMILE IN PARADISE LOST.

So when, from mountain tops, the dusky clouds
Ascending, &c.—(li. 488.)

QUALES aërii montis de vertice nubes
Cum surgunt, et jam Boreæ tumida ora quiêrunt,
Cælum hilares abdit, spissâ caligine, vultus :
Tum si jucundo tandem sol prodeat ore,
Et croceo montes et pascua lumine tingat,
Gaudent omnia, aves mulcent concentibus agros,
Balatuque ovium colles vallesque resultant.

TO WILLIAM HAYLEY, ESQ.

HAYLEY, thy tenderness fraternal, shown,
In our first interview, delightful guest !
To Mary, and me for her dear sake distressed,
Such as it is has made my heart thy own,
Though heedless now of new engagements grown :
For threescore winters make a wintry breast,
And I had purposed ne'er to go in quest
Of Friendship more, except with God alone.
But thou hast won me : nor is God my foe,
Who, ere this last afflictive scene began,
Sent thee to mitigate the dreadful blow,
My brother, by whose sympathy I know
Thy true deserts infallibly to scan,
Not more to admire the Bard than love the Man.

June 2, 1792.

C C

C

CATHARINA:

THE SECOND PART.

ON HER MARRIAGE TO GEORGE COURTENAY, ESQ.

BELIEVE it or not, as you chuse,
  The doctrine is certainly true,
That the future is known to the Muse,
  And poets are oracles too.
I did but express a desire
  To see Catharina at home,
At the side of my friend George's fire,
  And lo—she is actually come.

Such prophecy some may despise,
  But the wish of a poet and friend
Perhaps is approved in the skies,
  And therefore attains to its end.
'Twas a wish that flew ardently forth
  From a bosom effectually warmed
With the talents, the graces, and worth
  Of the person for whom it was formed.

June, 1792.

Maria* would leave us, I knew,
  To the grief and regret of us all,
But less to our grief, could we view
  Catharina the Queen of the Hall.
And therefore I wished as I did,
  And therefore this union of hands ;
Not a whisper was heard to forbid,
  But all cry, Amen ! to the banns.

Since therefore I seem to incur
  No danger of wishing in vain,
When making good wishes for her,
  I will e'en to my wishes again ;
With one I have made her a wife,
  And now I will try with another,
Which I cannot suppress for my life,—
  How soon I can make her a mother

LINES ADDRESSED TO DR. DARWIN,

AUTHOR OF "THE BOTANIC GARDEN."

TWO Poets,† (poets, by report,
  Not oft so well agree)
Sweet Harmonist of Flora's court !
  Conspire to honour thee.

They best can judge a poet's worth,
  Who oft themselves have known
The pangs of a poetic birth
  By labours of their own.

We therefore, pleased, extol thy song,
  Though various, yet complete,
Rich in embellishment, as strong
  And learnèd as 'tis sweet.

1792.

No envy mingles with our praise,
  Though, could our hearts repine
At any poet's happier lays,
  They would,—they must, at thine.

But we, in mutual bondage knit
  Of friendship's closest tie,
Can gaze on even Darwin's wit
  With an unjaundiced eye ;

And deem the bard, whoe'er he be,
  And howsoever known,
Who would not twine a wreath for thee,
  Unworthy of his own.

---

* Lady Throckmorton.
† Alluding to the poem by Mr. Hayley, which accompanied these lines.

ON HIS APPROACHING VISIT TO HAYLEY.

THROUGH floods and flames to your retreat
    I win my desperate way,
And when we meet, if e'er we meet,
    Will echo your huzza.

July 29, 1792.

TO GEORGE ROMNEY, ESQ.

ON HIS PICTURE OF ME IN CRAYONS, DRAWN AT EARTHAM IN THE SIXTY-FIRST YEAR OF MY AGE, AND IN THE MONTHS OF AUGUST AND SEPTEMBER, 1792.

ROMNEY, expert infallibly to trace
On chart or canvas, not the form alone
And semblance, but, however faintly shown,
The mind's impression too on every face,
With strokes that time ought never to erase ;
Thou hast so pencilled mine, that though I own
The subject worthless, I have never known
The artist shining with superior grace.
But this I mark,—that symptoms none of woe
In thy incomparable work appear.
Well ; I am satisfied it should be so,
Since, on maturer thought, the cause is clear ;
For in my looks what sorrow couldst thou see
When I was Hayley's guest, and sat to thee ?

October, 1792.

AN EPITAPH.

HERE lies one who never drew
Blood himself, yet many slew ;
Gave the gun its aim, and figure
Made in field, yet ne'er pulled trigger.
Armed men have gladly made
Him their guide, and him obeyed ;
At his signified desire,
Would advance, present, and fire.
Stout he was, and large of limb,
Scores have fled at sight of him !
And to all this fame he rose
Only following his nose.
Neptune was he called ; not he
Who controls the boisterous sea,
But of happier command,
Neptune of the furrowed land ;
And, your wonder vain to shorten,
Pointer to Sir John Throckmorton.

1792.

EPITAPH ON "FOP,"

A DOG BELONGING TO LADY THROCKMORTON.

THOUGH once a puppy, and though Fop by name,
Here moulders one whose bones some honour claim ;
No sycophant, although of spaniel race,
And though no hound, a martyr to the chase.
Ye squirrels, rabbits, leverets, rejoice !
Your haunts no longer echo to his voice ;
This record of his fate exulting view,
He died worn out with vain pursuit of you.
  " Yes "—the indignant shade of Fop replies—
  " And worn with vain pursuit man also dies."

August, 1792.

ON RECEIVING HAYLEY'S PICTURE.

IN language warm as could be breathed or penned,
Thy picture speaks the original my friend ;
Not by those looks that indicate thy mind,
They only speak thee friend of all mankind :
Expression here more soothing still I see,
That friend of *all* a partial friend to *me.*

January, 1793.

TO HIS COUSIN, LADY HESKETH.

REASONS WHY HE COULD NOT WRITE HER A GOOD LETTER.

MY pens are all split, and my ink-glass is dry ;
Neither wit, common sense, nor ideas, have I.

Feb. 10, 1793.

EPITAPH ON MR. CHESTER, OF CHICHELY.

TEARS flow, and cease not, where the good man lies,
Till all who know him follow to the skies.
Tears therefore fall where CHESTER's ashes sleep ;
Him wife, friends, brothers, children, servants, weep ;
And justly—few shall ever him transcend
As husband, parent, brother, master, friend.

April, 1793.

ON A PLANT OF VIRGIN'S BOWER,

DESIGNED TO COVER A GARDEN-SEAT.

THRIVE, gentle plant ! and weave a bower
　　For Mary and for me,
And deck with many a splendid flower
　　Thy foliage large and free.

Thou camest from Eartham, and wilt shade
　　(If truly I divine)
Some future day the illustrious head
　　Of him who made thee mine.

Should Daphne show a jealous frown,
　　And Envy seize the bay,
Affirming none so fit to crown
　　Such honoured brows as they,

Thy cause with zeal we shall defend,
　　And with convincing power ;
For why should not the Virgin's Friend
　　Be crowned with Virgin's Bower ?

Spring of 1793.

TO MY COUSIN, ANNE BODHAM,

ON RECEIVING FROM HER A NETWORK PURSE MADE BY HERSELF.

MY gentle Anne, whom heretofore,
When I was young, and thou no more
　　Than plaything for a nurse,
I danced and fondled on my knee,
A kitten both in size and glee,—
　　I thank thee for my purse.

Gold pays the worth of all things here ;
But not of love !—that gem's too dear
　　For richest rogues to win it :
I therefore, as a proof of love,
Esteem thy present far above
　　The best things kept within it.

May 4, 1793.

TO A YOUNG FRIEND,

ON HIS ARRIVING AT CAMBRIDGE WET WHEN NO RAIN HAD FALLEN THERE.

IF Gideon's fleece, which drenched with dew he found,
While moisture none refreshed the herbs around,
Might fitly represent the Church endowed
With heavenly gifts to heathens not allowed ;
In pledge, perhaps, of favours from on high,
Thy locks were wet when others' locks were dry.
Heaven grant us half the omen,—may we see
Not drought on others, but much dew on thee !

May, 1793.

INSCRIPTION

FOR A HERMITAGE IN THE AUTHOR'S GARDEN.

THIS cabin, Mary, in my sight appears,
Built as it has been in our waning years,
A rest afforded to our weary feet,
Preliminary to—the last retreat.

May, 1793.

TO MRS. UNWIN.

MARY ! I want a lyre with other strings,
Such aid from Heaven as some have feigned they drew,
An eloquence scarce given to mortals, new
And undebased by praise of meaner things,
That, ere through age or woe I shed my wings,
I may record thy worth with honour due,
In verse as musical as thou art true,
And that immortalizes whom it sings.
But thou hast little need.　　There is a book
By seraphs writ with beams of heavenly light,
On which the eyes of God not rarely look,
A chronicle of actions just and bright :
There all thy deeds, my faithful Mary, shine,
And, since thou own'st that praise, I spare thee mine.

May, 1793.

TO JOHN JOHNSON,

ON HIS PRESENTING ME WITH AN ANTIQUE BUST OF HOMER.

KINSMAN beloved, and as a son, by me !
When I behold this fruit of thy regard,
The sculptured form of my old favourite bard,
I reverence feel for him and love for thee.

Joy too, and grief. Much joy that there should be
Wise men and learned, who grudge not to reward
With some applause my bold attempt and hard,
Which others scorn; critics by courtesy.
The grief is this, that sunk in Homer's mine,
I lose my precious years, now soon to fail,
Handling his gold, which howsoe'er it shine,
Proves dross when balanced in the Christian scale.
Be wiser thou!—like our forefather DONNE,
Seek heavenly wealth, and work for God alone.

May, 1793.

INSCRIPTION FOR THE SAME BUST.

Εἰκόνα τίς ταύτην; κλυτὸν ἀνέρος οὔνομ' ὕλωλεν.
Οὔνομα δ' οὗτος ἀνὴρ ἄφθιτον αἰὲν ἔχει.

TRANSLATION BY THE AUTHOR.

THE Sculptor?—Nameless, though once dear to fame.
But this man bears an everlasting name.

ON A PORTRAIT OF HIMSELF,

(IN A LETTER TO HAYLEY.)

ABBOT is painting me so true
    That (trust me) you would stare,
And hardly know at the first view,
    If I were here or there.

THANKS FOR A PRESENT OF PHEASANTS.

IN Copeman's ear this truth let Echo tell,—
" Immortal bards like mortal pheasants well ; "
And when his clerkship's out, I wish him herds
Of golden clients, for his golden birds.

TO WILLIAM HAYLEY, ESQ.

DEAR architect of fine CHATEAUX in air,
Worthier to stand for ever, if they could,
Than any built of stone, or yet of wood,
For back of royal elephant to bear ;

Oh for permission from the skies to share,
Much to my own, though little to thy good,
With thee (not subject to the jealous mood !)
A partnership of literary ware !
But I am bankrupt now ; and doomed henceforth
To drudge, in descant dry, on others' lays ;
Bards, I acknowledge, of unequalled worth :
But what is commentator's happiest praise ?
That he has furnished lights for other eyes,
Which they who need them use, and then despise.

June 29, 1793.

A TALE.*

In Scotland's realm, where trees are few,
  Nor even shrubs abound ;
But where, however bleak the view,
  Some better things are found :

For husband there and wife may boast
  Their union undefiled,
And false ones are as rare almost
  As hedge-rows in the wild :

In Scotland's realm forlorn and bare
  This history chanced of late,—
This history of a wedded pair,
  A chaffinch and his mate.

The spring drew near, each felt a breast
  With genial instinct filled ;
They paired, and would have built a nest,
  But found not where to build.

The heaths uncovered and the moors
  Except with snow and sleet,
Sea-beaten rocks and naked shores,
  Could yield them no retreat.

Long time a breeding-place they sought,
  Till both grew vexed and tired ;
At length a ship arriving brought
  The good so long desired.

A ship !—could such a restless thing
  Afford them place of rest ?
Or was the merchant charged to bring
  The homeless birds a nest ?

Hush !—silent hearers profit most,—
  This racer of the sea
Proved kinder to them than the coast
  It served them with a tree.

But such a tree ! 'twas shaven deal,
  The tree they call a mast,
And had a hollow with a wheel
  Through which the tackle passed.

Within that cavity aloft
  Their roofless home they fixed,
Form'd with materials neat and soft,
  Bents, wool, and feathers mixed.

Four ivory eggs soon pave its floor,
  With russet specks bedight ;
The vessel weighs, forsakes the shore,
  And lessens to the sight.

The mother-bird is gone to sea
  As she had changed her kind ;
But goes the male ? Far wiser he
  Is doubtless left behind.

---

* This tale is founded on an article of intelligence which the author found in the "Buckingham-shire Herald," for Saturday, June 1, 1793, in the following words :—

"*Glasgow, May 23.*
"In a block, or pulley, near the head of the mast of a gabbert, now lying at the Broomielaw, there is a chaffinch's nest and four eggs. The nest was built while the vessel lay at Greenock, and was followed hither by both birds. Though the block is occasionally lowered for the inspection of the curious, the birds have not forsaken the nest. The cock, however, visits the nest but seldom ; while the hen never leaves it but when she descends to the hull for food."

No : soon as from ashore he saw
  The wingèd mansion move,
He flew to reach it, by a law
  Of never-failing love.

Then perching at his consort's side
  Was briskly borne along,
The billows and the blast defied,
  And cheered her with a song.

The seaman with sincere delight
  His feathered shipmates eyes,
Scarce less exulting in the sight
  Than when he tows a prize.

For seamen much believe in signs,
  And from a chance so new
Each some approaching good divines,—
  And may his hopes be true !

  June, 1793.

Hail, honoured land ! a desert where
  Not even birds can hide,
Yet parent of this loving pair
  Whom nothing could divide.

And ye who, rather than resign
  Your matrimonial plan,
Were not afraid to plough the brine
  In company with man ;

For whose lean country much disdain
  We English often show,
Yet from a richer nothing gain
  But wantonness and woe ;

Be it your fortune, year by year,
  The same resource to prove,
And may ye, sometimes landing here,
  Instruct us how to love !

ON A SPANIEL, CALLED "BEAU,"

KILLING A YOUNG BIRD.

A SPANIEL, Beau, that fares like you,
  Well fed, and at his ease,
Should wiser be than to pursue
  Each trifle that he sees.

But you have killed a tiny bird
  Which flew not till to-day,
Against my orders, whom you heard
  Forbidding you the prey.

Nor did you kill that you might eat
  And ease a doggish pain ;

  July 15, 1793.

For him, though chased with furious heat,
  You left where he was slain.

Nor was he of the thievish sort,
  Or one whom blood allures,
But innocent was all his sport
  Whom you have torn for yours.

My dog ! what remedy remains,
  Since, teach you all I can,
I see you, after all my pains,
  So much resemble man ?

BEAU'S REPLY.

SIR, when I flew to seize the bird
  In spite of your command,
A louder voice than yours I heard,
  And harder to withstand.

You cried "Forbear!"—but in my breast
  A mightier cried "Proceed !"—
'Twas Nature, sir, whose strong behest
  Impelled me to the deed.

Yet much as Nature I respect,
  I ventured once to break
(As you perhaps may recollect)
  Her precept for your sake ;

And when your linnet on a day,
  Passing his prison door,
Had fluttered all his strength away,
  And panting pressed the floor,

Well knowing him a sacred thing,
 Not destined to my tooth,
I only kissed his ruffled wing,
 And licked the feathers smooth.

Let my obedience then excuse
 My disobedience now,

Nor some reproof yourself refuse
 From your aggrieved Bow-wow ;

If killing birds be such a crime
 (Which I can hardly see),
What think you, sir, of killing Time
 With verse addressed to me ?

ANSWER TO STANZAS ADDRESSED TO LADY HESKETH,

BY MISS CATHARINE FANSHAWE.

To be remembered *thus* is Fame,
 And in the first degree ;
And did the few like her the same,
 The press might sleep for me.

So Homer, in the memory stored
 Of many a Grecian belle,
Was once preserved—a richer hoard,
 But never lodged so well.

1793.

ON A LETTER OF MISS FANSHAWE.

HER pen drops eloquence as sweet
 As any Muse's tongue can speak ;
Nor need a scribe, like her, regret
 Her want of Latin or of Greek.

Aug. 29, 1793.

TO THE SPANISH ADMIRAL COUNT GRAVINA,

ON HIS TRANSLATING THE AUTHOR'S SONG ON A ROSE INTO ITALIAN VERSE.

MY rose, Gravina, blooms anew ;
 And steeped not now in rain,
But in Castalian streams by you,
 Will never fade again.

1793.

ON FLAXMAN'S PENELOPE.

THE suitors sinned, but with a fair excuse,
Whom all this elegance might well seduce ;
Nor can our censure on the husband fall,
Who, for a wife so lovely, slew them all.

Sept. 1793

TO MARY.

THE twentieth year is well-nigh past,
Since first our sky was overcast ;
Ah, would that this might be the last !
    My Mary !

Thy spirits have a fainter flow,
I see thee daily weaker grow ;
'Twas my distress that brought thee low,
    My Mary !

Thy needles, once a shining store,
For my sake restless heretofore,
Now rust disused, and shine no more,
    My Mary !

For though thou gladly wouldst fulfil
The same kind office for me still,
Thy sight now seconds not thy will,
    My Mary !

But well thou playedst the housewife's part,
And all thy threads with magic art
Have wound themselves about this heart,
    My Mary !

Thy indistinct expressions seem
Like language uttered in a dream ;
Yet me they charm, whate'er the theme,
    My Mary !

Thy silver locks, once auburn bright,
Are still more lovely in my sight
Than golden beams of orient light,
    My Mary !

For, could I view nor them nor thee,
What sight worth seeing could I see ?
The sun would rise in vain for me,
    My Mary !

Partakers of thy sad decline,
Thy hands their little force resign ;
Yet, gently prest, press gently mine,
    My Mary !

Such feebleness of limbs thou provest.
That now at every step thou movest
Upheld by two, yet still thou lovest,
                    My Mary !

And still to love, though prest with ill,
In wintry age to feel no chill,
With me is to be lovely still,
                    My Mary !

But ah ! by constant heed I know,
How oft the sadness that I show
Transforms thy smiles to looks of woe,
                    My Mary !

And should my future lot be cast
With much resemblance of the past,
Thy worn-out heart will break at last,
                    My Mary !

Autumn of 1793.

ON RECEIVING HEYNE'S VIRGIL FROM MR. HAYLEY

I SHOULD have deemed it once an effort vain
To sweeten more sweet Maro's matchless strain,
But from that error now behold me free,
Since I received him as a gift from thee.

Oct. 1793.

MOTTO FOR A CLOCK.

QUÆ lenta accedit, quam velox præterit hora !
Ut capias, patiens esto, sed esto vigil !

Slow comes the hour ; its passing speed how great !
Waiting to seize it—vigilantly wait !

IN A TIME OF GREAT HEAT.

TO HAYLEY.

AH ! brother Poet, send me of your shade !
And bid the zephyrs hasten to my aid ;
Or, like a worm unearthed at noon, I go,
Despatched by sunshine, to the shades below.

EPIGRAMS ON HIS GARDEN-SHED.

I.

BEWARE of building! I intended
Rough logs and thatch,—and thus it ended.

II.

Instead of a pound or two, spending a mint
Must serve me at least, I believe, with a hint
That, building and building, a man may be driven
At last out of doors, and have no house to live in.

MONTES GLACIALES,

IN OCEANO GERMANICO NATANTES.

EN, quæ prodigia, ex oris allata remotis,
Oras adveniunt pavefacta per æquora nostras!
Non equidem priscæ sæclum rediisse videtur
Pyrrhæ, cum Proteus pecus altos visere montes
Et sylvas, egit. Sed tempora vix leviora
Adsunt, evulsi quando radicitùs alti
In mare descendunt montes, fluctusque pererrant.
Quid verò hoc monstri est magis et mirabile visu?
Splendentes video, ceu pulchro ex ære vel auro
Conflatos, rutilisque accinctos undique gemmis,
Baccâ cæruleâ, et flammas imitante pyropo.
Ex oriente adsunt, ubi gazas optima tellus
Parturit omnigenas, quibus æva per omnia sumptu
Ingenti finxêre sibi diademata reges?
Vix hoc crediderim. Non fallunt talia acutos
Mercatorum oculos: prius et quàm littora Gangis
Liquissent, avidis gratissima præda fuissent.
Ortos unde putemus? An illos Ves'vius atrox
Protulit, ignivomisve ejecit faucibus Ætna?
Luce micant propriâ, Phœbive, per aëra purum
Nunc stimulantis equos, argentea tela retorquent?
Phœbi luce micant. Ventis et fluctibus altis
Appulsi, et rapidis subter currentibus undis,
Tandem non fallunt oculos. Capita alta videre est
Multâ onerata nive et canis conspersa pruinis.
Cætera sunt glacies. Procul hinc, ubi Bruma ferè omnes
Contristat menses, portenta hæc horrida nobis
Illa strui voluit. Quoties de culmine summo

Clivorum fluerent in littora prona, solutæ
Sole, nives, propero tendentes in mare cursu,
Illa gelu fixit.   Paulatim attollere sese
Mirum cœpit opus ; glacieque ab origine rerum
In glaciem aggestâ sublimes vertice tandem
Æquavit montes, non crescere nescia moles.
Sic immensa diu stetit, æternumque stetisset
Congeries, hominum neque vi neque mobilis arte,
Littora ni tandem declivia deseruisset,
Pondere victa suo.   Dilabitur.   Omnia circum
Antra et saxa gemunt, subito concussa fragore,
Dum ruit in pelagum, tanquam studiosa natandi,
Ingens tota strues.   Sic Delos dicitur olim,
Insula, in Ægæo fluitâsse erratica ponto.
Sed non ex glacie Delos ; neque torpida Delum
Bruma inter rupes genuit nudum sterilemque.
Sed vestita herbis erat illa, ornataque nunquam
Deciduâ lauro ; et Delum dilexit Apollo.
At vos, errones horrendi, et caligine digni
Cimmeriâ, Deus idem odit.   Natalia vestra,
Nubibus involvens frontem, non ille tueri
Sustinuit.   Patrium vos ergo requirite cælum !
Ite ! Redite ! Timete moras ; ni lenitèr austro
Spirante, et nitidas Phœbo jaculante sagittas
Hostili vobis, pereatis gurgite misti !

March 11, 1799.

ON THE ICE ISLANDS,

SEEN FLOATING IN THE GERMAN OCEAN.

WHAT portents, from what distant region, ride,
Unseen till now in ours, the astonished tide?
In ages past, old Proteus, with his droves
Of sea-calves, sought the mountains and the groves ;
But now, descending whence of late they stood,
Themselves the mountains seem to rove the flood ;
Dire times were they, full-charged with human woes ;
And these, scarce less calamitous than those.
What view we now? More wondrous still ! Behold !
Like burnished brass they shine, or beaten gold ;
And all around the pearl's pure splendour show,
And all around the ruby's fiery glow.
Come they from India, where the burning earth,
All bounteous, gives her richest treasures birth ;
And where the costly gems that beam around
The brows of mightiest potentates are found ?
No.   Never such a countless dazzling store
Had left, unseen, the Ganges' peopled shore ;

Rapacious hands, and ever-watchful eyes,
Should sooner far have marked and seized the prize.
Whence sprang they then? Ejected have they come
From Ves'vius', or from Ætna's burning womb?
Thus shine they self-illumed, or but display
The borrowed splendours of a cloudless day?
With borrowed beams they shine. The gales, that breathe
Now landward, and the current's force beneath,
Have borne them nearer; and the nearer sight,
Advantaged more, contemplates them aright.
Their lofty summits crested high, they show,
With mingled sleet, and long-incumbent snow :
The rest is ice. Far hence, where, most severe,
Bleak Winter well-nigh saddens all the year,
Their infant growth began. He bade arise
Their uncouth forms, portentous in our eyes.
Oft as, dissolved by transient suns, the snow
Left the tall cliff to join the flood below,
He caught and curdled with a freezing blast
The current, ere it reached the boundless waste.
By slow degrees uprose the wondrous pile,
And long successive ages rolled the while,
Till, ceaseless in its growth, it claimed to stand
Tall as its rival mountains on the land.
Thus stood, and, unremovable by skill
Or force of man, had stood the structure still ;
But that, though firmly fixed, supplanted yet
By pressure of its own enormous weight,
It left the shelving beach, — and with a sound
That shook the bellowing waves and rocks around,
Self-launched, and swiftly, to the briny wave,
As if instinct with strong desire to lave,
Down went the ponderous mass. So bards of old
How Delos swam the Ægean deep have told.
But not of ice was Delos. Delos bore
Herb, fruit, and flower. She, crowned with laurel, wore,
Even under wintry skies, a summer smile ;
And Delos was Apollo's favourite isle.
But, horrid wanderers of the deep, to you
He deems Cimmerian darkness only due.
Your hated birth he deigned not to survey,
But, scornful, turned his glorious eyes away.
Hence ! Seek your home, nor longer rashly dare
The darts of Phœbus, and a softer air ;
Lest ye regret, too late, your native coast,
In no congenial gulf for ever lost !

March 19, 1799.

ON A MISTAKE IN HIS TRANSLATION OF HOMER.

COWPER had sinned with some excuse,
　　If, bound in rhyming tethers,
He had committed this abuse
　　Of changing ewes for wethers.

But male for female is a trope,
　　A rather bold misnomer,
That would have startled even Pope,
　　When he translated Homer.

THE CASTAWAY.

OBSCUREST night involved the sky,
　　The Atlantic billows roared,
When such a destined wretch as I,
　　Washed headlong from on board,
Of friends, of hope, of all bereft,
His floating home for ever left.

No braver chief could Albion boast
　　Than he with whom he went,
Nor ever ship left Albion's coast
　　With warmer wishes sent.
He loved them both, but both in vain,
Nor him beheld, nor her again.

Not long beneath the whelming brine,
　　Expert to swim, he lay;
Nor soon he felt his strength decline,
　　Or courage die away;
But waged with death a lasting strife,
Supported by despair of life.

He shouted : nor his friends had failed
　　To check the vessel's course,
But so the furious blast prevailed,
　　That, pitiless perforce,
They left their outcast mate behind,
And scudded still before the wind.

Some succour yet they could afford;
　　And such as storms allow,
The cask, the coop, the floated cord,
　　Delayed not to bestow.
But he (they knew) nor ship nor shore,
Whate'er they gave, should visit more.

Nor, cruel as it seemed, could he
　　Their haste himself condemn,
Aware that flight, in such a sea,

March 20, 1799.

Alone could rescue them ;
Yet bitter felt it still to die
Deserted, and his friends so nigh.

He long survives, who lives an hour
　　In ocean, self-upheld ;
And so long he, with unspent power,
　　His destiny repelled ;
And ever, as the minutes flew,
Entreated help, or cried " Adieu !"

At length, his transient respite past,
　　His comrades, who before
Had heard his voice in every blast,
　　Could catch the sound no more :
For then, by toil subdued, he drank
The stifling wave, and then he sank.

No poet wept him ; but the page
　　Of narrative sincere,
That tells his name, his worth, his age,
　　Is wet with Anson's tear :
And tears by bards or heroes shed
Alike immortalize the dead.

I therefore purpose not, or dream,
　　Descanting on his fate,
To give the melancholy theme
　　A more enduring date :
But misery still delights to trace
Its semblance in another's case.

No voice divine the storm allayed,
　　No light propitious shone,
When, snatched from all effectual aid,
　　We perished, each alone :
But I beneath a rougher sea,
And whelmed in deeper gulfs than he.

TRANSLATIONS.

TRANSLATIONS FROM THE FRENCH OF MADAME DE LA MOTTE GUYON.

THE NATIVITY.

'Tis folly all!—let me no more be told
Of Parian porticoes, and roofs of gold:
Delightful views of nature, dressed by art,
Enchant no longer this indifferent heart:
The Lord of all things, in His humble birth,
Makes mean the proud magnificence of earth;
The straw, the manger, and the mouldering wall,
Eclipse its lustre; and I scorn it all.
   Canals, and fountains, and delicious vales,
Green slopes, and plains whose plenty never fails;   10
Deep-rooted groves, whose heads sublimely rise,
Earth-born, and yet ambitious of the skies;
The abundant foliage of whose gloomy shades
Vainly the sun in all its power invades;
Where warbled airs of sprightly birds resound,
Whose verdure lives while winter scowls around;
Rocks, lofty mountains, caverns dark and deep,
And torrents raving down the rugged steep;
Smooth downs, whose fragrant herbs the spirits cheer;
Meads crowned with flowers; streams musical and clear, 20
Whose silver waters and whose murmurs join
Their artless charms, to make the scene divine;
The fruitful vineyard, and the furrowed plain
That seems a rolling sea of golden grain;
All, all have lost the charms they once possessed,
An infant God reigns sovereign in my breast;
From Bethlehem's bosom I no more will rove,
There dwells the Saviour, and there rests my love.
   Ye mightier rivers, that with sounding force
Urge down the valleys your impetuous course!   30
Winds, clouds, and lightnings! and, ye waves, whose heads,
Curled into monstrous forms, the seaman dreads!
Horrid abyss, where all experience fails,
Spread with the wreck of planks and shattered sails;
On whose broad back grim Death triumphant rides,
While havoc floats on all thy swelling tides,

Thy shores a scene of ruin, strewed around
With vessels bulged, and bodies of the drowned !
   Ye fish, that sport beneath the boundless waves,
And rest, secure from man, in rocky caves ;   40
Swift-darting sharks, and whales of hideous size,
Whom all the aquatic world with terror eyes !
Had I but faith immovable and true,
I might defy the fiercest storm, like you.
The world, a more disturbed and boisterous sea,
When Jesus shows a smile, affrights not me ;
He hides me, and in vain the billows roar,
Break harmless at my feet, and leave the shore.
   Thou azure vault, where through the gloom of night,
Thick sown, we see such countless worlds of light !   50
Thou moon, whose car, encompassing the skies,
Restores lost nature to our wondering eyes,
Again retiring when the brighter sun
Begins the course he seems in haste to run !
Behold him where he shines !   His rapid rays,
Themselves unmeasured, measure all our days ;
Nothing impedes the race he would pursue,
Nothing escapes his penetrating view,
A thousand lands confess his quickening heat,
And all he cheers are fruitful, fair, and sweet.   60
   Far from enjoying what these scenes disclose,
I feel the thorn, alas ! but miss the rose :
Too well I know this aching heart requires
More solid good to fill its vast desires ;
In vain they represent His matchless might,
Who called them out of deep primeval night ;
Their form and beauty but augment my woe :
I seek the Giver of those charms they show :
Nor, Him beside, throughout the world He made,
Lives there in whom I trust for cure or aid.   70
   Infinite God, thou great unrivalled ONE !
Whose glory makes a blot of yonder sun :
Compared with Thine, how dim his beauty seems,
How quenched the radiance of his golden beams !
Thou art my bliss, the light by which I move ;
In Thee alone dwells all that I can love ;
All darkness flies when Thou art pleased to appear,
A sudden spring renews the fading year ;
Where'er I turn I see Thy power and grace,
The watchful guardian of our heedless race ;   80
Thy various creatures in one strain agree,
All, in all times and places, speak of Thee ;
Even I, with trembling heart and stammering tongue,
Attempt thy praise, and join the general song.
   Almighty Former of this wondrous plan,
Faintly reflected in Thine image, Man,—
Holy and just,—the greatness of whose name
Fills and supports this universal frame,

Diffused throughout the infinitude of space,
Who art Thyself thine own vast dwelling-place ;   90
Soul of our soul, whom yet no sense of ours
Discerns, eluding our most active powers ;
Encircling shades attend Thine awful throne,
That veil thy face, and keep Thee still unknown ;
Unknown, though dwelling in our inmost part,
Lord of the thoughts, and Sovereign of the heart !
   Repeat the charming truth that never tires,
No God is like the God my soul desires !
He at whose voice heaven trembles, even He,
Great as He is, knows how to stoop to me.   100
Lo ! there He lies ;—that smiling infant said,
" Heaven, earth, and sea exist ! "—and they obeyed.
Even He, whose Being swells beyond the skies,
Is born of woman, lives, and mourns, and dies ;
Eternal and Immortal, seems to cast
That glory from His brows, and breathes His last.
Trivial and vain the works that man has wrought,
How do they shrink and vanish at the thought !
   Sweet solitude, and scene of my repose !
This rustic sight assuages all my woes.—   110
That crib contains the Lord, whom I adore ;
And earth's a shade, that I pursue no more.
He is my firm support, my rock, my tower,
I dwell secure beneath His sheltering power,
And hold this mean retreat for ever dear,
For all I love, my soul's delight, is here.
I see the Almighty swathed in infant bands,
Tied helpless down the Thunder-bearer's hands,
And in this shed that mystery discern,
Which faith and love, and they alone, can learn.   120
   Ye tempests, spare the slumbers of your Lord !
Ye zephyrs, all your whispered sweets afford !
Confess the God that guides the rolling year ;
Heaven, do Him homage ; and thou, Earth, revere !
Ye shepherds, monarchs, sages, hither bring
Your hearts an offering, and adore your King !
Pure be those hearts, and rich in Faith and Love ;
Join in His praise, the harmonious world above ;
To Bethlehem haste, rejoice in His repose,
And praise Him there for all that He bestows !   130
   Man, busy Man, alas ! can ill afford
To obey the summons, and attend the Lord ;
Perverted reason revels and runs wild,
By glittering shows of pomp and wealth beguiled ;
And, blind to genuine excellence and grace,
Finds not her Author in so mean a place.
Ye unbelieving ! learn a wiser part,
Distrust your erring sense, and search your heart ;
There, soon ye shall perceive a kindling flame
Glow for that infant God from whom it came ;   140

Resist not, quench not, that divine desire,
Melt all your adamant in heavenly fire !
Not so will I requite thee, gentle Love !
Yielding and soft this heart will ever prove ;
And every heart beneath thy power should fall,
Glad to submit, could mine contain them all.
But I am poor ; oblation I have none,
None for a Saviour, but Himself alone :
Whate'er I render Thee, from Thee it came ;
And if I give my body to the flame,   150
My patience, love, and energy divine
Of heart, and soul, and spirit, all are thine.
Ah, vain attempt to expunge the mighty score !
The more I pay, I owe Thee still the more.
    Upon my meanness, poverty, and guilt
The trophy of Thy glory shall be built ;
My self-disdain shall be the unshaken base,
And my deformity its fairest grace ;
For destitute of good, and rich in ill,
Must be my state and my description still.   160
    And do I grieve at such an humbling lot ?
Nay, but I cherish and enjoy the thought.
Vain pageantry and pomp of earth, adieu !
I have no wish, no memory for you :
The more I feel my misery, I adore
The sacred Inmate of my soul the more ;
Rich in His love, I feel my noblest pride
Spring from the sense of having nought beside.
    In Thee I find wealth, comfort, virtue, might ;
My wanderings prove Thy wisdom infinite ;   170
All that I have I give Thee ; and then see
All contrarieties unite in Thee ;
For Thou hast joined them, taking up our woe,
And pouring out Thy bliss on worms below,
By filling with Thy grace and love divine
A gulf of evil in this heart of mine.
This is, indeed, to bid the valleys rise,
And the hills sink,—'tis matching earth and skies !
I feel my weakness, thank Thee, and deplore
An aching heart, that throbs to thank Thee more ;   180
The more I love Thee, I the more reprove
A soul so lifeless, and so slow to love ;
Till, on a deluge of Thy mercy tossed,
I plunge into that sea, and there am lost.

GOD NEITHER KNOWN NOR LOVED BY THE WORLD.

YE linnets, let us try, beneath this grove,
Which shall be loudest in our Maker's praise !
In quest of some forlorn retreat I rove,
For all the world is blind, and wanders from His ways.

That God alone should prop the sinking soul,
Fills them with rage against His empire now :
   I traverse earth in vain from pole to pole,
To seek one simple heart, set free from all below.

   They speak of love, yet little feel its sway,
While in their bosoms many an idol lurks ;
   Their base desires, well-satisfied, obey,
Leave the Creator's hand, and lean upon His works.

   'Tis therefore I can dwell with man no more ;
Your fellowship, ye warblers ! suits me best :
   Pure love has lost its price, though prized of yore,
Profaned by modern tongues, and slighted as a jest.

   My God, who formed you for His praise alone,
Beholds His purpose well fulfilled in you :
   Come, let us join the choir before His throne,
Partaking in His praise with spirits just and true !

   Yes, I will always love ; and, as I ought,
Tune to the praise of Love my ceaseless voice ;
   Preferring Love too vast for human thought,
In spite of erring men, who cavil at my choice.

   Why have I not a thousand thousand hearts,
Lord of my soul ! that they might all be thine ?
   If Thou approve,—the zeal Thy smile imparts,
How should it ever fail ! can such a fire decline ?

   Love, pure and holy, is a deathless fire ;
Its object heavenly, it must ever blaze :
   Eternal Love a God must needs inspire,
When once He wins the heart, and fits it for His praise.

   Self-love dismissed,—'tis then we live indeed,—
In her embrace, death, only death is found ;
   Come, then, one noble effort, and succeed,
Cast off the chain of self with which thy soul is bound.

   Oh ! I could cry, that all the world might hear,
Ye self-tormentors, love your God alone ;
   Let His unequalled excellence be dear,
Dear to your inmost souls, and make Him all your own !

   They hear me not.—Alas ! how fond to rove
In endless chase of folly's specious lure !
   'Tis here alone, beneath this shady grove,
I taste the sweets of truth,—here only am secure.

THE SWALLOW.

I am fond of the swallow ;—I learn from her flight,
　Had I skill to improve it, a lesson of love :
How seldom on earth do we see her alight !
　She dwells in the skies, she is ever above.

It is on the wing that she takes her repose,
　Suspended and poised in the regions of air ;
'Tis not in our fields that her sustenance grows,
　It is winged like herself, 'tis ethereal fare.

She comes in the spring, all the summer she stays,
　And, dreading the cold, still follows the sun :—
So, true to our Love, we should covet his rays,
　And the place where he shines not, immediately shun.

Our light should be Love, and our nourishment prayer ;
　It is dangerous food that we find upon earth :
The fruit of this world is beset with a snare,
　In itself it is hurtful, as vile in its birth.

'Tis rarely, if ever, she settles below,
　And only when building a nest for her young ;
Were it not for her brood, she would never bestow
　A thought upon anything filthy as dung.

Let us leave it ourselves ('tis a mortal abode)
　To bask every moment in infinite Love ;
Let us fly the dark winter, and follow the road
　That leads to the Dayspring appearing above.

A FIGURATIVE DESCRIPTION OF THE PROCEDURE OF DIVINE LOVE,

IN BRINGING A SOUL TO THE POINT OF SELF-RENUNCIATION AND ABSOLUTE ACQUIESCENCE.

'Twas my purpose, on a day,
To embark and sail away ;
As I climbed the vessel's side,
Love was sporting in the tide ;
"Come," he said, "ascend ! make haste,
"Launch into the boundless waste."

Many mariners were there,
Having each his separate care ;
They that rowed us held their eyes
Fixed upon the starry skies ;
Others steered, or turned the sails
To receive the shifting gales.

Love, with power divine supplied,
Suddenly my courage tried ;
In a moment it was night,
Ship and skies were out of sight ;
On the briny wave I lay,
Floating rushes all my stay.

Did I with resentment burn
At this unexpected turn ?
Did I wish myself on shore,
Never to forsake it more ?
No :—" My soul," I cried, " be still !
" If I must be lost, I will."

Next he hastened to convey
Both my frail supports away ;
Seized my rushes ; bade the waves
Yawn into a thousand graves :
Down I went, and sunk as lead,
Ocean closing o'er my head.

Still, however, life was safe ;
And I saw him turn and laugh :
"Friend," he cried, "adieu ! lie low
"While the wintry storms shall blow ;
"When the spring has calmed the main,
"You shall rise and float again."

Soon I saw him, with dismay,
Spread his plumes and soar away ;
Now I mark his rapid flight,
Now he leaves my aching sight ;
He is gone whom I adore,
'Tis in vain to seek him more.

How I trembled then and feared,
When my Love had disappeared !
"Wilt thou leave me thus," I cried,
"Whelmed beneath the rolling tide ?"
Vain attempt to reach his ear !
Love was gone, and would not hear.

"Ah ! return, and love me still ;
"See me subject to thy will !
"Frown with wrath, or smile with grace
"Only let me see thy face !
"Evil I have none to fear,
"All is good, if Thou art near."

Yet he leaves me,—cruel fate !
Leaves me in my lost estate !
"Have I sinned ? Oh say wherein ?
"Tell me, and forgive my sin !
"King and Lord, whom I adore,
"Shall I see thy face no more ?

"Be not angry ; I resign,
"Henceforth, all my will to thine :
"I consent that Thou depart,
"Tho' thine absence breaks my heart ;
"Go then, and for ever too ;
"All is right that Thou wilt do."

This was just what Love intended,
He was now no more offended ;
Soon as I became a child,
Love returned to me and smiled ;
Never strife shall more betide
'Twixt the bridegroom and his bride.

A CHILD OF GOD LONGING TO SEE HIM BELOVED.

THERE'S not an echo round me,
  But I am glad should learn
How pure a fire has found me,
  The love with which I burn.
For none attends with pleasure
  To what I would reveal ;
They slight me out of measure,
  And laugh at all I feel.

The rocks receive less proudly
  The story of my flame ;
When I approach, they loudly
  Reverberate His name.
I speak to them of sadness,
  And comforts at a stand ;
They bid me look for gladness,
  And better days at hand.

Far from all habitation,
  I heard a happy sound,
Big with the consolation
  That I have often found :

I said, "My lot is sorrow,
  "My grief has no alloy ;"
The rocks replied—"To-morrow,
  "To-morrow brings thee joy."

These sweet and secret tidings
  What bliss it is to hear !
For, spite of all my chidings,
  My weakness and my fear,
No sooner I receive them,
  Than I forget my pain,
And, happy to believe them,
  I love as much again.

I fly to scenes romantic,
  Where never men resort ;
For in an age so frantic
  Impiety is sport ;
For riot and confusion
  They barter things above,
Condemning, as delusion,
  The joy of perfect love.

In this sequestered corner,
  None hears what I express ;
Delivered from the scorner,
  What peace do I possess !
Beneath the boughs reclining,
  Or roving o'er the wild,
I live as undesigning
  And harmless as a child.

No troubles here surprise me ;
  I innocently play,
While Providence supplies me,
  And guards me all the day :
My dear and kind Defender
  Preserves me safely here,
From men of pomp and splendour,
  Who fill a child with fear.

HAPPY SOLITUDE—UNHAPPY MEN.

My heart is easy, and my burthen light ;
I smile, though sad, when Thou art in my sight :
The more my woes in secret I deplore,
I taste Thy goodness, and I love Thee more.

There, while a solemn stillness reigns around,
Faith, Love, and Hope within my soul abound ;
And while the world suppose me lost in care,
The joys of angels, unperceived, I share.

Thy creatures wrong Thee, O Thou Sovereign Good !
Thou art not loved, because not understood ;
This grieves me most, that vain pursuits beguile
Ungrateful men, regardless of Thy smile.

Frail beauty and false honour are adored ;
While Thee they scorn, and trifle with Thy Word ;
Pass, unconcerned, a Saviour's sorrows by ;
And hunt their ruin with a zeal to die.

ASPIRATIONS OF THE SOUL AFTER GOD.

My Spouse ! in whose presence I live,
  Sole object of all my desires,
Who knowest what a flame I conceive
  And canst easily double its fires ;
How pleasant is all that I meet !
  From fear of adversity free,
I find even sorrow made sweet ;
  Because 'tis assigned me by Thee.

Transported I see Thee display
  Thy riches and glory divine ;
I have only my life to repay,
  Take what I would gladly resign.
Thy will is the treasure I seek,
  For Thou art as faithful as strong ;
There let me, obedient and meek,
  Repose myself all the day long.

My spirit and faculties fail ;
  Oh finish what love has begun !
Destroy what is sinful and frail,
  And dwell in the soul Thou hast won !
Dear theme of my wonder and praise,
  I cry, who is worthy as Thou !
I can only be silent and gaze :
  'Tis all that is left of me now.

O glory in which I am lost,
  Too deep for the plummet of thought!
On an ocean of deity tossed,
  I am swallowed, I sink into nought.
Yet lost and absorbed as I seem,
  I chant to the praise of my King :
And, though overwhelmed by the theme,
  Am happy whenever I sing.

DIVINE JUSTICE AMIABLE.

THOU hast no lightnings, O Thou Just!
  Or I their force should know ;
And if Thou strike me into dust,
  My soul approves the blow.

The heart, that values less its ease
  Than it adores Thy ways,
In Thine avenging anger sees
  A subject of its praise.

Pleased I could lie, concealed and lost,
  In shades of central night ;
Not to avoid Thy wrath, Thou knowest,
  But lest I grieve Thy sight.

Smite me, O Thou, whom I provoke ;
  And I will love Thee still ;
The well-deserved and righteous stroke
  Shall please me, though it kill.

Am I not worthy to sustain
  The worst Thou canst devise ?
And dare I seek Thy throne again,
  And meet Thy sacred eyes ?

Far from afflicting, Thou art kind ;
  And in my saddest hours
An unction of Thy grace I find,
  Pervading all my powers.

Alas ! Thou sparest me again ;
  And when Thy wrath should move,
Too gentle to endure my pain,
  Thou sooth'st me with Thy love.

I have no punishment to fear ;
  But, ah ! that smile from Thee
Imparts a pang far more severe
  Than woe itself would be.

THE TRIUMPH OF HEAVENLY LOVE DESIRED.

AH ! reign, wherever man is found,
  My Spouse, belovèd and divine !
Then I am rich, and I abound,
  When every human heart is Thine.

A thousand sorrows pierce my soul,
  To think that all are not Thine own :
Ah ! be adored from pole to pole ;
  Where is Thy zeal ? arise ; be known !

All hearts are cold, in every place,
  Yet earthly good with warmth pursue ;
Dissolve them with a flash of grace,
  Thaw these of ice, and give us new !

TRUTH AND DIVINE LOVE REJECTED BY THE WORLD.

O LOVE, of pure and heavenly birth !
O simple Truth, scarce known on earth !
Whom men resist with stubborn will ;
And, more perverse and daring still,
Smother and quench, with reasonings vain,
While error and deception reign.

Whence comes it, that, your power the same
As His on high, from whence you came,
Ye rarely find a listening ear,
Or heart that makes you welcome here?—
Because ye bring reproach and pain,
Where'er ye visit, in your train.

The world is proud, and cannot bear
The scorn and calumny ye share ;
The praise of men the mark they mean,
They fly the place where ye are seen ;
Pure Love, with scandal in the rear,
Suits not the vain ; it costs too dear.

Then, let the price be what it may,
Though poor, I am prepared to pay ;
Come shame, come sorrow ; spite of tears,
Weakness, and heart-oppressing fears ;
One soul, at least, shall not repine,
To give you room ; come, reign in mine !

LIVING WATER.

THE fountain in its source
    No drought of summer fears ;
The farther it pursues its course
    The nobler it appears.

But shallow cisterns yield
    A scanty short supply ;
The morning sees them amply filled,
    At evening they are dry.

THE SOUL THAT LOVES GOD FINDS HIM EVERYWHERE.

O Thou, by long experience tried,
Near whom no grief can long abide ;
My Love ! how full of sweet content
I pass my years of banishment !

All scenes alike engaging prove
To souls impressed with sacred Love !
Where'er they dwell, they dwell in
    Thee ;
In heaven, in earth, or on the sea.

To me remains nor place nor time !
My country is in every clime ;
I can be calm and free from care
On any shore, since God is there.

While place we seek, or place we shun,
The soul finds happiness in none ;
But, with a God to guide our way,
'Tis equal joy to go or stay.

Could I be cast where Thou art not,
That were indeed a dreadful lot ;
But regions none remote I call,
Secure of finding God in all.

My country, Lord, art Thou alone ;
Nor other can I claim or own ;
The point where all my wishes meet ;
My law, my love ; life's only sweet !

I hold by nothing here below ;
Appoint my journey, and I go ; [pride,
Though pierced by scorn, oppressed by
I feel Thee good, feel nought beside.

No frowns of men can hurtful prove
To souls on fire with heavenly Love !

Though men and devils both condemn,
No gloomy days arise from them.

Ah, then ! to His embrace repair ;
My soul, thou art no stranger there ;
There Love divine shall be thy guard,
And peace and safety thy reward.

GRATITUDE AND LOVE TO GOD.

ALL are indebted much to Thee,
But I far more than all,
From many a deadly snare set free,
And raised from many a fall.
Overwhelm me from above,
Daily, with Thy boundless love !

What bonds of gratitude I feel
No language can declare ;
Beneath the oppressive weight I reel,
'Tis more than I can bear :
When shall I that blessing prove,
To return Thee Love for Love ?

Spirit of Charity, dispense
Thy grace to every heart ;
Expel all other spirits thence,

Drive self from every part ;
Charity divine, draw nigh,
Break the chains in which we lie !

All selfish souls, whate'er they feign,
Have still a slavish lot ;
They boast of liberty in vain,
Of Love, and feel it not.
He whose bosom glows with Thee,
He, and he alone, is free.

O blessedness, all bliss above,
When thy pure fires prevail !
Love only teaches what is Love ;
All other lessons fail :
We learn its name, but not its powers,
Experience only makes it ours.

THE TESTIMONY OF DIVINE ADOPTION.

How happy are the new-born race ;
Partakers of adopting grace,
How pure the bliss they share !
Hid from the world and all its eyes,
Within their heart the blessing lies,
And conscience feels it there.

The moment we believe, 'tis ours ;
And if we love with all our powers
The God from whom it came,
And if we serve with hearts sincere,
'Tis still discernible and clear,
An undisputed claim.

But, ah ! if foul and wilful sin
Stain and dishonour us within,
Farewell the joy we knew ;

Again the slaves of Nature's sway,
In lab'rinths of our own we stray,
Without a guide or clue.

The chaste and pure, who fear to grieve
The gracious Spirit they receive,
His work distinctly trace ;
And, strong in undissembling love,
Boldly assert and clearly prove
Their hearts His dwelling-place.

O messenger of dear delight,
Whose voice dispels the deepest night,
Sweet peace-proclaiming Dove !
With Thee at hand to soothe our pains,
No wish unsatisfied remains,
No task but that of Love.

'Tis Love unites what sin divides ;
The centre, where all bliss resides ;
  To which the soul once brought,
Reclining on the first great Cause,
From His abounding sweetness draws
  Peace passing human thought.

Sorrow foregoes its nature there,
And life assumes a tranquil air,
  Divested of its woes ;   [breast,
There sovereign goodness soothes the
Till then incapable of rest,
  In sacred sure repose.

GOD HIDES HIS PEOPLE.

To lay the soul that loves him low
  Becomes the Only Wise :
To hide, beneath a veil of woe,
  The children of the skies.

Man, though a worm, would yet be
    great ;
  Though feeble, would seem strong ;
Assumes an independent state,
  By sacrilege and wrong.

Strange the reverse, which, once abased,
  The haughty creature proves !
He feels his soul a barren waste,
  Nor dares affirm he loves.

Scorn'd by the thoughtless and the vain,
  To God he presses near ;
Superior to the world's disdain,
  And happy in its sneer.

Oh welcome, in his heart he says,
  Humility and shame !
Farewell the wish for human praise,
  The music of a name !

But will not scandal mar the good
  That I might else perform ?
And can God work it, if he would,
  By so despised a worm ?

Ah, vainly anxious !—leave the Lord
  To rule thee, and dispose ;
Sweet is the mandate of His word,
  And gracious all He does.

He draws from human littleness
  His grandeur and renown ;
And generous hearts with joy confess
  The triumph all His own.

Down then with self-exalting thoughts !
  Thy faith and hope employ,
To welcome all that He allots,
  And suffer shame with joy.

No longer, then, thou wilt encroach
  On His eternal right ;
And He shall smile at thy approach,
  And make thee His delight.

SELF-DIFFIDENCE.

Source of love, and light of day,
Tear me from myself away ;
Every view and thought of mine
Cast into the mould of Thine ;
Teach, oh teach this faithless heart
A consistent, constant part ;
Or, if it must live to grow
More rebellious, break it now !

Is it thus that I requite
Grace and goodness infinite ?
Every trace of every boon
Cancelled and erased so soon !

Can I grieve Thee, whom I love ;
Thee, in whom I live and move ?
If my sorrow touch Thee still,
Save me from so great an ill !

Oh ! the oppressive, irksome weight,
Felt in an uncertain state ;
Comfort, peace, and rest, adieu,
Should I prove at last untrue !
Still I choose Thee, follow still
Every notice of Thy will ;
But, unstable, strangely weak,
Still let slip the good I seek.

Self-confiding wretch, I thought
I could serve Thee as I ought,
Win Thee, and deserve to feel
All the Love Thou canst reveal !
Trusting self, a bruisèd reed,
Is to be deceived indeed.
Save me from this harm and loss,
Lest my gold turn all to dross !

Self is earthly—Faith alone
Makes an unseen world our own ;
Faith relinquished, how we roam,
Feel our way, and leave our home !
Spurious gems our hopes entice,
While we scorn the pearl of price ;
And, preferring servants' pay,
Cast the children's bread away.

THE ACQUIESCENCE OF PURE LOVE.

LOVE ! if Thy destined sacrifice am I,
    Come, slay thy victim, and prepare Thy fires ;
Plunged in Thy depths of mercy, let me die
    The death which every soul that lives desires !

I watch my hours, and see them fleet away ;
    The time is long that I have languished here ;
Yet all my thoughts Thy purposes obey,
    With no reluctance, cheerful and sincere.

To me 'tis equal, whether Love ordain
    My life or death, appoint me pain or ease :
My soul perceives no real ill in pain ;
    In ease or health no real good she sees.

One Good she covets, and that Good alone ;
    To choose Thy will, from selfish bias free ;
And to prefer a cottage to a throne,
    And grief to comfort, if it pleases Thee.

That we should bear the cross is Thy command,
    Die to the world, and live to self no more ;
Suffer, unmoved, beneath the rudest hand,
    As pleased when shipwrecked as when safe on shore.

THE ENTIRE SURRENDER.

PEACE has unveiled her smiling face,
And woos thy soul to her embrace,
Enjoyed with ease, if thou refrain
From earthly love, else sought in vain ;
She dwells with all who Truth prefer,
But seeks not them who seek not her.

Yield to the Lord, with simple heart,
All that thou hast, and all thou art ;
Renounce all strength but strength divine,
And peace shall be for ever thine :
Behold the path which I have trod,
My path, till I go home to God.

GLORY TO GOD ALONE.

OH, loved ! but not enough—though dearer far
Than self and its most loved enjoyments are ;
None duly loves Thee, but who, nobly free
From sensual objects, finds his all in Thee.

Glory of God ! thou stranger here below,
Whom man nor knows, nor feels a wish to know ;
Our faith and reason are both shocked to find
Man in the post of honour—Thee behind.

Reason exclaims—" Let every creature fall,
" Ashamed, abased, before the Lord of all ! "
And faith, o'erwhelmed with such a dazzling blaze,
Feebly describes the beauty she surveys.

Yet man, dim-sighted man, and rash as blind,
Deaf to the dictates of his better mind,
In frantic competition dares the skies,
And claims precedence of the Only Wise.

Oh, lost in vanity, till once self-known !
Nothing is great, or good, but God alone ;
When thou shalt stand before His awful face,
Then, at the last, thy pride shall know his place.

Glorious, Almighty, First, and without end !
When wilt Thou melt the mountains and descend ?
When wilt Thou shoot abroad Thy conquering rays,
And teach these atoms Thou hast made Thy praise ?

Thy Glory is the sweetest heaven I feel ;
And, if I seek it with too fierce a zeal,
Thy Love, triumphant o'er a selfish will,
Taught me the passion, and inspires it still.

My reason, all my faculties, unite,
To make Thy Glory their supreme delight ;
Forbid it, Fountain of my brightest days,
That I should rob Thee, and usurp Thy praise !

My soul ! rest happy in thy low estate,
Nor hope, nor wish, to be esteemed or great ;
To take the impression of a will divine,
Be that thy glory, and those riches thine.

Confess Him righteous in His just decrees,
Love what He loves, and let His pleasure please ;
Die daily ; from the touch of sin recede ;
Then thou hast crowned Him, and He reigns indeed.

SELF-LOVE AND TRUTH INCOMPATIBLE.

FROM thorny wilds a monster came,
That filled my soul with fear and shame;
The birds, forgetful of their mirth,
Droop'd at the sight, and fell to earth;
When thus a sage addressed mine ear,
Himself unconscious of a fear:
   " Whence all this terror and surprise,
" Distracted looks and streaming eyes?
" Far from the world and its affairs,
" The joy it boasts, the pain it shares,
" Surrender, without guile or art,
" To God, an undivided heart;
" The savage form, so feared before,
" Shall scare your trembling soul no
      more;
" For loathsome as the sight may be,
" 'Tis but the *love of self* you see.

" Fix all your love on God alone,
" Chuse but His will, and hate your own,
" No fear shall in your path be found,
" The dreary waste shall bloom around,
" And you, through all your happy days,
" Shall bless His name, and sing His
      praise."
   O lovely solitude, how sweet
The silence of this calm retreat!
Here Truth, the fair whom I pursue,
Gives all her beauty to my view;
The simple unadorned display
Charms every pain and fear away.
O Truth, whom millions proudly slight;
O Truth, my treasure and delight!
Accept this tribute to thy name,
And this poor heart from which it came!

THE LOVE OF GOD THE END OF LIFE.

SINCE life in sorrow must be spent,
So be it—I am well content,
And meekly wait my last remove,
Seeking only growth in love.

No bliss I seek, but to fulfil
In life, in death, Thy lovely will;
No succours in my woes I want,
Save what Thou art pleased to grant.

Our days are numbered, let us spare
Our anxious hearts a needless care:
'Tis Thine to number out our days;
Ours to give them to Thy praise.

Love is our only business here,
Love, simple, constant, and sincere;
O blessed days Thy servants see,
Spent, O Lord! in pleasing Thee.

REPOSE IN GOD.

BLEST! who, far from all mankind,
This world's shadows left behind,
Hears from Heaven a gentle strain
Whispering Love, and loves again.

Blest! who, free from self-esteem,
Dives into the great Supreme,
All desire besides discards,
Joys inferior none regards.
  C

Blest! who in Thy bosom seeks
Rest that nothing earthly breaks,
Dead to self and worldly things,
Lost in Thee, Thou King of kings!

Ye that know my secret fire,
Softly speak and soon retire;
Favour my divine repose,
Spare the sleep a God bestows.

LOVE PURE AND FERVENT.

JEALOUS, and with love o'erflowing,
  God demands a fervent heart ;
Grace and bounty still bestowing,
  Calls us to a grateful part.

Oh, then, with supreme affection
  His paternal Will regard !
If it cost us some dejection,
  Every sigh has its reward.

Perfect Love has power to soften
  Cares that might our peace destroy;
Nay, does more—transforms them often,
  Changing sorrow into joy.

Sovereign Love appoints the measure
  And the number of our pains ;
And is pleased when we find pleasure
  In the trials He ordains.

THE PERFECT SACRIFICE.

I PLACE an offering at Thy shrine,
  From taint and blemish clear,
Simple and pure in its design,
  Of all that I hold dear.

I yield Thee back Thy gifts again,
  Thy gifts which most I prize ;
Desirous only to retain
  The notice of Thine eyes.

But if, by Thine adored decree,
  That blessing be denied ;
Resigned and unreluctant, see
  My every wish subside.

Thy will in all things I approve,
  Exalted or cast down !
Thy will in every state I love,
  And even in Thy frown.

DIVINE LOVE ENDURES NO RIVAL.

LOVE is the Lord whom I obey,
Whose will transported I perform ;
  The centre of my rest, my stay,
Love's all in all to me, myself a worm.

For uncreated charms I burn,
Oppressed by slavish fear no more ;
  For One in whom I may discern,
Even when He frowns, a sweetness I adore.

He little loves Him who complains,
And finds him rigorous and severe ;
  His heart is sordid, and he feigns,
Though loud in boasting of a soul sincere.

Love causes grief, but 'tis to move
And stimulate the slumbering mind ;
  And he has never tasted love
Who shuns a pang so graciously designed.

Sweet is the cross, above all sweets,
To souls enamoured with Thy smiles ;
The keenest woe life ever meets
Love strips of all its terrors, and beguiles.

'Tis just that God should not be dear
Where Self engrosses all the thought,
And groans and murmurs make it clear,
Whatever else is loved, the Lord is not.

The love of Thee flows just as much
As that of ebbing self subsides ;
Our hearts, their scantiness is such,
Bear not the conflict of two rival tides.

Both cannot govern in one soul ;
Then let self-love be dispossessed ;
The love of God deserves the whole,
And will not dwell with so despised a guest.

THE SECRETS OF DIVINE LOVE ARE TO BE KEPT.

SUN ! stay thy course, this moment
    stay—
Suspend the o'erflowing tide of day,
Divulge not such a love as mine,
Ah ! hide the mystery divine ;
Lest man, who deems my glory shame,
Should learn the secret of my flame.

O Night ! propitious to my views,
Thy sable awning wide diffuse :
Conceal alike my joy and pain,
Nor draw thy curtain back again,
Though morning, by the tears she shows,
Seems to participate my woes.

Ye Stars ! whose faint and feeble fires
Express my languishing desires,
Whose slender beams pervade the skies
As silent as my secret sighs,
Those emanations of a soul
That darts her fires beyond the pole ;

Your rays, that scarce assist the sight,
That pierce, but not displace, the night,
That shine indeed, but nothing show
Of all those various scenes below,
Bring no disturbance, rather prove
Incentives to a sacred love.

Thou Moon! whose never-failing course
Bespeaks a providential force,
Go, tell the tidings of my flame
To Him who calls the stars by name.
Whose absence kills, whose presence
    cheers,
Who blots or brightens all my years.

While, in the blue abyss of space,
Thine orb performs its rapid race,
Still whisper in his listening ears
The language of my sighs and tears ;
Tell him, I seek him, far below,
Lost in a wilderness of woe.

Ye thought-composing, silent Hours,
Diffusing peace o'er all my powers,
Friends of the pensive ! who conceal
In darkest shades the flames I feel ;
To you I trust, and safely may,
The love that wastes my strength away.

In sylvan scenes and caverns rude,
I taste the sweets of solitude ;
Retired indeed, but not alone,
I share them with a Spouse unknown,
Who hides me here, from envious eyes,
From all intrusion and surprise.

Imbowering Shades, and Dens pro-
found !
Where Echo rolls the voice around ;
Mountains ! whose elevated heads
A moist and misty veil o'erspreads ;
Disclose a solitary bride
To Him I love—to none beside.

Ye Rills ! that, murmuring all the way,
Among the polished pebbles stray ;
Creep silently along the ground,
Lest, drawn by that harmonious sound,
Some wanderer, whom I would not
meet,
Should stumble on my loved retreat.

Enamelled Meads, and Hillocks green,
And Streams that water all the scene !
Ye Torrents, loud in distant ears !
Ye Fountains ! that receive my tears !
Ah ! still conceal, with caution due,
A charge I trust with none but you.

If, when my pain and grief increase,
I seem to enjoy the sweetest peace,
It is because I find so fair
The charming object of my care,
That I can sport and pleasure make
Of torment suffered for His sake.

Ye Meads and Groves, unconscious
things !
Ye know not whence my pleasure
springs ;
Ye know not, and ye cannot know,
The source from which my sorrows flow:
The dear sole Cause of all I feel,—
He knows, and understands them well.

Ye Deserts ! where the wild beasts rove,
Scenes sacred to my hours of love ;
Ye Forests ! in whose shades I stray,
Benighted under burning day ;
Ah ! whisper not how blest am I,
Nor while I live, nor when I die.

Ye Lambs ! who sport beneath these
shades,
And bound along the mossy glades,
Be taught a salutary fear,
And cease to bleat when I am near :
The wolf may hear your harmless cry,
Whom ye should dread as much as I.

How calm, amid these scenes, my mind
How perfect is the peace I find !
Oh, hush, be still, my every part,
My tongue, my pulse, my beating heart
That Love, aspiring to its cause,
May suffer not a moment's pause.

Ye swift-finned nations, that abide
In seas as fathomless as wide ;
And, unsuspicious of a snare,
Pursue at large your pleasures there :
Poor sportive fools ! how soon does man
Your heedless ignorance trepan !

Away ! dive deep into the brine,
Where never yet sunk plummet-line ;
Trust me, the vast leviathan
Is merciful, compared with man ;
Avoid his arts, forsake the beach,
And never play within his reach !

My soul her bondage ill endures ;
I pant for liberty like yours ;
I long for that immense profound,
That knows no bottom and no bound
Lost in infinity, to prove
The incomprehensible of Love.

Ye Birds ! that lessen as ye fly,
And vanish in the distant sky ;
To whom yon airy waste belongs,
Resounding with your cheerful songs ;
Haste to escape from human sight !
Fear less the vulture and the kite.

How blest and how secure am I,
When, quitting earth, I soar on high ;
When, lost, like you I disappear,
And float in a sublimer sphere !
Whence falling, within human view,
I am ensnared, and caught like you.

Omniscient God, whose notice deigns
To try the heart and search the reins,
Compassionate the numerous woes
I dare not, even to Thee, disclose ;
Oh save me from the cruel hands
Of men, who fear not Thy commands

Love, all-subduing and divine,
Care for a creature truly Thine ;
Reign in a heart disposed to own
No sovereign but Thyself alone ;
Cherish a bride who cannot rove,
Nor quit Thee for a meaner love !

THE VICISSITUDES EXPERIENCED IN THE CHRISTIAN LIFE.

I SUFFER fruitless anguish day by day,
  Each moment, as it passes, marks my pain ;
Scarce knowing whither, doubtfully I stray,
  And see no end of all that I sustain.

The more I strive the more I am withstood ;
  Anxiety increasing every hour,
My spirit finds no rest, performs no good,
  And nought remains of all my former power.

My peace of heart is fled, I know not where ;
  My happy hours, like shadows, passed away ;
Their sweet remembrance doubles all my care,
  Night darker seems, succeeding such a day.

Dear faded joys, and impotent regret,
  What profit is there in incessant tears ?
O Thou, whom, once beheld, we ne'er forget,
  Reveal thy Love, and banish all my fears !

Alas ! He flies me—treats me as his foe,
  Views not my sorrows, hears not when I plead ;
Woe such as mine, despised, neglected woe,
  Unless it shortens life, is vain indeed.

Pierced with a thousand wounds, I yet survive ;
  My pangs are keen, but no complaint transpires ;
And while in terrors of Thy wrath I live,
  Hell seems to lose its less tremendous fires.

Has hell a pain I would not gladly bear,
  So thy severe displeasure might subside ?
Hopeless of ease, I seem already there,
  My life extinguished, and yet death denied.

Is this the joy so promised ?—this the love,
  The unchanging love, so sworn in better days ?
Ah ! dangerous glories ! shown me, but to prove
  How lovely Thou, and I how rash to gaze.

Why did I see them ? had I still remained
  Untaught, still ignorant how fair Thou art,
My humbler wishes I had soon obtained,
  Nor known the torments of a doubting heart.

Deprived of all, yet feeling no desires,
  Whence then, I cry, the pangs that I sustain ?
Dubious and uninformed, my soul inquires—
  Ought she to cherish or shake off her pain ?

Suffering, I suffer not ; sincerely love,
    Yet feel no touch of that enlivening flame ;
As chance inclines me, unconcerned I move,
    All times, and all events, to me the same.

I search my heart, and not a wish is there,
    But burns with zeal that hated self may fall ;
Such is the sad disquietude I share,
    A sea of doubts, and self the source of all.

I ask not life, nor do I wish to die ;
    And if thine hand accomplish not my cure,
I would not purchase with a single sigh
    A free discharge from all that I endure.

I groan in chains, yet want not a release ;
    Am sick, and know not the distempered part ;
Am just as void of purpose as of peace ;
    Have neither plan, nor fear, nor hope, nor heart.

My claim to life, though sought with earnest care,
    No light within me or without me shows ;
Once I had faith, but now in self-despair
    Find my chief cordial and my best repose.

My soul is a forgotten thing ; she sinks,
    Sinks and is lost, without a wish to rise ;
Feels an indifference she abhors, and thinks
    Her name erased for ever from the skies.

Language affords not my distress a name,—
    Yet is it real, and no sickly dream ;
'Tis Love inflicts it ; though to feel that flame
    Is all I know of happiness supreme.

When Love departs, a chaos wide and vast,
    And dark as hell, is opened in the soul ;
When Love returns, the gloomy scene is past,
    No tempests shake her, and no fears control.

Then tell me why these ages of delay ?
    O Love, all excellent, once more appear,
Disperse the shades, and snatch me into day,
    From this abyss of night, these floods of fear !

No—Love is angry, will not now endure
    A sigh of mine, or suffer a complaint ;
He smites me, wounds me, and withholds the cure ;
    Exhausts my powers, and leaves me sick and faint.

He wounds, and hides the hand that gave the blow ;
    He flies, he reappears, and wounds again ;—
Was ever heart that loved Thee treated so ?
    Yet I adore Thee, though it seem in vain.

And wilt Thou leave me, whom, when lost and blind,
　　Thou didst distinguish and vouchsafe to chuse,
Before Thy laws were written in my mind,
　　While yet the world had all my thoughts and views?

Now leave me? when, enamoured of Thy laws,
　　I make Thy glory my supreme delight;
Now blot me from Thy register, and cause
　　A faithful soul to perish from Thy sight?

What can have caused the change which I deplore?
　　Is it to prove me, if my heart be true?
Permit me then, while prostrate I adore,
　　To draw, and place its picture in Thy view.

'Tis Thine without reserve, most simply Thine;
　　So given to Thee, that it is not my own;
A willing captive of Thy grace divine;
　　And loves, and seeks Thee, for Thyself alone.

Pain cannot move it, danger cannot scare;
　　Pleasure and wealth, in its esteem, are dust;
It loves Thee, even when least inclined to spare
　　Its tenderest feelings, and avows Thee just.

'Tis all Thine own; my spirit is so too,
　　An undivided offering at Thy shrine;
It seeks Thy glory with no double view,
　　Thy glory, with no secret bent to mine.

Love, holy Love! and art Thou not severe,
　　To slight me, thus devoted and thus fixed?
Mine is an everlasting ardour, clear
　　From all self-bias, generous and unmixed.

But I am silent, seeing what I see,—
　　And fear, with cause, that I am self-deceived;
Not even my faith is from suspicion free,
　　And that I love seems not to be believed.

Live Thou, and reign for ever, glorious Lord!
　　My last, least offering, I present Thee now;—
Renounce me, leave me, and be still adored!
　　Slay me, my God, and I applaud the blow.

LOVE FAITHFUL IN THE ABSENCE OF THE BELOVED.

In vain ye woo me to your harmless joys,
Ye pleasant bowers, remote from strife and noise;
Your shades, the witnesses of many a vow
Breathed forth in happier days, are irksome now;
Denied that smile 'twas once my heaven to see,
Such scenes, such pleasures, are all past with me.

In vain He leaves me, I shall love Him still ;
And though I mourn, not murmur at His will;
I have no cause—an object all divine
Might well grow weary of a soul like mine ;
Yet pity me, great God ! forlorn, alone,
Heartless and hopeless, Life and Love all gone.

WATCHING UNTO GOD IN THE NIGHT SEASON.

SLEEP at last has fled these eyes,
  Nor do I regret his flight;
More alert my spirits rise,
  And my heart is free and light.

Nature silent all around,
  Not a single witness near ;
God as soon as sought is found,
  And the flame of love burns clear.

Interruption, all day long,
  Checks the current of my joys ;
Creatures press me with a throng,
  And perplex me with their noise.

Undisturbed I muse all night
  On the first Eternal Fair ;
Nothing there obstructs delight,
  Love is renovated there.

Life, with its perpetual stir,
  Proves a foe to Love and me ;

Fresh entanglements occur,—
  Comes the night, and sets me free.

Never more, sweet sleep, suspend
  My enjoyments, always new :
Leave me to possess my friend ;
  Other eyes and hearts subdue.

Hush the world, that I may wake
  To the taste of pure delights ;
Oh the pleasures I partake,—
  God the partner of my nights !

David, for the selfsame cause,
  Night preferred to busy day :
Hearts whom heavenly beauty draws
  Wish the glaring sun away.

Sleep, self-lovers, is for you ;—
  Souls, that love celestial know,
Fairer scenes by night can view
  Than the sun can ever show.

ON THE SAME.

SEASON of my purest pleasure,
  Sealer of observing eyes !
When, in larger, freer measure,
  I can commune with the skies ;
While, beneath thy shade extended,
  Weary man forgets his woes,
I, my daily trouble ended,
  Find, in watching, my repose.

Silence all around prevailing,
  Nature hushed in slumber sweet,
No rude noise mine ears assailing,
  Now my God and I can meet :

Universal nature slumbers,
  And my soul partakes the calm,
Breathes her ardour out in numbers,
  Plaintive song or lofty psalm.

Now my passion, pure and holy,
  Shines and burns without restraint,
Which the day's fatigue and folly
  Cause to languish, dim and faint :
Charming hours of relaxation !
  How I dread the ascending sun !
Surely idle conversation
  Is an evil, matched by none.

Worldly prate and babble hurt me;
   Unintelligible prove;
Neither teach me nor divert me;
   I have ears for none but Love.
Me they rude esteem, and foolish,
   Hearing my absurd replies;
I have neither art's fine polish
   Nor the knowledge of the wise.

Simple souls, and unpolluted
   By conversing with the great,
Have a mind and taste ill suited
   To their dignity and state;
All their talking, reading, writing,
   Are but talents misapplied;
Infants' prattle I delight in,
   Nothing human chuse beside.

'Tis the secret fear of sinning
   Checks my tongue, or I should say,
When I see the night beginning,
   I am glad of parting day:

Love this gentle admonition
   Whispers soft within my breast;
" Choice befits not thy condition,
   " Acquiescence suits thee best."

Henceforth, the repose and pleasure
   Night affords me I resign;
And Thy will shall be the measure,
   Wisdom Infinite! of mine:
Wishing is but inclination
   Quarrelling with Thy decrees;
Wayward nature finds the occasion,—
   'Tis her folly and disease.

Night, with its sublime enjoyments,
   Now no longer will I chuse;
Nor the day, with its employments,
   Irksome as they seem, refuse:
Lessons of a God's inspiring
   Neither time nor place impedes;
From our wishing and desiring
   Our unhappiness proceeds.

ON THE SAME.

Night! how I love thy silent shades,
   My spirits they compose;
The bliss of heaven my soul pervades,
   In spite of all my woes.

While sleep instils her poppy dews
   In every slumbering eye,
I watch, to meditate and muse,
   In blest tranquillity.

And when I feel a God immense
   Familiarly impart,
With every proof He can dispense,
   His favour to my heart;

My native meanness I lament,
   Though most divinely filled
With all the ineffable content
   That Deity can yield.

His purpose and His course he keeps;
   Treads all my reasonings down;
Commands me out of nature's deeps,
   And hides me in His own.

When in the dust, its proper place,
   Our pride of heart we lay,

'Tis then a deluge of His grace
   Bears all our sins away.

Thou whom I serve, and whose I am,
   Whose influence from on high
Refines, and still refines my flame,
   And makes my fetters fly;

How wretched is the creature's state
   Who thwarts Thy gracious power;
Crushed under sin's enormous weight,
   Increasing every hour!

The night, when passed entire with Thee,
   How luminous and clear;
Then sleep has no delights for me,
   Lest Thou shouldst disappear.

My Saviour! occupy me still
   In this secure recess;
Let reason slumber if she will,
   My joy shall not be less:

Let reason slumber out the night;
   But if Thou deign to make
My soul the abode of truth and light,
   Ah, keep my heart awake!

THE JOY OF THE CROSS.

Long plunged in sorrow, I resign
My soul to that dear hand of Thine,
    Without reserve or fear ;
That hand shall wipe my streaming eyes,
Or into smiles of glad surprise
    Transform the falling tear.

My sole possession is Thy love;
In earth beneath, or heaven above,
    I have no other store ;
And though with fervent suit I pray,
And importune Thee night and day,
    I ask Thee nothing more.

My rapid hours pursue the course
Prescribed them by love's sweetest force;
    And I Thy sovereign will,
Without a wish to escape my doom ;
Though still a sufferer from the womb,
    And doomed to suffer still.

By Thy command, where'er I stray,
Sorrow attends me all my way,
    A never-failing friend ;
And if my sufferings may augment
Thy praise, behold me well content,—
    Let sorrow still attend !

It costs me no regret, that she,
Who followed Christ, should follow me;
    And though, where'er she goes,
Thorns spring spontaneous at her feet,
I love her, and extract a sweet
    From all my bitter woes.

Adieu, ye vain delights of earth !
Insipid sports, and childish mirth,
    I taste no sweets in you ;
Unknown delights are in the Cross,
All joy beside to me is dross ;
    And Jesus thought so too.

The Cross ! oh, ravishment and bliss,—
How grateful even its anguish is,
    Its bitterness how sweet !
There every sense, and all the mind,
In all her faculties refined,
    Tastes happiness complete.

Souls once enabled to disdain
Base sublunary joys, maintain
    Their dignity secure ;
The fever of desire is passed,
And love has all its genuine taste,
    Is delicate and pure.

Self-love no grace in sorrow sees,
Consults her own peculiar ease ;
    'Tis all the bliss she knows :
But nobler aims true Love employ ;
In self-denial is her joy,
    In suffering her repose.

Sorrow and Love go side by side :
Nor height nor depth can e'er divide
    Their heaven-appointed bands ;
Those dear associates still are one,
Nor till the race of life is run
    Disjoin their wedded hands.

Jesus, avenger of our fall,
Thou faithful lover, above all
    The Cross hast ever borne !
Oh tell me,—life is in Thy voice,—
How much afflictions were Thy choice,
    And sloth and ease Thy scorn !

Thy choice and mine shall be the same,
Inspirer of that holy flame
    Which must for ever blaze !
To take the Cross and follow Thee,
Where love and duty lead, shall be
    My portion and my praise.

JOY IN MARTYRDOM.

Sweet tenants of this grove,
    Who sing, without design,
A song of artless love,
    In unison with mine :

These echoing shades return
    Full many a note of ours,
That wise ones cannot learn
    With all their boasted powers.

O Thou ! whose sacred charms
    These hearts so seldom love,
Although Thy beauty warms
    And blesses all above ;
How slow are human things
    To choose their happiest lot !
All-glorious King of kings,
    Say why we love Thee not ?

This heart, that cannot rest,
    Shall Thine for ever prove ;
Though bleeding and distressed,
    Yet joyful in Thy love :
'Tis happy, though it breaks
    Beneath Thy chastening hand ;
And speechless,—yet it speaks
    What Thou canst understand.

SIMPLE TRUST.

STILL, still, without ceasing
    I feel it increasing,
This fervour of holy desire ;
    And often exclaim,
    Let me die in the flame
Of a love that can never expire !

Had I words to explain
    What she must sustain
Who dies to the world and its ways :
    How joy and affright,
    Distress and delight,
Alternately chequer her days ;

Thou, sweetly severe !
    I would make Thee appear,
In all Thou art pleased to award,
    Not more in the sweet
    Than the bitter I meet
My tender and merciful Lord.

This faith, in the dark
    Pursuing its mark,
Through many sharp trials of love,
    Is the sorrowful waste
    That is to be passed
In the way to the Canaan above.

THE NECESSITY OF SELF-ABASEMENT.

SOURCE of Love, my brighter Sun,
    Thou alone my comfort art ;
See, my race is almost run ;
    Hast Thou left this trembling heart ?

In my youth Thy charming eyes
    Drew me from the ways of men ;
Then I drank unmingled joys ;
    Frown of Thine saw never then.

Spouse of Christ was then my name ;
    And devoted all to Thee,
Strangely jealous, I became
    Jealous of this self in me.

Thee to love, and none beside,
    Was my darling, sole employ ;
While alternately I died,
    Now of grief, and now of joy.

Through the dark and silent night
    On Thy radiant smiles I dwelt ;
And to see the dawning light
    Was the keenest pain I felt.

Thou my gracious teacher wert ;
    And Thine eye, so close applied,
While it watched thy pupil's heart,
    Seemed to look at none beside.

Conscious of no evil drift,
    This, I cried, is love indeed !—
'Tis the Giver, not the gift,
    Whence the joys I feel proceed.

But soon humbled, and laid low,
    Stript of all Thou hast conferred,
Nothing left but sin and woe,
    I perceived how I had erred.

Oh the vain conceit of man,
    Dreaming of a good his own,
Arrogating all he can,
    Though the Lord is good alone !

He the graces thou hast wrought
    Makes subservient to his pride ;
Ignorant, that one such thought
    Passes all his sin beside.

Such his folly—proved, at last,
    By the loss of that repose

Self-complacence cannot taste,
    Only Love Divine bestows.

'Tis by this reproof severe,
    And by this reproof alone,
His defects at last appear,
    Man is to himself made known.

Learn, all earth ! that feeble man,
    Sprung from this terrestrial clod,
Nothing is, and nothing can ;
    Life and power are all in God.

LOVE INCREASED BY SUFFERING.

" I LOVE the Lord " is still the strain
    This heart delights to sing ;
But I reply,—" Your thoughts are vain,
    " Perhaps 'tis no such thing."

Before the power of Love Divine
    Creation fades away ;
Till only God is seen to shine
    In all that we survey.

In gulfs of awful night we find
    The God of our desires ;
'Tis there He stamps the yielding mind,
    And doubles all its fires.

Flames of encircling love invest,
    And pierce it sweetly through ;
'Tis filled with sacred joy, yet pressed
    With sacred sorrow too.

Ah Love ! my heart is in the right—
    Amidst a thousand woes,
To Thee its ever new delight
    And all its peace it owes.

Fresh causes of distress occur
    Where'er I look or move ;

The comforts I to all prefer
    Are solitude and love.

Nor exile I, nor prison fear ;
    Love makes my courage great ;
I find a Saviour everywhere,
    His grace in every state.

Nor castle walls, nor dungeons deep,
    Exclude His quickening beams ;
There I can sit, and sing, and weep,
    And dwell on heavenly themes.

There sorrow, for His sake, is found
    A joy beyond compare ;
There no presumptuous thoughts abound,
    No pride can enter there.

A Saviour doubles all my joys,
    And sweetens all my pains,
His strength in my defence employs,
    Consoles me and sustains.

I fear no ill, resent no wrong,
    Nor feel a passion move,
When malice whets her slanderous
        tongue ;
    Such patience is in love.

SCENES FAVOURABLE TO MEDITATION.

WILDS horrid and dark with o'ershadowing trees,
    Rocks that ivy and briers infold,
Scenes Nature with dread and astonishment sees,
    But I with a pleasure untold ;

Though awfully silent, and shaggy, and rude,
  I am charmed with the peace ye afford ;
Your shades are a temple where none will intrude,
  The abode of my Lover and Lord.

I am sick of thy splendour, O fountain of day,
  And here I am hid from its beams ;
Here safely contemplate a brighter display
  Of the noblest and holiest of themes.

Ye forests, that yield me my sweetest repose,
  Where stillness and solitude reign,
To you I securely and boldly disclose
  The dear anguish of which I complain.

Here, sweetly forgetting, and wholly forgot
  By the world and its turbulent throng,
The birds and the streams lend me many a note
  That aids meditation and song.

Here, wandering in scenes that are sacred to night,
  Love wears me and wastes me away ;
And often the sun has spent much of his light
  Ere yet I perceive it is day.

While a mantle of darkness envelopes the sphere,
  My sorrows are sadly rehearsed ;
To me the dark hours are all equally dear,
  And the last is as sweet as the first.

Here I and the beasts of the desert agree ;
  Mankind are the wolves that I fear :
They grudge me my natural right to be free,
  But nobody questions it here.

Though little is found in this dreary abode
  That appetite wishes to find,
My spirit is soothed by the presence of God,
  And appetite wholly resigned.

Ye desolate scenes, to your solitude led,
  My life I in praises employ,
And scarce know the source of the tears that I shed,
  Proceed they from sorrow or joy.

There's nothing I seem to have skill to discern ;
  I feel out my way in the dark ;
Love reigns in my bosom, I constantly burn,
  Yet hardly distinguish a spark.

I live, yet I seem to myself to be dead ;
  Such a riddle is not to be found ;
I am nourished without knowing how I am fed,
  I have nothing, and yet I abound.

O Love ! who in darkness art pleased to abide,
　　Though dimly yet surely I see
That these contrarieties only reside
　　In the soul that is chosen of Thee.

Ah send me not back to the race of mankind,
　　Perversely by folly beguiled :
For where, in the crowds I have left, shall I find
　　The spirit and heart of a child ?

Here let me, though fixed in a desert, be free ;
　　A little one whom they despise,
Though lost to the world, if in union with Thee,
　　Shall be holy and happy and wise.

TRANSLATIONS OF THE LATIN POEMS OF MILTON.

ELEGIES.

ELEGY I.

TO CHARLES DEODATI.

AT length, my friend, the far-sent letters come,
Charged with thy kindness, to their destined home ;
They come, at length, from Deva's western side,
Where prone she seeks the salt Vergivian tide.
Trust me, my joy is great that thou shouldst be,
Though born of foreign race, yet born for me,
And that my sprightly friend, now free to roam,
Must seek again so soon his wonted home.
I well content, where Thames with influent tide
My native city laves, meantime reside,   10
Nor zeal nor duty now my steps impel
To reedy Cam, and my forbidden cell.
Nor aught of pleasure in those fields have I,
That, to the musing bard, all shade deny.
'Tis time that I a pedant's threats disdain,
And fly from wrongs my soul will ne'er sustain.
If peaceful days, in lettered leisure spent
Beneath my father's roof, be banishment,
Then call me banished, I will ne'er refuse
A name expressive of the lot I chuse.   20
I would that, exiled to the Pontic shore,
Rome's hapless bard had suffered nothing more ;
He then had equalled even Homer's lays,
And Virgil ! thou hadst won but second praise.
For here I woo the Muse, with no control ;
And here my books—my life—absorb me whole.
Here too I visit, or to smile, or weep,
The winding theatre's majestic sweep ;
The grave or gay colloquial scene recruits
My spirits, spent in learning's long pursuits,   30
Whether some senior shrewd, or spendthrift heir,
Suitor, or soldier now unarmed, be there ;
Or some coifed brooder o'er a ten years' cause
Thunder the Norman gibberish of the laws.
The lacquey there oft dupes the wary sire,
And artful speeds the enamoured son's desire.

There, virgins oft, unconscious what they prove,
What love is know not, yet, unknowing, love.
Or if impassioned Tragedy wield high
The bloody sceptre, give her locks to fly   40
Wild as the winds, and roll her haggard eye,
I gaze, and grieve, still cherishing my grief,
At times even bitter tears yield sweet relief :
As when, from bliss untasted torn away,
Some youth dies, hapless, on his bridal day ;—
Or when the ghost, sent back from shades below,
Fills the assassin's heart with vengeful woe,
When Troy, or Argos, the dire scene affords,
Or Creon's hall laments its guilty lords.
Nor always city-pent, or pent at home,   50
I dwell ; but when spring calls me forth to roam,
Expatiate in our proud suburban shades
Of branching elm, that never sun pervades.
Here many a virgin troop I may descry,
Like stars of mildest influence, gliding by.
Oh forms divine ! Oh looks that might inspire
Even Jove himself, grown old, with young desire !
Oft have I gazed on gem-surpassing eyes,
Outsparkling every star that gilds the skies,
Necks whiter than the ivory arm bestowed   60
By Jove on Pelops, or the Milky Road!
Bright locks, Love's golden snare ! these falling low,
Those playing wanton o'er the graceful brow !
Cheeks too, more winning sweet than after shower
Adonis turned to Flora's favourite flower !
Yield, heroines, yield, and ye who shared the embrace
Of Jupiter in ancient times, give place !
Give place, ye turbaned fair of Persia's coast !
And ye, not less renowned, Assyria's boast !
Submit, ye nymphs of Greece ! ye, once the bloom   70
Of Ilion ! and all ye of haughty Rome,
Who swept, of old, her theatres with trains
Redundant, and still live in classic strains !
To British damsels beauty's palm is due ;
Aliens ! to follow them is fame for you.
O city, founded by Dardanian hands,
Whose towering front the circling realms commands,
Too blest abode ! no loveliness we see
In all the earth, but it abounds in thee.
The virgin multitude that daily meets,   80
Radiant with gold and beauty, in thy streets,
Outnumbers all her train of starry fires,
With which Diana gilds thy lofty spires.
Fame says, that wafted hither by her doves,
With all her host of quiver-bearing loves,
Venus, preferring Paphian scenes no more,
Has fixed her empire on thy nobler shore.
But lest the sightless boy inforce my stay,

I leave these happy walls, while yet I may.
Immortal Moly shall secure my heart   90
From all the sorcery of Circæan art,
And I will e'en repass Cam's reedy pools
To face once more the warfare of the schools.
Meantime accept this trifle ! rhymes though few,
Yet such as prove thy Friend's remembrance true !

ELEGY II,

ON THE DEATH OF THE UNIVERSITY BEDEL AT CAMBRIDGE.

COMPOSED BY MILTON IN THE SEVENTEENTH YEAR OF HIS AGE.

THEE, whose refulgent staff, and summons clear,
    Minerva's flock long time was wont to obey,
Although thyself a herald, famous here,
    The last of heralds, Death, has snatched away.
He calls on all alike, nor even deigns
To spare the office that himself sustains.

Thy locks were whiter than the plumes displayed
    By Leda's paramour in ancient time,
But thou wast worthy ne'er to have decayed,
    Or Æson-like to know a second prime,
Worthy, for whom some goddess should have won
New life, oft kneeling to Apollo's son.

Commissioned to convene, with hasty call,
    The gownèd tribes, how graceful wouldst thou stand !
So stood Cyllenius erst in Priam's hall,
    Wing-footed messenger of Jove's command ;
And so Eurybates, when he addressed
To Peleus' son Atrides' proud behest.

Dread queen of sepulchres ! whose rigorous laws
    And watchful eyes run through the realms below ;
Oh, oft too adverse to Minerva's cause,
    Too often to the Muse not less a foe,
Chuse meaner marks, and with more equal aim
Pierce useless drones, earth's burden and its shame !

Flow, therefore, tears for him, from every eye ;
    All ye disciples of the Muses, weep !
Assembling all in robes of sable dye,
    Around his bier, lament his endless sleep !
And let complaining Elegy rehearse
In every school her sweetest, saddest verse.
    C   F F

ELEGY III.

ON THE DEATH OF THE BISHOP OF WINCHESTER.

COMPOSED IN THE AUTHOR'S SEVENTEENTH YEAR.

Silent I sat, dejected, and alone,
Making in thought the public woes my own,
When, first, arose the image in my breast
Of England's suffering by that scourge, the Pest !
How Death, his funeral torch and scythe in hand,
Entering the lordliest mansions of the land,
Has laid the gem-illumined palace low,
And levelled tribes of nobles at a blow.
I next deplored the famed fraternal pair,
Too soon to ashes turned, and empty air !   10
The heroes next, whom snatched into the skies
All Belgia saw, and followed with her sighs;
But thee far most I mourned, regretted most,
Winton's chief shepherd, and her worthiest boast !
Poured out in tears I thus complaining said :
" Death, next in power to him who rules the dead !
" Is't not enough that all the woodlands yield
" To thy fell force, and every verdant field ;
" That lilies, at one noisome blast of thine,
" And even the Cyprian queen's own roses, pine ;   20
" That oaks themselves, although the running rill
" Suckle their roots, must wither at thy will ;
" That all the wingèd nations, even those
" Whose heaven-directed flight the future shows,
" And all the beasts, that in dark forests stray,
" And all the herds of Proteus are thy prey?
" Ah, envious ! armed with powers so unconfined !
" Why stain thy hands with blood of human kind?
" Why take delight, with darts, that never roam,
" To chase a heaven-born spirit from her home?"   30
        While thus I mourned, the star of evening stood,
Now newly risen, above the western flood,
And Phœbus from his morning goal again
Had reached the gulfs of the Iberian main.
I wished repose, and on my couch reclined
Took early rest, to night and sleep resigned :
When—Oh for words to paint what I beheld !—
I seemed to wander in a spacious field,
Where all the champaign glowed with purple light
Like that o. sunrise on the mountain height ;   40
Flowers over all the field, of every hue
That ever Iris wore, luxuriant grew.
Nor Chloris, with whom amorous zephyrs play,
E'er dressed Alcinous' garden half so gay.

A silver current, like the Tagus, rolled
O'er golden sands, but sands of purer gold ;
With dewy airs Favonius fanned the flowers,
With airs awakened under rosy bowers :
Such, poets feign, irradiated all o'er
The sun's abode on India's utmost shore.   50
   While I that splendour and the mingled shade
Of fruitful vines with wonder fixt surveyed,
At once, with looks that beamed celestial grace,
The seer of Winton stood before my face.
His snowy vesture's hem descending low
His golden sandals swept ; and pure as snow
New-fallen shone the mitre on his brow.
Where'er he trod a tremulous sweet sound
Of gladness shook the flowery scene around :
Attendant angels clap their starry wings,   60
The trumpet shakes the sky, all æther rings ;
Each chants his welcome, folds him to his breast,
And thus a sweeter voice than all the rest :
" Ascend, my son ! thy Father's kingdom share !
" My son ! henceforth be freed from every care ! "
   So spake the voice, and at its tender close
With psaltry's sound the angelic band arose ;
Then night retired, and, chased by dawning day,
The visionary bliss passed all away.
I mourned my banished sleep, with fond concern ;   70
Frequent to me may dreams like this return !

ELEGY IV.

TO HIS TUTOR, THOMAS YOUNG,

CHAPLAIN TO THE ENGLISH FACTORY AT HAMBURGH,

WRITTEN IN THE AUTHOR'S EIGHTEENTH YEAR.

HENCE, my epistle—skim the deep—fly o'er
Yon smooth expanse to the Teutonic shore !
Haste—lest a friend should grieve for thy delay—
And the gods grant, that nothing thwart thy way !
I will myself invoke the king, who binds
In his Sicanian echoing vault the winds,
With Doris and her nymphs, and all the throng
Of azure gods, to speed thee safe along.
But rather to ensure thy happier haste,
Ascend Medea's chariot, if thou mayst ;   10
Or that, whence young Triptolemus of yore
Descended, welcome on the Scythian shore.
The sands, that line the German coast, descried,
To opulent Hamburga turn aside !

So called, if legendary fame be true,
From Hama, whom a club-armed Cimbrian slew.
There lives, deep-learned and primitively just,
A faithful steward of his Christian trust,
My friend, and favourite inmate of my heart,
That now is forced to want its better part.   20
What mountains now, and seas, alas, how wide!
From me this other, dearer self divide,
Dear as the sage renowned for moral truth
To the prime spirit of the Attic youth!
Dear as the Stagyrite to Ammon's son,
His pupil, who disdained the world he won!
Nor so did Chiron, or so Phœnix shine
In young Achilles' eyes, as he in mine.
First led by him through sweet Aonian shade,
Each sacred haunt of Pindus I surveyed;   30
And favoured by the Muse, whom I implored,
Thrice on my lip the hallowed stream I poured.
But thrice the sun's resplendent chariot, rolled
To Aries, has new-tinged his fleece with gold,
And Chloris twice has dressed the meadows gay,
And twice has summer parched their bloom away,
Since last delighted on his looks I hung,
Or my ear drank the music of his tongue:
Fly, therefore, and surpass the tempest's speed;
Aware thyself that there is urgent need!   40
Him, entering, thou shalt haply seated see
Beside his spouse, his infants on his knee;
Or turning, page by page, with studious look,
Some bulky Father, or God's holy book;
Or ministering (which is his weightiest care)
To Christ's assembled flock their heavenly fare.
Give him, whatever his employment be,
Such gratulation as he claims from me;
And, with a downcast eye, and carriage meek,
Addressing him, forget not thus to speak!   50
   " If, compassed round with arms, thou canst attend
To verse, verse greets thee from a distant friend.
Long due, and late, I left the English shore;
But make me welcome for that cause the more!
Such from Ulysses, his chaste wife to cheer,
The slow epistle came, though late, sincere.
But wherefore this? why palliate I the deed,
For which the culprit's self could hardly plead?
Self-charged, and self-condemned, his proper part
He feels neglected, with an aching heart;   60
But thou forgive : delinquents, who confess
And pray forgiveness, merit anger less;
From timid foes the lion turns away,
Nor yawns upon or rends a crouching prey;
Even pike-wielding Thracians learn to spare,
Won by soft influence of a suppliant prayer;

And Heaven's dread thunderbolt arrested stands
By a cheap victim, and uplifted hands.
Long had he wished to write, but was withheld,
And writes at last, by love alone compelled ;   70
For Fame, too often true when she alarms,
Reports thy neighbouring fields a scene of arms ;
Thy city against fierce besiegers barred,
And all the Saxon chiefs for fight prepared.
Enyo wastes thy country wide around,
And saturates with blood the tainted ground ;
Mars rests contented in his Thrace no more,
But goads his steeds to fields of German gore :
The ever-verdant olive fades and dies,
And Peace, the trumpet-hating goddess, flies,   80
Flies from that earth which Justice long had left,
And leaves the world of its last guard bereft.
    " Thus horror girds thee round.   Meantime alone
Thou dwell'st, and helpless, in a soil unknown ;
Poor, and receiving from a foreign hand
The aid denied thee in thy native land.
O ruthless country, and unfeeling more
Than thy own billow-beaten chalky shore !
Leavest thou to foreign care the worthies given
By Providence to guide thy steps to heaven ?   90
His ministers, commissioned to proclaim
Eternal blessings in a Saviour's name ?
Ah, then most worthy, with a soul unfed,
In Stygian night to lie for ever dead !
So once the venerable Tishbite strayed
An exiled fugitive from shade to shade,
When, flying Ahab and his fury wife,
In lone Arabian wilds he sheltered life ;
So from Philippi wandered forth forlorn
Cilician Paul, with sounding scourges torn ;   100
And Christ himself so left, and trod no more,
The thankless Gergesenes' forbidden shore.
    " But thou take courage ! strive against despair !
Quake not with dread, nor nourish anxious care !
Grim war indeed on every side appears,
And thou art menaced by a thousand spears ;
Yet none shall drink thy blood, or shall offend
Even the defenceless bosom of my friend.
For thee the Ægis of thy God shall hide,
Jehovah's self shall combat on thy side :   110
The same, who vanquished under Sion's towers,
At silent midnight, all Assyria's powers ;
The same, who overthrew in ages past
Damascus' sons that laid Samaria waste !
Their king he filled and them with fatal fears
By mimic sounds of clarions in their ears,
Of hoofs, and wheels, and neighings from afar,
Of clashing armour, and the din of war.

" Thou, therefore (as the most afflicted may),
Still hope, and triumph o'er thy evil day !   120
Look forth, expecting happier times to come,
And to enjoy, once more, thy native home ! "

ELEGY V.

ON THE APPROACH OF SPRING.

WRITTEN IN THE AUTHOR'S TWENTIETH YEAR.

Time, never wandering from his annual round,
Bids Zephyr breathe the Spring, and thaw the ground ;
Bleak Winter flies, new verdure clothes the plain,
And Earth assumes her transient youth again.
Dream I, or also to the Spring belong
Increase of genius, and new powers of song ?
Spring gives them, and, how strange soe'er it seems,
Impels me now to some harmonious themes.
Castalia's fountain and the forkèd hill.
By day, by night, my raptured fancy fill ;   10
My bosom burns and heaves, I hear within
A sacred sound that prompts me to begin.
Lo, Phœbus comes ! with his bright hair he blends
The radiant laurel wreath ; Phœbus descends :
I mount, and undepressed by cumbrous clay
Through cloudy regions win my easy way ;
Rapt, through poetic shadowy haunts I fly ;
The shrines all open to my dauntless eye,
My spirit searches all the realms of light,
And no Tartarean gulfs elude my sight.   20
But this ecstatic trance—this glorious storm
Of inspiration—what will it perform ?
Spring claims the verse, that with his influence glows,
And shall be paid with what himself bestows.
    Thou, veiled with opening foliage, lead'st the throng
Of feathered minstrels, Philomel ! in song ;
Let us, in concert, to the season sing,
Civic and sylvan heralds of the Spring !
    With notes triumphant Spring's approach declare !
To Spring, ye Muses, annual tribute bear !   30
The Orient left and Æthiopia's plains,
The Sun now northward turns his golden reins ;
Night creeps not now, yet rules with gentle sway,
And drives her dusky horrors swift away ;
Now less fatigued, on this ethereal plain
Boötes follows his celestial wain ;
And now the radiant sentinels above,
Less numerous, watch around the courts of Jove.

For, with the night, force, ambush, slaughter fly,
And no gigantic guilt alarms the sky. 40
Now haply says some shepherd, while he views,
Recumbent on a rock, the reddening dews,
This night, this surely, Phœbus missed the Fair,
Who stops his chariot by her amorous care.
Cynthia, delighted by the morning's glow,
Speeds to the woodland, and resumes her bow ;
Resigns her beams, and, glad to disappear,
Blesses his aid who shortens her career.
Come—Phœbus cries—Aurora come—too late
Thou lingerest, slumbering, with thy withered mate ! 50
Leave him, and to Hymettus' top repair !
Thy darling Cephalus expects thee there.
The goddess, with a blush, her love betrays,
But mounts, and, driving rapidly, obeys.
Earth now desires thee, Phœbus ! and to engage
Thy warm embrace, casts off the guise of age ;
Desires thee, and deserves ; for who so sweet,
When her rich bosom courts thy genial heat ?
Her breath imparts to every breeze that blows
Arabia's harvest, and the Paphian rose. 60
Her lofty fronts she diadems around
With sacred pines, like Ops on Ida crowned ;
Her dewy locks with various flowers new-blown
She interweaves, various, and all her own,
For Proserpine, in such a wreath attired,
Tænarian Dis himself with love inspired.
Fear not, lest, cold and coy, the nymph refuse !
Herself, with all her sighing Zephyrs, sues ;
Each courts thee, fanning soft his scented wing,
And all her groves with warbled wishes ring. 70
Nor, unendowed and indigent, aspires
The amorous Earth to engage thy warm desires,
But, rich in balmy drugs, assists thy claim,
Divine Physician ! to that glorious name.
If splendid recompense, if gifts can move
Desire in thee (gifts often purchase love),
She offers all the wealth her mountains hide,
And all that rests beneath the boundless tide.
How oft, when headlong from the heavenly steep
She sees thee playing in the western deep, 80
How oft she cries—" Ah Phœbus ! why repair
Thy wasted force, why seek refreshment there ?
Can Tethys win thee ? wherefore shouldst thou lave
A face so fair in her unpleasant wave ?
Come, seek my green retreats, and rather chuse
To cool thy tresses in my crystal dews,
The grassy turf shall yield thee sweeter rest ;
Come, lay thy evening glories on my breast,
And breathing fresh, through many a humid rose,
Soft whispering airs shall lull thee to repose ! 90

No fears I feel like Semele to die,
Nor lest thy burning wheels approach too nigh,—
For thou canst govern them ; here therefore rest,
And lay thy evening glories on my breast ! ”
    Thus breathes the wanton Earth her amorous flame,
And all her countless offspring feel the same ;
For Cupid now through every region strays,
Brightening his faded fires with solar rays ;
His new-strung bow sends forth a deadlier sound,
And his new-pointed shafts more deeply wound ;   100
Nor Dian's self escapes him now untried,
Nor even Vesta at her altar-side ;
His mother too repairs her beauty's wane,
And seems sprung newly from the deep again.
Exulting youths the Hymeneal sing,
With Hymen's name roofs, rocks, and valleys ring ;
He, new-attired, and by the season drest,
Proceeds, all fragrant, in his saffron vest.
Now, many a golden-cinctured virgin roves
To taste the pleasures of the fields and groves ;   110
All wish, and each alike, some favourite youth
Hers, in the bonds of Hymeneal truth.
Now pipes the shepherd through his reeds again,
Nor Phillis wants a song that suits the strain ;
With songs the seaman hails the starry sphere,
And dolphins rise from the abyss to hear ;
Jove feels himself the season, sports again
With his fair spouse, and banquets all his train.
Now too the Satyrs, in the dusk of eve,
Their mazy dance through flowery meadows weave,   120
And neither god nor goat, but both in kind,
Silvanus, wreathed with cypress, skips behind.
The Dryads leave their hollow sylvan cells
To roam the banks and solitary dells ;
Pan riots now, and from his amorous chafe
Ceres and Cybele seem hardly safe ;
And Faunus, all on fire to reach the prize,
In chase of some enticing Oread flies ;
She bounds before, but fears too swift a bound,
And hidden lies, but wishes to be found.   130
Our shades entice the Immortals from above,
And some kind power presides o'er every grove ;
And long, ye Powers, o'er every grove preside,
For all is safe and blest, where ye abide !
Return, O Jove ! the age of gold restore—
Why choose to dwell where storms and thunder roar ?
At least, thou, Phœbus ! moderate thy speed !
Let not the vernal hours too swift proceed,
Command rough Winter back, nor yield the pole
Too soon to Night's encroaching, long control !   140

ELEGY VI.

TO CHARLES DEODATI,

Who, while he spent his Christmas in the country, sent the Author a poetical Epistle, in which he requested that his verses, if not so good as usual, might be excused on account of the many feasts to which his friends had invited him, and which would not allow him leisure to finish them as he wished.

WITH no rich viands overcharged, I send
Health, which perchance you want, my pampered friend ;
But wherefore should thy muse tempt mine away
From what she loves, from darkness into day ?
Art thou desirous to be told how well
I love thee, and in verse ? verse cannot tell,
For verse has bounds, and must in measure move
But neither bounds nor measure knows my love.
How pleasant, in thy lines described, appear
December's harmless sports, and rural cheer !   10
French spirits kindling with cærulean fires,
And all such gambols as the time inspires !
    Think not that wine against good verse offends ;
The Muse and Bacchus have been always friends,
Nor Phœbus blushes sometimes to be found
With ivy, rather than with laurel, crowned.
The Nine themselves ofttimes have joined the song
And revels of the Bacchanalian throng ;
Not even Ovid could in Scythian air
Sing sweetly—why ? no vine would flourish there,   20
What in brief numbers sung Anacreon's muse ?
Wine, and the rose, that sparkling wine bedews.
Pindar with Bacchus glows—his every line
Breathes the rich fragrance of inspiring wine,
While, with loud crash o'erturned, the chariot lies
And brown with dust the fiery courser flies.
The Roman lyrist steeped in wine his lays,
So sweet in Glycera's and Chloe's praise.
Now too the plenteous feast and mantling bowl
Nourish the vigour of thy sprightly soul ;   30
The flowing goblet makes thy numbers flow,
And casks not wine alone, but verse bestow.
Thus Phœbus favours, and the arts attend,
Whom Bacchus, and whom Ceres, both befriend :
What wonder, then, thy verses are so sweet,
In which these triple powers so kindly meet ?
The lute now also sounds, with gold inwrought,
And touched with flying fingers, nicely taught ;
In tapestried halls, high-roofed, the sprightly lyre
Directs the dancers of the virgin choir.   40
If dull repletion fright the muse away,
Sights, gay as these, may more invite her stay :

And, trust me, while the ivory keys resound,
Fair damsels sport, and perfumes steam around,
Apollo's influence, like ethereal flame,
Shall animate, at once, thy glowing frame,
And all the Muse shall rush into thy breast,
By love and music's blended powers possest.
For numerous powers light Elegy befriend,
Hear her sweet voice, and at her call attend ;   50
Her Bacchus, Ceres, Venus, all approve,
And, with his blushing mother, gentle Love.
Hence to such bards we grant the copious use
Of banquets, and the vine's delicious juice.
But they, who demi-gods and heroes praise,
And feats performed in Jove's more youthful days,
Who now the counsels of high heaven explore,
Now shades, that echo the Cerberean roar,
Simply let these, like him of Samos, live ;
Let herbs to them a bloodless banquet give ;   60
In beechen goblets let their beverage shine,
Cool from the crystal spring, their sober wine !
Their youth should pass in innocence, secure
From stain licentious, and in manners pure,
Pure as the priest, when robed in white he stands,
The fresh lustration ready in his hands.
Thus Linus lived, and thus, as poets write,
Tiresias, wiser for his loss of sight ;
Thus exiled Chalcas, thus the bard of Thrace,
Melodious *tamer* of the savage race ;   70
Thus, trained by temperance, Homer led, of yore,
His chief of Ithaca from shore to shore,
Through magic Circe's monster-peopled reign,
And shoals insidious with the Siren train ;
And through the realms where grizly spectres dwell,
Whose tribes he fettered in a gory spell :
For these are sacred bards, and, from above,
Drink large infusions from the mind of Jove.
    Wouldst thou, (perhaps 'tis hardly worth thine ear)
Wouldst thou be told my occupation here ?   80
The promised King of peace employs my pen,
The eternal covenant made for guilty men,
The new-born Deity with infant cries
Filling the sordid hovel, where he lies ;
The hymning Angels, and the herald star,
That led the Wise, who sought him from afar,
And idols on their own unhallowed shore
Dashed, at his birth, to be revered no more !
    This theme on reeds of Albion I rehearse :
The dawn of that blest day inspired the verse ;   90
Verse that, reserved in secret, shall attend
Thy candid voice, my critic, and my friend !

ELEGY VII.

COMPOSED IN THE AUTHOR'S NINETEENTH YEAR.

As yet a stranger to the gentle fires
That Amathusia's smiling queen inspires,
Not seldom I derided Cupid's darts,
And scorned his claim to rule all human hearts.
" Go, child," I said, " transfix the timorous dove !
" An easy conquest suits an infant love ;
" Enslave the sparrow, for such prize shall be
" Sufficient triumph to a chief like thee !
" Why aim thy idle arms at human kind ?
" Thy shafts prevail not 'gainst the noble mind."   10
    The Cyprian heard, and, kindling into ire,
(None kindles sooner) burned with double fire.
    It was the spring, and newly-risen day
Peeped o'er the hamlets on the first of May ;
My eyes, too tender for the blaze of light,
Still sought the shelter of retiring night,
When Love approached : in painted plumes arrayed
The insidious god his rattling darts betrayed,
Nor less his infant features, and the sly
Sweet intimations of his threatening eye.   20
    Such the Sigean boy is seen above,
Filling the goblet for imperial Jove ;
Such he, on whom the nymphs bestowed their charms,
Hylas, who perished in a Naiad's arms.
Angry he seemed, yet graceful in his ire,
And added threats, not destitute of fire.
" My power," he said, " by others' pain alone
" 'Twere best to learn ; now learn it by thy own !
" With those who feel my power that power attest,
" And in thy anguish be my sway confest !   30
" I vanquished Phœbus, though returning vain
" From his new triumph o'er the Python slain,
" And when he thinks on Daphne, even he
" Will yield the prize of archery to me.
" A dart less true the Parthian horseman sped,
" Behind him killed, and conquered as he fled :
" Less true the expert Cydonian, and less true
" The youth whose shaft his latent Procris slew.
" Vanquished by me see huge Orion bend,
" By me Alcides, and Alcides' friend.   40
" At me should Jove himself a bolt design,
" His bosom first should bleed transfixt by mine.
" But all thy doubts this shaft will best explain,
" Nor shall it reach thee with a trivial pain.
" Thy muse, vain youth ! shall not thy peace ensure,
" Nor Phœbus' serpent yield thy wound a cure."

He spoke, and, waving a bright shaft in air
Sought the warm bosom of the Cyprian fair.
That thus a child should bluster in my ear
Provoked my laughter, more than moved my fear. 50
I shunned not, therefore, public haunts, but strayed
Careless in city or suburban shade,
And passing, and repassing, nymphs that moved
With grace divine, beheld where'er I roved.
Bright shone the vernal day, with double blaze,
As beauty gave new force to Phœbus' rays.
By no grave scruples checked, I freely eyed
The dangerous show, rash youth my only guide,
And many a look of many a Fair unknown
Met full, unable to control my own. 60
But one I marked (then peace forsook my breast)—
One—oh how far superior to the rest !
What lovely features ! such the Cyprian queen
Herself might wish, and Juno wish her mien.
The very nymph was she, whom, when I dared
His arrows, Love had even then prepared ;
Nor was himself remote, nor unsupplied
With torch well-trimmed and quiver at his side ;
Now to her lips he clung, her eyelids now,
Then settled on her cheeks, or on her brow ; 70
And with a thousand wounds from every part
Pierced, and transpierced, my undefended heart.
A fever, new to me, of fierce desire
Now seized my soul, and I was all on fire ;
But she, the while, whom only I adore,
Was gone, and vanished, to appear no more.
In silent sadness I pursue my way ;
I pause, I turn, proceed, yet wish to stay,
And while I follow her in thought, bemoan,
With tears, my soul's delight so quickly flown. 80
When Jove had hurled him to the Lemnian coast,
So Vulcan sorrowed for Olympus lost,
And so Œclides, sinking into night,
From the deep gulf looked up to distant light.
Wretch that I am, what hopes for me remain,
Who cannot cease to love, yet love in vain ?
Oh could I once, once more behold the Fair,
Speak to her, tell her, of the pangs I bear,
Perhaps she is not adamant, would show
Perhaps some pity at my tale of woe. 90
O inauspicious flame !—'tis mine to prove
A matchless instance of disastrous love.
Ah spare me, gentle Power !—If such thou be,
Let not thy deeds and nature disagree.
Spare me, and I will worship at no shrine
With vow and sacrifice, save only thine.
Now I revere thy fires, thy bow, thy darts,
Now own thee sovereign of all human hearts.

Remove ! no—grant me still this raging woe !
Sweet is the wretchedness that lovers know :   100
But pierce hereafter (should I chance to see
One destined mine) at once both her and me.
    Such were the trophies, that, in earlier days,
By vanity seduced, I toiled to raise,
Studious, yet indolent, and urged by youth,
That worst of teachers ! from the ways of truth ;
Till learning taught me, in his shady bower,
To quit Love's servile yoke, and spurn his power.
Then, on a sudden, the fierce flame supprest,
A frost continual settled on my breast,   110
Whence Cupid fears his flames extinct to see,
And Venus dreads a Diomede in me.

EPIGRAMS.

ON THE INVENTOR OF GUNS.

PRAISE in old times the sage Prometheus won,
Who stole æthereal radiance from the sun ;
But greater he, whose bold invention strove
To emulate the fiery bolts of Jove.

The Poems on the subject of the Gunpowder Treason I have not translated, both because the matter of them is unpleasant, and because they are written with an asperity, which, however it might be warranted in Milton's day, would be extremely unseasonable now.—C.

TO LEONORA SINGING AT ROME.

[I have translated only two of the three poetical compliments addressed to Leonora, as they appear to me far superior to what I have omitted.—C.]

ANOTHER Leonora once inspired
Tasso, with fatal love to frenzy fired ;
But how much happier, lived he now, were he,
Pierced with whatever pangs for love of thee !
Since could he hear that heavenly voice of thine,
With Adriana's lute of sound divine,
Fiercer than Pentheus' though his eye might roll,
Or idiot apathy benumb his soul,
You still with medicinal sounds might cheer
His senses wandering in a blind career ;
And, sweetly breathing through his wounded breast,
Charm, with soul-soothing song, his thoughts to rest.

TO THE SAME.

NAPLES, too credulous, ah! boast no more
The sweet-voiced Siren buried on thy shore,
That, when Parthenope deceased, she gave
Her sacred dust to a Chalcidic grave,
For still she lives, but has exchanged the hoarse
Pausilipo for Tiber's placid course,
Where, idol of all Rome, she now in chains
Of magic song both gods and men detains.

THE COTTAGER AND HIS LANDLORD.

A FABLE.

A PEASANT to his lord paid yearly court,
Presenting pippins of so rich a sort
That he, displeased to have a part alone,
Removed the tree, that all might be his own.
The tree, too old to travel, though before
So fruitful, withered, and would yield no more.
The 'squire, perceiving all his labour void,
Cursed his own pains, so foolishly employed,
And " Oh," he cried, " that I had lived content
" With tribute, small indeed, but kindly meant !
" My avarice has expensive proved to me,
" Has cost me both my pippins and my tree."

TO CHRISTINA, QUEEN OF SWEDEN.

WRITTEN IN CROMWELL'S NAME, AND SENT WITH THE PROTECTOR'S PICTURE.

CHRISTINA, maiden of heroic mien !
Star of the North ! of northern stars the queen !
Behold what wrinkles I have earned, and how
The iron casque still chafes my veteran brow,
While, following Fate's dark footsteps, I fulfil
The dictates of a hardy people's will.
But softened, in thy sight, my looks appear,
Not to all queens or kings alike severe.

MISCELLANEOUS POEMS.

ON THE DEATH OF THE VICE-CHANCELLOR,

A PHYSICIAN.

LEARN, ye nations of the earth,
The condition of your birth ;
Now be taught your feeble state ;
Know, that all must yield to Fate !

If the mournful, rover, Death,
Say but once—" Resign your breath ! "
Vainly of escape you dream,
You must pass the Stygian stream.

Could the stoutest overcome
Death's assault, and baffle doom,
Hercules had both withstood,
Undiseased by Nessus' blood.

Ne'er had Hector pressed the plain
By a trick of Pallas slain,
Nor the chief to Jove allied
By Achilles' phantom died.

Could enchantments life prolong,
Circe, saved by magic song,
Still had lived, and equal skill
Had preserved Medea still.

Dwelt in herbs and drugs a power
To avert man's destined hour,
Learn'd Machaon should have known
Doubtless to avert his own :

Chiron had survived the smart
Of the hydra-tainted dart,
And Jove's bolt had been, with ease,
Foiled by Asclepiades.

Thou too, sage ! of whom forlorn
Helicon and Cirrha mourn,
Still hadst filled thy princely place,
Regent of the gownèd race ;

Hadst advanced to higher fame
Still thy much-ennobled name,
Nor in Charon's skiff explored
The Tartarean gulf abhorred.

But resentful Proserpine,
Jealous of thy skill divine,
Snapping short thy vital thread,
Thee too numbered with the dead.

Wise and good ! untroubled be
The green turf that covers thee !
Thence, in gay profusion, grow
All the sweetest flowers that blow !

Pluto's consort bid thee rest !
Æacus pronounce thee blest,
To her home thy shade consign,
Make Elysium ever thine!

ON THE DEATH OF THE BISHOP OF ELY.

WRITTEN IN THE AUTHOR'S SEVENTEENTH YEAR.

MY lids with grief were tumid yet,
And still my sullied cheek was wet
With briny tears, profusely shed
For venerable Winton dead ;
When Fame, whose tales of saddest
    sound,
Alas ! are ever truest found,

The news through all our cities spread
Of yet another mitred head
By ruthless Fate to death consigned—
Ely, the honour of his kind !
    At once a storm of passion heaved
My boiling bosom ; much I grieved,
But more I raged, at every breath

Devoting Death himself to death.
With less revenge did Naso teem,
When hated Ibis was his theme ;
With less Archilochus denied
The lovely Greek, his promised bride.
But lo ! while thus I execrate,
Incensed, the minister of fate,
Wondrous accents, soft, yet clear,
Wafted on the gale I hear.
　　" Ah, much deluded ! lay aside
" Thy threats, and anger misapplied !
" Art not afraid with sounds like these
" To offend, where thou canst not ap-
　　pease ?
" Death is not (wherefore dream'st thou
　　thus ?)
" The son of Night and Erebus ;
" Nor was of fell Erinnys born
" On gulfs where Chaos rules forlorn :
" But, sent from God, His presence
　　leaves,
" To gather home His ripened sheaves,
" To call encumbered souls away
" From fleshly bonds to boundless day,
" (As when the winged Hours excite
" And summon forth the morning light)
" And each to convoy to her place
" Before the Eternal Father's face.
" But not the wicked :—them, severe
" Yet just, from all their pleasures here

" He hurries to the realms below,
" Terrific realms of penal woe !
" Myself no sooner heard his call,
" Than, 'scaping through my prison
　　wall,
" I bade adieu to bolts and bars,
" And soared, with angels, to the stars,
" Like him of old, to whom 'twas given
" To mount on fiery wheels to heaven.
" Boötes' waggon, slow with cold,
" Appalled me not; nor to behold
" The sword that vast Orion draws,
" Or even the Scorpion's horrid claws.
" Beyond the Sun's bright orb I fly,
" And far beneath my feet descry
" Night's dread goddess, seen with awe,
" Whom her winged dragons draw.
" Thus, ever wondering at my speed,
" Augmented still as I proceed,
" I pass the planetary sphere,
" The Milky Way—and now appear
" Heaven's crystal battlements, her
　　door
" Of massy pearl, and emerald floor.
　　" But here I cease.　For never can
" The tongue of once a mortal man
" In suitable description trace
" The pleasures of that happy place ;
" Suffice it, that those joys divine
" Are all, and all for ever, mine ! "

NATURE UNIMPAIRED BY TIME.

Ah, how the human mind wearies herself
With her own wanderings, and, involved in gloom
Impenetrable, speculates amiss !
Measuring, in her folly, things divine
By human ; laws inscribed on adamant
By laws of man's device, and counsels fixt
For ever by the hours that pass and die.
　　How ?—shall the face of Nature then be ploughed
Into deep wrinkles, and shall years at last
On the great parent fix a sterile curse ?　　　　　　　　10
Shall even she confess old age, and halt,
And, palsy-smitten, shake her starry brows ?
Shall foul Antiquity with Rust, and Drought,
And Famine, vex the radiant worlds above ?
Shall Time's unsated maw crave and ingulf
The very heavens, that regulate his flight ?
And was the Sire of all able to fence

His works, and to uphold the circling worlds,
But, through improvident and heedless haste,
Let slip the occasion ?—so, then, all is lost—   20
And in some future evil hour yon arch
Shall crumble and come thundering down, the poles
Jar in collision, the Olympian king
Fall with his throne, and Pallas, holding forth
The terrors of the Gorgon shield in vain,
Shall rush to the abyss, like Vulcan hurled
Down into Lemnos, through the gate of heaven.
Thou also, with precipitated wheels,
Phœbus, thy own son's fall shalt imitate,
With hideous ruin shalt impress the deep   30
Suddenly, and the flood shall reek, and hiss,
At the extinction of the lamp of day.
Then too shall Hæmus, cloven to his base,
Be shattered, and the huge Ceraunian hills,
Once weapons of Tartarean Dis, immersed
In Erebus, shall fill himself with fear.
    No.   The Almighty Father surer laid
His deep foundations, and, providing well
For the event of all, the scales of fate
Suspended in just equipoise, and bade   40
His universal works, from age to age,
One tenor hold, perpetual, undisturbed.
    Hence the prime mover wheels itself about
Continual, day by day, and with it bears
In social measure swift the heavens around.
Not tardier now is Saturn than of old,
Nor radiant less the burning casque of Mars.
Phœbus, his vigour unimpaired, still shows
The effulgence of his youth, nor needs the god
A downward course, that he may warm the vales ;   5c
But, ever rich in influence, runs his road,
Sign after sign, through all the heavenly zone.
Beautiful, as at first, ascends the star
From odoriferous Ind, whose office is
To gather home betimes the ethereal flock,
To pour them o'er the skies again at eve,
And to discriminate the night and day.
Still Cynthia's changeful horn waxes and wanes
Alternate, and, with arms extended still,
She welcomes to her breast her brother's beams.   6c
Nor have the elements deserted yet
Their functions : thunder, with as loud a stroke
As erst, smites through the rocks, and scatters them.
The East still howls, still the relentless North
Invades the shuddering Scythian, still he breathes
The winter, and still rolls the storms along.
The king of ocean, with his wonted force,
Beats on Pelorus ; o'er the deep is heard
The hoarse alarm of Triton's sounding shell ;

Nor swim the monsters of the Ægean sea   70
In shallows, or beneath diminished waves.
Thou, too, thy ancient vegetative power
Enjoyest, O earth! Narcissus still is sweet;
And, Phœbus! still thy favourite, and still
Thy favourite Cytherea! both retain
Their beauty; nor the mountains, ore-enriched
For punishment of man, with purer gold
Teemed ever, or with brighter gems the deep.
      Thus in unbroken series all proceeds;
And shall, till wide involving either pole,   80
And the immensity of yonder heaven,
The final flames of destiny absorb
The world, consumed in one enormous pyre!

ON THE PLATONIC IDEA,

AS IT WAS UNDERSTOOD BY ARISTOTLE.

YE sister powers, who o'er the sacred groves
Preside, and thou, fair mother of them all,
Mnemosyne! and thou who, in thy grot
Immense, reclined at leisure, hast in charge
The archives, and the ordinances of Jove,
And dost record the festivals of heaven,
Eternity!—inform us who is He,
That great original by nature chosen
To be the archetype of human kind,
Unchangeable, immortal, with the poles   10
Themselves coeval, one, yet everywhere,
An image of the god who gave him being?
Twin-brother of the goddess born from Jove,
He dwells not in his father's mind, but, though
Of common nature with ourselves, exists
Apart, and occupies a local home.
Whether, companion of the stars, he spend
Eternal ages, roaming at his will
From sphere to sphere the tenfold heavens; or dwell
On the moon's side that nearest neighbours earth;   20
Or torpid on the banks of Lethe sit
Among the multitude of souls ordained
To flesh and blood, or whether (as may chance)
That vast and giant model of our kind
In some far distant region of this globe
Sequestered stalk, with lifted head on high
O'ertowering Atlas, on whose shoulders rest
The stars, terrific even to the gods.
Never the Theban seer, whose blindness proved

His best illumination, him beheld   30
In secret vision : never him the son
Of Pleione, amid the noiseless night
Descending, to the prophet-choir revealed ;
Him never knew the Assyrian priest, who yet
The ancestry of Ninus chronicles,
And Belus, and Osiris far-renowned ;
Nor even thrice great Hermes, although skilled
So deep in mystery, to the worshippers
Of Isis showed a prodigy like him.
    And thou, who hast immortalised the shades   40
Of Academus,—if the schools received
This monster of the fancy first from thee,—
Either recall at once the banished bards
To thy republic, or, thyself evinced
A wilder fabulist, go also forth.

TO HIS FATHER.

OH that Pieria's spring would through my breast
Pour its inspiring influence, and rush
No rill, but rather an o'erflowing flood !
That, for my venerable father's sake
All meaner themes renounced, my muse, on wings
Of duty borne, might reach a loftier strain.
For thee, my father ! howsoe'er it please,
She frames this slender work ; nor know I aught
That may thy gifts more suitably requite ;
Though to requite them suitably would ask   10
Returns much nobler, and surpassing far
The meagre stores of verbal gratitude :
But, such as I possess, I send thee all.
This page presents thee in their full amount
With thy son's treasures, and the sum is nought ;
Nought, save the riches that from airy dream
In secret grottoes, and in laurel bowers,
I have, by golden Clio's gift, acquired.
    Verse is a work divine ; despise not thou
Verse therefore, which evinces (nothing more)   20
Man's heavenly source, and which, retaining still
Some scintillations of Promethean fire,
Bespeaks him animated from above.
The gods love verse ; the infernal powers themselves
Confess the influence of verse, which stirs
The lowest deep, and binds in triple chains
Of adamant both Pluto and the Shades.
In verse the Delphic priestess, and the pale
Tremulous Sibyl, make the future known ;

And he who sacrifices, on the shrine　　　　　　　30
Hangs verse, both when he smites the threatening bull,
And when he spreads his reeking entrails wide
To scrutinize the fates enveloped there.
We too, ourselves, what time we seek again
Our native skies, and one eternal now
Shall be the only measure of our being,
Crowned all with gold, and chanting to the lyre
Harmonious verse, shall range the courts above,
And make the starry firmament resound.
And, even now, the fiery spirit pure　　　　　　　40
That wheels yon circling orbs, directs, himself,
Their mazy dance with melody of verse
Unutterable, immortal, hearing which
Huge Ophiuchus holds his hiss suppressed;
Orion, softened, drops his ardent blade;
And Atlas stands unconscious of his load.
Verse graced of old the feasts of kings, ere yet
Luxurious dainties, destined to the gulf
Immense of gluttony, were known, and ere
Lyæus deluged yet the temperate board.　　　　　50
Then sat the bard a customary guest
To share the banquet, and, his length of locks
With beechen honours bound, proposed in verse
The characters of heroes and their deeds
To imitation; sang of Chaos old,
Of Nature's birth, of gods that crept in search
Of acorns fallen, and of the thunder-bolt
Not yet produced from Ætna's fiery cave.
And what avails, at last, tune without voice,
Devoid of matter? Such may suit perhaps　　　　60
The rural dance, but such was ne'er the song
Of Orpheus, whom the streams stood still to hear,
And the oaks followed. Not by chords alone
Well touched, but by resistless accents more,
To sympathetic tears the ghosts themselves
He moved: these praises to his verse he owes.
　Nor thou persist, I pray thee, still to slight
The sacred Nine, and to imagine vain
And useless, powers, by whom inspired, thyself
Art skilful to associate verse with airs　　　　　70
Harmonious, and to give the human voice
A thousand modulations, heir by right
Indisputable of Arion's fame.
Now say, what wonder is it if a son
Of thine delight in verse, if, so conjoined
In close affinity, we sympathise
In social arts, and kindred studies sweet?
Such distribution of himself to us
Was Phœbus' choice; thou hast thy gift, and I
Mine also, and between us we receive,　　　　　80
Father and son, the whole inspiring god.

No! howsoe'er the semblance thou assume
Of hate, thou hatest not the gentle Muse,
My father! for thou never badest me tread
The beaten path, and broad, that leads right on
To opulence, nor didst condemn thy son
To the insipid clamours of the bar,
To laws voluminous, and ill observed ;
But, wishing to enrich me more, to fill
My mind with treasure, led'st me far away   90
From city din to deep retreats, to banks
And streams Aonian, and, with free consent,
Didst place me happy at Apollo's side.
I speak not now, on more important themes
Intent, of common benefits, and such
As nature bids, but of thy larger gifts,
My father! who, when I had opened once
The stores of Roman rhetoric, and learned
The full-toned language of the eloquent Greeks,
Whose lofty music graced the lips of Jove,   100
Thyself didst counsel me to add the flowers
That Gallia boasts ; those too with which the smooth
Italian his degenerate speech adorns,
That witnesses his mixture with the Goth ;
And Palestine's prophetic songs divine.
To sum the whole, whate'er the heaven contains,
The earth beneath it, and the air between,
The rivers and the restless deep, may all
Prove intellectual gain to me, my wish
Concurring with thy will ; Science herself,   110
All cloud removed, inclines her beauteous head,
And offers me the lip, if, dull of heart,
I shrink not, and decline her gracious boon.
   Go now and gather dross, ye sordid minds
That covet it ; what could my father more ?
What more could Jove himself, unless he gave
His own abode, the heaven in which he reigns ?
More eligible gifts than these were not
Apollo's to his son, had they been safe
As they were insecure, who made the boy   120
The world's vice-luminary, bade him rule
The radiant chariot of the day, and bind
To his young brows his own all-dazzling wreath ?
I therefore, although last and least, my place
Among the learned in the laurel grove
Will hold, and where the conqueror's ivy twines,
Henceforth exempt from the unlettered throng
Profane, nor even to be seen by such.
Away, then, sleepless Care ; Complaint, away ;
And, Envy, with thy "jealous leer malign !"   130
Nor let the monster Calumny shoot forth
Her venomed tongue at me. Detested foes !
Ye all are impotent against my peace,

For I am privileged, and bear my breast
Safe, and too high for your viperean wound.
    But thou, my father ! since to render thanks
Equivalent, and to requite by deeds
Thy liberality, exceeds my power,
Suffice it that I thus record thy gifts,
And bear them treasured in a grateful mind !   140
Ye too, the favourite pastime of my youth,
My voluntary numbers, if ye dare
To hope longevity, and to survive
Your master's funeral, not soon absorbed
In the oblivious Lethæan gulf,
Shall to futurity perhaps convey
This theme, and by these praises of my sire
Improve the fathers of a distant age !

TO SALSILLUS,

A ROMAN POET, MUCH INDISPOSED.

The original is written in a measure called *Scazon*, which signifies *limping*, and the measure
is so denominated because, though in other respects Iambic, it terminates with a Spondee, and
has consequently a more tardy movement.
    The reader will immediately see that this property of the Latin verse cannot be imitated
in English.

My halting Muse, that dragg'st by choice along
Thy slow, slow step, in melancholy song,
And likest that pace, expressive of thy cares,
Not less than Deiopeia's sprightlier airs,
When in the dance she beats with measured tread
Heaven's floor, in front of Juno's golden bed ;
Salute Salsillus, who to verse divine
Prefers, with partial love, such lays as mine.
Thus writes that Milton, then, who, wafted o'er
From his own nest on Albion's stormy shore,   10
Where Eurus, fiercest of the Æolian band,
Sweeps with ungoverned rage the blasted land,
Of late to more serene Ausonia came
To view her cities of illustrious name,
To prove, himself a witness of the truth,
How wise her elders, and how learned her youth.
Much good, Salsillus ! and a body free
From all disease, that Milton asks for thee,
Who now endurest the languor, and the pains,
That bile inflicts, diffused through all thy veins,   20
Relentless malady ! not moved to spare
By thy sweet Roman voice, and Lesbian air !
    Health, Hebe's sister, sent us from the skies,
And thou, Apollo, whom all sickness flies,

Pythius, or Pæan, or what name divine
Soe'er thou choose, haste, heal a priest of thine !
Ye groves of Faunus, and ye hills that melt
With vinous dews, where meek Evander dwelt,
If aught salubrious in your confines grow,
Strive which shall soonest heal your poet's woe,   30
That, rendered to the Muse he loves, again
He may enchant the meadows with his strain.
Numa, reclined in everlasting ease,
Amid the shade of dark embowering trees,
Viewing with eyes of unabated fire
His loved Ægeria, shall that strain admire :
So soothed, the tumid Tiber shall revere
The tombs of kings, nor desolate the year,
Shall curb his waters with a friendly rein,
And guide them harmless, till they meet the main.   40

TO GIOVANNI BATTISTA MANSO,

MARQUIS OF VILLA.

MILTON'S ACCOUNT OF MANSO.

Giovanni Battista Manso, Marquis of Villa, is an Italian nobleman of the highest estimation
among his countrymen, for genius, literature, and military accomplishments. To him Torquato
Tasso addressed his "Dialogues on Friendship," for he was much the friend of Tasso, who has
also celebrated him among the other princes of his country, in his poem entitled "Gerusalemme
Conquistata," book xx.

> *Fra cavalier magnanimi, e cortesi,*
> *Risplende il Manso.*

During the Author's stay at Naples, he received at the hands of the Marquis a thousand kind
offices and civilities, and, desirous not to appear ungrateful, sent him this poem a short time before
his departure from that city.

THESE verses also to thy praise the Nine—
O Manso ! happy in that theme—design,
For, Gallus and Mæcenas gone, they see
None such besides, or whom they love as thee ;
And if my verse may give the meed of fame,
Thine too shall prove an everlasting name.
Already such, it shines in Tasso's page
(For thou wast Tasso's friend) from age to age,
And, next, the Muse consigned (not unaware
How high the charge) Marino to thy care,   10
Who, singing to the nymphs Adonis' praise,
Boasts thee the patron of his copious lays.
To thee alone the poet would entrust
His latest vows, to thee alone his dust ;

And thou with punctual piety hast paid,
In laboured brass, thy tribute to his shade.
Nor this contented thee,—but lest the grave
Should aught absorb of theirs which thou couldst save,
All future ages thou hast deigned to teach
The life, lot, genius, character of each,   20
Eloquent as the Carian sage, who, true
To his great theme, the life of Homer drew.
    I, therefore, though a stranger youth, who come
Chilled by rude blasts that freeze my northern home,
Thee dear to Clio, confident proclaim,
And thine, for Phœbus' sake, a deathless name.
Nor thou, so kind, wilt view with scornful eye
A Muse scarce reared beneath our sullen sky,
Who fears not, indiscreet as she is young,
To seek in Latium hearers of her song.   30
We too, where Thames with his unsullied waves
The tresses of the blue-haired Ocean laves,
Hear oft by night, or slumbering seem to hear,
O'er his wide stream, the swan's voice warbling clear,
And we could boast a Tityrus of yore,
Who trod, a welcome guest, your happy shore.
    Yes, dreary as we own our northern clime,
Even we to Phœbus raise the polished rhyme.
We too serve Phœbus; Phœbus has received
(If legends old may claim to be believed)   40
No sordid gifts from us, the golden ear,
The burnished apple, ruddiest of the year,
The fragrant crocus, and, to grace his fane,
Fair damsels chosen from the Druid train ;
Druids, our native bards in ancient time,
Who gods and heroes praised in hallowed rhyme.
Hence, often as the maids of Greece surround
Apollo's shrine with hymns of festive sound,
They name the virgins, who arrived of yore,
With British offerings, on the Delian shore ;   50
Loxo, from giant Corineus sprung,
Upis, on whose blest lips the future hung,
And Hecaerge, with the golden hair,
All decked with Pictish hues, and all with bosoms bare.
    Thou, therefore, happy sage, whatever clime
Shall ring with Tasso's praise in after time,
Or with Marino's, shalt be known their friend,
And with an equal flight to fame ascend.
The world shall hear how Phœbus and the Nine
Were inmates once, and willing guests of thine.   60
Yet Phœbus, when of old constrained to roam
The earth, an exile from his heavenly home,
Entered, no willing guest, Admetus' door,
Though Hercules had ventured there before.
But gentle Chiron's cave was near, a scene
Of rural peace, clothed with perpetual green,

And thither, oft as respite he required
From rustic clamours loud, the god retired.
There, many a time, on Peneus' bank reclined
At some oak's root, with ivy thick entwined,   70
Won by his hospitable friend's desire,
He soothed his pains of exile with the lyre.
Then shook the hills, then trembled Peneus' shore,
Nor Œta felt his load of forests more ;
The upland elms descended to the plain,
And softened lynxes wondered at the strain.
  Well may we think, O dear to all above !
Thy birth distinguished by the smile of Jove,
And that Apollo shed his kindliest power,
And Maia's son, on that propitious hour,   80
Since only minds so born can comprehend
A poet's worth, or yield that worth a friend.
Hence on thy yet unfaded cheek appears
The lingering freshness of thy greener years ;
Hence, in thy front and features we admire
Nature unwithered and a mind entire.
Oh might so true a friend to me belong,
So skilled to grace the votaries of song,
Should I recall hereafter into rhyme
The kings and heroes of my native clime,   90
Arthur the chief, who even now prepares,
In subterraneous being, future wars,
With all his martial knights, to be restored
Each to his seat around the federal board ;
And oh, if spirit fail me not, disperse
Our Saxon plunderers, in triumphant verse :
Then, after all, when, with the past content,
A life I finish, not in silence spent,
Should he, kind mourner, o'er my death-bed bend,
I shall but need to say—" Be yet my friend ! "   100
He, too, perhaps, shall bid the marble breathe
To honour me, and with the graceful wreath,
Or of Parnassus or the Paphian isle,
Shall bind my brows,—but I shall rest the while.
Then also, if the fruits of faith endure,
And virtue's promised recompense be sure,
Borne to those seats to which the blest aspire
By purity of soul and virtuous fire,
These rites, as fate permits, I shall survey
With eyes illumined by celestial day,   110
And, every cloud from my pure spirit driven,
Joy in the bright beatitude of heaven !

ON THE DEATH OF DAMON.

THE ARGUMENT.

Thyrsis and Damon, shepherds and neighbours, had always pursued the same studies, and had, from their earliest days, been united in the closest friendship. Thyrsis, while travelling for improvement, received intelligence of the death of Damon, and, after a time, returning and finding it true, deplores himself, and his solitary condition, in this poem.

By Damon is to be understood Charles Deodati, connected with the Italian city of Lucca by his father's side, in other respects an Englishman; a youth of uncommon genius, erudition, and virtue.

YE nymphs of Himera (for ye have shed
Erewhile for Daphnis, and for Hylas dead,
And over Bion's long-lamented bier,
The fruitless meed of many a sacred tear),
Now through the villas laved by Thames rehearse
The woes of Thyrsis in Sicilian verse,
What sighs he heaved, and how with groans profound
He made the woods and hollow rocks resound,
Young Damon dead; nor even ceased to pour
His lonely sorrows at the midnight hour.   10
   The green wheat twice had nodded in the ear,
And golden harvest twice enriched the year,
Since Damon's lips had gasped for vital air
The last, last time, nor Thyrsis yet was there;
For he, enamoured of the Muse, remained
In Tuscan Fiorenza long detained,
But, stored at length with all he wished to learn,
For his flock's sake now hasted to return;
And when the shepherd had resumed his seat
At the elm's root, within his own retreat,   20
Then 'twas his lot, then, all his loss to know,
And, from his burthened heart, he vented thus his woe:
   " Go, seek your home, my lambs; my thoughts are due
" To other cares than those of feeding you.
" Alas! what deities shall I suppose
" In heaven, or earth, concerned for human woes,
" Since, O my Damon! their severe decree
" So soon condemns me to regret of thee!
" Departest thou thus, thy virtues unrepaid
" With fame and honour, like a vulgar shade?   30
" Let him forbid it whose bright rod controls
" And separates sordid from illustrious souls,
" Drive far the rabble, and to thee assign
" A happier lot, with spirits worthy thine!
   " Go, seek your home, my lambs; my thoughts are due
" To other cares than those of feeding you.
" Whate'er befall, unless by cruel chance
" The wolf first give me a forbidding glance,
" Thou shalt not moulder undeplored, but long
" Thy praise shall dwell on every shepherd's tongue;   40

" To Daphnis first they shall delight to pay,
" And, after him, to thee, the votive lay,
" While Pales shall the flocks and pastures love,
" Or Faunus to frequent the field or grove,
" At least, if ancient piety and truth,
" With all the learned labours of thy youth,
" May serve thee aught, or to have left behind
" A sorrowing friend, and of the tuneful kind.

    " Go, seek your home, my lambs ; my thoughts are due
" To other cares than those of feeding you.   50
" Yes, Damon ! such thy sure reward shall be ;
" But ah, what doom awaits unhappy me ?
" Who now my pains and perils shall divide,
" As thou wast wont, for ever at my side,
" Both when the rugged frost annoyed our feet,
" And when the herbage all was parched with heat ;
" Whether the grim wolf's ravage to prevent,
" Or the huge lion's, armed with darts we went ?
" Whose converse, now, shall calm my stormy day,
" With charming song who now beguile my way ?   60
    " Go, seek your home, my lambs ; my thoughts are due
" To other cares than those of feeding you.
" In whom shall I confide ? whose counsel find
" A balmy medicine for my troubled mind ?
" Or whose discourse with innocent delight
" Shall fill me now, and cheat the wintry night,
" While hisses on my hearth the pulpy pear,
" And blackening chestnuts start and crackle there,
" While storms abroad the dreary meadows whelm,
" And the wind thunders through the neighbouring elm ? 70
    " Go, seek your home, my lambs ; my thoughts are due
" To other cares than those of feeding you.
" Or who, when summer suns their summit reach,
" And Pan sleeps hidden by the sheltering beech,
" When shepherds disappear, nymphs seek the sedge,
" And the stretched rustic snores beneath the hedge,
" Who then shall render me thy pleasant vein
" Of Attic wit, thy jests, thy smiles, again ?
    " Go, seek your home, my lambs ; my thoughts are due
" To other cares than those of feeding you.   80
" Where glens and vales are thickest overgrown
" With tangled boughs, I wander now alone,
" Till night descend, while blustering wind and shower
" Beat on my temples through the shattered bower.
    " Go, seek your home, my lambs ; my thoughts are due
" To other cares than those of feeding you.
" Alas ! what rampant weeds now shame my fields,
" And what a mildewed crop the furrow yields !
" My rambling vines, unwedded to the trees,
" Bear shrivelled grapes ; my myrtles fail to please ;   90
" Nor please me more my flocks ; they, slighted, turn
" Their unavailing looks on me, and mourn.

" Go, seek your home, my lambs; my thoughts are due
" To other cares than those of feeding you.
" Ægon invites me to the hazel grove,
" Amyntas, on the river's bank to rove,
" And young Alphesibœus to a seat
" Where branching elms exclude the mid-day heat.
" ' Here fountains spring,—here mossy hillocks rise;
" ' Here Zephyr whispers, and the stream replies.'   100
" Thus each persuades, but, deaf to every call,
" I gain the thickets, and escape them all.
      " Go, seek your home, my lambs; my thoughts are due
" To other cares than those of feeding you.
" Then Mopsus said, (the same who reads so well
" The voice of birds, and what the stars foretell,
" For he by chance had noticed my return,)
" ' What means thy sullen mood, this deep concern?
" ' Ah, Thyrsis! thou art either crazed with love,
" ' Or some sinister influence from above;   110
" ' Dull Saturn's influence oft the shepherds rue;
" ' His leaden shaft oblique has pierced thee through.'
      " Go, go, my lambs, unpastured as ye are,
" My thoughts are all now due to other care.
" The nymphs, amazed, my melancholy see,
" And 'Thyrsis!' cry, ' what will become of thee?
" ' What wouldst thou, Thyrsis? such should not appear
" ' The brow of youth, stern, gloomy, and severe;
" ' Brisk youth should laugh and love,—ah, shun the fate
" ' Of those twice wretched mopes who love too late!'   120
      " Go, go, my lambs, unpastured as ye are;
" My thoughts are all now due to other care.
" Ægle with Hyas came, to soothe my pain,
" And Baucis' daughter, Dryope the vain,
" Fair Dryope, for voice and finger neat
" Known far and near, and for her self-conceit;
" Chloris too came, whose cottage on the lands
" That skirt the Idumanian current stands;
" But all in vain they came, and but to see
" Kind words, and comfortable, lost on me.   130
      " Go, go, my lambs, unpastured as ye are;
" My thoughts are all now due to other care.
" Ah, blest indifference of the playful herd,
" None by his fellow chosen, or preferred!
" No bonds of amity the flocks enthral,
" But each associates and is pleased with all;
" So graze the dappled deer in numerous droves,
" And all his kind alike the zebra loves;
" The same law governs where the billows roar,
" And Proteus' shoals o'erspread the desert shore;   140
" The sparrow, meanest of the feathered race,
" His fit companion finds in every place,
" With whom he picks the grain that suits him best,
" Flirts here and there, and late returns to rest,

" And whom, if chance the falcon make his prey,
" Or hedger with his well-aimed arrow slay,
" For no such loss the gay survivor grieves,
" New love he seeks, and new delight receives.
" We only, an obdurate kind, rejoice,
" Scorning all others, in a single choice.   150
" We scarce in thousands meet one kindred mind ;
" And if the long-sought good at last we find,
" When least we fear it, Death our treasure steals,
" And gives our heart a wound that nothing heals.
 " Go, go, my lambs, unpastured as ye are ;
" My thoughts are all now due to other care.
" Ah, what delusion lured me from my flocks,
" To traverse Alpine snows and rugged rocks !
" What need so great had I to visit Rome,
" Now sunk in ruins, and herself a tomb ?   160
" Or, had she flourished still as when of old
" For her sake Tityrus forsook his fold,
" What need so great had I to incur a pause
" Of thy sweet intercourse for such a cause,
" For such a cause to place the roaring sea,
" Rocks, mountains, woods, between my friend and me ?
" Else, had I grasped thy feeble hand, composed
" Thy decent limbs, thy drooping eyelids closed,
" And, at the last, had said—' Farewell,—ascend,—
" ' Nor even in the skies forget thy friend !'   170
 " Go, go, my lambs, untended homeward fare ;
" My thoughts are all now due to other care.
" Although well pleased, ye tuneful Tuscan swains !
" My mind the memory of your worth retains,
" Yet not your worth can teach me less to mourn
" My Damon lost ;—he too was Tuscan born,
" Born in your Lucca, city of renown !
" And wit possessed, and genius, like your own.
" Oh, how elate was I, when stretched beside
" The murmuring course of Arno's breezy tide,   180
" Beneath the poplar grove I passed my hours,
" Now cropping myrtles, and now vernal flowers,
" And hearing, as I lay at ease along,
" Your swains contending for the prize of song !
" I also dared attempt (and, as it seems,
" Not much displeased attempting) various themes,
" For even I can presents boast from you,
" The shepherd's pipe, and osier basket too ;
" And Dati, and Francini, both have made
" My name familiar to the beechen shade,   190
" And they are learned, and each in every place
" Renowned for song, and both of Lydian race.
 " Go, go, my lambs, untended homeward fare ;
" My thoughts are all now due to other care.
" While bright the dewy grass with moonbeams shone,
" And I stood hurdling in my kids alone,

" How often have I said (but thou hadst found
" Ere then thy dark cold lodgment under ground),
" Now Damon sings, or springes sets for hares,
" Or wickerwork for various use prepares !   200
" How oft, indulging fancy, have I planned
" New scenes of pleasure that I hoped at hand,
" Called thee abroad as I was wont, and cried,
" ' What, hoa ! my friend,—come lay thy task aside,
" ' Haste, let us forth together, and beguile
" ' The heat beneath yon whispering shades awhile,
" ' Or on the margin stray of Colne's clear flood,
" ' Or where Cassibelan's grey turrets stood !
" ' There thou shalt cull me simples, and shalt teach
" ' Thy friend the name and healing powers of each,   210
" ' From the tall bluebell to the dwarfish weed,
" ' What the dry land and what the marshes breed,
" ' For all their kinds alike to thee are known,
" ' And the whole art of Galen is thy own.'
" Ah, perish Galen's art, and withered be
" The useless herbs that gave not health to thee !
" Twelve evenings since, as in poetic dream
" I meditating sat some statelier theme,
" The reeds no sooner touched my lip, though new
" And unessayed before, than wide they flew,   220
" Bursting their waxen bands, nor could sustain
" The deep-toned music of the solemn strain ;
" And I am vain perhaps, but I will tell
" How proud a theme I chose,—ye groves, farewell !
     " Go, go, my lambs, untended homeward fare ;
" My thoughts are all now due to other care.
" Of Brutus, Dardan chief, my song shall be,
" How with his barks he ploughed the British sea,
" First from Rutupia's towering headland seen,
" And of his consort's reign, fair Imogen ;   230
" Of Brennus and Belinus, brothers bold,
" And of Arviragus, and how of old
" Our hardy sires the Armorican controlled,
" And of the wife of Gorloïs, who, surprised
" By Uther, in her husband's form disguised
" (Such was the force of Merlin's art), became
" Pregnant with Arthur of heroic fame.
" These themes I now revolve,—and oh, if Fate
" Proportion to these themes my lengthened date,
" Adieu my shepherd's reed ! yon pine-tree bough   240
" Shall be thy future home ; there dangle thou
" Forgotten and disused, unless ere long
" Thou change thy Latian for a British song ;
" A British ?—even so,—the powers of man
" Are bounded ; little is the most he can :
" And it shall well suffice me, and shall be
" Fame, and proud recompense enough for me,
" If Usa, golden-haired, my verse may learn.

" If Alain bending o'er his crystal urn,
" Swift-whirling Abra, Trent's o'ershadowed stream,   250
" Thames, lovelier far than all in my esteem,
" Tamar's ore-tinctured flood, and, after these,
" The wave-worn shores of utmost Orcades.
    " Go, go, my lambs, untended homeward fare ;
" My thoughts are all now due to other care.
" All this I kept in leaves of laurel-rind
" Enfolded safe, and for thy view designed
" This, and a gift from Manso's hand beside
" (Manso, not least his native city's pride),
" Two cups that radiant as their giver shone,   260
" Adorned by sculpture with a double zone.
" The spring was graven there ; here slowly wind
" The Red-sea shores, with groves of spices lined ;
" Her plumes of various hues amid the boughs
" The sacred, solitary Phœnix shows,
" And, watchful of the dawn, reverts her head
" To see Aurora leave her watery bed.—
" In other part, the expansive vault above,
" And there too, even there, the god of love ;
" With quiver armed he mounts, his torch displays   270
" A vivid light, his gem-tipt arrows blaze,
" Around his bright and fiery eyes he rolls,
" Nor aims at vulgar minds or little souls,
" Nor deigns one look below, but aiming high
" Sends every arrow to the lofty sky ;
" Hence forms divine, and minds immortal, learn
" The power of Cupid, and enamoured burn.
    " Thou, also, Damon (neither need I fear
" That hope delusive), thou art also there ;
" For whither should simplicity like thine   280
" Retire ? where else such spotless virtue shine ?
" Thou dwellest not (thought profane) in shades below,
" Nor tears suit thee ;—cease then my tears to flow !
" Away with grief, on Damon ill bestowed !
" Who, pure himself, has found a pure abode,
" Has passed the showery arch, henceforth resides
" With saints and heroes, and from flowing tides
" Quaffs copious immortality and joy,
" With hallowed lips !—Oh ! blest without alloy,
" And now enriched with all that faith can claim,   290
" Look down, entreated by whatever name,
" If Damon please thee most (that rural sound
" Shall oft with echoes fill the groves around)
" Or if Deodatus, by which alone
" In those ethereal mansions thou art known.
" Thy blush was maiden, and thy youth the taste
" Of wedded bliss knew never, pure and chaste :
" The honours, therefore, by divine decree
" The lot of virgin worth, are given to thee ;
" Thy brows encircled with a radiant band,   300

" And the green palm-branch waving in thy hand,
" Thou in immortal nuptials shalt rejoice,
" And join with seraphs thy according voice,
" Where rapture reigns, and the ecstatic lyre
" Guides the blest orgies of the blazing quire."

AN ODE ADDRESSED TO MR. JOHN ROUSE

LIBRARIAN OF THE UNIVERSITY OF OXFORD,

ON A LOST VOLUME OF MY POEMS, WHICH HE DESIRED ME TO REPLACE, THAT HE MIGHT ADD THEM TO MY OTHER WORKS DEPOSITED IN THE LIBRARY.

This Ode is rendered without rhyme, that it might more adequately represent the original, which, as Milton himself informs us, is of no certain measure. It may possibly for this reason disappoint the reader, though it cost the writer more labour than the translation of any other piece in the whole collection.—C.

STROPHE.

MY twofold book! single in show,
　　But double in contents,
Neat, but not curiously adorned,
　　Which, in his early youth,
A poet gave, no lofty one in truth,
Although an earnest wooer of the muse—
　　Say while in cool Ausonian shades
　　Or British wilds he roamed,
　　Striking by turns his native lyre,
　　　By turns the Daunian lute,　　　　　　10
　　　And stepped almost in air;

ANTISTROPHE.

Say, little book, what furtive hand
Thee from thy fellow-books conveyed,
　　What time, at the repeated suit
　　Of my most learned friend,
I sent thee forth, an honoured traveller,
From our great city to the source of Thames,
　　　　Cærulean sire;
Where rise the fountains, and the raptures ring
　　Of the Aonian choir,　　　　　　　　20
　　　Durable as yonder spheres,
　　And through the endless lapse of years
　　　Secure to be admired?

STROPHE II.

Now what god, or demigod,
For Britain's ancient genius moved
　　(If our afflicted land

Have expiated at length the guilty sloth
    Of her degenerate sons)
   Shall terminate our impious feuds,
And discipline, with hallowed voice, recall ?   30
     Recall the Muses too,
     Driven from their ancient seats
In Albion, and well-nigh from Albion's shore,
    And with keen Phœbean shafts
    Piercing the unseemly birds,
      Whose talons menace us,
Shall drive the harpy race from Helicon afar ?

ANTISTROPHE.

But thou, my book, though thou hast strayed,
    Whether by treachery lost,
Or indolent neglect, thy bearer's fault,   40
    From all thy kindred books,
To some dark cell, or cave forlorn,
    Where thou endurest, perhaps,
The chafing of some hard untutored hand,
     Be comforted—
For lo ! again the splendid hope appears
    That thou mayest yet escape
The gulfs of Lethe, and on oary wings
Mount to the everlasting courts of Jove !

STROPHE III.

Since Rouse desires thee, and complains   50
    That though by promise his,
Thou yet appearest not in thy place
Among the literary noble stores
     Given to his care,
But, absent, leavest his numbers incomplete
    He, therefore, guardian vigilant
    Of that unperishing wealth,
Calls thee to the interior shrine, his charge,
Where he intends a richer treasure far
Than Ion kept (Ion, Erectheus' son   60
Illustrious, of the fair Creüsa born)
In the resplendent temple of his god,
Tripods of gold, and Delphic gifts divine.

ANTISTROPHE.

Haste, then, to the pleasant groves,
    The Muses' favourite haunt ;
Resume thy station in Apollo's dome,
    Dearer to him
Than Delos, or the forked Parnassian hill !
    Exulting go,

Since now a splendid lot is also thine,   70
And thou art sought by my propitious friend ;
    For there thou shalt be read
    With authors of exalted note,
The ancient glorious lights of Greece and Rome.

EPODE.

    Ye then, my works, no longer vain
    And worthless deemed by me !
Whate.er this steril genius has produced
Expect, at last, the rage of Envy spent,
    An unmolested happy home,
Gift of kind Hermes, and my watchful friend ;   80
    Where never flippant tongue profane
      Shall entrance find,
And whence the coarse unlettered multitude
    Shall babble far remote.
    Perhaps some future distant age,
Less tinged with prejudice, and better taught,
    Shall furnish minds of power
    To judge more equally.
    Then, Malice silenced in the tomb,
    Cooler heads and sounder hearts,   90
      Thanks to Rouse, if aught of praise
I merit, shall with candour weigh the claim.

TRANSLATIONS OF THE ITALIAN POEMS.

SONNET.

FAIR Lady ! whose harmonious name the Rhine,
  Through all his grassy vale, delights to hear,
  Base were indeed the wretch who could forbear
  To love a spirit elegant as thine,
That manifests a sweetness all divine,
  Nor knows a thousand winning acts to spare,
  And graces, which Love's bow and arrows are,
  Tempering thy virtues to a softer shine.
When gracefully thou speakest, or singest gay,
  Such strains as might the senseless forest move,
  Ah then—turn each his eyes and ears away,
Who feels himself unworthy of thy love !
  Grace can alone preserve him, ere the dart
  Of fond desire yet reach his inmost heart.

SONNET.

As on a hill-top rude, when closing day
  Imbrowns the scene, some pastoral maiden fair
  Waters a lovely foreign plant with care,
  Borne from its native genial airs away,
That scarcely can its tender bud display;
  So on my tongue these accents, new and rare,
  Are flowers exotic, which Love waters there.
  While thus, O sweetly scornful! I essay
Thy praise in verse to British ears unknown,
  And Thames exchange for Arno's fair domain;
  So Love has willed, and ofttimes Love has shown
That what he wills he never wills in vain.
  Oh that this hard and steril breast might be
  To Him, who plants from heaven, a soil as free!

CANZONE.

They mock my toil—the nymphs and amorous swains—
" And whence this fond attempt to write," they cry,
" Love-songs in language that thou little knowest?
" How darest thou risk to sing these foreign strains?
" Say truly,—findest not oft thy purpose crossed,
" And that thy fairest flowers here fade and die?"
Then, with pretence of admiration high—
" Thee other shores expect, and other tides;
" Rivers, on whose grassy sides
" Her deathless laurel leaf, with which to bind
" Thy flowing locks, already Fame provides;
" Why then this burthen, better far declined?"
  Speak, Muse! for me.—The fair one said, who guides
My willing heart, and all my fancy's flights,
" This is the language in which Love delights."

SONNET.

TO CHARLES DIODATA.

Charles—and I say it wondering—thou must know
  That I, who once assumed a scornful air,
  And scoffed at Love, am fallen in his snare;
  (Full many an upright man has fallen so.)

Yet think me not thus dazzled by the flow
   Of golden locks, or damask cheek ; more rare
   The heartfelt beauties of my foreign fair,
   A mien majestic, with dark brows that show
The tranquil lustre of a lofty mind ; .
   Words exquisite, of idioms more than one,
   And song, whose fascinating power might bind,
And from her sphere draw down, the labouring moon ;
   With such fire-darting eyes, that should I fill
   My ears with wax, she would enchant me still.

SONNET.

LADY ! it cannot be but that thine eyes
   Must be my sun, such radiance they display,
   And strike me even as Phœbus him whose way
   Through horrid Libya's sandy desert lies.
Meantime, on that side steamy vapours rise
   Where most I suffer. Of what kind are they,
   New as to me they are, I cannot say,
   But deem them, in the lover's language—sighs.
Some, though with pain, my bosom close conceals,
   Which, if in part escaping thence, they tend
   To soften thine, thy coldness soon congeals.
While others to my tearful eyes ascend,
   Whence my sad nights in showers are ever drowned,
   Till my Aurora comes, her brow with roses bound.

SONNET.

ENAMOURED, artless, young, on foreign ground,
   Uncertain whither from myself to fly,
   To thee, dear Lady, with an humble sigh
   Let me devote my heart, which I have found
By certain proofs, not few, intrepid, sound,
   Good, and addicted to conceptions high :
   When tempests shake the world, and fire the sky,
   It rests in adamant self-wrapt around,
As safe from envy, and from outrage rude,
   From hopes and fears that vulgar minds abuse,
   As fond of genius and fixed fortitude,
Of the resounding lyre, and every muse.
   Weak you will find it in one only part,
   Now pierced by Love's immedicable dart.

COMPLIMENTARY POEMS TO MILTON.

FROM THE LATIN AND ITALIAN.

THE NEAPOLITAN, JOHN BAPTIST MANSO,

MARQUIS OF VILLA,

TO THE ENGLISHMAN, JOHN MILTON.

WHAT features, form, mien, manners, with a mind
Oh how intelligent ! and how refined !
Were but thy piety from fault as free,
Thou wouldest no Angle but an Angel be.

AN EPIGRAM,

ADDRESSED TO THE ENGLISHMAN, JOHN MILTON, A POET WORTHY OF THREE LAURELS, THE GRECIAN, LATIN, AND ETRUSCAN, BY JOHN SALSILLI, OF ROME.

MELES* and Mincio,† both, your urns depress !
Sebetus,‡ boast henceforth thy Tasso less !
But let the Thames o'erpeer all floods, since he
For Milton famed shall, single, match the three.

TO JOHN MILTON.

GREECE, sound thy Homer's, Rome, thy Virgil's name,
But England's Milton equals both in fame.

SELVAGGI.

AN ODE,

ADDRESSED TO THE ILLUSTRIOUS ENGLISHMAN, MR. JOHN MILTON, BY SIGNOR ANTONIO FRANCINI, GENTLEMAN, OF FLORENCE.

EXALT me, Clio, to the skies,
   That I may form a starry crown,
Beyond what Helicon supplies
   In laureate garlands of renown ;
To nobler worth be brighter glory given,
And to a heavenly mind a recompense from heaven.

---

* Meles is a river of Ionia, in the neighbourhood of Smyrna, whence Homer is called Melesigenes.
† The Mincio watered the city of Mantua, famous as the birthplace of Virgil.
‡ Sebetus is now the *Fiume della Maddalena ;* it runs through Naples.

Time's wasteful hunger cannot prey
　　On everlasting high desert,
Nor can Oblivion steal away
　　Its record graven on the heart ;
Lodge but an arrow, Virtue, on the bow
That binds my lyre, and death shall be a vanquished foe.

In Ocean's blazing flood enshrined,
　　Whose vassal tide around her swells,
Albion, from other climes disjoined,
　　The prowess of the world excels ;
She teems with heroes that to glory rise,
With more than human force in our astonished eyes.

To Virtue, driven from other lands,
　　Their bosoms yield a safe retreat ;
Her law alone their deed commands ;
　　Her smiles they feel divinely sweet.
Confirm my record, Milton, generous youth !
And by true virtue prove thy virtue's praise a truth.

Zeuxis, all energy and flame,
　　Set ardent forth in his career ;
Urged to his task by Helen's fame
　　Resounding ever in his ear ;
To make his image to her beauty true,
From the collected fair each sovereign charm he drew.

The bee, with subtlest skill endued.
　　Thus toils to earn her precious juice
From all the flowery myriads strewed
　　O'er meadow and parterre profuse ;
Confederate voices one sweet air compound,
And various chords consent in one harmonious sound.

An artist of celestial aim,
　　Thy genius, caught by moral grace,
With ardent emulation's flame
　　The steps of Virtue toiled to trace,
Observed in every land who brightest shone,
And, blending all their best, made perfect good thy own.

From all in Florence born, or taught
　　Our country's sweetest accent there,
Whose works, with learned labour wrought,
　　Immortal honours justly share,
Thou hast such treasure drawn of purest ore,
That not even Tuscan bards can boast a richer store.

Babel confused, and with her towers
　　Unfinished spreading wide the plain,
Has served but to evince thy powers
　　With all her tongues confused in vain,
Since not alone thy England's purest phrase
But every polished realm thy various speech displays.

The secret things of heaven and earth
    By Nature, too reserved, concealed
From other minds of highest worth,
    To thee are copiously revealed ;
Thou knowest them clearly, and thy views attain
The utmost bounds prescribed to moral truths' domain.

Let Time no more his wing display,
    And boast his ruinous career,
For Virtue, rescued from his sway,
    His injuries may cease to fear ;
Since all events that claim remembrance find
A chronicle exact in thy capacious mind.

Give me, that I may praise thy song,
    Thy lyre, by which alone I can,
Which, placing thee the stars among,
    Already proves thee more than man ;
And Thames shall seem Permessus, while his stream,
Graced with a swan like thee, shall be my favourite theme.

I who beside the Arno strain
    To match thy merit with my lays,
Learn, after many an effort vain,
    To admire thee rather than to praise,
And that by mute astonishment alone,
Not by the faltering tongue, thy worth may best be shown.

TRANSLATION OF DRYDEN'S POEM ON MILTON.

TRES tria, sed longè distantia, sæcula vates
    Ostentant tribus è gentibus eximios.
Græcia sublimem, cum majestate disertum
    Roma tulit, felix Anglia utrique parem.
Partubus ex binis Natura exhausta, coacta est,
    Tertius ut fieret, consociare duos.

July, 1780.

TRANSLATIONS FROM VINCENT BOURNE.

ON THE PICTURE OF A SLEEPING CHILD.

SWEET babe, whose image here expressed
　　Does thy peaceful slumbers show;
Guilt or fear, to break thy rest,
　　Never did thy spirit know.

Soothing slumbers, soft repose,
　　Such as mock the painter's skill,
Such as innocence bestows,
　　Harmless infant, lull thee still !

THE THRACIAN.

THRACIAN parents, at his birth,
　　Mourn their babe with many a tear,
But with undissembled mirth
　　Place him breathless on his bier.

Greece and Rome with equal scorn,
　　" O the savages !" exclaim ;
" Whether they rejoice or mourn,
　" Well entitled to the name !"

But the cause of this concern
　　And this pleasure would they trace,
Even they might somewhat learn
　　From the savages of Thrace.

RECIPROCAL KINDNESS THE PRIMARY LAW OF NATURE.

ANDROCLES from his injured lord, in dread
Of instant death, to Libya's desert fled.
Tired with his toilsome flight, and parched with heat,
He spied, at length, a cavern's cool retreat ;
But scarce had given to rest his weary frame,
When, hugest of his kind, a lion came :

He roared approaching ; but the savage din
To plaintive murmurs changed,—arrived within,
And with expressive looks, his lifted paw
Presenting, aid implored from whom he saw.   10
The fugitive, through terror at a stand,
Dared not awhile afford his trembling hand ;
But bolder grown, at length inherent found
A pointed thorn, and drew it from the wound.
The cure was wrought ; he wiped the sanious blood,
And firm and free from pain the lion stood.
Again he seeks the wilds, and day by day
Regales his inmate with the parted prey ;
Nor he disdains the dole, though humble, unprepared,
Spread on the ground, and with a lion shared.   20
But thus to live—still lost—sequestered still—
Scarce seemed his lord's revenge a heavier ill.
Home ! native home ! oh might he but repair !
He must, he will, though death attends him there.
He goes, and doomed to perish, on the sands
Of the full theatre unpitied stands ;
When lo ! the self-same lion from his cage
Flies to devour him, famished into rage.
He flies, but viewing in his purposed prey
The man, his healer, pauses on his way,   30
And, softened by remembrance into sweet
And kind composure, crouches at his feet.
   Mute with astonishment the assembly gaze :
But why, ye Romans ? Whence your mute amaze ?
All this is natural : Nature bade him rend
An enemy ; she bids him spare a friend.

A MANUAL,

MORE ANCIENT THAN THE ART OF PRINTING, AND NOT TO BE
FOUND IN ANY CATALOGUE.

THERE is a book, which we may call
   (Its excellence is such)
Alone a library, though small ;
   The ladies thumb it much.

Words none, things numerous, it contains ;
   And, things with words compared,
Who needs be told, that has his brains,
   Which merits most regard ?

Ofttimes its leaves of scarlet hue
   A golden edging boast ;
And, opened, it displays to view
   Twelve pages at the most.

Nor name, nor title, stamped behind,
   Adorns its outer part ;
But all within 'tis richly lined,
   A magazine of art.

The whitest hands that secret hoard
   Oft visit ; and the fair
Preserve it in their bosoms stored,
   As with a miser's care.

Thence implements of every size,
   And formed for various use,
(They need but to consult their eyes,)
   They readily produce.

The largest and the longest kind
  Possess the foremost page,
A sort most needed by the blind,
  Or nearly such from age.

The full-charged leaf, which next en-
      sues,
  Presents in bright array
The smaller sort, which matrons use,
  Not quite so blind as they.

The third, the fourth, the fifth supply
  What their occasions ask,
Who with a more discerning eye
  Perform a nicer task.

But still with regular decrease
  From size to size they fall,
In every leaf grow less and less ;
  The last are least of all.

Oh ! what a fund of genius, pent
  In narrow space, is here !
This volume's method and intent
  How luminous and clear !

It leaves no reader at a loss
  Or posed, whoever reads :
No commentator's tedious gloss,
  Nor even index needs.

Search Bodley's many thousands o'er !
  No book is treasured there,
Nor yet in Granta's numerous store,
  That may with this compare.

No !—rival none in either host
  Of this was ever seen,
Or, that contents could justly boast,
  So brilliant and so keen.

AN ENIGMA.

A NEEDLE, small as small can be,
In bulk and use surpasses me,
  Nor is my purchase dear ;
For little, and almost for nought,
As many of my kind are bought
  As days are in the year.

Yet though but little use we boast,
And are procured at little cost,
  The labour is not light ;
Nor few artificers it asks,
All skilful in their several tasks,
  To fashion us aright.

One fuses metal o'er the fire,
A second draws it into wire,
  The shears another plies,

Who clips in lengths the brazen thread
  For him who, chafing every shred,
    Gives all an equal size.

A fifth prepares, exact and round,
The knob with which it must be crowned;
  His follower makes it fast :
And with his mallet and his file
To shape the point, employs awhile
  The seventh and the last.

Now therefore, Œdipus ! declare
What creature, wonderful and rare,
  A process that obtains
Its purpose with so much ado
At last produces !—tell me true,
  And take me for your pains !

SPARROWS SELF-DOMESTICATED

IN TRINITY COLLEGE, CAMBRIDGE.

NONE ever shared the social feast,
Or as an inmate or a guest,
Beneath the celebrated dome
Where once Sir Isaac had his home,
Who saw not (and with some delight
Perhaps he viewed the novel sight)

How numerous at the tables there
The sparrows beg their daily fare.
For there, in every nook and cell,
Where such a family may dwell,
Sure as the vernal season comes
Their nests they weave in hope of crumbs,

Which kindly given, may serve with food
Convenient their unfeathered brood ;
And oft as with its summons clear
The warning bell salutes their ear,
Sagacious listeners to the sound,
They flock from all the fields around,
To reach the hospitable hall,
None more attentive to the call.
Arrived, the pensionary band,

Hopping and chirping, close at hand,
Solicit what they soon receive,
The sprinkled, plenteous donative.
Thus is a multitude, though large,
Supported at a trivial charge ;
A single doit would overpay
The expenditure of every day,
And who can grudge so small a grace
To suppliants, natives of the place ?

FAMILIARITY DANGEROUS.

As in her ancient mistress' lap
  The youthful Tabby lay,
They gave each other many a tap,
  Alike disposed to play.

But strife ensues.   Puss waxes warm,
  And with protruded claws
Ploughs all the length of Lydia's arm,
  Mere wantonness the cause.

At once, resentful of the deed,
  She shakes her to the ground,
With many a threat that she shall bleed
  With still a deeper wound.

But, Lydia, bid thy fury rest ;
  It was a venial stroke :
For she that will with kittens jest
  Should bear a kitten's joke.

INVITATION TO THE REDBREAST.

SWEET bird, whom the Winter constrains—
  And seldom another it can—
To seek a retreat while he reigns,
  In the well-sheltered dwellings of man,
Who never can seem to intrude,
  Though in all places equally free,
Come ! oft as the season is rude,
  Thou art sure to be welcome to me.

At sight of the first feeble ray
  That pierces the clouds of the east,
To inveigle thee every day
  My windows shall show thee a feast;
For, taught by experience, I know
  Thee mindful of benefit long,
And that, thankful for all I bestow,
  Thou wilt pay me with many a song.

Then soon as the swell of the buds
  Bespeaks the renewal of Spring,
Fly hence, if thou wilt, to the woods,
  Or where it shall please thee to sing :
And shouldst thou, compelled by a frost,
  Come again to my window or door,
Doubt not an affectionate host,
  Only pay, as thou payedst me before.

Thus music must needs be confest
　　To flow from a fountain above ;
Else how should it work in the breast
　　Unchangeable friendship and love ?
And who on the globe can be found,
　　Save your generation and ours,
That can be delighted by sound,
　　Or boasts any musical powers ?

STRADA'S NIGHTINGALE.

THE shepherd touched his reed ; sweet Philomel
　　Essayed, and oft essayed to catch the strain,
And treasuring, as on her ear they fell,
　　The numbers, echoed note for note again.

The peevish youth, who ne'er had found before
　　A rival of his skill, indignant heard,
And soon (for various was his tuneful store)
　　In loftier tones defied the simple bird.

She dared the task, and rising, as he rose,
　　With all the force that passion gives inspired,
Returned the sounds awhile, but in the close,
　　Exhausted fell, and at his feet expired.

Thus strength, not skill, prevailed.　O fatal strife,
　　By thee, poor songstress, playfully begun !
And oh, sad victory, which cost thy life,
　　And he may wish that he had never won.

ODE ON THE DEATH OF A LADY

WHO LIVED ONE HUNDRED YEARS, AND DIED ON HER BIRTHDAY, 1728.

ANCIENT dame, how wide and vast,
　　To a race like ours, appears,
Rounded to an orb at last,
　　All thy multitude of years !

We, the herd of human kind,
　　Frailer and of feebler powers ;
We, to narrow bounds confined,
　　Soon exhaust the sum of ours.

Death's delicious banquet, we
　　Perish even from the womb,
Swifter than a shadow flee,
　　Nourished but to feed the tomb.

Seeds of merciless disease
　　Lurk in all that we enjoy ;
Some that waste us by degrees,
　　Some that suddenly destroy.

And if life o'erleap the bourn
　　Common to the sons of men,
What remains, but that we mourn,
　　Dream, and dote, and drivel then ?

Fast as moons can wax and wane,
　　Sorrow comes ; and while we groan,
Pant with anguish and complain,
　　Half our years are fled and gone.

If a few (to few 'tis given),
  Lingering on this earthly stage,
Creep and halt with steps uneven
  To the period of an age,

Wherefore live they, but to see
  Cunning, arrogance, and force,
Sights lamented much by thee,
  Holding their accustomed course?

Oft was seen, in ages past,
  All that we with wonder view;
Often shall be to the last;
  Earth produces nothing new.

Thee we gratulate; content
  Should propitious Heaven design
Life for us, as calmly spent,
  Though but half the length of thine.

THE CAUSE WON.

Two neighbours furiously dispute;
A field the subject of the suit.
Trivial the spot, yet such the rage
With which the combatants engage,
'Twere hard to tell, who covets most
The prize—at whatsoever cost.
The pleadings swell.   Words still suffice;
No single word but has its price:
No term but yields some fair pretence
For novel and increased expense.
   Defendant thus becomes a name
Which he that bore it may disclaim;
Since both, in one description blended,
Are plaintiffs—when the suit is ended.

THE SILKWORM.

The beams of April, ere it goes,
A worm, scarce visible, disclose;
All winter long content to dwell
The tenant of his native shell.
The same prolific season gives
The sustenance by which he lives,
The mulberry-leaf, a simple store,
That serves him—till he needs no more!
For, his dimensions once complete,
Thenceforth none ever sees him eat;
Though, till his growing time be past,
Scarce ever is he seen to fast.
That hour arrived, his work begins;
He spins and weaves, and weaves and
    spins;
Till circle upon circle wound
Careless around him and around,
Conceals him with a veil, though slight,
Impervious to the keenest sight.
Thus self-inclosed, as in a cask,
At length he finishes his task:
And, though a worm when he was lost,
Or caterpillar at the most,
When next we see him, wings he wears,
And in papilio-pomp appears;
Becomes oviparous; supplies
With future worms and future flies
The next ensuing year—and dies!
Well were it for the world, if all
Who creep about this earthly ball,
Though shorter-lived than most he be,
Were useful in their kind as he.

THE INNOCENT THIEF.

Not a flower can be found in the fields,
　Or the spot that we till for our pleasure,
From the largest to least, but it yields
　The Bee, never wearied, a treasure.

Scarce any she quits unexplored,
　With a diligence truly exact ;
Yet, steal what she may for her hoard,
　Leaves evidence none of the fact.

Her lucrative task she pursues,
　And pilfers with so much address,
That none of their odour they lose,
　Nor charm by their beauty the less.

Not thus inoffensively preys
　The canker-worm, indwelling foe !
His voracity not thus allays
　The sparrow, the finch, or the crow.

The worm, more expensively fed,
　The pride of the garden devours ;
And birds peck the seed from the bed,
　Still less to be spared than the flowers.

But she, with such delicate skill,
　Her pillage so fits for her use,
That the chemist in vain with his still
　Would labour the like to produce.

Then grudge not her temperate meals,
　Nor a benefit blame as a theft ;
Since, stole she not all that she steals,
　Neither honey nor wax would be left.

DENNER'S OLD WOMAN.

In this mimic form of a matron in years,
How plainly the pencil of Denner appears !
The matron herself, in whose old age we see
Not a trace of decline, what a wonder is she !
No dimness of eye, and no cheek hanging low,
No wrinkle, or deep-furrowed frown on the brow !
Her forehead indeed is here circled around
With locks like the riband with which they are bound ;
While glossy and smooth, and as soft as the skin
Of a delicate peach, is the down of her chin ;
But nothing unpleasant, or sad, or severe,
Or that indicates life in its winter, is here.
Yet all is expressed, with fidelity due,
Nor a pimple or freckle concealed from the view.
　Many, fond of new sights, or who cherish a taste
For the labours of art, to the spectacle haste ;
The youths all agree, that could old age inspire
The passion of love, hers would kindle the fire,
And the matrons with pleasure confess that they see
Ridiculous nothing or hideous in thee.
The nymphs for themselves scarcely hope a decline,
O wonderful woman ! as placid as thine.
　Strange magic of art ! which the youth can engage
To peruse, half-enamoured, the features of age ;
And force from the virgin a sigh of despair,
That she, when as old, shall be equally fair !
How great is the glory that Denner has gained,
Since Apelles not more for his Venus obtained !

THE TEARS OF A PAINTER.

APELLES, hearing that his boy
Had just expired, his only joy !   [him,
Although the sight with anguish tore
Bade place his dear remains before him.
He seized his brush, his colours spread ;
And—" Oh ! my child, accept,"—he said,
" ('Tis all that I can now bestow,)
" This tribute of a father's woe ! "
Then, faithful to the twofold part,
Both of his feelings and his art,
He closed his eyes with tender care,
And formed at once a fellow pair.
His brow with amber locks beset,
And lips he drew, not livid yet ;
And shaded all that he had done
To a just image of his son.

Thus far is well.   But view again
The cause of thy paternal pain !
Thy melancholy task fulfil !
It needs the last, last touches still.
Again his pencil's powers he tries,
For on his lips a smile he spies :
And still his cheek unfaded shows
The deepest damask of the rose.
Then, heedful to the finished whole,
With fondest eagerness he stole,
Till scarce himself distinctly knew
The cherub copied from the true.
    Now, painter, cease !   Thy task is done.
Long lives this image of thy son ;
Nor short-lived shall the glory prove,
Or of thy labour or thy love.

THE MAZE.

FROM right to left, and to and fro,
Caught in a labyrinth, you go,
And turn, and turn, and turn again,
To solve the mystery, but in vain ;
Stand still and breathe, and take from me
A clue, that soon shall set you free !
Not Ariadne, if you met her,
Herself could serve you with a better.
You entered easily—find where—
And make, with ease, your exit there !

THE SNAIL.

To grass, or leaf, or fruit, or wall,
The Snail sticks close, nor fears to fall,
As if he grew there, house and all
                    Together.

Within that house secure he hides,
When danger imminent betides
Of storm, or other harm besides
                    Of weather.

Give but his horns the slightest touch,
His self-collecting power is such,
He shrinks into his house with much
                    Displeasure.

Where'er he dwells, he dwells alone,
Except himself has chattels none,
Well satisfied to be his own
                    Whole treasure.

Thus, hermit-like, his life he leads,
Nor partner of his banquet needs,
And if he meets one, only feeds
                    The faster.

Who seeks him must be worse than blind
(He and his house are so combined)
If, finding it, he fails to find
                    Its master.

NO SORROW PECULIAR TO THE SUFFERER.

THE lover, in melodious verses,
His singular distress rehearses,
Still closing with a rueful cry,
" Was ever such a wretch as I ?"
Yes ! thousands have endured before
All thy distress ; some, haply more.
Unnumbered Corydons complain,
And Strephons, of the like disdain :
And if thy Chloe be of steel,
Too deaf to hear, too hard to feel ;
Not her alone that censure fits,
Nor thou alone hast lost thy wits.

THE CANTAB.

WITH two spurs, or one, and no great matter which,
Boots bought, or boots borrowed, a whip or a switch,
Five shillings or less for the hire of his beast,
Paid part into hand ;—you must wait for the rest.
Thus equipt, Academicus climbs up his horse,
And out they both sally for better or worse ;
His heart void of fear, and as light as a feather ;
And in violent haste to go not knowing whither :
Through the fields and the towns (see !) he scampers along,
And is looked at and laughed at by old and by young.
Till at length overspent, and his sides smeared with blood,
Down tumbles his horse, man and all, in the mud.
In a waggon or chaise shall he finish his route ?
Oh ! scandalous fate ! he must do it on foot.
　Young gentlemen, hear !—I am older than you !
The advice that I give I have proved to be true :
Wherever your journey may be, never doubt it,
The faster you ride, you're the longer about it.

TRANSLATIONS FROM THE LATIN CLASSICS.

VIRGIL'S ÆNEID, Book VIII. Line 18.

THUS Italy was moved ;—nor did the chief
Æneas in his mind less tumult feel.
On every side his anxious thought he turns,
Restless, unfixed, not knowing what to chuse.
And as a cistern that in brim of brass
Confines the crystal flood, if chance the sun
Smite on it, or the moon's resplendent orb,
The quivering light now flashes on the walls,
Now leaps uncertain to the vaulted roof :
Such were the wavering motions of his mind.　　　　　　10
'Twas night—and weary Nature sunk to rest ;
The birds, the bleating flocks, were heard no more.
At length, on the cold ground, beneath the damp
And dewy vault, fast by the river's brink,
The Father of this country sought repose.
When lo ! among the spreading poplar boughs,
Forth from his pleasant stream, propitious rose
The god of Tiber : clear transparent gauze
Infolds his loins, his brows with reeds are crowned ;
And these his gracious words to soothe his care :　　　　20
　　" Heaven-born, who bring'st our kindred home again
" Rescued, and givest eternity to Troy,
" Long have Laurentum and the Latian plains
" Expected thee ; behold thy fixed abode.
" Fear not the threats of war, the storm is passed,
" The gods appeased.　For proof that what thou hearest
" Is no vain forgery or delusive dream,
" Beneath the grove that borders my green bank,
" A milk-white swine, with thirty milk-white young,
" Shall greet thy wondering eyes.　Mark well the place ; 30
" For 'tis thy place of rest, there end thy toils :
" There, twice ten years elapsed, fair Alba's walls
" Shall rise, fair Alba, by Ascanius' hand.
" Thus shall it be ;—now listen, while I teach
" The means to accomplish these events at hand.
" The Arcadians here, a race from Pallas sprung,
" Following Evander's standard and his fate,
" High on these mountains, a well-chosen spot,
" Have built a city, for their grandsire's sake
" Named Pallanteum.　These perpetual war　　　　　　40
　　C　　　　　　I I

" Wage with the Latians : joined in faithful league
" And arms confederate, add them to your camp.
" Myself between my winding banks will speed
" Your well-oared barks to stem the opposing tide.
" Rise, goddess-born, arise ; and with the first
" Declining stars, seek Juno in thy prayer,
" And vanquish all her wrath with suppliant vows.
" When conquest crowns thee, then remember Me.
" I am the Tiber, whose cærulean stream
" Heaven favours ; I with copious flood divide   50
" These grassy banks, and cleave the fruitful meads ;
" My mansion, this,—and lofty cities crown
" My fountain head."—He spoke, and sought the deep,
And plunged his form beneath the closing flood.
     Æneas at the morning dawn awoke,
And, rising, with uplifted eye beheld
The orient sun, then dipped his palms, and scooped
The brimming stream, and thus addressed the skies :
     " Ye nymphs, Laurentian nymphs, who feed the source
" Of many a stream, and thou, with thy blest flood,   60
" O Tiber ! hear, accept me, and afford,
" At length afford, a shelter from my woes.
" Where'er in secret cavern under ground
" Thy waters sleep, where'er they spring to light,
" Since thou hast pity for a wretch like me,
" My offerings and my vows shall wait thee still :
" Great horned Father of Hesperian floods,
" Be gracious now and ratify thy word !"
He said, and chose two galleys from his fleet,
Fits them with oars, and clothes the crew in arms.   70
When lo ! astonishing and pleasing sight,
The milk-white dam, with her unspotted brood,
Lay stretched upon the bank, beneath the grove.
To thee, the pious prince, Juno, to thee
Devotes them all, all on thine altar bleed.
That livelong night old Tiber smoothed his flood,
And so restrained it that it seemed to stand
Motionless as a pool, or silent lake,
That not a billow might resist their oars.
With cheerful sound of exhortation soon   80
Their voyage they begin ; the pitchy keel
Slides through the gentle deep ; the quiet stream
Admires the unwonted burthen that it bears,
Well polished arms, and vessels painted gay.
Beneath the shade of various trees, between
The umbrageous branches of the spreading groves,
They cut their liquid way, nor day nor night
They slack their course, unwinding as they go
The long meanders of the peaceful tide.
     The glowing sun was in meridian height,   90
When from afar they saw the humble walls
And the few scattered cottages, which now

The Roman power has equalled with the clouds;
But such was then Evander's scant domain.
They steer to shore, and hasten to the town.
  It chanced the Arcadian monarch on that day,
Before the walls, beneath a shady grove,
Was celebrating high, in solemn feast,
Alcides and his tutelary gods.
Pallas, his son, was there, and there the chief   100
Of all his youth ; with these, a worthy tribe,
His poor but venerable senate, burned
Sweet incense, and their altars smoked with blood.
Soon as they saw the towering masts approach,
Sliding between the trees, while the crew rest
Upon their silent oars, amazed they rose,
Not without fear, and all forsook the feast.
But Pallas, undismayed, his javelin seized,
Rushed to the bank, and from a rising ground
Forbade them to disturb the sacred rites.   110
" Ye stranger youth ! what prompts you to explore
" This untried way ? and whither do ye steer?
" Whence, and who are ye ? Bring ye peace or war?"
Æneas from his lofty deck holds forth
The peaceful olive branch, and thus replies :
" Trojans and enemies to the Latian state,
" Whom they with unprovoked hostilities
" Have driven away, thou seest. We seek Evander ;
" Say this,—and say beside, the Trojan chiefs
" Are come, and seek his friendship and his aid."   120
Pallas with wonder heard that awful name,
And "Whosoe'er thou art," he cried, "come forth ;
" Bear thine own tidings to my father's ear,
" And be a welcome guest beneath our roof,"
He said, and pressed the stranger to his breast ;
Then led him from the river to the grove,
Where, courteous, thus Æneas greets the king :
" Best of the Grecian race, to whom I bow
" (So wills my fortune) suppliant, and stretch forth
" In sign of amity this peaceful branch,   130
" I feared thee not, although I knew thee well
" A Grecian leader, born in Arcady,
" And kinsman of the Atridæ. Me my virtue,
" That means no wrong to thee,—the Oracles,
" Our kindred families allied of old,
" And thy renown diffused through every land,
" Have all conspired to bind in friendship to thee,
" And send me not unwilling to thy shores.
" Dardanus, author of the Trojan state
" (So say the Greeks), was fair Electra's son ;   140
" Electra boasted Atlas for her sire,
" Whose shoulders high sustain the æthereal orbs.
" Your sire is Mercury, who Maia bore,
" Sweet Maia, on Cyllene's hoary top.

" Her, if we credit aught tradition old,
" Atlas of yore, the selfsame Atlas, claimed
" His daughter. Thus united close in blood,
" Thy race and ours one common sire confess.
" With these credentials fraught, I would not send
" Ambassadors with artful phrase to sound   150
" And win thee by degrees, but came myself;
" Me, therefore, me thou seest; my life the stake :
" 'Tis I, Æneas, who implore thine aid.
" Should Daunia, that now aims the blow at thee,
" Prevail to conquer us, nought then, they think,
" Will hinder, but Hesperia must be theirs,
" All theirs, from the upper to the nether sea.
" Take then our friendship, and return us thine !
" We too have courage, we have noble minds,
" And youth well tried and exercised in arms."   160
      Thus spoke Æneas. He with fixed regard
Surveyed him speaking, features, form and mien.
Then briefly thus,—" Thou noblest of thy name,
" How gladly do I take thee to my heart,
" How gladly thus confess thee for a friend !
" In thee I trace Anchises ; his thy speech,
" Thy voice, thy countenance. For I well remember
" Many a day since, when Priam journeyed forth
" To Salamis, to see the land where dwelt
" Hesione, his sister, he pushed on   170
" E'en to Arcadia's frozen bounds. 'Twas then
" The bloom of youth was glowing on my cheek ;
" Much I admired the Trojan chiefs, and much
" Their king, the son of great Laomedon,
" But most Anchises, towering o'er them all.
" A youthful longing seized me to accost
" The hero, and embrace him ; I drew near,
" And gladly led him to the walls of Pheneus.
" Departing, he distinguished me with gifts,
" A costly quiver stored with Lycian darts,   180
" A robe inwove with gold, with gold embossed
" Two bridles, those which Pallas uses now.
" The friendly league thou hast solicited
" I give thee therefore, and to-morrow all
" My chosen youth shall wait on your return.
" Meanwhile, since thus in friendship ye are come,
" Rejoice with us, and join to celebrate
" These annual rites, which may not be delayed,
" And be at once familiar at our board."
      He said, and bade replace the feast removed ;   190
Himself upon a grassy bank disposed
The crew ; but for Æneas ordered forth
A couch spread with a lion's tawny shag,
And bade him share the honours of his throne,
The appointed youth with glad alacrity
Assist the labouring priest to load the board

With roasted entrails of the slaughtered beeves,
Well-kneaded bread and mantling bowls.   Well pleased,
Æneas and the Trojan youth regale
On the huge length of a well-pastured chine.   200
    Hunger appeased, and tables all despatched,
Thus spake Evander : " Superstition here,
" In this old solemn feasting, has no part.
" No, Trojan friend, from utmost danger saved,
" In gratitude this worship we renew.
" Behold that rock which nods above the vale,
" Those bulks of broken stone dispersed around ;
" How desolate the shattered cave appears,
" And what a ruin spreads the incumbered plain.
" Within this pile, but far within, was once   210
" The den of Cacus ; dire his hateful form,
" That shunned the day, half monster and half man.
" Blood newly shed streamed ever on the ground
" Smoking, and many a visage pale and wan,
" Nailed at his gate, hung hideous to the sight.
" Vulcan begot the brute : vast was his size,
" And from his throat he belched his father's fires.
" But the day came that brought us what we wished,
" The assistance and the presence of a god.
" Flushed with his victory and the spoils he won   220
" From triple-formed Geryon lately slain,
" The great avenger, Hercules, appeared.
" Hither he drove his stately bulls, and poured
" His herds along the vale.   But the sly thief,
" Cacus, that nothing might escape his hand
" Of villany or fraud, drove from the stalls
" Four of the lordliest of his bulls, and four
" The fairest of his heifers ; by the tail
" He dragged them to his den, that, there concealed,
" No footsteps might betray the dark abode.   230
" And now, his herd with provender sufficed,
" Alcides would be gone ; they as they went
" Still bellowing loud, made the deep-echoing woods
" And distant hills resound : when hark ! one ox,
" Imprisoned close within the vast recess,
" Lows in return, and frustrates all his hope.
" Then fury seized Alcides, and his breast
" With indignation heaved : grasping his club
" Of knotted oak, swift to the mountain top
" He ran, he flew.   Then first was Cacus seen   240
" To tremble, and his eyes bespoke his fears.
" Swift as an eastern blast he sought his den,
" And dread, increasing, winged him as he went.
" Drawn up in iron slings above the gate,
" A rock was hung enormous.   Such his haste,
" He burst the chains, and dropped it at the door,
" Then grappled it with ironwork within
" Of bolts and bars by Vulcan's art contrived.

" Scarce was he fast, when panting for revenge
" Came Hercules ; he gnashed his teeth with rage,   250
" And quick as lightning glanced his eyes around,
" In quest of entrance.   Fiery red and stung
" With indignation, thrice he wheeled his course
" About the mountain ; thrice, but thrice in vain,
" He strove to force the quarry at the gate,
" And thrice sat down o'erwearied in the vale.
" There stood a pointed rock, abrupt and rude,
" That high o'erlooked the rest, close at the back
" Of the fell monster's den, where birds obscene
" Of ominous note resorted, choughs and daws.   260
" This, as it leaned obliquely to the left,
" Threatening the stream below, he from the right
" Pushed with his utmost strength, and to and fro
" He shook the mass, loosening its lowest base ;
" Then shoved it from its seat ; down fell the pile ;
" Sky thundered at the fall ; the banks give way,
" The affrighted stream flows upward to his source.
" Behold the kennel of the brute exposed,
" The gloomy vault laid open.   So, if chance
" Earth yawning to the centre should disclose   270
" The mansions, the pale mansions of the dead,
" Loathed by the gods, such would the gulf appear,
" And the ghosts tremble at the sight of day.
" The monster braying with unusual din
" Within his hollow lair, and sore amazed
" To see such sudden inroads of the light,
" Alcides pressed him close with what at hand
" Lay readiest, stumps of trees, and fragments huge
" Of millstone size. He (for escape was none),
" Wondrous to tell ! forth from his gorge discharged   28c
" A smoky cloud that darkened all the den ;
" Wreath after wreath he vomited amain
" The smothering vapour mixed with fiery sparks :
" No sight could penetrate the veil obscure.
" The hero, more provoked, endured not this,
" But with a headlong leap he rushed to where
" The thickest cloud enveloped his abode ;
" There grasped he Cacus, spite of all his fires,
" Till, crushed within his arms, the monster shows
" His bloodless throat, now dry with panting hard,   290
" And his pressed eyeballs start.   Soon he tears down
" The barricade of rock, the dark abyss
" Lies open ; and the imprisoned bulls, the theft
" He had with oaths denied, are brought to light ;
" By the heels the miscreant carcase is dragged forth,
" His face, his eyes, all terrible, his breast
" Beset with bristles, and his sooty jaws
" Are viewed with wonder never to be cloyed.
" Hence the celebrity thou seest, and hence
" This festal day.   Potitius first enjoined   300

" Posterity these solemn rites ; he first
" With those who bear the great Pinarian name,
" To Hercules devoted, in the grove
" This altar built, deemed sacred in the highest
" By us, and sacred ever to be deemed.
" Come then, my friends, and bind your youthful brows
" In praise of such deliverance, and hold forth
" The brimming cup ; your deities and ours
" Are now the same ; then drink, and freely too."
So saying, he twisted round his reverend locks   310
A variegated poplar wreath, and filled
His right hand with a consecrated bowl.
At once all pour libations on the board,
All offer prayer. And now, the radiant sphere
Of day descending, eventide drew near ;
When first Potitius with the priests advanced,
Begirt with skins, and torches in their hands.
High piled with meats of savoury taste, they ranged
The chargers, and renewed the grateful feast.
Then came the Salii, crowned with poplar too,   320
Circling the blazing altars : here the youth
Advanced, a choir harmonious ; there were heard
The reverend seers responsive : praise they sung,
Much praise in honour of Alcides' deeds ;
How first with infant gripe two serpents huge
He strangled, sent from Juno ; next they sung
How Troja and Œchalia he destroyed,
Fair cities both, and many a toilsome task
Beneath Eurystheus (so his stepdame willed)
Achieved victorious.   " Thou, the cloud-born pair,   330
" Hylæus fierce and Pholus, monstrous twins,
" Thou slewest the minotaur, the plague of Crete,
" And the vast lion of the Nemean rock.
" Thee Hell, and Cerberus, Hell's porter, feared,
" Stretched in his den upon his half-gnawed bones.
" Thee no abhorred form, not even the vast
" Typhœus, could appal, though clad in arms.
" Hail, true-born son of Jove, among the gods
" At length enrolled, nor least illustrious thou,
" Haste thee propitious, and approve our songs !"—   340
Thus hymned the chorus ; above all they sing
The cave of Cacus, and the flames he breathed.
The whole grove echoes, and the hills rebound.
    The rites performed, all hasten to the town ;
The king, bending with age, held as he went
Æneas and his Pallas by the hand,
With much variety of pleasing talk
Shortening the way.   Æneas, with a smile,
Looks round him, charmed with the delightful scene,
And many a question asks, and much he learns   350
Of heroes far renowned in ancient times.
Then spake Evander : " These extensive groves

" Were once inhabited by fauns and nymphs
" Produced beneath their shades, and a rude race
" Of men, the progeny uncouth of elms
" And knotted oaks.   They no refinement knew
" Of laws or manners civilized, to yoke
" The steer, with forecast provident to store
" The hoarded grain, or manage what they had,
" But browsed like beasts upon the leafy boughs,   360
" Or fed voracious on their hunted prey.
" An exile from Olympus, and expelled
" His native realm by thunder-bearing Jove,
" First Saturn came.   He from the mountains drew
" This herd of men untractable and fierce,
" And gave them laws ; and called his hiding-place,
" This growth of forests, Latium. Such the peace
" His land possessed, the golden age was then,
" So famed in story ; till by slow degrees
" Far other times, and of far different hue,   370
" Succeeded, thirst of gold and thirst of blood.
" Then came Ausonian bands, and armed hosts
" From Sicily ; and Latium often changed
" Her master and her name.   At length arose
" Kings, of whom Tybris of gigantic form
" Was chief ; and we Italians since have called
" The river by his name ; thus Albula
" (So was the country called in ancient days)
" Was quite forgot.   Me from my native land
" An exile, through the dangerous ocean driven,   380
" Resistless fortune and relentless fate
" Placed where thou seest me.   Phœbus, and
" The nymph Carmentis, with maternal care
" Attendant on my wanderings, fixed me here. "

[Ten lines omitted.]

He said, and showed him the Tarpeian rock,
And the rude spot where now the capitol
Stands all magnificent and bright with gold,
Then overgrown with thorns.   And yet even then
The swains beheld that sacred scene with awe ;
The grove, the rock, inspired religious fear.   390
" This grove (he said) that crowns the lofty top
" Of this fair hill, some deity, we know,
" Inhabits, but what deity we doubt.
" The Arcadians speak of Jupiter himself,
" That they have often seen him, shaking here
" His gloomy ægis, while the thunder-storms
" Came rolling all around him.   Turn thine eyes,
" Behold that ruin ; those dismantled walls,
" Where once two towns, Janiculum——,
" By Janus this, and that by Saturn built,   400
" Saturnia."   Such discourse brought them beneath
The roof of poor Evander ; thence they saw,

Where now the proud and stately Forum stands,
The grazing herds wide scattered o'er the field.
Soon as he entered—" Hercules," he said,
" Victorious Hercules, on this threshold trod,
" These walls contained him, humble as they are.
" Dare to despise magnificence, my friend,
" Prove thy divine descent by worth divine,
" Nor view with haughty scorn this mean abode."   410
So saying, he led Æneas by the hand,
And placed him on a cushion stuffed with leaves,
Spread with the skin of a Lybistian bear.

[The Episode of Venus and Vulcan omitted]

While thus in Lemnos Vulcan was employed.
Awakened by the gentle dawn of day,
And the shrill song of birds beneath the eaves
Of his low mansion, old Evander rose.
His tunic and the sandals on his feet,
And his good sword well girded to his side,
A panther's skin dependent from his left,   420
And over his right shoulder thrown aslant,
Thus was he clad.   Two mastiffs followed him,
His whole retinue and his nightly guard.

THE SALAD.

THE winter night now well-nigh worn away,
The wakeful cock proclaimed approaching day,
When Simulus, poor tenant of a farm
Of narrowest limits, heard the shrill alarm,
Yawned, stretched his limbs, and anxious to provide
Against the pangs of hunger unsupplied,
By slow degrees his tattered bed forsook,
And poking in the dark, explored the nook
Where embers slept with ashes heaped around,
And with burnt finger-ends the treasure found.   10
   It chanced that from a brand beneath his nose,
Sure proof of latent fire, some smoke arose ;
When trimming with a pin the incrusted tow,
And stooping it towards the coals below,
He toils, with cheeks distended, to excite
The lingering flame, and gains at length a light.
With prudent heed he spreads his hand before
The quivering lamp, and opes his granary door.
Small was his stock, but taking for the day
A measured stint of twice eight pounds away,   20

With these his mill he seeks.   A shelf at hand,
Fixt in the wall, affords his lamp a stand :
Then baring both his arms, a sleeveless coat
He girds, the rough exuviæ of a goat ;
And with a rubber, for that use designed,
Cleansing his mill within, begins to grind :
Each hand has its employ ; labouring amain,
This turns the winch, while that supplies the grain.
The stone revolving rapidly, now glows,
And the bruised corn a mealy current flows ;   30
While he, to make his heavy labour light,
Tasks oft his left hand to relieve his right ;
And chants with rudest accent, to beguile
His ceaseless toil, as rude a strain the while.
And now " Dame Cybale, come forth ! " he cries ;
But Cybale, still slumbering, nought replies.
   From Afric she, the swain's sole serving-maid,
Whose face and form alike her birth betrayed ;
With woolly locks, lips tumid, sable skin,
Wide bosom, udders flaccid, belly thin,   40
Legs slender, broad and most misshapen feet,
Chapped into chinks, and parched with solar heat.
Such, summoned oft, she came ; at his command
Fresh fuel heaped, the sleeping embers fanned,
And made in haste her simmering skillet steam,
Replenished newly from the neighbouring stream.
   The labours of the mill performed, a sieve
The mingled flour and bran must next receive,
Which shaken oft, shoots Ceres through refined,
And better dressed, her husks all left behind.   50
This done, at once his future plain repast,
Unleavened, on a shaven board he cast,
With tepid lymph first largely soaked it all,
Then gathered it with both hands to a ball,
And spreading it again with both hands wide,
With sprinkled salt the stiffened mass supplied ;
At length, the stubborn substance, duly wrought,
Takes from his palms impressed the shape it ought,
Becomes an orb, and quartered into shares,
The faithful mark of just division bears.   60
Last, on his hearth it finds convenient space,
For Cybale before had swept the place,
And there, with tiles and embers overspread,
She leaves it,—reeking in its sultry bed.
   Nor Simulus, while Vulcan thus, alone,
His part performed, proves heedless of his own,
But sedulous, not merely to subdue
His hunger, but to please his palate too,
Prepares more savoury food.   His chimney-side
Could boast no gammon, salted well, and dried,   70
And hooked behind him : but sufficient store
Of bundled anise, and a cheese it bore ;

A broad round cheese, which, through its centre strung
With a tough broom-twig, in the corner hung ;
The prudent hero therefore, with address
And quick despatch, now seeks another mess.
  Close to his cottage lay a garden-ground,
With reeds and osiers sparely girt around ;
Small was the spot, but liberal to produce,
Nor wanted aught that serves a peasant's use ;   80
And sometimes even the rich would borrow thence,
Although its tillage was his sole expense.
For oft, as from his toils abroad he ceased,
Home-bound by weather or some stated feast,
His debt of culture here he duly paid,
And only left the plough to wield the spade.
He knew to give each plant the soil it needs,
To drill the ground, and cover close the seeds ;
And could with ease compel the wanton rill
To turn, and wind, obedient to his will.   90
There flourished starwort, and the branching beet,
The sorel acid, and the mallow sweet,
The skirret, and the leek's aspiring kind,
The noxious poppy—quencher of the mind !
Salubrious sequel of a sumptuous board,
The lettuce, and the long huge-bellied gourd ;
But these (for none his appetite controlled
With stricter sway) the thrifty rustic sold ;
With broom-twigs neatly bound, each kind apart
He bore them ever to the public mart ;   100
Whence, laden still, but with a lighter load,
Of cash well earned, he took his homeward road,
Expending seldom, ere he quitted Rome,
His gains, in flesh-meat for a feast at home.
There, at no cost, on onions rank and red,
Or the curled endive's bitter leaf, he fed :
On scallions sliced, or with a sensual gust
On rockets—foul provocatives of lust ;
Nor even shunned, with smarting gums, to press
Nasturtium, pungent face-distorting mess !   110
  Some such regale, now also in his thought,
With hasty steps his garden-ground he sought :
There delving with his hands, he first displaced
Four plants of garlick, large, and rooted fast ;
The tender tops of parsley next he culls,
Then the old rue-bush shudders as he pulls,
And coriander last to these succeeds,
That hangs on slightest threads her trembling seeds.
  Placed near his sprightly fire he now demands
The mortar at his sable servant's hands ;   120
When stripping all his garlick first, he tore
The exterior coats, and cast them on the floor,
Then cast away with like contempt the skin,
Flimsier concealment of the cloves within.

These searched, and perfect found, he one by one
Rinsed, and disposed within the hollow stone ;
Salt added, and a lump of salted cheese,
With his injected herbs he covered these,
And tucking with his left his tunic tight,
And seizing fast the pestle with his right,   130
The garlick bruising first he soon expressed,
And mixed the various juices of the rest.
He grinds, and by degrees his herbs below,
Lost in each other, their own powers forego,
And with the cheese in compound, to the sight
Nor wholly green appear, nor wholly white.
His nostrils oft the forceful fume resent ;
He cursed full oft his dinner for its scent,
Or with wry faces, wiping as he spoke
The trickling tears, cried—" Vengeance on the smoke ! " 140
The work proceeds : not roughly turns he now
The pestle, but in circles smooth and slow ;
With cautious hand that grudges what it spills,
Some drops of olive-oil he next instils ;
Then vinegar with caution scarcely less ;
And gathering to a ball the medley mess,
Last, with two fingers frugally applied,
Sweeps the small remnant from the mortar's side :
And thus, complete in figure and in kind,
Obtains at length the Salad he designed.   150
   And now black Cybale before him stands,
The cake drawn newly glowing in her hands :
He glad receives it, chasing far away
All fears of famine for the passing day ;
His legs enclosed in buskins, and his head
In its tough casque of leather, forth he led
And yoked his steers, a dull obedient pair,
Then drove afield, and plunged the pointed share.

June 8, 1799.

FROM OVID.

OVID. TRIST. LIB. V. ELEG. XII.

Scribis, ut oblectem.

You bid me write to amuse the tedious hours,
And save from withering my poetic powers.
Hard is the task, my friend, for verse should flow
From the free mind, not fettered down by woe.
Restless amidst unceasing tempests tossed,
Whoe'er has cause for sorrow, I have most.

Would you bid Priam laugh, his sons all slain ;
Or childless Niobe from tears refrain,
Join the gay dance, and lead the festive train ?
Does grief or study most befit the mind,   10
To this remote, this barbarous nook confined ?
Could you impart to my unshaken breast
The fortitude by Socrates possessed,
Soon would it sink beneath such woes as mine ;
For what is human strength to wrath divine ?
Wise as he was, and Heaven pronounced him so,
My sufferings would have laid that wisdom low.
Could I forget my country, thee and all,
And even the offence to which I owe my fall,
Yet fear alone would freeze the poet's vein,   20
While hostile troops swarm o'er the dreary plain.
Add that the fatal rust of long disuse
Unfits me for the service of the Muse.
Thistles and weeds are all we can expect
From the best soil impoverished by neglect ;
Unexercised, and to his stall confined,
The fleetest racer would be left behind ;
The best built bark that cleaves the watery way,
Laid useless by, would moulder and decay ; —
No hope remains that time shall me restore,   30
Mean as I was, to what I was before.
Think how a series of desponding cares
Benumbs the genius and its force impairs.
How oft, as now, on this devoted sheet,
My verse constrained to move with measured feet,
Reluctant and laborious limps along,
And proves itself a wretched exile's song.
What is it tunes the most melodious lays ?
'Tis emulation and the thirst of praise ;
A noble thirst, and not unknown to me,   40
While smoothly wafted on a calmer sea.
But can a wretch like Ovid pant for fame ?
No, rather let the world forget my name.
Is it because that world approved my strain,
You prompt me to the same pursuit again ?
No, let the Nine the ungrateful truth excuse,
I charge my hopeless ruin on the Muse,
And, like Perillus, meet my just desert,
The victim of my own pernicious art.
Fool that I was to be so warned in vain,   50
And, shipwrecked once, to tempt the deep again !
Ill fares the bard in this unlettered land,
None to consult, and none to understand.
The purest verse has no admirers here,
Their own rude language only suits their ear.
Rude as it is, at length familiar grown,
I learn it, and almost unlearn my own.
Yet to say truth, even here the Muse disdains

Confinement, and attempts her former strains,
But finds the strong desire is not the power,   60
And what her taste condemns, the flames devour.
A part, perhaps, like this, escapes the doom,
And though unworthy, finds a friend at Rome ;
But oh the cruel art, that could undo
Its votary thus ! would that could perish too !

HOR. LIB. I. ODE IX.

Vides, ut altâ stet nive candidum
Soracte ; . . . . .

SEEST thou yon mountain laden with deep snow,
The groves beneath their fleecy burthen bow,
    The streams, congealed, forget to flow?
Come, thaw the cold, and lay a cheerful pile
        Of fuel on the hearth ;
Broach the best cask, and make old Winter smile
        With seasonable mirth.

This be our part,—let heaven dispose the rest ;
    If Jove command, the winds shall sleep,
    That now wage war upon the foamy deep,
And gentle gales spring from the balmy west.

        Even let us shift to-morrow as we may ;
            When to-morrow's passed away,
            We at least shall have to say,
            We have lived another day ;
Your auburn locks will soon be silvered o'er,
Old age is at our heels, and youth returns no more.

HOR. LIB. I. ODE XXXVIII.

Persicos odi, puer, apparatus.

BOY, I hate their empty shows,
    Persian garlands I detest,
Bring not me the late-blown rose,
    Lingering after all the rest.

Plainer myrtle pleases me,
    Thus outstretched beneath my vine,
Myrtle more becoming thee,
    Waiting with thy master's wine.

ANOTHER TRANSLATION OF THE SAME ODE.

[English Sapphics have been attempted, but with little success, because in our language we have no certain rules by which to determine the quantity. The following version was made merely in the way of experiment how far it might be possible to imitate Latin Sapphic in English without any attention to that circumstance.]

> Boy! I detest all Persian fopperies,
> Fillet-bound garlands are to me disgusting;
> Task not thyself with any search, I charge thee,
>   Where latest roses linger.
>
> Bring me alone (for thou wilt find that readily)
> Plain myrtle.   Myrtle neither will disparage
> Thee occupied to serve me, or me drinking
>   Beneath my vine's cool shelter.

HOR. LIB. II.   ODE XV.

Otium Divos rogat in patenti.

> EASE is the weary merchant's prayer,
>   Who ploughs by night the Ægean flood,
> When neither moon nor stars appear,
>   Or faintly glimmer through the cloud.
>
> For ease the Mede with quiver graced,
>   For ease the Thracian hero sighs;
> Delightful ease all pant to taste,
>   A blessing which no treasure buys.
>
> For neither gold can lull to rest,
>   Nor all a Consul's guard beat off
> The tumults of a troubled breast,
>   The cares that haunt a gilded roof.
>
> Happy the man whose table shows
>   A few clean ounces of old plate;
> No fear intrudes on his repose,
>   No sordid wishes to be great.
>
> Poor short-lived things, what plans we lay!
>   Ah, why forsake our native home,
> To distant climates speed away?
>   For self sticks close where'er we roam!

Care follows hard, and soon o'ertakes
  The well-rigged ship, the warlike steed ;
Her destined quarry ne'er forsakes ;
  Not the wind flies with half her speed.

From anxious fears of future ill
  Guard well the cheerful, happy now ;
Gild e'en your sorrows with a smile,
  No blessing is unmixed below.

Thy neighing steeds and lowing herds,
  Thy numerous flocks around thee graze,
And the best purple Tyre affords
  Thy robe magnificent displays.

On me indulgent Heaven bestowed
  A rural mansion, neat and small ;
This lyre ;—and as for yonder crowd,
  The happiness to hate them all.

EPIGRAMS, TRANSLATED FROM THE LATIN OF OWEN.

ON ONE IGNORANT AND ARROGANT.

THOU mayst of double ignorance boast,
Who know'st not that thou nothing know'st.

PRUDENT SIMPLICITY.

THAT thou mayst injure no man, dove-like be,
And serpent-like, that none may injure thee !

TO A FRIEND IN DISTRESS.

I WISH thy lot, now bad, still worse, my friend ;
For when at worst, they say, things always mend.

RETALIATION.

THE works of ancient bards divine,
   Aulus, thou scorn'st to read ;
And should posterity read thine,
   It would be strange indeed !

SELF-KNOWLEDGE.

WHEN little more than boy in age,
I deemed myself almost a sage ;
But now seem worthier to be styled,
For ignorance, almost a child.

SUNSET AND SUNRISE.

CONTEMPLATE, when the sun declines,
   Thy death, with deep reflection ;
And when again he rising shines,
   Thy day of resurrection !

TRANSLATIONS OF GREEK VERSES.

FROM THE GREEK OF JULIANUS.

A SPARTAN, his companion slain,
　Alone from battle fled ;
His mother, kindling with disdain
　That she had borne him, struck him dead ;
For courage, and not birth alone,
In Sparta, testifies a son !

ON THE SAME, BY PALLADAS.

A SPARTAN 'scaping from the fight,
His mother met him in his flight,
Upheld a falchion to his breast,
And thus the fugitive addressed :
" Thou canst but live to blot with shame
" Indelible thy mother's name,
" While every breath that thou shalt draw
" Offends against thy country's law :
" But, if thou perish by this hand,
" Myself indeed throughout the land,
" To my dishonour, shall be known
" The mother still of such a son ;
" But Sparta will be safe and free,
" And that shall serve to comfort me."

AN EPITAPH.

MY name—my country—what are they to thee ?
What, whether base or proud my pedigree ?
Perhaps I far surpassed all other men ;
Perhaps I fell below them all ; what then ?
Suffice it, stranger ! that thou seest a tomb ;
Thou know'st its use ; it hides—no matter whom.

ANOTHER.

TAKE to thy bosom, gentle Earth ! a swain
　With much hard labour in thy service worn ;
He set the vines that clothe yon ample plain,
　And he these olives that the vale adorn.

He filled with grain the glebe ; the rills he led
　Through this green herbage, and those fruitful bowers ;
Thou, therefore, Earth ! lie lightly on his head,
　His hoary head, and deck his grave with flowers.

ANOTHER.

PAINTER, this likeness is too strong,
And we shall mourn the dead too long.

ANOTHER.

AT threescore winters' end I died,
　A cheerless being, sole and sad ;
The nuptial knot I never tied,
　And wish my father never had.

BY CALLIMACHUS.

AT morn we placed on his funereal bier
　Young Melanippus ; and at eventide,
Unable to sustain a loss so dear,
　By her own hand his blooming sister died.

Thus Aristippus mourned his noble race,
　Annihilated by a double blow,
Nor son could hope, nor daughter more to embrace,
　And all Cyrene saddened at his woe.

ON AN UGLY FELLOW.

BEWARE, my friend ! of crystal brook,
Or fountain, lest that hideous hook,
　Thy nose, thou chance to see ;
Narcissus' fate would then be thine,
And self-detested thou wouldst pine,
　As self-enamoured he.

BY HERACLIDES.

IN Cnidus born, the consort I became
Of Euphron. Aretimias was my name.
His bed I shared, nor proved a barren bride,
But bore two children at a birth, and died.
One child I leave to solace and uphold
Euphron hereafter, when infirm and old,
And one, for his remembrance' sake, I bear
To Pluto's realm, till he shall join me there.

ON THE REED.

I WAS of late a barren plant,
Useless, insignificant,
Nor fig, nor grape, nor apple bore,
A native of the marshy shore ;
But gathered for poetic use,
And plunged into a sable juice,
Of which my modicum I sip
With narrow mouth and slender lip,
At once, although by nature dumb,
All eloquent I have become,
And speak with fluency untired,
As if by Phœbus' self inspired.

TO HEALTH.

ELDEST born of powers divine !
Blessed Hygeia ! be it mine
To enjoy what thou canst give,
And henceforth with thee to live :
For in power if pleasure be,
Wealth or numerous progeny,
Or in amorous embrace,
Where no spy infests the place ;
Or in aught that Heaven bestows
To alleviate human woes,
When the wearied heart despairs
Of a respite from its cares ;
These and every true delight
Flourish only in thy sight ;
And the sister Graces three
Owe, themselves, their youth to thee,
Without whom we may possess
Much, but never happiness.

ON AN INFANT.

BEWAIL not much, my parents ! me, the prey
Of ruthless Hades, and sepulchred here.
An infant, in my fifth scarce finished year,
He found all sportive, innocent, and gay,
Your young Callimachus ; and if I knew
Not many joys, my griefs were also few.

ON THE ASTROLOGERS.

THE astrologers did all alike presage
My uncle's dying in extreme old age ;
One only disagreed.   But he was wise,
And spoke not till he heard the funeral cries.

ON AN OLD WOMAN.

MYCILLA dyes her locks, 'tis said ;
    But 'tis a foul aspersion :
She buys them black ; they therefore need
    No subsequent immersion.

ON INVALIDS.

FAR happier are the dead, methinks, than they
Who look for death, and fear it every day.

ON FLATTERERS.

No mischief worthier of our fear
    In nature can be found
Than friendship, in ostent sincere,
    But hollow and unsound ;
For lulled into a dangerous dream
    We close infold a foe,
Who strikes, when most secure we seem,
    The inevitable blow.

ON A TRUE FRIEND.

HAST thou a friend ?   Thou hast indeed
    A rich and large supply,
Treasure to serve your every need,
    Well managed, till you die.

TO THE SWALLOW.

ATTIC maid! with honey fed,
　　Bearest thou to thy callow brood
Yonder locust from the mead,
　　Destined their delicious food?

Ye have kindred voices clear,
　　Ye alike unfold the wing,
Migrate hither, sojourn here,
　　Both attendant on the spring!

Ah, for pity drop the prize;
　　Let it not with truth be said
That a songster gasps and dies
　　That a songster may be fed.

ON LATE-ACQUIRED WEALTH.

POOR in my youth, and in life's later scenes
　　Rich to no end, I curse my natal hour,
Who nought enjoyed while young, denied the means;
　　And nought when old enjoyed, denied the power.

ON A BATH, BY PLATO.

DID Cytherea to the skies
From this pellucid lymph arise?
Or was it Cytherea's touch,
When bathing here, that made it such?

ON A FOWLER, BY ISIODORUS.

WITH seeds and birdlime, from the desert air,
Eumelus gathered free, though scanty, fare.
No lordly patron's hand he deigned to kiss,
Nor luxury knew, save liberty, nor bliss.
Thrice thirty years he lived, and to his heirs
His seeds bequeathed, his birdlime, and his snares.

ON NIOBE.

CHARON! receive a family on board,
　　Itself sufficient for thy crazy yawl;
Apollo and Diana, for a word
　　By me too proudly spoken, slew us all.

ON A GOOD MAN.

TRAVELLER, regret me not ; for thou shalt find
　　Just cause of sorrow none in my decease,
Who, dying, children's children left behind,
　　And with one wife lived many a year in peace :
Three virtuous youths espoused my daughters three,
　　And oft their infants in my bosom lay,
Nor saw I one, of all derived from me,
　　Touched with disease, or torn by death away.
Their duteous hands my funeral rites bestowed,
　　And me, by blameless manners fitted well
To seek it, sent to the serene abode
　　Where shades of pious men for ever dwell.

ON A MISER.

THEY call thee rich !—I deem thee poor,
　Since, if thou darest not use thy store,
　But savest it only for thine heirs,
　The treasure is not thine, but theirs.

ANOTHER.

A MISER, traversing his house,
Espied, unusual there, a mouse,
And thus his uninvited guest
Briskly inquisitive addressed :
" Tell me, my dear, to what cause is it
" I owe this unexpected visit ?"
The mouse her host obliquely eyed,
And, smiling, pleasantly replied :
" Fear not, good fellow, for your hoard !
" I come to lodge, and not to board."

ANOTHER.

ART thou some individual of a kind
Long-lived by nature as the rook or hind ?
Heap treasure, then ; for if thy need be such,
Thou hast excuse, and scarce canst heap too much.
But man thou seem'st : clear therefore from thy breast
This lust of treasure—folly at the best !
For why shouldst thou go wasted to the tomb,
To fatten with thy spoils thou know'st not whom ?

ON FEMALE INCONSTANCY.

RICH, thou hadst many lovers;—poor, hast none:
　　So surely want extinguishes the flame,
And she who called thee once her pretty one,
　　And her Adonis, now inquires thy name.

Where wast thou born, Sosicrates, and where,
　　In what strange country, can thy parents live,
Who seem'st, by thy complaints, not yet aware
　　That want's a crime no woman can forgive?

ON HERMOCRATIA.

HERMOCRATIA named—save only one,
Twice fifteen births I bore, and buried none;
For neither Phœbus pierced my thriving joys,
Nor Dian—she my girls, or he my boys.
But Dian rather, when my daughters lay
In parturition, chased their pangs away.
And all my sons, by Phœbus' bounty, shared
A vigorous youth, by sickness unimpaired.
O Niobe! far less prolific! see
Thy boast against Latona shamed by me!

FROM MENANDER.

FOND youth! who dream'st that hoarded gold
　　Is needful, not alone to pay
For all thy various items sold,
　　To serve the wants of every day;

Bread, vinegar, and oil, and meat,
　　For savoury viands seasoned high;
But somewhat more important yet—
　　I tell thee what it cannot buy.

No treasure, hadst thou more amassed
　　Than fame to Tantalus assigned,
Would save thee from a tomb at last,
　　But thou must leave it all behind.

I give thee, therefore, counsel wise;
　　Confide not vainly in thy store,
However large—much less despise
　　Others comparatively poor;

But in thy more exalted state
　　A just and equal temper show,
That all who see thee rich and great
　　May deem thee worthy to be so.

ON THE GRASSHOPPER.

HAPPY songster, perched above,
On the summit of the grove,
Whom a dewdrop cheers to sing
With the freedom of a king !
From thy perch survey the fields
Where prolific nature yields
Nought that, willingly as she,
Man surrenders not to thee.
For hostility or hate
None thy pleasures can create.
Thee it satisfies to sing
Sweetly the return of spring,
Herald of the genial hours,
Harming neither herbs nor flowers.
Therefore man thy voice attends
Gladly,—thou and he are friends ;
Nor thy never-ceasing strains
Phœbus or the Muse disdains
As too simple or too long,
For themselves inspire the song.
Earth-born, bloodless, undecaying,
Ever singing, sporting, playing,
What has nature else to show
Godlike in its kind as thou ?

ON A THIEF.

WHEN Aulus, the nocturnal thief, made prize
Of Hermes, swift-winged envoy of the skies,
Hermes, Arcadia's king, the thief divine,
Who when an infant stole Apollo's kine,
And whom, as arbiter and overseer
Of our gymnastic sports, we planted here ;
" Hermes," he cried, " you meet no new disaster ;
" Ofttimes the pupil goes beyond his master."

ON PALLAS BATHING.

FROM A HYMN OF CALLIMACHUS.

NOR oils of balmy scent produce,
Nor mirror for Minerva's use,
Ye nymphs who lave her ; she, arrayed
In genuine beauty, scorns their aid.
Not even when they left the skies
To seek on Ida's head the prize

From Paris' hand, did Juno deign,
Or Pallas in the crystal plain
Of Simois' stream her locks to trace,
Or in the mirror's polished face,
Though Venus oft with anxious care
Adjusted twice a single hair.

TO DEMOSTHENES,

ON A FLATTERING MIRROR.

It flatters and deceives thy view,
  This mirror of ill-polished ore;
For were it just, and told thee true,
  Thou wouldst consult it never more.

ON A SIMILAR CHARACTER.

You give your cheeks a rosy stain,
  With washes dye your hair;
But paint and washes both are vain
  To give a youthful air.

Those wrinkles mock your daily toil,
  No labour will efface 'em,
You wear a mask of smoothest oil,
  Yet still with ease we trace 'em.

An art so fruitless then forsake,
  Which though you much excel in,
You never can contrive to make
  Old Hecuba young Helen.

ON MILTIADES.

Miltiades! thy valour best
(Although in every region known)
The men of Persia can attest,
Taught by thyself at Marathon.

ON A BATTERED BEAUTY.

Hair, wax, rouge, honey, teeth you buy,
  A multifarious store!
A mask at once would all supply,
  No   would it cost you more.

ON PEDIGREE.

FROM EPICHARMUS.

MY mother! if thou love me, name no more
My noble birth! Sounding at every breath
My noble birth, thou kill'st me.   Thither fly,
As to their only refuge, all from whom
Nature withholds all good besides; they boast
Their noble birth, conduct us to the tombs
Of their forefathers, and from age to age
Ascending, trumpet their illustrious race:
But whom hast thou beheld, or canst thou name,
Derived from no forefathers?   Such a man
Lives not; for how could such be born at all
And if it chance that, native of a land
Far distant, or in infancy deprived
Of all his kindred, one, who cannot trace
His origin, exist, why deem him sprung
From baser ancestry than theirs who can?
My mother! he whom nature at his birth
Endowed with virtuous qualities, although
An Æthiop and a slave, is nobly born.

ON ENVY.

PITY, says the Theban bard,
From my wishes I discard;
Envy, let me rather be,
Rather far, a theme for thee!
Pity to distress is shown,
Envy to the great alone.
So the Theban: but to shine
Less conspicuous be mine!
I prefer the golden mean,
Pomp and penury between;
For alarm and peril wait
Ever on the loftiest state,
And the lowest, to the end,
Obloquy and scorn attend.

TRANSLATION OF AN EPIGRAM OF HOMER.

PAY me my price, potters! and I will sing.
Attend, O Pallas! and with lifted arm
Protect their oven; let the cups and all

---

* No title is prefixed to this piece, but it appears to be a translation of one of the Ἐπ γράμματα of Homer called Ὁ Κάμινος, or The Furnace.   Herodotus, or whoever was the author of the Life of Homer ascribed to him, observes: "Certain potters, while they were busy in baking their ware, seeing Homer at a small distance, and having heard much said of his wisdom, called to him, and promised him a present of their commodity and of such other things as they could afford, if he would sing to them; when he sang as follows."

The sacred vessels blacken well, and, baked
With good success, yield them both fair renown
And profit, whether in the market sold
Or streets, and let no strife ensue between us.
But oh, ye potters ! if with shameless front
Ye falsify your promise, then I leave
No mischief uninvoked to avenge the wrong.
Come Syntrips, Smaragus, Sabactes, come,
And Asbetus ; nor let your direst dread,
Omodamus, delay !   Fire seize your house !
May neither house nor vestibule escape !
May ye lament to see confusion mar
And mingle the whole labour of your hands,
And may a sound fill all your oven, such
As of a horse grinding his provender,
While all your pots and flagons bounce within.
Come hither also, daughter of the sun,
Circe the sorceress, and with thy drugs
Poison themselves, and all that they have made !
Come also, Chiron, with thy numerous troop
Of Centaurs, as well those who died beneath
The club of Hercules, as who escaped,
And stamp their crockery to dust ; down fal!
Their chimney ; let them see it with their eyes,
And howl to see the ruin of their art,
While I rejoice ; and if a potter stoop
To peep into his furnace, may the fire
Flash in his face and scorch it, that all men
Observe, thenceforth, equity and good faith

BY PHILEMON.

OFT we enhance our ills by discontent,
And give them bulk beyond what Nature meant.
A parent, brother, friend deceased, to cry,
" He's dead indeed, but he was born to die "—
Such temperate grief is suited to the size
And burthen of the loss ; is just and wise :
But to exclaim, " Ah ! wherefore was I born,
" Thus to be left for ever thus forlorn ? "
Who thus laments his loss invites distress,
And magnifies a woe that might be less,
Through dull despondence to his lot resigned,
And leaving reason's remedy behind.

BY MOSCHUS.

I SLEPT when Venus entered : to my bed
A Cupid in her beauteous hand she led,
A bashful seeming boy, and thus she said :
    " Shepherd, receive my little one ! I bring
" An untaught love, whom thou must teach to sing."
She said, and left him.   I, suspecting nought,
Many a sweet strain my subtle pupil taught,
How reed to reed Pan first with osier bound,
How Pallas formed the pipe of softest sound,
How Hermes gave the lute, and how the quire
Of Phœbus owe to Phœbus' self the lyre.
Such were my themes ; my themes nought heeded he,
But ditties sang of amorous sort to me,
The pangs that mortals and immortals prove
From Venus' influence, and the darts of love.
Thus was the teacher by the pupil taught ;
His lessons I retained, and mine forgot.

TRANSLATIONS OF ENGLISH VERSES.

FROM THE FABLES OF GAY.

LEPUS MULTIS AMICUS.

Lusus amicitia est, uni nisi dedita, ceu fit,
  Simplice ni nexus fœdere, lusus amor.
Incerto genitore puer, non sæpe paternæ
  Tutamen novit, deliciasque domûs :
Quique sibi fidos fore multos sperat, amicus,
  Mirum est huic misero si ferat ullus opem.

Comis erat, mitisque, et nolle et velle paratus
  Cum quovis, Gaii more modoque, Lepus.
Ille, quot in sylvis et quot spatiantur in agris
  Quadrupedes, nôrat conciliare sibi ;   10
Et quisque innocuo, invitoque lacessere quenquam
  Labra tenus saltem fidus amicus erat.
Ortum sub lucis dum pressa cubilia linquit,
  Rorantes herbas, pabula sueta, petens,
Venatorum audit clangores ponè sequentum,
  Fulmineumque sonum territus erro fugit.
Corda pavor pulsat, sursum sedet, erigit aures,
  Respicit, et sentit jam prope adesse necem.
Utque canes fallat, latè circumvagus, illuc,
  Unde abiit, mirâ calliditate redit ;   20
Viribus at fractis tandem se projicit ultro
  In mediâ miserum semianimemque viâ.
Vix ibi stratus, equi sonitum pedis audit, et, oh spe
  Quam lætâ adventu cor agitatur equi !
Dorsum (inquit) mihi, chare, tuum concede, tuoque
  Auxilio nares fallere, vimque canum.
Me meus, ut nôsti, pes prodit—fidus amicus
  Fert quodcunque lubens, nec grave sentit, onus.
Belle miselle lepuscule (equus respondet), amara
  Omnia quæ tibi sunt, sunt et amara mihi.   30
Verum age—sume animos—multi, me pone, bonique
  Adveniunt, quorum sis citò salvus ope.
Proximus armenti dominus bos solicitatus
  Auxilium his verbis se dare posse negat.
Quando quadrupedum, quot vivunt, nullus amicum
  Me nescire potest usque fuisse tibi,

Libertate æquus, quam cedit amicus amico,
　Utar, et absque metu ne tibi displiceam ;
Hinc me mandat amor.　Juxta istum messis acervum
　Me mea, præ cunctis chara, juvenca manet ;　　　　40
Et quis non ultro quæcunque negotia linquit,
　Pareat ut dominæ, cum vocat ipsa suæ ?
Neu me crudelem dicas—discedo—sed hircus,
　Cujus ope effugias integer, hircus adest.
Febrem (ait hircus) habes.　Heu, sicca ut lumina languent !
　Utque caput, collo deficiente, jacet !
Hirsutum mihi tergum ;　et forsan læserit ægrum ;
　Vellere eris melius fultus, ovisque venit.
Me mihi fecit onus natura, ovis inquit, anhelans
　Sustineo lanæ pondera tanta meæ ;　　　　　　50
Me nec velocem nec fortem jacto, solentque
　Nos etiam sævi dilacerare canes.
Ultimus accedit vitulus, vitulumque precatur
　Ut periturum alias ocyus eripiat.
Remne ego, respondet vitulus, suscepero tantam,
　Non depulsus adhuc ubere, natus heri ?
Te, quem maturi canibus validique relinquunt,
　Incolumem potero reddere parvus ego ?
Præterea tollens quem illi aversantur, amicis
　Forte parum videar consuluisse meis.　　　　60
Ignoscas oro.　Fidissima dissociantur
　Corda, et tale tibi sat liquet esse meum.
Ecce autem ad calces canis est ! te quanta perempto
　Tristitia est nobis ingruitura !—Vale !

AVARUS ET PLUTUS.

Icta fenestra Euri flatu stridebat, avarus
　Ex somno trepidus surgit, opumque memor.
Lata silenter humi ponit vestigia, quemque
　Respicit ad sonitum respiciensque tremit ;
Angustissima quæque foramina lampade visit,
　Ad vectes, obices, fertque refertque manum.
Dein reserat crebris junctam compagibus arcam,
　Exultansque omnes conspicit intus opes.
Sed tandem furiis ultricibus actus ob artes
　Queîs sua res tenuis creverat in cumulum,　　　10
Contortis manibus nunc stat, nunc pectora pulsans
　Aurum execratur, perniciemque vocat ;
O mihi, ait, misero mens quam tranquilla fuisset,
　Hoc celâsset adhuc si modo terra malum !
Nunc autem virtus ipsa est venalis ; et aurum
　Quid contra vitii tormina sæva valet ?
O inimicum aurum ! O homini infestissima pestis,
　Cui datur illecebras vincere posse tuas ?

Aurum homines suasit contemnere quicquid honestum est,
    Et præter nomen nil retinere boni.   20
Aurum cuncta mali per terras semina sparsit ;
    Aurum nocturnis furibus arma dedit.
Bella docet fortes, timidosque ad pessima ducit,
    Fœdifragas artes, multiplicesque dolos,
Nec vitii quicquam est, quod non inveneris ortum
    Ex malesuadâ auri sacrilegâque fame.
Dixit, et ingemuit ; Plutusque suum sibi numen
    Ante oculos, irâ fervidus, ipse stetit.
Arcam clausit avarus, et ora horrentia rugis
    Ostendens, trimulum sic Deus increpuit.   30
Questibus his raucis mihi cur, stulte, obstrepis aures ?
    Ista tui similis tristia quisque canit.
Commaculavi egone humanum genus, improbe ? Culpa,
    Dum rapis, et captas omnia, culpa tua est.
Mene execrandum censes, quia tum pretiosa
    Criminibus fiunt perniciosa tuis ?
Virtutis specie, pulchro ceu pallio amictus
    Quisque catus nebulo sordida facta tegit.
Atque suis manibus commissa potentia, durum
    Et dirum subito vergit ad imperium.   40
Hinc, nimium dum latro aurum detrudit in arcam,
    Idem aurum latet in pectore pestis edax ;
Nutrit avaritiam et fastum, suspendere adunco
    Suadet naso inopes, et vitium omne docet.
Auri at larga probo si copia contigit, instar
    Roris dilapsi ex æthere cuncta beat :
Tum, quasi numen inesset, alit, fovet, educat orbos,
    Et viduas lacrymis ora rigare vetat.
Quo sua crimina jure auro derivet avarus,
    Aurum animæ pretium qui cupit atque capit ?   50
Lege pari gladium incuset sicarius atrox
    Cæso homine, et ferrum judicet esse reum.

PAPILIO ET LIMAX.

QUI subito ex imis, rerum in fastigia surgit
    Nativas sordes, quicquid agitur, olet.

NOTES.

[*The authorities for those poems which were not published by the author himself, are given between brackets in small capitals.*]

Page 1 (HAYLEY, i. 89), *l* 17. "Exhale," to draw out: meaning now obsolete. So Shak-speare :—

> "See, dead Henry's wounds
> Open their congealed mouths and bleed afresh !
> Blush, blush, thou lump of foul deformity ;
> For 'tis thy presence that exhales this blood."

The allusion at the end of this poem is probably to Lord Chesterfield, who resigned the Seals of Secretary of State, Feb. 6th, 1748. See Mahon's Hist. ch. xxx., or Student's Hume, p. 608.

Page 2. All the pieces from this to p. 8 are from EARLY POEMS.

Page 3. Cowper is curiously defective in his rhymes. The following rhymes will be found in this one page :—*Death, beneath ; fled, speed ; prey, sea ; wretch, beach ; guard, prepared ; spirit, bear it ; had, said ; perter, smarter ; do, so ; shapes, relapse ; foolish, polish ; alone, gun.*

Page 4. Cutfield, or rather Catfield, was the parish of Cowper's uncle, Rev. Roger Donne. Cowper visited it often in youth.

Page 6. "Sir C. Grandison" was published in the autumn of 1753.

Page 8, last stanza. "*Prune*, to dress, to prink. A ludicrous word." (Johnson's Dictionary.)

> "Every scribbling man
> Grows a fop as fast as e'er he can,
> Prunes up, and asks his valet, the glass,
> If pink or purple best become his face."—*Dryden.*

Page 9. (HAYLEY, i. 82.) Written the year he was called to the bar, 1754. Contains the first allusion to his fits of melancholy.

"*Pitch-kettled,* a favourite phrase at the time this Epistle was written, expressive of being puzzled, or what in the *Spectator's* time would have been called *bamboozled.*" (Hayley.)

The illustration of Dame Gurton and her son is taken from the celebrated comedy of Gammer Gurton's needle, said to have been written by Bishop Still, about the year 1565.

Pages 10—14. (All from EARLY POEMS.)

Page 10, 1st and 2nd stanzas. Hebrus was the principal river in Thrace. On its banks

Orpheus was torn in pieces by the Thracian women, because of his grief for his lost Eurydice.

Page 12. R. S. S. I have not a notion of the meaning of these letters.

Page 15. (HAYLEY, i. 79.) Sir William Russell was drowned whilst bathing in the Thames, 1757.

Page 16. (This and the following Satire were printed in Duncombe's Horace, 1757. The Duncombes, father and son, were of Hertford-shire, and the elder was an intimate friend of Cowper's father. At the time this translation was made, its author was leading a dilettante life at the Temple, amusing himself with such matters, and always ready to furnish them to any friend who asked his help.)

Mæcenas was sent to Brundusium A.U.C. 715, to arrange differences between Augustus and M. Antony, and, in order to beguile the tedi-ousness of the expedition, summoned Horace and other literary friends. Horace wrote this account of his own journey to amuse Mæcenas.

Of Heliodorus nothing is known.

Aricia was 16 miles from Rome, and Appii Forum 20 miles further on. Here they take barges on the canal for 20 miles to Terracina.

Page 17, *col.* 1. *Feronia,* an ancient Sabine goddess, introduced by the Sabines among the Romans. Her chief temple was at Terracina where a well of pure water, sacred to her, flowed down Mount Soracte. It is "the pure and glassy stream" here referred to.

Cocceius was a common friend of Cæsar and Antony. His presence with Mæcenas was there-fore a sign of peace. They had already effected the treaty of Brundusium.

"My eyes, by watery," &c. This was owing to having slept in the open air, in the marshes.

Capito Fonteius was Antony's legate in Asia.

Fundi, 9 miles from Terracina.

Aufidius, prætor of Fundi. The original here is very humorous and sarcastic. A scribe was a clerk.

Muræna was Mæcenas' brother-in-law.

Plotius and *Varius,* the two most intimate friends of "the bard of Mantua," Virgil.

Formia is the modern Gaeta, 80 miles from Rome

L L

Sinuessa, 18 miles from Formia, on the coast.

Page 17, *col.* 2. *Caudium* was the scene of the celebrated humiliation of the Roman army, known as the "Caudine Forks." The "tavern" probably lay beside the road ; and the villa of Cocceius on the hill above.

Oscian, that is, Campanian. "True Oscian breed" is a satirical way of saying that he was a low and mean fellow—just as we might talk of "genuine Seven Dials poetry."

"For carbuncles," &c. The people of Campania were subject to the growth of great warts or wens on their foreheads, which, when cut out, left great scars behind.

Page 18, *col.* 1. "Nor does your phiz," &c., *i. e.* because your face is so ugly.

"Of you, sir," &c. It was the custom, when any one had received any deliverance or other piece of good fortune, to leave some offering representing it in the temple of the gods. Boys and girls, on growing up, are said to have left their toys and dolls as offerings to the Lares, or household gods. Cicirrus jocosely asks Sarmentus when he hung up his chains, implying that he is a runaway slave, and that his former mistress has still a title to him.

Trivicus, a little village still called Trivico.

col. 2. "Whose name my verse," &c. The name was *Equotuticum*, which could not anyhow be got into an hexameter verse.

Fishy Barium. On the Adriatic. The inhabitants still live by fishing.

"That incense," &c. Pliny, in his Natural History (ii. 111), mentions this supposed miracle, and believes in it. It was not likely to find favour with Epicurean Horace.

Page 19, *col.* 1. *Beard*, manager of Covent Garden Theatre. He had just achieved great success with his "Opera of Artaxerxes."

"Well, I'm convinced my time is come," &c. The poet has hitherto tried to be civil, but, finding this of no use, tries insulting his tormentor, by inventing this prophecy for the nonce.

col. 2. "Rufus Hall." In the original, "Temple of Vesta," which was by the Forum, as Westminster Hall was by the law courts.

Newcastle, the then Prime Minister, is in the original "Mæcenas."

Page 20. (JOHNSON'S COWPER, iii. 27.) The Prayer for Indifference appeared in the *Annual Register* for 1762, p. 202. The writer addresses it to Oberon, and declares that she prays not for love-charms, nor ease, nor peace, but for the nymph Indifference. The following extract will convey a fair idea of it, and shew the point of Cowper's reply :—

"At her approach, see hope, see fear,
    See expectation fly ;
With disappointment in the rear,
    That blasts the purposed joy.

"The tears which pity taught to flow
    My eyes shall then disown ;
The heart which throbbed for others' woe
    Shall then scarce feel its own.

"The wounds which now each moment bleed,
    Each moment then shall close ;
And peaceful days shall still succeed
    To nights of sweet repose."

Page 21. *An Ode*, &c. This Mock Ode appeared in the *St. James' Magazine* for Nov. 1763, where it was signed "L." Lloyd was the editor of that magazine, and his old Westminster friends contributed. At the beginning Cowper wrote nothing for it, being at Brighton ; but soon he furnished a paper, signed "W. C.," on English Pindaric odes, and promised to furnish one according to rule. On this ground Southey identified the present ode as his, which appeared a few months after ; but there is no further proof of the authorship.

Page 23. (COWPER'S AUTOBIOGRAPHY.) The circumstances under which he wrote these appalling sapphics are told in the Introductory Memoir, p. xxx. Southey says of the third lines in the two last stanzas respectively, that they are both "evidently corrupt," and suggests that in the former, instead of "if vanquished," the author may have written "in anguish." But the text is probably right. He had an idea that there was a bare chance for him in the strife with the Avenging Deity. The expression, "fed with judgment," is taken from Ezek. xxxiv. 16.

Page 24. On the OLNEY HYMNS generally, see Introductory Memoir, p. xxxviii.

H. i. 5th stanza. Several modern editions have altered "thy throne," in the third line, to "*its* throne." But this is quite wrong. The poet is regarding his own heart as the rightful throne of the Holy Ghost, and the idol as usurping it.

H. ii. 3rd stanza ; 1 Sam. xxiii. 27.

Page 27. H. xi. was certainly written at Huntingdon, being exactly like a letter which he wrote to Mrs. Cowper from thence.

Page 30. H. xx. 2nd stanza. "The paschal sacrifice," &c. Exod. xii. 13.

3rd stanza. "The Lamb," &c. Lev. xii. 6.

4th stanza. "The scape-goat," &c. Lev. xvi. 21.

5th stanza. "Dipt in his fellow's blood," &c. Lev. xiv. 51.

Page 31. H. xxvi. was written for the opening service at "the Great House." See Memoir, p. xxiv.

Page 32. H. xxviii. 2nd stan. Luke xii. 50.

Page 34. H. xxxiv. last stan. Cant. v. 8.

H. xxxv. was written on the very eve of his second attack of insanity, Jan. 1773.

Page 36. H. xliv. 3rd stan. Josh. xii. 11.

Page 37. H. xlvi. was written at Dr. Cotton's, whilst he was recovering from his first attack. H. xlvii. was written when he was on the point of leaving Dr. Cotton's, and forming the resolution not to return to London.

Page 49. On TABLE TALK, see Memoir, p. xlvi. It was begun at the end of 1780. Though not first written, it was placed first, because it had less of religion than the rest of the larger poems, and he wished not to discourage readers by beginning too seriously. "I am merry," he writes, "that I may decoy people into my company; and grave, that they may be the better for it."

l 6. There was a very old but erroneous idea that lightning will not strike laurel. The Emperor Tiberius used to wear a wreath of it when a thunderstorm threatened. Byron cleverly throws a symbolical meaning into this notion :—

" For the true laurel-wreath which glory weaves
Is of the tree no bolt of thunder cleaves."
Childe Harold, iv. 41.

ll 13-46. These lines were added by the author after the MS. had been sent to the printer.

l. 29. The author is writing generally, but probably he has Frederick the Great in his mind especially.

Page 50, *ll* 65-82. Intended as a description of George III.

l 83. See Macaulay's Essays, i. 279-281.

Page 51, *l* 93. Quevedo de Villagas died at Madrid in 1635, aged 65. His "Visions of Hell" have been translated into English.

l 110. A quit-rent was the nominal rent (it might be a handful of corn, or a peppercorn, or a flower) by the payment of which the tenant of an old manor was able to go *quiet* and free. The satire of this and the following lines will be abundantly illustrated by the Poetical pages of any old magazine.

Page 52, *l* 182. Francis, third and last Duke of Bridgewater, is called the father of British internal navigation. He was living quietly at a retired country house at Worsley, near Manchester, when his attention was called to the difficulties of transporting the coal of which the surrounding soil was full. He met with James Brindley, who undertook to make a canal to Manchester, and with great engineering skill, backed by brave support from the Duke, he accomplished the design in 1760. Six years later, Brindley began the "Grand Trunk Canal" from the Trent to the Mersey, and before his death in 1772 drew the plan for the Oxfordshire Canal, connecting the Trent with the Thames. (Mahon's History, ch. xli.)

Page 53, *l* 192. "When admirals," &c. Probably referring to Admiral Keppel. For an account of the popular *furore* after the court-martial on him, see Mahon, vi. 269. The generals are those of the American war.

Page 53, *l* 237. "*Frisk,* a frolic—an act of wanton gaiety." (Johnson.) Compare these lines with the events nine years later.

l 318. The Gordon riots of 1780. Mahon, vi. 23.

l 339. Chatham died May 11, 1778.

Page 56, *l* 361. "Subserviency," obedience to God's will. The unfavourable meaning which we now almost invariably give this word is not found in Johnson's Dictionary.

l 362. This alludes to the "Armed Neutrality" of 1780, an alliance between Russia, Sweden, and Denmark (afterwards joined by Prussia and Holland), to maintain, in opposition to the principles of British maritime law and the decisions of her Admiralty courts, that neutral ships make free goods. England thus stood at bay against all the nations of Europe as well as against her insurgent colonies in America. But the combination wrought her but slight injury. See Lord Stanhope's History of England, chaps. lxii. and lxiii.

l 384. John Brown, D.D., Vicar of New-castle-on-Tyne, a voluminous writer, popular in his time, but now forgotten. The work here referred to, " An Estimate of the Manners and Principles of the Time," made a vast sensation when it appeared, and went through many editions. He depicts England as sunk into a hopeless condition, and at the point of utter ruin as a nation. The rest of George the Second's reign, from the very year of this publication, is a chronicle of glorious victories both by land and sea, planned and executed by the genius of Chatham. See Macaulay's Essays, i. 307.

Page 58, *l* 500. "The graceful name," *i.e.* Vates.

Page 59, *l* 509. Southey says that this was the custom still at Westminster School in his time. But I believe it is so no longer. The head-master was sub-almoner to the Queen, and used to present the good boys with Maundy money.

l 519. "Morris-dance," a corruption of " Moorish dance," a fantastic performance, accompanied with the sound of bells and waving of ribbons.

l 527. The following description is taken from Northouck's " History of London " (1773):—" The dial of the clock projects over the street at the extremity of a beam ; and over it by a kind of whimsical conceit, calculated only for the amusement of countrymen and children, is an Ionic porch, containing the figures of two savages, carved and painted, as big as life, which with knotted clubs alternately strike the hours and quarters on two bells hung between them." The church was rebuilt in 1831, and the figures were not restored. They now ornament a house near the Regent's Park.

Page 59, *l* 553. " Pounce," to seize with the *pounces* or talons. The expression, " pounce upon," is quite modern.

Page 60, *l* 559. This is borrowed from Dryden's Epigram on Milton, Globe Edition, p. 652.

l 566. The ancients believed that, during the seven days before, and the seven after the shortest day, the halcyon, or kingfisher, was breeding on the waters, and that during that time there was always calm at sea.

l 603. The thyrsus was a staff bound round with ivy and vine leaves, supposed to be borne by Bacchus.

Page 62, *l* 670. See Memoir, p. xxv.

Page 63, *l* 716. This thought was suggested to him by reading Johnson's " Lives of the Poets." He says in a letter that it was a melancholy reflection, forced upon him by that work, that nearly all poets were wicked men.

l 760. Sternhold and Hopkins, authors of the " Old Version" of the Psalms, middle of 16th century.

Page 64. THE PROGRESS OF ERROR was the first written of this series of Poems. See Memoir, p. xlv. Its versification is harsh, but it is full of pithy sayings.

Page 66, *l* 94. " *Tumbrel*, a dung-cart." (Johnson.)

l 121. Monmouth Street, in St. Giles', was chiefly occupied by old clothes shops.

l 124. All the commentators have taken "Occiduus" to be a punning nickname for Wesley. If this is so, it must have been Charles. The proceedings here satirized seem altogether at variance with what we know of John Wesley. But Charles was cheerful and joyous in his habits, and his musical talents were very great. It is, therefore, most likely that it is really he who is the subject of this satire, though I have failed to find any direct evidence of it. Mr. Bruce had seen a copy of the poems, belonging to Mr. Gough, annotated by some neighbours of Cowper, in which it was stated that " Occiduus" was a clergyman near Olney. A letter of Cowper to Newton, dated Sept. 9, 1781, speaks of this matter further, but without enlightening us as to the name.

Page 67, *l* 156. Is. lviii. 13, lvi. 2, 6.

Page 70, *l* 332. " *Quarry*, game flown at by a hawk." (Johnson.)

l 336. Lord Chesterfield, who is referred to here under the name of " Petronius," resigned the office of Secretary of State in 1748. Three years after he proposed and carried the Reform of the Calendar. This was his last public work: he became deaf, and retired into private life. During this time he wrote his " Letters to his Son," Philip, born illegitimately in 1732. The latter, however, died in 1768, leaving his father to languish cheerlessly for five years longer. On the old man's death, Philip Stanhope's widow published the whole correspondence.

" It had appeared, on the death of Chesterfield's son, that he had secretly married without his father's consent, or even knowledge ; and the widow, upon Chesterfield's own demise, published for profit the whole correspondence of the Earl with her late husband ;—a correspondence written in the closest confidence and unreserve, and without the slightest idea of ever meeting the public eye. It is, however, by these Letters that Chesterfield's character, as an author, must stand or fall. Viewed as composition, they appear almost unrivalled as models for a serious epistolary style, clear, elegant, and terse, never straining at effect, and yet never hurried into carelessness. While constantly urging the same topics, so great is their variety of argument and illustration that, in one sense, they appear always different, in another sense, always the same. They have already incurred strong reprehension on two separate grounds : first because some of their maxims are repugnant to good morals ; and secondly, as insisting too much on manners and graces, instead of more solid acquirements. On the first charge I have no defence to offer ; but the second is certainly erroneous, and arises only from the idea and expectation of finding a general system of education in letters that were intended solely for the improvement of one man. Young Stanhope was sufficiently inclined to study, and imbued with knowledge ; the difficulty lay in his awkward address and indifference to pleasing. It is against these faults, therefore, and these faults only, that Chesterfield points his battery of eloquence. Had he found his son, on the contrary, a graceful but superficial trifler, his Letters would no doubt have urged, with equal zeal, how vain are all accomplishments when not supported by sterling information. In one word, he intended to write for Mr. Philip Stanhope, and not for any other person. And yet even after this great deduction from general utility, it was still the opinion of a most eminent man, no friend of Chesterfield, and no proficient in the graces—the opinion of Dr. Johnson—Take out the immorality, and the book should be put into the hands of every young gentleman." (Lord Stanhope, iii. p. 360.)

Page 71, *l* 373. This couplet originally stood,

" With memorandum book to minute down
The several posts, and where the chain broke down."

He saw the oversight of making " down " rhyme to itself in correcting the proof. " This," he said, is not only down, but down derry-down."

Page 72, *l* 441. Wheels were greased with tar in Cowper's time. Coachmen used to carry it with them.

l 490. Another attack on his cousin, Madan,

whom he had already vituperated in *Antithe-lyphthora*. See Memoir, p. xliii.

Page 73, *l* 485. Antony von Leuwenhoek, born at Delft, 1632, and died there, 1723. Remarkable for his skill with the microscope, which made him also a good physiologist ; and some of his discoveries were of great importance. His works occupy four 4to. vols.

Page 74, *l* 526. Pygmalion, a celebrated statuary of Cyprus, chiselled a statue of such exquisite beauty that he fell in love with it, and Venus, at his earnest request, endowed it with life. He married it, and became the father of Paphus, the founder of the city of that name in Cyprus.

Page 76. TRUTH. It was the Author's fear that this poem would give offence to "unenlightened readers" which induced him to ask Newton to write his Preface.

Page 78, *l* 83. " Adust," burnt, scorched.

l 119. Spencer Cowper, son of the Lord Chancellor, Dean of Durham 1745-1774. The poet says " Second stall," because the first was the Bishop's. There is an uninteresting pamphlet by him in the British Museum, and a volume of good Sermons on Church Festivals, the following extract from which will show that he was no Calvinist:—

" That predestination to eternal life is the arbitrary choice of a despotic Power determined by no rule, but that of an uncontrollable will, and independent of any preceding merit or worth in the persons so predestinated, is a doctrine unworthy of God, and destructive of all moral goodness."

l 131. This description is a description, to the minutest detail, of the two prominent figures in Hogarth's " Morning."

Page 80, *l* 201. Geta is a laughter-moving servant in Terence's two plays *Adelphi* and *Phormio*.

Page 82, *l* 311. This was in Feb. 1778. " Nobles disguised themselves as tavern-waiters to obtain sight of him : the loveliest of France would lay their hair beneath his feet. His chariot is the nucleus of a comet whose train filled whole streets : they crown him in the theatre, with immortal *vivats ;* finally stifle him under roses, for old Richelieu recommended opium in such state of the nerves, and the excessive patriarch took too much." (Carlyle's French Revolution.)

Page 83, *l* 358. Dr. Richard Conyers, Rector of St. Paul's, Deptford, was the brother-in-law of Thornton, and was the means of introducing Newton to Cowper. (Memoir, p. xxxvi.) It is needless to add that he was a zealous evangelical preacher.

ll 364 and 379. In these two lines the poet has broken through one of his own canons, and, venturing out of England, has tried to describe what he has never seen. In the first line

he errs as to the fact. And the second, I am told, is not at all a description of the olive. Its small clustering berries grow sessile along the branches. The line is a mistaken gloss on Isaiah xxiv. 13.

Page 83, *l* 378. " And one who," &c. The Earl of Dartmouth, the patron of Olney, and a fast friend of Newton.

Page 87. On EXPOSTULATION, see Memoir, p. xliv.

Page 88, *l* 33. Jer. ix. 1.

Page 91, *l* 190. Joshua v. 14.

Page 92, *l* 246. " Peeled," plundered. So in Milton, "Paradise Regained."

Page 93, *l* 283. Cowper, though professedly a Whig, always regarded the Americans as rebels, and believed that George III. was right in his persistent endeavours to conquer them.

l 292. Various naval engagements were fought in 1780, with great bravery, but indecisive results. Such were Rodney's in the West Indies, April 17 ; Parker's, off the Dogger Bank ; and Graves', with the French, in the *Chesapeake*. See Lord Stanhope's Hist., chaps. lxii. lxiii.

l 293. On the violence of the political strifes of that time, see the opening of ch. lxi. of Lord Stanhope. " Mean, shabby, pitiful, and unwarrantable," were epithets used by one speaker in the House of Lords.

l 309. The National Debt was nearly doubled during the American War. In 1775 it was £124,000,000 ; in 1783, £238,000,000. But it is now £740,000,000.

Page 95, *l* 374. "Trucked," trafficked away.

l 376. The Test Act was passed in 1673, with a view of excluding Papists from power. Under its provisions, all persons holding any position of trust, civil or military, or admitted of the Royal Household, were to receive the Sacrament of the Lord's Supper, according to the usage of the Church of England, declaring at the same time that they had no belief in Transubstantiation. One therefore meets in the newspapers of that day with notices like this :—" Yesterday his Royal Highness Prince Frederick received the Communion, having been appointed Ranger of Richmond Park." The Act was repealed in 1828. The bishop here referred to is Warburton (Gloucester 1760—1779) ; and the works, Essays " On the Alliance between Church and State," and " The Necessity and Equity of a Test Law."

l 390. At the first printing of these Poems, the following passage followed *l* 389. After the edition was printed off, the author came to the conclusion that it was objectionable, and finding Newton agreeing with him, had the leaf cancelled, and substituted lines 390-413 for the omitted passage. I have a copy of the first edition lying before me, with the cancel perfectly visible. A few copies are in existence, containing both the cancelled leaf and that substituted for it. Here is the passage. Few will doubt that the second thoughts were best, though there are modern editions in which the passage is reprehensibly retained, without a word about the author's omission of it :—

> " Hast thou admitted with a blind, fond trust,
> The lie that burn'd thy fathers' bones to dust,
> That first adjudged them heretics, then sent
> Their souls to heav'n and cursed them as they went?
> The lie that Scripture writes in its disguise,
> And execrates above all other lies,
> The lie that claps a lock on mercy's plan,
> And gives the key to yon infirm old man,
> Who once insconced in apostolic chair
> Is deified and sits omniscient there;
> The lie that knows no kindred, owns no friend
> But him that makes its progress his chief end,
> That having spilt much blood, makes that a boast,
> And canonizes him that sheds the most?
> Away with charity that sooths a lie,
> And thrusts the truth with scorn and anger by ;
> Shame on the candour and the gracious smile
> Bestow'd on them that light the martyr's pile,
> While insolent disdain in frowns express'd
> Attends the tenets that endured that test :
> Grant them the rights of men, and while they cease
> To vex the peace of others, grant them peace ;
> But trusting bigots whose false zeal has made
> Treach'ry their duty, thou art self-betray'd."

Page 96, *l* 423. Jude, verse 7.

Page 97, *l* 480. The absurdity of the idea that the Latin element in our tongue comes from the Roman occupation of Britain needs no comment. Cowper knew almost nothing of history. He seems, further on, to think that Woden and Thor were British deities.

l 517. "Which may be found at Doctors' Commons," Cowper adds in a note.

Page 98, *l* 550. Alluding to the reign of Charles II. See Macaulay's Hist. ch. iii., "State of the Navy."

l 574. Prince Charles's march to Derby.

l 598. "That immortal plain," namely, Runnymede. The barons there surpassed Phœbus, because he found only a laurel instead of the nymph Daphne ; they gained both the laurel of victory, and the liberty which was the subject of the warfare.

Page 101, *l* 694. See note on p. 56, *l* 362.

Page 103, *l* 46. "Tilth," tillage, husbandry (Shakspeare and others).

Page 106, *l* 205. On Dr. Cotton, see Memoir, p. xxx. He died in extreme old age, in 1788.

Page 110, *l* 459. Cowper has this note : "The Moravian Missionaries in Greenland. *Vide* Krantz." The work thus referred to is the English translation, by La Trobe, of David Krantz's "History of the Moravian Brethren," published in 1780. A copy of this work lies before us ; and we extract from it the passage referred to :—

" The second mission was undertaken on the 19th of January, 1733, to *Greenland.* The brethren, *Christian David, Matthew Stach,* and *Christian Stach,* having met with many friends and patrons at Copenhagen, set sail on the 10th of April. Soon after their arrival, on the 20th of May, they built a house not far from the Colony of *Godhaab.* They endeavoured to learn the language, and to enter into a useful intercourse with the heathen, but met with many difficulties ; among which, that which seemed the most distressing was, that almost all the Greenlanders of that district had been carried off by the small-pox. In the year 1734 they received two assistants, and agreed with one another that they would faithfully hold out, in hunger and distress, by hard and hazardous labour, amidst contempt on all sides, in danger of life among the incensed savages, by a supposed desertion of their friends at Copenhagen, by an apparent unfruitfulness, nay, impossibility of access to the hearts of the heathen, and in many other hardships and difficulties attending the mission in the first years. They had, indeed, the joy of baptizing, in the year 1739, the first-fruits, *Samuel Kajarnak,* and family ; but he was soon obliged to flee from murderers. Yet he returned again in the year 1740, and drew many Greenlanders after him, to whom he, on his flight, had preached the gospel. A great awakening arose, soon after, among the Greenlanders ; and in a few years the congregation of the baptized, regulated so orderly as could hardly have been thought possible among savages, increased to such a degree that they were obliged to think of a second congregation from among the heathen, which in 1758 was begun at Fishers' Bay, and which is yet flourishing." The whole history of this mission, as well as that of the same body to the West Indies, is one of the most self-denying and beautiful on record. It was this which made Greenland a Christian country.

Page 112, *l* 554. "Leuconomus," George Whitefield. Born at Gloucester, Dec. 1714; educated at Oxford ; ordained 1736, and immediately became famous as a preacher. He could be heard, it is said, at a mile distance (Eng. Cyclopædia). Was a most intimate friend of the Wesleys, both at Oxford and afterwards, until he quarrelled with them on the question of predestination, Whitefield taking Calvinistic views. The personal breach soon healed, but from that time they never worked in concert again. He died at Boston, in America, Dec. 1770.

Page 116, *l* 754. The last lines, in all probability, refer to Newton.

Page 117. CHARITY may be said to complete the series of "Christian Poems." It was written in a fortnight, and completed on the 12th of July, 1781.

l 23. Captain Cook was killed at Owhyee (Hawaii), Feb. 14, 1779, and the news was received in England with profound grief.

Page 117, *ll* 51—64. There is confusion in Cowper's historical memory here. Cortez conquered Mexico in 1519-20, and therefore in the reign, not of Philip, but of Charles V. In the course of the war, the Mexican king, Montezuma, in trying to persuade his subjects to submit to the conquest which he saw to be inevitable, was mortally wounded by them, to the great chagrin of Cortez. In his last hours, we are told, "Cortez joined with Father Bartholomew in persuading him renounce his idolatry ; but all their arguments were to no purpose, and he expired, after having conjured the general to avenge his death." Francis Pizarro, in 1531, achieved the conquest of Peru. By acts of treachery unparalleled even by Spaniards, he gained possession of the Inca, Atahualpa, and having led him to pay an enormous ransom, had him tried by Father Vincent for idolatry, avarice (!), and other offences. He was condemned to be burnt alive. The pious priest afterwards "undertook the Inca's conversion ; and his arguments were worthy of himself. He promised that if he would die a Christian, instead of being burned, he should be only strangled, which had the desired effect, and, to the eternal dishonour of all concerned in this iniquitous proceeding, he was baptized in the evening and strangled next morning."

l 66. Is. xiv. 10, 11.

l 230. Is. lxvi. 3.

l 253. Thornton. See Memoir, xxiii. note.

ll 290-311. John Howard, born in London, 1726. After the earthquake at Lisbon, he determined, being a rich man, to go thither to help the sufferers, but was captured by a French privateer. The sights which he saw in the prison helped to shape his future career of philanthropy. A few years later he visited the town and country jails in England and Wales, and laid a report before the House of Commons. Afterwards (in 1777) he published his "Account of the State of Prisons," astonishing the world by the value of his researches, by his prodigious labour, hazard, and self-devotion. He was immediately felt to be not only one of the greatest, but one of the noblest characters of the age. In the same pious labour he then visited the Netherlands, Germany, France, Italy, Sweden, Poland, Russia, Spain, and Portugal. Dangers or disgust never turned him from his path : he visited Constantinople and Smyrna because they were plague-stricken, and he desired to know the state of the lazarettos. Pushing eastwards, he was seized with fever in the Crimea, and died at Cherson in 1790.

Page 125, *l* 432. 1 Cor. xiii.

Page 126, *l* 499. Dean Swift.

Page 128, *l* 609. The Baptists are dipped : all other Christians are commonly sprinkled. "Love," says Cowper, "might make them tolerant of each other."

Page 128, *l* 613. The "Prince" of Machiavel, full of "projects dark and deep for the statesman," is the work referred to here. See Macaulay's Essay on it.

Page 129. CONVERSATION was originally intended for the introduction to a second volume. "I am in the middle of an affair called 'Conversation,' which, as 'Table Talk' serves in the present volume by way of introductory fiddle, I design shall perform the same office in a second." (Letter to Newton.)

Page 130, *l* 57. Vestris was an Italian stage-dancer of wonderful skill. He took a farewell of the stage in 1781, and was succeeded by his son.

Page 133, *l* 198. Dares was one of the companions of Æneas, and Entellus a Sicilian. The fierce combat between these two pugilists is described in the Æneid, v. 362-472

Page 134, *l* 243. Guy is supposed to have flourished in the reign of Æthelstan, and, besides many victories over dragons, he is said to have decided the fate of the kingdom by fighting an enormous Danish giant on Magdalen Hill, near Winchester.

Page 135, *l* 299. "Budge," *i. e.* wearing a fur robe to look like a philosopher. Cp. *Comus*, l. 707.

Page 136, *l* 352. "Il n'est jamais plus difficile de bien parler que quand on a honte de se taire." (Rochefoucauld.)

l 358. There was an idea that the ancients had the art of making lamps which would burn for a thousand years, and placed them in sepulchres.

Page 139, *l* 505. Luke xxiv. 13-31.

"*Exact,* v. n., to practise extortion." (Johnson.) So in Ps. lxxx. 22.

Page 140, *l* 590. "Fixed fee-simple," exclusive possession.

Page 145, *l* 824. Allusion to the profane orgies of Medmenham Abbey. A picture is still in existence in which the chief actor in these evil deeds, Sir F. Dashwood, is represented as adoring the Venus de Medici. See Mahon's Hist., ch. xxxvii.

l 850. 1 Kings xviii. 21.

Page 147. RETIREMENT. "My view, in choosing this subject, is to direct to the proper use of the opportunities it affords for the cultivation of a man's best interests ; to censure the vices and follies which people carry with them into their retreats, where they make no other use of their leisure than to gratify themselves with the indulgence of their favourite appetites, and to pay themselves, by a life of pleasure, for a life of business." (Letter to Newton.)

Page 149, *l* 106. In the first two editions this line ran, "Whatever is, seems formed indeed for us." It was altered to its present form in 1793.

Page 151, l 278. Cowper's own love, as we have seen, was doomed to end in sorrow and disappointment. From that time he never wrote on Love, except in these bitter lines.

Page 152, l 279. Dr. William Heberden. This most amiable and admirable man was born in 1710, and was Cowper's medical friend in London. The present passage is inexpressibly affecting, so earnest and true is the poet's sympathy with him on the cause of his retirement. He lived, however, twenty years after this, and died at the age of ninety. He is said to have spoken often of his affection for Cowper.

Page 155, l 421. "Balk," the unploughed ridges between the furrows, or at the ends of the field.

Page 157, l 137. "Nereids," sea nymphs; "Dryads," wood nymphs.

Page 160, l 688. Voltaire, at his retreat at Ferney, built a church, and inscribed on the porch, "Deo erexit Voltaire."

Page 161, l 691. Allusion to Horne Tooke's Letter to Dunning, which contained the germs of the "Diversions of Purley."

Page 163. The Doves. Written in May 1780, and sent to Mrs. Newton, with this explanatory note:—"The male dove was smoking a pipe, and the female dove was sewing, while she delivered herself as above. This little circumstance may lead you perhaps to guess what pair I had in my eye." Of course he means Mr. and Mrs. Bull.

The fable of *The Raven* was also sent to Newton about the same time, with a letter describing the circumstance which suggested it.

"'Twas April, as the bumpkins say," &c. The change of style had been made in 1752, but the common people for many years pertinaciously held that they had been cheated of eleven days of their life, and were furious with the promoters of the change. I have myself heard an old woman descanting on the impiety of it; she "had heard her mother say so."

"Dray," the local name for a squirrel's nest.

Page 164. "Sweet stream," &c. Addressed to Miss Shuttleworth, Mrs. W. Unwin's sister.

Alexander Selkirk was born in Fifeshire in 1676, quarrelled with his family and went to sea, and his adventures on the island of Juan Fernandez are said to have furnished the materials for Defoe's great fiction. Some relics of his "solitary abode," a gun and cup, are still in the possession of the family. But, after his return home, he pined for his island again, and would see no one, only going out of doors after dark. After staying nine months at home, he went away again, and was never more heard of.

Page 165. On the Promotion of Thurlow. This was written for Hill, and sent to him in a letter, dated Nov. 14, 1779, no doubt with a natural desire to recall himself and his prophecy to the memory of his old friend. See Memoir, p. xxvi.

The *Ode to Peace* was written at the beginning of his second attack of insanity, 1773. Memoir, p. xl.

Page 166. The Modern Patriot was intended for a description of Burke on account of his friendship with Fox, and the line which he took on the American and Roman Catholic questions. A few days afterwards, however, Cowper saw how unjust his poem was. "I was so well pleased with his proposals for a Reformation [Economical Reform Speech, Feb. 9, 1780], that I thought better of his cause, and burnt my verses." He must have kept a copy.

On observing some Names of Note. Cowper had borrowed the book from Unwin, and sent it back with these lines.

Page 167. Report, &c., sent both to Unwin and Hill in letters. See Memoir, p. xlii. The original MS. is in the Brit. Mus., with the following heading :—

Nose Plf., Eyes Deft.
Vid. Plowden,
folio 6,000.

The house of Lord Mansfield, which was burnt by the Golden Rioters, was in Bloomsbury Square. See Mahon, ch. lxi.
"The Vandals," alluding to the terrible havoc and destruction wrought by the Vandals when they sacked Rome in 455.

Page 168. The Love of the World, &c. Newton told Cowper this story, and he versified it in about an hour. Newton sent the verses to Mr. Thornton, having inserted some lines of his own. With this insertion, as Cowper's note shows, they appeared in the *Leeds Journal,* he not being aware who put them in print, or made the additions. Lines 9–14 appear to be those added by Newton, and in many editions they are printed in brackets; but as there are no brackets in Cowper's own edition, I have printed none.

Southey supposes that the expression, "going the whole hog," is derived from this fable.

Page 170. In the letter forwarding *The Nightingale and Glow-worm* to Unwin, Cowper writes, "I only premise that in the philosophical tract in the *Register,* I found it asserted that the glow-worm is the nightingale's food."

Votum. The following translation is offered merely for the information of those who do not read Latin.

A WISH.

Ye morning dews, ye breezes bringing health,
Ye groves, ye meads enriched by gentle streams,
Ye grassy knolls, ye shades in deep-sunk vales ;
Oh that those days might come again when I
At my dear birth-place rambled midst ye all !

Ah happy days! For then no fears oppressed,
No wish for better things, no thought of change.
And now what would I but that, all unknown,
I might grow old beside my cottage hearth,
And sleep in peace beneath an unmarked turf.

Page 170, *l* 170. The poor little Goldfinch died next door to Cowper's house. He kept this poem by him for several months, continually retouching it.

Page 171. *The Pineapples and the Bee.* Written September 1779, and addressed to Mrs. Hill, who had given the poet the seeds from which he produced his pineapples.

The *Translation of Horace* was inserted by him among his original poems for the sake of the *Reflection* which follows it.

Page 172. Vincent Bourne was usher of the fifth form at Westminster when Cowper passed through it. He was famous for his skill in Latin poetry, and is described as slovenly, dirty, and good-natured. One of his pupils, the Duke of Richmond, once set fire to his greasy wig, and then boxed his ears to put it out. " I have an affection for the memory of Vinny Bourne," says Cowper in one of his letters. But he says also : " I lost more than I got by him, for he made me as idle as himself. He was so inattentive to his boys, and so indifferent whether they brought him good or bad exercises, or none at all, that he seemed determined, as he was the best, so to be the last Latin poet of the Westminster line."

Page 173. *The Shrubbery* was written soon after the *Ode to Peace.* (See note, p. 165.) The Shrubbery is at Weston. It was afterwards cut down by a stupid bailiff, who misunderstood an order of Mr. Throckmorton.

Page 174. *The Winter Nosegay.* "That sunny shed," viz. in the author's garden, summerhouse and greenhouse by turns. (Memoir, p. xlv.)

Page 175. *Prior's Poem* is in Anderson's Poets, vii. p. 405.

Boadicea was written after reading Hume's History, in 1780.

Page 181. In a letter to Unwin, announcing the transmission of the MS. of this volume, Cowper writes :—

"The motto of the whole is *Fit surculus arbor.* If you can put the author's name under it, do so ; if not, it must go without one. For I know not to whom to ascribe it. It was a motto taken by a certain Prince of Orange, in the year 1733, but not to his own writing, or indeed to any poem at all, but, as I think, to a medal."

Page 183, *l* 9. "Our sires had none." Our author has again confounded Britons with Englishmen.

Page 184, *l* 54. "Crewel," a knot.

Page 184, *l* 58. "Lumber." Every edition published in the author's lifetime read *Umber.* The correction was never made until 1803.

l 78. It is said that a Saxon king conferred the distinction of royalty upon the two chief magistrates of this ancient town, who were originally elected from the two principal crafts, viz. millers and tanners. The first notice of them in literature is in the Duke of Buckingham's Play of the *Rehearsal.*

Page 186, *l* 154. "Yon eminence." A hill on the grounds of Weston House, two or three fields west of Cowper's residence.

l 173-6. The square tower of Clifton ; the tall spire, Olney ; the villages remote, Emberton, Steventon.

Page 187, *l* 227. "The peasant's nest," a better sort of farm cottage ; now, however, tiled instead of thatched, and the trees are all cut down.

Page 188, *l* 253. "A colonnade," a fine avenue of chesnuts in Weston Park, ending at the rustic bridge.

l 278. "The Alcove" is beyond the rustic bridge, a view seat of six sides, three of them open. Only a visit to the place can enable the reader to realize the wonderful truthfulness of the whole description.

Page 193, *l* 534. This was a portrait from life. An engraving taken from this description was sent to Cowper, who replied : " I cannot say that poor Kate much resembles the original, who was neither so young nor so handsome as here represented ; but she has a figure well suited to the account given in *The Task*, and a face exceedingly expressive of despairing melancholy."

Page 195, *l* 621. The Society and Friendly Islands.

l 633. "Omai" was a native of the Friendly Islands. He acted as interpreter to Captain Cook in his third voyage, and came to England with him in 1775. He was naturally an object of very great interest in London circles, and charmed everybody by his intelligence, modesty, and self-reliance. Dr. Johnson was delighted with him ; and Reynolds painted him. Cowper was correct in supposing that he pined after English refinement after his return home, though it was only a guess introduced as a vehicle for satire on our own frivolity. It was afterwards related that he entreated pathetically to be carried back to England again.

Page 197, *l* 700. Four years after this was written, Reynolds had to give up painting, owing to failing sight.

l 702. Bacon was a friend of Newton, and, on the strength of this, took the opportunity of expressing to the poet his admiration of his first volume, and also sent him a print of his newly finished monument to Chatham. Cowper returned the civility by introducing the present lines. Bacon's letters to him are almost the only ones which have survived amongst those which he received.

Page 197, *l* 736. Another severe thrust at Clive.

Page 198. Cowper thus explains the Title of *The Timepiece* in a letter to Newton :— "The book to which it belongs is intended to strike the hour that gives notice of approaching judgment." (Dec. 13, 1784.)

Page 199, *l* 40. The decision, that "slaves cannot breathe in England," was given by the Judges, June 22, 1772, on the case of Somerset. A poor slave, of that name, was brought to England, but on account of ill-health was turned adrift by his master. By the charity of Granville Sharpe he was restored to health, on which his brutal master reclaimed him. The claim was resisted: a trial ensued in the Queen's Bench, and the decision was given as stated here. In 1786, the year after these lines were written, England was employing 130 ships, which carried 42,000 slaves ; but in the following year the Society for the Suppression of the Slave Trade was instituted, and the question was opened in Parliament. In April 1791, Wilberforce made a direct motion for abolition, which was lost by 88 to 83. Lord Grenville and Fox took up the question as Ministers in 1806, and the slave trade was abolished in 1807.

Page 200, *l* 64. There was great alarm felt about this fog, apprehensions being felt that it portended an earthquake. The great astronomer Lalande wrote a letter from Paris to compose the public mind. It seems to have been caused by great heat following heavy rains.

l 74. The calamity which is described in the lines which follow took place in Feb. 1782. (See *Ann. Reg.*) Thousands of persons perished in Messina ; and the aged Prince of the place persuaded a great number of the survivors that they would be safer on the open sea. Accordingly they went out in fishing boats ; but the sea was suddenly lashed into violence, the boats were swamped, and fresh multitudes perished, the Prince among them. See line 121.

Page 203, *l* 214. *Ausonia*, poetic name for Italy.

l 242. Wolfe was killed in the moment of victory, at Quebec, Sept. 13, 1759.

Page 205, *l* 351. The subject of this satire is Dr. Trusler, who, besides making a large income by writing compendiums of popular books, such as Cook's Voyages, abridged the sermons of eminent divines and printed the residuum in MS. character for use in the pulpit. The degrading trade, unhappily, still flourishes.

l 360. "In score," *i.e.* with marks of accent, &c., attached to the words.

Page 206, *l* 369. "To droll," to play the buffoon. Now obsolete.

Page 210, *l* 579. *Lustrum*, a period of five years.

l 595. *Mentor*, the confidential friend of Ulysses. (Odyssey, ii. 390.)

l 596. *Lucullus*, a celebrated Roman commander, famous, on his return from his command in Asia, for his luxurious living. Plutarch tells how an actor once asked him for a hundred purple robes ; Lucullus replied, that he might have twice as many.

Page 211, *l* 652. "Hackneyed," *i.e.* taken home in a hackney-coach.

Page 213, *l* 774. "Oscitancy," sleepiness, state of yawning.

l 780. See Memoir, p. xxxviii.

Page 215, *l* 32. "Nitrous air," the name given by Priestley to oxygen gas, whose researches into its nature were nearly contemporaneous with the writing of these lines.

Page 219, *l* 215. "Parallax," the apparent change in position of a star when viewed from different points.

Page 220, *l* 251. "Castalia," the fountain on Mount Parnassus, sacred to Apollo and the Muses.

l 257. "Themis," was the goddess of law, order, and equity.

Newton (Sir I.) 1642-1727, Milton 1608-1674, Hale (Sir M.) 1609-1676.

Page 221, *l* 334. The "one hare" was "Puss." See his celebrated account.

Page 224, *l* 452. Alluding to the *Culex* and *Batrachomyomachia*, poems attributed respectively to Virgil and Homer.

l 456. "The Splendid Shilling" written by John Phillips, born 1676, died 1708 (Anderson's Poets, vol. vi. p. 539) Cowper was a warm admirer of this poem.

Page 226, *l* 579. "Ficoides," the Ice-plant.

Page 230. "Voluble," rolling. So used in Milton. This meaning is now obsolete.

l 766. "Capability Brown" realized a handsome fortune by his successes in landscape gardening, and died just before these lines were written.

Page 231, *l* 2. This bridge bestrides the whole valley between Olney and Emberton, this being needful in consequence of winter floods, which frequently lay the whole ground under water.

Page 233, *l* 86. Katerfelto was a quack who used to exhibit in London in company with a black cat, and began his advertisements with "Wonders ! wonders !"

l 86. "Skillet," a small kettle.

Page 233, *l* 86. "Plashed," that is, with the branches half broken, and then interwoven with other branches.

Page 238, *l* 364. "East, that breathes the spleen," that infuses melancholy and irritability into the infirm. The allusion is to the old conjecture that the spleen is the seat of vexation and despondency. Compare *Sofa*, l. 455.

Page 240, *l* 428. Mr. Smith, the first Lord Carrington, is the benefactor here referred to. Cowper says so in a letter to Unwin. He writes: "How I love and honour that man ! For many reasons I dare not tell him how much. That line of Horace, ' *Dii tibi divitias dederunt artemque fruendi*,' was never half so applicable to the poet's friend as to Mr. Smith. My bosom burns to immortalize him."

l 101. This is a description of Lavendon Mill, about two miles from Olney. It was destroyed about twenty years after these lines were written, and its place is now filled by a cotton-mill.

Page 250, *l* 126, *ff.* The ice-palace of St. Petersburg was constructed by the Empress Anna in the very cold winter of 1740. Large blocks of ice were cut from the Neva, squared with rule and compass, and carved with figures. When each was ready, it was moved to its place with cranes and pulleys, and at the instant of fitting it a little water was thrown upon the block to which it was joined. This instantly freezing, the whole was literally one block of ice, "producing, without contradiction, an effect infinitely more beautiful than if it had been built of the most costly marble, its transparency and bluish tint giving it rather the appearance of a precious stone." See an article in the *Penny Magazine* for 1837 (p. 459). extracted from an account published at the time at St. Petersburg. There is an engraving of it in the same page, from the same source. The toy lasted from January till March.

l 135. Virgil, Georg. iv. 317.

Page 251, *l* 178. Probably alludes to an intention in ancient times, which was abandoned, to hew Mount Athos into a statue of Alexander. The Egyptian Sphinx is the nearest approach to what has actually been done in this way. The next line, of course, refers to the Pyramids.

Page 253, *l* 322. Judges ix. 6, *ff.*

Page 254, *l* 361. A foolish distinction. Enlightened patriotism is attachment to *institutions*, and therefore is not impatient of shortcomings in those who represent them. A letter to Newton, written just at this time, speaks with some severity of George III. for his conduct in the overthrow of the Fox and North coalition.

Page 256, *l* 444. Manes, the founder of the Manicheans, lived in the third century. He taught that there were two gods of equal power,

the one good, the other evil. It is merely the belief of all ignorant and superstitious minds. The god of evil is of course dreaded for the harm he can do, and his wrath is deprecated by his terror-stricken votaries, as in the case of Baal and Moloch in Holy Scripture.

Page 257, *l* 486. John Hampden born 1594, killed at the battle of Chalgrove Field, 1643; Algernon Sidney born 1620 ; executed 1683.

Page 260, *l* 675. The τὸ καλόν of the Greek philosophy.

Page 266, *l* 66. "The embattled tower"—of Emberton Church.

Page 267, *l* 84. "Meditation," &c., *i.e.* Earnest thought causes hours to seem but as moments.

l 98. *I.e.* Books often exert a deceptive influence on an unthinking, undiscerning reader.

Page 268, *l* 165. "Hypericum," St. John's wort ; "Mezereon," spurge laurel ; "Althæa," marsh-mallow.

Page 271, *l* 287. Langford, a famous auctioneer in articles of *vertu.*

Page 274, 443. Deut. xxii. 4, 6, 7.

Page 275, *l* 485. The story of Misagathus (*Greek*, signifying "hater of good") is disagreeable and very improbable.

Page 278, *l* 637. The Handel Commemoration held in Westminster Abbey in June 1784. The lines were added during the revisal of the proofs. There were thousands of listeners and "525 voices and instruments."

l 658. The news of the battle of Culloden is said to have reached the London congregations on Sunday, during morning service.

l 660. William, Duke of Cumberland.

l 678. Alluding to the Stratford Jubilee of 1769.

Page 280, *l* 773. "Libbard," old form of "leopard," found in Shakspeare and Spenser.

Page 282, *l* 884. The Unitarian seceders from the Church of England.

Page 286. See Memoir, p. liv. In a letter to Unwin, November 24, 1784, Cowper says, "I wrote this Epistle to Hill on Wednesday last. A tribute so due, that I must have disgraced myself if I had not payed it. He ever serves me in all that he can, though he has not seen me these twenty years."

Page 288. There is an able criticism on this Poem, answering Cowper's strictures, and pointing out the impracticability of some of his own ideas, in the *Pamphleteer*, vol. iv., Lond. 1814.

Page 291, *l* 131. John Bunyan.

Page 306. The original John Gilpin is said to have been a Mr. Beyer, a linendraper living at the corner of Paternoster Row and Cheapside. He died in 1791, at the age of 98. See *Notes and Queries*, 2nd series, viii. 110.

Of the wonderful popularity of this poem we have spoken in the Memoir. The original MS. and the first printed copy are in Brit. Mus., and the Catalogue has several pages devoted to different editions, translations, and continuations of it. The latter, as might be expected, are mere rubbish.

In *Hone's Table Book*, p. 454, there is a ludicrous engraving of an old woman with a huge bonnet, in the style of Mrs. Gamp's, sitting astride a gate, and underneath it is said, " The sketch here engraved (probably from the poet's friend Romney) was found, with these three stanzas in the hand-writing of Cowper, among the papers of the late Mrs. Unwin :—

> " Then Mrs. Gilpin sweetly said
>   Unto her children three,
> ' I'll clamber o er this style so high,
>   And you climb after me.
>
> But having climbed unto the top,
>   She could no further go,
> But sate, to every passer-by,
>   A spectacle and show :
>
> Who said, ' Your spouse and you this day
>   Both show your horsemanship ;
> And if you stay till he comes back,
>   Your horse will need no whip.'"

Hone goes on to say, that probably Cowper intended this as part of a continuation of his ballad. Mrs. G., finding time hang heavy on her hands during her husband's involuntary excursion, goes out for a walk, and thus comes to grief, in a manner the very contrary to her husband.

" Merry pin," *i.e.* merry humour. The expression was derived from the custom of drinking from mugs with pins fixed in them, to regulate the quantity to be drunk.

Page 311. (POEMS, 1794.) Written September 1788. Mrs. T. was the wife of Mr. (afterwards Sir George).

Page 312. *The Rose* (GENT. MAG., 1785, and POEMS, 1794). Written June 8, 1783. Sir J. Stephen thinks that this was a gentle rebuke of Newton, " whose ungentle touch was occasionally put forth at the vicarage to dry up his tears." (Essays, vol. ii. p. 113.) He is right undoubtedly. This was just the time when Cowper felt Newton's roughness most.

When this poem appeared in the *Gent. Mag.*, signed with initials only, some foolish woman told her friends that it was hers. Cowper heard of the larceny, and was very angry, and wrote to a friend, when about to publish it among his works, that he was going to teach her that his rose had thorns.

Ode to Apollo. (POEMS, 1794.)

Page 313. *The Poet's New Year's Gift*, written for New Year's Day, 1788.

Page 315. *The Dog and Water-lily*. The incident is also told in a letter to Lady Hesketh (June 27, 1788).

Catharina (POEMS, 1794). Written in 1790. She became Lady Throckmorton on the death of Sir John, her husband's eldest brother. Grimshawe's edition of Cowper is dedicated to her, with warm encomiums.

Page 316. (POEMS, 1794.)

Page 317. (Ibid. both pieces.)
The last stanza but one of *The Faithful Bird* originally stood thus :—

> " For, setting on his grated roof,
> He chirped and kissed him, giving proof
>   That he desired no more ;
> Nor would forsake his cage at last,
> Till gently seized, I shut him up
>   A prisoner as before."

Page 320. (Published with *The Dog and Water-lily* in separate form, price 6d., in 1798, as well as in the collected edition of that year.) See Memoir, p. lxv.

Page 323. (GENT. MAG., January 1785, and POEMS, 1800.) These poplars were at Lavendon Mill, near Olney. Fresh trees have since grown up from the old roots.

Page 324. The epitaph on Mr. Thomas Hamilton (POEMS, 1800) was written for his tombstone in Newport Pagnell Churchyard. He died in 1788, aged thirty-two.

Page 325. The *Epitaph on a Hare* (POEMS, 1800). It was written in March, 1783. The MS. is in the Brit. Mus. Poor Puss, who is referred to here, lived three years longer, as the following memorandum shows, found among Cowper's papers after his death:—

" Tuesday, March 9, 1786 : This day died poor Puss, aged eleven years, eleven months. He died between twelve and one at noon, of mere old age, apparently without pain."

Page 327. (H. iv. 266.) The awe-inspiring incident here described took place at Leeds. The preacher was a Wesleyan, Mr. Edwards, who preached from Isaiah iv. 2.

Page 328. (Both these pieces are from HAYLEY, i. 257, 262.) The Latin inscription was written by Unwin, and sent to Cowper for his opinion. He returned it with the translation.

Page 329. (H. i. 270.) This riddle was sent to several friends, as the letters show, but was first published in the *Gentleman's Magazine* for 1806. In the following number it was answered thus :

> " A riddle by Cowper
> Made me swear like a trooper,
> But my anger, alas ! was in vain ;
>   For remembering the bliss
>   Of beauty's soft kiss,
> I now long for such riddles again.
>
>   J. T.

Page 329. *To Sir J. Reynolds.* (PRIVATE CORRESPONDENCE.) The author intended to place this in his first volume , but its prediction being falsified by the miscarriage of the royal cause in America, he threw it aside. " It was produced," he says, "by the successes we met with about three years ago. But, unhappily, the ardour I felt upon the occasion, disdaining to be confined within the bounds of fact, pushed me upon uniting the prophetical with the poetical character, and defeated its own purpose." " Iberia " is Spain.

Page 330 *Impromptu.* (GENT. MAG., 1781. Said there to be "by a gentleman.") Sent in a letter to Newton.
On a Review. Also sent to Newton, and first published in Cowper's Letters. The *Review* here referred to was the *Monthly ;* the article was written by a Mr. Badcock.
On *Madan's Answer.* In a letter to Newton, May 13, 1781. A great portion of the third volume of Madan's book is occupied with replying to Newton's comments.
Antithelyphthora. See Memoir, p. xliii.

Page 335. *Love abused.* (HAYLEY, v. 261.) The thought was, of course, suggested by Thelyphthora.
In seditionem horrendam. (H. i. 250.) Cowper had read in the newspaper the foolish suggestion that the Gordon riots were really planned by France, and set on foot with French bribes. It is a pity he gave another thought to such an absurd surmise. But the wickedness of the plot so horrified him that he wrote these verses. He always wrote verses, he says, when violently moved, because his prose was apt, under such circumstances, to be " verbose, inflated, and disgusting."

Page 336. *A Card.* Vestris, as we have elsewhere said, was a celebrated dancer of the time. The present poem was written when he took leave of the stage in favour of his son, being unable to perform as heretofore. The lines were sent to Unwin, Feb. 27, 1781.
On the High Price, &c. Sent in a letter to Newton. The cocoa-nuts were naught indeed : " they contained nothing but a putrid liquor, with a round white lump, which in taste and substance much resembled tallow, and was of the size of a small walnut."

Page 337. (HAYLEY, ii. 3.) Written soon after the acquaintance with Lady Austen began. See Memoir, p. l.

Page 338. "*Silver-End,*" a part of Olney adjoining Cowper's residence.
"*Sancerre,*" Lady Austen's residence in France.

Page 339. *The Flatting Mill.* (JOHNSON'S COWPER, 1815.) Written in Dec. 1781, and intended for the first volume of poems, but omitted by Newton's advice.

Page 340. (JOHNSON'S COWPER.) Enclosed in a letter.
The simile which Cowper has here latinised was by the Curate of Olney, as Cowper tells Unwin in the letter which contained it.

Page 341. The note from Cowper, at the bottom of the page, is addressed to Unwin. The original copy is in the British Museum. The Latin verses were by Dr. Vincent, who succeeded Lloyd, and was afterwards head-master.

Page 342. This poem also was intended for the first volume, but Johnson did not like it. " I shall not humble him for finding fault with it," said Cowper (Dec. 31, 1781), "though I have a better opinion of it myself." (First published by Bull, with the translations from Madame Guyon. Hayley printed another version, differing in many places from the present ; and among the Unwin MSS. in the Brit. Mus. is a third. It shows how much labour the Poet bestowed on his work.)

Page 343, *col.* 2. "Tattlers." Prov. xvi. 28.
" Hand-in-Hand insurance plates." The " Hand-in-Hand," which still issues these plates, is the oldest of the insurance companies, dating from 1696.

Page 344. "The Chymist's Golden Dream," Alchemy.

Page 345. *To Lady Austen.* (HAYLEY, ii. 18.) The benevolent plans of Lady Austen to dispel Cowper's melancholy led her to present him with a small printing-press. During a flood which prevented intercourse between Clifton and Olney, he wrote these lines, printed them himself, and sent them to her.

Page 346. *The Colubriad.* (HAYLEY ii. 49.) " Colubriad " is from " coluber," a snake. The circumstance is described in a letter to Unwin, Aug. 3. 1782. *Count de Grasse* was the French admiral defeated by Lord Rodney, in April 1782. The present comparison was no doubt suggested by the caricatures of him which were in circulation at this time.

Page 347. The *young lady* to whom the *cockscombs* were sent was, according to Mr. Bruce, Miss Green, Lady Austen's niece. Except in the Aldine edition, these verses have not been printed before. Their appearance in the present edition is explained in the Preface, p. xix. There are a few variations between our copy and the Aldine.
The *Songs* (HAYLEY, ii. 51) were written for Lady Austen to sing to airs which she was accustomed to play on the harpsichord.

Page 348. (H. ii. 53. The original MS. of the poem, and the Latin translation which follows it, are in the Brit. Mus.) Written for the same purpose as the preceding. Cowper did not like the metre which the air compelled him to use ; but, by common consent, he has produced one of the noblest songs in the language. The sad event occurred on the 12th of August, 1782. The editor has heard his grandfather, who was one of the witnesses, describe it. It is well described by Lord Stanhope, ch. lxvi.

Page 349. This humorous piece was discovered by Hayley, rolled up with the MSS. of the other songs written at Lady Austen's request, as if the author wished to lay aside, but not to destroy, the memories of their friendship. Written 1783. Clifton Reynes was about a mile from Olney, the residence of Mr. Jones, Lady Austen's brother-in-law.

Page 351. *In Brevitatem*, &c., with *Translation.* (HAYLEY, ii. 157.) Enclosed in a letter to Newton, Jan. 24, 1784, prefaced by the following jingle :—

> "The late Dr. Jortin
> Had the good fortune
> To write these verses
> Upon tombs and hearses;
> Which I, being jinglish,
> Have done into English."

Page 352. The circumstances which produced this effusion are recorded in the Memoir, p. xlix. The verses were sent to Unwin, November 10, 1783, with no other injunction than that he was not to print them. Hayley printed the latter portion (from the top of p. 353). After the death of Thurlow (Colman had died in 1794), there was no reason for suppressing the remainder.

Page 354. (BULL.) This lady was a Mrs. Billacoys.

Page 355. *To the Immortal*, &c. (PRIVATE CORRESPONDENCE.) Sent in a letter to Unwin, April 25, 1784.
To a Lady. Printed here for the first time. Of great interest, as being the verses which led Lady Austen to think that Cowper loved her. See Memoir, p. liv.

Page 356. The poem at the top is here placed for the first time among Cowper's Poems. It appeared in the *Record* newspaper of Feb. 20, 1867, and was sent by a correspondent who copied it from the poet's MS.
In 1784 Newton published his *Apologia*, a defence of his position as a clergyman of the Established Church. A reply soon followed, entitled *An Apology for Protestant Dissenters.* This was noticed in the *Monthly Review*, in which the critic said :—"In reply to Mr. Newton's fourth argument, in which he pleads, in the usual cant of these Reformers," &c. The *Monthly Review* was then read at Olney, passing from hand to hand in a small circle of friends. Cowper being of the number, he marked his disapprobation of the sentiment, and his regard for Newton, by writing these lines on the offensive page.
Epitaph on Johnson (H. ii. 275), written

January 15, 1785, just a month after the philosopher's death. Sent to Unwin.
On the Author, &c. There is a long letter of Cowper to Newton, speaking of this writer with mingled indignation and contempt. He had asserted that "Virgil never wrote a line worth reading," whereupon Cowper compares "the unfortunate man" to Erostratus (the incendiary of the Temple of Ephesus), and to Empedocles, who threw himself down the crater of Etna, both ready to do anything to get talked about.

Page 357. (H. iii. 17.) Miss C—— was Miss Creuzé. The name is given in full in the original MS. now in the British Museum. It was written at Unwin's request. In the letter containing it, Cowper says, "It is serious, but epigrammatic, like a bishop at a ball."
Gratitude. (H. ii.) See Memoir, p. lxiv.

Page 358. (POEMS, 1803.) Written to Unwin, Dec. 1779, in reference to his complaint of the disagreeableness of collecting his dues.

Page 359. The *Sonnet to Henry Cowper* (his first cousin) was sent by the author anonymously to the *Gentleman's Magazine* with a view to getting the unbiassed opinions of his relatives upon it. The ruse was successful, for the General copied and sent the lines to Cowper, saying that he thought them good. H. C. was reading-clerk to the House of Lords.

Page 360. (GENT. MAG. 1788.) Mrs. Montague (1720–1800) was the author of "Dialogues of the Dead" and the "Defence of Shakspeare." The Blue Stocking Club met at her house in Leicester Square. Cowper knew her through Lady Hesketh, of whom she was an intimate friend.

Page 361. This and the two following poems were written in 1788. The agitation on the slave trade was now in full force. Cowper, in his poem *Charity*, had written on the righteous side. His relatives now begged him to write a poem on the subject. He declined this, but wrote the following ballads, with a view to getting them sung to popular airs. "The Morning Dream," for example, was intended to be sung to the tune of "Tweeddale." None of these were published until 1803, after the poet's death.

Page 363. (POEMS, 1808.) The *mischievous bull* was Mr. Throckmorton's, and had, of course, been dwelling in Weston Park.

Page 364. (POEMS, 1808.) *Annus Mirabilis* was written in March of the year spoken of.

Page 365. *Hymn.* (JOHNSON.) He had been applied to, some little time before, by Mr. Bull to write a hymn of this character, but the application reached him in one of his melancholy hours, and he declared it to be impossible. Next year, however, the curate of

Olney, Mr. Bean, made another application, and was successful, for this was the result.

Stanzas, &c. (BULL, and POEMS, 1803.) The origin of this poem, and of the five which follow, forms one of the most amusing episodes in the poet's life. He thus describes it in a letter to Lady Hesketh:

"On Monday morning last, Sam brought me word that there was a man in the kitchen who desired to speak with me. I ordered him in. A plain, decent, elderly figure made its appearance, and, being desired to sit, spoke as follows: 'Sir, I am clerk of the parish of All-Saints, in Northampton, brother of Mr. Cox, the upholsterer. It is customary for the person in my office to annex to a bill of mortality, which he publishes at Christmas, a copy of verses. You will do me a great favour, sir, if you would furnish me with one.' To this I replied, 'Mr. Cox, you have several men of genius in your town; why have you not applied to some of them? There is a namesake of yours in particular—Cox, the statuary, who, everybody knows, is a first-rate maker of verses. He surely is the man of all the world for your purpose.' 'Alas! sir, I have heretofore borrowed help from him; but he is a gentleman of so much reading that the people of our town cannot understand him.' I confess to you, my dear, I felt all the force of the compliment implied in this speech, and was almost ready to answer, 'Perhaps, my good friend, they may find me unintelligible too, for the same reason.' But on asking him whether he had walked over to Weston on purpose to implore the assistance of my muse, and on his replying in the affirmative, I felt my mortified vanity a little consoled, and pitying the poor man's distress, which appeared to be considerable, promised to supply him. The waggon has accordingly gone this day to Northampton loaded in part with my effusions in the mortuary style."

It will be noticed that there is no poem for 1791. The old clerk died, and Cowper hoped that this would put himself "out of office." After a year's interval, however, the new clerk came to beseech a continuance.

Page 370. *Impromptu.* (HAYLEY, iii. 21.) In a humorous letter to Unwin. He begins by saying that he has been trying again and again to find something to write about, and then goes off into these lines.

The *Lines on the Queen's Visit to London*, to see the illuminations, after the king's recovery, were written at the request of Lady Hesketh, and presented to the Princess Augusta, in the expectation that they would be shown to her Majesty; but Cowper never heard any more of them.

Page 371. (JOHNSON, iii.) This circumstance is narrated in the *Gentleman's Magazine* for April 1789, but contradicted in the following month. However, it is admitted that the subject concerned did throw

an unsuccessful bird on the fire, but it escaped "by its natural, unconfined agility." He soon afterwards drank himself into a fatal fever.

Page 372. *Lines*, &c. (HAYLEY, iii. 188.) In a letter to Rose. "My cousin and I diverted ourselves by imagining the manner in which Homer would have described the scene."

Page 373. *To Mrs. T.* (H. iii. 203.) The Ode of Horace was found in one of the Roman libraries in 1788. Cowper asked Mrs. T. to copy it into the fly-leaf of his Horace, and her execution of the task procured her this compliment, which he wrote in a blank page of the same book.

Page 374. (PRIV. CORRESPONDENCE.) Mrs. King, wife of the rector of Pertenhall, introduced herself to him on the ground of being a friend of his brother. He gladly opened correspondence with her, and it was warm and constant on both sides. They never met.

Stanzas on the late, &c. (HAYLEY, iv. 264.) The coffin of Milton, buried at Cripplegate Church, was opened, and a pamphlet published, describing the appearance of the body.

Page 375. On Thornton, see Memoir, p. xxxvi. note.

Page 376. *To Mr. Bagot.* (HAYLEY, iii. 269.) This is the opening of a letter.

The *Four Ages* (HAYLEY, iv. 121) was suggested by his neighbour, Mr. Buchanan, curate of Ravenstone, who sketched out his idea of what the work should be. Cowper replied, "You have sent me a beautiful poem, wanting nothing but metre." Cowper tried, as we see, to write it, but the troubles which came upon him forced him to abandon the idea.

Page 377. (HAYLEY, iii. 294.) The "two nymphs" were May and June, and the poem was written in consequence of the inclemency of the former month in 1791. "Oh! what a month of May this has been!" he says, in a letter to John Johnson. "Let never poet, English poet at least, give himself to the praises of May again."

Page 378. *On the Refusal*, &c. occurs in a letter to Mrs. Throckmorton. Some friend of Mr. Throckmorton's had made the application, and Cowper felt the refusal keenly. "It seems not a little extraordinary that persons so nobly patronised themselves on the score of literature should resolve to give no encouragement to it in return. Should I find a fair opportunity to thank them hereafter, I will not neglect it."

The *retired Cat.* (HAYLEY, iii. 72.)

Page 380. *Yardley Oak* (H. iv. 423) was in Yardley Chase, near Olney. A memorandum in Cowper's handwriting says, "Yardley Oak is 22 feet 6½ inches in girth." It is said to have been planted by Judith, daughter of William the Conqueror, and wife of Earl Waltheof.

Page 380, *l* 35. "The Fabled Twins," Castor and Pollux, sons of Leda.

l 41. At Dodona was an oracle of Jupiter, the responses of which were given from a hollow oak tree.

Page 383. *To the Nightingale.* (H. iii. 261.) The author mentions the circumstance in a letter to Johnson, and, as in the poem, hopes it is a happy omen. But it was unfulfilled ; for he says afterwards that 1792 is the saddest year he has yet known.

Page 384. The *Lines written for Insertion* &c., were altered more than once. The original form was—

" In vain to live from age to age
  We modern bards endeavour ;
  But write in Patty's book one page,
  You gain your point for ever."

The final version was due to the suggestion of Lady Hesketh.

To Wilberforce. (H. iii. 275.) It had been rumoured about in the county that Cowper's views upon the slave trade were questionable. He refuted the charge by merely inserting the present sonnet in the *Northampton Mercury*, and took no further notice. The last two lines originally stood thus :—

"Then let them scoff—two prizes thou hast won,
 Freedom for captives, and thy God's—' Well done !'"

Dr. Austen (H. iii. 391), a friend of Hayley's, gave gratuitous assistance to Mrs. Unwin in her illness. He died in 1793, and Cowper wrote a very touching letter of sympathy to Hayley, in which he calls him "our good Samaritan."

Page 385. Miss Sally Hurdis was sister of Rev. James Hurdis, a minor poet (and Professor of Poetry at Oxford), and one of Cowper's correspondents.

Concerning his friendship with Hayley, see Memoir, p. lxviii. Hayley, as seen by the Sonnet, had just visited him, and during his visit Mrs. Unwin's attack had taken place, and he had been most kind and useful in the emergency.

Page 386. (HAYLEY, iii. 406.) Mr. Courtenay was Sir John Throckmorton's brother, and succeeded him in the title.

(HAYLEY, iii. 399.) The lines to Dr. Darwin were written at Eartham in August, 1792. He was a warm friend of Hayley.

Page 387. *On his approaching*, &c. (HAYLEY, iii. 413.) The opening of a letter to him.) The floods and flames refer to the dreadful nervous fits he had had concerning this journey, which are described in the letter.

(HAYLEY, iii. 23.) The Sonnet to Romney occupied three months in writing, so depressed were the poet's spirits.

To George Romney. This picture is now in the possession of Mr. H. R. Vaughan Johnson. It appeared in the Exhibition of Portraits in 1868, beside the portrait of his mother which his lines have made so famous.

Page 388. *Epitaph on Fop* (HAYLEY, iv. 2), written at Eartham, and sent to Mrs. Courtenay.

The two lines to Lady Hesketh (HAYLEY, iv. 39) are the heading of a letter, describing his condition. Without his nightly dose of twelve drops of laudanum, he says, he is devoured by melancholy.

Epitaph on Mr. Chester (HAYLEY, iv. 262).

Page 389. *On a Plant*, &c. (JOHNSON, iii. 249.)

Page 390. The *young friend* (HAYLEY, iv. 67) was John Johnson.

Inscription, &c. (HAYLEY, iv. 264.) This was written for a rough house which he intended building, but his intention was frustrated by a much finer one being built, for which these lines would have been unfitting. See his humorous account in the note to the Epigrams at p. 397.

To Mrs. Unwin. When this exquisite sonnet (HAYLEY, ii.) was written, Mrs. Unwin was a sad wreck. Cowper describes, at the time of Hayley's visit, how they sit reading together, and adds, " Poor Mrs. Unwin, in the meantime, sits quiet in her corner, occasionally laughing at us both, and not seldom interrupting me with some remark, for which she is rewarded by me with ' Hush, hold your peace.' "

To John Johnson, &c. (H. iv. 258.) Cowper had expressed a wish for a bust of Homer, and Johnson made several attempts to procure one, and at length succeeded. It still stands in the grounds at Weston, with Cowper's inscription. See p. 391.

... *Page* 391. *On a Portrait of Himself* (HAYLEY iii. 410). Written July 15, 1792, shortly before starting for Eartham. The portrait was taken at the request of John Johnson, who wanted it for his aunt, Mrs. Bodham. By universal consent, it was pronounced an excellent likeness.

The *Thanks for a Present*, &c., was sent in a letter to Johnson, December 31, 1793. Copeman was a friend of Johnson.

The sonnet *to Hayley* (H. iv. 68) was in answer to a proposal that they should undertake a joint literary work. Cowper added, that he had other reasons for not entertaining the proposal. " I am nobody in verse, unless in a corner and alone, and unconnected in my operations." He afterwards, however, entertained a proposal that he and Hayley should complete " The Four Ages " between them, as a vehicle for illustrations by Flaxman and Lawrence. See his letter to Hayley of July 7, 1793. But the increased gloominess which fell on him, at the end of the year, put the whole plan out of possibility.

Page 393. (HAYLEY, iii. 160.)

Page 394. (HAYLEY, iv. 272.) Catharine Fanshawe was a co-heiress with two sisters, and was known among her friends for her talent for graceful pleasantry, both in prose and verse, as well as for her skill in art. She was the authoress of the well-known riddle on the letter H—

"'Twas whispered in Heaven, 'twas muttered in Hell," &c.

There is a laughable mock ode of hers in Miss Berry's Journal, and an equally laughable letter with it, vol. ii. pp. 298—301.

The "stanzas" which she had addressed to Lady Hesketh were produced under the following circumstances. Lady Hesketh had lent her a MS. poem of Cowper's, on condition that she should neither show nor copy it. Miss Fanshawe kept her promise in the letter, but sent it back with the following stanzas :—

" What wonder if my wavering hand
    Had dared to disobey,
When Hesketh gave a harsh command,
    And Cowper led astray ?

Then take this tempting gift of thine,
    By pen uncopied yet ;
But, canst thou memory confine,
    Or teach me to forget ?

More lasting than the touch of art
    Her characters remain,
When written by a feeling heart
    On tablets of the brain."

The "*Letter*" was one which Miss Fanshawe wrote to Lady Hesketh, who sent Cowper an extract from it—doubtless some pretty compliment on his "Stanzas."

Page 394. *On Flaxman's Penelope.* (HAYLEY, iv. 92.) Sent in a letter to H.

Page 395. (HAYLEY, iv. 145.) The calm of passionate despair seems to reign over these exquisite verses. They were written shortly before leaving Weston for ever.

Page 396. *On receiving,* &c. (JOHNSON, iii. 265.)

Motto for a Clock. This was a clock sculptured by Bacon for King George III. It is now in the Presence Chamber at Windsor Castle. The translation is by Hayley.

In a time, &c. (HAYLEY, ii. 135.) Written July 7, 1793. Hayley was a man who sought much after shade ; he "could not bear a sunbeam."

Page 397. (HAYLEY, iv. 77 and 99.) On his return from Eartham, Cowper said to his favourite domestic, "Sam, build me a shed in the garden, with anything you can find, and make it rude and rough, like one of those at Eartham." "Yes, sir," said Sam, and straightway, laying his own noddle with the village carpenter's, built a thing fit for Stowe Gardens. (Letter to Hayley, July 24, 1793.) The poet was going to put the first of the epigrams over the door, but that he feared to "break Sam's heart, and the carpenter's too."

Montes Glaciales. (H. iv. 367.)

Page 400. "I have heard of my *wether mutton* from many quarters," he writes ; "I have accordingly satirized myself in two stanzas which I composed last night, while I lay awake, tormented with pain, and dosed with laudanum."

The Castaway. On this terrible but grand poem, see Memoir, p. lxxii.

Page 403. Jeanne Marie Bouvières de la Mothe was born in April, 1648, at Montargis, a town about 50 miles south of Paris, in the province of Orleanois. Little is known of her parents but that they were well-to-do people, and of pious life. They had both been married before, and each had a family ; and one of her half-sisters, a nun in the Ursuline convent at Montargis, was the cause of her being placed for education in the same convent. Whilst there, the widowed English queen, Henrietta Maria, wished her to become maid of honour to her daughter ; but her father refused the offer. She early formed the resolution of giving herself to God, and has recorded her endeavours to do so, her successes and failures, in her autobiography. In 1663 her father removed with his family to Paris, and the following year she was married to a rich gentleman of the court, M. Guyon, thirty-eight years old, she being but just sixteen. Her mother-in-law disliked her heartily, and lost no opportunity of insulting her ; and her husband, though sometimes kind, was more often cold and harsh with her ; but these sorrows did but decide her the more earnestly to seek rest in religion. The views which she ultimately took up, and found sufficient for her spiritual needs, were given to her by a Fransciscan (his name does not appear), who had spent five years in solitude, and to whom she now resorted for confession. On telling her self-dissatisfaction to him, he "remained silent for some time in meditation and prayer," and then said, "Your efforts have been unsuccessful because you have sought without, what you can only find within. Accustom yourself to seek God in your heart, and you will not fail to find Him." She says that these words darted into her soul like lightning, and she never lost sight of them. The poem entitled "Love and Gratitude" (p. 413) was written when the effect of them was still upon her. From the day of this speech, July 22, 1668, she always dated her conversion.

It would be out of the question here to give a detailed account of her views, or extracts from her prose writings. Cowper's beautiful translations of her verses will amply answer the purpose of showing what her theology was. *Quietism* is the name which was given to it. It might be summed up in the words, "Deus est summum bonum. Rest is to be found in the mind reposing itself upon the love of God." It belongs to the same class as S. Augustine's Confessions, or Thomas à Kempis's "Imitatio Christi," or Leighton's Commentary—not to name living writers.

Her increased fervour met with little favour from her husband. When she went to her private devotions, she complains, he would time her with his watch, and if she was more than half-an-hour at a time he would be vexed. Her only worldly joy was in her three children—two

M M

sons and a daughter. Of these the eldest son was for a while alienated from her through the influence of her mother-in-law, and the small-pox, after destroying her own great beauty of face, carried off her younger and best-loved boy. "I loved my boy tenderly," she writes: "but though I was greatly afflicted, I saw the hand of the Lord so clearly that I shed no tears. I offered him up to God." It was now that she wrote "Divine Justice Amiable" (p. 411). It was nearly at the same time that she first became acquainted with Francis de la Combe, an eloquent Barnabite friar, who had been introduced to her by her cousin. She was the means of inspiring him with her views, and he became the foremost preacher of Quietism in France. After a few years he was seized by a *lettre de cachet*, and sent to the Bastille for heresy. He was afterwards placed in another prison; but a prisoner he remained until his death, twenty-two years after his first arrest.

In 1672 another heavy blow fell upon her—a twofold blow. Her father and little daughter died nearly together. Becoming convinced more and more that it was God's will to perfect her by afflictions, she resolved, by the advice of a nun, to mark the fourth anniversary of her conversion by drawing up and signing what she called a "marriage covenant with the Saviour." Here it is :—

"I henceforth take Jesus Christ to be mine. I promise to receive Him as a husband to me. And I give myself to Him, unworthy though I am, to be His spouse. I ask of Him, in this marriage of spirit with spirit, that I may be of the same mind with Him—meek, pure, nothing in myself, and united in God's will. And, pledged as I am to be His, I accept, as a part of my marriage portion, the temptations and sorrows, the crosses and the contempt, which fell to Him.

"JEANNE M. B. DE LA MOTHE GUYON. "Sealed with her ring."

This document is a sufficient explanation of the poem entitled "Aspirations," &c. (p. 410).

Soon after came on what she calls a "state of deprivation," which lasted for six years—a deprivation not of holy desire or purpose, or faith or hope, but of *consolation* in religion. It was to teach her, as she afterwards believed, that religious joy must not be sought for its own sake; that it can only be possessed with safety when its possessor cares not for it, but only for God. The poems at pp. 408, 421, 423, are descriptive of this phase of her experience, and there are many other references to it. "The Joy of the Cross," at p. 426, was written as the sorrow was passing away. The mention, from time to time, of the forest and its songsters is explained by her frequent retirement for prayer to a forest near her home, where, more than anywhere, as she writes, her soul found peace.

Her husband died in 1676. They had been much estranged, but not separated; but they were entirely reconciled in his last days. She soon after left her mother-in-law, and devoted herself to almsdeeds and works of love in different parts of France, afterwards in Italy, being forced to move constantly in consequence of the persecutions of the Bishop of Geneva, whose request that she would go into a convent she had refused. This is the "Banishment" to which she refers in the last poem in p. 412. That in p. 410, "Happy Solitude," is said to have been written on the Lake of Geneva immediately after her success in freeing a girl from the temptations of a wicked ecclesiastic; and that in the following page, "The Triumph," &c., was the outpouring of her heart on crossing the Alps, and looking down for the first time on the land of the Po and Adige.

In July 1686 she returned to Paris, and soon after occurred the arrest and imprisonment of La Combe, already mentioned. Soon after she herself was seized, and confined for eight months. Several poems belonging to this imprisonment have not been translated by Cowper. She appealed to her enemies, but they replied with taunts; then to Père la Chaise, the King's confessor, but no answer was returned. An application by her friend Madame de Miramion to Madame de Maintenon was more successful, and she regained her liberty. Almost immediately after this she began her acquaintance and correspondence with the Abbé Fenelon. As this correspondence does not bear upon her poetry, we pass it by. But it was apparently the influence which she exerted over Fenelon which led Bossuet to uneasiness and suspicion of her, ending in his bringing the matter before the king, and being appointed, with two others, commissioners to examine her writings. Whilst waiting in suspense, and expecting an unfavourable judgment, she wrote "The Acquiescence," &c., at p. 415. No judgment was pronounced at this time; and after the trial she retired for a season to a convent at Meaux, where her life and conversation won her such love and reverence, that the prioress entreated her to stay for life. She returned, however, to Paris; but soon after, the opposition continuing, she was imprisoned at Vincennes. The following poems belong to this imprisonment :— "The Entire Surrender" (p. 415), "Glory to God alone" (p. 416), "Self-love and Truth," &c. (p. 417), "The Love of God," &c. (p. 417), "The Secrets," &c. (p. 419), and several not translated by Cowper.

Just at the same time Fenelon was made Archbishop of Cambray. Louis XIV. did not like him; but the appointment was urged upon him by the Duke of Burgundy, and Fenelon's high position made refusal difficult. Probably, too, the king expected to win him over to his side. The hope, however, was vain. Fenelon published his *Explication des Maximes des Saints*, in which the principles of Quietism were avowed, and it was immediately attacked as heretical by Bossuet. That great orator and controversialist was now at the height of his reputation ; and though Fenelon had written little, all men knew that the controversy would be a battle between giants. It does not fall within the limits of the present note, except that, as it progressed, Bossuet, irritated at being foiled by his opponent, lost his temper, and actually descended to throwing out insinuations concerning the relations of Fenelon and Madame Guyon, and compared the two to the heretic Montanus and Priscilla. Fenelon doubted whether to answer this ; but his friends were urgent that he should do so, and accordingly he produced a reply, of which Charles Butler says, " A nobler effusion of the indignation of insulted virtue and genius, eloquence has never produced." Public opinion declared that the great Bossuet himself had found his match. But this did not meet the king's views, and he appealed to the Pope. Innocent XII. was an amiable and pious man, and desired and entreated that conciliatory measures might prevail. But the king was too urgent for this, and demanded a censure almost with menaces. So it was pronounced, and Fenelon accepted it so far as to cease from controversy any further. He certainly never changed his views ; but in his preaching he avoided forms of expression which were likely to be called Quietist. His latest writings are some of his most beautiful. He died in 1715, at the age of sixty-five.

Madame Guyon was removed to the Bastille in 1698, after having had shameful indignities to bear ; and in this terrible place she wrote "Truth and Divine Love," &c. (p. 411) and "The Testimony," &c. (p. 413). She was released in 1702, but banished to Blois. Her constitution, however, was broken, and her life was from this time uneventful. Her eldest son was living in the neighbourhood, and seems to have treated her dutifully. She spoke as fervently as ever of the love of God, but strength for active work was gone. She died on the 9th of June, 1717, after drawing up a will, the piety of which proves that He whom her soul loved was sustaining her unto the end.

Page 431. See list of books, p. xviii. No. 7, and Memoir, p. lxvii.

Deodati was not only a college friend of Milton, but they saw much of each other in London, and were frequent correspondents. Two letters from Deodati to Milton are in the British Museum. The second of them was sent from Cheshire, whither Deodati had removed after taking his degree in 1625, and is probably that referred to in Milton's answer, written in the spring of 1626.

ll 3, 4. Deva, the Dee. *Vergivium* is the Latin name of the Irish Sea.

l 12. *My forbidden cell.* This refers to some incident in Milton's college life, the nature of which has caused a controversy too complicated to be discussed here. See Masson's Life of Milton, pp. 135-141. All that need be

said here is that Milton and his tutor, Chappell, had some quarrel, that the Master of the college had to interfere, and that Milton was " rusticated"—sent away for awhile. He appears, however, to have soon come back, and to have been placed under another tutor.

Page 431, *l* 52. Ovid, who was banished by Augustus to Tomi, on the Euxine. Milton probably rates him too highly in the lines which follow.

l 31, *ff*. These characters are all of them from Terence ; except the " coifed brooder," or lawyer, who is taken from a modern Latin play, *Ignoramus*, which was extremely popular at Cambridge. (Masson, p. 186.)

Page 432, *ll* 45, 46. Romeo and Macbeth, or Richard III.

l 49. Eteocles and Polynices. See Sophocles' "Antigone."

l 52. Cheyne Walk, Chelsea, or Gray's Inn Gardens.

l 76. Alluding to the legend that London was founded by the Trojans, under Brut—a legend which Milton's " History of England " showed that he half believed.

l 88. " The sightless boy," Cupid.

Page 433, *Elegy* ii. This Bedel was Richard Redding, M.A. Died Oct. 1626.

1st stanza " Summons clear," refers to the practice of Bedels giving public notice of Convocations.

2nd stanza. " Leda's paramour," the swan. *Æson* was, according to the legend, made young again by his daughter Medea. (Ov. Met. vii.) *Apollo's son* was Æsculapius.

3rd stanza. Cyllenius, Hermes (Mercury), who dwelt on Mount Cyllene. *Eurybates,* one of the heralds sent by Agamemnon to Achilles. (Iliad, i. 320.)

Page 434. The Bishop was Lancelot Andrewes, who died Sept. 21, 1626.

l 4. The Plague raged this year so fiercely that Parliament was adjourned from London to Oxford : 10,000 persons died of it in London.

l 9. The "fraternal pair" (brothers in arms) were Prince Christian of Brunswick and Count Mansfeld, the two ablest supporters of the Elector Palatine in the Thirty Years' War. They both died in 1626. See Dyer's Modern Europe, ii. 550. The " heroes " are apparently the large number of rank and file who died in the same campaign.

l 26. The creatures of the sea.

l 34. *Iberian,* Spanish.

l 43. *Chloris,* goddess of flowers ; identical with the Roman Flora. *Alcinous,* the happy ruler of the Phæacians in the isle of Scheria. See the description of his gardens in the Odyssey.

Page 435, *Elegy* iv. Thomas Young soon afterwards returned to England, and became vicar of Stowmarket. He died there in 1655.

Page 435, *l* 5. "The king," Æolus, who kept the winds imprisoned in a mountain in Sicily, for which *Sicania* was another name.

l 7. *Doris*, mother of the Nereids, or sea nymphs.

l 10. "Medea's chariot" was drawn by winged dragons. Triptolemus, the inventor of the plough and agriculture, and of the civilization which springs from it, was presented by the goddess. Demeter (Ceres) with a winged chariot wherewith to travel over the earth and give men the blessings of agriculture.

Page 436, *l* 16. *Hama*, a puissant Saxon, was said to have been killed here by Starköder, a Cimbrian (Danish) giant.

l 23. "The sage," Socrates. The "Stagyrite," Aristotle. "Ammon's son," Alexander the Great, whose mother, Olympias, was reputed the daughter of Jupiter Ammon.

l 26. The tutors of Achilles.

l 29. *Aonia*, that part of Bœotia in which was Helicon, the Muses' fountain.

l 55. Penelope.

Page 437, *l* 72. Battles between the German Protestant League and the Imperialists under Tilly. See Schiller's Thirty Years' War, Bohn's Translation, p. 101.

l 75. *Enyo*, the goddess of war.

l 97. 1 Kings xix. There is a covert allusion to Charles I. and his wife.

l 100. Acts xvi. There is an allusion here to the whippings inflicted by the Star-chamber.

l 102. Matt. viii. 34.

l 112. 2 Kings xix. 35.

ll 114, 115. 2 Kings vii. 6.

Page 438. The 5th Elegy was written just after he had taken his B.A. degree. It was written in London. See *l* 28.

l 9. "The forkèd hill." Helicon.

l 36. *Boötes*, the constellation before the Great Bear, imagined to be the waggoner driving "Charles' Wain." "Less fatigued," that is, he rises higher in the sky.

l 37–40. The stars appear less numerous because the light increases. He gives as poetic reason, that there is less danger of midnight attacks.

Page 439, *l* 45. *Cynthia* was both the moon and the huntress-goddess.

l 50. "Thy withered mate," Tithonus. Aurora was represented as leaving his side each morning to proclaim the coming day. She carried away the youth Cephalus, through admiration of his beauty.

l 62. *Ops*, i.e. Cybele, who was represented with a crown.

Page 439, *l* 65. While Proserpine was gathering flowers, Pluto came up from the earth and carried her away. He is called "Tænarian Dis," because a cavern in Tænarum (south of Peloponnesus) was supposed to belong to him.

l 83. *Tethys*, wife of Oceanus, mother of the river-gods.

Page 440, *l* 91. *Semele*, being beloved by Zeus, became the object of Hera's jealousy, who therefore took the form of Semele's old nurse, and recommended her to ask Zeus to appear to her in all his splendour. The god unwillingly did so, and she was in a moment consumed by the lightnings.

l 92. "Lest." Every edition hitherto has read *let*. I have altered it, because *let* makes no meaning : "lest" represents the original accurately.

> "Nec me —crede mihi—terrent Semelëia fata,
> Nec Fhaetonteo fumidus axis equo ;
> Cum tu, Phœbe, tuo sapientius uteris igni."

He means, of course, that there is no danger of Phœbus setting the earth on fire, as Phaeton did ; for Phœbus has the mastery over his horses.

l 122. *Silvanus*, the wood-god.

l 127. *Faunus*, the god of shepherds. *Oreads*, nymphs. The conclusion is not very easy. The poet, in lines 135-6, calls on Jove to restore the golden age, where there is perpetual spring, and to return as of old to earth again. If that is impossible, he goes on, at least let not the year hasten too quickly. Give us time to enjoy the delights of nature before Winter comes.

This is one of Milton's most beautiful poems, and had it been written in English would probably have been second to none in popularity.

Page 441, *l* 4. "Darkness," retirement.

l 11. The game of "snapdragon."

l 27. Horace. For Glycera, see Od. i. 19, and for Chloë, i. 23.

Page 442, *l* 49. That is, Elegiac poetry is used for all sorts of subjects.

l 55. "But they," &c., *i.e.* epic poets.

l 59. Homer.

l 67. *Linus*, the son of Apollo, personification of a dirge or lamentation.

l 68. *Tiresias* having become blind in youth, Athena was entreated to restore his sight. She was unable to do so, and therefore gave him as compensation the power of understanding the voice of birds, and also a staff by which he could walk without stumbling.

l 69. *Calchas*, the soothsayer of the Greeks in the siege of Troy. "The bard of Thrace" was Orpheus.

l 72. The "chief of Ithaca" was Odysseus, or Ulysses, the hero of the Odyssey, whence the stories referred to in the following lines are all taken.

The conclusion, of course, refers to his magnificent "Ode on the Nativity," with which he tells us here he was inspired as he lay awake on Christmas morning. It is unpublished yet, he adds ; it waits for Deodati's judgment.

" Reeds of Albion," *i.e.* in the vernacular tongue, not in Latin, like this.

Page 443. An interesting piece of auto-biography. It must have occurred on the 1st or 2nd of May, 1628.

l 2. *Amathusia*, Aphrodite (Venus). So called from Amathus, a town in Cyprus, where was a temple to her.

l 15. His eyes were already weak, evidently. His blindness came on about 1654.

l 21. " The Sigean boy," Ganymede, the god's cupbearer.

l 24. Hylas went to draw water from a fountain, when the Nymphs fell in love with him and drew him in, and he was never seen again. Daphne was chased by Phœbus Apollo, and when on the point of being caught was turned into a laurel, which thenceforward became Apollo's favourite tree. *Cydonia*, one of the chief cities of Crete. Its inhabitants were famous for their skill in archery.

l 38. " Latent," *i.e.* unknown. Cephalus was the husband of Procris. He had been presented with a javelin which was never to miss its mark, and one day, when out hunting, he killed her, not knowing her.

l 39. There are many legends concerning the giant hunter, Orion, but all agree that he was deprived of sight, in consequence of the violence of his love.

l 40. *Alcides* was Hercules ; his friend, Telamon the hunter.

l 46. " Phœbus' serpent," *i.e.* Æsculapius, the god of healing, who came to Rome disguised in the form of a snake.

l 83. *Œclides*, Amphiaraus, one of the Argonauts. He fought in the war against Thebes, but was defeated, and whilst he was fleeing the earth swallowed him up before he could be overtaken.

Page 445, *l* 103. These lines seem to have been added at a later date, after he got over his love-attack.

1st Epigram. The first line alludes to the legend that Zeus, in displeasure, withheld fire from men, but Prometheus stole it in a hollow tube.

2nd Epigram. Leonora Baroni was the Jenny Lind of her age. Milton heard her for the first time at a magnificent concert at the Cardinal Barberini's, which he describes in one of his Epistles. A French writer, quoted by Warton, who had heard Leonora sing, accompanied by her mother, Adriana, on the lute, says that it threw him into such raptures that he " forgot his mortality."

Pentheus, King of Thebes, was driven mad by Dionysus, for resisting the introduction of his worship into the kingdom.

Page 446. *Naples*, &c. Parthenope was one of the Sirens, said to be buried at Naples. *Chalcidic*, a name sometimes given to the Greek colonies in South Italy, from Chalcis, whence the colonists came.

" The hoarse Pausilipo," alluding to the murmur of the waves at the foot of the Mount of that name.

Christina, Queen of Sweden, the daughter of Gustavus Adolphus, was only six years old at the time of her father's death. She was elected queen then, and assumed the government in 1644. For an account of her life and character, see *Dyer's Mod. Europe*, vol. iii. p. 36. She abdicated in 1654, and soon after joined the Roman Catholic Church. There is some reason for thinking that the lines here translated were written, not by Milton, but by Marvell.

Page 447. The Vice-Chancellor was Dr. John Goslyn, Master of Caius, and Professor of Medicine. Died 1626.

Nessus was a Centaur, whom Hercules shot with a poisoned arrow. Hercules was afterwards induced to put on a robe which had been dipped in Nessus' blood, and the poison penetrated all his limbs. At the moment of his death he was caught up to the gods.

" Ne'er had Hector," &c. Iliad xxii. 226. (Pope, *l* 401.)

" Nor the chief"—namely, Sarpedon. Il. xvi. 452. (Pope, *l* 580.)

Machaon, surgeon of the Greeks in the Trojan war, son of Æsculapius. He was killed by Eurypylus.

Chiron, the wisest of the Centaurs, instructed in medicine by Apollo. While fighting with the other Centaurs, Hercules accidentally hit him with a poisoned arrow.

Asclepiades, Æsculapius. He was slain by Zeus with a flash of lightning, lest men should escape death altogether through his skill.

Cirrha, Delphi. Put here poetically for Cambridge.

Æacus, so renowned for his justice and piety that he was called upon to settle disputes, not only among men, but among the gods, and after his death was appointed judge of the dead.

The Bishop of Ely was Nicholas Felton, who died a few days after Bishop Andrewes.

Page 448, *1st col.* *Naso*, Ovid. In his poem entitled *Ibis* he furiously lashes an unknown enemy.

Archilochus was an early Greek poet. He was a suitor to the daughter of Lycambes, who at first consented, then refused, to give his daughter. In his rage, Archilochus wrote a poem, not only accusing him of perjury, but lampooning the whole family so ferociously, that when the verses were recited at a public festival the daughters of Lycambes hung themselves through shame.

Page 449, *l* 24. Pallas had the head of Medusa in the centre of her shield, which had the terrible power of turning all who looked upon it into stone.

Page 449, *l* 25. "Hurled," *i.e.* by Zeus.

l 29. "Thy own son," Phaeton.

l 33. *Hæmus,* now Balkan.

l 34-5. The Ceraunian hills were said to have been used as missiles in the war of the Titans.

l 43. "The prime mover," Primum mobile, the external sphere, which, according to the Ptolemaic system, set all the others in motion.

l 46. *Saturn,* god of the seasons, which, says the poet, keep on their round as of old. "The burning casque of Mars," the abode of the lightning.

l 49. *Phœbus,* the sun, which needs not, through weakness, to draw nearer to the earth, in order to give it warmth.

l 53. "The star," Venus, sometimes a morning, sometimes an evening star.

l 58. *Cynthia,* the moon.

l 60. The moon is supposed to hold out her arms to catch the first beams of the sun.

l 68. *Pelorus,* N.E. promontory of Sicily.

l 69. The shell blown by the Tritons was supposed to have the effect of soothing the restless waves of the ocean.

Page 450, *l* 74. Hyacinth was the favourite of Apollo; Adonis of Cytherea (Venus). The poet, of course, means that the flowers bearing these names are still as sweet and beautiful as ever. The anemone was said to have sprung from the blood of Adonis.

l 80. 2 S. Peter iii. 7.

l 3. *On the Platonic Idea. Mnemosyne,* mother of the Muses.

l 7. Alludes to the Platonic doctrine that there is in the divine regions an archetype of man, an original perfect model of what man was intended to be.

l 13. "The goddess born," Pallas.

l 21. *Lethe,* the river of forgetfulness. See Virg. Æn. vi. 713. (Dryden, *l* 955.)

l 29. Tiresias.

l 32. Hermes. "The prophet-choir," the Soothsayers.

l 34. Sanchoniathon. There are only fragments of an ancient history said to have been written by him. But modern examination has led to the opinion that they are forgeries.

l 37. Hermes Trismegistus, the author of works much valued by the Neo-Platonists of Alexandria.

Page 451, *l* 40. Plato. *Academus* was the grove, near Athens, in which Plato taught.

l 1. *To his Father.* "Pieria's stream," sacred to the Muses.

l 18. *Clio,* the muse of history.

Page 452, *l* 40. Alluding to the belief in the

"music of the spheres." By *Ophiuchus* (*i.e.* the serpent), *Orion,* and *Atlas,* are meant the constellations of that name.

Page 452, *l* 50. *Lyæus,* Bacchus. From a word signifying "to loosen."

l 55. It was Orpheus who sang these things. See Apoll. Rhod. i. 277 (Fawkes' Translation, *l* 620).

l 70. Milton's father was a good musical composer, and had written some pieces of great intricacy.

Page 453, *l* 82. His father had evidently tried to persuade him that literature was a thankless profession, but, on finding that he was bent on it, did not object further.

l 91. "Deep retreats," namely Horton.

l 112. "Offers me," &c., offers to kiss me.

l 120. Alluding again to Apollo and Phaeton.

Page 454. Hardly anything is known of Salsillus. He appears to have been a poet of much promise, but to have died early. (See Masson, p. 754.)

l 4. The fairest nymph that attended on Juno.

l 7. "Verse divine," Italian poetry.

l 11. *Eurus,* the east wind.

l 13. *Ausonia,* Italy.

Page 455, *l* 28. *Evander* is said to have built a town under the Aventine hill, and to have taught his neighbours meekness and justice. It was here that Salsillus was now living. The venerable Manso, the generous patron of the stricken Tasso and of Marini, was now in his 78th year, having been born in 1561. His whole character seems to have been a most beautiful one. See Masson, pp. 756-761. He died at the age of 84.

l 3. That is, since Virgil celebrated Gallus and Mæcenas, there has been no patron who so deserved praise.

l 10. Tasso (1544-1595). Marini (1569-1625). He wrote the long poem *Adone,* which is referred to in the next line.

Page 456, *l* 19. Manso had built monuments to them, and had also written the Life of Tasso.

l 21. Herodotus, to whom a Life of Homer, still extant, has been ascribed.

l 35. *Tityrus* is a poet in the opening Eclogue of Virgil, and therefore often put for any writer of song. The allusion here is to Chaucer.

l 50. Herodotus describes the Hyperboreans, who lived beyond the north wind, as coming to make their offerings at Delos; and Milton identifies these with the British Druids. Loxo was the maiden who brought the offerings, and Milton makes her the daughter of Corineus, a giant who, according to Geoffry of Monmouth, lived in Cornwall. The other maidens here mentioned accompanied Loxo.

l 63. Apollo, banished from heaven for slaying the Cyclops, kept the herds of Admetus king of Thessaly, for a year, and, during that time, the god used to repair to the cavern of Chiron, the wise and good Centaur, for relaxation.

Page 457, *l* 69. *Peneus*, a river of Elis.

l 75. *Œta*, a pile of mountains south of Thessaly.

l 80. *Maia's son*, Hermes.

l 94. The Round Table. The poet here and in the following poem intimates a long-cherished intention of writing a poem on King Arthur. How he changed his purpose we know, but he left this work to not unworthy hands.

Page 458. Deodati died in Aug. or Sept. 1638, whilst Milton was in Italy. The latter, whilst in ignorance of his loss, wrote the Sonnet at p. 466. He heard of it on his way home.

l 1. *Himera* was in Sicily. Theocritus and Moschus, Sicilian poets, sang, one the fates of Daphnis and Hylas, the other that of Bion.

l 6. *Thyrsis*, Milton.

l 37. "Unless, by chance," &c.; alluding to the superstition of the ancients that, if any one was seen by a wolf before the wolf was seen by him, he lost the use of his voice.

Page 459, *l* 43. *Pales*, Roman god of flocks and sheep.

Page 460, *l* 105. *Mopsus*, a prophet during the Trojan war. No doubt the poet means some friend here. And so in lines 123–6, he doubtless means some ladies of his acquaintance : the last, Chloris, must have lived in Essex ; for "the Idumanian current" was the river Chelmer.

l 140. *Proteus*, the prophetic old man of the sea, kept the flocks of Neptune.

Page 461, *l* 189. See p. 469. Dati's tribute, being in prose, does not appear in this volume.

Page 462, *l* 207. Horton, Milton's residence, was near the Colne.

l 208. Deodati lived for a while at St. Albans, the ancient capital of Cassibelan.

l 209. "Simples," herbs.

l 224. "Ye groves, farewell." That is, I am quitting pastoral for heroic poetry.

l 227. *Dardan*, Trojan. *Rutupia*, Richborough, in Kent.

l 231. The two brothers invaded Gaul and Italy, and Brennus conquered Rome.

l 232. *Arviragus*, son of Cunobelin, Shakspeare's Cymbeline.

l 233. "Our hardy sires." The blunder here is Cowper's again (see note on p. 97). Milton, in the original, does not call the Britons our sires. *Armorica*, Britanny. Gorlois, king of Cornwall ; *Uther Pendragon* became ena-

moured of his wife Iogerne. See Tennyson's "Coming of Arthur."

Page 462, *l* 248. *Usa*, the Ouse. It is probably the Yorkshire river which the poet means

Page 463, *l* 249. The *Alne*, by Alnwick.

l 250. *Abra*, the Humber.

l 256. He means that, whilst he was abroad, he used to please himself by thinking how he would recite these heroic verses to his friend on their reunion. But the exact meaning of the original is not very clear :—

> " Hæc tibi servabam lenta sub cortice lauri ;
> Hæc, et plura simul."

Does it not mean, "in my laurel-crowned head"?—he having been admitted as a poet.

l 258. Manso had given these two cups after the reception of Milton's Poem to him.

Page 464. Dr. John Rouse, Librarian of the Bodleian, 1620–5.

l 1. "Twofold." He published his poems in 1645, half English, half Latin, with separate title-pages.

l 5. Milton himself.

l 10. *Daunian*, Italian.

l 17. From London to Oxford, near which the Thames and Isis join.

Page 465, *l* 60. *Ion*, son of Creüsa, daughter of Erectheus, king of Attica. Ion was reared at the Temple of Delphi, and on being grown up was made treasurer there.

Pages 466–67, *1st Sonnet*. "The Rhine." This is a mistake of the translator. The river spoken of is the Reno, which flows past Bologna. Nothing is known concerning the lady, or ladies, who inspired the tender feelings described in these Sonnets.

Milton found, not long after this, that at the time when he wrote his Sonnet to Deodati, his friend was dead. See note on p. 458, *l* 1.

Page 472. On Vincent Bourne, see note on p. 172.

Page 473, *l* 13. "Inherent," sticking in. Used, therefore, in the sense of the Latin word from which it is derived.

l 15. "Sanious blood," the thin serous blood which runs from a wound.

There is probably no need to give the answers to the enigmas.

Page 478. *Denner's Old Woman*. The picture was exhibited for a long time in Westminster Hall.

Page 481, *l* 21. "Heaven-born," being the son of Venus and Anchises.

l 37. *Pallas*, king of Arcadia, great grandsire of Evander. The latter, son of the nymph Carmentis (*l* 383), migrated to Italy sixty years before the Trojan war.

Page 482, *l* 57. "Dipped his palms," *i.e.* offered a libation.

Page 483, *l* 99. *Alcides*, Hercules, grandson of Alcæus.

l 133. *Atridæ*, Agamemnon and Menelaus.

Page 484, *l* 154. *Daunia*, part of Apulia ; so called from Daunus, the ancestor of Turnus, now rival of Æneas for the hand of Lavinia, daughter of the Latin king, Latinus.

l 168. Hesione and Priam were the only children of Laomedon who survived the capture of Troy. Hesione married Telamon, king of Salamis.

Page 486, *l* 297. "Sooty jaws," because Hercules, by squeezing his throat, had put the flames out.

Page 488, *l* 396. "Ægis," Jupiter's shield. In the middle of it was the Gorgon head, and it was bordered with golden tassels.

Page 493, *l* 11. "This remote," &c. ; viz. Tomi, on the Euxine Sea, whither he was banished by Augustus.

l 48. *Perillus* was the inventor of the brazen bull in which Phalaris, tyrant of Agrigentum, burnt his victims alive. Perillus is said to have been the first to perish by his own invention.

Page 497. "John Owen, Latin poet and epigrammatist, 1560—1622." (Hole's Biographical Dictionary.) " Nothing good, and hardly tolerable, in a poetical sense, had appeared in Latin verse among ourselves till this period. Owen's Epigrams (Audoeni Epigrammata), a well-known collection, were published in 1607. Unequal enough, they are sometimes neat, and more often witty ; but they scarcely aspire to the name of poetry." (Hallam's Literary History, iii. 277.)

Page 498. There are several stories which illustrate the first two pieces. One will suffice. At the battle of Thermopylæ, two Spartans were absent, sick. But when one of them heard that the struggle was begun, he hastened thither, sick as he was, and fell fighting. The other returned to Sparta, where he was treated as a coward ; and though he afterwards fell in the thickest of the fight at Platæa, covered with wounds, he was not buried with the same honours as the rest.

Palladas was an Alexandrian epigrammatist in the fifth century.

Page 499. *Callimachus*, Alexandrian poet, lived in the third century B.C., favoured by Ptolemy Philadelphus. Very few of his writings are extant.

Page 502. *Cytherea*, Venus. She is said to have risen out of the foam of the sea.

Niobe, by glorifying herself over her numerous offspring, provoked Apollo and Diana, the children of Latona, to kill them all.

Page 504. *Menander* flor. B.C. 342.

Page 505. The story of Hermes stealing Apollo's oxen within a few hours of his birth is told by Horace.

Page 506. *Simois* was the river of Troas beside which Paris assigned the prize of beauty to Venus in preference to Juno and Minerva.

Page 507. *Epicharmus*, the first Greek comic writer, B.C. 480.

The Theban bard, Pindar.

For the original of the "Epigram of Homer," see Herodotus, Vita Homeri : Oxford Pocket Classics.

Page 508. The names *Syntrips, Smaragus, Sabactes*, signify, "Smasher, Crasher, Dasher." They were lubber-fiends, who broke all the pots in the kitchen.

Philemon, an Athenian comic poet B.C. 330.

Page 509. *Moschus*, of Cyracuse, a pastoral poet.

Page 510. "*The Hare and many Friends*," Gay, i. 50. (Anderson's Poets, viii. 364.) "*The Miser and Plutus*," Book i. 6 (Anderson 347).

Page 511. The two first lines only of "*The Butterfly and Snail*" (i. 24) :—

> "All upstarts, insolent in place,
> Remind us of their vulgar race."

THE END.

R. CLAY AND SONS, LTD., BREAD ST. HILL, E.C., AND BUNGAY, SUFFOLK.

Macmillan's
GLOBE LIBRARY

Crown 8vo.   Cloth.   3s. 6d. each

The volumes marked with an asterisk (*) are also issued in green limp leather, with full gilt backs and gilt edges, price 5s. net each

BOSWELL

* BOSWELL'S LIFE OF JOHNSON.   Edited with an Introduction by MOWBRAY MORRIS.

BURNS

* POEMS, SONGS, AND LETTERS, being the complete Works of Robert Burns, edited from the best printed and manuscript authorities, with Glossarial Index and a Biographical Memoir by ALEXANDER SMITH.

CHAUCER

* THE WORKS OF GEOFFREY CHAUCER. Edited by ALFRED W. POLLARD, W. FRANK HEATH. MARK H. LIDDELL and W. S. McCORMICK.

COWPER

* THE POETICAL WORKS OF WILLIAM COWPER. Edited with Notes and Biographical Introduction by W. BENHAM, B.D.

DEFOE

ROBINSON CRUSOE.   Edited after the Original Editions, with a Biographical Introduction by HENRY KINGSLEY, F.R.G.S.

MILTON

*THE POETICAL WORKS OF JOHN MILTON. With Introductions by Professor MASSON.

PEPYS

THE DIARY OF SAMUEL PEPYS. With Introduction and Notes by G. GREGORY SMITH.

POPE

*THE POETICAL WORKS OF ALEXANDER POPE. Edited, with Notes and Introductory Memoir, by Dr. A. W. WARD.

SCOTT

*POETICAL WORKS OF SIR WALTER SCOTT. With a Biographical and Critical Memoir by F. T. PALGRAVE.

SHAKESPEARE

*THE WORKS OF WILLIAM SHAKESPEARE. Edited by W. G. CLARK, M.A., and W. ALDIS WRIGHT, M.A.

SPENSER

*THE COMPLETE WORKS OF EDMUND SPENSER. Edited from the original editions and manuscripts by R. MORRIS. With a Memoir by J. W. HALES, M.A.

TENNYSON

*THE POETICAL WORKS OF ALFRED, LORD TENNYSON. Also in extra cloth, gilt edges. 4s. 6d.

VIRGIL

THE WORKS OF VIRGIL, rendered into English Prose. With Introductions, Running Analysis, Notes, and Index. By J. LONSDALE, M.A., and S. LEE, M.A.

The Globe Library

SOME PRESS OPINIONS OF THE SERIES

THE SATURDAY REVIEW

" The 'Globe' Editions are admirable for their scholarly editing, their typographical excellence, their compendious form and their cheapness."

THE DAILY TELEGRAPH

"The 'Globe' Editions are unmatched for their combination of editorial capability and care with excellence of production and lowness of price."

THE LITERARY WORLD

" These ' Globe ' Editions are not only truly cheap, which many so-called cheap editions are not, but excellent in every way. The matter is of the very best, being reproductions of old standard authors, the type is remarkably clear and pleasant to the eye, and the volumes are handsomely though not showily got up. They are just the books which a young man, with only a limited sum to spend on literary purchases, must rejoice to add to his own select library."

THE BRITISH QUARTERLY

" In elegance and scholarliness the ' Globe ' Editions of Messrs. Macmillan surpass any popular series of our classics hitherto given to the public. Wonderfully beautiful, distinct and compendious, as near an approach to miniature perfection as has ever been made."

THE GLASGOW HERALD

" The famous, accurate and marvellously cheap editions for which the people are indebted to Messrs. Macmillan & Co."

MACMILLAN & CO., LTD.
ST. MARTIN'S STREET
LONDON
W.C.

S.5.12.13